"A masterful book on the important biblical concept of the *imago Dei,* which has too often received cursory treatment. The breadth and depth of Kilner's scholarship are impressive, and his carefully crafted work is simultaneously astute and engaging. . . . Students and theologians will be consulting his *Dignity and Destiny* for years to come."

— BRENT WATERS
Garrett-Evangelical Theological Seminary

"Kilner carefully demonstrates how theological convictions about the image of God matter profoundly for Christian life and witness. . . . Convincingly shows how poorly conceived or sloppy exegesis not only hampers an individual's love for God and others but also creates an ethos that reinforces broad injustices ranging from racism to disregard for those with disabilities."

— ERIN DUFAULT-HUNTER
Fuller Theological Seminary

"A well-analyzed, nicely written study of the single most important truth undergirding respect for human life. . . . Our society, including the church, has a spotty record dealing with moral challenges — racism, poverty, gender roles, abortion — which are skewed by distorted views of what it means for us to bear the image of God. Kilner's book gives a soundly biblical understanding that can address these shortcomings."

— DANIEL R. HEIMBACH
Southeastern Baptist Theological Seminary

Dignity and Destiny

Humanity in the Image of God

John F. Kilner

WILLIAM B. EERDMANS PUBLISHING COMPANY
GRAND RAPIDS, MICHIGAN / CAMBRIDGE, U.K.

Published 2015 by

Wm. B. Eerdmans Publishing Co.

2140 Oak Industrial Drive N.E., Grand Rapids, Michigan 49505 /
P.O. Box 163, Cambridge CB3 9PU U.K.

Printed in the United States of America

21 20 19 18 17 16 15   7 6 5 4 3 2 1

Library of Congress Cataloging-in-Publication Data

Kilner, John Frederic.
Dignity and destiny: humanity in the image of God / John F. Kilner.
pages   cm
Includes bibliographical references and index.
ISBN 978-0-8028-6764-3 (pbk.: alk. paper)
1. Image of God. 2. Theological anthropology — Christianity   I. Title.

BT103.K4647   2015
233´.5 — dc23

2014036009

www.eerdmans.com

For Beth and Marvin,
gifts of God's goodness

Contents

Introduction

Why another book on the image of God? If nothing else, there is great value in the notes here, which connect readers to many of the thousands of discussions of this important topic!

As those notes document, vast speculation about God's image has appeared over the centuries. Apparently most people never got the memo — the one a Desert Father reportedly wrote: "Don't speculate about the image."[1]

If only such speculation were always benign; however, many people have invoked this concept to perpetrate some of the worst oppression in history. Others, often unintentionally, have promoted views of God's image that have undermined the idea's ability to inspire the church's outreach to unbelievers and engagement with challenges to human life and dignity.

This needs to change.

The present book aspires to contribute to that end. Among other things, it shows the dangers of understanding humanity's creation in God's image primarily in terms of ways that people are presently like God. Relatedly, it explains why it is unwise to think that God's image can be damaged. People are damaged, but even the Bible never says that God's image is.[2] Great devastation can be avoided, and liberation gained, by speaking of God's image in the way that the biblical authors do.

---

1. Merriell (1990: 2) traces this statement back to the apostle Paul's contemporary, Sopater, in "Apophthegmata Patrum."

2. In this book, "biblical" and "Bible" will refer to the sacred book of Christianity, including the Old and New Testaments, not including the Apocrypha — though the discussion here will periodically include relevant material from the Apocrypha identified as such.

Ultimately, the image of God is Jesus Christ. People are first created and later renewed according to that image. Image involves connection and reflection. Creation in God's image entails a special connection with God and an intended reflection of God. Renewal in God's image entails a more intimate connection with God through Christ and an increasingly actual reflection of God in Christ, to God's glory. This connection with God is the basis of human dignity. This reflection of God is the beauty of human destiny. All of humanity participates in human dignity. All of humanity is offered human destiny, though only some embrace and will experience it. Christ and humanity, connection and reflection, dignity and destiny — these lie at the heart of what God's image is all about.

As with any work of this magnitude, there are more people to credit than I could possibly name here. In particular, I am painfully aware of the many authors and Christian communities I have *not* had the space or time to cite in the notes. So many of these, along with so many cited, warrant deep appreciation for struggling to understand what humanity's creation and renewal in God's image mean — and for helping others to do so.

Trinity International University, an anonymous foundation, my colleague John Dunlop, and my family provided the time and means necessary for me to do the research and writing of this book. Special thanks go to Trinity deans Tite Tienou and Jeanette Hsieh; associate deans Jim Moore and Don Hedges; my departmental colleagues; the head of the foundation; and my wife Suzanne — for their personal encouragement and support. I am grateful for the graduate students who provided assistance along the way — notably Brian Tung, Armida Stephens, Jonathan King, Austin Freeman, and Sarah Abbey. The labors of graduate assistant Madison Pierce were particularly noteworthy — without them this book would have been greatly delayed and impoverished. Throughout, the editorial and production staff at Eerdmans were a delight to work with and exceptionally skilled.

So many of my colleagues deserve special thanks for their contributions to this project. Some, like Kevin Vanhoozer, Richard Averbeck, Te-Li Lau, Joshua Jipp, Greg Strand, Bill Kynes, Donal O'Mathuna, and Marvin Wickware graciously provided detailed written critique. Many others, such as David Pao, Eric Tully, Doug Sweeney, Scott Manetsch, and Peter Kilner, engaged in fruitful discussions. Still others, like Darrell Bock, kindly took the time to offer a vital insight at the conclusion of one of my presentations of a portion of this book — in Darrell's case, after the plenary address I gave at the U.S. national meeting of the Evangelical Theological Society.

Such presentations at educational institutions including Trinity, Talbot, Wheaton, Harvard, and Johns Hopkins, not to mention addresses in many church and denominational settings, such as Harvest Bible Chapel, Willow Creek, and the EFCA, generated innumerable helpful conversations.

I am more aware now than ever that so much of the value of projects like this is due to people other than their authors, and that credit for everything belongs to the ultimate Author of all.

For God's glory,
J.F.K.

PART I

The Human and Divine Context

CHAPTER ONE

Much Is at Stake:
The Liberation and Devastation of God's Image

How can something foster both liberation and devastation? The answer lies in the possibility of co-opting, for evil, a powerful idea that has the potential to inspire great good. Co-opting is much easier if the idea is inadequately formulated in a way that lends itself to misuse. Such has often been the case with the idea that humanity is in God's image.

Viewing people in terms of the image of God has fostered magnificent efforts to protect and redeem people. It has also encouraged oppressing and even destroying people. All this has been possible simultaneously because of a common misconception that being in God's image is about how people are (actually) "like God" and "unlike animals." This view understands being in God's image in terms of attributes that people have now, most commonly people's ability to reason, rule over (manage) creation, be righteous, or be in relationship. In this view, sin can damage such attributes and thus damage God's image. Accordingly, people vary in the extent to which they have these attributes — and are in God's image. For many, that means how much people warrant respect and protection varies from person to person. The door to devastation is open as soon as people begin to define being in God's image in terms of currently having attributes of God.

The problem here is not that a biblical idea has proven to be destructive, but that an unbiblical idea masquerading as a biblical idea has proven to be destructive. This unbiblical idea is at odds with what the Bible's authors mean by being created in God's image and how they employ this concept in life situations. So this book's primary purpose will be to clarify what the Bible itself teaches about humanity being in God's image, with no governing agenda other than that. The widely known concept of humanity's creation in God's image is indeed a concept that has reached the contemporary world largely via the Bible. Accordingly, clarity regarding biblical teaching on this idea is essential before further theological and cultural development of the idea is on sound footing.

Nevertheless, to appreciate the importance of doing this biblical study, it *is* helpful to note first how much is at stake. The idea of the image of God is quite influential in theology and in everyday life, and it is a huge loss to misunderstand it in a way that undermines its power to liberate. Moreover, misunderstandings of being in God's image have contributed to some of the greatest atrocities in history, and it is a great gain to understand it in a way that is not conducive to such devastation. We will consider in this chapter both the potential of humanity's creation in God's image to inspire great good and how, if misunderstood, this idea can foster terrible evil. The chapter will conclude with a consideration of why such disagreement has surrounded this idea through the centuries.

Image-Inspired Liberation

Simply the amount of writing devoted to humanity's creation and renewal in God's image through the ages attests eloquently to the potential of these ideas to inspire great good. Biblical scholar Claus Westermann and theologian Stanley Grenz call this literature "limitless," while a chronicler of that literature, Gunnlaugur Jónsson, describes it as "nearly infinite."[1] Few biblical ideas have stirred as much interest or prompted as much study.[2]

As Christian theologians have often acknowledged, the impact of the image-of-God idea has reached way beyond the bounds of their own field. Observes Emil Brunner (with later support from Hermann Häring and George Kelsey), "The history of this idea is the history of . . . Western understanding" when it comes to the meaning of being human.[3] "It is doubtful if there is any one concept more basic for democracy and Western civilization in general," concurs T. B. Maston.[4] "Not only is theology involved," echoes Charles Feinberg, "but reason, law, and civilization as

1. Westermann, 1994: 148; Grenz, 2001: 184-85; Jónsson, 1988: 1.

2. So Berman, 2008: 22; Crouch, 2010: 2.

3. Brunner, 1947: 92-93. Häring, 2001: 3 similarly underscores the importance of this idea for "Western culture," and G. Kelsey, 1965: 87 for "Western democracies."

4. Maston, 1959: 13. McReynolds (2013: 26) similarly notes "the enormous influence the image of God has had in the West."

a whole."[5] Human rights analyst Roger Ruston similarly underscores "the debt that secular thought owes to theology" for the illuminating idea of humanity in God's image.[6] In terms of religious thinking, members of the Muslim, Jewish, and Christian communities all consider the image of God concept to be particularly important.[7]

At the same time, Christian theologians are quick to acknowledge how influential the ideas of humanity's creation and renewal in God's image have been in Christian theology and ethics. According to Carl Henry, with a second from Charles Sherlock, the image-of-God concept is "determinative for the entire gamut of doctrinal affirmation."[8] That includes not just humanity's creation but also humanity's redemption and eternal destination.[9] The image of God is a "starting point" (Michelle Gonzalez) with "orienting power . . . for Christian theology" (J. Wentzel van Huyssteen) — "the necessary bridging concept" (Ben Witherington III), which makes it part of "the essence of Christianity" (Vladimir Lossky).[10] Many others concur that God's image plays a pivotal role in a Christian understanding of God and all of life.[11]

Humanity's existence in God's image is particularly important for understanding who people are. Theologians Louis Berkhof and Philip Hughes see it as the "essence" of humanity.[12] It is God's "final vocabulary" (Mark Talbot) for what makes humans human (Millard Erickson) — a view shared

5. Feinberg, 1972: 236.

6. Ruston, 2004: 287.

7. See Umar, 2004; Stendahl, 1992: 141; Hefner, 2000: 87-88; Reinders, 2006: 124. For more on Islam's view, see Soskice, 2011: 297; Melchert, 2011; on Judaism's view, see Matt, 1987; Reiss, 2011.

8. Henry, 1973: 339; Sherlock, 1996: 17.

9. Chafer, 1947: v. 2, 169; Hopkins, 2005: 33.

10. Gonzalez, 2007: 132; van Huyssteen, 2006: 116 (cf. 162); Witherington, 2009: v. 2, 5; Lossky, 1985: 126. Schönborn (2011: 41) even goes so far as to claim that "we may say without exaggerating that the great eras of theological renewal have also been the high points of the image of God."

11. E.g., Hilkert, 1995: 192 (feminist and womanist theology); Howe, 1995: 38 (human relationships); Bray, 1998: 42 (the church); Häring, 2001: 3 (contemporary theology); Gelernter, 2008: 396 (biblical religion); Mangano, 2008: Preface (all revelation, invoking James Orr). Thus Grenz (2001: 15) concludes that the image of God has "far-reaching implications for Christian thought and practice — for both theological construction and theological praxis."

12. L. Berkhof, 1949: 205; Hughes, 1989: 4. Cf. Hollinger, 2009: 74 ("most fundamental dimension"); Cortez, 2010: 10 ("starting point"); Rakestraw, 1992: 402 ("key").

by many in theological, biblical, and ministry fields alike.[13] In fact, many see humanity's creation in God's image as "central," "at the heart of" — in fact, "the most important matter in" — theological anthropology.[14] From this perspective, humanity in God's image is this discipline's "foundation" and "controlling concept."[15]

Many scholars, studying how Christians have viewed human beings through the centuries, have remarked over the "enduring" and "indestructible" influence of the idea of being created in God's image.[16] This "comprehensively normative" role is rather surprising to some, primarily because of the huge disagreement today and throughout history regarding what it means for humanity to be in God's image.[17] However, the enduring centrality of the image idea and the scope of the disagreement only serve to underscore the importance of the ongoing effort to gain greater clarity.

The need for greater clarity, though, is far from merely a conceptual or academic challenge. How people have understood being in God's image has had a "tremendous impact" on human well-being, for better and for worse.[18] Much of this impact has been hugely positive.

The understanding that humanity is in God's image has played a liberating role in "Christian tradition" by encouraging Christians to respect and protect the dignity and life of all human beings.[19] This influence has been so widespread that it continues to shape the guiding documents of

13. Talbot, 2006: 176; Erickson, 2013: 457 (drawing on Rad, 1964b: 390-92 and Eichrodt, 1967: 122). Cf. van Huyssteen, 2006: 321; Crouch, 2010: 2; Balswick et al., 2005: 31.

14. Central: Breck, 1998: 145; Woodhead, 2006: 234; Gonzalez, 2007: 26, 124; Mahoney, 2010: 682. At the heart of: van Huyssteen, 2006: 126. Most important: Bray, 2001: 575; Gardoski, 2007: 5. John Wesley (1985o: 355) specifies that humanity fulfilling its purpose as created in God's image "is the one thing needful upon earth."

15. Foundation: Grenz, 2001: 183 (cf. 2002: 42). Controlling concept: Lints, 2006b: 4. Similarly, Pope, 1875: v. 1, 6; Haering, 1915: v. 1, 390; John Paul II, 1997a: 454; Balswick et al., 2005: 30.

16. Enduring: Robinson, 2011: 162, 166. Indestructible: Hall, 1986: 63-64 (reflecting on the "wealth of meaning" that Ricoeur [1965: 110] finds in the concept of God's image). Similarly, Clines, 1968: 98-99; Pannenberg, 1985: 20; Schwöbel, 2006: 50; Cortez, 2010: 15.

17. Comprehensive: Jenson, 1999: 53. Normative: van Huyssteen, 2006: 149. Cf. B. Ware, 2002: 14; McFarland, 2005: 1.

18. See J. Johnson, 2005: 176.

19. To illustrate this, Pannenberg, 1991: 176 draws upon the teaching and impact of Theophilus of Antioch, Gregory of Nyssa, Ambrose, Leo the Great, Gregory the Great, Bonaventura, and Aquinas. Soulen and Woodhead, 2006: 4 similarly draw upon Theophilus of Antioch and Augustine. A World Council of Churches report (World, 2005: par. 12) reaches a similar conclusion, as does Schönborn's (2011: 40) assessment of Christian tradition.

a wide range of Christian traditions and denominations, including Protestant, Orthodox, and Catholic.[20] However, such influence has extended far beyond the church. The biblically based notion that all people have a special status by virtue of their creation in God's image has inspired much secular work on behalf of human dignity and human rights.[21]

Admittedly, some look to early Roman and Greek philosophy rather than to the biblical image of God idea for the roots of present understandings of human dignity. However, the dignity that the classical world recognized was primarily the dignity of the virtuous person — not a dignity intrinsic to humanity per se that could undergird respect and protection for all people.[22] Others incline toward the Enlightenment, especially the writings of Immanuel Kant, as the primary source of contemporary views of human dignity. However, these defenses of human dignity more plausibly constitute attempts to explain in nonreligious terms a persuasive concept that had long before come to light through biblical revelation.[23] Many have expressed doubt that such a view of human dignity could have emerged — or is lastingly sustainable — apart from its connection with a creator God.[24] One could argue that some past violations of human dignity, such as the mass manufacture of nerve toxins, court-mandated sterilizations, and harmful experimentation on prison populations, have only become thinkable once the perpetrators have set aside the protective view that all human beings are in God's image.[25]

Recognizing humanity's creation in God's image has played a significant role historically in freeing people from the ravages of need and oppression.[26] The outlook of Clement of Rome charted this course in the earliest centuries of the church:

---

20. See discussions in Moltmann, 1984: 12 (Protestant et al.); Habib, 1998: 36 (Orthodox et al.); Ruston, 2004: 270 (Catholic et al.).

21. Baker, 1991: 35; Bayertz, 1996: xiii-xiv; Stackhouse, 2005: 38; Botman, 2006: 83-84.

22. Ferngren, 1987: 34-36 favorably reviews two studies documenting this conclusion, by Den Boer (1979) and Rist (1982). See also Dover, 1974: 273-88; Merriell, 1990: 243-44; Pigeaud, 1997: 266-90.

23. On the role of the Enlightenment, see Ruston, 2004: 286-87. After considering competing historical claims, Stackhouse (2005: 29) concludes: "I deny that it was Kant's immaculate conception of human dignity that served as the root of human rights ideas, as a number of secularist advocates of human rights have claimed. He was not in that way Immanuel."

24. For example, Ferngren, 1987: 42; Ruston, 2004: 287-88; Schulman, 2008: 10.

25. As explained in D. Hart (2009: 232).

26. For illustrations from other arenas such as immigration, the use of violence, and

You should do good to and pay honour and reverence to man, who is made in the image of God: ... minister food to the hungry, drink to the thirsty, clothing to the naked, hospitality to the stranger, and necessary things to the prisoner; and that is what will be regarded as truly bestowed upon God.[27]

Both this perspective of needy people as created in God's image and that of Christian service as conforming to the image of Christ became powerful motivators for helping people in poverty.[28] In contrast, people outside the church during its earliest years exhibited relatively little concern to help poor individuals.[29]

By the twentieth century of the church, North American Christian leaders such as Martin Luther King Jr. were still mobilizing efforts to care for impoverished people by making countercultural appeals to their status as "in God's image."[30] King and others also saw that this status mandates not just helping to meet people's needs but learning from them as well. In King's words:

Sometimes Aunt Jane on her knees can get more truth than the philosopher on his tiptoes. And this is what "all men are made in the image of God" tells us. We must believe this and we must live by it.[31]

At the same time, Latin American Christian leaders in international gatherings such as the Puebla Conference were similarly calling for much greater attention to the needs and perspectives of impoverished people precisely because they are "made in the image and likeness of God."[32]

The recognition that sick people, too, are in God's image has similarly benefited those incapacitated by illness. Again, from the earliest centuries of the church, Christians cared for those who were sick because "every

---

the commodification of the human body, see McKanan, 2002: 63, 230; Ferngren, 2009: 100; World, 2005: par. 119.

27. Clement, 1885: bk. 5, ch. 23.

28. See Ferngren, 1987: 32-33; 2009: 103 and other sources on care for needy persons that Ferngren identifies, some of which are noted below; cf. Holman, 2001: 149-51.

29. Winslow, 1965: 348-59; Downey, 1965: 3-15; Kudlien, 1970: 91-97; Den Boer, 1979: 62-72; Veyne, 1990: 23, 30; P. Brown, 1992: 91-93; Ferngren, 2009: 98-99.

30. King, 1968: 180. See discussion in Wills, 2009: 26-27.

31. King, 1965.

32. Eagleson and Scharper, 1979: par. 1142; S. Pope, 1993: 259; Hicks, 2000: 145.

stranger in need was a neighbor who bore the image of God."[33] This care, which extended to each person in need and not just to generic support for public programs, distinguished the church from the surrounding Roman and Greek culture.[34] It motivated Christians to refuse to participate in the common practice of infanticide (frequently in the form of abandoning deformed or unwanted infants outdoors).[35] In this regard, early church practice was much closer to that of Hebrew culture, which was also nourished by the notion of every person being created in God's image.[36] This notion spurred the early church, in fact, to go beyond nonparticipation in infanticide to rescuing abandoned infants and caring for them.[37] More recently it has inspired Christian efforts to care for people with disabilities,[38] and for those with socially stigmatized diseases such as HIV/AIDS.[39]

Humanity's creation in God's image, then, has inspired initiatives to meet the needs of those who are neediest. It has also inspired efforts to overcome the oppression of other groups, such as Native Americans,[40] enslaved Africans[41] and their descendants, and women. Consider a few representative examples. Regarding Native Americans, the Spanish colonization of the West Indies and other areas of the Americas during the sixteenth century provides an excellent illustration.[42] In the face of much oppression and brutality, many Spanish friars risked their lives for the benefit of indigenous people there. Their motivation was simply "the abiding confidence that they would not encounter any human being in

33. Ferngren, 2009: 145.

34. Hands, 1968: 77-88; Ferngren, 1987: 31-32; 2009: 101; R. Garland, 1995: 11-18; Kapparis, 2002: 54-62.

35. Amundsen, 1996: 50-69; Ferngren, 1987: 36; 2009: 101 (drawing on the early Christian writings of Minucius Felix and Lactantius).

36. Rist, 1982: 129-31; Ferngren, 2009: 97-98.

37. Collste, 2002: 45.

38. A good example is the multi-campus Harvest Bible Chapel in Chicago, where the name of the fellowship of people with disabilities is "In His Image." See http://www .harvestbiblechapel.org/ministry.aspx?ministry_id=290654&site_id=10780.

39. Catholic, 1987; Hilkert, 1995: 194; World, 2005: par. 119.

40. This category does not indicate that all native peoples in the Americas are the same people group. Rather, it indicates that the examples in this section of the chapter all involve people in groups native to the Americas.

41. This category does not indicate that all people from Africa enslaved elsewhere are the same people group. Rather, it indicates that the examples in this section of the chapter all involve people forcibly removed from some part of Africa.

42. D. Davis (2008: 143) cites the belief that all people are in God's image as a "crucial variable" in undermining slavery in Venezuela and some other parts of Hispanic America.

any rural compound or village or city who was not created in the image and likeness of the God and Father of Jesus Christ."[43] Back in Spain, leaders in the church and legal system such as Francisco de Vitoria were inspired by the same confidence. Recognizing that Native Americans, like Europeans, were in God's image served as "the doctrinal starting point" for Vitoria and his colleagues to challenge attempts to justify the domination of indigenous peoples.[44]

Among the most ardent defenders of such people in the West Indies and beyond was Bartholomé de las Casas, the first officially appointed "Protector of the Indians." Again, his driving inspiration was that God deeply cares for all people, "formed in his image and likeness."[45] As South American theologian Gustavo Gutiérrez notes, Las Casas stood up even for "the least" of the Native Americans: "The image of God, in which they have been created, is present in all of them. This is the root of their most elementary human rights."[46] In harmony with Genesis 9:6 and James 3:9, Las Casas realized that to abuse what is in God's image was tantamount to abusing God, who for Las Casas was most visibly God-in-Christ. So upon returning to Spain, he responded to questions from a lawyer of the Inquisition by saying "I left Christ in the Indies not once, but a thousand times beaten, afflicted, insulted and crucified by those Spaniards who destroy and ravage the Indians."[47]

Ample evidence is also available to illustrate the impetus that humanity's creation in God's image provided for efforts to free enslaved Africans in the United States. The rationale for such efforts goes back to early leaders in the church such as Gregory of Nyssa, who demanded of slaveholders:

> What price did you put on . . . the likeness of God? . . . Who is his seller? To God alone belongs this power; or rather, not even to God himself. For his gracious gifts, it says, are irrevocable (Rom. 11:29). . . . God does not enslave what is free.[48]

---

43. Elliot, 1993: 38; Mouw, 2012: 264.

44. Vitoria, 1917; Ruston, 2004: 63, 86.

45. Las Casas, 1958: 357; Ruston, 2004: 126-27.

46. Gutiérrez, 1993: 296-97 (where he quotes from Las Casas' *Apologia*); cf. 1993: 82-83 and Ruston, 2010: 389.

47. As quoted in Pierce, 1992: 6-7, 9.

48. See Gregory, 1993: 74, and discussions in Maxwell, 1975: 32-33; Collste, 2002: 45; D. Hart, 2009: 178-79. As Collste observes, "a new view of the slaves that would undermine slavery as a social institution was introduced."

The liberating influence of the idea that all humanity is in God's image was hardly confined to the United States.[49] However, it was particularly evident there in the anti-slavery and anti-oppression efforts of the nineteenth century and beyond.

While there is evidence near the beginning of the century of powerful appeals to God's image,[50] by the 1830s illustrations abound. Writings such as the letters of revivalist Theodore Dwight Weld and the book *Slavery* by distinguished Boston minister William Ellery Channing made compelling cases that nothing "can annul the birth-right charter, which God has bequeathed to every being upon whom he has stamped his own image."[51] Similarly moving were national image-of-God–based appeals to the nation such as those by William Whipper of the American Moral Reform Society.[52]

During the 1840s and 1850s debates over the slavery issue intensified. In 1841, when former slave Frederick Douglass first told his story in public, people were "well prepared to see both his sufferings and his survival as evidence of the *imago dei*."[53] Leading abolitionist William Garrison singles out this event as more motivating than any other experience of his life.[54] When the U.S. Supreme Court upheld slavery practices in the notorious Dred Scott decision of 1857, Douglass appealed to a higher court regarding this decision:

> It is an attempt to undo what God has done, to blot out the broad distinction instituted by the *Allwise* between men and things, and to change

49. See D. Davis, 2008: 239 (cf. 2001: 198) on the British abolitionists' "deep faith that all human beings are created in the image of God, and that we therefore have a compelling duty to overcome institutions that dehumanize groups of people by treating them as exploitable animals." Davis (2008: 394) observes a similar outlook in the French king Philippe the Fair, who explained his liberating initiatives by maintaining that "since all human beings are created in the image of God, they must be free."

50. For example, efforts to outlaw slavery in new U.S. states, as described in David Rice's publication in which he argued that "inasmuch as all men were created in the image of God, every man, regardless of race, has a God-given right to freedom." See Rice, 1956: 4-6, 12 and discussion in H. S. Smith, 1972: 56.

51. The quotation is from Weld's January 2, 1833 letter to William Lloyd Garrison (in Barnes and Dumond, 1965: 97-98; cf. discussion in D. Davis, 2008: 252-53). Channing (1836: 25; cf. 9-10, 76-77) considered slaves' creation in "God's image" to be "the great argument against seizing and using a man as property"; cf. discussion in H. S. Smith, 1972: 137.

52. On Whipper's 1837 national address, see Glaude, 2000: 131; Wills, 2009: 16.

53. McKanan, 2002: 129.

54. In his "Preface" to the 1845 written version of Douglass's narrative (see Douglass, 1994: 3-4; and discussion in McKanan, 2002: 129).

the image and superscription of the everliving God into a speechless piece of merchandise. Such a decision cannot stand. God will be true though every man be a liar.[55]

Douglass was not without support even in the judicial system, for Judge Nathan Green of the Tennessee Supreme Court had argued years earlier that "a slave is not in the condition of a horse. The slave . . . is made in the image of the Creator."[56] Meanwhile, a wide range of other reformers, from Henry Garnet (who escaped from slavery) to wealthy land speculator Gerrit Smith, also influentially critiqued slavery. They labeled it a violation of enslaved people's divine creation in God's image.[57]

During this period, appeals to the image of God served not only to discourage slaveholders from practicing slavery but also to encourage enslaved people to resist such subjection. African American activists such as Maria Stewart reminded those in bondage that God "hath formed and fashioned you in his own glorious image."[58] As a result, enslaved people "began to get the notion that they were created in the image of God. This confirmed their sense of human worth and reaffirmed their awareness that being a slave was a contradiction to their dignity as human beings."[59] Fugitives from slavery "discovered the *imago dei* in their own capacity to expose slavery's violence."[60] Enslaved women gained strength to nurture their families and reject oppressive ideas "because of their fundamental belief in their rights as human beings created in the image of God."[61]

As the Civil War got underway early in the 1860s, the appeals to the image of God as a basis for ending slavery became increasingly public and prominent. Journalist Orestes Brownson decried the way that slaveholders "stifle what is human in [enslaved people], and prevent the development in them of that 'image and likeness' of God in which they were created."[62]

55. Douglass, 1992a: 250-51. See also Douglass, 1992b: 217 ("The slave is a man, 'the image of God'"); and discussion in Ruston, 2004: 269-70; Wills, 2009: 17-18.

56. In the case *Ford v. Ford* (1846). See Howington, 1975; Genovese, 2000: 226; Wills, 2009: 19.

57. Garnet, 1999: 296; Ge. Smith, 1859: 37-38. For discussion, see Wills, 2009: 15-16; McKanan, 2002: 49.

58. McKanan, 2002: 48-49.

59. Ellis, 1996: 44.

60. McKanan, 2002: 150.

61. Weems, 2003: 25 (rejecting oppressive ideas). On nurturing families, see Douglas, 1995: 77.

62. Brownson, 1861. See discussion in Maxwell, 1975: 108-9.

Meanwhile, Senator Charles Sumner was arguing in the U.S. Senate against slavery because of its dehumanizing impact on "man, created in the image of God."[63] Historian Goldwin Smith challenged Christians to consider not only creation but also redemption — that a Christian slaveholder should free those he has enslaved "for the transforming of his and their life into the image of their Maker."[64] Surveying the many arguments made against slavery in the decades leading up to the Civil War, pastor-educator Richard Wills concludes:

> More than the secular rationale could admit, freedom had a moral quality that grew out of a theological worldview that sought to articulate what it meant to have been created in God's image. . . . It was this theological idea that rallied the social resistance against the forces of slavery so all those created in God's image might be included in "We the people."[65]

The legacy of this outlook is evident a century later in the civil rights activism of Howard Thurman and Martin Luther King Jr. According to theologian Karen Teel, "For Thurman and King, the image of God applies to all human persons and legitimates black people's struggle for equality. . . . The image of God thus provides the theological basis for black people's struggle for survival."[66] King in particular "ultimately lodged his appeal for civil rights in an interpretation of *imago Dei* that was grounded in the claims of scripture. . . . In sync with the abolitionists who employed an image of God rationale in their struggle against the throes of slavery, King engaged similar language to defend his civil rights message and methodology."[67] The idea of all people being in God's image was primarily an appeal that a leader would make to others, to challenge their racism. However, African American leader John Perkins found that the idea first had to work within him, to change his own racist attitudes — a necessary precursor to his later work in racial reconciliation.[68]

Recognition of humanity's creation in God's image, then, has made a significant contribution to efforts to end slavery and racism, as various

---

63. Sumner, 1860: 129. See discussion in Ruston, 2004: 269-70.
64. Go. Smith, 1863: 6.
65. Wills, 2009: 13, 15. For a similar analysis, see Dyck, 1990: 39.
66. Teel, 2010: 72. Cf. Cannon, 1988: 160-63.
67. Wills, 2009: 23, 28.
68. Marsh, 2005: 171.

historical commentators have concluded.[69] Not only has it convicted the oppressors, but it has also uplifted and sustained the oppressed. This powerful work has been evident

- in the "black church's . . . historic mission to rescue man as the image of God,"[70]
- in the "language of power and survival [in the music of African American spirituals] that celebrates African Americans as *imago Dei*,"[71] and
- in a "black theology" in which "one's blackness signifies being created in God's image."[72]

A society "that does not know how to value anyone as . . . a person made in God's image" is missing what historically has been one of the greatest protections against the dehumanization and corruption of African American men and women.[73]

Sadly, women of all races have been subject to demeaning, not necessarily because of their skin color but due to their gender. Historically they have often discovered that their creation in God's image is one of the most powerful protections against such demeaning. Scholar Anne Clifford applauds the way that women's "struggle against the dehumanizing forces of patriarchy" has been undergirded by "the recognition that females are *imago Dei*."[74] Mercy Amba Oduyoye, with affirmations from fellow theologians Mary Catherine Hilkert and Lisa Sowle Cahill, even maintains that around the world

> many women have claimed the biblical affirmation of our being created "in the Image of God" both for the protection of women's self-worth and self-esteem and to protest dehumanization by others. . . . Without it the whole edifice of human relations seems to crumble and fall.[75]

According to Palestinian Jean Zaru, the "truth that we are made in the image and likeness of God" has emerged for women in her part of the

69. E.g., Hilkert, 1995: 194; McKanan, 2002: 46.

70. C. E. Lincoln, 1999: 266. Cf. Lincoln and Mamiya, 1990: 4.

71. Kirk-Duggan, 1993: 164. Cf. Gonzalez, 2007: 126.

72. Hopkins, 2005: 8.

73. Usry and Keener, 1996: 56, drawing on the analysis of African American scholar Cornel West.

74. Clifford, 1995: 183.

75. Oduyoye, 1996: 170; Hilkert, 2002: 9; Cahill, 2006b: 60.

world as the greatest hope for overcoming "injustice, exploitation, oppression, and everything that comes from false beliefs."[76] The international Mexico Conference on Doing Theology from Third World Women's Perspective similarly affirmed the importance of living out the implications of "being created in God's image . . . in order to build an egalitarian society." However, it noted that this has been happening differently in Latin America, Africa, and Asia.[77]

In Latin America, survival strategies are key. Milagros Peña, an author of books on Mexico and Peru, provides a telling example of this in her report of an interview with Alma Tamez. Tamez found over time that the most effective way to challenge male oppression was to appeal to the fact that "women and men were both made in the same image of God."[78] For the women of Nicaragua, observes Latin American author Luz Beatriz Arellano, "the starting point for demanding their own rights and their own opportunities" was their discovery "that they had been created in the image of God just as much as men."[79] Meanwhile, in Africa, women's struggle is with elements of traditional African culture and colonialism. Ghanaian theologian Mercy Amba Oduyoye observes that women there have appropriated "the 'image of God' motif to stake a claim to freedom from oppression, to full humanity."[80]

In Asia, the challenge for women has more to do with rediscovering the dignity of being women and fighting injustices. To meet this challenge, according to Korean theologian Chung Hyun Kyung, "Asian women use most frequently the teaching from Genesis that contains the message that men and women are created equally in God's image."[81] A key resource for them has been the journal *In God's Image.* According to Hope Antone of Indonesia's Asian Women's Resource Centre, since 1982 this journal has been "a product of the solidarity of a group of women in Asia who dreamt a world that was free from oppression and discrimination, a world where the image of God was not violated or abused."[82]

In light of the global impact of the affirmation that all people are in God's image, the conclusion of Cambridge's Zoe Bennett Moore is per-

---

76. Zaru, 1994: 230-31.
77. "Mexico," 1994: 37-38.
78. Peña, 2007: 122.
79. Arellano, 1994: 324.
80. Oduyoye, 2001: 50.
81. Kyung, 1994: 252, 258; cf. Gonzalez, 2007: 130.
82. Antone, 2007: 1; cf. Kyung, 1990: 21.

haps not surprising: "[T]here is a direct connection between the value given to human life and that life seen as made in the image of God."[83] No more surprising is the prominence that U.S.-based feminist theologians have attached to all of humanity's elevated status rooted in God's image. Michelle Gonzalez, whose introductory theology book is titled *Created in God's Image,* explains that "feminist theologians use the *imago Dei* to reclaim the full humanity of women."[84] Letty Russell similarly acknowledges that the purpose of her book on biblical interpretation is "to affirm women so that they are acknowledged as fully human partners with men, sharing in the image of God."[85] For University of Chicago professor Anne Carr, "the critical principle of the promotion of the full humanity of women is the ancient principle of the *imago dei.*"[86] Adding that "women are claiming that principle," she underscores a point made by many others: All humanity's creation in God's image is not just a written ideal — it has made a concrete, liberating difference in the lives of countless women around the globe.

This image-of-God understanding has also served to inspire care for the natural world in which humanity lives. Much of this discussion will have to await Chapter 5,[87] which addresses God's intention for those in the divine image to "rule" over creation. However, it is worth noting here, with theologian Wolfhart Pannenberg, that the recognition of humanity's creation in God's image effectively encouraged care for the natural environment throughout the first seventeen centuries of the church.

> Only beginning in the eighteenth century did the commission given to human beings to represent God in their dominion over nature turn into a claim that they have unlimited power to dispose of nature. This happened, in other words, at the very time when modern humanity in its self-understanding was cutting its ties with the creator God of the Bible.[88]

British professor Stephen Wright agrees:

83. See her presentation at the December 1998 World Council of Churches Consultation in England, as discussed in Mayland, 1999: 61.
84. Gonzalez, 2007: 125.
85. Russell, 1985: 13.
86. Carr, 1993: 14.
87. In the present work, reference to "Chapter" or its abbreviation "Ch." — with a capital "C" — will always refer to a chapter in this work.
88. Pannenberg, 1985: 78.

The disorder and imbalance in the world and in humanity itself can be traced to humanity's repudiation of [its] pivotal role . . . as the image of God. . . . A constructive relationship with the created order, allowing us to make "useful alterations" without violating its essential nature, has been replaced by one in which it is seen . . . as an enemy to be tamed.[89]

Humanity's status in God's image, then, has served historically as a compelling impetus toward liberation. It has fostered respect and protection for those who have been wrongly oppressed, including impoverished, ill, and disabled people, as well as Native Americans, enslaved Africans and their descendants, and women. It has also inspired care for the natural environment. Where attention to it has waned, this influence has tended to weaken and needs restoration. However, for that restoration to be effective, it should involve a biblically sound understanding of what it means to be in God's image. Ironically, misunderstandings of God's image have had precisely the opposite effect. They have fostered the very sort of devastation that humanity's creation in God's image should prevent.

So it will be important, before proceeding further, to take a careful look at ways that the idea of God's image has been misunderstood and misused in history — and how that has occurred. Such awareness will help guard against reading into the Bible understandings of God's image that contradict the Bible's own teaching.

Image-Inspired Devastation

Surprisingly, the damage done by misusing the idea of God's image ranges as widely as the idea's liberating effects. As McGill University professor Douglas Hall has observed, "[T]he dominant historical deployment of the imago Dei symbol is misleading and even — given our present socio-historical context — dangerous."[90] It has led to the oppression of all of the groups discussed above, and more. Typically, the problem involves people's tendency to view being in God's image in terms of ways that people presently are most excellent — most like God and most unlike animals. That has commonly involved equating being in God's image with engaging in human relationships and/or manifesting human capacities such as

---

89. S. Wright, 2003: 34. Cf. B. Childs, 1993: 400; Horton, 2005: 105.
90. Hall, 1986: 55-56.

reason, human virtues such as righteousness, or human functions such as rulership over creation.

The result has been "problematic if not disastrous, time and again," notes ethicist David Gushee.[91] People who are lowest on the reason, righteousness, rulership, or relationship scale are deemed least like God and least worthy of respect and protection — a conclusion that makes good sense if being in God's image is about current capacities, virtues, functions, and/or relationships. This approach to God's image began in the early days of the church, side by side with more biblically sound understandings of God's image. At that early point, without good biblical grounding some divided the concept into two separate concepts. One concept was "image," which is constant in all people; the other was "likeness," which changes and varies from person to person (see Ch. 3 here). People's value — and thus the respect they were due — differed according to their degree of God-likeness (see Ch. 5).[92]

The particular God-likeness considered central to God's image has changed over time as the values in the surrounding culture have changed (see more on this later in the chapter). Reason was primary in the Greek culture of much of the early church, with righteousness and rulership gaining in importance later, and relationship becoming more culturally prominent recently. However, the common theme has been that having such attributes is what being in God's image is about; and since human significance is grounded in being created in God's image, people must have more or less significance if they have more or less likeness to God — are more or less in God's image.[93] This way of thinking has encouraged such abuses as mistreatment of impoverished and disabled people, the Nazi holocaust and exterminations of Native American groups, oppression of enslaved Africans (and their descendants) and women, and damaging of the natural environment.

First, consider people who are impoverished and as a result, often relatively uneducated as well. Where people have understood being in God's image (and thus human worth) in terms of the rational capacities

91. Gushee, 2012: 44.

92. See Rist, 1982: 161 regarding the persuasiveness of this logic in history, and Z. Moore, 2003: 106 for the many different groups who have suffered as a result.

93. Understanding being in God's image in terms of relationship with God has especially exacerbated the difficulty here. If what matters is only one's relationship with God, worldly matters such as how people treat each other and the natural environment become relatively unimportant. See discussion in Collste, 2002: 45-46.

that humans possess, "much damage has been done."[94] Societies have devalued those who evidence limited rational capacities, such as those who are relatively uneducated. A "shrunken form of *imago Dei*" has promoted further disadvantaging of groups already marginalized through economic poverty.[95] One particularly vivid example of this is the way that the understanding of being in God's image current in the eleventh through seventeenth centuries skewed the selection of saints in the Catholic Church. A detailed sociological study of these saints shows that, at a time when the well-to-do made up only a tiny fraction of the overall population, more than 60 percent of saints came from the "upper" classes of society.[96] As the study indicates, "the dominance of persons from the upper classes as objects of cultic veneration is indicative of the degree to which popular visions of the divine image were far more inclined to reflect established social norms than challenge them."[97]

For analogous reasons, a shrunken *imago Dei* has resulted in similar disadvantaging of people with disabilities, particularly mental disabilities.[98] Various Christian leaders in the history of the church, such as Thomas Aquinas, have considered the image of God in mentally compromised people to be "practically nonexistent."[99] The result has been a degrading of people with disabilities — a denial of their dignity.[100] This has led to their exclusion from activities and communities in which they ought to be able to participate.[101] They have been viewed at best as "marred images," resulting in "perilous" outcomes.[102] So it was not surprising that when disabled people gathered at a symposium in Sheffield, England to compare their experiences, they repeatedly reported not being viewed or treated as "made in God's image" the way that other people are.[103] As one partic-

94. Hall, 1986: 108-9; Brink, 2001: 93.

95. Grey, 2003: 231. See Ruston, 2010: 388 for the way that John Locke's economic-abilities view of the image of God led to the "disinheritance of many" impoverished people during the Industrial Revolution.

96. Weinstein and Bell, 1982: 143.

97. So McFarland, 2005: 68.

98. Hall, 1986: 108-9; Brink, 2001: 93; Grey, 2003: 231.

99. Aquinas, 1947: pt. I, Q. 93, art. 8. See discussion in Hoekema, 1994: 37.

100. Primavesi, 2003: 187 (degrading); Hilkert, 2002: 7-8 (denial of dignity). Cf. Yong, 2007: 172.

101. Z. Moore, 2003: 106.

102. Reynolds, 2008: 177.

103. This symposium, a fruit of a World Council of Churches initiative, is discussed in Mayland, 1999; Macaskill, 2003: 211; Rogerson, 2010: 192.

ipant painfully tried to understand the source of the discrimination that she regularly experiences: "I became disabled — so was I once in God's image, but am no longer?"[104]

Her experience is one fruit of a long history in which some Christian leaders such as Emil Brunner have denied that normal protections apply to people with serious disabilities (e.g., those who are "grossly retarded") because of the compromise to God's image that has taken place.[105] Apparently Martin Luther even advocated drowning a "feebleminded" twelve-year-old child because his limited mental capacities appeared to evidence corruption of his reason and soul.[106] Such treatment of people with disabilities was characteristic of the culture in which the early church developed,[107] and has offered an influential pattern for the church's treatment of people with disabilities whenever Christians have reduced being in God's image to particular attributes. At particular risk have been people at the beginning and end of their lives. Some leaders have declared them to be void of God's image before they have developed rational attributes or after they have lost them.[108]

The Nazi holocaust is another powerful historical illustration of how the idea of humanity in God's image invites destructive misuse when people understand it to be referring to current human attributes (whether capacities, virtues, functions, or relationships). Adolf Hitler, as part of developing his approach to the weaker members of society in his 1927 book *Mein Kampf*, identifies the stronger members of society as "images of the Lord." In contrast, the weaker members for Hitler are mere "deformities" of that image to be "cleansed" from society.[109] Dietrich von Hildebrand

104. Davies-John, 2003: 124.

105. For Emil Brunner (1952: 57), the protection of being in the image of God "ceases where true human living ceases — on the borderline of imbecility or madness." Robert Wennberg (1985: 131), reflecting on whether all people are fully in God's image and so have full moral standing, concludes: "the grossly retarded . . . need not be assumed to possess a moral standing as full as that of a normal human adult."

106. Luther (1952: 387) reports this in a write-up of one of his famous "Table Talks." See discussions in Kanner, 1964: 7; Towns and Groff, 1972: 38-39.

107. As Seneca (1995: 32) affirmed in the first century: "We destroy abnormal offspring at birth; children, too, if they are born weak or deformed, we drown." Cf. discussion in Ferngren, 2009: 101.

108. Regarding children and the beginning of life, see Hall, 1986: 108-9; Z. Moore, 2003: 106. Regarding elderly people and the end of life, see Grey, 2003: 231; Fletcher, 1954: 218 (and the discussion of Fletcher in Verhey, 2003: 73).

109. Hitler, 1939: 606.

was one of a relative few in Germany at the time who recognized that it was precisely the biblical teaching that all of humanity continues in the *undeformed* image of God that offered the greatest defense against Hitler's destructive initiatives. As he wrote, soon after being forced to flee Nazi Germany in 1933: "All of Western Christian civilization stands and falls with the words of Genesis, 'God made man in His image.' "[110]

The problem, then, was understanding God's image in terms of something that can be deformed by sin or other causes, as can any human attribute. That understanding logically invited the conclusion that some people can be more in God's image than others and so warrant greater respect and protection. What resulted in Nazi Germany were categories of people who were *untermenschen* (subhuman), those in whom the attributes that constituted God's image were most deformed, marred, distorted, etc. They became the targets of Nazi efforts, first to eliminate people with disabilities or other frailties through neglect, forced sterilization, or killing. Later the focus turned to exterminating gypsies and Jews.[111]

Hildebrand was exceptional among Christians in his recognition of the importance of understanding God's image in a way that excluded the possibility of it being diminished. Sad, laments Cahill, has been "the devastating refusal by Christian theology to attribute the fullness of the imago Dei" to groups such as the millions exterminated by the Nazis.[112] Others have noted that the very same idea so captivating to Hitler — that God's image can be damaged — has continued to be influential up to the present, to the detriment of the weakest people in society.[113]

There were many influences that helped shape Hitler's thinking. One was the government-run program of forced sterilizations in the United States. During the Nuremburg Trials, that program was a primary precedent to which those defending the actions of Hitler and his followers appealed. They made special reference to the U.S. Supreme Court decision defending that program *(Buck v. Bell)*, written by Chief Justice Oliver Wendell Holmes Jr.[114] Another significant influence on Hitler was the

---

110. Von Hildebrand, 1934, as translated in Crosby, 2006: 9.

111. Davies-John, 2003: 121.

112. Cahill, 2006b: 58.

113. E.g., Yong, 2007: 173.

114. For the relevant Nuremburg documents, see http://buckvbell.com. For an analysis of the *Buck v. Bell* case, which set the stage for more than sixty thousand forced sterilizations in the U.S. (occurring as recently as the latter half of the twentieth century), see Lombardo, 2008.

government effort in the United States to suppress and exploit the Native American people, as portrayed in the novels of Karl May that Hitler devotedly read.[115]

Interestingly, one of the greatest champions of such governmental efforts was Harvard professor Oliver Wendell Holmes Sr. (father of the pro-eugenics Supreme Court justice). Holmes Sr. argued that Native Americans were not as fully "God's image" as the so-called "white man" was, and so it would be appropriate for the "red man" to be "rubbed out."[116] One widely influential source of this sort of outlook was John Locke's philosophy defining "what it is to be human — and therefore God-like" in terms of "the busy improvement of wealth-producing capacity." Native Americans did not appear to be very God-like and so "the result was again a violent one."[117] In recent decades, many commentators have decried mistakenly using the idea of creation in God's image to suggest that only "white humanity is humanity as God intended it to be" — a view that led to "the extermination of Amerindians."[118]

Native Americans in Latin America in many ways shared the predicament of Native Americans in the United States. Europeans teaching the creation of all people in God's image were nevertheless able to enslave these indigenous peoples by questioning their full humanity and thus their image-of-God status.[119] As Ruston observes, "The institutions of Spanish Catholicism predetermined what it meant to be human and God-like according to its own image."[120] Latino/Hispanic Studies professor Nelson Maldonado-Torres concurs that white European colonizers formulated a view of God that was like who they were. Then they concluded that those who were like God — who were in God's image — looked and acted like white European colonizers. Native Americans were thus subhuman and could be exploited.[121]

115. See Plischke, 1951; G. Brooks, 1967; Cracroft, 1967; and discussion in Berkhofer, 1978: 101.

116. O. Holmes, 1901: 298. See discussion in Gossett, 1997: 243; Gould, 1993: 87.

117. Ruston (2004: 283; 2010: 386-87) summarizes Locke's image-related influence in these terms.

118. E.g., Cone, 1986: 7; Bradley, 2010: 66-67.

119. Gutiérrez (1993: 293) notes that conqueror Juan Gines de Sepulveda, for example, felt justified in enslaving Native Americans because "they are as inferior to the Spaniards as ... monkeys to human beings." See discussion in Cahill, 2006b: 58.

120. Ruston, 2004: 283; 2010: 388-89.

121. Maldonado-Torres, 2008: 113-14. Similarly Teel, 2010: 43; Z. Moore, 2003: 106. D. Kelsey, 2009: v. 2, 1014-15 offers a related analysis of how people form their understanding of the image of Christ that in turn becomes normative for humanity.

As Teel summarizes after reviewing the extensive evidence in her book *Racism and the Image of God:*

> The notion of the human person as made in the image and likeness of God . . . [at times] has been disastrous: . . . [it has made it] dangerously easy to dismiss some individual persons and groups of people as less human than others. . . . This reasoning has had terrible consequences: it is the appalling history of . . . racism in all its forms.[122]

Part of the problem here was the self-serving bias toward the human traits that the colonizers saw in themselves and not in those they oppressed. However, that probably would not have been sufficient to high-jack the idea of creation in God's image had they not understood being in that image in terms of ways that people are presently like God. Once that mindset was in place, colonizers could read any of their own traits into God, including whiteness. For some, viewing God as white was too much of a stretch. However, even many of them were able to see such divine traits as reason and rulership as justification that they represented God's image on earth and that the "illiterates" they enslaved did not. In this way, observes Cahill, those in power were granted the license "to colonize and exploit other groups deemed not to reflect God's image or not to reflect it in the same way or to the same extent."[123] The result of such exploitation, according to Teel, has been "the death and enslavement of millions and the imperialistic domination of millions more."[124]

Victims of this massive abuse include not only Native Americans but also enslaved Africans and their descendants. According to the research of Christian ethicist Kyle Fedler, "[D]uring America's early years, many theologians, both northern and southern, held that black men and women were not made in the image of God."[125] Cahill adds that the full problem was actually even greater, because denying that some people had any connection with the image flowed from the view that God's image is variable. Due to sin or other factors, it might not be present at all in some people, or at least might not be fully present in them. This way of thinking led to

---

122. Teel, 2010: 2-3, 43, 166. Also Hilkert, 2002: 7-8.

123. Cahill, 2006a: 211. Verduin (1970: 42-43) calls the gospel they promoted a "truncated gospel" because it lacked the foundation of all people as created in God's image.

124. Teel, 2010: 166.

125. Fedler, 2006: 82.

the oppression of huge categories of people whom some judged to lack "the fullness of the *imago Dei.*"[126]

By 1853, the problem had become sufficiently widespread that some prominent figures in the church such as William Hosmer, author of *Slavery and the Church,* recognized the need to address it directly. They were deeply concerned that the idea of humanity "made in the image of God . . . [w]as patronizing such a shameless crime as slavery."[127] Shortly before that in an address to the Presbyterian Church, national church leader James Thornwell had similarly deplored efforts to deny enslaved Africans the image-of-God status of white people — efforts denying them "the same humanity in which we glory as the image of God."[128] Nevertheless, soon thereafter even someone as prominent as Oliver Wendell Holmes Sr. was still accepting the idea that "the white race" was "more like God's image" than "the black race."[129]

Some of those who invoked God's image in support of slavery appealed to white people's intuitions that white bodies and characteristics were more godlike than black people's.[130] Others appealed to the idea that being in God's image was about traits that distinguish people from animals and that African slaves had certain traits closer to animals than to what constituted being in God's image.[131] Still others, in language similar to that which colonizers of Native Americans used, appealed to divine traits like reason and rulership in "whites" as evidence that they better represented God's image on earth than did the illiterate people they enslaved.[132]

Ironically, a prominent way of opposing these views ultimately contributed to the plausibility of invoking God's image in support of slavery. That opposing viewpoint maintained that the evils of slavery "degrade the image of God in man, stunting or corrupting the individual's capacities."[133] This way of speaking reinforced the ideas both that God's image is a matter

---

126. Cahill, 2006b: 58-59.

127. Hosmer, 1853: 122.

128. Thornwell, 1850: 11. See discussion in Jenkins, 1935: 230.

129. In an address delivered in 1855; see O. Holmes, 1901: 298.

130. See analysis in Copeland, 2010: 27, 51; Teel, 2010: 127. Ruchames, 1967: 272 notes "the white man's enslavement of the African Negro, as a being obviously different from himself."

131. So D. Davis, 2008: 32. For the European roots of this outlook, see Teel, 2010: 22. Unlike white slaveholders who were in God's image/likeness, "blacks were described as a people created by nature in the likeness of beasts" — Bruns, 1971: 45; Scott, 2008: 95.

132. See D. Davis, 2008: 54; Teel, 2010: 43, 166.

133. D. Davis, 2008: 253.

of present human capacities and that sin can corrupt such capacities. Once people accepted the idea of a corruptible image, the idea of humanity's original creation in God's image was no longer sufficient to uphold human dignity. Sin could considerably weaken that image, and thus the protection it afforded.

Perverting the idea of God's image in order to demean and oppress African Americans in the United States by no means ended with the Civil War. In 1900 Charles Carroll's influential book *"The Negro a Beast" or "In the Image of God"* appeared. There Carroll argued that the first affirmation in the title was true, rather than the second: "If the White was created 'in the image of God,' then the Negro was made after some other model." Accordingly, he explained, with the protection of God's image irrelevant, "extermination" of black people (and for related reasons all nonwhite peoples) was reasonable.[134]

This book received exceptional support from its publisher, the American Book and Bible House, with the publisher including the following notice in the book itself:

In placing this book entitled *"The Negro a Beast" or "In the Image of God"* upon the American market, we do so knowing that there will be many learned men who will take issue with us, but while we are fully convinced of this, we are also convinced that when this book is read and its contents duly weighed and considered in an intelligent and prayerful manner, that it will be to the minds of the American people like unto the voice of God from the clouds appealing unto Paul on his way to Damascus.

There was such wide circulation of the book that a statewide church denominational gathering found it necessary to address its unusually great influence.[135] Moreover, Carroll's book stimulated the writing of at least three entire books to engage with its claims, one of which observed that "the book is sold all over the country . . . and many are led to believe its arguments unanswerable. . . . [These arguments] must prove disastrous."[136] The Jim Crow Museum of Racist Memorabilia at Ferris State University

---

134. Carroll, 1969: 90. 311. For further description, see McKitrick, 1963: 94.

135. On the Texas Baptist response to the book, see Jenkins, 1935: ch. 5; Posey, 1952: ch. 7; and discussion in Reimers, 1965: 28.

136. Eastman, 1905: 14-15. The other two books were Armistead, 1903 and Schell, 1901.

25

suggests that the teaching of Carroll's book on the deficiency of God's image in African Americans turned out to play a significant role in fostering the thousands of lynchings of African Americans between 1882 and 1951.[137] Martin Luther King Jr. later acknowledged the influence of this line of thinking and expressed particular exasperation over it.[138]

The publication of an edited and updated version of this book in 1967 by a different publisher, under the title *In the Image of God,* evidences the persistent influence of this book and the image-of-God argument that is its central thrust. Another exceptional affirmation of support from the publisher opens this updated edition: "The Publisher's Announcement, made in the year 1900, is as germane today as when first released and is fittingly applicable to the present endeavor to edit and reprint the salient points of the original publication. It is, therefore, being quoted here. . . ." The book then ironically goes on to insist that "to properly evaluate the causes of racial problems, one must rightly understand what God means by saying 'Let us make man in our image, after our likeness' (Gen. 1:26)."[139] Carroll's book provides compelling evidence that having an accurate understanding of the image of God is indeed crucial — and that misunderstanding God's image can foster rather than alleviate racial problems.

Some of the refutations of the book fell short because they shared the same starting assumption as the book itself: the idea that being in God's image is about current human attributes. One refutation argues that African Americans really have more attributes than Carroll credits to them.[140] Another argues that African Americans measure up to "whites" better when different attributes are recognized as more central to creation in God's image.[141] However, by leaving unchallenged the idea that being in God's image is about current attributes, the most persuasive aspect of Carroll's book was allowed to stand: only those who sufficiently manifest the traits, capabilities, etc. that constitute being in God's image warrant respect and protection. Two years after the 1967 edition, a third publisher issued a version of the book which was simply a republication of the original.[142] As recently as 2012, still another publisher has republished both Carroll's

---

137. See http://www.ferris.edu/jimcrow/brute.
138. King, 1961b: 211. According to Wills, 2009: 22, King saw this as the "prevailing logic of . . . counterabolitionist thought."
139. *In the Image,* 1967: 1.
140. Eastman, 1905: 39-40.
141. Armistead, 1903: 509-15.
142. Carroll, 1969.

book and one of the refutation books.[143] Moreover, the "Biblical-Truth" website continues to promote Carroll's message under the title "In the Image of God," alongside other recommended documents such as the U.S. Constitution.[144]

Against this backdrop has arisen the so-called "Christian Identity" movement, which developed significant and increasing popularity during the latter half of the twentieth century through such groups as the Ku Klux Klan, Aryan Nations, and CSA ("Covenant, Sword, and Arm of the Lord").[145] People associated with this movement give multiple accounts of why only white people are in God's image. For example, some say that certain races are related to creatures that pre-date Adam (one of Carroll's arguments). Others maintain that certain races descend from Cain, who was the offspring of Eve and Satan and so was "made in the image and likeness of Satan."[146] The common theme, as CSA puts it, is that only white people "walk in [God's] image upon this earth."[147] The Christian Identity movement is another graphic example of how invoking the image of God can lead to atrocities, as Klan lynchings and Aryan Nations' celebrations of racially motivated murders illustrate.[148]

Not surprisingly, then, African Americans who spoke more recently at a symposium on the image of God have directly connected people's understanding of being in God's image with the racism they have experienced personally.[149] When some people questioned whether it was valid to make this connection, they insisted that the connection is real.[150] So have commentators who have studied the matter on a much larger scale. In their view, some contemporary societies accord African Americans no more than a diminished image-of-God status at best,[151] leading directly to their "degrading" and "marginalizing."[152]

143. Ulan Press has republished both Carroll's and Eastman's books.

144. See the "literature" section of http://biblical-truth.info/Main.htm.

145. Zeskind, 1986: 7; Abanes, 1996: 154-55; Walters, 2001: 12.

146. Gayman, 1994: 210. See discussion in Walters, 2001: 15-16. On the historical roots of this idea, see Ruchames, 1967: 257; Scott, 2008: 95.

147. The Covenant, 1995: 329-30. See discussion in Zeskind, 1986: 45.

148. Abanes (1996: 166-68) describes an Aryan Nations publication that celebrates members involved in "murderous exploits" as "Aryan Heroes" in the footsteps of "Heroes of the Confederate States" and "Heroes of the Third Reich."

149. Rogerson, 2010: 192.

150. Mayland, 2003: 14.

151. Maston, 1959: 7; Teel, 2010: 109.

152. Primavesi, 2003: 187 (degrading); Grey, 2003: 231 (marginalizing).

THE HUMAN AND DIVINE CONTEXT

The misuse of God's image here follows a pattern similar to that in the case of Native Americans. People see African Americans simultaneously as subhuman and not really/fully in God's image. Accordingly, the respect due to those in God's image does not apply to them.[153] As communications professional Joan Harrell describes the predicament, "negative images cannot help but affect how some American Christians interpret the meaning of Imago Dei in relationship to people of color."[154]

What makes the image of God so susceptible to manipulation in this way is the common tendency to think of being in God's image in terms of having attributes today (i.e., traits, virtues, functions, capacities, etc.) that are like God's attributes. To the degree that one's attributes fall short of the way that God intends human attributes to be, God's image is supposedly damaged or deficient. The cause of that damage most commonly is sin, directly or indirectly. As with other things in life, a more-damaged image is not worth as much as a less-damaged image.

What complicates this scenario, however, is that sin disposes people to see themselves (and those like them) as better than they are, and to see other people who are very different from them as the ones who are damaged. "Damaged" means "fallen short of God's standards for humanity," and God's standards reflect God's own attributes. Therefore, God's standards (i.e., God's image) become precisely what one has and others lack. God has made humanity in the divine image, but as biblical scholar Gosnell Yorke explains, "we inevitably end up, to varying degrees, making God in our image as well — be it consciously or subconsciously."[155] Voltaire put this succinctly: "If God has made us in his image, we have returned him the favor."[156] Being aware of this tendency does not necessarily protect against it, in that Voltaire himself appears to have looked down on "blacks" on the grounds that they did not image God well.[157]

When something as peripheral to the common essence of humanity

153. So Verduin, 1970: 37; Bradley, 2010: 66-67, 129 (drawing on Cone, 1979: 120-21; 1986: 7).

154. Harrell, 2008: 15.

155. Yorke, 1995: 3. See elaboration in Z. Moore, 2003: 106 and Bradley, 2010: 132. Cf. the analysis in D. Kelsey, 2009: v. 2, 1014-15 where the image of Christ is in view.

156. Voltaire, 1880.

157. See Cohen, 2003: 86, 88, who sees a statement Voltaire wrote in a fictional work (Voltaire, 1961) as reflecting not just a view held in his day, but his own view as well: "Our wise men have said that man was created in the image of God. Now here is a lovely image of the Divine Maker — a flat and black nose with little or hardly any intelligence."

as a particular skin color is in view, the problem with this way of thinking is evident to many.[158] However, the tendency is to argue in response that a spurned skin color is really as godlike as any other skin color.[159] This response leaves intact the notion that being in God's image is about the degree to which people line up on some sort of traits/capabilities scale. It is that very notion that opens the door to viewing and treating some individuals and groups as better than others. Even powerful anti-slavery arguments such as John Wesley's, which maintained that slavery dehumanizes the slaveholder most, kept the debate in the realm of who is least human (least manifesting God's image).[160] They could have instead questioned whether God's image is something that can be damaged by sin and thus can vary in degree from person to person. Not having done so, as formidable a theology as that of Wesley's contemporary Jonathan Edwards and Edwards's Puritan theological tradition was able to condone some form of slavery — a development lamented by hip-hop artist and scholar alike.[161]

In an analogous way, otherwise formidable theologies have also led to support for the demeaning and oppression of women. Men, with their "superior" godlike attributes such as reasoning and rulership (without serious regard for the degree to which those are socially developed rather than inherent), have often determined that men are the norm of humanity. They are the ones truly in the image of God.[162] Women, then, in this outlook are at best deficient in terms of God's image. Many theologians have gone so far as to suggest that women lack God's image entirely, perhaps having

158. E.g., see Ruchames, 1967: 272; Ellis, 1996: 43; Bradley, 2010: 127.

159. Fields, 2001: 100 and Bradley, 2010: 173-74 observe this in much of black liberation theology. Teel, 2010: 163 discusses some problems with this approach.

160. For Wesley's views of God's image as holiness and love, see his "The Image of God" (J. Wesley, 1985k) and *Thoughts Upon Slavery* (J. Wesley, 2011), and discussion in Scott, 2008: 98-99.

161. Hip-hop artist Propaganda, in the song "Precious Puritans" on his 2012 album *Excellent,* conveys the distrust that some African Americans have for Puritan theology, despite its many strengths, because of its contamination by an understanding of God's image in which there are in effect "multiple images." (Some people are more in God's image than others — thereby opening the door to justifying slavery.) In the words of the song, addressed to those promoting Puritan theology without sufficient attention to its image-of-God concept: "Your precious Puritans . . . taught a gospel that says God had multiple images in mind when he created us in it. Their fore-destined salvation contains a contentment in the stage they were given, which is to be owned by your forefathers' superior, image-bearing face — says your precious Puritans." See discussion in Bradley, 2013: 8.

162. See Carr, 1993: 14; Gonzalez, 2007: 161.

lost it in "the Fall" (the Fall, as described in Genesis 3, being Adam's and Eve's first disobedience of God and resulting separation from God).[163] Consequently, according to such theologians, women are not really human.[164]

As Yale professor Margaret Farley observes, "[N]umerous studies have already documented the tendency of Christian theology to . . . [refuse] to ascribe to women the fullness of the *imago dei.*"[165] Theologian Stanley Grenz and others see this problem "throughout church history."[166] It has had quite a destructive impact on women. A consultation of the World Council of Churches in the late twentieth century concluded that "the doctrine of God's image *(imago Dei)* has by tradition been a source of oppression and discrimination against women."[167] Many commentators since then have echoed their assessment.[168] This image-related oppression of women has taken the form of exclusion, exploitation, degrading, indignity, marginalization, and violence.[169]

As will become evident below, there are plenty of Christian leaders through the ages who have explicitly affirmed that women are not — or are not fully — in God's image. The authors of the Bible, however, are not among them. In Chapters 3-4 we will be considering what Genesis 2–3 and 1 Corinthians 11 contribute to an understanding of a missing, lost, or damaged image of God. To anticipate: they simply do not speak to that issue, though they have provided fertile opportunities for people to read into them various theological and cultural assumptions.

Genesis 2–3 addresses many important matters, though there is no mention of the Genesis 1 image-of-God status of humanity. Nevertheless, from an early date, some people have altered the meaning of Genesis 1 by considering the material in Genesis 2–3 to be contradictory to it rather than complementary. This approach has allowed people to choose one teaching and reject another — a veritable invitation to import personal

163. See Børresen, 1995: 187; Fedler, 2006: 82; Gonzalez, 2007: 28.

164. For a historical review of such theologians, see A. Schmidt, 1989: 69-95 and discussion in M. O'Neill, 1993: 148.

165. Farley, 1975: 629, citing: Daly, 1975; Tavard, 1973; Ruether, 1974.

166. Grenz, 2001: 290. Also Farley, 1976: 166; Cahill, 2006b: 58-59.

167. See "Image of God Source of Oppression, Says Consultation," 1981: 77; and discussion in Hilkert, 2002: 4.

168. E.g., Stark, 2007: 237 ("destructive effects"); Teel, 2010: 43 ("terrible consequences"); Brink, 2001: 93 ("drastic results").

169. Hall, 1986: 109 (oppression); Macaskill, 2003: 211 (exclusion); Cahill, 2006a: 211 (exploitation); Primavesi, 2003: 187 (degrading); Hilkert, 2002: 7-8 (denial of dignity); Garner, 2007: 128 (marginalization); Z. Moore, 2003: 104 (violence).

assumptions and preferences rather than holding different teachings in tension. Even the translators who produced the historically influential Greek version of the Old Testament, the Septuagint, display this tendency to adjust the meaning of one text in favor of another. Whether intentionally or not, they appear to have slightly altered the meaning of the Genesis text at several points in a way that encourages reading the inferiority of women into the image-of-God affirmations of Genesis 1.[170]

As for Paul in 1 Corinthians 11:7, he affirms that males are God's image and glory. Then, in order to explain how women are different from men, he adds that women are men's glory. What it means to Paul for women to be men's glory is an interesting topic, as is the topic of what men are for women. However, as many have noted,[171] Paul says nothing here about woman not being God's image or God's glory (though some read that into Paul's statement here[172]). At most there is a contrast between different ways of manifesting glory, as Chapter 3 will explain.

Image and glory are related but quite distinct concepts (see multiple discussions in Chs. 2, 6, and 7). Conflating them leads to the position that Paul teaches that women are the "image of men"[173] (whereas men are the image of God) — which is not the actual language in Paul's text. Those who understand Paul to be denying God's image to women understandably complain that Paul is not doing justice but rather doing violence to biblical teaching.[174] He is supposedly creating a theological quagmire that has brought the image-of-God concept under heavy attack.[175] Such harsh charges are not surprising in light of history, for the stakes turned out to be quite high. Where the protection of being in God's image was removed, women became more vulnerable to serious oppression.

After the first century, among the earliest evidence of a connection

---

170. See detailed documentation in Loader, 2004: 57; cf. Clifford, 1995: 179.

171. Scholars who derive from the Bible a range of views concerning roles of women in the church and home acknowledge that Paul does not deny that women are in God's image here. E.g., see Ware, 2002: 20; S. Wright, 2003: 35; Ruston, 2004: 281; Fee, 1987: 516; and many others cited on this point in Chapter 2.

172. E.g., many of the historical figures highlighted below. Also Kümmel, 1963: 69; Conzelmann, 1975: 186; Cook, 1975: 92; Beckwith, 1978: 57; Børresen, 1982: 360; E. Ross, 1990: 97, 100; J. Barr, 1993: 165-67; Ruether, 1995: 275; Arx, 2002: 530 (citing other examples); Jastram, 2004: 32-33; Gonzalez, 2007: 15. As van Vliet, 2009: 61 observes, "the stumbling block upon which nearly everyone tripped was 1 Corinthians 11:7."

173. As in McCasland, 1950: 86; Wilson, 1973: 358; Tavard, 1973;29; Bray, 2001: 575.

174. See Schnelle, 1996: 101 (justice); McCasland, 1950: 86 (violence).

175. See Hays, 1997: 186 (quagmire); G. Peterson, 1996: 222 (attack).

between the image of God and second-class status for women is the writing of Tertullian at the beginning of the third century. Tertullian suggests that man rather than woman is God's image, and that woman "destroyed so easily God's image, man."[176] The implications of this outlook become more apparent late in the fourth century in the writings of Ambrosiaster, Diodore of Tarsus, and Chrysostom. Ambrosiaster explicitly maintains that women are not God's image, and his influence helped ensure that women would receive inferior status in canon law.[177] Diodore and Chrysostom from the school of Antioch similarly deny image-of-God status to women, thus maintaining that God has placed women, like everything else in the created order, under the dominion of men.[178]

Early in the fifth century, Augustine finds a way to connect women with God's image, so he is not as dismissive of women as some of those who addressed the matter before him.[179] However, he in effect divides life into two realms — the life of the spirit in relation to God, and the life of worldly matters. In the former realm women and men are both in God's image; in the latter only men, in themselves, can be so. Because of Augustine's huge theological influence throughout the centuries, his conclusion that women are not fully in God's image has fostered viewing women as inferior to men in church and society.[180]

This inferiority has to do with both mind and body. Augustine invokes women's supposedly rational inferiority as manifested in the temporal realm to explain how Paul both maintains the truth of Genesis 1 and "assigns the image of God only to the man, and not to the woman."[181] Not only did this view hinge on a dubious understanding of Paul on this particular point (see above), but it also promoted the idea that women per se did not have the same rational ability as men to exercise responsibility even in societal

176. Tertullian, 2002:bk. I, ch. 1. See discussion in Ruether, 1974: 157.

177. On this view of women in Ambrosiaster, see D. Hunter, 1992 and discussion in Ruston, 2004: 280; Matter, 2007: 204.

178. Diodore, 1860: 1564-65; Chrysostom, 1862: 73 (though also in homilies 3 and 9). See discussion in Tavard, 1973: 85; Hilkert, 1995: 192; and the fuller analysis in Horowitz, 1979.

179. So Lloyd, 1984: 30-31; van Bavel, 1989: 281-82, 286; Hilkert, 1995: 192-93; Meconi, 2000: 47-62; Matter, 2000: 170-74; Stark, 2007: 216.

180. See Clanton, 1990: 41; A. Schmidt, 1989: 83; Stark, 2007: 223; Bowery, 2007: 91; and the long-term impact described in Lloyd, 1984.

181. Augustine, 1963: bk. XII, ch. 19; Stark, 2007: 232. Regarding Paul, Augustine (1963: bk. XII, ch. 12) writes: "The Apostle . . . assigns the image of God only to the man, and not to the woman."

matters.[182] Perhaps reflecting the dualistic Manichean philosophy (the inferiority of the physical) that he held before conversion to Christ, Augustine tended to associate women and women's bodies with emotion, sexuality, and other nonrational traits that he considered unreflective of God.[183]

If a woman was to be seen in conjunction with God's image, it was only derivatively and in association with a man. As Augustine scholar Judith Stark summarizes: "Only when woman is joined to the man is she considered to be the image of God, just as only when the lower intellect is joined to the higher is it considered to be the image of God. . . . The imago status of women is acknowledged, but only after they have paid the price" of having to detach from their bodies and their sexuality.[184] Augustine, then, encouraged the basic approach to God's image that this image does not characterize all people equally, due to certain differences in their traits and capacities. The door was open wide for image-of-God teaching to perpetuate rather than undermine oppressive societal hierarchies, especially where single women were concerned.[185]

During the centuries from Augustine to Aquinas, there is recurring evidence that such views persisted. Sixth-century archbishop Isadore taught that women were in the image of men rather than in the image of God.[186] Since being in God's image was central to being human, it was inevitable that some would come to question the full humanity of women. At the second council of Macon in 585, a bishop did just that.[187] By the twelfth century, Augustinian views continued to echo in such master teachers as Gratian (women are not God's image), Peter Abelard (women are the image of men rather than of God), and Ernaud of Bonneval (women have a lower rational capacity than men).[188] The serious implications of such teaching became clearer in church law as contained in the Decretum of 1140, which reads:

182. See Gonzalez, 2007: 38-40 and Børresen's (1982: 361) analysis of Augustine, 1963: bk. XII, ch. 7 and 1982: ch. 3, sect. 23.

183. Farley, 1976: 167-68; Børresen, 1982: 361; Clanton, 1990: 41.

184. Stark, 2007: 228 (cf. 216, 227, 235), discussing Augustine, 1963: bk. XII, ch. 7. Similarly Ruether, 1974: 156; 2007: 55-56; A. Schmidt, 1989: 134.

185. Oduyoye, 1995: 5 develops this critique. For its broader implications, see K. Power, 1996 (esp. 221-22); Stark, 2007: 235.

186. See A. Schmidt's (1989: 83-84) commentary on Isadore's *Sententiae* 10:4-6.

187. Hefele, 1877: 41. See discussion in A. Schmidt, 1989: 84.

188. See commentaries by Hilkert (1995: 192), Horowitz, 1979: 177-80, and A. Schmidt (1989: 84) on Gratian's *Decretum*, Abelard's *Introductio ad Theologiam,* and Ernaud's *Hexameron.*

Women were drawn from man, who has God's jurisdiction as if he were God's vicar, because he has the image of the One God. Therefore woman is not made in God's image. . . . Neither can she teach, nor be a witness, nor give a guarantee, nor sit in judgement.[189]

In the Middle Ages, women who refused to conform to such mandates "ended up at the stake, burnt for being witches."[190]

In the thirteenth century, Thomas Aquinas takes up the question of women's image-of-God status in order to refute the idea of some in his day that women are not at all in God's image. However, he does so in a way reminiscent of Augustine, by acknowledging that in the temporal sphere women are not as fully God's image as men are.[191] In fact, drawing on Aristotelian arguments for the inferiority of women's souls as well as bodies, Aquinas characterizes a female as a defective, undeveloped male.[192] Accordingly, he advises: Except in the area of procreation, "man can be more efficiently helped by another man."[193] As Roman Catholic ethicist Margaret Farley concludes, during the time of Aquinas "the inferior fate of women was more and more theologically sealed."[194]

By the mid-sixteenth century, somewhat similar categories were still in place, as indicated by the writings of John Calvin. Like Aquinas, Calvin was arguing against those who maintained that women were in no sense God's image. However, like many before him, Calvin also distinguished two aspects or spheres of God's image. One had to do with "spiritual and eternal life" and the other had to do with "the political order." In the first sphere for Calvin, men and women were both in God's image, but in the latter sphere, only men were.[195] Thus Calvin could say that "the woman was created in the image of God, albeit in a secondary degree."[196] The practical implications of this were considerable for the public realm in which so

189. For text and discussion, see Oduyoye, 1982: 49.

190. Oduyoye, 1982: 49.

191. Aquinas, 1947: pt. I, Q. 93, art. 4-5. For discussion see Gonzalez, 2007: 43-44.

192. Aquinas, 1947: pt. I, Q. 92, art. 1. Cf. pt. II-II, Q. 70, art. 2 and discussion in Børresen, 1982: 362-63.

193. Aquinas, 1947: pt. II, Q. 156, art. 1. See discussion in Lloyd, 1984: 35.

194. Farley, 1976: 168.

195. Calvin, 1960a: bk. I, ch. 15, sec. 4. For analysis, see J. Thompson, 1988: 131; Ruether, 2007: 55; van Vliet, 2009: 28.

196. See Calvin's commentary on Genesis 2:18 and discussion in DeBoer, 1976; J. Thompson, 1988: 125, 143.

much of life takes place. Explains Calvin, "Any unmarried man . . . is the head. Of whom? Of women, for we must not pay attention to this only within a household, but within the whole order that God has established in this world."[197]

In late sixteenth- and early seventeenth-century Europe, again the logical implications of women not being fully in God's image began to surface. According to some, lacking the fullness of God's image entailed not being fully human — meaning that women need not be respected and protected as much as men. In Germany, renowned author Valens Acidalius published a significant work arguing just that. The public debates it sparked, its print run of 174 years, and the way it was widely imitated and plagiarized testify to its popularity.[198] Years later the famous British poet and chaplain to King James I, John Donne, captured a similar sentiment in one of his poems: "Man to God's image, Eve to man's was made. Nor find we that God breathed a soul in her."[199]

In light of these and many other illustrations, it is no wonder that Julia O'Faolain and Lauro Martines have titled their book about women in the last two millennia *Not in God's Image*.[200] Moreover, women continue to bear the brunt of not being considered as fully in God's image as men are, as a series of consultations in Europe has discovered. The testimony of numerous women from various settings confirmed the research findings prior to these events — that "worldwide . . . many women are oppressed and marginalized in our churches because of an underlying belief (usually unspoken but occasionally voiced openly) that women are secondary and . . . not as completely in the image of God."[201] Latino scholar Rubén Rodríguez echoes that "many in the church still have a difficult time accepting that women . . . share equally in the imago Dei" and that this is "the greatest challenge facing U.S. Latino/a theology today."[202] Denying women full image-of-God status has fostered "the deep alienation that many Christian

---

197. See Calvin's sermon on 1 Corinthians 11:4-10, as translated in DeBoer, 1976: 245; also J. Thompson, 1988: 142.

198. Fleischer, 1981: 107-20; A. Schmidt, 1989: 84-85.

199. For text and analysis of the poem "To the Countess of Huntingdon," see Donne, 1896b; A. Schmidt, 1989: 85.

200. O'Faolain and Martines, 1973.

201. Mayland, 2003: 11, 14; Rogerson, 2010: 192. For a still-influential example of teaching that women are not fully God's image, see Hodge, 1976: 210.

202. Rodríguez, 2008: 172.

35

women feel toward Christianity as a religion that fails to affirm . . . their female humanity as 'image of God.' "[203]

What warrants special notice here is the way of thinking about God's image that has led to harmfully prioritizing men over women in all spheres of temporal existence. The key has most often been the idea that God's image can be damaged or lost. Admittedly, some people have attributed maleness itself to God so comprehensively that it is impossible to conceive of women as created in God's image.[204] However, more often people have defined being in God's image in terms of attributes that tend to render men more godlike than women, at least in many cultural settings.[205] The problem consistently has to do with understanding God's image as something that can characterize some people more than others because there is less image where a person manifests certain attributes to a lesser degree. Such diminishing can be due either to sin or to God's intention. We have already noted a similar dynamic leading to the mistreatment of impoverished and disabled people, the Nazi holocaust, attempted exterminations of Native American groups, and oppression of enslaved Africans and their descendants.

A similar dynamic is at work regarding humanity's relationship with the natural world. Again, much of this discussion will have to await Chapter 5, which addresses God's intention for those in the divine image to "rule" over creation. However, in sum, where people have understood being in God's image as humanity's present ability to rule over creation, some have seen a license to exploit whatever is not in God's image.[206] Where people have seen rationality as a central aspect of being in God's image, some have claimed absolute power to denigrate whatever is not

---

203. Hilkert, 1995: 203.

204. See analysis in Farley, 1976: 167; E. Johnson, 1984: 464; Meyer-Wilmes, 1987: 96-97; Z. Moore, 2003: 106; Fernandez, 2004: 122-23. For the resulting "domination" of men over "deficient or defective" women, see P. Hunter, 1993: 190-91; Gonzalez, 2007: 86. The situation becomes even more problematic when Jesus' maleness is seen as normative for all who would be in God's image — see Hilkert, 1995: 202; D. Kelsey, 2009: v. 2, 1014-15; T. Peters, 2010: 220.

205. See analysis in Hall, 1986: 109; Sherlock, 1996: 87; van Huyssteen, 2006: 127; Gonzalez, 2007: x; Teel, 2010: 43.

206. As discussed in Hilkert, 2002: 7-8; Cahill, 2006a: 211; 2006b: 58-59; Garner, 2007: 128. Lynn White (1967: 1205) advanced an influential thesis that the idea of humanity "made in God's image" inclined many people to believe "that it is God's will that man exploit nature for his proper ends." See Ch. 5 for an explanation of how this belief flowed from a misunderstanding of God's image.

in God's image.[207] That God's image could be invoked to justify such behavior cries out for a careful biblical investigation of whether or not being in God's image really consists of current attributes such as rulership and reason.

Such an investigation must await later chapters in the present work. However, if being in God's image is indeed rooted in current human attributes — or in anything that can vary among people because it is changeable due to sin — history teaches an important lesson. The idea that humanity is created in God's image will not just be a source of great liberation, it will continue to invite terrible devastation. It will be fair to say regarding this idea what some have said regarding religion in general: It is "high voltage; it can energize much or electrocute many."[208]

Why Such Disagreement

Contradictory views of what it means for humanity to be in God's image have long flourished. Before attempting to clarify the meaning of this idea, it will be helpful to unpack why there has been so much disagreement surrounding it. The problem is partly due to expecting too little of the concept and partly due to expecting too much. Those inclined to expect too little devote insufficient attention to it, either because it seems to receive relatively little attention in the Bible or because it seems to receive relatively little definition in the Bible. Those inclined to expect too much of it read all sorts of theological and cultural ideas into it without sufficient biblical warrant.

Little Attention in the Bible

Some people do not give humanity's creation in God's image careful consideration because they see relatively few direct references to it in the Bible. While their observation is true, the conclusion they draw from it does not necessarily follow. The particular places where references to God's image appear are unusually significant in the Bible.[209] The first appear-

---

207. Regarding absolute power, see Primavesi, 2003: 189; regarding denigration, see Hall, 1986: 108-9.

208. Stackhouse (2005: 27) attributes this expression to George Williams.

209. For more on this observation, see Berkouwer, 1975: 67 and Grenz, 2001: 14.

ance, in Genesis 1, is at the very creation of humanity, where being in God's image stands out as a key statement about who human beings are. Extraordinarily, in the space of two verses there are three statements of the divine intention and action to create humanity in God's image. This is not an incidental matter but something that readers of the Bible are to notice and remember.[210]

The image again appears in Genesis at two other pivotal points in human history. At the start of Genesis 5, the Fall has occurred, radically affecting humanity. Also the genealogies are about to begin, specifically identifying humanity. For humanity again to be freshly identified as being in God's image at this pivotal point is particularly significant. Then early in Genesis 9, right after the flood wipes out virtually all of the human race and humanity receives a fresh (albeit still fallen) start, humanity's image-of-God status yet again appears in order to reiterate what is irremovable from who human beings are. This is the place where God characterizes murder as a uniquely destructive action that one human being takes against another. God's justification for the serious punishment that murder warrants focuses squarely on humanity's creation in God's image.[211]

A fourth pivotal point in human history is the coming of Jesus Christ as God incarnate. Not only does the New Testament identify Christ as God's image (see Ch. 2), but humanity's dignity and destiny are also freshly defined in terms of that image (see Chs. 6 and 7). At the same time, both Pauline and non-Pauline books of the New Testament reaffirm humanity's creational association with God's image (e.g., 1 Cor. 11:7; James 3:9). Accordingly, the vast amount of Christian literature devoted to the topic of God's image is not surprising.[212] No less surprising is the significance that much Jewish literature accords to God's image.[213] The passages in the

---

210. S. Holmes, 2005: 318 and Smail, 2006: 43-44 develop this theme.

211. Sherlock, 1996: 31 emphasizes the importance of the post-Fall and post-flood locations in the Bible, whereas Bray, 1991: 201 and Gardoski, 2007: 6 emphasize the locations where the Bible explains the initial genealogies and the significance of murder.

212. See the "Resources Cited" section at the end of this book for a portion of that literature.

213. George Moore's *Judaism* (1944: 447) discusses Jewish perspective on this topic, concluding that humanity's status as created in God's image becomes in "Jewish thought . . . a universal principle of conduct." For example, R. Simeon b. Azzai considered due reverence for people because of their image-related status to be "the most comprehensive principle in the Law" (see Laws, 1993, 155-56). For more examples and analysis, see Scroggs, 1966: 68; Altmann, 1968: 235.

Bible that address God's image may not be large in number, but they are huge in significance and warrant careful attention.

There are "very powerful reasons" why a detailed development of humanity's creation in God's image is not explicitly present in the Old Testament.[214] As Old Testament scholar Gerhard von Rad observes, "The central point in OT anthropology is that man is dust and ashes before God."[215] Against that backdrop, any idea that might be construed — even if misunderstood — as implying the actual likeness of people to God would be confusing. What is striking is that reference to humanity's existence in God's image appears at all.[216]

The limited number of references, without much detail and at key points in the biblical text, suggest an attempt to affirm a core idea or two here rather than suggesting that people and God are actually alike in particular ways. To a certain degree, the lack of detail is not surprising. God is largely ineffable, so it is not surprising that God's image would be difficult to describe as well.[217] As fourth-century church leaders Epiphanius and Gregory pondered the answer to the question "What is the full meaning of God's image?," they concluded: "God alone knows" it.[218] On the other hand, there is a strategic attempt in the Bible to use the image of God concept as a "gravitational force" or "seedbed" to anchor and stimulate some understanding of humanity.[219]

As Chapter 3 will discuss, being in the image/likeness of God involves humanity's *connection with God,* which commentators have variously described in terms of "covenant," "calling," etc.[220] It also has something to do with the *reflection of God* — with God's intention for humanity to be the "crowning glory" of creation, reflecting certain aspects of who God is and what God does.[221] For the Bible's authors, how much people *actually* are unlike God is painfully visible. However, God's *intention* that people

214. J. Barr, 1968: 13. See also Kraynak, 2008: 74.

215. Rad, 1964b: 390.

216. Rad, 1964b: 390; Grenz, 2001: 185.

217. So Rad, 1964b: 392; Thielicke, 1966: 159-60 (who draws upon Martin Luther).

218. The statement is from Epiphanius, in his *Haereses* III:1, as discussed in Maloney, 1973: 188. Gregory of Nyssa (1972: 553) put it similarly: "The true answer to this question, indeed, perhaps only the very Truth knows." See also Chafer, 1947: v. 2, 162 (who draws upon John Howe).

219. Van Huyssteen, 2006: 124 (gravitational force); Mathews, 1995: 163 (seedbed).

220. Shepherd, 1988: 1020 (covenant); Mays, 2006: 39 (calling).

221. For the notion of "crowning glory," see Sawyer, 1974: 426.

become like God is just as visible — something that the Genesis teaching of humanity's creation in God's image introduces and grounds.

In other words, the image of God is not something per se that the Bible defines in any detail. It is more of a "placeholder" — a "hermeneutical lens" through which the reader is better able to understand the significance of what happens in history and where God's people are headed.[222] By itself, other than conveying the ideas of connection and reflection just noted, it is open-ended and suspenseful.[223] It invites the reader still today to read on, to learn what it could look like to understand people in terms of God's image, and God's people more specifically in terms of the image of God in Christ.[224]

The Old Testament authors are at a particular disadvantage here. They have God's revelation that humanity is in God's image, but they lack the definitive statement of what its fulfillment looks like, as God later reveals it in Christ. Accordingly, further image-of-God terminology understandably awaits the New Testament after its introduction in the opening chapters of Genesis.[225] By no means is the concept lost in the meantime, as describers of the New Testament thought world such as biblical scholars Eugene Merrill and Ben Witherington have elaborated.[226] Nevertheless, there remains a sense, even within the New Testament, that the image-of-God concept is somewhat of a placeholder in terms of detail about who human beings are. As the apostle John writes, Christians can know that they will ultimately be like Christ, but there is much about what that will entail that they cannot know now (1 John 3:2).[227]

Little Definition in the Bible

Some people, then, attribute less significance than they should to humanity's creation in God's image simply because the divine image seems

222. So Briggs, 2010: 112, 123-24. For a related but different use of the lens metaphor, see Towner, 2005: 350.

223. On this theme, see Grenz, 2004: 622; Sexton, 2010: 204; E. Davis, 2009: 55-56; Vorster, 2011: 12.

224. For further discussion, see Rad, 1972: 59; Grenz, 2001: 202-3; Fields, 2001: 98; Briggs, 2010: 122-26. On appropriate and inappropriate ways to bring New Testament perspective to bear on the interpretation of Genesis, see Cortez, 2010: 27.

225. For similar observations, see Irenaeus, 1867: bk. V, ch. 16; McLeod, 1999: 54; Gunton, 2002: 122; McFarland, 2005: 4.

226. Merrill, 2003: 445; Witherington, 2009: v. 2, 98.

227. See also Smalley, 1984: 144-45; Painter, 2002: 221; McFarland, 2005: 9.

to receive relatively little attention in the Bible. Others may recognize the great importance of God's image, but they despair of knowing what it means because the Bible says so little to define it. Admittedly, the image is "conceptually obscure," "not very clear," and "never fully grasp-able."[228] The subject requires more than "a pinch of humility," for "we will never fully understand or define it."[229] As Old Testament scholar Christopher Wright wisely observes, "Since the Bible nowhere defines the term, it is probably futile to attempt to do so very precisely."[230] Nevertheless, as noted above (and see Ch. 3 for detail), readers can recognize broad themes intrinsic in how the Bible's authors invoke God's image, such as humanity's special connection with God and intended reflection of God.[231]

The texts manifestly have *some* meaning, which the authors expect to make sense to readers. Apparently neither fallen humanity's compromised intelligence nor the inadequacy of human language has convinced the authors that communication about God's image is futile.[232] They use the Genesis 1 Hebrew terms for image and likeness, and the Greek New Testament equivalents, as if the terms themselves are understandable vocabulary for readers. Accordingly, investigating both the biblical context of relevant verses and broader cultural contexts will be important and legitimate in order to discern what the authors were taking for granted about the meaning of these terms.[233] Yet we must always remain alert for ways that the Bible's authors are not just adopting but also adapting culturally familiar concepts to convey new ideas. Again, we can expect such investigation to yield some legitimate understanding, as long as we are careful not to read

228. Black, 2006: 179 (conceptually obscure); Welker, 2006: 327 (not very clear); Yong, 2007: 182 (never fully graspable). Similarly, Reynolds, 2008: 178-79; Teel, 2010: 41.

229. Wells, 2004: 23 (humility); Gonzalez, 2007: 125 (never fully define). Similarly McFarland, 2005: 22.

230. C. Wright, 2004: 119. Similarly Middleton, 2005: 44, drawing on J. Barr, 1968 and Sawyer, 1974; and Sherlock, 1996: 33.

231. As Mouw (2012: 266) notes, "We can be confident that . . . we are being given a piece of supremely important information, and that we ought not to grow 'weary in seeking' to understand [God's image] more clearly."

232. So Crouch, 2010: 7-8. Luther (1958: 61, cf. 62-65) was "afraid that since the loss of this image through sin we cannot understand it to any extent." However, that pessimistic conclusion flowed from his questionable view that humanity lost God's image at the Fall (see Ch. 4).

233. For further development of this outlook, see McCasland, 1950: 93; Rad, 1962: 144; W. Schmidt, 1983: 195; B. Ware, 2002: 17; Frame, 2006: 234.

detailed meanings into the texts that reflect agendas other than those of the authors (more on this below).

One reason people should not expect to find too much detail conveyed by the image-of-God term per se is that there is unavoidably an element of mystery to it.[234] Indeed, God is largely a mystery, so one would expect some element of mystery to attend to anyone created in God's image.[235] The same goes for the believer's being conformed to Christ's image, in that there is far more to Christ than human minds can understand.[236] In other words, the reluctance of the Bible's authors to provide complete details about what constitutes being in God's image may well be intentional[237] — even a model for how to think and communicate about the divine image appropriately.

Much of the commentary on God's image to date simply starts with a different assumption. It assumes that there must be one or more details about humanity — capabilities, traits, capacities, etc. — that define the image and explain why humanity warrants such a status. According to biblical scholar James Barr, the quest for the meaning of "the image of God" begins by assuming that there is a

> thing to which the phrase refers. The exegetical operation then tries to identify this entity. From this operation, which from its effects in this instance might be termed the blood-out-of-a-stone process, it comes to be decided that the image of God in man consists in . . .[238]

This process typically goes beyond what the Bible warrants (see illustrations below).[239] The many conflicting conclusions themselves suggest that something is wrong with the process by which people often attempt to understand God's image.[240] The end result is exasperating, with some

234. Horst, 1950: 264; Berkouwer, 1975: 74; Woodhead, 2006: 233; Gonzalez, 2007: ix-x; Stein, 2008: 314.

235. So Fichtner, 1978: 170; Nellas, 1987: 22 (drawing on Gregory, 1972); Woodland, 2006: 234-35; Cortez, 2010: 38.

236. So World, 2005: par. 77; D. Kelsey, 2009: v. 2, 1045.

237. So Beyreuther and Finkenrath, 1976: 502; Carlson, 2008: 92 (drawing on John Scotus Eriugena). On mystery as an ally of religious belief in the battle against atheism, see Watts, 2006: 253.

238. J. Barr, 1968: 12-13.

239. On the general point, see Bajema, 1974: 30; Pannenberg, 1991: v. 2, 205.

240. So Piper, 1971: 25; Grenz, 2001: 200. On the unending conflicts between explanations of God's image, see Tigay, 1984: 170; B. Childs, 1993: 567-68; Hefner, 2000: 88; Crouch, 2010: 2.

theologians even suggesting "that the term be excised from the theological vocabulary, so frustrating is its interpretation."[241] As the next chapter will explain, however, some of this frustration is due to overlooking the clearest insight that the Bible provides into what being God's image means. Christ *is* God's image, according to the New Testament, and there is enough explanatory material in the relevant passages to offer many insights into what it means for humanity to be created *in* God's image.

Overlooking such material, or exasperation over the relative paucity of material elsewhere in the Bible, can render one susceptible to a serious temptation. The temptation is to import definitions that are far afield from the relevant biblical texts into the idea of God's image. The most common sources of such imports are theology and culture.

Importing Theological Ideas

Over the centuries, in response to finding relatively little definition of God's image in the biblical texts, some commentators have filled the perceived void by reading into the idea whatever is central to their theology. Biblical interpretation expert Richard Briggs describes the process this way:

> When theologians have stared down the well at the possibilities for understanding the phrase "image of God" in Gen. 1, they have seen something rather like a reflection of their own image, or rather what they already understand the notion of "image" to be. The point of the passage has in effect been reversed: in the image of their human preunderstanding readers have created the meaning of this text.[242]

"Like Humpty-Dumpty [in Lewis Carroll's *Through the Looking-Glass*], they have made the word mean just what they choose it to mean," agrees Old Testament scholar Norman Snaith.[243] More specifically, adds theological historian John Thompson, "Gen. 1:26 does, in fact, serve usefully as a 'weathervane.' An interpreter's explanation of the *imago dei* often points to his or her larger theological agenda" rather than to the explicit teaching of the Bible regarding God's image.[244]

241. Hefner, 1984: 330.
242. Briggs, 2010: 113.
243. Snaith, 1974: 24. Similarly Middleton, 2005: 18.
244. J. Thompson, 1988: 125. Similarly Canceran, 2011: 11; Peterson, 2011: 20.

Since theological agendas can be all over the map, no wonder an examination of the resulting views of God's image can lead one in exasperation to describe many of those views as "exotically baroque, . . . esoteric, speculative . . . metaphysical pyrotechnics of the first degree."[245] Where more sound theologies are involved, the problem here is more subtle. People may transfer to God's image characteristics or capacities that the Bible actually does attribute to humanity. Accordingly, the resulting definitions may appear intuitively plausible.

Discovering definitions in this way, though, is not logically sound. People are many things from creation onward. Those include, for instance, being in God's image and being potential sinners. There is no reason to assume that one such term defines the other — that people are potential sinners, for instance, because they are in God's image. Similarly, if the Bible affirms that people were created as rational creatures, righteous beings, in God's image, rulers over the natural order, and relational entities, it is not legitimate to conclude that any of those things is what any other of those things *means* — even if an author in the Bible refers to them side by side as does this sentence.[246] They are simply all things that are true of persons. Being rational does not necessarily mean being righteous, just as being in God's image does not necessarily mean being any of these other aspects of who people are.[247]

It can easily seem plausible to suggest that being in God's image is about, for example, ruling over the natural world or relating to God and others; God does indeed tell people to do such things and people do indeed do them to a degree. However, as we search for the meaning of humanity's creation in God's image, we must be wary of the tendency to import sound theological ideas that are valid descriptions of people and assume that they largely explain what God's image means. Just because they help explain who people are does not necessarily entail that they define what being in God's image means. People are more than just "in God's image," as important as being in God's image is.[248]

Something significant is lost when people conflate humanity and God's

245. Van Huyssteen, 2006: 149.

246. On the logical fallacy of this common practice, see J. Barr, 1993: 160; Cortez, 2010: 25.

247. On the methodological challenge here, see Wilson and Bloomberg, 1993: 8-9; I. H. Marshall, 2001: 53. Cf. Piper, 1971: 26-27.

248. For more on the problem of conflating people and God's image, see Henriksen, 2011: 268-69; also Chapters 3 and 7 in the present work.

image, such that anything true of people is true of God's image. If the image is everything that people are, then it is nothing in particular. Being in God's image adds nothing to what is known about people from other sources. God affirms humanity's creation not simply to be "creation," but to be "creation *in God's image.*" God means to communicate something in particular here about humanity that will have concrete implications. If that is the case, then all that is true about humanity is not necessarily true about God's image.

For instance, just because sin has damaged humanity does not logically require that it has damaged God's image. Everything that is true of one is not necessarily true of the other. Recognizing this is important, because it means that being in God's image can tell us something about humanity that we do not otherwise know. It may have more to do with what God intends for humanity than about the actual attributes of people living today. Of course, whether God's intentions or actual human attributes are central to being in God's image is dependent on what the Bible actually says. In this early chapter of our investigation, the challenge is to try to understand how people could have imported so many conflicting theological assumptions into God's image, so that we can endeavor as best we can to stay out of the import business.

Perhaps several examples of such importing will help illustrate the problem. Some commentators see the Gospel of John commending reason and so argue that God's image has to do with reason — even though John does not mention God's image there.[249] Others find appreciation for righteousness in Matthew 5, Luke 17, or Romans 2 and so argue that God's image has to do with righteousness — though these chapters do not discuss God's image.[250] Many see the idea of rulership appearing side by side with God's image in Genesis 1:26 (and Sir. 17:3 in the Apocrypha) and so assume that rulership defines God's image — even though the idea of rulership is not consistently present in other biblical passages about God's image.[251] Still others define God's image in terms of relationship with God and people since those themes are present in Genesis 2, Genesis 4, Prov-

249. See Clark, 1984: 17 invoking John 1; Lewis and Demarest, 1987: v. 2, 141 invoking John 7; and Boer, 1990: 51 citing Calvin on John 1.

250. See Machen, 1947: 177-78 on Matthew 5; Gregory of Nyssa, 1954: 148 on Luke 17; Lewis and Demarest, 1987: v. 2, 139 on Romans 2.

251. On Genesis 1, see sources discussing rulership in Chapter 4; on Sirach 17, see Murphy-O'Connor, 1982: 50.

erbs 1, and Revelation 21 — though again God's image is not the subject of those chapters.[252]

Because reason, righteousness, rulership, and relationship are all important aspects of who people are, using their (degree of) presence in people today to define God's image can be appealing. However, when commentators rather than the Bible's authors themselves make such connections, these connections can appear more to serve a particular theology than to convey biblical teaching. Particularly when commentators end up reaching contradictory conclusions about what constitutes God's image, it appears that at least some of these commentators are inappropriately conflating God's image with other legitimate biblical ideas.

Similar theological importing can lead not only to conflicting definitions of God's image but also to unwarranted conclusions about God's image. Again, several examples may prove helpful. Each involves a conclusion about God's image that a later chapter here will demonstrate to be biblically unsound.

For instance, conflating the biblical ideas of "image" and "glory" makes it considerably more difficult to understand what God's image is (see Chs. 2, 6, and 7). However, that can happen if one assumes that discussions of glory in 2 Peter and Revelation are about God's image per se.[253] Viewing "image" and "likeness" as constituting two separate things can similarly lead investigations of God's image to unwarranted conclusions (see Ch. 3).[254] So can seeing only humanity as a whole and not particular people as being in God's image (see Ch. 3), based on conflating with God's image both body and vine metaphors in the gospels.[255] Perhaps the most common conflation of all, as previously noted, involves equating people and God's image (see Ch. 7). That can easily lead to understanding virtually every biblical passage on regeneration as talking about restoring a damaged image of God, in a way quite different from the way that the Bible consistently talks about God's image.[256]

The point here is not that humanity's creation in God's image is dis-

---

252. Regarding Genesis 2, note assumptions about God's image in Sherlock, 1996: 40-41; Smail, 2006: 42. See also Sawyer, 1974: 425 on Genesis 4; Towner, 2005: 352 on Proverbs 1; and Grenz, 1998: 621-22 on Revelation 21.

253. As in Kline, 1980: 26, 29.

254. Pannenberg, 1991: v. 2, 207-8 critiques this in the earliest centuries of the church.

255. As in Boer, 1990: 171-72.

256. Re. Niebuhr, 1964: 160-61 critiques this in Martin Luther. Note John Calvin's (1960a: bk. III, ch. 3, sec. 9) similar tendency.

connected from most other theological doctrines in the Bible. Quite the opposite is the case, as this book will demonstrate. Humanity's creation in God's image, for example, is "the foundation of the fittingness of the Incarnation" (Thomas Aquinas).[257] As theologian Anthony Hoekema and others elaborate, "it was only because man had been created in the image of God that the Second Person of the Trinity could assume human nature."[258] The same reason helps account for why God in Christ was willing to suffer so much for humanity on the cross.[259] God's image thus becomes connected with the redemption, justification, regeneration, reconciliation, adoption, election, and resurrection of God's people.[260] Nevertheless, there is a big difference between recognizing the many ways that the Bible works out the implications of creation/renewal in God's image, and *defining* God's image in terms of selected implications. The latter approach has helped produce the huge array of conflicting views of God's image.

Importing Cultural Ideas

If it is easy unknowingly to read other theological ideas into God's image, in a way that alters the meaning of the term, it is just as easy to import cultural ideas without being aware of doing so. As theologian Karl Barth assesses the history of writing about God's image, "[A]uthors merely found the concept in the text and then proceeded to pure invention in accordance with the requirements of contemporary anthropology."[261] Many resonate with Barth's assessment.[262] Some see authors relying, often unconsciously, on insights about humanity that are representative of their own culture rather than the text of the Bible.[263] In other words, the dominant mindset

257. Aquinas, 1947: pt. III, Q. 4, art. 1. See also discussion in Pinckaers, 2005: 153-54.

258. Hoekema, 1994: 22. Similarly Orr, 1948: 268; Buswell, 1962: 232; Goldingay, 2003: 223; Kraynak, 2008: 78.

259. See Thomas, 1949: 163.

260. Chafer, 1947: v. 2: 167 and I. H. Marshall, 2001: 61 (redemption); Thielicke, 1966: 162, 195-96, drawing on Martin Luther (justification); Orr, 1948: 278-79 (regeneration); Hoekema, 1994: 55-56 (reconciliation); Aquinas, 1947: pt. III, Q. 23, art. 2 (adoption); MacDonald, 2008: 325-26 (election); Clines, 1968: 87 (resurrection).

261. K. Barth, 1958a: 193.

262. E.g., see acknowledgments in Clines, 1968: 54-55; Boer, 1990: 8; Bird, 1997: 126; Crouch, 2010: 3. As Cortez, 2010: 19 puts it, "Barth speaks for many" in this matter.

263. So H. Berkhof, 1979: 179; Middleton, 2005: 18; Balswick et al., 2005: 30; van Huyssteen, 2006: 159.

at the time, or *Zeitgeist,* is what has shaped many understandings of God's image.[264] Notes Genesis scholar J. Richard Middleton: "[M]any interpreters turn to extrabiblical, usually philosophical, sources to interpret the image and end up reading contemporaneous conceptions of being human back into the Genesis text."[265]

Other observers see more individual influences at work here, albeit influences conditioned to some degree by cultural norms. These are the personal beliefs and values — some would call them prejudices — that prompt people to assume that one thing about humanity is more "godlike" than another.[266] Sometimes it is not the "likeness" term in the biblical "likeness-image" concept but instead the "image" term that prompts people to make assumptions. "Image" suggests different things to people in different cultural contexts.[267] So the situation is ripe for a vast array of interpretations to emerge due to a wide range of cultural influences.

Historical examples abound. In the earliest centuries of the church, Greek (especially Stoic and neo-Platonic) thinking — with its emphasis on reason — understandably inclined many to view God's image as something related to reason.[268] This influence is still evident in the early fifth century in the writings of Augustine, as is Aristotle's influence much later in Aquinas.[269] The culture-engaging energies of the Renaissance similarly yielded many defenses of God's image as rulership over the natural world (Pico della Mirandola et al.), just as the Reformation's reaction to Roman Catholic natural theology predictably prompted viewing God's image in terms of God-imparted righteousness (Luther et al.).[270] Of par-

---

264. Curtis, 1992: 389-90; Black, 2006: 180; J. Strong, 2008: 629; Cortez, 2010: 15; and Vainio, 2014: 123.

265. Middleton, 2005: 17. On the influence of contemporary "philosophy" on authors' understanding of God's image, see Brink, 2001: 88; van Huyssteen, 2006: 126. Cf. Green, 1999: 59 in terms of contemporary "worldviews."

266. P. Ramsey, 1950: 265 (beliefs); Wenham, 1987: 30 (values); Oduyoye, 1982: 51-52 (prejudices).

267. Welz, 2011: 75.

268. K. Schmidt, 1947: 158-62; Clines, 1968: 54-55; Rist, 1982: 155; Sherlock, 1996: 79. See also the section on reason and God's image in Chapter 5 of the present work.

269. See Sullivan, 1963; Squire, 1951; and Pelikan, 1978: ch. 2 plus discussion in Middleton, 2005: 20; also Treier, 2008: 73. Grenz (2001: 183; 2002: 41) sees individualism accompanying rationalism in Augustine's work. See also discussions of Augustine and Aquinas in Chapter 4 of the present work.

270. See Trinkaus, 1995 and discussion in Middleton, 2005: 22, 28-29 and the section on righteousness and God's image in Chapter 5 of the present work.

ticular interest in light of his critique of such cultural influences is Karl Barth himself. Barth's emphasis on God's image as relationship evidences the influence of Martin Buber's existential I-Thou concept, among other influences.[271] As Chapter 5 will discuss, current relational emphases and environmental concerns may well underlie inclinations toward understanding God's image as relationship or rulership in theology and biblical studies today.[272]

Such examples notwithstanding, it can often be difficult to identify the cultural influences at work in any person or generation. The greatest cultural influences are not necessarily what are prominent in the culture of the day. People frequently form their views of God's image based on what they read, and those writings may be influenced by cultural trends that were prominent when their authors wrote them. In fact, people's views may not affirm present or previous culture, but may instead constitute a reaction against one of them. Nevertheless, affirmation and rejection of constantly changing cultural values both constitute formidable influences that help explain the huge range of conflicting views of God's image over time and in the present day.[273]

Not surprisingly, the very approach to God's image that has rendered it most susceptible to destructive applications (see earlier in this chapter) makes it most susceptible to cultural influence. When people assume that being in God's image is about ways that people are presently like God, they are disposed to read into God's image whatever traits or capacities their contemporary culture admires.[274] For some, that is enjoying pizzas.[275] For others, it is exterminating certain groups of people (see earlier in this chapter). As political scientist Paul Brink notes, "Christians risk merely 'baptizing' those qualities lauded by the dominant culture, thus sacrific-

---

271. Buber, 1958, as discussed in Jónsson, 1988: 74-75 (drawing on Cairns). J. Barr, 1993: 161; Middleton, 2005: 23-24; and van Huyssteen, 2006: 137 view Barth's concept of God's image as also profoundly shaped by reaction to common appeals to nature in Emil Brunner's writings and in German National Socialism. See Rumscheidt, 1972 on Barth and Nazism, plus the section on relationship and God's image in Chapter 5 of the present work. Meanwhile, Niskanen, 2009: 417-18 and Price, 2002: 197 discuss the connections between Barth and sexuality-oriented Freudian psychology.

272. In addition to the sources and discussion in Chapter 5, see H. McDonald, 1981: 35 and Jónsson, 1988: 221 regarding the influence of environmental sensitivities.

273. See Lazenby, 1987: 67-68; Hughes, 1989: 61; B. Childs, 1993: 567; Briggs, 2010: 113.

274. See Westermann, 1974: 58; D. Hall, 1986: 74, 91; Grenz, 2001: 143; van Huyssteen, 2006: 315.

275. E.g., see D. G. Jones, 2002: 100.

ing a uniquely Christian understanding of the doctrine" of God's image.[276] People also risk baptizing their own personal values by conceiving of God's image in terms of ways people are currently like God.[277] Commentators throughout the centuries (typically the most educated of people) often incline toward understanding God's image in terms of reason, while others promote their own gender as central to God's image.[278] Rather than people being in the image of God, God is remade in the image of people.[279]

The big question, then, is what is the likelihood that this book is anything other than a promotion of cultural or theological ideas that strike the author as most attractive, even personally beneficial? As multiple commentators have noted, "interpreters typically see the interpretations of others as hopelessly subjective and their own as objectively true."[280] I am not one of them, because I do not pretend to be immune from such influences. Nevertheless, a high priority in the writing of this book has been to identify and minimize them where possible. While the result is not perfect, I have purposely not been tentative in the language used in this book. Readers are arguably best served by being able to read the strongest possible case for a view, so that they can assess for themselves if the approach better accounts for all of the biblical data than other available approaches. If some find any claim in the book too strong, I only hope that it will be received in the same constructive spirit that it is given. Response is welcome. There is a pressing need to bring greater clarity to the topic of God's image, and any ways that people can work together to that end are valuable.

One strategy to guard against personal bias in this book has been to attend carefully to what the relevant biblical texts actually say about God's image, rather than substituting other ideas for this concept and discussing their biblical and cultural meanings instead.[281] Another strategy has been to consider carefully the wide range of meanings people throughout his-

---

276. Brink, 2001: 89.

277. For development of this theme, see McFarland, 2005: 166.

278. Regarding reason, so observes Erickson, 2013: 461. Philosopher Gordon Clark (1969: 218) may provide an example by not just concluding that God's image is reason but by insisting that "the solution of this paradox [of the meaning of God's image] is very easy and very clear." Regarding gender, see Woodhead, 2006: 235.

279. On this theme, see previous discussion earlier in this chapter; also Ruether, 1995: 286-87.

280. N. Wright, 1992b: 51, as affirmed by Middleton, 2005: 34.

281. In line with Schmutzer's challenge (2009: 227).

tory have given to God's image, noting especially when such definitions are more definitive than the biblical data will allow.[282] There has been a special effort to include the writings of large numbers of commentators in both biblical studies and theology, in light of the long history of conflict between these two fields regarding the meaning of God's image.[283] Still another strategy has been to have countless discussions and invite numerous written critiques of this material in order to weed out as many personal biases and theological/cultural assumptions as possible.

One final strategy emerged from the study, rather than guiding it from the outset. As careful study of the biblical texts proceeded, one point emerged again and again. The Bible's authors do not define God's image by ways that people are especially like God, that is, in terms of present human attributes. This somewhat surprising conclusion ended up offering protection against prioritizing as "God's image" some culturally approved or theologically attractive human attributes over others. However, I am jumping ahead: this is the very thing that must be demonstrated from the biblical texts. We cannot assume it at the outset because it provides a convenient way to lessen theological/cultural bias. To the biblical texts, then, we must turn.

282. In line with Hoekema's challenge (1994: 100).
283. On this history, see P. Bird, 1981: 130-31; Middleton, 2005: 24; Cortez, 2010: 30.

CHAPTER TWO

Much Is Known: Christ as God's Image

Discussions of topics usually begin at the beginning. The Bible begins with Genesis 1 ("In the beginning . . ."). Therefore, biblical discussions of humanity's existence "in God's image" commonly begin with Genesis 1. Is Genesis 1 really the beginning though?

The New Testament reveals that God was engaged in planning *before* the beginning (e.g., see Titus 1:2; 2 Tim. 1:9; 1 Cor. 2:7). In fact, God had a "purpose" (the language of Rom. 8:28 and elsewhere) that included creating humanity with a dignity and a destiny bound closely with Christ, whom the Bible calls God's "Son." God intended that people would fulfill their purpose as created "in" God's image by developing toward the fullness of what God's image entails (see Ch. 3). This was God's desire — that none would perish (1 Tim. 2:4; 2 Pet. 3:9) — in a way that was in harmony with God's own sovereign will.[1] God foreknew that all people would reject the divine purpose for them, yet God would not let people, sin, or Satan have the last word. God would do whatever it took — even the death of an only Son on a cross — to enable all who were willing to become members of God's eternal family to complete their development into God's image.

The New Testament also reveals that God's purpose all along has not been for humanity to develop into some sort of generic "God's image,"

---

1. Exactly how this desire that none would perish squares with the certainty that God's sovereign plan for humanity cannot be thwarted is the subject of many theological debates between such theological camps as Calvinists and Arminians, and even between subgroups within traditions such as Reformed Protestants. Such debates are beyond the scope of the present work. The point here is that it is possible to affirm with the Bible that God created all people in the divine image and to understand this as expressing God's intention for all people, regardless of one's theological camp.

but to be conformed specifically to the image of Christ. "For those whom [God] foreknew [God] also predestined to be conformed to the image of [God's] Son, in order that he might be the firstborn within a large family" (Rom. 8:29).[2] However, since Christ *is* God's image (2 Cor. 4:4; Col. 1:15), conforming to the model of Christ's being and doing is tantamount to conforming to God's image. It is the fulfillment of God's determination at creation that people would be "in" God's image, living and growing in reference to God's standard for humanity. That image/standard is Christ, whose God-given glory — a manifestation of being God's image — was present "before the beginning" (John 17:5; cf. Jude 25).

Accordingly, although a discussion of humanity's creation "in God's image" could begin with the pithy references to that idea in Genesis 1, beginning there has led people in all sorts of conflicting directions (see Ch. 5). If today's discussion took place at a time before the New Testament was available, then perhaps one could do no better than to begin with Genesis. This is not our point in history though. Since Genesis indicates that humanity stands in some sort of relationship with God's image — by using different prepositions to describe that relationship (see Ch. 3) — we would do well first to obtain as much clarity as the Bible provides on what God's image is. We can then examine what it means for humanity to be "in" or "according to" that image.

The New Testament affirms explicitly that Christ *is* God's image, so unpacking the meaning of that affirmation is the surest place to begin. Then we will be in a better position to consider the meaning of the Genesis and other biblical texts. We cannot interpret Old Testament texts as if the authors had New Testament ideas in view. However, we can interpret them with the expectation that they do not contradict what the New Testament reveals were God's purposes from "before the beginning."

Since Christ is so central to understanding what God's image is all about, one can understand why theologian Stanley Grenz felt compelled to point out that his own published systematic theology is deficient on this score. He recognized that it fails to give sufficient attention to Christ as the image of God as part of explaining what it means for people to be in God's image. He also faults other major systematic theologies on the

---

2. Throughout this book, as here, a noun in brackets will replace a pronoun in a quotation where that helps to clarify precisely to what the pronoun is referring. Unless stated otherwise, biblical quotations in this book are from the New Revised Standard Version of the Bible.

same grounds.[3] If Christ is the "primary and true image" of God, then understanding what that affirmation means is indeed essential for accurately interpreting humanity's status as created in God's image.[4]

The Term "Image"

Simply put, image is about *connection* in a way that may also involve *reflection*. Being the image of God turns out to mean having a special connection with God and indeed being a meaningful reflection of God. "Image" is the most common translation of the Hebrew word *tselem* and the Greek word *eikon,* which appear in various biblical passages addressing humanity's creation in the image of God. *Eikon* also is the primary New Testament term for Christ as God's "image." One may well wonder why the Bible's authors employed these terms for "image" as part of describing humanity and Christ. The answer most likely has to do not with the terms' precision, but with their flexibility and range. Authors in the Bible also employ other Hebrew nouns such as *pesel* (Exod. 20:4; Isa. 40:20) and *masseka* (e.g., Exod. 34:17; Isa. 30:22) to mean "image." However, those terms have focused negative connotations due to their frequent association with forbidden idols.[5]

Tselem also can refer to idols in the Bible (e.g., Num. 33:52; 2 Kgs. 11:18), but it can be used in a more descriptive way without such negative connotations in different contexts. In 1 Samuel 6:5 it refers to images of mice and tumors that priests tell the Philistine lords to send back to Israel as a guilt offering with the stolen ark, to "give glory to the God of Israel." In the Psalms, it refers to people as mere shadows (39:6) and to some as mere phantoms in a dream (73:20). These last two instances illustrate how the word — normally referring to something quite materially solid — can also refer to something far from such. Its range of meaning extends all the way from the very physical to the completely nonmaterial.[6] As such, along with

---

3. Grenz, 2004: 625, critiquing Grenz, 1994. He cites Grudem, 1994 and an earlier edition of Erickson, 2013 as examples, but notes that there are many others.

4. So Watson, 1997: 282-83; Jeeves, 2005: 183; Treier, 2008: 153-54; also Kreitzer, 1989: 84, and Cortez, 2010: 17, regarding Paul's emphasis on Christ.

5. On the problems that using such a word would have caused for the image-of-God concept, see discussion of terms in A. A. Jones, 1962: 556; J. Barr, 1968: 19-24; McFarland, 2005: 21-22.

6. As will be discussed in the next chapter where humanity is the focus, some com-

its Greek counterpart *eikon,* it ended up working well in reference to both Christ and humanity as a whole, who have physical form but are more than material.[7] As discussion below will document, the Bible's authors using the term do indeed have the visible, physical form of Christ in view, but also far more than physical traits and capacities.

The idea that being an image signifies having a special connection is evident, for example, in Daniel 3:1-7, which reports the Babylonian King Nebuchadnezzar erecting a large *tselem* in the province of Babylonia. Anyone who spurned the image was to be thrown into a blazing furnace (v. 6) — a threat that Nebuchadnezzar acted on in the case of Shadrach, Meshach, and Abednego (v. 21). The purpose of this image was to represent the original in a way so closely connected to it that honoring it was to honor the original and dishonoring it was to dishonor the original.

As in Daniel 3, kings in the ancient Near East would periodically erect an image *(tselem)* in order to establish their presence as rulers where they were not physically present.[8] Evidence exists of this practice in Mesopotamia, the setting of Daniel 3. For instance, the ruler Ashur-nasir-pal II writes in his annals after defeating king Haiani: "At that time I fashioned a heroic image of my royal self, my power and my glory I inscribed thereon. . . . I fashioned memorial steles and inscribed thereon my glory and my prowess, and I set them up by his city gate."[9] Such images could sometimes serve to represent the ruler prayerfully before a god. However, even then the reminder of the ruler's political sovereignty was generally present.[10]

---

mentators, focusing primarily on the connection of the term with physical objects, conclude that the term refers primarily to the physical aspect of humanity (e.g., Cook, 1975: 87; Callender, 2000: 25; Crouch, 2010: 4; see discussion of Humbert, 1940 and Koehler, 1948 in Eichrodt, 1967: 122). Others are more impressed by the term's nonmaterial connections and see those as primary in reference to humanity (e.g., Cassuto, 1989: 56; Sawyer, 1992: 66). This range of views is itself reflective of how effectively the term can convey such a wide range of reference points.

7. Wildberger, 1997: 1081 notes the "remarkable flexibility" of this term. Others who comment on the wide range of the term's reference points include Piper, 1971: 16; P. Bird, 1981: 139-40; Hamilton, 1990: 134-35; Curtis, 1992: 389; Mathews, 1995: 167-68; van Leeuwen, 1997: 645-46; Garr, 2003: 136; Middleton, 2005: 45-46.

8. See discussions in Rad, 1962: 146-47; Clines, 1968: 87-88; Birch, 1984: 14; Jónsson, 1988: 57; Bray, 2001: 576; Gunton, 2002: 40; Garr, 2003: 163-64; Youngblood, 2006: 7.

9. Grenz, 2001: 198-99; Middleton, 2005: 104-7; J. Strong, 2005: 94-96; and the numerous earlier sources and specific examples cited therein.

10. See analysis in Albrektson, 1976: 43; Curtis, 1984: 119; Garr, 2000: 231; Middleton, 2005: 106-7. A good example where both purposes are explicit is the statue of King Had-yisi from Tell Fakhariyeh, discussed below.

Images representing rulers also occurred in Egypt, as when Pharaoh Ramses II had his image hewn out of rock on the Mediterranean coast north of Beirut as a sign of his rule there.[11]

While images could directly represent human rulers — reminding people of the rulers they represented — images could just as easily have a god as the reference point. Constructed images could be in places where people regularly worship, such that honoring the image was to honor the god.[12] This concept of the image representing a god, common in the ancient Near East, surfaces in Amos 5:26 (cited also in Acts 7:43), where even the house of Israel appears to be worshiping Mesopotamian gods by worshiping their images *(tselem)*. Alternatively, a human ruler could be seen as a god's living image. In that case, as in Daniel 3, crafted material images could represent both the ruler and the god since the ruler represented the god. (Nebuchadnezzar not only incorporates the god Nabu's name in his own, but he claims "glorious majesty" for himself in Dan. 4:30 — similar to the claims of the Mesopotamian king Shalmaneser.)[13]

The view of kings as images of gods is well attested in the ancient Near East.[14] For example, in Mesopotamia, a king could be an image *(tsalmu)* of such gods as Bel, Enlil, or Marduk.[15] In Egypt, where the names for the primary deity varied, viewing kings as divine images was even more common — for example, Amenophis III as image of the god Amon-Re, Tutankhamen as image of the god Amun, or Thutmose IV as image of the god Re.[16]

There are various differences between practices in Mesopotamia and Egypt. Moreover, debates continue over which setting is the more imme-

11. Wolff, 1974: 160-61; S. Wright, 2003: 32-33; and the numerous earlier sources and specific examples cited therein.

12. For example, see Beale, 2004: 88-90, and the discussion of idolatry in Chapter 3 of the present book.

13. Shalmaneser "fashioned a mighty image of my majesty" and virtually equates this image with "the glory of Assur" his god. See Frankfort, 1954: 90; Beale 2004: 82.

14. See discussions in Konkel, 1992: 3; P. Bird, 1981: 140-43; Westermann, 1994: 151-52; Dumbrell, 2002: 16.

15. Tigay, 1984: 171-72; Callender, 2000: 27-28. Cf. Walton, 2000: 519-20; Middleton, 2005: 111-22; Herring, 2008: 487; and the numerous earlier sources and specific examples cited therein.

16. W. Schmidt, 1983: 195; Sarna, 1989: 12; van Leeuwen, 1997: 643. Cf. Wildberger, 1965; Clines, 1968: 85; Jónsson, 1988: 207-8; J. Strong, 2005: 94-95; Niehaus, 2008: 99-100; and the numerous earlier sources and specific examples cited therein.

diate cultural backdrop to the writing of the Old Testament[17] — or if the immediate cultural backdrop to the Genesis passages on God's image is a missing "Canaanite" tradition that incorporated both Mesopotamian and Egyptian concepts of "image."[18] As biblical scholar J. Richard Middleton observes, "the meaning of the image, thus, cannot be made to depend on something as tenuous as a particular historical reconstruction."[19] However, the basic themes found in both regions (and echoed in the Apocrypha)[20] do resonate with the core Daniel 3 idea that "image" signals a close connection between original and image. In the next chapter we will give more attention to how the Bible's authors adopted and adapted terms such as "image" from the cultures of the ancient Near East. The element of "connection" in "image" worked well for the authors' purposes, with little adaptation necessary.

Another element often but not necessarily present in an image is a resemblance between the image and certain attributes of the original. To be sure, such resemblance need not characterize an image. Many images in Mesopotamia could be mere lumps of rock.[21] In Egypt, the same pharaoh could be the image of both a male and a female deity, just as the same god could have both a human and an animal as an image.[22] The primary point of an image was the way it was connected with the original, whether in the present, past, or both.[23] However, images often displayed visually something about a king. In Daniel 3 the great height and gold surface of the image reflected the king's grandeur and wealth. Similarly, the images

---

17. These debates are described and documented in Stendebach, 2003: 389-90; Curtis, 1992: 391; Garr, 2003: 136-37. See esp. Middleton, 2005: ch. 3 for greater detail.

18. So P. Bird, 1981: 143. Cf. Horton, 2006: 186.

19. Middleton, 2005: 93.

20. The Wisdom of Solomon (14:17) explains it this way: "When people could not honor monarchs in their presence, since they lived at a distance, they imagined their appearance far away, and made a visible image of the king whom they honored." Thus, as Kümmel (1963: 86) observes, when Slovonic Enoch (44:1) reflects on humanity's creation in God's image, it concludes: "He who abhors the countenance of a man, abhors the countenance of the Lord."

21. Bernhardt, 1956: 31-33, 55; Clines, 1968: 92; Grenz, 2001: 199.

22. W. Schmidt, 1983: 196; van Leeuwen, 1997: 643-44. Smail (2006: 45) affirms the general conclusion that "being like" a god was not a necessary part of being an image of that god.

23. An image could as easily memorialize something done in the past as it could signify the authority of the original in the present; often both were in view. See Miller, 1972: 296; Jónsson, 1988: 58.

of Ramses II and Ashur-nasir-pal II mentioned earlier appear to have been fashioned to look like those rulers, with size or attached words impressing the observer with some of the ruler's noteworthy attributes.

Accordingly, the Bible's authors would likely have assumed the core ideas of connection — with possible reflection — as the reader's basic understanding of the term. As with any term in the Bible, these authors were then able to adopt those aspects of it that were theologically sound regarding Christ as God's image. They did the same regarding humanity's creation in God's image. In each case, they not only adopted the term but also adapted its meaning to do justice to the differences between Christ and created humanity.

A good example of where the Bible's authors needed to provide further definition concerns the degree of connection to God involved here. Outside of the Bible, an image could have a "spiritual union" with a divinity that the image represents — resulting in the divine presence or even the divine essence in the image.[24] While that idea is appropriate when speaking of Christ as God's image, a clearer element of separation is necessary when applying the image-of-God concept to people, as the next chapter will explain.

Not surprisingly, the primary Greek translation of *tselem* in the Septuagint and primary word for "image" in the New Testament — *eikon* — can have as wide a range of meaning as *tselem*. In the New Testament, *eikon* most often refers to physical representations; but what they represent is far more than physical in nature.[25] Furthermore, the idea that the original is closely connected with or somehow present in the image — already suggested in the term *tselem*[26] — becomes even more evident in the term *eikon*.[27] This renders the latter a particularly appropriate term for talking about Christ's identity as the image of God.

24. On spiritual union, see Schmutzer, 2009: 178-79; on divine presence, see Clines, 1968: 87-88; Pannenberg, 1985: 20-21; Schüle, 2005: 6; Herring, 2008: 480-81; Cortez, 2010: 35; on divine essence, see Conzelmann, 1975: 288; Walton, 2001: 131.

25. See McCasland, 1950: 92; Piper, 1971: 20; Barrett, 1993: 132-33; I. H. Marshall, 2001: 50-51; M. Harris, 2005: 331.

26. See Wildberger, 1997: 1081; Garr, 2003: 134-35.

27. The closeness of this connection is noted in Lenski, 1946b: 949-50; K. Barth, 1958a: 201; Kleinknecht, 1964: 389; Kittel, 1964d: 395; Flender, 1976: 287-88; Fichtner, 1978: 35; Ra. Martin, 1981: 52; Grenz, 2001: 209-10; Vorster, 2011: 22. For example, when Hebrews 10:1 describes the law as only a shadow *(skia)* of the good things to come and not the *eikon* of things, the author employs *eikon* to denote something that would have a much more substantial connection with the original.

Evil powers in the New Testament can have an image as well, and the concept similarly suggests the idea of a close connection. In Revelation 13, the dragon gives a beast the power and throne (v. 2) of Satan (cf. 12:9), and an image *(eikon)* of the beast is made and given breath to speak and to kill (v. 15). (Interestingly, speaking badly and killing are two of the most prominent violations of God's image found elsewhere in the Bible — see discussion below.) Refusing to worship the image is a fatal offense because of the close connection of the image to the beast and, ultimately, to Satan (v. 15).

Humanity and Christ both have a special connection with God. They also presently (Christ) or ultimately (humanity) are a reflection of God. However, there are important differences between humanity and Christ. As Chapter 3 will discuss, people "in God's image" are not so thoroughly identified with God that they *are* God. God intends people ultimately to become the "likeness" of God, where the special connection with God and the reflection involved entail similarity rather than identity. Christ, however, is an "exact imprint" of God (*"charakter,"* Heb. 1:3). So whereas God intends people ultimately to be a "likeness-image," Christ is an "imprint-image." In other words, the term "image" in the Bible varies somewhat in meaning according to its context — especially according to the person or thing to which it refers.[28] As Augustine and Aquinas wisely observed, there can be different types of image.[29]

Chapter 3 will detail how the likeness-image concept connecting God and people is within the range of meanings of each term, "likeness" and "image." So either term alone can accurately refer to who God intends people to be — as each does in the Bible. Nevertheless, likeness-image is a single concept designating an image that is similar to, but not an exact representation of, the original.

Similarly, as explained below, the imprint-image concept connecting God and Christ is within the range of meanings of each term, "imprint" and "image." So either term alone can accurately refer to Christ — as each does in the Bible. Nevertheless, imprint-image is a single concept designating an image that is identical to — an exact representation of — the original.

According to the relevant biblical texts, Christ being the exact image

28. As has long been observed: See, e.g., A. Strong, 1907: 515; Lightfoot, 1927: 143; M. Harris, 2005: 331.

29. "Equality does not belong to the essence of an image; for as Augustine says: Where there is an image there is not necessarily equality" (Aquinas, 1947: pt. I, Q. 93, art. 1; cf. pt. I, Q. 36, art. 1). For related insights see Chafer, 1947: v. 2, 172-73; D. Kelsey, 2009: v. 2, 956.

of God means that there is so close a connection between the two that they are essentially one. It also means that Christ constitutes a complete picture of what God intends for people in God's image to be and to do. This picture is nothing less than a reflection of who God is and what God does. For Christ and humanity alike, then, God's image has to do with connection and reflection. There is a special connection with God — a connection involving similarity in the case of humanity, a connection of identity in the case of Christ. A meaningful reflection of God is also at issue — *present* through Christ *as* God's image and *intended* for humanity *in* God's image.

The Primary New Testament Passages

A good place to begin an investigation of Christ as the image *(eikon)* of God is Colossians 1:15. There Paul (as the author identifies himself in v. 1)[30] straightforwardly affirms that Christ "is the image of the invisible God," thereby signaling both special connection and meaningful reflection. This affirmation appears in the middle of a long sentence running from verse 9 to 20. In this sentence, Paul identifies Christ as the "firstborn" *(prototokos)* in two respects: the firstborn of all creation (v. 15) and the firstborn from the dead (v. 18). However, the redemptive aspect of Jesus' resurrection is not merely a later thought added well after Paul's reference to Christ as God's image in verse 15. The very words leading up to this reference praise God's "beloved Son, in whom we have redemption, the forgiveness of sins" (vv. 13-14).

The point of this long sentence in Colossians 1, then, is not to separate Jesus and the pre-incarnate Christ, but to identify Jesus with Christ and ultimately with God. Moreover, this identification is particularly intimate — not just a matter of "image" but of a particularly personal type of image — one that involves firstborn sonship. As the image and firstborn son, Christ *is* God at work in creation and redemption.

The very wording of this extended sentence reinforces such an understanding. After identifying Christ as God's image in verse 15, not only does the next verse begin with the word "for" (or "because" — *hoti*), but so also does verse 19. The first instance introduces a string of reasons that Christ

30. Whenever a book of the Bible names someone as its author, the present work will simply refer to the author of that book by using the same name. When the point being made depends on who authored the book in view, more discussion will be included.

warrants the exalted status of being the "image of God"; and the second summarizes the implication that all these reasons point to: "in him all the fullness of God was pleased to dwell" (v. 19).[31]

In other words, as the image of the invisible God, Christ gives people the opportunity actually to see God.[32] Jesus himself had previously observed: "Whoever has seen me has seen the Father" (John 14:9; 12:45), for "the Father is in me and I am in the Father" (John 10:38) — so much so that "the Father and I are one" (John 10:30). Christ, as God's image in Colossians 1, is the "exact representation," "manifestation," "essence," or "substance" of God, in the sense of truly being God "revealed."[33] While humanity's significance also is rooted in a special connection with God, the connection of Jesus with the Father is of a unique kind.

In light of this emphasis in Colossians 1, many commentators not surprisingly end up concluding that the uniquely close connection of Christ with God is central to what it means for Christ to be the image of God. For some, Christ as God's image is fully divine, equal with God.[34] Christ is the very presence of God[35] — some would say God's substance or essence.[36] Others emphasize the visible connotation of being an image.[37] Christ then becomes the revelation or embodiment of God.[38] In Christ there is finally an opportunity to see God.[39] Being God's image then becomes an echo of John's affirmation that "[n]o one has ever seen God. It is God the only Son, who is close to the Father's heart, who has made him known" (John 1:18).

While the emphasis of Christ as the image of God in Colossians 1 might be Christ's uniquely close connection with God, some understand this text also to be suggesting Christ's magnificent reflection of God. After all, the contrast here is between God as invisible and Christ as image (i.e., as visible). When people look at Christ they see an expression of all the divine attributes in a way that reveals who God is and models how God intends for

31. On the "fullness of God" as an explanation of what the image of God involves, see Gardoski, 2007: 18; Smail, 2006: 58; Witherington, 2009: v. 2, 122-23.

32. So Cairns, 1973: 42; Hoekema, 1994: 21; Patzia, 1990: 29-30; World, 2005: par. 75.

33. M. Harris, 2005: 315 (exact representation); Schweizer, 1982: 66 (manifestation); Wells, 2004: 38 (essence); Ra. Martin, 1981: 57 (substance); Kleinknecht, 1964: 389 and Lohse, 1971: 46 (revealed).

34. Kittel, 1964d: 395; Spicq, 1982: 208; Hughes, 1989: 25; Bray, 2001: 576.

35. K. Barth, 1958b: 219; Barrett, 1993: 132; McFarland, 2005: 16; Cortez, 2010: 32-33.

36. Substance: Maloney, 1973: 90 (citing Athanasius); essence: Ra. Martin, 1996: 500.

37. Lightfoot, 1927: 143-44; Clines, 1993: 427.

38. Lohse, 1971: 48; Ra. Martin, 1986: 71; Mangano, 2008: 169.

39. Clines, 1968: 102; Witherington, 2009: v. 1, 20.

people to be in the world.[40] What is implicit here regarding Christ as God's image, the New Testament better develops elsewhere, both directly (see below) and indirectly in passages addressing how the image that is Christ serves as a model and goal of human existence (see Ch. 6).

The second of the two New Testament verses that explicitly identify Christ as "the image [*eikon*] of God" is 2 Corinthians 4:4. Here the idea of close connection is also present, again to the ultimate degree in which two are really one. Whereas in verse 4 the focus is on "the glory of Christ, who is the image of God," verse 6 explains that this glory is "glory of God in the face of Jesus Christ." Because Christ is God's image, God and Christ are so closely associated that the glory of one is essentially the glory of the other.[41] As the image of God, Christ is the expression, revelation, and very presence of God.[42] Yet the close association of glory *(doxa)* with image suggests something else about what it means to be God's image.

To be an image of God is not just about the fact that a close connection is present; it also implies that the image shows something about what it images. The image-glory passage in view here runs from the mention of "glory" in 2 Corinthians 3:7 to the reference to what is "visible" in 4:11. In 3:7, Paul introduces glory by talking about how visible it was on the face of Moses. But now there is a "greater glory" (3:10), the "glory of God in the face of Jesus Christ" (4:6). In a contrast with unbelievers, who cannot see this glory because a veil is in the way (3:13-15), Paul describes believers, who have "unveiled faces, seeing the glory of the Lord" (3:18). This "seeing," says Paul, involves an image-related renewal that transforms them "from one degree of glory to another" (3:18).

While more detailed attention to this transformation must await Chapter 6, the important point here is that glory is changing, not image. Glory can be greater or lesser — can be a matter of degree. Image is something that one simply is (Christ) or is oriented to (humanity). In view here, as Paul explains four verses later (4:4), is Christ's status as "the image of God." That status — that image — is the standard of what humanity should be, toward which people are being transformed. The increasing degrees of glory

40. For example, see discussion in McCasland, 1950: 87-88; S. Wright, 2003: 36; Schumacher, 2008: 371; D. Kelsey, 2009: v. 2, 966.

41. For elaboration, see Hoekema, 1994: 21; Gardoski, 2007: 18; Vorster, 2011: 17. Cf. Golitzin, 2003: 340.

42. On expression, see Ra. Martin, 1986: 79; on revelation, see Wilson, 1973: 357; on presence, see Witherington, 1995: 386.

that correspond to this transformation reflect ways that Jesus is becoming more visible in believers. For example, Paul notes that he and his fellow believers endeavor to deal with suffering in a godly way by identifying with Christ's suffering, "so that the life of Jesus may also be made visible in our bodies" (4:10-11).

In 2 Corinthians 3-4, then, Paul suggests that Christ as God's image entails not only the closest connection with God but also the greatest manifestation of God's glory. That glory is a visible expression or reflection of who God is and how God acts.[43] It radiates the splendor of the very attributes of God.[44] According to 4:6, this is a fulfillment of the intention of "God who said 'Let light shine out of darkness.'" God also said in Genesis 1: "Let us make humanity in our image." As 2 Corinthians 3-4 suggests, then, whereas God intended humanity to increasingly express God's glory by growing ever closer to the standard God established for humanity, a veil of sin prevented that intention from being fulfilled apart from the liberating work of Christ. Moreover, Christ, as the image of God, makes visible what fulfilling the intention of God looks like.

Lack of clarity regarding what God's image is, how sin affects it, etc., is sometimes due to overlooking the distinction between image and glory. Many commentators see the two terms as largely synonymous.[45] It is better to see the two as sometimes connected, yet distinct in important respects.[46] What, then, does "glory" mean? Defining this word precisely is notoriously difficult.[47] "Glory," often translating the Hebrew *kabod* in the Old Testament, carries a sense of weightiness and thus importance, in a way that calls forth praise from others.[48] The original Greek translation of the Old Testament used *doxa* to translate *kabod.* The New Testament then employs *doxa* in a way harmonious with the Old Testament's use of the term.[49]

43. On expression, see Clines, 1993: 427; on reflection, see Matera, 2003: 97 and Black, 2006: 191. Gaffin, 2010: 147 speaks in terms of revelation.

44. See Grenz, 2001: 211; 2004: 619 (radiates); Furnish, 1984: 249 (splendor); Wilson and Blomberg, 1993: 9 (attributes).

45. So Hughes, 1989: 26; Keener, 2005: 170; Bray, 1991: 219 — the last of whom observes this understanding as "commonly accepted" in New Testament scholarship.

46. So Wilson, 1973: 357; H. D. McDonald, 1981: 40; Bockmuehl, 1997: 8; Lambrecht, 1999: 56; Schwöbel, 2006: 55.

47. As Gordon Fee (1987: 515-16) puts it, "To define this term is like trying to pick up mercury between one's fingers."

48. See Rad, 1964a: 238; 1964b: 391.

49. On the relation of *doxa* to *kabod,* see Kittel, 1964a: 242.

So for Paul, no two things have the same glory. Celestial bodies like the sun, moon, and stars differ from each other in glory and from things of the earth in glory. In fact, even two stars do not have the same glory (1 Cor. 15:40-41). Not surprisingly, the greatest glory of all belongs to God. Because God has so much glory, in fact, the Bible often refers to God's glory as simply an unwavering characteristic of who God is.[50] There is commonly a visible radiance to it, which suggests not only something praiseworthy but also something that is praiseworthy for recognizable reasons.[51] Many commentators identify these reasons as God's attributes, including both what God is and does.[52] Such attributes are made manifest in Christ.

To cite but a few examples: These attributes include wisdom, which encompasses and goes far beyond the attribute of reason.[53] Christ is the "Lord of glory" because he has a wisdom far beyond that of this world (1 Cor. 2:6-8). Christ's glory also flows from being righteous, from being "full of truth" (John 1:14).[54] Moreover, God in Christ gloriously demonstrates supreme rulership and relationship attributes.[55] Christ has a "throne of glory" (Matt. 19:28; 25:31) from which to rule.[56] Yet God commonly exercises power in the form of Christ's love.[57] Jesus' earthly public ministry begins with his special blessing and provision for a common wedding, which "revealed his glory" (John 2:11). Later highlights include Jesus raising Lazarus from the dead "for God's glory" (John 11:4). Such concrete acts of love are reminiscent of God's provision of manna each morning for the wandering Israelites, thereby enabling them to "see the glory of the Lord" (Exod. 16:7).

God's glory in Christ is not only manifested through God's attributes; it also can be greater or lesser in a sense, depending on how people respond to those attributes. People can "give" or "not give" glory *(doxa)* to God, meaning that God can be more — or less — "glorified" *(doxadzom-*

---

50. For elaboration of this aspect, see Nixon, 1962: 472; Buchanan, 1972: 6.

51. On this visible radiance, see H. Carson, 1960: 42; Belleville, 1995: 116; Grenz, 2001: 206; L. T. Johnson, 2006: 69; M. Bird, 2009: 52, Ciampa and Rosner, 2010: 526.

52. E.g., Westcott, 1950: 11-12; Wilson and Blomberg, 1993: 9; Morgan, 2010: 157; Melick, 2010: 94.

53. See Witherington, 1995: 382.

54. Kline, 1980: 27 unpacks some of the ethical dimensions of God's glory.

55. This combination is highlighted in Thrall, 1994: 309 and Grenz, 2001: 206.

56. On glory and Christ's rule, see Vorster, 2011: 17.

57. See Lenski, 1946b: 964; Thiselton, 2000: 836.

enos). Jesus' teaching, for instance, causes him to be glorified by people (Luke 4:15). Often, when Jesus would heal people, onlookers would glorify God (e.g., Matt. 9:8; 15:31; Mark 2:12; Luke 5:25; 7:16; 13:13; 18:43). However, sometimes they would not, as in the case of nine of the ten lepers Jesus healed who did not give glory to God. This omission concerns Jesus because he knows his actions and character are supposed to glorify God. As he explains to his disciples regarding his post-resurrection work: "I will do whatever you ask in my name, so that the Father may be glorified in the Son" (John 14:13). This continues his earthly ministry where, as he observes to the Father: "I glorified you on earth by finishing the work that you gave me to do" (John 17:4).

Image and glory, then, are connected, but they are not the same thing. Being God's image is something that Christ is, exactly and unchangeably. Christ is intimately connected with God and completely fulfills God's intentions for how humanity is to reflect God's attributes. Particularly to the extent that these intentions are fulfilled in Christ and recognized by people, there is glory. Ultimately, and most importantly, there is God's glory. Being God's image is designed to magnify God's glory, though that glory, manifested in people, is diminished when sin intervenes.[58] In humanity, sin seriously impacts glory, so people need restoring from one degree of glory to another (see Ch. 6). In sinless God, and specifically in Christ, glory is securely rooted in who God is and what God does. Nevertheless, the intervention of sin can limit glory even then by preventing people from "glorifying" God, as noted above.

The glory that Christ has, as God's image, gives an indication of the glory — the glorification — that God has planned for people who have trusted in Christ to liberate them from the devastation of sin.[59] Not only has God created them in the divine image — intending them to become the full humanity that Christ models for them — but God removes the impediment of sin so that God's intention can be fulfilled. Glory, then, comes from the manifestation of God's attributes. And Christ's existence as God's image exemplifies God's intention that such attributes become visible as God-glorifying attributes.[60] Since Christ is the image of God, and

---

58. On this association of image and glory, see Collins, 1999: 409-10; Niehaus, 2008: 113-14. The impact of sin is discussed in Chapter 3 of the present work.

59. For further development of this theme, see Scroggs, 1966: 95-96; Attridge, 1989: 43; Grenz, 2004: 618-19; Lints, 2006a: 222; Vorster, 2011: 18.

60. So Aquinas, 1947: pt. I, Q. 34, art. 2; D. Garland, 1999: 212; D. Kelsey, 2009: v. 2, 915, 961-62, 1004.

is unspoiled by sin, what God is[61] and does[62] can truly be seen in Christ's person and actions.

The discussion above underscores the importance of not equating different biblical terms too quickly. Just because the words are closely related, a pair of terms do not necessarily mean the same thing. In Hebrews 1, there is another pair of terms where recognizing the difference can help clarify what God's image involves. According to verse 3, Christ, God's son, "is the radiance[63] [*apaugasma*] of God's glory and the exact imprint [*charakter*] of God's very being." This language picks up on the two central themes of what it means to be God's image: connection and reflection. Christ is intimately connected with God as God's exact imprint; and Christ, as the radiance of God's glory, magnificently reflects who God is and what God does.

As noted at the outset of this chapter, "exact imprint" suggests where to locate Christ in the range of the meaning of *eikon*. Christ is the "imprint-image" or exact image of God. Moreover, Christ is sinless, which Hebrews affirms a few chapters later (4:15). Paul affirms the same a chapter after he declares Christ to be God's image (2 Cor. 5:21). Because Christ is sinless, Christ reflects God's attributes exactly.

Accordingly, many commentators not surprisingly see in Hebrews 1:3 essentially the same affirmation about Christ as calling Christ "the image of God."[64] Some focus on the closeness between the Hebrews affirmation and that found in 2 Corinthians 4:4.[65] Others similarly connect the affirmation about Christ in Hebrews 1:3 with that in Colossians 1:15.[66] As in Colossians 1, identifying Christ as the exact imprint is not a way to separate the pre-incarnate Christ from Jesus. Rather, the son of which the author speaks is God's word to humanity "in these last days" (as opposed to the days of the

---

61. In this context, D. Garland (1998: 87; 1999: 212-13) discusses both what God is and does, while the focus is more on what God is in Ambrose, 1961: 254; Hafemann, 2000: 177; Grenz, 2001: 214.

62. On this emphasis, see Ra. Martin, 1981: 57; Zachman, 1990: 49; Dehsen, 1997: 270; Watson, 1997: 291.

63. Although the NRSV has "reflection" where the NIV and other translations have "radiance," radiance is preferable, as explained below.

64. E.g., McCasland, 1950: 94; Clines, 1968: 102; Wilson, 1973: 357; Mitton, 1981: 166; Hughes, 1989: 45; Attridge, 1989: 43-44; Hagner, 1990: 24; Ellingworth, 1993: 99; I. H. Marshall, 2001: 56; A. Mitchell, 2007: 42.

65. E.g., Hughes, 1977: 43-44; M. Bird, 2009: 51-52; D. Kelsey, 2009: v. 2, 985.

66. E.g., Cairns, 1973: 41; Grenz, 2004: 620; Smail, 2006: 59; D. Kelsey, 2009: v. 2, 987.

prophets long ago — vv. 1-2) — the son who not only "created the worlds" (v. 1) but also "made purification for sins" (v. 3).

In the language of Hebrews 1:3, then, Christ is the exact imprint of God's "very being" *(hupostaseos).* The term *hupostaseos* anchors this expression by indicating that in view here is God's essential being — God's essence, substance, or nature.[67] Christ is the exact imprint of that essence.

In other words, the core image-of-God theme of connection is squarely in view here. By using *charakter* rather than *eikon,* the author clarifies that Christ is the strongest form of image — an exact image — of God.[68] Christ is uniquely connected, in fact one, with God.[69] The term *charakter* does not appear elsewhere in the New Testament. However, it appears fifty-one times in the writings of Philo, which would have been well known when Hebrews was written. For Philo, God is *aneu* [without] *charakteros* — nothing can be an exact imprint of God's very being. To identify Christ as exactly that, then, is quite a claim regarding the connection of God and Christ.[70]

Although the idea of connection is dominant here due to the combination of *charakter* and *hupostaseos,* the former term offers a hint of the other core image-of-God theme, reflection. God intends images of God to reflect distinctive particulars of what God is and does. Identifying Christ as *charakter* of God evokes a picture of a stamp producing a coin or a wax seal. There are generally details involved in the stamp that make it distinctive and communicate its identity.[71] Even more intriguing is the fact that in other settings *charakter* can mean either that which does the stamping or what results from the stamping (i.e., the thing stamped). In other words, Christ's status as God's image, as well as the standard that Christ provides for people whom God is conforming to that image, may well both be in view here.[72]

67. A. Mitchell, 2007: 42 (essential being); Westcott, 1950: 13 and Hagner, 1990: 24 (essence); Bruce, 1964: 5-6 (substance); Witherington, 2009: v. 1, 401-2 (nature).

68. So Gess, 1976: 288; Kistemaker, 1997: 140; I. H. Marshall, 2001: 56-57; L. T. Johnson, 2006: 69; O'Brien, 2010: 55. Accordingly, Haering (1915: v. 1, 391), Vorster (2007a: 331), and Gushee (2013: 108) call Christ the "perfect" image.

69. On the close connection in view here, see Montefiore, 1964: 35; Gess, 1976: 288-89; Hall, 1986: 79-80; Long, 1997: 15; Witherington, 2009: v. 1, 401-2.

70. For more detail regarding the use of *charakter* in Philo and Hebrews, see Lane, 1991: 13.

71. For elaboration and examples, see Westcott, 1950: 12; Wilckens, 1967: 421; Buchanan, 1972: 6-7; Hoekema, 1994: 21; S. Wright, 2003: 38; D. Kelsey, 2009: v. 2, 983 (who draws upon Koester, 2001).

72. So Lenski, 1946c: 38; Grenz, 2001: 221; Smail, 2006: 59; Gushee, 2013: 109.

The second pair of terms in Hebrews 1:3 that helps fill out the image of God concept in relation to Christ identifies Christ as the "radiance [*apaugasma*] of God's glory." There is some debate as to whether "radiance" or "reflection" is the best translation for *apaugasma*.[73] As many have noted, the two alternatives are not necessarily all that different in meaning.[74] Both convey the visibility of God's glory *(doxa)*. However, "radiance" may be preferable simply because it underscores that the reflection involved here is a particularly intense one.

Christ's connection with God's glory is extremely close. In harmony with the closeness between God and Christ heralded in the expression that follows (see discussion above), radiance intimately expresses what glory itself is. Accordingly, many leaders in the early church favored the "radiance" translation, and the wording of the Nicene Creed echoes it.

There is no parallel in the New Testament since the term does not appear there apart from Hebrews 1:3. However, the term does appear once in the Septuagint in a passage about divine Wisdom (Wisdom of Solomon 7:26), which describes a similar closeness with God. Many commentators see there a meaning that the word "radiance" captures well.[75] The author of Hebrews, then, is trying to communicate that Christ is (radiates) the very glory of God.[76]

As noted above, glory in the Bible involves the manifestation of God's attributes. Humanity's creation in God's image entails God's intention that such attributes become visible as God-glorifying attributes in Christ. So the affirmation in Hebrews 1:3 that Christ radiates God's glory meshes well with Paul's affirmation that Christ is God's image. By radiating God's glory, Christ reflects many aspects of who God is in particularly striking fashion.[77] The connection here with the wisdom of God has already been noted.[78] Verse 3 identifies other attributes by way of illustration. Christ's

73. Attridge, 1989: 42-43 and Ellingworth, 1993: 98-99 lay out most of the arguments on each side.

74. See discussions in Westcott, 1950: 11; Montefiore, 1964: 34-35; L. T. Johnson, 2006: 69; D. Kelsey, 2009: v. 2, 982.

75. E.g., Bruce, 1964: 5; Hagner, 1990: 23-24; Lane, 1991: 13; Witherington, 2009: v. 1, 401.

76. So Lenski, 1946c: 36; Gess, 1976: 289; Hughes, 1977: 42; I. H. Marshall, 2001: 56; Mangano, 2008: 171.

77. On the manifesting of God's attributes here, see Lenski, 1946c: 37; Westcott, 1950: 10; I. H. Marshall, 2001: 57; Vorster, 2011: 18. Cf. Boer, 1990: 63 on the way that God's glory in Christ expresses God's autonomy.

78. See also Hughes, 1977: 43; Ellingworth, 1993: 99.

righteousness is manifest in making "purification for sins," and Christ's rulership is evident in "his powerful word." Moreover, relationship is also central to who Christ is, for it is Christ as son of God (v. 2) who is God's exact imprint and radiance.

Christ as Enabler and Standard of God's Image

Because of sin, humanity is not able to live out God's intentions for people created in God's likeness-image (see Chs. 3-4). Christ, however, can live them out precisely because Christ is fully God and free from sin. If humanity is not only to be created according to the standard of God's image but is also actually to fulfill God's intention for people, something must be done about sin. Christ is God's gift to humanity, not simply as the image of God, but also as the likeness of humanity and provision for sin. Without Christ as the image of God and the likeness of humanity, humanity's destiny as God's likeness-image could never be fulfilled. As John Donne has put it:

> 'Twas much, that man was made like God before,
> But that God should be made like man, much more.[79]

The crucial identity of Christ as the likeness of humanity is spelled out in several New Testament passages, the first of which is Philippians 2:6-8. Here Paul celebrates Christ as being "in human likeness" — literally in the likeness of humanity (*en homoiomati anthropon*, v. 7). The emphasis here is on the vast difference between God and people. To take on human form, Christ had to do far more than give up some things: Christ "emptied himself" (*heauton ekenosen*, v. 6). This difference between humanity and Christ/God will need further attention near the end of this chapter. It is grounded in Christ's unique connection with God as God's image. While in Hebrews Christ is "the exact imprint of God's very being" (1:3), here Christ is "in the form of God" and has "equality with God."[80]

Being in the likeness-image of God has always been a source of great dignity for humanity. However, becoming the likeness of humanity was a source of great humility for Christ. Christ "took the form of a slave" (v. 7)

---

79. Donne, 1609; and see related discussion in Canadian, 2005: 10.

80. On this theme, see Altmann, 1968: 244-45; Reule, 1971: 82; Wilson, 1973: 357; Furnish, 1984: 249; Witherington, 2009: v. 1, 237.

and experienced humbling (v. 8). That humbling included many things, but its focus involved "becoming obedient to death — even death on a cross!" (v. 8). As Jesus himself had already put it, "the Son of Man came not to be served but to serve, and to give his life a ransom for many" (Mark 10:45). Christ's identification with the lowliest state of human existence serves as a confirmation that God highly esteems every single human being (indeed, all are in the divine image).[81]

Sin is squarely in view here. It has imprisoned all people and stymied the fulfillment of God's intentions for those created in God's image, just as it enticed Adam and Eve in Eden. As Chapter 4 will discuss, sin inclined Adam and Eve to reach for the forbidden fruit because it represented a way to be like God. Christ, in contrast, demonstrates that holding on to equality with God for self-serving purposes is not God's way[82] — is not, ironically, to be like God. God is a God of loving sacrifice. God's glory is at stake here — as the culmination of verses 6-11 indicates is the case. But such glory is not something contrary to sacrificial humility. At times glory can only be manifested through humility.[83] Where humanity is concerned, only by Christ becoming the likeness of humanity and dying a slave's death to pay the price for humanity's sin can people become free to fulfill their God-given destiny to become (conformed to) God's image.

The book of Hebrews adds confirming detail to what Philippians describes. Christ did not just take on a general likeness of humanity; Christ "had to become like his brothers and sisters in every respect [kata panta]" (2:17). The reason was human sin, which thoroughly infects every aspect of human beings. As that verse concludes, Christ assumed human likeness "to make a sacrifice of atonement for the sins of the people." Christ becomes humanity's high priest.[84] For those who have been freed from sin, Christ also demonstrates how God intends for godly people to endure suffering. In fact, Christ stands ready to enable them to do so: "Because he himself was tested by what he suffered, he is able to help those who are being tested" (v. 18).

81. For further development of this theme, see D. Hart, 2009: 174. Schumacher (2008: 360) ties Christ's love for humanity to Christ's recognition that humanity is in God's image.

82. On this contrast, see Ridderbos, 1975: 74-75; Hughes, 1989: 50; C. Brown, 1991: 91-92; Dumbrell, 2002: 23.

83. On humility as a manifestation of who God is here, see Brueggemann, 1982: 34; B. Childs, 1993: 584; Clines, 1993: 427; Kilcrease, 2010: 31.

84. On Christ becoming sufficiently like people to become their high priest, see Bruce, 1964: 52-53; Buchanan, 1972: 36; Hughes, 1977: 119-20; Attridge, 1989: 95; Lane, 1991: 64; Ellingworth, 1993: 181; Guthrie, 1998: 116; Koester, 2001: 241; O'Brien, 2010: 199.

Two chapters later (4:15), Hebrews adds an important clarification. Whereas Christ took on the likeness of humanity "in every respect" in the face of life's challenges, he did so without sinning. He was *"kata panta* [in every respect] *kath homoioteta* [according to a likeness] *choris hamartias* [apart from sin]." Christ's sinlessness is an important qualification because it confirms Christ's divinity and ensures that Christ is the perfect, unblemished sacrifice which alone can permanently rescue from sin those who trust in God's only begotten son (7:26-28). It also is an important backdrop to the fullest description of what it means for Christ to be humanity's likeness, i.e., Paul's explanation of that in his letter to the Romans.

According to Romans 8:3, by sending God's son, Christ, "in the likeness of sinful flesh, and to deal with sin, [God] condemned sin in the flesh." Christ here is in the likeness of flesh, and that flesh is identified as the flesh of sin *(homoiomati sarkos hamartias).* This expression provides more detail regarding the expression *homoiomati anthropon,* which Paul employs in Philippians 2 (see above). Flesh is the human form, and to say that Christ became this likeness of humanity is to echo John's statement that "the Word became flesh [*sarx*]" (John 1:14). This flesh of humanity has a crucial and fatal characteristic — sin — which is why Christ takes on flesh. Christ has come to deal with sin, in fact, to remove it (actually, to condemn it to prison permanently the way that sin had previously imprisoned people).

This is not to say that Christ becomes sinful as part of taking on flesh.[85] Not only Hebrews 4:15 but also Paul's own acknowledgment in 2 Corinthians 5:21 preclude that possibility. Rather, Christ has come to sin's own turf, to human flesh. There Christ will fight the extraordinary battle in which the loser becomes the winner, where death gives way to life. As death draws near, on the cross, Christ becomes sin (again 2 Cor. 5:21). Christ assumes the sin of all whom God forgives and dies to pay the penalty that a just God, in accordance with a just law, must require of those who sin.[86]

The affirmation in Romans 8:3 that Christ has become humanity's

85. Although some have argued that Christ takes on sin at the Incarnation (e.g., Branick, 1985), Gillman, 1987: 600-604 and Dunn, 1988: 439, among others, have effectively countered that argument. However, there is broader agreement that in the resurrection God cleanses Christ from humanity's sin, which Christ bears on the cross (e.g., Branick, 1985: 259).

86. For more on Christ as the likeness of humanity yet sinless, see J. Murray, 1968: v. 1, 278-79; Cranfield, 1985: 382; Fitzmyer, 1993: 485; Mounce, 1995: 175-76; Moo, 1996: 479-80; Hultgren, 2011: 299.

likeness "to deal with sin" *(peri hamartias)* uses the same two words that the Old Testament (in the Septuagint's Greek translation, Lev. 6:25; Num. 8:8) and the book of Hebrews (10:6, 8) use to signify sin offerings. Christ, however, is the ultimate sin offering.[87] In submitting to the limitations of human flesh, Christ frees people from the limitations of the flesh so that they may live instead according to God's Spirit. As Paul explains it, Christ becomes the likeness of flesh "so that the just requirement of the law might be fulfilled in us, who walk not according to the flesh but according to the Spirit" (Rom. 8:4).

Christ is also the image of God, as Paul goes on to remind his readers in Romans 8.[88] Because Christ has become the likeness of humanity, humanity can now become the likeness of God that God has always intended them to be. This likeness involves conforming to the image of Christ (8:29), who is the exact image of God, as Chapters 6-7 of the present work will discuss. Christ, then, as the likeness of humanity, frees people from the sin that prevents them from fulfilling God's intentions for them as God's likeness-image. Christ as the image of God, meanwhile, is the standard for what being God's image should look like.

Christ's role as standard warrants further development here. Because biblical passages discussing Christ as the image of God most obviously present Christ as the revelation of who God is, it is easy to miss how important they are for people's identity. However, this is not an either-or interpretive choice.[89] As discussed earlier in this chapter, Christ's *connection* with God is one essential aspect of what it means for Christ to be God's image. Yet Christ's *reflection* of God demonstrates what God intends for humanity to be as well.

There are various ways to formulate a summary of how Christ as God's image serves as a revelation (or epiphany or other communication) of who people are to be because they are in God's image.[90] At issue here is what it means to be "human" — what "true humanity" entails.[91] Some see in

---

87. For elaboration, see Hodge, 1950: 253; Bruce, 1963: 161; J. Murray, 1968: 280-81; 1977: 34; Mounce, 1995: 176.

88. Bonhoeffer (1959b: 271) in particular is impressed with the connection of likeness and image here.

89. Scroggs, 1966: 98 and Walsh and Middleton, 1984: 83 emphasize this point.

90. As revelation, see Steenberg, 2009: 8; as epiphany, see Fichtner, 1978: 171; as other communication, see Lossky, 1985: 136-37 and Watson, 1997: 284-85.

91. "Human": Holmes, 2005: 319; Smail, 2005: 62. "True humanity": N. Wright, 1992b: 416; Canadian, 2005: 4; World, 2005: par. 127.

Christ a "pattern" for true humanity.[92] Others similarly see Christ as the "model," "prototype," "paradigmatic case," or "norm" for what it means to be human.[93] Still others prefer the term "ideal" as a reminder that Christ does not display what people actually are (in their sinfulness) but what God intends them to be.[94]

Whatever the terminology, the point is that Christ as the image of God is a reflection of God that demonstrates God's intentions for humanity.[95] Christ illustrates God's purposes and goals for humanity.[96] As the fulfillment of humanity's vocation — of God's call upon people[97] — Christ demonstrates who people can be.[98] Christ both is and illustrates human destiny.[99]

One way that the New Testament develops this theme is to portray Christ as the "ultimate Adam."[100] In 1 Corinthians 15:42-49 (cf. Rom. 5:12-21), for example, Paul brings together image language and the language of the ultimate (*eschatos*, v. 45) Adam. All people have borne the image of Adam (v. 49) — a reference not to the image of God but to Adam's human fallenness and aspects of his finiteness (see Ch. 4 in the present work). Those who "belong to Christ" (v. 23) can bear an image of a different Adam — Christ.

Paul uses the unusual expression of "bearing" Christ's image rather than "being" Christ's image to signify that he is talking about the characteristics that people actually manifest. Paul knows that people are not living out the attributes that should characterize those created in God's

92. E.g., Wilkins, 1997: 119; Grenz, 2002: 45.

93. E.g., Stanley, 1984: 130; Byrne, 1996: 272-73; Blackwell, 2011: 162 (model). Richardson, 2004 (prototype). Watson, 1997: 291 (paradigmatic case). Black, 2006: 181 (norm).

94. E.g., Bonhoeffer, 1959a: 37; Beale, 2011: 445-56.

95. For the language of intention in this context, see Mitton, 1981: 166; Ra. Martin, 1983: xxi; Hoekema, 1994: 22; D. Garland, 1998: 87; Grenz, 2004: 618; Reynolds, 2008: 199-200; Erickson, 2013: 464; Cortez, 2010: 17.

96. So Clines, 1968: 103; Cairns, 1973: 56; N. Wright, 1986: 274-75; Nellas, 1987: 34-35; Grudem, 1994: 445; Grenz, 2004: 627; Deane-Drummond, 2012: 944.

97. For the language of vocation in this context, see Ro. Martin, 2002: 86; Grenz, 2004: 621, 628; Green, 2011: 277.

98. On this future orientation, see Nellas, 1987: 33; McLeod, 1999: 72-73 (drawing on Narsai); T. Peters, 2010: 221.

99. For the language of destiny/destination in this context, see Mays, 2006: 41; Jersild, 2008: 43; Witherington, 2009: v. 2, 150; Vorster, 2011: 20.

100. See Scroggs, 1966: 97-98; Altmann, 1968: 245; Ridderbos, 1975: 70-76; McClendon, 1991: 442; Moo, 1996: 534; Grenz, 2004: 619; Gaffin, 2010: 137. Irenaeus also makes much of this theme; see Maloney, 1973: 44.

image. The reason for this is that people presently bear the image of finite and fallen Adam.

That, however, can change. By following Christ, people can live out the attributes that should characterize being in God's image. They can begin even now the process of bearing the image of Christ — actually living out who Christ is and what Christ does. That is what God intended for the first Adam in the beginning, by creating Adam in the divine image, but because of sin it is something that can only be fulfilled in Christ, the one who *is* God's image.

Significantly, Paul does not just lift up Christ as divine and therefore worthy of following, as he does elsewhere. Instead, he refers to Christ even in his resurrected and glorified state as human (an *anthropos* "of heaven" vs. the first Adam, the *anthropos* "of dust," v. 49). To appreciate who (the first) Adam was, one must look to another *adam*, Christ.[101] Through this eschatological or ultimate Adam, one understands God's intentions for humanity.[102] The fulfillment of those intentions in Christ displays God's image exactly.[103] Christ is thus the model of humanity — truly image of God, truly human.[104]

To affirm that Christ is the standard for who people are to be is not yet to say anything specific regarding what that includes. In fact, generating a definitive list of specifics is impossible. As previously discussed, the New Testament teaches that Christ as God's image reveals who God is, with the intention that this revelation will serve as a standard for who people are to be. Yet nowhere does the text claim that Christ reveals everything about God — just that Christ does truly represent many things about God. There are mysteries about God that people do not understand, some characteristics of Christ (e.g., his Jewishness) that do not reveal characteristics of God per se, and some aspects of God in Christ that await Christ's return before people can understand them.[105] However, while they wait, Christians can be confident that they will ultimately become more like Christ — more

101. See McFarland, 1999: 107.

102. So Kittel, 1964d: 395-96; Murphy-O'Connor, 1982: 42-44; Dunn, 1988: 483; Smail, 2006: 59.

103. So Orr, 1948: 272; Pannenberg, 1985: 79; Grenz, 2001: 216-17; Vorster, 2011: 17.

104. Byrne, 1996: 272-73 (model); Fichtner, 1978: 63-64 (image); Scroggs, 1966: 93-94 (human). K. Barth, 1958a: 203 explores the close connection between true image and true human.

105. For elaboration, see Balthasar, 1967: 86; McFarland, 2005: 4, 8; D. Kelsey, 2009: v. 2, 1009.

conformed to Christ's image — than they could possibly describe now (1 John 3:2; see discussion in Ch. 6).

Some things, then, though not everything, can be said about what Christ being God's image and thus the standard for humanity entails. As the discussion above suggests, these things are expressions of God's glory and include various divine attributes involving both who God is and what God does.[106] God's intention is that such attributes become visible as God-glorifying attributes first in Christ and ultimately in all humanity.

One example of such attributes is God's wisdom. As noted above, terminology that is uniquely shared by 2 Corinthians 4 and the Wisdom of Solomon 7 in the Greek Bible, the Septuagint, suggests to many (some would say most) scholars a likely connection between the two passages.[107] Presenting Christ as God's image could in part be Paul's way of adapting the familiar Hellenistic-Jewish notion of personified Wisdom for his purposes.

Paul is well aware of the Old Testament personification of wisdom as one who "was there when [God] made the world" (Prov. 8:26), and he readily identifies Christ as God's wisdom (e.g., 1 Cor. 1:24, 30). So chapter 7 of the Wisdom of Solomon may have suggested to Paul a way to connect wisdom and image with the person of Christ: Wisdom is "a pure emanation of the glory of the Almighty . . . a reflection of eternal light, a spotless mirror of the working of God, and an image of his goodness" (vv. 25-26). Glory, reflection, light, mirror, goodness, eternal, spotless — these are all ideas connected with the image of God as embodied by Christ according to 2 Corinthians 4, Colossians 1, and Hebrews 1.

Paul, however, is not letting Greek rationalistic concepts shape his account of Christ. Rather, he is presenting Christ as encompassing selected, true characteristics of God already familiar to his readers and adding much more. For instance, neither Paul nor others would see all things as created for wisdom, the way that Paul sees everything created for Christ (Col. 1:15-16).[108] Instead, wisdom is one of many attributes that God intends for

---

106. Horton, 2006: 187, 190 and Cortez, 2010: 38, for example, acknowledge the inclusion of both aspects.

107. O'Brien, 1987: 43 says "many"; Köstenberger et al., 2009: 615 says "most"; and Witherington, 2009: v. 1, 400 (invoking early church support from Clement of Alexandria) says that the connection is "clear." For other examples of those making this connection, see Stendebach, 2003: 395; Thrall, 1994: 310; M. Harris, 2005: 331; Thompson, 2005: 30; Minor, 2009: 80-81. Cf. Keener, 2005: 16.

108. As Ra. Martin, 1981: 58 has observed. See also Wilson, 1973: 360.

Christ to manifest, as God's image, to God's glory.[109] God's wisdom is not self-centered or prideful, in the way that human wisdom shaped by sin is (cf. the contrast between human and godly wisdom in 1 Cor. 1:19-25). As will become clearer in Chapters 6-7, Christ's wisdom is not merely abstract but ultimately provides concrete guidance for godly living.[110] To "learn Christ" is to develop minds that are not futile or darkened (Eph. 4:17, 18, 20). Christ, as God's image, is the model and enabler of freedom (2 Cor. 3:17-18).

A second, and perhaps more obvious, example of an attribute that God intends for Christ to manifest as God's image is righteousness. Christ, as one who has never sinned, is *the* example of what God intends for true humanity.[111] Christ's righteousness is not only an aspect of being God, but it is also a genuine human attribute that is part of God's intention for the divine image.[112] Accordingly, "learning Christ" involves foreswearing licentiousness and impurity (Eph. 4:19-20). When Paul lifts up Christ as God's image (2 Cor. 4:4), according to which believers are to be transformed (2 Cor. 3:18), it is in terms of a particular manifestation of glory — justification (2 Cor. 3:9). Justification is not the end of Christ's righteousness-related work in Christians for God's glory, but a step toward their full glorification. In that glorification the full implications of what it means for Christ and ultimately the church to bear God's image become clear.[113]

A third example of Christ's image-related attributes involves rulership. As noted in Chapter 5, Hebrews 2:8-9 indicates that God's intentions for people's rulership since the beginning have not come to fruition . . . "but we do see Jesus." Christ's life, death, and glorification are all mentioned here as part of describing the power Christ successfully exercised over the "suffering of death."[114] Christ demonstrates what rulership can be when sin no longer has control. Rulership, though, as a fulfillment of God's purposes

---

109. See Conzelmann, 1975: 187; Schweizer, 1982: 65-66; Dunn, 1996: 88; Matera, 2003: 102; Keener, 2005: 169-70.

110. On this theme related to Christ as God's image, see Mangano, 2008: 171-72.

111. See Orr, 1948: 271-72; Mahoney, 2011: 44.

112. John Wesley (1985l: 452-53) explains further the difference between Christ's human and divine natures in relation to Christ being the image of God, and how righteousness is involved.

113. The central place of Christ's glorification, as God's image, is developed in Dunn, 1973: 140-41.

114. On the connection of Hebrews 2 here with Christ as God's image, see Orr, 1948: 272; O'Donovan, 1986: 24, 53; Grenz, 2001: 208-9; Horton, 2006: 190.

for Christ as God's image, extends much farther. According to Colossians 1:15, Christ fulfills God's image-related intentions by holding together all of creation (v. 17), serving as head of the church (v. 18), and reconciling all things to God (v. 20).[115] As Jesus frequently said, he was about promoting a kingdom (or better, a rulership), one in which God's values and ways were manifest. Jesus' life, culminating most prominently in his death, illustrates the servant-leadership kind of rulership that God intends.[116]

While many other attributes of Christ illustrate God's intentions, one particularly significant further example involves relationship. As introduced earlier in this chapter, to be explained further in Chapter 3, being God's image means that there is a close connection with God. However, it also has to do with attributes that God intends the divine image to reflect — attributes that Christ manifests exactly without the hindrance of sin.

Christ is the supreme model, for instance, of what God intends for relationships with people.[117] Jesus sacrifices himself for the good of others and relates to all as if oppressive human distinctions among types of people are irrelevant. According to Colossians 3:10, when Christ serves as the image according to which Christians are renewed, that renewal does away with prioritizing people on the basis of their being Greek or Jew, circumcised or uncircumcised, slave or free. Christ as God's image demonstrates God's commitment to reconciling relationships that have been broken for whatever reasons, including relationships with the non-human creation.[118]

Romans 8:29 offers a compelling picture of some of the key relationships involved here. Paul lifts up Christ as the image to which God's people are to conform. What is most exemplary about Christ in this context is that Christ — in Paul's words — is the Son of God. If people are to take this image as the pattern for their own existence, then they too are to be, as Paul would put it, children of their heavenly Father and so be members of the same family. In other words, the reason for believers conforming to

---

115. For further discussion, see Jervell, 1960: 333; Wildberger, 1965: 500; Barth and Blanke, 1994: 249; Vorster, 2011: 17.

116. Verhey, 2003: 90 and S. Wright, 2003: 43; C. Wright, 2004: 125 further develops this kingdom/rulership and servant-leadership in relation to God's image. Also see Ch. 5.

117. On relationship and being God's image, see S. Wright, 2003: 36; Gonzalez, 2007: 64.

118. Sherlock, 1996: 69 develops this theme further on the human plane. Vorster, 2011: 24 expands it to include the nonhuman creation.

the image of Christ is "in order that he might be the firstborn within a large family." Christ's identity is humanity's destiny.[119]

Paul does not always connect image language with sonship. For example, in 2 Corinthians 3-4 Christ as God's image is "Lord" (3:16, 17, 18; 4:5). But sonship is one important aspect of what it entails for Christ to be the image of God in the New Testament.[120] The author of Hebrews similarly connects image-related language in the first chapter (see above) to Christ as the "Son" (v. 2). In view here is not just Christ's divinity, where "Son" refers to one member of the Trinity. Rather, in the biblical passages noted above, sonship is also a characterization of Jesus as human among people in his earthly life, in death and resurrection, and among brothers and sisters in eternal glory. It refers to God's relational intentions for Christ as the image of God.[121]

Just as Christ is God's unique image, so the New Testament authors call Christ God's son in a special way. For instance, John 3:16 reports that God's "only Son" was God's gift to the world. Whether "only" or "only begotten" is the best translation of *monogene* here, the point is that Jesus has a unique family connection with God. Not even angels are special children in this sense, according to Hebrews (1:5). Nevertheless, when the image concept is under consideration, as in Romans 8:29, Christ is specifically the firstborn *(prototokos)* of many.[122] In other words, Christ as the image of God demonstrates the close familial relationship that God intends for all people.

Many of the attributes of Christ are the model and standard for attributes that people, created in the divine image, are increasingly to manifest even before Christ's return. However, some attributes of Christ that God intends for people ultimately to manifest are attributes that even Adam and Eve did not manifest before the Fall — so people cannot manifest them until after their glorification when Christ returns. Those include imperishability (being unable to die) and a glorified, spiritual body (see Ch. 7). Christ, as the one who has the power to destroy death itself, is imperishable (1 Cor.

119. See related discussion in McFadyen, 1990: 46-47; Pannenberg, 1991: v. 2, 176; Schnelle, 1996: 101-2.

120. So Cairns, 1973: 41; Kline, 1980: 30; H. D. McDonald, 1981: 39-40; Baker, 1991: 38.

121. See O'Brien, 1987: 44; C. Brown, 1991: 88, 98; Mathews, 1995: 164; Horton, 2005: 107; 2006: 186-87; Beale, 2011: 446.

122. R. Jewett (2007: 529) is one of many scholars who understand *prototokos* here, as in another image-related passage, Colossians 1:15, to signify not merely first in order but also first in significance.

15:25-26); and Christ now has a spiritual body (1 Cor. 15:44-47). "Just as we have borne the image of the man of dust, we will also bear the image of the man of heaven" (1 Cor. 15:49) — including an imperishable spiritual body.

To be sure, there are those who separate Christ and humanity more than this discussion would suggest is biblically warranted. In many cases, they are really just stating vigorously a point that the present work affirms as well — that only Christ *is* the image of God (as opposed to created according to that image).[123] However, some are making the stronger claim that people are not associated with the image of God in any meaningful sense; only Christ is.[124] Without being God one cannot be God's image.[125] So, according to this view, the New Testament and Old Testament may not even be talking about the same thing when they refer to the image of God.[126]

There are several major reasons why disconnecting Christ and humanity completely when it comes to God's image is unwarranted. The first is that doing so typically flows from the common but inadequate assumption that being in God's image is about how people are actually like God. Indeed, Christ is actually so much more like God than people are that the same term really cannot meaningfully apply to them both. For example, Christ and God are uncreated and divine; humanity is neither.

However, as this book will demonstrate in great detail (see especially Chs. 3, 4, and 5), *actual* likeness to God is not what being created in God's image involves. Creation *in* God's image is God's expressed *intention* that people evidence the special connection they have with God through a meaningful reflection of God.

In humanity, because of sin, there is a huge disconnect between what God intends people to be and what they actually are. However, in Christ, with no sin present, God's intentions are fulfilled and manifested exactly. Language of connection and reflection, then, fit well both with Christ as God's image and with humanity as created in that image. There is no need to think that different concepts are involved here.

---

123. See H. Carson, 1960: 42; John Paul II, 1997b: 521; I. H. Marshall, 2001: 58; World, 2005: par. 78; Pinckaers, 2005: 157 (drawing on Aquinas); Mahoney, 2010: 679.

124. E.g., Thielicke, 1966: 171; Pannenberg, 1985: 238, 498; Grenz, 2001: 217; Wells, 2004: 31-32; McFarland, 2005: 57.

125. E.g., Augustine, 1990: 267; K. Barth, 1958b: 222; Bray, 1991: 211-14; Baker, 1991: 40; Ra. Martin, 1996: 500; Smail, 2003: 24-25; Gardoski, 2007: 18; Vorster, 2011: 18-19.

126. Eltester (1958: 148) and J. Barr (1993: 164) are two who maintain that there is a complete disconnect here.

The second reason why disconnecting Christ and humanity completely is unwarranted, where God's image is concerned, is that doing so overlooks the ways that the relevant New Testament passages build on and help explain image-of-God creational language in Genesis, together with redemptional themes also set in motion in Genesis.[127] As already explained, the key passages in 2 Corinthians, Colossians, and Hebrews, plus the Christ-as-Ultimate-Adam passages, elaborate the Old Testament image-of-God concept in ways that many find "difficult to deny."[128]

The third problem with totally separating Christ as God's image from humanity being in God's image is that doing so neglects the common language that the Bible uses to describe both. As documented in this chapter and Chapter 6, God intends for people and Christ to manifest the glory of God in specific ways that include various attributes reflecting who God is and what God does. Reason/wisdom, righteousness, rulership, and relationship/family are examples of attributes that the Bible identifies with Christ as God's image. They are also examples of what God intends people to develop because they are created according to that image — that is, according to Christ. While Christ fulfills God's intentions exactly, and is the very embodiment of those intentions, humanity fails miserably. But that is not the end of the human story, as Chapters 6-7 explain.

Rather than being unrelated, Christ as the image of God and humanity as created in the image of God are profoundly related. Christ has always been God's image, from before the creation of humanity (see discussion of relevant New Testament verses above). In other words, God knew the standard for what humanity was to be — the humanity of Christ — before creating Adam/*adam*.[129] The Ultimate Adam, Jesus Christ, is a fulfillment

127. On creational connections, see McCasland, 1950: 87; Kline, 1977: 266; Grenz, 2004: 626; McDonough, 2009: 90; D. Kelsey, 2009: v. 2, 905, 961; Briggs, 2010: 118; Oberdorfer, 2010: 238. On redemptional connections, see Athanasius, 1885: chs. 11, 13; Wilson and Blomberg, 1993: 9; McLeod, 1999: 49; D. Kelsey, 2009: v. 2, 905, 962-63.

128. So Ridderbos, 1975: 70-73, who notes in particular the dependence of 2 Corinthians 4 (e.g., v. 6) and Colossians 1 on creation and cites Jervell's (1960: 174) claim that "we have before us [in Col. 1], therefore, a christological interpretation of Genesis 1." Watson, 1997: 281-82, and S. Wright, 2003: 38 reach the same conclusion. On the mutual interdependence of the Genesis and Christological (New Testament) accounts of God's image, see Smail, 2003: 24; Mangano, 2008: Preface; Vorster, 2011: 4, 16.

129. So Kümmel, 1963: 86; Maloney, 1973: 36, 39 (discussing the view of Irenaeus); Ridderbos, 1975: 73; Kline, 1977: 261; Hughes, 1985: 20; Golitzin, 2003: 349; Grenz, 2004: 626; Holmes, 2005: 319; Smail, 2006: 63-64; Behr, 2013: 27; Gushee, 2013: 108.

of who God has always intended people to be.[130] But that is not because Christ becomes something new. Christ is the same yesterday, today, and forever (Heb. 13:8). In one sense, the Ultimate Adam is really the first — the one who not only created *adam* but also was the God-intended standard for *adam*.[131]

> In his own image God created man,
> And when from dust he fashioned Adam's face,
> The likeness of his only Son was formed:
> His Word incarnate, filled with truth and grace.[132]

How this all fits together becomes more understandable in light of the Incarnation. Christ becoming flesh and blood is not a new initiative that God develops to restore a wayward humanity.[133] God has always intended Christ to be the image of God, the standard of humanity, and the perfect lamb whose blood redeems believers. As the first letter of the apostle Peter puts it, for this redemptive task Christ "was destined before the foundation of the world, but was revealed at the end of the ages" (1 Pet. 1:20).[134] Ephesians adds that God "before the foundation of the world . . . destined [believers] for adoption as his children through Jesus Christ" (Eph. 1:4-5). This is an echo of the Romans 8:29 image passage (see Ch. 6), according to which God "predestined [believers] to be conformed to the image of his Son, in order that he might be the firstborn within a large family."

God created humanity at the outset in the image of God, in harmony with Christ as God's image. This paved the way for Christ, in the Incarnation, to take on the likeness of humanity, as discussed earlier in this chapter.[135] One might even say that humanity's creation in the image of God was the reason the Incarnation was possible, as part of God's eternal

---

130. Boer, 1990: 160 develops this theme.

131. See Krause, 2005: 366; McDonough, 2009: 89-90; Harrison, 2010: 35; Tanner, 2010: 14. Behr (2013: 27) notes that a close connection between Christ as the image of God and the creation of humanity in the image of God was "the predominant perspective of the Christian tradition in the first millennium."

132. This "traditional hymn" is reprinted in Soskice, 2011: 295.

133. For an elaboration of this theme, see T. Ware, 1974: 94; Steenberg, 2009: 7-8. Cf. Goodman, 2008: 146.

134. According to some translations such as the NIV, Revelation 13:8 reflects a similar understanding in its description of "the Lamb who was slain from the creation of the world."

135. So N. Wright, 1986: 274; Gonzalez, 2007: 48.

purposes.[136] This creation also established Christ, God's image, as the standard for humanity's transformation (2 Cor. 3:18; Col. 3:10; again see Ch. 6).

The recognition of Christ as the image of God — the standard of what God has always intended people in God's image to be — had a powerful effect on the early church. Various commentators have remarked on the relatively little concern about making images or prohibiting images of God in the New Testament.[137] At the time of its writing, the church had just experienced the image of God visibly in their very midst. Christ had shown them their destiny and reminded them of their dignity as God's creation in the divine image. As Chapter 4 will note, images must be God's work and must glorify God, rather than displacing God. So the New Testament remains opposed to human-constructed idols. But people can fulfill the divine intention for them as made in God's image through their renewal in Christ. That is God's work, to God's glory. For humanity's renewal to make sense, though, we first need to consider humanity's original creation in God's image.

136. So Bruce, 1957: 194; Cameron, 1989: 27; Mangano, 2008: 169-70; cf. van Leeuwen, 1997: 647.

137. E.g., K. Barth, 1958a: 201-2; Lints, 2006a: 222.

PART II

Human Dignity

Humanity's Creation in God's Image

Although the concept of humanity's creation in the image of God is vitally important, its exact meaning has always been controversial (Ch. 1). Accordingly, the discussion here has begun with a consideration of the clearest affirmation about the image of God in the Bible — Christ "is" God's image (Ch. 2). We are now in a better position to consider what it means for humanity to be "created in" God's image. This task will not be complete until we consider what it means for people to be renewed in God's image, that is, to be renewed in Christ (Chs. 6-7).

Who Is Identified with the Image of God

According to Genesis 1, God created *adam*. Who exactly is this *adam* that Genesis 1 describes using "image of God" language? *Adam* here refers not only to a single man named Adam but also to humanity as a whole. Contemporary readers can easily miss this point if they are located in societies like the United States that emphasize individualism, personal freedom, and autonomy. *Adam* is more than one human being or even one collection of human beings; there is also a corporate entity somehow involved in the image of God.[1] Overlooking that can lead to a truncated view of God's

---

1. On the importance of not neglecting this corporate aspect of the image, see Brunner, 1952: 64-65; Wolff, 1974: 161; Berkouwer, 1975: 98-99; Brueggemann, 1982: 33-34; Mouw, 1983: 47; Moltmann, 1984: 17; Greidanus, 1984: 15; Boer, 1990: 171-72; Hoekema, 1994: 99-100 (citing Herman Bavinck in support); Jenson, 1999: 59; Grenz, 2002: 43; and Bradley, 2010: 26. As will be discussed below, some commentators place too exclusive an emphasis

image, which can reinforce rather than critique unhealthy individualism.[2] When that occurs, the dignity of being in God's image sometimes ends up protecting only particular individuals rather than extending to the human community in its entirety (see Ch. 1).

Genesis 1:26 introduces the creation of humanity using a singular noun, *adam,* to which verse 27 refers by using both a singular and a plural pronoun. In other words, there is a tension between the singularity and plurality of humankind. Many translations obscure the fact that the first reference to this "humankind" in verse 27 employs a singular pronoun,[3] by which the Hebrew text indicates that in some sense it is the single entity, humanity as a whole, that is associated with God's image.[4] As we will see, New Testament passages connecting people with the image of Christ also tend to have a corporate entity (group) in view rather than just separate human beings. For instance, Paul connects all believers to the image of Christ in Romans 8:29 (cf. "we all" in 1 Cor. 3:18), explaining that God had this corporate connection in mind from the beginning.[5]

At the same time, the verbs describing humanity's ruling over creation in Genesis 1:26 and 1:28 are plural. Moreover, Genesis 1:27 does indeed associate "humankind"/*adam* with a plural pronoun as well as a singular pronoun. The author here suggests that male and female components of the whole (plural) — not just the whole itself represented by Adam (singular) — are directly involved with the image-of-God designation. Later passages that associate people and God's image, such as Genesis 9:6 and

---

on the corporate dimension (e.g., Boer, 1990: 7: "No one person . . . only mankind, whether as two or as many, is *imago Dei*").

2. This caution is developed in Richard, 1986: 165; LaCugna, 1993: 109; and Sherlock, 1996: 84.

3. The reference here may be to the particular man Adam; however, the text presents Adam's creation in verse 27 as the fulfillment of God's intention in verse 26 to create humanity, so Adam must at least represent humanity.

4. For instance, both the NRSV and the NIV translate verse 27b "in the image of God he created them." However, "them" is translating a singular pronoun indicating in the original text that humanity is not just a collection of human beings but also an integrated entity. The same translational obscuring occurs in Genesis 5:1. A clearer translation here would either use a singular pronoun such as "it" to translate the singular Hebrew pronoun or would repeat the singular noun ("humanity" or "humankind") in place of the singular pronoun.

5. Gregory of Nyssa (1972: 555) adds that the same foreknowledge of God that sees the church as a whole in conjunction with the image of Christ in the new creation also sees humanity as a whole in conjunction with the image of God in the initial creation. See also Maloney, 1973: 142-43; D. Hart, 2002: 548-49.

James 3:9, more directly suggest that particular people have "image" status, with the protections that affords, in that people are often killed or cursed one at a time.[6] The basis for that status is that they are members of *adam,* but the text accords this status to particular human beings (e.g., the plural *anthropous* in James 3:9; for more on particular human beings and God's image, see discussion of relationship in Ch. 5). Genesis 5:1-2 reflects both the plural and the singular nature of humanity, referring back to the original creation and again using both a singular and a plural pronoun to refer to the same word *adam.*[7]

In some passages, *adam* refers to a particular human being whose name is Adam. Often the definite article ("the") is used to clarify when Adam the particular person is in view, rather than humanity in general. But that convention is not always maintained. It is possible the author intentionally fosters some ambiguity as to whether an individual or corporate human(ity) is in view, since both the individual and corporate aspects of human existence are so important.[8]

As Chapter 1 has already illustrated, recent history demonstrates the significance and power of holding together the communal and individual ways that people are associated with God's image. This dynamic, a major affirmation of the Catholic International Theological Commission's document "Communion and Stewardship: Human Persons Created in the Image of God," was also central to the liberating efforts of Martin Luther King Jr.[9] Other commentators have noticed the appropriateness of this dynamic in conjunction with a God who is three in one — multiple persons and yet a unity at the same time.[10]

Thus referring to particular people as being in God's image is legiti-

---

6. Mulzac (2001: 74) and Oberdorfer, 2010: 232 develop this theme from Genesis 9; Niskanen, 2009: 428 roots it in Genesis 1; Mathews (1995: 173) and I. H. Marshall (2001: 54) appeal to biblical language generally; and Benedict XVI (1995: 45) invokes broader theological grounds. For historical support, see Horowitz, 1979: 204.

7. There is no distinction here between *hadam* and *adam,* as sometimes occurs in Genesis 1. Simply *"adam"* refers to both an individual man and to the entire community of people created.

8. As Gordon Wenham (1987: 32) has noted on exegetical grounds. Cf. Verduin, 1970: 72.

9. On King, see Wills, 2009: 140; on the Commission, see Mahoney, 2010: 683 (cf. Hittinger, 2013: 44 on Catholic thought generally regarding God's image). On the general point, see Haering, 1915: v. 1, 394; Marshall, 2001: 62; Plantinga, 2002: 40; Mays, 2006: 36-37; Rogerson, 2010: 193; Mitchell, 2013: 86.

10. E.g., see Green, 1999: 54-55; Frame, 2006: 232.

mate; but that is always in the context of — and never separate from — their identity as (members of) humanity. Speaking of all humanity as created in God's image is legitimate as well; but that is inclusive of — not to the exclusion of — particular human beings. Connecting God's image both to humankind as a whole and to each of the humans who constitute that "kind" guards against destructive overemphasis on individuals *or* collectives.[11]

To sustain this dynamic even in the language for God's image, adopting flexible terminology is crucial. It must be able to refer to the totality of humanity and yet immediately also suggest the plurality of individuals who make up that totality. The word "people" meets these criteria particularly well and so will generally be used throughout this book to identify those who are in God's image.

How People Are Related to the Image of God

"The image of God" would not have been a strange concept to readers and hearers of the Old Testament, as explained in the previous chapter. In various parts of the ancient Near East, people considered kings, priests, and monuments, among other things, to be images of gods or kings. The biblical writings adopt the general concept but adapt it in various ways to fit the biblical message. For example, in the Bible not merely the king is involved in God's image, but even the lowliest of people are involved as well (see discussion below).

Another important adaptation of the Bible's authors is the way they normally avoid stating that people simply *are* the image of God.[12] Rather, these authors insert a preposition indicating that people stand in some relationship with God's image.[13] Various translations indicate that people

11. For elaborations of this observation, see Moltmann, 1976: 63-64; Faus, 1993: 517-18; Gunton, 1999: 59.

12. On the importance of paying careful attention to the ways that the authors of the Bible adjust ideas they employ from their contemporary cultural context, see Niskanen, 2009: 420. For example, as Di Vito, 2010: 172 notes, it is "hardly thinkable" that the author of the statements in Genesis about humanity being in the image of God — who "takes considerable pains . . . to assert the fundamental distance between God and humankind" — would ever suggest that humanity *is* the image of God, in the manner of the Egyptian pharaoh or certain Assyrian or neo-Babylonian kings. Cf. Mathews, 1995: 168.

13. On prepositions in the Bible as basically signifying relationships between things, see M. Harris, 2012: 27.

are created "in" or "according to" God's image. Christ, in the words of the New Testament (e.g., 2 Cor. 4:4; Col. 1:15) simply *is* the image of God (no preposition). In contrast, image-related passages in Genesis (1:26; 1:27; 5:1; 9:6) consistently insert a preposition — and not always the same one — between people and the image. Image-related passages in the New Testament directly or indirectly referring to Genesis (e.g., James 3:9; Col. 3:10) also insert a preposition.

It is not plausible that the author in each passage is simply saying that people are God's image, as if there were no prepositions there, and no need to add them. What makes more sense is that the Bible's authors recognize a difference between Christ and the rest of humanity. With Christ not overtly in view as a reference point in the Old Testament, the recognition there would simply have been that people are not yet God's image but are intended ultimately to be so.[14] In the New Testament it will become clearer that Christ as God's image is the standard to which people still need to conform. Even Adam and Eve before the Fall needed further development — they were not already God's image (see Ch. 7). They were created according to that image. James 3:9 is particularly significant on this point since it conveys a New Testament author's summary of how the Genesis idea should be understood — not just as reinterpreted in Christ, but in its own right applying to all people.[15] In the words of James, people are made *kata* (according to) the likeness-image of God,[16] just as Paul explains that people need further making *kata* (according to or toward) the image of their Creator (see below and Ch. 6).

In Genesis, the image-related prepositions are *be* and *ke*. *Be* is often translated "in" — hence the familiar expression "in God's image." Some scholars, particularly since the influential analysis of D. J. A. Clines in 1968 (which drew on the lexical work of Gesenius), have noted that *be* can occasionally mean "as" in the unusual sense of "is." The idea would be that humanity is created as God's image, meaning that it *is* God's image.[17]

However, "the majority of contemporary exegetes" and "most com-

---

14. On the importance of this distinction see, for example, Feinberg, 1972: 244; Bird, 1981: 138; Hughes, 1989: 17; Pannenberg, 1991: 215-16; Smail, 2006: 57; McFarland, 2005: 4; McDonough, 2009: 91.

15. On James 3:9 as describing the image-related concept of Genesis 1:26-27, see Ra. Martin, 1988: 119; Richardson, 1997: 157; McKnight, 2011: 294.

16. As Richardson (1997: 157) explains, the idea here is that a key purpose of people's creation by God is "to reflect the attributes of God in a creaturely way."

17. Clines, 1968: 75-76, introduces his position by referencing Gesenius.

mentators" disagree with this conclusion.[18] One reason is that *ke* is much less likely to have that meaning (and *kata* in the New Testament even less so).[19] In other words, regardless of how one translates *be*, the meaning throughout the Bible hardly can be that people "are" God's image.[20] Accordingly, the Old Testament lexicon by Brown, Driver, and Briggs, which updates the work of Gesenius, concludes that *be* in Genesis 1:26 serves to relate something (here humanity) to a model (here the image of God).[21] More recently the standard *Hebrew and Aramaic Lexicon of the Old Testament* by Koehler and Baumgartner specifies that "according to" is the best rendering of both *be* and *ke* in image passages in Genesis 1 and 5.[22] Genesis, then, records that God has created humanity "according to" the divine image.

A review of the way that Genesis uses *be* and *ke* confirms that — like the terms "image" and "likeness" (see below) — the two prepositions are essentially interchangeable in the image-of-God concept.[23] For instance, the Hebrew preposition *be* goes with "image" and the preposition *ke* goes with "likeness" in Genesis 1:26-27; but *be* goes with "likeness" and *ke* goes with "image" in Genesis 5:1-3. In other words, while the two prepositions can mean different things, they also have a meaning in common that describes people's relationship to God's image.[24] *Be* commonly means "in"

---

18. This is the observation that Grenz, 2001: 189 reaches after assessing the relevant literature. Emphatic statements of disagreement with the view espoused by Clines date all the way back to early church leaders such as Athanasius (see Maloney, 1973: xii, 8, 97-98) and Augustine (see D. Robinson, 2011: 8-9), are prominent later in Aquinas (1947: pt. I, q. 36, art. 1 and pt. I, q. 93, art. 1), and are found more recently in K. Barth, 1958a: 197, D. Kelsey, 2009: v. 2, 956, and numerous authors cited in the next dozen notes below.

19. E.g., Humbert, 1940: 159; Miller, 1972: 296; Harland, 1996: 187.

20. For additional linguistic and other reasons why *be* cannot be signifying that people *are* God's image, see J. Barr, 1968: 17; Mettinger, 1974: 406; Sawyer, 1974: 421; Wenham, 1987: 29; Hamilton, 1990: 137; Schmutzer, 2009: 173.

21. Brown, Driver, and Briggs, 1966: 90. Similarly, Eichrodt, 1967: 122.

22. Koehler and Baumgartner, 2001: 104.

23. Later acknowledged by Clines himself (1993: 427). See also Humbert (1940: 159); W. Schmidt (1964: 133); Rad (1972: 58); Sawyer (1974: 421); Wenham (1987: 29); Barentsen (1988: 31-32); Westermann (1994: 145); Vogels (1994: 190-92); Wildberger (1997: 1082); Mathews (1995: 167); Gardoski (2007: 11); and Middleton (2005: 47-48). W. Randall Garr (2003: 6-7) documents many others who agree, though he himself is sympathetic to the way that distinguishing between prepositions can lead to the view that children are less God's image than their father is (2003: 176) — a view whose merits hinge on whether or not the image is a variable status (see later in this chapter).

24. See Wenham, 1987: 28-29 on the overlapping meanings of *be* and *ke*, drawing on the analysis of Brown, Driver, and Briggs, 1996: 88-91, 453-55. Similarly, see Waltke, 1989: 10.

or "according to."[25] Since *ke* commonly means "according to" or "toward," something close to "according to" appears to be the overlapping meaning in view here.[26]

This meaning is confirmed by the corresponding use of *kata* (normally "according to")[27] in the New Testament. In fact, the Greek Old Testament, the Septuagint, most often uses *kata* to translate both *be* and *ke;* the Latin Vulgate always uses *ad* ("toward") for both. Reference to early Greek translations of the Hebrew Bible and to Greek New Testament summaries of Hebrew Old Testament teaching on God's image can help add precision to translation. The Greek language has many more — and so more nuanced — prepositions than the Hebrew language has.[28]

There are two New Testament books that comment on the image status of both Christ and people, and they consistently distinguish between Christ, who is God's image, and people who need transformative growth according to the standard of that image. In Colossians 1, Christ straightforwardly *is* the image of God (v. 15). However, two chapters later, when people are in view, they are not God's image but they need renewal according to God's image in Christ (3:10).[29] (The parallel passage, Eph. 4:24, similarly includes the preposition *kata,* suggesting that it is central to the concept.)[30] Similarly, according to 2 Corinthians 4:4, Christ *is* God's image. Yet four verses earlier (3:18), when people are in view, they need transformation into the divine image. God's intention from the beginning has been to conform people to God's image — to Christ (Rom. 8:29).

25. For this range of meaning in *be,* see Charlesworth, 1990: 68.

26. For further justification of *be* in Genesis 1 as meaning something like "according to," see Vriezen, 1943: 93; Berkhof, 1949: 204; Hamilton, 1990: 137. Westermann, 1994: 145, drawing on the work of K. L. Schmidt, W. Baumgartner, and A. Kropat, further explains the rendering of *ke* in Genesis 1 as "according to" and supports the same translation of *be* in Genesis 1. See also Gardoski, 2007: 10, drawing on Waltke and O'Connor, 1990: 196-203. Some commentators, such as Merrill (2003: 444), have appropriately observed that the prepositions can be translated using various words including "in," so long as neither equation nor too great a distance are in view between people and the image of God.

27. As Bortone (2010: 117, 190) and M. Harris (2012: 147, 152) explain in their monumental works on Greek prepositions, *kata* followed by the accusative case normally has a meaning of "according to" or something closely related to that.

28. See Charlesworth, 1990: 68.

29. In support of translating *kata* in Col. 3:10 as "according to" the model/pattern of Christ — and for the renewal here as parallel to the original creation "according to" the image of God in Genesis 1:27 — see O'Brien, 1987: 191; McDonough, 2009: 90-91; M. Harris, 2010: 133.

30. On the meaning here of *kata,* again as "according to," see O'Brien, 1987: 191.

In summary, then, people are not God's image now the way that Christ is; however, they are intimately connected with God because God's image is the very blueprint for humanity. Describing humanity as "the image of the image" risks suggesting too great an eternal distance between people and God.[31] The distance is great now, but because God is transforming people into the very image of God in Christ (2 Cor. 3:18), that distance will eventually decrease substantially. The basic idea here is that God has a likeness-image, and God has created people with that in view. It is a standard for what God intends humanity ultimately to be. It is the goal toward which humanity is to develop. As the New Testament clarifies, sin prevents people from developing as God intends — in fact, it damages people so badly that they are much farther from God's standard after their "fall" into sin than before it (see Ch. 4). However, Christ, as both the standard and the source of humanity's renewal, breaks the power of sin and liberates people to resume their God-intended development to become fully conformed to Christ — to God's image who is Christ.

As noted at the start of the previous chapter, the apostle Paul appears to have an exceptionally complete view of God's image — from "before the beginning" to "after the end" of the current material world. He has less to contribute than other authors of the Bible regarding what takes place at creation because he is focused on God's goal for everything, including its final form. From the perspective of eternity, he speaks of Christ's followers as effectively already conformed to God's image in Christ, in addition to being justified and glorified (Rom. 8:29). As his other statements on these subjects confirm, he does not literally mean that right now people are already (conformed to) God's image or already (fully) glorified. Rather, being God's "image" and "glory" are what God intends humanity fundamentally to be. Their destiny involves becoming that, though at present they are only en route.[32]

In terms of glory, Paul can envision people as "glorified" and so can

---

31. Versions of this expression can be found, for example, in W. Pope, 1875: v. 1, 427; Maloney, 1973: 39; M. O'Neill, 1999: 81, 86; Dumbrell, 2002: 16; Lints, 2006a: 221; McKenna, 2008: 350; Mangano, 2008: 2-3; D. Kelsey, 2009: v. 2, 1010. As Hughes (1989: 15-16) notes, this idea is very close to Philo's concept of "the image of the Image," a view many find closer to Greek Platonic thinking than to the outlook of the Old Testament. See Aalders, 1981: 70-71; Barentsen, 1988: 32; cf. Clines, 1968: 73-75.

32. Even Clines, who previously had connected people and God's image more closely than most, later recognized the appropriateness of including the preposition when summarizing Paul's overall view underlying 1 Corinthians 11. Clines (1993: 427) notes that for Paul here: "every male 'is' God's image . . . presumably meaning he is created after God's image."

refer to them as if they are "the glory of God" (1 Cor. 11:7), but he knows all too well that "all have sinned and fall short of the glory of God" (Rom. 3:23) and that even Christians can fail to glorify God (e.g., 1 Cor. 6:19-20). Similarly he can envision people as "the image of God" (1 Cor. 11:7). However, he knows all too well that their transformation into that image is far from complete (2 Cor. 3:18), and that it is Christ who is truly the image of God right now (four verses later, 2 Cor. 4:4).[33] So 1 Corinthians 11:7 does not contradict the teaching throughout the rest of the Bible — that people are not God's image but are created "in" (according to) God's image. Rather, it illustrates an appreciation for the wonderful dignity and destiny that attend human existence, from an eternal perspective.

It is appropriate for people today occasionally to join Paul in such appreciation, heralding humanity as being God's image — as long as it does not obscure an important reality.[34] Humanity's status as created in God's image is rooted in the purpose and standard of human creation, not in what is descriptively true about people today. Saying that people "are" God's image all too often leads to the idea that being God's image is about how people are like God today. Whatever those traits or capacities are, some people inevitably demonstrate them more than others, leading to the conclusions that some people are more God's image than others are, and that sin damages God's image (more in some than in others) — neither of which the Bible ever affirms (see later in this chapter, plus Ch. 4). It is generally safer, then, to speak as the authors of the Bible normally do — saying that people are created in (or according to) God's image — and will be transformed into that image in (or according to) Christ.

By affirming only that men are God's image in 1 Corinthians 11, Paul might appear to be suggesting that women are not God's image. To avoid that conclusion, some commentators have suggested that he is talking here about Adam or Christ only — or not really about God's image.[35] However,

---

33. As biblical scholar M. Harris notes (2012: 65), there are multiple concepts in Paul's writings, including "transformation" and "salvation," that Paul sometimes speaks of in present tense, even though Paul reveals elsewhere that he knows that far more than a present-tense affirmation is necessary to convey the fullness of the concept. For example, transformation is "past (Gal 2:20; 3:27), present (Ro 12:2), and future (1Co 15:51; Php 3:21)."

34. Hughes (1989: 21-22) concurs with this balance, noting that even theologians as sophisticated as Karl Barth (1958a: 197) affirm that people are created according to, rather than as, God's image; yet Barth occasionally refers to people as God's image.

35. E.g., Murphy-O'Connor, 1982: 54 (Adam); K. Barth, 1958a: 203 (Christ); Gardoski, 2007: 17 (image).

there is no need to circumvent the straightforward connection of men and God's image in this text. Paul does affirm that men are God's image;[36] but he does not say that *only* men are involved in the image and glory of God. He affirms this status of men and then makes a different affirmation of women — that a woman is a glory of a man.

The contrast here between men and women involves glory only, with the understanding that God's image encompasses both male and female being so obvious from Genesis 1:27 that Paul does not need to re-state the woman's image status here.[37] As noted in Chapter 2, for Paul different creations of God can have different glories. If two stars can have different glories (four chapters later, in 1 Cor. 15:41), there is nothing surprising about men and women being God's glory in different ways.[38] Although a fuller discussion of "glory" and its relation to "image" must await Chapters 6 and 7 (see also Ch. 2), it is worth noting here that Paul is careful in verses 11-12 to guard against the misunderstanding that being someone's glory involves anything demeaning.[39] The failure to uphold the consistent biblical teaching on image and glory has led to the tragic misuse of the image-of-God concept to oppress women, as we saw in Chapter 1.

What Creation in God's Image Is Not

After examining who is identified with the image of God and how they are related to it, we are now in a better position to consider more specifically what it means for humanity to be created in God's image. As explained in

36. So Scroggs, 1966: 70; Ridderbos, 1975: 72; J. Murray, 1977: 36; Clark, 1984: 9; Lewis and Demarest, 1994: v. 2, 134; Roy, 2009: 10; and many earlier examples such as Augustine and Peter Lombard cited in Hughes, 1989: 16.

37. So Barentsen, 1988: 34-35; Thiselton, 2000: 837; Black, 2006: 191. A similar position — that the focus of the discussion is glory, not image — is affirmed in Barrett, 1993: 252; Grenz, 2001: 204; D. Garland, 2003: 522-23; Lakey, 2010: 112.

38. Somewhat similarly, Paul has just noted that the head *(kephale)* of every man (male) is Christ and the head of a woman is the man (v. 3). Few would take that to mean that Christ is not the head of both women and men, especially in light of teachings elsewhere that Christ is the head *(kephale)* of all (e.g. Eph. 1:22). For the conclusion that Paul is assuming that women, like men, are an image and glory of God, see Fee, 1987: 516; Sherlock, 1996: 254; Frame, 2006: 230; D. Kelsey, 2009: v. 2, 943.

39. An observation echoed by Fee, 1987: 516-17; Hays, 1997: 183; Collins, 1999: 402-3; D. Garland, 2003: 523.

Chapter 1, the history of interpretation of the image-of-God concept is significantly hampered by cultural and theological assumptions. Since the Bible nowhere fully defines what it means for people to be created in the image of God, conflicting interpretations abound. Reading into this idea other concepts that may be related to it, but are not what it is, has been all too easy. Accordingly, careful regard for how the Bible's authors do talk about being in God's image is vital, so that the understanding of the image that one adopts is what fits best with that language.

Perhaps the most important clue to gain from the biblical text regarding what being in the image of God refers to is that being in God's image has to do with people as entire beings (whether humanity as a whole or its component members are in view). There is no suggestion that being in the image is constituted only by current human "attributes" (i.e., abilities, traits, capacities, and other things that people have, are, do, etc.). Select attributes (even if God-like) are not what are in God's image — persons as a whole are.

A few biblical examples can help illustrate this observation. Genesis 1 portrays God talking about making humanity in the divine image (v. 26) and then doing so. Each image statement is simply about "humanity" (*adam,* as discussed above), with appropriate activities/blessings/commands following or flowing from that statement. Such outflows are appropriate because of what it means to be in the image of God, which will be addressed below. Genesis 5:1-2 reflects this same identification of *adam* per se, not a particular aspect of *adam,* as being in God's image — followed by other affirmations. The analogous language in verse 3 identifying Seth as being in the image of Adam similarly says nothing about particular attributes of Seth but refers to his entire person.

As soon as we move beyond the first five chapters of Genesis, and creation in the image of God becomes the basis for other appeals in the Bible, the wholistic nature of what God's image is about becomes more evident. In Genesis 9:6, creation in God's image becomes a basis for punishing the evil of murder: *adam* (as an entity — not some aspect of humanity) is in the image of God. There is no suggestion that some attribute of people is at issue here.

The outlook in James 3 is similar with regard to the evil of cursing. It is wrong because it tears down people who are in the image of God. People themselves — not anything in particular about them — are connected with God's image and so, in a special way, with God. The appeal to God's image in 1 Corinthians 11:7 also simply identifies God's image with a particular group of people, as discussed above, with no particular attributes in view.[40]

The widespread support for this understanding that God's image has to do with people in their entirety is not surprising. In fact, this view has been heralded as "a new consensus."[41] Some arrive at this position via a careful review of the relevant biblical texts, especially the seminal verses in Genesis 1.[42] Others recognize that biblical anthropology is so consistently wholistic that it is hard to imagine such an essential characterization of humanity as being anything else.[43]

Regardless, the mistake in view here is to associate God's image with only the "material" or "spiritual" aspect of people,[44] with only their structure or function,[45] or with one side of any such dichotomy, trichotomy, or other subdivision within people.[46] Focusing on different parts of the human being has its place, especially where they have been damaged by sin and need restoring.[47] But the creation of people in the image of God concerns humanity as a whole and human beings in their entirety.[48]

40. As will be examined in detail in Chapter 6, other New Testament passages overtly connecting people with God's image are not talking about people *as* God's image. Instead they are talking about people growing closer to God in Christ by becoming more like Christ, who is the image of God. Humanity in God's image and Christ as God's image are not unrelated ideas, but the distinctions are so significant that the relevant passages need careful attention before identifying their relevance to the matter at hand here.

41. E.g., by Stanley Grenz (2001: 193-94). Clines (1968: 59) and McLeod (1999: 48-51) similarly identify lists of significant contemporary and ancient authors in addition to those noted here below who support this view.

42. E.g., see Pannenberg, 1991: 206-7; Hoekema, 1994: 64-65; Schüle, 2005: 7; Cortez, 2010: 28.

43. Regarding the Old Testament in particular, see Rad, 1972: 58-59; Standebach, 1974: 392; Westermann, 1984: 392; Wenham, 1987: 30; Curtis, 1992: 390. Clines (1968: 57) and B. Childs (1993: 569) locate God's image in the context of anthropological assumptions that are consistent throughout the Bible.

44. Many lament how often connecting God's image with one side of a "spiritual vs. material" dichotomy has led astray analyses of the "image of God" concept — see Ramsey, 1950: 284; Rad, 1962: 144-45; J. Murray, 1977: 39; Gill, 1978: 392; Jónsson, 1988: 118; Hilkert, 1995: 197-98; Gunton, 2002: 41, 154; I. H. Marshall, 2001: 60-62; Horton, 2006: 182; Cortez, 2010: 39.

45. Berkouwer (1975: 40), Hoekema (1994: 69-70), and Wells (2004: 27) warn against such other dichotomies.

46. So J. Childs, 1982: 230; International, 2004: par. 9; Berry and Jeeves, 2008: 4.

47. See Chapters 6-7 on the restoration of specific attributes in people through Christ, and the acknowledgments in Hughes, 1989: 200; and Waltke, 1989: 3.

48. For further development of this idea, cf. Berkouwer, 1975: 63; John Paul II, 1979:

Accordingly, many authors have been outspoken in their criticism of viewing creation in God's image in terms of one or more current human attributes.[49] For some, the primary problem is that no biblical passage discussing humanity's creation in the image of God indicates that this image is a matter of attributes that people presently have.[50] In fact, some of the psalms suggest quite the opposite. Whereas various authors of the Bible teach that creation in the divine image warrants protection from harm (e.g., Genesis 9; James 3), the psalmist David asks "What are human beings that you are mindful of them?" (e.g., 8:4; cf. 144:3). For him, no current human attributes warrant such concern about human well-being — a point overlooked by some commentators.[51]

Were God's image to be a matter of specific attributes that people actually have — which warrant speaking of people as being in God's image — then that image would be a matter of degree. People with better attributes would in some sense be more in the image of God, and people themselves would vary over time in terms of how much they are in God's image. But as Martin Luther King Jr. once famously observed, "there are no gradations in the image of God."[52] By the way the biblical texts invoke God's image, the authors of the Bible appear to agree. They never attach an adjective to the Hebrew or Greek terms for God's likeness-image in order to indicate how much of God's image is present — just pronouns identifying whose image is in view. Another distinctive of the biblical use of God's image — compared with some other common uses of the term in the ancient Near East — is

---

64; H. D. McDonald, 1981: 35; W. Barr, 1982: 475, 484; Oduyoye, 1982: 53; Ryrie, 1986: 192; Shepherd, 1988: 1019; Weinandy, 2000: 148; International, 2004: par. 31; Jeeves, 2005: 182; Gonzalez, 2007: 130-31; Berry and Jeeves, 2008: 26, 37 (drawing on C. Wright, 2004: 119); Driscoll and Breshears, 2010: 132; Sands, 2010: 34; Koyzis, 2014: 136. See Chapter 7 regarding the importance of recognizing the place of the human body in the concept of God's image.

49. E.g., Thielicke, 1966: 151-52; Zizioulas, 1975: 407-9; Berkouwer, 1975: 60; Yannaras, 1984: 26-27; Hamilton, 1990: 137; Tanner, 1994: 573; Rae and Cox, 1999: 131-32; Budziszewski, 2002: 30; McFarland, 2005: 60; P. Peterson, 2008: 34-35; D. Kelsey, 2009: v. 2, 906-7; Cortez, 2010: 36; Gushee, 2013: 46. See also other examples in Hoekema, 1994: 49, 60, etc.

50. So K. Barth, 1958a: 185; Thielicke, 1966: 166; Jenson, 1999: 55; Erickson, 2013: 469.

51. For example, Hoekema (1994: 44) observes that Calvin (in his Commentary on Psalm 8) sees various human attributes as constituting God's image here, whereas Hoekema himself (81) sees primarily the attribute of relationship. For efforts to identify God's image with the attribute of rulership, see Chapter 5.

52. King, 1965; cf. Fields, 2001: 59. Moreland and Rae (2000: 335) add a philosophical analysis in harmony with King's theological understanding. See also the bioethical analysis in Bajema, 1974: 59.

that it applies to humanity in general, without qualification, rather than only to people like kings who have exceptional traits or characteristics.[53]

An illustration here may help. Consider the denarius coin that Jesus asked people to look at when he addressed people's obligation to pay taxes (Matt. 22:15-22; Mark 12:13-17; Luke 20:20-26).[54] That denarius was likely rather worn. Any such damage to the coin, however, was irrelevant, and Jesus does not mention it here. A worn coin was no less of a coin because of such damage. It was still a denarius and was still known to bear the image of Caesar. The coin itself was not the image; but the coin, notes Jesus and the people, had at least two things on it, an image and an inscription (Matt. 22:20). In modern U.S. coinage, were it a quarter, it wouldn't be worth 22 cents or 15 cents, depending on how unrecognizable the face was on it. If it was a denarius it bore the image of Caesar by definition and its worth and purpose were determined by that.

After asking the people whose image *(eikon)* was on the denarius, Jesus advised them to "render to Caesar the things that are Caesar's and to God the things that are God's" (Matt. 22:21, ESV). Some see in this passage a definite[55] or possible[56] reference to people being in the image of God. As association with Caesar's image entails an obligation to Caesar,[57] so association with God's image entails an obligation to God. People owe merely coins to Caesar; they owe their entire selves to God. Since Jesus does not explicitly associate people with the image of God here, one should be care-

---

53. See Clines (1968: 93-94), who draws upon Eichrodt (1967: 128). For a fuller discussion of the relevance of the ancient Near East as a context for the Old Testament, see Chapter 2 as well as later in the present chapter.

54. Background information on this coin is provided in Geldenhuys, 1951: 504; Lane, 1974: 423-24; Flender, 1976: 288; Fitzmyer, 1981: 1296; Beare, 1982: 439; Keener, 1999: 525; Luz, 2001: 65-66.

55. E.g., Augustine, 1960: 47; Lenski, 1946a: 991; Giblin, 1971: 525; Cairns, 1973: 43; J. Brooks, 1991: 193; Owen-Ball, 1993: 10-12; Sherlock, 1996: 33; Davies and Allison, 2004: 375. Nolland originally (1989) doubted this connection but changed his position (2005: 898-99) after further consideration.

56. E.g., Hooker, 1991: 281; Moule, 1965: 97; Green, 1997: 715-16; Keener, 1999: 526; Grenz, 2001: 203.

57. Many find the idea of obligation in the change of verbs in Matthew 22 (and parallels) from "give" *(dounai* in v. 17) to "give back" (i.e., what is owed, *apodote* in v. 21), and in mention of the "things that are Caesar's" (v. 21) — see Cranfield, 1977: 371-72; Mann, 1986: 470; Harrington, 1991: 310-11; Mounce, 1991: 208; Morris, 1992: 557; Blomberg, 1992: 331; Bock, 1994: 1613. Carson (1988: 460) cautions against too great a reliance on the distinction between verbs.

ful not to look for details regarding God's image here.[58] However, Jesus does challenge people to give God what God is due; and he does connect the ideas of "obligation" and "image" regarding Caesar. So at a minimum this passage appears to be an invitation to consider who or what is closely associated with God's image and the implications of that association.[59] The answers to these questions, though, lie elsewhere in the Bible.

Being created in God's image, then, is not a matter of human attributes, which people have to varying degrees. A possible rejoinder here is that being in God's image is not about attributes in general but specifically about ways that people are like God. However, understanding being in God's image in terms of current likenesses fares no better, as many have also observed, partly because likenesses are merely examples of attributes (abilities, traits, capacities, and other things that people have, are, do, etc.).[60] Bearing certain likenesses to God has its important place in the life of a believer (e.g., see John 13:15; Eph. 5:1; Phil. 2:5; 1 Pet. 1:16). But where the Bible speaks of that, there is implicitly or explicitly the accompanying recognition that one who is "a child of the devil" (1 John 3:8) instead does not bear such likenesses. The creational status of all people in God's image, then, must be referring to something other than the presence of such likenesses.

Moreover, likenesses to God in the Bible are not a basis of human significance in the way that people's status as being in the likeness-image of God is. Otherwise, law would replace gospel, with demonstrating like-

---

58. On the importance of not concluding too much about God's image here, see I. H. Marshall, 1978: 736; Bray, 1991: 209-10, 2001: 576; France, 2002: 469. After all, Jesus did not explicitly say that all coins bearing Caesar's image belonged to Caesar (a concern of Stein, 1992: 498; Gundry, 1993: 694; and Buchanan, 1996: 853), or that only people belong to God (a concern of Luz, 2001: 67).

59. Many of those who see Jesus implicitly making a connection here between people and God's image speak of people as "bearing" God's image (e.g., J. Wesley, 1985h: 117; Kidner, 1967: 51; Lane, 1974: 425; R. Smith, 1988: 261; Evans, 1990: 300; I. H. Marshall, 2001: 51; Krause, 2005: 367: Schmutzer, 2009: 178; also Hughes, 1989: 46 [approvingly] citing Tertullian, and Fitzmyer, 1981: 1292-93 [approvingly] citing Völkl, 1961: 113-16; Schnackenburg, 1965: 117-18; Cairns, 1973: 38; Bornkamm, 1975: 123). For the difference between "bearing" and "being" God's image see discussion of 1 Corinthians 15:49 in Chapter 4.

60. See, for example, Berkouwer, 1975: 62; Yannaras, 1984: 19; J. Barr, 1993: 169; Krause, 2005: 361; H. Reinders, 2008: 220; Carlson, 2008: 107; Treier, 2008: 180-81 discussing McFarland, 2005: 3-6. Brink (2001: 87) and Middleton (1994: 10) lament that such efforts to equate being in God's image with ways that people are like God are "blissfully unconcerned with authorial intent."

nesses the necessary basis for right standing with God.[61] This distinction between being in the likeness-image of God and presently being like God should not be surprising in light of the Bible's emphasis on the dissimilarity of people and God.[62]

According to Isaiah 40, people are mere grass that withers before God (vv. 6-7). "All the nations are as nothing before him; they are accounted by him as less than nothing and emptiness. To whom then will you liken God?" (vv. 17-18). Even the most capable of people, "the rulers of the earth," are "as nothing" (v. 23). "To whom then will you compare me?" says God (v. 25). Six chapters later God takes up the theme again: "To whom will you liken me?" (46:5) for "there is no one like me" (v. 9). To illustrate his point God adds several examples, the last (v. 11) being the vast difference between God (the Lord) and a human (the led). The psalmist echoes this observation to the Lord: "[W]ho in the skies can be compared to the Lord?" for "the heavens are yours" (Ps. 89:6, 11). The psalmist then immediately extends his observation to "the world and all that is in it" (v. 11).

The point here is not that there are no similarities of any kind between God and anything else. There can be similarities between God and people, as noted above. God is also "like a lion," "like a leopard," and "like a bear" (Hos. 13:7-8), as Christ is "like a sheep" (Acts 8:32). For that matter, people are "like the animals" (Ps. 49:12, 20) and "like a breath" (Ps. 144:4). But to observe specific similarities is no more to affirm a fundamental present "likeness" between God and people than it is similarly to connect people with animals or God with animals. In even the similarities between God and people, the dissimilarity is preeminent.[63]

Viewing attributes (likenesses to God) as the basis of human worth opens the door to reductionism — focusing only on those characteristics of people that one thinks are most important.[64] Such an outlook in turn

61. Thielicke (1966: 166). See also Hull, 2001: 222-23; Ware, 2002: 16; Overstreet, 2005: 68. Augustine's (1982: ch. 16, sec. 57) distinction between "like" (i.e., likenesses) and "likeness" — albeit in a somewhat different context — is potentially helpful here.

62. Although the aspiration to be "like God" can afflict believers and nonbelievers alike, H. R. Niebuhr (1996: 72) observes that, ideally, "the important difference between the church and the world is that the church knows itself to be 'world' before God while the world does not know this but thinks that it can be like God."

63. So Augustine (1963: bk. 15, sec. 39), discussed in Treier (2008: 75), and variously formulated in Ramsey, 1950: 252; Crawford, 1966: 233; Berkouwer, 1975: 62-63; Waltke, 1989: 4; R. Otto, 1992: 508 (drawing on Emil Brunner); Häring, 2001: 4; Merrill, 2006: 169-70.

64. For this concern, see P. Peterson, 2008: 29-30; Cortez, 2010: 21; Erickson, 2013: 469.

can all too easily lead to devaluing those who do not manifest those characteristics sufficiently. From that logically (though perhaps unconsciously) flows the demeaning and oppression of particular groups of people.[65] The tragedy that this logic has actually fostered in history was documented in the opening chapter of this book.

Regarding people with disabilities, the (generally unspoken) logic is that since attributes like reason, sensory abilities, and strength are what make people in the likeness of God and thus worthy of protection, those deficient in such attributes are not as worthy as others.[66] If maleness is thought to be a particularly significant attribute of God, then it is not hard to see how that (subtly or not so subtly) leads to privileging men over women in all aspects of life.[67] A similar logic is at work concerning degree of wealth, color of skin, etc. Biblical affirmations that all people are created in the image of God provide a ringing denunciation of basing people's significance on their particular attributes — precisely because that image is not a matter of their current attributes.[68]

People who want to justify benefiting one type of person over another would understandably gravitate toward a view of God's image defined in terms of present human attributes and likenesses to God. But they are not the only people. The illusion that human significance is rooted in ways that people are like God is as old as the Garden of Eden (Gen. 3:5). Because Genesis indicates that Adam and Eve are in the likeness-image of God at their initial creation, the enticement to become "like God" suggests that something else is in view. Whereas the initial creation is about a status not made up of specific current attributes, the temptation is about gaining a specific attribute and finding new significance in that.[69]

---

65. Regarding this logic, see Ruston, 2004: 282-83; McFarland, 2005: 9-10; H. Reinders, 2006: 128; Yong, 2007: 172; Gonzalez, 2007: 147; Cortez, 2010: 20. Hefner (1984: 337) sees this logic ultimately bringing into question the worth of humanity as a whole.

66. Bajema, 1974: 38-39; Ferngren, 1987: 27; H. Reinders, 2006: 128; Polkinghorne, 2006: 97. Reynolds (2008: 179) observes that "the results have been catastrophic."

67. McFarland, 2005: 3; Gonzalez, 2007: 145-45 (and other sources cited therein).

68. Abraham Lincoln (1953: 546) and Martin Luther King Jr. (1991b: 118-19) both identified the U.S. Declaration of Independence as a particularly powerful contemporary restatement of the biblical "image of God" doctrine. As Lincoln put it: In opposition to "the doctrine that none but rich men, or none but white men, were entitled to life, liberty and the pursuit of happiness," the authors of the Declaration insist that "nothing stamped with the Divine image and likeness was sent into the world to be trodden on, and degraded, and imbruted by its fellows." For further development of this theme, see McKanan, 2002: 57; Wills, 2009: 25-26.

69. On this contrast between achieving a particular likeness and being in God's likeness-

By yielding to the temptation, Adam and Eve do indeed become like God, knowing good and evil (Gen. 3:22). In context, this appears to be a reference to gaining a form of autonomy — taking upon themselves responsibility for distinguishing good and evil.[70] Human history eloquently testifies that people do this poorly on their own, apart from God. Prophets in every age have had ample opportunity to lament "those who call evil good and good evil" (e.g., Isa. 5:20). People have a form of knowledge/autonomy, but "there is no one who has understanding" (Rom. 3:11; closely connected in the Bible with "wisdom"). For the apostle Paul and the psalmist David on whom he draws (Ps. 14:2-3), this predicament is intimately associated with people's failure to seek God for the understanding/ wisdom they need (same verses). Such neglect is tantamount to saying "there is no God" (Ps. 14:1).

As we will see later in this chapter, dependence on God is central to what creation in God's image entails.[71] Rather than "deifying human capabilities," dependence reminds people that God is God.[72] Human significance does not lie fundamentally in striving to be like God, which all too easily becomes an aspiration to *be* God.[73] Current likenesses to God, as we will see, must play a more secondary (though important) role.

Genesis 3 warns against the enterprise to establish humanity as "like God," which is primarily about promoting people's interests and rooting their significance in their current attributes. This stands in stark contrast to Genesis 1, which is primarily about promoting God and rooting people's significance in their special connection with God, as created in God's image.

The temptations of Genesis 3 arise whenever people consider justi-

---

image in Genesis, see Bonhoeffer, 1959b: 269; Sherlock, 1996: 42. The idea (suggested, e.g., in Sawyer, 1992: 66; van Huyssteen, 2006: 160; cf. Stendahl, 1992: 142) — that the becoming "like God" described in Genesis 3 is a part of what God intended by creating humanity in the likeness-image of God in Genesis 1 — is at odds with the text itself. The serpent is suggesting that humanity pursue something that God does not intend for people to pursue. Moreover, God punishes Adam and Eve for pursuing it. For more on this matter, see Hughes, 1989: 117.

70. So Aquinas, 1947: pt. II-II, Q. 163, art. 2; Towner, 2001: 44; Dumbrell, 2002: 23; Kass, 2003: 68; Gardoski, 2007: 11; C. Wright, 2006: 164; Cahill, 2006b: 67.

71. For this link in the context of Genesis 1–3, see Waltke, 1989: 7; Hughes, 1989: 195; B. Childs, 1993: 570; Callender, 2000: 69; M. Williams, 2014: 87.

72. The expression is from Beale (2008: 135), echoing C. Wright, 2006: 164 — both of whom critique preoccupation with current human attributes when endeavoring to understand what being in God's image means.

73. As Bonhoeffer (1959a: 73) observes, it "makes a creator out of the creature." Cf. Bayertz, 1996: 77; Smail, 2006: 201-2; Schwöbel, 2006: 52-53.

fying their actions solely on the basis of what appears best to them (as in autonomy-based ethics) or beneficial to humanity (as in utilitarian ethics). Again, there is a role for such considerations, but it is secondary. When it becomes primary, then the alluring benefits of eating the fruit (Gen. 3:6) are replaced with pain (v. 16) — just as the alluring freedom to eat from one more tree in the garden (v. 3) ends up leading to the loss of freedom to eat from any of the garden's trees at all (v. 23).

It has always been tempting for people to think that ways they are presently "like God" is the basis of their significance (i.e., what being in God's image is about, since that is so bound up biblically with human significance). If that is the basis, then significance resides in one or more human attributes — things people in fact are, have, or do. People can then trust in themselves rather than having to depend on God. This is the antithesis of the apostle Paul's mindset that "when I am weak, then I am strong" (2 Cor. 12:10) — a mindset that even he arrived at only after much struggle with the way that he and most others commonly view human significance as a function of human strengths.[74]

People who view and value themselves in terms of their attributes are not necessarily nonreligious. They may still recognize their limitations and their need for help. But they devise god(s) based on likenesses to themselves — based on what they value. They create God in/as their own image — with "image" misconceived to mean "likenesses."[75] Some people value gold, silver, and stone, so they "think that the deity is like gold, or silver, or stone, an image formed by the art and imagination of mortals" (Acts 17:29). Others value other things and therefore devise their gods accordingly. Such idolatry will receive more scrutiny later in Chapter 4.

As Adam and Eve succumbed to the temptation to aspire to be "like God" (Gen. 3:5, 22), so did the builders of Babel, with aspirations to dwell in the heavens like God (Gen. 11:4). Since then outspoken people such

---

74. For further discussion of how viewing being in God's image in terms of current attributes leads people mistakenly to baptize qualities lauded by the dominant culture of one's society and to exalt themselves, see Hall, 1986: 91-92 (baptize) and Gibbs, 1984: 190, 197 (exalt).

75. On the reversal of who creates whom when God's image is understood in terms of actual likenesses to God, see R. Niebuhr, 1964: v. 1, 166; Häring, 2001: 9; Z. Moore, 2003: 106. Oduyoye (1995: 111) observes this reversal to be "common." Mays (2006: 37-38) suggests that it opens the door to all sorts of idolatry. A similar mindset underlies the quip of Comte-Sponville (2006: 119): " 'God created man in his own image,' we read in Genesis. This should cast doubt on the original." See further discussion in T. Peters, 2010: 218.

as the king of Babylon have similarly voiced the aspiration to "ascend to heaven," by which they mean to be "like the Most High" (Isa. 14:13-14). Countless others, in the pride that is our common lot as human beings, have harbored similar unspoken aspirations.

Rarely formulated so explicitly in thought — much less in speech — such aspirations are embedded in the comforting notion that one is "like God." When this idea is connected with the image of God, the thought becomes that one has worth and significance rooted in various current attributes.[76] Such a motivation does not necessarily lie behind viewing creation in God's image in terms of ways people are currently like God. But it does constitute one reason why that view is so appealing, despite all of the problems with it described above.

There are better ways to understand the relation between present human attributes (i.e., likenesses to God) and God's image. A detailed description of that will have to await the discussion of the term "likeness" later in this chapter and the examination of important particular likenesses to God in Chapter 5. However, simply put, current human attributes have more to do with the purposes and consequences of being *in* the image of God than with what actually defines being in God's image. Attributes are evidences of what it would look like to manifest God's image fully. As explained earlier, humanity's creation in God's image means people are created according to the standard of who God is in Christ. In fact, even before the Fall, people were not all that this standard entailed they would ultimately be (see Ch. 7). After the Fall, people were much farther from fulfilling this standard. Nevertheless, at both points they were "in God's image" — a status that has reference to the standard according to which God intended them to live.

Genesis 1 indicates that humanity's creation in the image of God displays God's intentions for humanity — it is not merely a description of how people "turned out." Before describing humanity's creation in verse 27, the author adds an unusual description of the deliberative process on God's part that led to this aspect of creation (v. 26). What unfolds are God's intentions for who people are to be and what they are to do. The two are intertwined, for people must have the ability to do what God calls upon them to do.[77]

76. For critiques of the human inclination to think this way, see Ramsey, 1950: 254; Bajema, 1974: 41; Schwöbel, 2006: 56.

77. So Lazenby, 1987: 66; Tanner, 1994: 574; Moreland and Rae, 2000: 378; Horton, 2006: 184.

However, having the ability does not necessarily mean having an attribute resident in oneself. God often works through people who lack normal attributes in order to demonstrate that God is at work through them in a more immediate way. Thus God calls Moses (Exod. 4:10-12), Isaiah (Isa. 6:5-7), Jeremiah (Jer. 1:6-9), Paul (2 Cor. 12:7-9), and others to do things they are incapable of doing. Yet this is not an oversight on God's part, as if God has mistakenly created or allowed them to be the wrong people. God's purposes for people can reach beyond the attributes with which God has created them. The wonder of being in God's image is about people's special connection with God and how that will enable all who wish, to be a reflection of God in Christ. It is not about how far people are along the course God has set for humanity. In fact, some of God's purposes are for humanity as a whole, and not just for particular people. So God has purposes that can be fulfilled by humanity even when some members of humanity lack the attributes to contribute to the achievement of those purposes. All people, with and without the best attributes, are in God's image.

Another way to explain what God-likenesses are is to describe them as flowing from being in God's image. People do have abilities to be like God in certain ways because God has created them in the divine image. Getting the logical flow here is important. Such likenesses are not what it means to be in the image of God. Instead they are intended consequences of being in that image.[78] They are among the purposes for which God has created humanity.[79] Considering having godly human attributes to be what being in God's image *is* does indeed conflict with biblical teaching in all the ways explained in this chapter. But it also leads to a confusing way of thinking about the impact of sin on God's image (see Ch. 4) and has fostered the destructive misapplication of the image-of-God concept in the life of the church and the world (see Ch. 1).

Inadequate Assumptions

Since identifying being in God's image with current human attributes is one of several significant ways that discussions of the divine image get off course, it is worth taking some space here to examine how that occurs.

---

78. Regarding this distinction, see Thielicke, 1966: 193-94 (drawing upon Martin Luther); O'Mathuna, 1995: 202; Rae and Cox, 1999: 132; Walton, 2001: 132.

79. So Beyreuther and Finkenrath, 1976: 502; P. Bird, 1981: 145; Erickson, 2013: 470-71.

This misstep results directly from one or more of three understandable but ultimately inadequate assumptions. Those assumptions are that being in God's likeness-image is about how people currently are excellent,[80] how they are like God,[81] and how they are unlike animals.[82] Each of the three basic assumptions warrants consideration here.

How People Are Excellent

Some commentators assume that being in God's image has to do with how people today are excellent to some degree. They are aware that the concept of being in God's image provides grounding for human life and dignity in the Bible, so it is understandable for them to assume that what is excellent about people is what gives them their dignity, and therefore what constitutes being in God's image. A number of these commentators think of excellence in terms of what they identify as the "best" traits of most human beings.[83] Others, appropriately aware that being in God's image connects to the whole person, as discussed above, appear to assume that all actual positive human traits of people constitute human excellence and thus being in God's image.[84] This can lead to connecting God's image with eyesight greater than that of a lynx or eagle or with being "incorruptible"

80. Mays (2006: 35) observes that the inclination has been to define the humanity-in-God's-image concept in terms of attributes. H. Reinders (2006: 127) agrees that "the Christian tradition has by and large adhered to" this approach, noting (2008: 229) that theological reflection has always been tempted to explain being in the divine image in terms of human attributes.

81. According to Walsh and Middleton (1984: 52-53), "The image has usually been linked to some feature, or constellation of features, thought to be shared by God and humanity." Cf. Middleton, 2005: 18-19; Merrill, 2003: 443. Grenz (2001: 193) identifies this as "historically the most widely held conjecture" regarding God's image. Its more recent popularity is evidenced by the many references to God's image in a U.S. President's Council on Bioethics collection of essays on human dignity (2008), which promote this view (e.g., see the book's introduction: Schulman, 2008: 8).

82. As Sunderland (2003: 192) notes, "Much theological and social thought has been focused on defining our specialness, looking for qualitative, all or nothing, distinctions from animal nature." Cf. Waltke, 1989: 4; G. Peterson, 1996: 15; Spanner, 1998: 219; Ware, 2002: 15; McKnight, 2005: 31-32.

83. E.g., Nellas, 1987: 27; Plantinga, 2002: 41; Gardoski, 2007: 16; Schmutzer, 2009: 168.

84. In the words of Rakestraw (1992: 400): God's image includes "all that we are and do as human beings." Cf. Wilson and Blomberg, 1993: 9-10; Hilkert, 1995: 202-3; Dumbrell, 2002: 16; Frame, 2006: 16; Briggs, 2010: 123.

— traits that go far beyond (and in some cases conflict with) the testimony of the Bible.[85]

Assuming that God's image has to do with current human excellences, in fact, is based on two other equally inadequate assumptions. One involves the individualistic notion that being in God's image is primarily about differences among people rather than something involving humanity as a whole and each member of humanity (see earlier discussion). Such a focus on difference easily causes one to understand being in God's image in terms of a range of different current attributes.[86] The other assumption is that particular people who lack normal human excellences can reliably be included in the protection due to those in the image of God, if being in God's image means having human excellences.[87] The necessity of such inclusion is rather implausible. If what warrants protection is being in God's image, and that is about having certain excellences, then by definition the lack of such excellences would seem to invalidate inclusion in the protection. History attests to how many have borne the brunt of such exclusion (see Ch. 1).

How People Are Like God

Some people assume that being in God's image has more to do with how people are presently like God than simply how people are excellent. Being in God's image may to them "obviously" mean having current likenesses to God.[88] (It is often not clear if they have considered the more biblically

---

85. Luther (1958: 62) draws the conclusion regarding eyesight; Habermas (2008: 49-50) regarding people not being corruptible.

86. "We image God precisely in our differences" (Teel, 2010: 164). Cf. Goodman, 2008: 156.

87. Collste, 2002: 168-69, is an example of this assumption. Wennberg (1985: 135-36) illustrates the invalidity of this assumption by arguing that those with insufficient attributes do not warrant the protections that others receive as created in God's image. Gushee, 2013: 43, affirms the assumption's invalidity.

88. Whereas Dabney, 1878: 293, uses this term overtly, many others simply affirm that actual likenesses to God are (at least a major part of) what constitute God's likeness-image (e.g., A. Strong, 1907: 7; Thomas, 1949: 154; Arminius, 1986: 363; Wenham, 1987: 32; Grudem, 1994: 443-49; S. Hall, 1995: 40; G. Peterson, 1996: 229-31; Cooper, 1998: 185; Collste, 2002: 38; D. G. Jones, 2002: 95; Jastram, 2004: 47; Gardoski, 2007: 12-13; M. Smith, 2007: 1; Goodman, 2008: 46-47; Mangano, 2008: 6; Moreland, 2009: 4-5; Schönborn, 2011: 31 [drawing on Aquinas]). See also discussion of Theodoret's similar view in McLeod, 1999: 80. Ferngren (2009: 97) notes the influence of this view in the early church.

sound view that being in God's likeness-image has to do with who God in Christ is rather than who people presently are.) Alternatively, from the mere fact that certain likenesses to God (however small) exist, one may make the unfounded assumption that those are what being in the likeness-image of God must mean.[89] This assumption then often leads to the idea that since God does X and people are "like God," then to be in the image of God means that people do X.[90] That does not logically follow. What follows is that we may see some attributes in some people that are in some measure "like" attributes in God. However, this says nothing about whether or not those attributes have any place in the definition of the term "image of God."

Preoccupation with how people are presently like God, when explaining what God's image means, has led to the unbiblical idea (recall above) that people are significant because they are so much like God. This inflated view of current humanity can in turn lead to the ideas that nothing in humanity is unlike God or that if something is of the essence of God, it must be characteristic of humans as well.[91] Then if the Bible acknowledges a particular characteristic in both God and people (as, e.g., Psalms 111–12 do), the Bible must be talking there about the image of God.[92] So everything from walking on water to the capacity to be infinite can become associated with what it means for humanity to be in God's image.[93] The concept rapidly loses all meaningful and biblically grounded definition.

This inadequate assumption linking being in God's image with ways people are currently like God itself commonly flows from three additional assumptions. First is the assumption that it makes no difference to use "image" as a verb, rather than following the Bible's preference (see later in this chapter) for a noun.[94] The prepositional phrase (that employs the

89. E.g., Hoekema (1994: 71): "Why should the gifts and capacities just mentioned be thought of as belonging to the image of God? The answer is that in all of these capacities man is like God."

90. So McKnight, 2005: 32-33. Similarly, Gregory of Nyssa, 1972: 542; Smail, 2006: 157-58.

91. For the first idea, see Chafer, 1947: v. 2, 163; for the second, see W. Pope, 1875: v. 1, 428; Gerhard, 1962: 32-33; McMinn and Campbell, 2007: 115.

92. So, e.g., Mangano, 2008: 6.

93. Regarding walking on water, see Balswick et al., 2005: 30. Regarding the human capacity to be infinite, see Nellas, 1987: 28.

94. This verbal form of image is common when ways that people are like God are in view. For example, McFadyen, 1990: 24; McClendon, 1991: 443; Hoekema, 1994: 28; Hilkert, 2002: 18; Dixon, 2003: 119; Verhey, 2003: 85; Fernandez, 2004: 174; Ecumenical, 2004: 512; Smail, 2006: 162-63; Driscoll and Breshears, 2010: 120; Mahoney, 2010: 700.

noun) "in God's image" has to do with an intended standard rather than present human attributes. However, talking about "imaging God" all too easily inclines the speaker and hearer to think in terms of particular aspects of specific people (or humanity as a whole) that are currently like God. Second, not only can using "image" as a verb be misleading, but so can using the wrong verb in connection with "image" as a noun. For example, talking about people "possessing" God's image misleadingly suggests that this image is not what people "are" but is something that people have — an attribute of some sort.[95]

A third inadequate assumption prompting people to think of being in God's image in terms of present likeness to God is the idea that humanity's creation in God's image does not end until Adam and Eve eat from the forbidden tree in Genesis 3. Because the couple becomes more "like God" (v. 22) as a result, this supposed extension of the creation narrative defines being in God's image in some people's minds in terms of likeness to God.[96] However, the creation of humanity, as overviewed in Genesis 1, ends with God's pronouncement that everything was "very good" (1:31). That was hardly the state of things when the couple ate from the tree (3:16-19), indicating that the eating was something separate from and subsequent to creation.

How People Are Unlike Animals

Meanwhile, many commentators supplement or replace the above primary assumptions with the assumption that being in God's image is about how people are unlike animals. The Bible indeed identifies only people, not animals, as being in the image of God. However, that does not mean that every way people and animals differ is what being in God's image is about. The Bible also does not identify rocks as being in the image of God; but that does not mean that every way people and rocks differ is what it means to be in God's image.

Some commentators — from Augustine to Aquinas to Calvin to others more recently — explicitly affirm that differences from animals are a

---

95. For an example, see Barentsen, 1988: 37.

96. For example, Sawyer, 1992: 69; Kass, 2003: 96, 185. Many others, such as Kline (1980: 27), see Genesis 3 not as a part of the original creation but nevertheless as addressing the image of God idea.

defining characteristic of being in God's image.[97] Others employ this as a consideration to help determine or confirm what being in God's image is.[98] Genesis does indeed describe various differences between people and animals. For instance, a divine deliberation is ascribed only to the creation of humanity and people are commanded to rule over animals (Gen. 1:26, 28). Other examples of people-animal differences include Adam naming the animals (vs. God naming humanity in Gen. 5:2) and finding no helper fit for him (Gen. 2:19, 20), Abel sacrificing animals as offerings to God (Gen. 4:4), and the covenantal relationship between God and humanity forbidding the killing of humans but allowing the killing of animals (Gen. 9:3, 6, 9).[99]

Nevertheless, Genesis also notes the commonality between people and animals (especially in contrast with God). People and many animals share the same day of creation, and they all are to eat the same food and multiply to fill the earth (Gen. 1:22, 24, 28-30). God forms them all from the ground, and animates them to become living beings/souls (*nephesh,* Gen. 2:7, 19, cf. 1:28). Indeed, all share the "breath of life" (Gen. 6:17; 7:21, 22).[100] Moreover, science is discovering that certain animals have some (degree of) attributes traditionally ascribed exclusively to humans.[101] Such teachings and findings can understandably be threatening to those who assume that human significance depends on how people are unlike animals. The Bible itself, though, does not define being in God's image in terms of such present differences.[102]

---

97. "God's image . . . ought to be sought only in those marks of excellence with which God had distinguished Adam over all other living creatures" (Calvin, 1960a: bk. II, ch. 12, sec. 6). Cf. Augustine, 1991: bk. I, ch. 17; Aquinas, 1947: pt. I, Q. 3, art. 2; Purkiser, 1960: 213; Phelps, 2004: 351; Duncan, 2008; De Cruz and De Maeseneer, 2014: 95.

98. E.g., Brunner, 1947: 98; Orr, 1948: 64-65; Clark, 1969: 215; Feinberg, 1972: 246; Bajema, 1974: 38; Sarna, 1989: 12; Kass, 1990: 37; J. Barrett, 1993: 252; Rae and Cox, 1999: 131; Treier, 2008: 195-96; Vorster, 2007b: 368.

99. These matters are discussed in Chrysostom, 1986: 107; Thielicke, 1966: 154-55; Shedd, 1980: v. 2, 5-6; Hughes, 1989: 4-6; Pannenberg, 1991: 189; Hoekema, 1994: 11-12; Vanhoozer, 1997: 163.

100. For elaboration, see Buswell, 1962: 241-42; Stendahl, 1992: 143; Green, 1999: 53; C. Wright, 2004: 117-18.

101. For details, see Zizioulas, 1975: 405-7; Case-Winters, 2004; van Huyssteen, 2006; G. Peterson, 2008: 473; Cortez, 2010: 19-20; Briggs, 2010: 119; Fisher, 2010: 203.

102. Regarding the inadequacy of understanding God's image in terms of differences from animals, see Clines, 1968: 98; Lossky, 1985: 138; C. Wright, 2004: 117; H. Reinders, 2008: 238; Briggs, 2010: 119-21; Cortez, 2010: 14; Moritz, 2011: 319.

Understanding creation in the image of God in terms of the ways that people are unlike animals commonly flows from three additional inadequate assumptions. One is that being in God's image is primarily about the difference between people and the rest of creation. However, that is to overlook the obvious: that the very wording of the image-of-God concept signals that it is about what people *are,* in a way somehow connected with God, rather than what they *are not.*[103]

The second underlying assumption is that because humanity's status in the image of God grounds human significance, and animals lack that particular status, animals are insignificant. A logical error is involved here. Just because the Bible states that humanity is in the image of God, and does not say the same about animals, does not imply that animals are insignificant.[104] The significance of animals rests on its own basis, which is something other than being in God's image. That recognition is important. Otherwise, defining humanity's image-related status in terms of differences from animals can become a thinly disguised way simply to (ab)use animals for human purposes.

A third assumption — that the way to protect against such abuse is to view animals (and all creation) as in God's image as well[105] — is ultimately not helpful.[106] It accepts the premise that the value of animals resides in their place on the same ("image") scale as humans. That comparison is inherently stacked against animals, a fact to which the history of animal and other environmental abuse testifies (see Ch. 1). Jesus does indeed compare people with animals at times (e.g., Luke 13:15-16; 14:3-5). But that is typically to argue that people should not be accorded *less* value than animals, and animals are very important to God and people alike. Moreover, Jesus never connects such comparisons with God's image.

In fact, the tendency to misinterpret being in God's image in terms of current attributes has led to connecting it not only to animals but also to

103. For elaboration, see Cairns, 1973: 118; Barentsen, 1988: 32; Hoekema, 1994: 22; Jewett with Shuster, 1996: 54; Jennings, 2003: 109; H. Reinders, 2006: 124; Cortez, 2010: 38. Thus to suggest that humanity's status as an image of God means that a person is "a deified animal" (e.g., Nellas, 1987: 15) inappropriately implies that humanity's primary identity consists in a connection with animals (albeit an elevated one).

104. Berkouwer, 1975: 358-59; Hall, 1986: 106-7; D. Kelsey, 2009: v. 1, 30; Deane-Drummond, 2012: 943 all develop this point. See also the rulership section in Chapter 4.

105. For examples of this assumption at work, see Gilkey, 1993: 150, 175; 1994; G. Peterson, 1996: 214; Hilkert, 2002: 2; Kraynak, 2008: 76; Putz, 2009: 620; Cortez, 2010: 19.

106. So Berkouwer, 1975: 84-85; van Huyssteen, 2006: 314, 322.

angels, including Satan. Many theologians have been quick to dismiss such connections as unbiblical, since the Bible only identifies humans as created in "God's image."[107] However, others are more open to using this terminology, precisely because they see that humans and angels have certain attributes in common. Regarding unfallen angels, they cite such attributes as rational knowledge, morality, and rulership.[108] Regarding Satan, they suggest that the perversion of such attributes makes people more an image of Satan than of God.[109]

While noting these similarities is legitimate, there is no biblical warrant for maintaining that angels are in the image of God, as people are, or that people are in the image of Satan rather than of God. The Bible does not talk in such terms because doing so reflects an unbiblical understanding of what it means for humanity to be in the image of God. Biblically, people are created to develop according to God's image in Christ. Being in that image is not a matter of the attributes that people currently have.

Common Themes

The assumption that being in God's image is a matter of present human excellences, likenesses to God, or differences from animals, then, commonly flows from a host of other inadequate assumptions. Moreover, it reinforces other equally unbiblical assumptions. For example, being in God's image becomes a matter of degree (contrary to the view of the Bible's authors — see above), since people differ in terms of their excellences, how much they are like God, and how different they are from animals.[110] Meanwhile, sin is assumed to damage God's image substantially (which is at odds with the language of the Bible — see Ch. 4), since authors of the Bible do teach

107. E.g., Gregory of Nyssa, 1972: 528; L. Berkhof, 1949: 206; Berkouwer, 1975: 86.

108. E.g., Aquinas, 1947: pt. I, Q. 59, art. 2 and pt. I, Q. 93, art. 4; Calvin, 1960a: bk. I, ch. 15, sec. 3; Clark, 1984: 15; Wenham, 1987: 32; Shepherd, 1988: 1017; Merriell, 1990: 160-61.

109. E.g., J. Wesley, 1985g: 179; Gerhard, 1962: 63; Hoeksema, 1966: 213; Altmann, 1968: 246; Dehsen, 1997: 268; Packer, 2003: 56.

110. For examples of such degreed language, see Thomas, 1949: 159; Wolterstorff, 1985: 70; Grudem, 1994: 449; Watson, 1997: 291; Driscoll and Breshears, 2010: 119; Visala, 2014: 117. Theoretically, it is possible to argue that there is some point at which human excellences become so great, or likenesses to God so significant, or differences from animals so pronounced, that a status of "God's image" is reached. However, as previously explained, the Bible does not indicate that this status is a matter of falling high enough on a continuum; rather, it is something categorically connected with humanity (see later in this chapter).

that sin badly damages these excellences, likenesses, and differences.[111] As such assumptions compound, the resulting view of being in God's image becomes increasingly far removed from the way that the Bible employs this idea.

Because being in God's image is not a matter of current variable attributes such as reason, righteousness, rulership, or relationship (see Ch. 5), all people without exception can be — and are — in the image of God. This glorious truth grounds human dignity and human destiny, and requires respect and protection for every human being (see Conclusion). Sin has badly damaged human *attributes,* and they need restoration in Christ. But sin has not damaged God's *image* — which is why the New Testament only says that *humanity,* not God's image, needs restoration (see Ch. 7). Without clarity on these various points, based on a careful reading of the Bible, it will be next to impossible to discern from the limited biblical data available what it means for humanity to be in the image of God. Circumstances will be ripe for smuggling into the text whatever theological convictions or cultural values seem most important at the time (see Ch. 1). However, with such understandings as guide rails, a picture of being in God's image emerges that is in line with everything the Bible says about what God's image is and what being created in that image means.

Creation in God's Image

Although the summary expression "God's image" commonly identifies the concept in view here, two closely related terms are actually involved. God determines in Genesis 1:26 to create humanity in the divine "image" and "likeness." The present discussion will first consider the term "image" because in the next verse describing God's actual creation of humanity, the text simply states that God created humanity in the "image" *(tselem)* of God. There is no mention there of "likeness" *(demuth).* Nevertheless, since God's intentions in creation somehow involve "likeness," according to the previous verse and later references to humanity in God's image, that term will be discussed second. As we will see, the two together make up

111. Most documentation must await Chapter 4. But examples of understanding being in God's likeness-image in terms of variable attributes, leading to the view that sin damages not just the attributes but also the likeness-image, include Gregory of Nyssa, 1972: 553; Luther, 1958: 62; Hughes, 1989: 55; Grudem, 1994: 450; J. Strong, 2005: 98; Driscoll and Breshears, 2010: 139.

a single concept. God creates humanity in reference to (according to) the likeness-image of God. That concept involves humanity's special *connection* with God, which makes it possible for humanity to become a meaningful *reflection* of God.

As noted in Chapter 2, "image" is the most common translation of the Hebrew word *tselem* and the Greek word *eikon,* which appear in the biblical passages addressing humanity in the image of God. Although the English term is familiar to most people, that very familiarity can be a liability. Readers can easily give it a meaning that the Bible's authors did not intend, as has been discussed and illustrated in Chapter 1. For example, in line with English usage, where "image" is often a verb, it is not unusual to encounter the explanation that *tselem* comes from the verb meaning "to cut."[112] However, there is no such verb in biblical Hebrew.[113] The concept appears to be fundamentally a noun concept, contrary to its common English counterpart, as noted above.

One may well wonder, then, why the authors of the Bible employed this term for "image" as part of describing humanity. The answer most likely has to do not with the word's precision, but with its flexibility and range. As already explained in Chapter 2, regarding the biblical background to Christ as God's image, its range of meaning extends all the way from the very physical to the completely nonmaterial.[114] As such, it ended up working well in reference to humanity, whom God intended at creation to be material but more than material.[115]

Some commentators, focusing primarily on the association of the term with physical objects, conclude that the term refers primarily to

112. E.g., Cook, 1975: 87, following Koehler, 1948; Towner, 2005: 345.

113. J. Barr (1968: 24) notes that the Arabic verb alleged to be a parallel to the hypothetical Hebrew verb in view here apparently did not lend itself to the formation of a corresponding noun, such that the noun for "image" in Arabic was connected with a different verb. Cf. Wenham, 1987: 29.

114. Some commentators, focusing primarily on the connection of the term with physical objects, conclude that the term refers primarily to the physical aspect of humanity (e.g., Cook, 1975: 87; Callender, 2000: 25; Crouch, 2010: 4; see discussion of Humbert, 1940 and Koehler, 1948 in Eichrodt, 1967: 122). Others are more impressed by the term's nonmaterial connections and see those as primary in reference to humanity (e.g., Cassuto, 1989: 56; Sawyer, 1992: 66).

115. Wildberger, 1997: 1081, notes the "remarkable flexibility" of this term. Others who comment on the wide range of the term's reference points include Piper, 1971: 16; P. Bird, 1981: 139-40; Hamilton, 1990: 134-35; Curtis, 1992: 389; Mathews, 1995: 167-68; van Leeuwen, 1997: 645-46; Garr, 2003: 136; Middleton, 2005: 45-46.

the physical aspect of humanity.[116] This view emphasizes that Genesis 1 is primarily about the material world and humanity's part in it. Others are more impressed by the term's nonmaterial associations and see those as primary in reference to humanity.[117] This view often notes that the explicit introduction of God as Spirit in Genesis 1:2 signals that if people are in the image of God, it must at least include a spiritual aspect. This range of views is reflective of how effectively the term can convey such a wide range of reference points.

Just because a word has a wide range of meanings in the Bible does not mean that all of those meanings are present in any particular use of the word. However, in the case of the term as a connector term between humanity and God — and especially God in Christ — there is ample evidence throughout the Bible (see below) that the image-of-God term encompasses both physical and nonphysical aspects of humanity. As noted in Chapter 2, *eikon,* the primary Greek translation of *tselem* in the Septuagint and primary word for "image" in the New Testament, has a similarly wide range of meaning. Moreover, its use in image-of-God passages confirms that both physical and nonphysical aspects of humanity are in view when authors of the Bible employ the term.

To the consternation of many in recent centuries, the Bible never provides a definition of the concept "image of God." Nevertheless, the Bible does offer some important clues to help guide the search for the concept's meaning.

First of all, as we have seen, the biblical texts provide evidence that humanity's creation in God's image is not about actual human attributes (including ways that people are presently like God or unlike animals). Rather, it has to do with being created to conform to who Christ is as the image of God. That conformation takes place over time and involves all types of human attributes, as Chapter 5 will discuss in detail. None of these attributes, including reason, righteousness, rulership, and relationship, is the "essence" of what being in God's image is about. Each of them appears in some biblical references to God's image but not in others. What is the common link among all of these passages? What is the core idea operative in all references to God's image if it is not any of these attributes individually or present attributes as a whole?

---

116. E.g., Cook, 1975: 87; Callender, 2000: 25; Crouch, 2010: 4; see discussion of Humbert, 1940 and Koehler, 1948 in Eichrodt, 1967: 122.

117. E.g., Cassuto, 1989: 56; Sawyer, 1992: 66.

Image as Connection

Simply put, first of all, some sort of special connection between God and people is in view here. Understanding who people are is not possible without recognizing this connection.[118] Passages about God's image do not define "image," but they do suggest something essential about it. According to Genesis 9:6, for instance, murdering a human being is forbidden not simply because God forbids it, but for a deeper and even more motivating reason as well. Human beings are connected with God in a profoundly significant way: they are created in God's image. God has a very personal stake in the life of a human being. When one destroys (or badly damages)[119] a human being, one is affronting God.

Verse 6 begins: "Whoever sheds the blood of a human, by a human shall that person's blood be shed." *Adam* is the Hebrew word for "human" in both instances. The second part of the verse adds the explanation ". . . for in the image of God has God made humankind [again, *adam*]."[120] In other words, God gives a reason for the previous statement about (the various members of) *adam* that is rooted in who people are. Murdering *adam* is wrong because of the significance of people as created in God's image. And *adam*, created in God's image, is to bear the responsibility for punishing one who has violated *adam*.[121]

118. See Brunner, 1947: 102; G. Kelsey, 1965: 76-77; K. Peters, 1974: 99; Otto, 1992: 511; Fields, 2001: 98; Reiss, 2011: 186.

119. Gushee, 2012: 51-52 suggests that the metaphorical expression "shedding blood" could plausibly encompass other serious "blood-spilling" crimes such as violent rape and the worst forms of torture.

120. TNIV.

121. While there is no indication in Genesis 9:6b that the rationale of being created in God's image applies more prominently to one member of *adam* in 9:6a than to the other, the preceding context explains why so many biblical (e.g., Kidner, 1967: 101; Sawyer, 1974: 425-26; Brueggemann, 1982: 83; Wenham, 1987: 193-4; Sarna, 1989: 59, 62; Mathews, 1995: 405-6; Walton, 2001: 343; Merrill, 2003: 444; Youngblood, 2006: 18) and theological (Calvin, 1948: Gen. 9:6; Chafer, 1947: v. 2, 168; Berkhof, 1949: 204; K. Barth, 1958a: 198; Murray, 1977: 36; Wolterstorff, 1985: 68-69; Ferngren, 1987: 26; Dyck, 1990: 38; Hoekema, 1994: 16; John Paul II, 1997b: 523, 535-36; Kass, 2003: 184, 186; Ware, 2002: 20) commentators emphasize creation in the image here as the basis for the great significance of human lives. In verse 5 God has indicated that for the life of every human being an accounting will be required. So verse 6 then describes the mechanism God will use for that accounting: God entrusts to human beings the responsibility to punish murderers. Since the reason for the first part of verse 6 (capital punishment) has already been given in verse 5, what follows in the second part of verse 6 is not likely to be merely another rationale for the first part of

According to James 3:9, not just murdering but even cursing a person is wrong because a person is in the image of God.[122] The same sort of connection with God requires such restraint.[123] Cursing people is tantamount to cursing God. In other words, when one damages or dishonors people, one is acting in the same way toward God.[124] Or, more positively, treating people well is a way to honor or glorify God.[125] Numerous commentators have noted the importance of this biblical basis for verbally treating people with respect.[126] There is almost certainly a reference here to the original creation of the human race in Genesis 1.[127] People may be sinful and unworthy of attention, but that does not diminish the fact that they are still in God's image and therefore warrant respect.

As William Ellery Channing once put it, "God's throne in heaven is unassailable. The only war against God is against his image."[128] Accordingly, it is not surprising to see Satan attacking Adam and Eve soon after they are created in God's image — in a way that brings into question whether they really are "like God" in the way they ought to be (Gen. 3:5). Throughout the Pentateuch, in fact, there is a two-way form of this battle raging. Just as the "pretender to the throne" is attacking those who are in God's image, so God through God's people is attacking the images *(tselem)* of other gods (Num. 33:52).

---

the verse — i.e., it would naturally be added to provide more than the reason why human beings will be the ones to punish murderers. Rather, the second part of the verse appears to take a step back and ground the entire teaching about the importance of not killing human beings (including the consequences of doing so) in an appeal related to the image of God.

122. Although this passage refers to God's "likeness," it is addressing the same "image" concept in view here, as will be explained later in this chapter.

123. This parallel between Genesis 9 and James 3 is noted by many commentators, including Hartin, 2003: 187; Allen, 2000: 95; Bray, 1991: 210; Adamson, 1976: 146; Chafer, 1947: v. 2, 167-68.

124. Davids (1989: 85) and Schmutzer (2009: 177) put this in terms of injuring and defacing, respectively; Wenham (1987: 31-32) and D. Kelsey (2009: v. 2, 945) in terms of affronting and dishonoring. Wolterstorff (1985: 68) discusses the similar language of abusing in Calvin. See also Maston, 1959: 15.

125. McLeod (1999: 66) and Berkouwer (1975: 115), respectively, adopt these terms. A fuller development of the connection between "image" and "glory" must await Chapter 6.

126. For example, on James 3:9 see Hartin, 2003: 187; Marshall, 2001: 55; Moo, 2000: 163; Hoekema, 1994: 20; Murray, 1977: 37; Buswell, 1962: 236. For a wider biblical view, see Wolterstorff, 1985: 68; Calvin, 1960 *(Institutes):* III, 7:6.

127. For example, see Hartin, 2003: 187; L. Johnson, 1995: 262; Laws, 1993: 156; Cook, 1975: 92.

128. Channing, 1841: 76.

As noted in Chapter 2, evil powers in the New Testament such as the beast in Revelation 13 can have an image as well; and the concept similarly suggests the idea of a close connection. Refusing to worship the image of the beast is a fatal offense, because of the close connection of the image to the beast and, ultimately, to Satan (v. 15). This worship is required to take the form of, in effect, attempting to hide one's connection to God as one who is in God's image by more visibly displaying the evidence that one is in the image of (is connected to) Satan. This evidence is the "mark of the beast" (vv. 16-17).

Capturing in a single word the nature of the connection involved in being created in God's image is quite challenging. One common approach is to speak of people as "representing" God before other people and/or all of creation.[129] Both terms for image, *tselem*[130] and *eikon*,[131] incline toward this meaning. Accordingly, some commentators call people in the image of God "representatives" of God;[132] others call them "representations."[133]

Two ideas are embedded here, whether or not they neatly correspond with these two English terms. To represent can mean either to "stand for something" or to "present a likeness of something." As explained above, biblical use of the term "image" involves the idea of "standing for" to some degree, since in treating people with honor or dishonor, one is honoring or dishonoring God. Analogies such as being "agents," "ambassadors," or other emissaries of God presumably attempt to convey a sense of this concept.[134]

---

129. G. Peterson (2008: 471), following van Huyssteen (2006), identifies this as the "consensus" view of those seeking to understand what the term meant "in its original Hebraic context." Westermann (with J. Reinders, 1997: 194, in support) objects that there is no one before whom humanity can represent God. Representing God to all of creation may be embedded in the "likeness" aspect of "image," to be discussed below. However, even on the human level alone, there is no difficulty here unless one overlooks the dual sense in which humanity is an image of God (explained above). Because "image" involves individuals as well as humanity corporately, people are to recognize individuals as created in God's image and treat them in ways appropriate to those representing God.

130. See R. Harris, 1980: 767; Westermann, 1994: 146; Curtis, 1992: 389; Mays, 2006: 35.

131. See Lightfoot, 1927: 143; Ra. Martin, 1981: 57; Black, 2006: 191.

132. E.g., Waltke, 1989: 3; McLeod, 1999: 51; Schillebeeckx, 1990: 245.

133. E.g., Berkouwer, 1975: 114-15; Harrelson, 1980: 64; Furnish, 1984: 248; Sharp, 1995: 307; Wernow, 1995: 104; Hefner, 2000: 88; Canceran, 2011: 7.

134. So in Brueggemann, 1997: 452; D. T. Williams, 1999: 183-84; Horton, 2005: 108; Merrill, 2006: 342; cf. Gushee, 2013: 46. Cortez (2010: 31) relates the idea to a national flag (where to defile a nation's flag is to defile the nation itself) or a national ruler (where this same dynamic is intensified).

The idea of "presenting a likeness" is also relevant to the notion of "image," but in a particular way. The Bible does not employ the concept of being in God's image to refer to actual current likenesses to God, though the English term "represent" can imply that. Rather, "being in the image" refers to intended likenesses, as will be explained shortly. So one must be careful not to infer too much from the English term "image." The biblical terms for image do indeed convey a sense of "visibility" — a sense that an image represents in visible form something else.[135] In that sense, people in God's image are indeed visible beings with a connection to someone invisible.[136] This does not necessarily mean that an image portrays particular characteristics of the original,[137] as explained in Chapter 2. Nevertheless, images often do so (see Ch. 5).

The present and previous chapters have documented substantial evidence that the understanding of a *tselem* reflected in the Bible (e.g., in Daniel 3) was widespread in the ancient Near East. But making explicit here what has been implicit to this point may be helpful regarding the relevance of such an extrabiblical cultural understanding for understanding a term's meaning in the Bible. There is a risk in considering the meaning of biblical terms outside of the biblical context. Moving directly from understanding the meaning of a term in the broader culture to a mistaken assumption that it means the same thing in the Bible is all too easy.[138] On the other hand, authors have to use the common language of their day. They must work with terms that have meaningful content, while identifying any ways in which they are giving terms distinctive new meanings or implications. In fact, the Bible's authors are particularly prone to give added or altered meaning to familiar concepts.

So there is an important but limited place for understanding what authors and readers of biblical texts would likely have understood terms to mean outside of a biblical context. For example, words like *tselem* had a common meaning during the period when Genesis was written. So the word did not need to be defined by the author of Genesis unless its intended meaning was substantially different from what people would assume by

---

135. See Leitch, 1975: 257; Conzelmann, 1975: 187; I. H. Marshall, 2001: 51.

136. See H. R. Niebuhr, 1996: 81; Allen, 2000: 88; McKnight, 2005: 18.

137. As Robert Browning (2004: XVII) writes in his poem "Christmas Eve": "Though he is so bright, and we so dim, We are made in his image to witness him."

138. For the risks involved here, particularly related to establishing what the Bible means by affirming that humanity is in the image of God, see Miller, 1972: 289; Stendebach, 2003: 392; B. Childs, 1993: 567-68; Briggs, 2010: 118.

hearing it. As many have noted, the very fact that so little is said in Genesis, to explain what "image" means, argues strongly that readers already had a basic understanding of the term.[139] From a providential perspective, one might even say that God had prepared the way for the crucial revelation that humanity is in God's image by ensuring that a basic understanding of the term "image" developed in the ancient Near East before the writing of Genesis.[140] Others have observed a similar cultural understanding working in conjunction with the Old Testament to provide the familiarity necessary for New Testament readers to understand the term *eikon*.[141]

Since the term "image" apparently did not require radical redefinition for the Bible's authors, it remained for them to use the term in ways that reflected common understanding of the term, while giving it explicit new meaning and implications where theologically necessary. We should not be surprised, then, to find that the basic idea of image, as the authors of the Bible use it, is in line with how people would have understood it in their cultural setting. "Image" was a word signifying close connection, but in a particular direction: the image represented someone or something, with significant implications for how the image should be viewed and treated. Chapter 2 has already discussed the Mesopotamian, Egyptian, and Canaanite backdrops to this term and illustrations of where they are reflected in the Old and New Testament. The idea that people who dishonor the image dishonor the original does not need correcting in the Bible, but simply application.[142]

The connection between image and original in the ancient Near East could be quite close. In light of the distance that the Bible is always careful to maintain between God and people, care is necessary lest the extrabiblical cultural context mislead biblical interpretation at this point. As noted in Chapter 2, outside of the Bible an image could have a "spiritual union" with a divinity that the image represents — resulting in the divine presence or even the divine essence in the image.[143] If such language means to affirm

---

139. So Clines, 1968: 85; Rad, 1972: 58; Tigay, 1984: 173; Curtis, 1992: 390; Callender, 2000: 28-29; Grenz, 2001: 190; Shults, 2003: 231; J. Strong, 2005: 93-94; Cortez, 2010: 22-23.

140. As, for example, Niehaus (2008: 29-30) suggests.

141. For instance, McCasland, 1950: 92.

142. For further discussion of this feature attached to images of rulers, see Clines, 1968: 83; J. Strong, 2005: 104-5; Merrill, 2006: 170. Regarding images of a god, see Clines, 1968: 82; Herring, 2008: 492.

143. On spiritual union, see Schmutzer, 2009: 178-79; on divine presence, see Clines, 1968: 87-88; Pannenberg, 1985: 20-21; Schüle, 2005: 6; Herring, 2008: 480-81; Cortez, 2010: 35; on divine essence, see Conzelmann, 1975: 288; Walton, 2001: 131.

a close connection between God and people, it may be on the right track, as long as it does not claim *too* close a connection or sharing of identity.[144] Only Christ is God's image in that sense.

Furthermore, if such language means to suggest that people are presently like God in many ways, it is at odds with the way in which the Bible speaks of people being in God's image. To be sure, there sometimes were specific resemblances in form or function between image and original in the ancient Near East. But it is easy to overemphasize those.[145] One may miss something crucial in the process. Exactly how "likeness" relates to the concept of "image" and people relate to the concept of "likeness-image" is one of the ways that the Bible's authors are careful to distinguish their view from the looser usage of the term in the broader culture. As will be explained below, the need for that was rooted in a distinctive understanding of sin and the Fall.

Before discussing that matter, though, it is important to note two other distinctive ways that the authors of the Bible use the term "image." Whereas both Mesopotamia and Egypt were familiar with the idea that people could be images of a god, only special people like rulers for the most part were seen as such. In contrast, the Bible portrays all human beings (e.g., *adam* [singular] in Genesis 1; *anthropous* [plural] in James 3) as being in God's image.[146]

Many refer to this change as the Bible's "democratizing" of the image concept,[147] although some have taken issue with this term because of its

144. Westermann (1994: 153) has rightly warned against understanding humanity's status in God's image in a way that diminishes the holiness and transcendence of God. Similarly, see Horton, 2005: 185-86. Conceiving of image in terms of connection need not do that. See critique of Westermann in Grenz, 2001: 200; Treier, 2008: 122; D. Kelsey, 2009: v. 2, 928. Cf. Mathews, 1995: 168, on recognizing appropriate distance between God on the one hand and humanity in God's image on the other.

145. For critiques of overemphasizing various similarities between image and original in the ancient Near East, see Curtis, 1992: 390; Konkel, 1992: 2-3; McLeod, 1999: 45-47; Walton, 2001: 130; Herring, 2008: 485; Schmutzer, 2009: 176-77.

146. As noted in Pannenberg, 1991: v. 2, 203; Ware, 2002: 17; S. Wright, 2003: 33; Horton, 2005: 107; Schüle, 2005: 5-6; World, 2005: par. 85; Garner, 2007: 98; Vorster, 2007b: 368; Cortez, 2010: 21-22.

147. E.g., W. Schmidt, 1983: 197; Wenham, 1987: 30-31; Waltke, 1989: 6; Hamilton, 1990: 135; I. Hart, 1995: 318-19; Harland, 1996: 180; Ruston, 2004: 277-78; Mangano, 2008: 9; Sands, 2010: 37; Bosman, 2010: 569; Bradshaw, 2010: 114; Oberdorfer, 2010: 232; McReynolds, 2013: 32; Koyzis, 2014: 22. Jónsson (1988: 143) calls this the "dominant opinion" among Old Testament scholars. R. Jewett (2007: 529) emphasizes that just as the Old Testament democratizes the understanding of "image" familiar in the surrounding cultures, so does the

individualistic connotations. A term like "universalizing," they maintain, would better convey the idea that humanity as a whole (rather than particular people) is in the image of God.[148] However, as explained above, this concern assumes an either/or mentality whereas the Bible affirms a both/and approach. In both a corporate and particular sense, all people are in God's image. Something important is lost by neglecting either of these two aspects.

Affirming all people and not just rulers as being in God's image in effect counters the tendency in the ancient Near East (as in many other eras and places) to think too highly of rulers and too lowly of everyone else. Rulers in Israel as well as in the broader ancient Near East could readily be exalted to godlike status at the expense of other people. Biblical teaching on God's image runs counter to that tendency.[149] People in the ancient Near East, on the other hand, were commonly viewed as mere slaves of the god(s). The Bible undermines that view as well by combining the servant/slave status of people in relation to God with a much higher evaluation of people's significance in relation to God and creation.[150]

There are only a few known references in the ancient Near East that associate all of humanity with God's image.[151] Their rarity underscores the distinctive contribution of the Bible in connecting all people and God via the concept of "image." At the same time, the existence of such references outside the Bible confirms that the "image" terminology is flexible enough to be applied to more than select human beings — perhaps another indication of why the term was so useful for the Bible's authors. As noted above, we must be careful not to let the meaning of the term "image" in

New. Levenson (1994: 115) recognizes such a "democratization of offices" as part of a larger biblical trend, in which God's promises to David eventually extend to all Israel, while God's priests are not just those who descend from Levi but eventually include all Israelites (and ultimately all believers, Jew and Gentile alike).

148. So Grenz, 2001: 201; 2002: 43; Smail, 2006: 45-46.

149. See discussions in Dehsen, 1997: 265; Assmann, 2000: 46-49; Häring, 2001: 4-5.

150. Regarding Mesopotamia, see P. Bird, 1981: 142; Grenz, 2001: 200-201; Horton, 2006: 186. Beale (2004: 82) considers the related view of people in Egypt.

151. Wildberger (1997: 1083) cites Mesopotamian evidence in Maag, 1954: 85-116, 1955: 15-44, in Westermann, 1994: 154, plus Egyptian evidence in Hornung, 1967: 123-26, and E. Otto, 1971: 335-48. The best-known examples are the Egyptian *Instruction of Merikare* (see Lichtheim, 1976: v. 1, 106; Tigay, 1984: 173; Konkel, 1992: 3; Walton, 2001: 130), and the Egyptian *Instruction for Ani* (see Williams, 1972: 221; Lichtheim, 1976: v. 2, 145; Tigay, 1984: 173; Curtis, 1984: 196). Middleton (2005: 99-104) discusses both and finds it unlikely that their ideas directly influenced the author of Genesis.

the ancient Near East dictate what the Bible means by the term. Still, it can alert us to the basic understanding that initial readers likely brought to the text to help us look for ways that this understanding is affirmed and altered in the Bible.

One final way that authors of the Bible alter the meaning of the image-of-God concept is to add the prepositions. As explained earlier in this chapter, people are not created simply as images of God; they are created in — according to — God's image. The New Testament reveals that this image is Christ and that God had in view people conforming to God's image in Christ from before the beginning of creation (see Ch. 2).

However, even the Old Testament authors apparently sensed that claiming people *are* God's image — particularly in their sinfulness — went too far. Since God's image involves a special connection with God and meaningful reflection of God, affirming the latter of people would have contradicted the whole thrust of the Old Testament. As noted earlier, the psalmist could not see anything in people to explain God's favor. ("What are human beings, that you are mindful of them?" — Ps. 8:4.) If people were God's image, reflecting various attributes of God, the answers would have been evident; however, "there is no one like" God (Isa. 46:9).

Nevertheless, the Old Testament authors perceived that humanity is profoundly connected with God by virtue of God's eternal purposes for humanity. God intends for people to reflect who God is and what God does, though they may fall far short of actually doing so now. While they do not warrant the title of "God's image" yet, they have dignity grounded in their destiny to become God's image — and so warrant that title once they are fully conformed to Christ.[152] Until then, people are just "in" or "according to" God's image — always accountable to the standard of God's image, and developing toward that image as God enables and people endeavor.

People are not just stone statues the way that so many ancient images were — created in the final form of the image they were intended to be. Rather, they are living beings who must grow before they are what the Creator intended them to become. Perceiving this and altering the ancient Near Eastern concept to communicate it is one of the great contributions of the Old Testament.

---

152. On the need for people to become God's image — something that they are not yet but that God intends them to be — see International, 2004: par. 12. As Chapter 6 will discuss, the New Testament (e.g., 2 Cor. 3:18) accordingly speaks of the need for people to be "transformed into" a divine image that they are not yet.

Image as Reflection

We can now at last take up the question of the relationship of "likeness" and "image." After all, God's original intention, as recorded in Genesis 1:26, is to create people in a way that they are in "God's likeness" as well as "God's image." Are there two concepts here or one — and what does the idea of likeness add to or clarify about the idea of image?

The first indication that there is just one concept here comes in the very next verse. Whereas both image *(tselem)* and likeness *(demuth)* are involved in God's intention (v. 26), the author considers *tselem* alone to be sufficient to describe God's acting on that intention (and similarly in 9:6). God creates humanity in, or according to, God's *tselem*.[153] Several chapters later (5:1), when summarizing that creative action, the author simply says that God has created humanity in (according to) God's *demuth*.

Similarly, New Testament authors can reference people's creational status in terms of either "image" *(eikon)* alone — as in 1 Corinthians 11:7 — or "likeness" *(homoiosis)* alone — as in James 3:9. In the biblical context, therefore, it is common to find commentators concluding that there is no meaningful difference between the terms[154] — they represent the same idea.[155] Once Genesis has introduced the likeness-image concept, later references to it in Genesis and the New Testament need only involve one term or the other. Either term alone is sufficient to refer to humanity's status bestowed through creation by God.

Accordingly, many biblical scholars conclude that the two terms point to the same idea[156] and should not be employed to distinguish two different aspects of who people are.[157] Using two terms like this for a single concept is a form of parallelism common in biblical Hebrew.[158] As some put it, the terms are virtually "synonymous"[159] or "interchange-

153. Pieper (1950: 515), Piper (1971: 17), and Hughes (1989: 7) are among the many who find that this use of one term in place of the two indicates that there is just one concept here.

154. See Clark, 1984: 13-14; Ryrie, 1986: 190; Boyce, 1990: 213; Clines, 1993: 426-27; B. Childs, 1993: 567; M. Williams, 2014: 82.

155. See L. Berkhof, 1949: 203-4; Gerhard, 1962: 34; Youngblood, 2006: 7.

156. E.g., Gill, 1978: 392; Sarna, 1989: 12; Hughes, 1989: 7.

157. E.g., Brunner, 1947: 111; Orr, 1948: 36; Thiessen, 1949: 219; Gerhard, 1962: 33-34; Shepherd, 1988: 1017; Hoekema, 1994: 13; Mangano, 2008: 2.

158. Thomas, 1949: 154; Buswell, 1962: 232; D. Hall, 1986: 70; Barentsen, 1988: 31; McLeod, 1999: 44-45; Smail, 2003: 25; Crouch, 2010: 3.

159. So A. Strong, 1907: 521; Mueller, 1934: 205; L. Berkhof, 1949: 203; Oduyoye, 1982:

able."[160] Such appears to be the view of the translators who produced the early major Greek translation of the Old Testament known as the Septuagint. In Genesis 1:26 they translate *tselem* as *eikon* and *demuth* as *homoiosis;* but in 5:1 they translate *demuth* as *eikon,* thereby suggesting that when *tselem* or *demuth* appears alone to describe humanity's creational status, either word is referring to the same single likeness-image concept.[161]

Further evidence that this is the case appears in early Genesis, later in the Old Testament, and elsewhere. In early Genesis, the author indicates a similar proclivity to use different terms to refer to a single creation-related idea, in the very verbs that describe creation. God "creates" *(bara)* and "makes" *('asa)* things in Genesis 1–5, though the author appears not to have two different concepts in view. In Genesis 1 the author states God's intention to "make" *('asa)* humanity (v. 26) and then describes God acting on that intention by saying that God "creates" *(bara)* humanity (v. 27). In Genesis 5, when the author looks back to God's bringing humanity into existence (v. 1), both *bara* and *'asa* describe that action. Similarly, in Genesis 2, when all of God's creative activity is done, both verbs appear in verse 3 to describe that activity.[162]

Tselem and *demuth* similarly appear together in early Genesis, as we have seen, to refer to the same people. This pairing occurs outside of Genesis as well. In Ezekiel 23:14-15, both terms describe the same human figures on a wall.[163] So it is not surprising to find that the same pairing appears outside of the Bible in the ancient Near East context of the Old Testament.

The most celebrated instance of that is on the ninth-century BC statue of King Had-yisi from Tell Fakhariyeh (in modern-day Syria).[164] The inscription on the statue is in two languages, Aramaic and Assyrian. In Aramaic, the equivalents *(slm* and *dmwt)* of the two Hebrew terms refer to the statue

---

45; I. Hart, 1995: 321; Watson, 1997: 280; Horton, 2006: 185; Roy, 2009: 9; Cortez, 2010: 16; Gushee, 2013: 42.

160. So Barabas, 1963: 370-71; Klug, 1984: 146; Stendebach, 2003: 394; Garr, 2003: 3-5.

161. On the Septuagint's translation of Genesis 5:1, see Hamilton, 1980: 192; Merrill, 2003: 442; Loader, 2004: 51.

162. For more examples, see J. Barr, 1968: 25.

163. Westermann (1994: 146) finds the two words here to have the "same meaning."

164. For more information on this statue, see Abon-Assaf, Bordreuil, and Millard, 1982; Millard and Bordreuil, 1982: 135-41; Greenfield and Shaffer, 1983: 109-16; Angerstorfer, 1984: 7-11; Gropp and Lewis, 1985: 45-61; Callender, 2000: 26-27; Schüle, 2005: 9-10; Herring, 2008: 487.

in a way that makes them essentially "synonymous,"[165] "parallel,"[166] "interchangeable"[167] — they refer to the same concept.[168] Attempts to find significant differences between the terms have proven unsatisfactory.[169] That is not surprising in light of a clue from the Assyrian version of the inscription. Its author considers the single word *tsalmu* to be an adequate equivalent for both Aramaic terms[170] (much as *tselem* alone in Gen. 1:27 and 9:6 conveys the same concept that *tselem* and *demuth* together refer to in Gen. 1:26).

With such overwhelming evidence suggesting that humanity in God's "likeness-image" refers to a single concept, one may wonder why some people throughout history have found two different concepts here. One major reason goes back to the primary Greek translation (Septuagint) and Latin translation (Vulgate) of the Old Testament, which were so influential particularly during the formative centuries of the church. Although the Hebrew text of Genesis 1:26 simply puts the "image" and "likeness" words side by side, these two translations inserted the word "and" between them. This gave the impression that two separate concepts are involved here, rather than one concept with two ways to refer to it.[171] Some also consider intertestamental Jewish speculation about possible differences between "image" and "likeness" to be a significant reason for this departure from the teaching of Genesis.[172]

Others have probably assumed that two different words entail two different concepts — an unsafe assumption in general. In this case, that assumption, plus overlooking the way that the Hebrew language uses two words in parallel to describe a single concept, can readily lead to the false expectation of finding two concepts rather than one.

165. So Grenz, 2001: 187; Middleton, 2005: 107.

166. So Jónsson, 1988: 206; van Leeuwen, 1997: 644.

167. So Sarna, 1989: 12; Konkel, 1992: 2.

168. So Mathews, 1995: 167; Mangano, 2008: 2.

169. For example, both Angerstorfer (1984: 9-10) and Stendebach (2003: 393) find Dohmen's attempt (1983: 91-106) unsuccessful since it does not account for the way that the two terms are nearly interchangeable. However, Dohmen's analysis does helpfully indicate that the use of two terms may suggest that the single concept in view here is complex. See elaboration of this complexity below in the context of biblical terminology.

170. See Dehsen, 1997: 260-61; Garr, 2000: 227-28; Crouch, 2010: 6-7.

171. For the contribution of this addition to the misunderstanding of the concept, see Clines, 1968: 91-92; Berkouwer, 1975: 69; Hoekema, 1994: 13; Lewis and Demarest, 1994: v. 2, 134; Mathews, 1995: 164; Loader, 2004: 27-28. Even today, translators often insert a comma (if not a full "and") between the two terms.

172. E.g., Bray, 2001: 575.

Still others have likely promoted the two-concept approach because it conveniently supports other affirmations they want to make about the image. The likeness-image concept then becomes just another way to promote that theological system. (We have already discussed in Chapter 1 the common methodological problem of reading one's theological "system" into the likeness-image concept rather than allowing what the Bible says about the concept to establish its meaning more directly.)

For example, many systems include the idea that while sin does not change people from human beings to something else, it makes them much less like God. So it is not hard to imagine how useful the image and likeness terms have been as vehicles for conveying these ideas. People continue in God's image, they suggest, but the likeness is damaged. The human capacity for reason, for example, continues, but sin damages or even obliterates human righteousness.

This distinction was common in the earliest centuries of the church.[173] Irenaeus became particularly well known for it,[174] while Clement of Alexandria,[175] Origen,[176] and Augustine among many others[177] affirmed it as well. Medieval theologians,[178] Aquinas prominent among them,[179] were active supporters of it. Accordingly, it has significantly influenced Roman Catholic and Greek Orthodox thinking about humanity in God's image — and certain strands of Protestant and other Christian thinking as well (Calvin, Brunner, et al.).[180] Even in the early church, though, there were major lead-

173. See Thielicke, 1966: 202-3; Crawford, 1966: 233; H. D. McDonald, 1981: 56; Miley, 1989: 406-7; Treier, 2008: 74.

174. Irenaeus (1867) sees many sinful people "possessing indeed the image . . . but not receiving the similitude." For discussion of his views, see Maloney, 1973: 37, 73; Osborn, 2003: 256; Gonzalez, 2007: 30-31. For people influenced by his views, see Maloney, 1973: 188-90; Shults, 2003: 221; Mahoney, 2010: 679.

175. See discussions in L. Berkhof, 1949: 202; Hughes, 1989: 8.

176. See discussions in H. W. Robinson, 1926: 165; Maloney, 1973: 74; Hughes, 1989: 8.

177. L. Berkhof (1949: 202, 205) discusses Augustine and others such as Athanasius and Ambrose. On Gregory of Nyssa, see Schneider, 1967: 191; on John of Damascus, see Baker, 1991: 98; on early Christian ascetics, see Woodhead, 2006: 238; on Diadochus of Photiki, see Breck, 1998: 29.

178. See discussions in Brunner, 1952: 76; Lewis and Demarest, 1994: v. 2, 125-26; Erickson, 2013: 462.

179. Aquinas, 1947: pt. I, Q. 93, art. 9; cf. analysis in D. Hall, 1986: 60.

180. Although Protestants have not always used the image vs. likeness terminology in the same way, the distinction involved there is often evident. For example, Boer (1990: 50-51) critiques it in Calvin; Kaufman (1956: 158) in other Reformers; G. Peterson (1996: 224) in Brunner; and Power (1997: 131, 139) provides a more recent illustration of it.

ers who recognized that this distinction was contrary to biblical teaching.[181] In recent centuries, the recognition has become more widespread.[182]

This separation of "image" and "likeness" emerges, among other ways, from the misconception that being "in the likeness of God" is a matter of ways that people are actually like God — a misconception discussed above. The biblical insufficiency of this view is particularly evident in the primary New Testament reference to people being in God's "likeness," James 3:9. It is precisely those who apparently warrant cursing most — those with the least God-like attributes — whom James is identifying as being in God's likeness. The passage appears to be stressing that the reason for respecting people is rooted in something other than their attractive attributes.

To be clear: Sin has badly damaged people in many ways, and the Bible uses many different terms to convey that. But humanity's status in the likeness-image of God is not one of them (Ch. 4). As we have seen, employing a supposed difference between "image" and "likeness" in such passages as Genesis 1:26-27 to describe the damage of sin, is at odds with the way that the Bible itself uses these terms. To use biblical terms in creative new ways can be stimulating. But if that obscures or even contradicts what the Bible intends for those terms to convey, then something vital is at risk. In the case of the likeness-image term, nothing less than human dignity and human destiny are on the line. Clarity here is essential.

The biblical evidence, then, points to there being a single concept involving the terms "image" and "likeness."[183] This is a view with which many concur.[184] Nevertheless, the question remains as to what the term "likeness" contributes to this concept. If the term "image" sufficiently conveyed the concept, it is hard to imagine why the Bible's authors would have involved another term.

181. Maloney discusses several of them at length. Interestingly, even some of the major early church theologians, who employed a supposed image vs. likeness terminology to explain certain concepts in their theological systems, often reverted to using the two terms synonymously in their writings. Maloney (1973) cites numerous examples in the writings of Origen (p. 74) and Irenaeus (p. 202). See also Gonzalez, 2007: 28-29, on Irenaeus.

182. See Kaufman, 1956: 158; Clark, 1969: 216; Feinberg, 1972: 237; H. D. McDonald, 1981: 33-34; Wildberger, 1997: 1082.

183. In addition to the evidence noted above, Romans 1:23 is an example of where "image" *(eikon)* and "likeness" *(homoioma,* a term similar to *homoiosis)* are employed together to describe a single concept rather than two separate concepts: People have exchanged the glory of God for "a likeness of an image of" various things.

184. Westermann (1994: 146) affirms the "widespread agreement." For elaborations, see K. Barth, 1958a: 198; and Cook, 1975: 86-87.

Commentators frequently note that at the heart of the Hebrew word *demuth* and the Greek word *homoiosis* is the idea of likeness.[185] But the debate is unending over whether "likeness" modifies what "image" means, or "image" modifies what "likeness" means. Support for both positions is understandable, since the analysis above suggests that both are valid. There is a single concept at issue here. Either term is sufficient to refer to it, so the concept must reside in the common ground that these two terms share.[186] Each term modifies (i.e., helps to focus and explain) the other.

The term "image," as we have seen, indicates the presence of a connection between an image and an original. We have also seen that an image may or may not have anything to do with being like (i.e., sharing the traits or other attributes of) the original. Including "likeness" with "image" communicates that the kind of image in view here somehow has to do with likeness to the original.[187] It does not so much strengthen or weaken any similarity implied in the word "image" as it simply ensures that similarity is understood to be in some way a part of the concept in view.[188]

This likeness can involve more than the visible, physical likeness that many see as most characteristic of the term "image."[189] While "like-

185. E.g., see Wenham, 1987: 29; Bray, 1991: 196; Hoekema, 1994: 13; Grudem, 1994: 442-43; Konkel, 1997: 968; Callender, 2000: 25; Garr, 2003: 118; Towner, 2005: 346-47; Middleton, 2005: 46; Merrill, 2006: 169; Smail, 2006: 45; Mangano, 2008: 2. However, these and other commentators differ over exactly how "likeness" connects God and humanity.

186. See discussions in Aquinas (1947: pt. I, Q. 93, art. 1), who cites Augustine in support; Lenski, 1946a: 989; 1946b: 949-50; Schneider, 1967: 190; C. Carter, 1983a: 206; cf. van Huyssteen (2006: 156), who cites Middleton in support. Kidner, 1967: 50-51, and Hodge, 1982: v. 2, 96, developing the idea of the two terms reinforcing and explaining each other.

187. See discussions in Gerhard, 1962: 34; Hoeksema, 1966: 204; J. Barr, 1968: 24; Clines, 1968: 92; Rad, 1972: 57-58; Hughes, 1989: 7-8; Grenz, 2001: 202. On the more general idea that "likeness" in some way explains "image," see Calvin, 1960a: bk. I, ch. 15, sec. 3; L. Berkhof, 1949: 206; J. Murray, 1977: 34; Waltke, 1989: 3; Garr, 2003: 5.

188. Whereas some commentators such as Aalders (1981: 71) and Westermann (1994: 146-47) perceive strengthening here, many others perceive weakening: e.g., Horst, 1950: 261; Eichrodt, 1967: 123; Wilson, 1973: 356; P. Bird, 1981: 139; Curtis, 1992: 386; Dumbrell, 2002: 16; Goldingay, 2003: 223. As Konkel (1997: 969) has noted, *demuth* can have either effect, depending on the context; cf. Middleton, 2005: 48-49. In one sense, broadening the concept beyond the physical focus of "image" does constitute a "weakening" of sorts, just as the affirmation that similarity is indeed involved constitutes a sort of "strengthening."

189. For elaboration on this point, see Leitch, 1975: 256; Hamilton, 1990: 135-36; Dehsen, 1997: 260; Garr, 2003: 120.

ness" (i.e., *homoiosis*) does not appear in the New Testament outside of James 3:9, there is ample evidence in the Old Testament regarding the meaning of likeness *(demuth)* apart from any connection with image *(tselem)*. Most often *demuth* does refer to something visible, such as a sketch (2 Kgs. 16:10) or a physical object (2 Chron. 4:3), though its many appearances in the visions of Ezekiel suggest that it need not refer to something with solid substance (e.g., the radiance of God's glory in Ezek. 1:28). The term's wide range is evident in its use to refer to sound (Isa. 13:4) and moral character (Ps. 58:4). So the range of the term renders it potentially suitable for describing human beings. Ultimately, though, it is the actual range of human attributes associated in some way with the likeness-image concept that confirms the flexibility of the term in the image-of-God concept.

"Likeness" simply indicates that similarity between two things is somehow involved. A similarity may or may not indicate that there is a reason for the similarity — that there is a connection between the two things that are similar. A rock in a river and an egg at a store may look nearly identical, but there may be no connection between the two things. Including "image" with "likeness" communicates that the kind of likeness in view is because of a connection between two things, where one is the original.

The likeness-image concept connecting God and people, then, is within the range of meanings of each term individually (hence either term alone can accurately refer to it). Accordingly, it falls within the range of meanings that the two terms have in common. At this point, we might be tempted to conclude the following about the likeness-image concept: that using it to describe humanity basically signals that people are connected to God in a way that makes them like God. However, we have already seen that this concept cannot have such a meaning because there is ample evidence that the concept is not about actual human traits, capacities, or abilities that make all people like God.

This impasse suggests the need to return to the biblical text. We must determine if there is something special about references to the "likeness-image" concept when it connects people and God, compared to the way the term "likeness" commonly appears elsewhere in the Bible. Indeed there is.

Whenever the "likeness" term appears in reference to humanity and God's "likeness-image," it is explicitly in the context of how God created people to be. There is a verb and a preposition. People are "created in [or according to]" the likeness of God. That is not the case where "likeness" appears elsewhere (e.g., in the passages cited above). In these latter instances, one thing is simply stated to be a likeness of something else. It is not just created with the *intention* that it be like it. It simply *is* like it. By contrast, in Genesis 1:26, God's *intention* for humanity is at the heart of what creation in the likeness-image of God entails. Later references to people created in God's likeness in Genesis 5:1 and James 3:9 mention the same creational intention since that is a necessary context for understanding the meaning of the term.[190]

Analogous language appears in Genesis 5:3, where the text says Adam begets Seth in or according to his image. Is this a statement that baby Seth looks just like his father? (Babies rarely do right away.) Or is it a statement that he has a special connection to his father, such that he normally over time would reflect many of the attributes of his father (as fathers normally intend). The latter much better describes what it means for a living being to be made in the image of someone else. It is about an orientation — having a model according to which one is expected to develop. People understand that, and it served wonderfully in Genesis 5 to help readers understand what it means for people to be created in God's likeness-image.

In other words, the likeness involved in being created in God's likeness-image is about the likeness that God is intending at creation, not a descriptive statement about the way that people actually are. Not only is this understanding flagged by the language (verb and preposition) in the key passages themselves, but it is also the best way to make sense of all the previously discussed evidence indicating that God's image cannot be about ways that people are actually like God. The expectation at creation is that the creational intent of likeness to God will increasingly become a reality in the lives of people.

Humanity was intended to be like God, but is basically not like God due to sin. Truly there is no mortal human who is actually living as a likeness *(demuth)* of God, as Isaiah 40:18 explicitly observes (see above). However, God created people with the intention that they would be God's *demuth,* and God's intentions will not be thwarted. So God went on to

---

190. Theologians ranging from Karl Barth (1958a: 200) to various Eastern Orthodox leaders (see Woodhead, 2006: 237-38) recognize the central place of "intention" here, though their theologies differ in many other ways. See also Kuitert, 1972: 32; Mouw, 2012: 257. Rakestraw (1997: 261) and Eibach (2008: 68) describe this intention for humanity in terms of God's calling of humanity.

provide a way through Christ by which intended likeness could become actual likeness, as we saw in Chapter 2.[191]

Humanity's creation, then, in the "likeness-image" (or simply "likeness" or simply "image" — this book will tend to use the latter, for simplicity's sake) means the following. All people are created according to God's image, which the New Testament identifies as Jesus Christ. As Chapters 6 and 7 document: from before the beginning of creation, God intended that humanity should conform to the divine image, to Christ. So God created humanity well along the way toward that end. Even before the Fall, humanity had a further way to go before becoming a full reflection of Christ, having a transformed spiritual body and imperishability (not able to die). However, after the Fall people lost most of their ability to reflect God. As Chapter 4 explains, they continue to be in God's image, unique among creation as those whom God intends to become conformed to the divine image. No image has been damaged, for God's image is Christ — it is the standard of what God intends humanity to become. Nevertheless, sin has severely damaged people, who desperately need renewal according to the image of Christ.

Only Christ, then, currently *is* God's image in the complete sense of what it means to be the image of God: embodying a special connection with God and a glorifying reflection of God. People are created *in* (according to) that image. Simply by virtue of being in God's image, people do have a special connection with God. But it is not a connection of identity, as Christ (who *is* God) has. Rather, it is a connection of similarity (of likeness, as the Bible puts it). Simply by virtue of being in God's image, people can manifest some reflection of God (see Ch. 5); but it is far from all the reflection that God intends. Only after death will people's transformation into the image of God in Christ be complete. Until then they are in (according to) that image, accountable to God to develop increasing likeness to God.

Because there is already connection and some reflection, occasionally saying that people *are* God's image is not inappropriate. However, since doing so conveys only a partial truth, it is risky. All too readily it leads to the assumption that being God's likeness-image is defined by how much people are currently like God, with the implications that all are not equally God's likeness and that God's image has been damaged

---

191. On image as rooted in God's purpose, shown supremely in Christ, see Painter, 2001: 45.

by sin. This assumption and these implications have contributed to the devastation documented in Chapter 1. For the most part, then, it is wiser to speak of people as created "in" God's image, as a reminder that God's image is Christ, the standard "according to" or "in" which all people were created. Simply by being "in" the image of God — being en route to a glorious destiny as God's image in Christ — people have an impressive God-given dignity.

CHAPTER FOUR

The Impact of Sin on God's Image

The creation of humanity in God's image involves connection and reflection (Ch. 3). People have a special connection to God, and God's intention is that a variety of human attributes (somehow reflecting God's own attributes) ought to evidence such a connection. However, almost from the start, sin intervenes. People, including all of their various attributes — traits, capacities, functions, etc. — are badly damaged.

There is ample discussion and documentation in the Bible regarding the destructive impact of sin on people. Yet at the same time there is every indication that people remain "in God's image" — that no harm has been done to this status or to the image on which it is based. People retain a special connection with God (though their relationship with God is badly damaged), and God still intends for people to reflect likenesses to God (though in actuality they largely fail to do so). The image of God is the standard of who people are created to be — embodied in the person of Christ — and that standard is not diminished in any way because of sin. Clarity on this point is crucial, since it will combine with other biblical evidence to demonstrate where many popular but inadequate views of the image of God have gotten off course (Ch. 5).

Two sets of biblical passages need careful consideration here. First are those passages throughout the Bible that discuss God's image and all people. Next are the New Testament passages that focus on people experiencing new life in Christ.

Humanity as a Whole

In Genesis 3, what later became known as "the Fall" takes place. It is the subjugation of humanity, in the persons of Adam and Eve, to sin. Many assume that sin and the Fall damage God's image, simply because they damage people. However, Genesis 3 is about human beings, not their status in the image of God. Neither of the primary Hebrew terms *(tselem and demuth)* used for the image in Genesis 1 — or their equivalents — are mentioned in Chapter 3. Plenty is said about the people involved, including what about *them* has been lost or damaged; but nothing about God's image.

Many interpreters of the Bible have conflated the image of God with the human being, embarking on the wrong path at the outset. One reason such conflation is dangerous is that it can connect God too closely with human sin. Since God has created people in the divine image and they end up sinning, some will conclude that a tendency to sin is a part of what it means to be in God's image.[1] This comes very close to ascribing sin directly to God.

More often, conflating people with the image of God instead leads to the biblically unsound[2] assumption that if the human being changes, God's image does also. When people are undamaged, so is God's image; but when people are damaged, God's image is also. The logical fallacy here becomes clearer by considering the difference between an object and the standard according to which it is made. A blueprint for a building may call for a high-quality structure. Just because the building has suffered damage does not mean that the standard — the blueprint — has changed as well.

As explained in previous chapters, the Bible indicates that God created humanity according to a standard embodied by Christ. Just because sin has badly damaged people, that does not mean that the standard, the image of God, has been damaged. The image "of God" involves the attributes of God — not the damaged attributes of fallen people. People created according to that image are to reflect godly attributes, even if it takes the death of God's Son to enable people to conform to God's image in Christ.

Connecting God's image with sin would only make sense if one has smuggled in an understanding of what constitutes that image — something that sin necessarily damages. But one cannot conclude what constitutes

---

1. For example, Robinson, 2011: 7-8 understands "the Christian tradition" to teach that "our being created in God's image, because of that first sin, entails our tendency to sin."

2. This book will refer to an idea as "biblically unsound" if it is an idea that the Bible never teaches (e.g., that God's image is damaged by sin) and it does not fit well with what the Bible does teach on related matters.

God's image until after gathering all of the biblical evidence regarding what that image is, and what it means to be "in" or "according to" that image. Whether or not the Bible sees God's image as damaged by sin is an important clue to what being — and being "in" — God's image means.

Conflating people and God's image has predisposed some to equate that image with every way that people are actually like God. There are no passages in the Bible, as we have already noted in Chapter 3, that explicate the meaning of God's image in terms of actual current human attributes (e.g., capacities, functions, or relationships). If no biblical passage affirms that any such resemblance is what constitutes God's image, we are on precarious ground to equate the two.

In fact, in light of teachings later in the Bible that root people's significance and dignity in their image-of-God status, given by God, the first few chapters of Genesis may imply a subtle warning. From the beginning, what God has given people has not satisfied them. They want to have a hand in their status. In Genesis 3 they come to think of that status in terms of how they are like God and try to increase that likeness by coming to "know good and evil."

The entire enterprise of people trying to establish their status by breaking it down into ways they are presently like God is misguided. The attraction of this enterprise is understandable. If human status (grounded in being in God's image) is a matter of present characteristics or capacities or relationships that people have, then they can somehow take credit for them. Though God originally gave them those attributes, the source is forgotten because what matters is possession. Others who lack those attributes then become inferior to them. The biblical writings paint a very different picture than this by consistently refraining from explicating God's image in terms of current likenesses to God. There is good reason to consider that to be more than accidental.

Those who tend to view being in God's image in terms of presently being "like God" may understandably see image-of-God language in Genesis 3. In verse 5 the serpent tells Eve that eating the forbidden fruit will make her "like God, knowing good and evil." Then in verse 22, after she and Adam eat the fruit, God observes with concern that humanity "has become like one of us, knowing good and evil." However, this passage addresses a problematic way of becoming like God, not the image/likeness in which God previously created humanity. Moreover, the concern here is not that a likeness is decreasing due to sin but that it is increasing.

Whatever else is going on in Genesis 3, there appears to be no evidence here of God's image being damaged by the Fall. Much is said about people, including their attributes. Their righteousness and relational ability are compromised, and the rest of Genesis goes on to document much other damage as well. However, there is no indication in the text that God's image, according to which people are created, has suffered damage. Were the standard itself damaged, then people would no longer be accountable to be better than they are. It is precisely the continuing standard of God's image, embodied in Christ, that requires people to be more and points to an eternal future in Christ when they will be so.

Two chapters later, in Genesis 5, further generations of fallen humanity come into view. After the reaffirmation that God created Adam and Eve in the image of God (v. 1), the text notes that Adam in turn fathered a son, Seth, in his image. Again there is no indication of any loss or damage to God's image. This speaks volumes, in light of how central it is for humanity to be in the image of God in Genesis 1, and how radical the impact of sin is in Genesis 3-4. Were the image damaged by sin, it would not make sense for the author simply to reaffirm humanity's creational status "in God's image" in chapter 5. Admittedly a damaged image would still be an image. However, neither here nor anywhere else in the Bible is the concept of God's image associated with damage — any more than any of God's standards for humanity are.

Genesis 9 contains the clearest statement in the Old Testament regarding God's image after the Fall. According to verse 6, people are to act (or not act) in certain ways precisely because they are in God's image. The wording (preposition + *tselem*) echoes that in Genesis 1:27. There is some debate over whether this rationale explains why people should not be killed or why people can inflict capital punishment on murderers. Some would say the rationale applies to both (or even to everything discussed in vv. 1-6a).[3] In any case, the rationale and the image apply to people currently alive, those killed and/or those doing the killing. So the text constitutes a direct affirmation that God's image was not lost due to the Fall. Moreover, there is not the slightest indication of any damage to God's image.

Admittedly, one might wonder if this text could be referring only to Adam's original creation in God's image, with the prospect of that image's restoration in Christ in view. There are several problems with such an interpretation. First, it is highly unlikely that the author of Genesis had in mind the prospect of restoring the image in Christ. Without that prospect

---

3. See sources on this passage cited in the Conclusion, esp. discussion in Aalders, 1981: 186-88.

explicitly in view, a lost image would provide no rationale for punishing murder at the time of the author.

Those who see the New Testament as teaching the restoration of a lost image understandably feel compelled to read the idea of a lost image back into the Old Testament. However, because it turns out that a restored image is not the New Testament teaching, as will be discussed below, the felt need to import the idea of a lost image into Genesis is unfounded.

The closest New Testament parallel to Genesis 9:6, regarding whether or not people after the Fall are still in God's image, appears to be James 3:9. That passage similarly grounds a current standard of moral conduct directly in humanity's creation according to the image of God. As discussed immediately below, the text identifies the people being cursed as created in the image of God. There is no indication that re-creation in Christ is in view or that it was their ancestor Adam alone who was in God's image. So the most plausible understanding of Genesis 9:6 is that it invokes the continuing post-Fall image-of-God status of human beings as the basis for punishing murder.

The James 3 passage is one of the only two direct New Testament statements that humanity in general is in God's image. In verse 7, James notes the role that human beings have played in taming all kinds of land, air, and sea animals. That observation is reminiscent of the role God gave to human beings regarding all three types of creatures in Genesis 1:28, immediately after creating humanity according to the divine image in 1:27. So it is not surprising to find the affirmation that human beings are created according to God's image in verse 9 of James 3.

There are multiple indications that James is speaking of all people being in God's image today. The humanity *(anthropos)* that tames creatures in verse 7 shows no evidence of being a reference only to Christians. That same humanity is then referred to as the humanity who is according to God's image in verse 9. They have become *(gegonotas)* that way, because God has made them so.

The point that James is making here requires this affirmation of the current status of human beings. Long after the author of Genesis 9 employed this affirmation to forbid murder, James has heard Jesus teach that if murder (angry action) is wrong, so are angry words (Matt. 5:21-22).[4]

4. Although Jesus was only addressing implications for the community of believers, James applies the expansive principle to the wider human context that both he and the author of Genesis 9:6 had in view.

Accordingly, he updates the image-of-God teaching of Genesis here. In order to explain why his readers are not to curse human beings, he must affirm who human beings are today. They are specially connected with God by virtue of being made in God's image.

James addresses the recipients of his letter as "brothers and sisters" (*adelphoi,* v. 10) — language appropriate when Christians alone are in view. But since James is concerned about their speech not just toward one another but toward people in general, he uses different language to refer to those being cursed — the more generic *anthropous* in verse 9. In other words, there is no suggestion here that God's image has been lost or damaged or that only Christians are in the image of God.

Imagining why James, like other authors of the Bible, would avoid any suggestion that God's image has been damaged is not difficult. After all, what can realistically be expected from those who think that such damage has occurred? It would be logical for people's respect for the dignity of all human beings to be diminished, along with people's sensitivity to the wrong of verbally abusing others. The ultimate basis for such respect and restraint would be diminished by sin. The more apparent a particular person's fallenness, the more damaged the image would be and the less basis there would be for respecting the person. Quite literally, the standard itself for the godliness God expected of people at creation would be lowered.

As noted earlier, there is one other direct biblical reference to humanity in general being in God's image: Paul's brief and cryptic affirmation in 1 Corinthians 11. While arguing that a man ought not wear something on his head while praying or prophesying, Paul invokes the man's image-of-God status. He does not say anything one way or the other regarding a woman and the image of God. Instead he talks about "glory" in relation to her — a different matter discussed below in relation to 2 Corinthians 3. So rather than putting words in Paul's mouth, it is probably best here to confine our discussion to the questions of whether the image of God that Paul invokes in verse 7 applies to people today and, if so, whether only Christians are in view. (See Ch. 3 regarding other peculiarities of this passage, such as why the preposition before "image" is absent.)

First, the discussion of the creation of human beings in verses 8-9 strongly suggests that the reference to a man as an image of God in verse 7 refers to the image in Genesis 1 according to which God created him. In fact, the word "indeed" or "for" *(gar)* that begins verse 8 explicitly indicates that what follows is an explanation of what precedes. However, Paul does not leave the reference to God's image in the past, as merely part of

God's original creation. He uses the causal participle *huparchon* to affirm that a man's current image-related status has implications for how he is to act now. In other words, nothing has transpired or intervened since the original creation to change that status.

As was the case in the James passage, the audience to which Paul is speaking appears to be exclusively Christian. Here they are those involved in or concerned about praying and prophesying. They are the "church of God that is in Corinth" (1:2), expected to live as do the other "churches of God" (11:16). But as in James, Paul here grounds what their view of other people should be in humanity's creation, not in people's re-creation in Christ. In other words, a man's image-of-God status has the particular implications for Christians noted here, just as it has the broader implications for non-Christians noted in James 3 and Genesis 9. Most importantly for our purposes, there is no indication that any image has been damaged or lost — regardless of who is in view here.

No other biblical texts refer directly to all of humanity as being in God's image. However, because more than a few interpreters invoke Psalm 8 and a story in the life of Jesus as sources for insight regarding this image, a few comments about those texts are in order here. Even in these instances, there is no indication that God's image has been lost or damaged.

When Psalm 8 reminds some readers that humanity is created in God's image, it is generally because verse 5 says that God made humanity with an exalted status (a little lower than *elohim* — i.e., "God" or the "heavenly beings"). Some hear an echo of the pinnacle of God's creation in Genesis 1 when God creates humanity in the divine image.

There is no indication here in Psalm 8 that this status has been reduced since that original creation. To the contrary, the praise due to God is linked to it and would be compromised if humanity's status were compromised. The exalted status the psalmist has in mind is a current status: "What *are* human beings . . ." (v. 4, italics added) — not what *were* they only in the original creation. As noted previously, the psalmist can find no reasons — no current godly attributes — that warrant humanity's lofty status. Were humanity's status to be rooted in ways that people presently are like God, then those likenesses and humanity's status would indeed be damaged by sin. However, the exalted status continues, even though all the likenesses have not. That observation is amazing to the psalmist, since people so often think of status as rooted in the attributes one actually has. Humanity's status, though, is rooted instead in the special connection people have with God and the standard according to which

God intends them to live and grow. That standard is as unchanging as the very person of God.

Another possible indirect reference to God's image occurs when Jesus addresses people's obligation to pay taxes (Matt. 22:15-22; Mark 12:13-17; Luke 20:20-26). There Jesus teaches that people have an obligation to give the denarius (tax) coin to Caesar because it is his. It is his — suggests Jesus by pointing to the coin — because of its association with Caesar's image (see discussion of this passage in Ch. 3). Jesus adds that people have a parallel obligation to give to God what is God's. While he does not explicitly explain any identifying features of what belongs to God, the parallel to Caesar suggests that anything associated with God's image is owed to God.

If Jesus is grounding this obligation in people's creation in God's image, then there is no indication here that God's image has been lost or damaged. Such damage would imply that the obligation itself has lessened — hardly the point Jesus is making.

People Experiencing New Life in Christ

As we turn from texts addressing humanity as a whole to texts addressing those with new life in Christ, we will do well to remember the previously discussed difference between "human beings" and "God's image." People are many things in addition to having a status related to God's image. Accordingly, when we read in both the Old and New Testament writings about the terrible damage that sin has done to human beings, that damage does not necessarily imply anything about the image of God. Acknowledging that the biblical writings recognize no damage done to God's image does not weaken or question the gravity of sin and its devastating effect on the human race and beyond. If anything, sin is all the more heinous because of the way that it causes people to contradict who their Creator intends them to be.

Recognizing the distinction here between human beings and God's image makes it easier to see that it is humanity, not God's image, which has been damaged according to the consistent teaching throughout the Bible. A more careful examination of the texts that address those experiencing new life in Christ is then necessary to confirm or oppose that view. Is a damaged image restored, or are damaged human beings restored? It is important to read the texts carefully and not to read into them ideas that are not there. The same can be said of church doctrinal statements.[5] A detailed examination of the relevant New Testament texts must await Chapter 6. However, some preliminary observations are in order here.

One prominent biblical text addressing God's image and people experiencing new life in Christ is in Romans 8. In verse 29 Paul explains the end to which God has predestined Christians: conformity to the image of Christ. Most importantly for our present purposes, people — not God's image — are what the text says a process of justification and glorification is restoring (v. 30).

No language here indicates that any sort of image is changing. Rather, God is changing people, and the image of Christ is that to which people are being conformed. If anything, it is the constancy of that image that provides a sure goal for all believers. Interestingly, the text consistently refers to that goal in terms of Christ's image, not the broader term "God's image" — suggesting that there may be present here a development or glorification beyond what Adam and Eve experienced as originally created in the image of God before the Fall (more on this in Ch. 7).

We turn next to 2 Corinthians 3, where Paul writes in verse 18 that believers are being transformed into the image of the Lord. As in Romans 8, there is neither language indicating that any harm has been done to the image in which people were originally created, nor a suggestion of an image changing in any way. According to this text, the Lord provides (or is) the *goal* and the *means* of people's growth.

While the image does not change, believers as people change. Accordingly, the biblical writers use a term other than image — glory — to refer to that which changes. As verse 18 puts it, people are transformed "from one degree of glory to another." It is the (degree of) glory that changes, not the image. Discussions of God's image often confuse or conflate the terms "glory" and "image," resulting in the biblically unsound assumption that God's image can be damaged or lost, and then restored, the way that glory can. However, the biblical writers consistently reserve language of change for the term "glory" (as in 2 Cor. 3:18).

Instead of a damaged or lost image being restored, Paul writes in terms

5. If one begins with the assumption that God's image has been damaged by sin, it is all too easy to assume that documents roundly denouncing sin support the idea that God's image in fallen humanity is damaged. For example, see Towner, 2005: 351, which cites the strong statements on sin in the 1647 Westminster Confession (VI, 4) and in the Council of Trent's 1546 Decree Concerning Original Sin as affirming that God's image is damaged, though they actually do not mention God's image.

of something new happening because of Christ. The people of Israel were under the "old covenant" (v. 14) and their minds were hardened (v. 14). But now they are able to understand and accept the gospel message "in Christ" (v. 14). There was glory in the old covenant, but the glory of the new is so much greater that the old has lost its glory (vv. 9-10). Whereas Moses was incapable of retaining the glory he gained from his personal encounter with God (v. 13), believers now have a new capacity for ever-increasing glory (v. 18). Shortly thereafter, Paul describes what is happening in believers as a "new creation" (5:17).

The problem at hand is not a corrupted image but sinful people whom the "god of this world" (4:4) oppresses. Paul recognizes that one reason people need something new is that they are unable to be and live as God intends. When people turn to the Lord, notes Paul, there is a veil over their inner selves that is removed (3:15). They then at last have the "freedom" (v. 17) to begin a growth in glory whose standard is the Lord's image. As noted in Chapters 2, 3, and 6, God's image in the Old and New Testament alike is consistently about humanity's and Christ's connection with God and reflection of God. If there is a difference in emphasis between the Testaments, the discussions of humanity in the image of God begun in the Old Testament emphasize the *status* of humanity, whereas discussions of the image of (God-in-)Christ concept introduced first in the New Testament, with Christ revealed, emphasize the *standard* for humanity.

The image of Christ provides the standard for how God intended and intends humanity to live out its status. In Christ alone, as perfect God and human being, not only the status of God's image but also the standard of God's image are completely fulfilled. That is why Christ is the only one the Bible's authors consistently affirm *is* the image of God (4:4; cf. Col. 1:15) — the "exact representation" of God (Heb. 1:3), as Chapter 2 has explained.

Again, as always, there is nothing about this image of God that is deficient or damaged in any way. God's image, whether in reference to Christ or human beings, is something that the Bible contrasts with human sinfulness — not something that sin ever alters.

A third key passage addressing people redeemed in Christ occurs in Colossians 3. There Paul writes that Christians (people "raised with Christ" — v. 1) are now clothed with a "new self, which is being renewed in knowledge according to the image of its creator" (v. 10). Again, there is no indication of any damaged or lost image here. The image is not being renewed, people are. The image is the standard or goal according to which people are being renewed.

As discussed in Chapter 2, the subject here is not merely individual "selves" but also humanity in a corporate sense, sometimes the entire human race in Adam and sometimes the church in Christ. So "self" as a translation of *anthropos* here in verses 9-10 is misleading, with its exclusively individualistic connotation. A better translation for *anthropos* is "humanity." Paul is telling Christians to put off the old humanity and put on the new. What that entails will be the subject of Chapters 6-7. However, the basic idea is to set aside an old way of being and doing in favor of a new way of being truly human.

Instead of Colossians 3:9-10 specifying or implying a lost or damaged image, there is an emphasis here on something new happening. Not merely a restoration of something old (whether an image or people) is underway. A damaged "old humanity" is not being renewed. That has been discarded completely (v. 9) — it has "died" (v. 3).

A new humanity has replaced it, which is now capable of being renewed according to the image of its creator (v. 10). The creator mentioned here is not identified as the creator of the original creation, only as the creator of this new humanity. Even if "creator" here refers more precisely to God than to Christ, it is the new work of God in Christ — the new humanity being renewed — that Paul has in view. As he explains it, "in that renewal . . . Christ is all and in all" (v. 11).

At the same time as something new in Christ is underway, there is an element of continuity here. Paul is addressing a plural "you" who have taken off the old humanity and put on the new. So there is no reason to think that the status of all human beings created in God's image ever changed. Rather, a new possibility for human existence has come to the fore in Christ: living out the intended implications of being in (according to) God's image.

Ephesians 4 includes a related teaching from Paul — that Christians have a new humanity created to be "according to God" (*kata theon,* v. 24). There are important similarities and differences here compared with the passage in Colossians 3. In both places Paul refrains from any indication that the image of God has been damaged or lost, or that it is being renewed. It is people who are being renewed, not the image. The directive to "be renewed," in fact, appears earlier, in a separate verse (v. 23) talking about people rather than the image. The next verse is often said to be talking about the image. In fact, though, the word never appears in verse 24, as will be discussed below. In any case, that verse refers to a standard or goal that the text never characterizes as damaged.

Another similarity between the Ephesians and Colossians passages is that Ephesians 4 also locates the problem in sin rather than in a damaged image. With language reminiscent of 2 Corinthians 3, Paul observes that people without God are "darkened in their understanding" (v. 18). The only way to see the light, Paul reminds his readers, is to "put away" the old humanity (v. 22) and "clothe" themselves with the new humanity (v. 24). Again, although human participation is required, human effort alone would never be sufficient. The new humanity must be "created" (v. 24) by God, since the "life of God" (v. 18) is what unbelievers lack.

As in Colossians 3, the language here suggests that something new — corporately and not just with particular people — is happening in Christ. Not merely a restoration of an image that has been damaged is underway. A damaged "old humanity" is not being renewed. That has been put away (v. 22). A new humanity has replaced it.

However, the language describing the new humanity here is somewhat different than in the parallel passage in Colossians, and it accentuates the newness of what is happening in Christ. Paul here drops the "image" term entirely. That does not mean that he has an entirely different concept in view. In light of what he goes on to say, it appears instead that he just wants to focus on one aspect of the image concept: that believers are to imitate God in certain ways.

This idea of imitating God and reflecting aspects of God's character to the world appears at the beginning, middle, and end of chapter 4. Chapter 5 then summarizes the general point in its opening two verses: "Therefore be imitators of God, as beloved children, and live in love, as Christ loved us." Ever since the initial creation, God has intended that people would exhibit various God-like attributes. The intended standard for humanity, God's image, has never been lost or damaged. But as we will see in Chapters 6-7, it is only in Christ that God's intention becomes much more than an intention — it becomes a glorious reality.

Two other passages particularly warrant consideration when evaluating whether or not sin has damaged God's image. In 1 John 3, first of all, John writes that believers "are God's children now" and that "when he is revealed, we will be like him" (v. 2). There is no mention here of the "image of God." However, the idea that believers will actually be like God in the future once God is revealed to all suggests a connection to the image-of-God theme.

The important point for our present purposes is that no hint of any damage to God's image is evident here. Rather, there is an affirmation of human destiny that has been sure from before the moment of God's creation of humanity in the likeness-image of God. What the actual likeness to God will look like is unknown (it "has not been revealed," v. 2), for humanity's existence in God's image is about God's intentions, not actual likeness per se.

The other remaining passage is in 1 Corinthians 15. In this chapter Paul repeatedly contrasts dying natural bodies with resurrected spiritual bodies. He uses this contrast to explain the progression in the life of Christians. Like all human beings, they "have borne the image of the man of dust" (v. 49). But unlike others, Christians are not "of the dust" but are "of heaven" (v. 48). Accordingly, they will "bear the image of the man of heaven" (v. 49 — see discussion in Ch. 6). One important aspect of this, Paul explains, is that the perishable cannot "inherit the imperishable" (v. 50), but the "perishable body must put on imperishability" (v. 53).

Since the presence of the term "image" in association with Christ (the man of heaven) suggests to many a connection with the image-of-God/Christ idea (see Ch. 2), it is worth noting what the text says about that image. There is no hint that this image has been lost or damaged. The only thing that is flawed and limited is Adam, the man of dust. It is the people who are limited, not the image of God/Christ.

Instead, there appears to be a suggestion here that because the first Adam, and humanity in general, was but dust, a bodily transformation would have been necessary even had humanity never sinned. Regardless, a new body is necessary now and Christ with his spiritual body is the first fruits of what dying accomplishes for believers. This does not imply that there is no continuity from the beginning of human creation to the end of human resurrection. The dying seed metaphor here (vv. 36-38) does suggest that much which is useless and covering the core must be stripped away. Yet there is something there (as in Colossians) that can be transformed into new life because of how God has made it to be.

From elsewhere in the New Testament, as discussed above, it appears that the status of being in the image of God is included with what continues. But for God's intentions to become reality, human transformation is essential. As in 1 John, such transformation ensures that believers will be like God (which is what the unique wording "bear the image" appears to be emphasizing here). While this transformation begins in the present, it is not primarily about a present, actual likeness to God. The bodily transformation of believers is one of many indications that God's image has to do with God's intention, not with merely who people already are.

146

The Undamaged Image of God

All people, then, have the uncompromised status of being in the image of God. Everyone, including Christians, can fail to live up to the standard that their status should entail, but that does not mean that any status itself has been reduced. Nor does it imply that "restoring" people is all that is going on in Christ's renewing work. All that God intends people to be (e.g., "imperishable," 1 Cor. 15:52) was not evident in the Garden of Eden. What God is doing in Christ does indeed heal the damage that humanity has suffered due to sin; however, more than restoration is at issue. We must await Chapters 6-7 for a fuller account of what else human destiny entails.

In light of the analysis of relevant biblical passages above, many scholars have appropriately insisted that the Fall and ongoing sin have not damaged God's image. Some reach this conclusion on theological grounds,[6] others on the basis of a wide range of Old and New Testament teachings.[7] Still others find Genesis 9:6 and James 3:9 particularly compelling on this score.[8] Those who focus on the Old Testament are particularly supportive of this view,[9] to the point that some have claimed "widespread consensus" regarding it.[10] To be clear: No one claims that the Bible explicitly teaches that God's image remains undamaged. Instead they make a different argument. They observe that what the Bible says about God's image does not consistently make sense unless it is true that God's image remains undamaged.

Without that understanding there are numerous problems. In Genesis 1, for instance, being created in the image of God is the first and foremost descriptor of being human. Some commentators understandably worry that for this to be lost or damaged would be for humanity to lose its distinct identity.[11]

---

6. For example, see W. Pope, 1875: v. 1, 423; Kittel, 1964c: 393; Breck, 1998: 8; Bray, 1998: 49-50; Mangano, 2008: 11; Roy, 2009: 11; Bori, 2010: 43; Mitchell, 2013: 92.

7. E.g., L. Berkhof, 1949: 204; Kidner, 1967: 51; Clines, 1968: 100; Mathews, 1995: 170-71; Mangano, 2008: 10.

8. See Porteous, 1962: 683; Piper, 1971: 20; Huebscher, 1988: 3; Hoekema, 1994: 18-20; Erickson, 2013: 470; Bray, 2001: 575; Mays, 2006: 36.

9. E.g., Flender, 1976: 287; Johnston, 1998: 138; Garr, 2003: 153; Towner, 2005: 351; Schmutzer, 2009: 177. Cf. van Huyssteen, 2006: 135.

10. For such claims, see J. Childs, 1982: 230-31; Jónsson, 1988: 224-25; B. Childs, 1993: 569; Westermann, 1994: 148; Grenz, 2001: 185; cf. Maston, 1959: 8.

11. E.g., Kaufman, 1956: 158; J. Murray, 1977: 37; Mangano, 2008: 11.

A bigger problem concerns the role that humanity's status "in God's image" plays in human moral responsibility. As already noted, people must be treated properly because they are in God's image — they have a close connection with God and are intended to be a meaningful reflection of God. They must not abuse or be abused because both abuser and abused are in the image of God. Removing or reducing this status puts humanity itself in jeopardy.[12] This is no mere theoretical concern, as Chapter 1 has demonstrated. Considering God's image to be damaged undermines the protections against some of humanity's worst behavior. It also undermines the importance of viewing and treating people with due respect in everyday interactions.

Understanding God's image to be damaged is not as problematic as understanding it to be lost entirely. But the predicament is akin to a badly damaged foundation of a building. The weakness is not as great as having no foundation at all. But it is a serious problem nonetheless in the face of life's storms. Furthermore, perception is key in terms of how people view and treat others. If God's image is a crucial basis for human significance, and that basis is damaged, people cannot help but have less respect for the "least lovely" among them. No wonder the Bible's authors never even hint that the image of God has been damaged.

Part of the outrageousness of sin, then, is that it causes people to contradict who they are (i.e., who they are created to be). God created people with the intention that they bring glory to their Creator. They are closely identified with God and so are to manifest various attributes to some degree reflective of God's own. However, sin prevents the fulfillment of those intentions. Though people remain in God's image, and neither the fact of connection with God nor the intention that there should be reflection of God has changed, what actually appears is far from what God intends.

From the earliest stages of humanity, "the Lord saw that the wickedness of humankind was great in the earth, and that every inclination of the thoughts of their hearts was only evil continually" (Gen. 6:5). The great flood follows. Yet no sooner has the flood ended than God reaffirms that "the inclination of the human heart is evil from youth" (Gen. 8:21), for no amount of water is sufficient to wash away human sin. Sin's presence is as surely a continuing feature of human existence as is humanity's status in

---

12. So argue Berkouwer, 1975: 127; H. D. McDonald, 1981: 122; Bray, 1991: 224; Horton, 2005: 118. See also Schwöbel, 2006: 51 on the connection between God's image and moral responsibility.

God's image, which the text also affirms just seven verses later (9:6). The picture is no different by the time of the New Testament. Humanity has passed through much more water — the Red Sea, the Jordan River, and beyond — but never has humanity's burden of sin been greater. "Ungodliness and wickedness" still mark life apart from God (Rom. 1:18), with no one seeking God and all being "under the power of sin" (Rom. 3:9-11).[13] What water cannot cleanse, only the blood of Christ has the power to wash away (as Chs. 6-7 will elaborate).

To speak metaphorically, it is as if sin covers most of the evidence that people are in God's image — that they have any connection with God.[14] Sin prevents godly human attributes from developing as they should, such that what is so often visible in the world today is corruption rather than the God-glorifying human attributes God intends. God's image is not damaged, but its existence is obscured by sin.[15] It can become hidden from view not only as people look at others, but also in the way they see themselves.[16]

Maintaining that God's image is not damaged by sin does not minimize the significance of sin — it heightens it.[17] People are not off the hook in terms of moral responsibility. Were God's image largely gone, then so would be the connection with God and God's expectations for humanity that attach to being in God's image. Sin would be more normal, more appropriate to who people are. It is the view that God's image has been lost or damaged that ends up minimizing sin.

Some, especially in the Roman Catholic, Greek Orthodox, and certain

---

13. Others have detailed the Bible's voluminous teaching on the seriousness and pervasiveness of sin (e.g., Berkouwer, 1975: chs. 4-5; Grudem, 1994: ch. 24; Erickson, 2013), so that will not be repeated here.

14. This idea is developed in Origen, 1982: 193; Gregory of Nyssa, 1952: 149; 1972: 558-59, 573. Cf. Hoehner, 2002: 611 and the discussion of Ambrose in McCool, 1959: 67. For example, a large mask can cover a face, and the moon can cover the light of the sun in an eclipse. The face or the sun are not damaged in the process, though what they look like is quite different from how they were created to look normally.

15. For this terminology in the early church, see Maloney's discussion (1973: 95) of Athanasius' *Contra Gentes* and Merriell's analysis (1990: 32) of Augustine's *The Trinity* (1963); cf. Aquinas, 1947: pt. 1, Q. 93, art. 8. More recent examples include A. Strong, 1907: 515; Leitch, 1975: 257; Ferngren, 1987: 30; John Paul II, 1997a: 455; D. Kelsey, 2009: v. 2, 1044; Reitman, 2010: 125.

16. As Teel (2010: 116-17) observes, these are among the most destructive aspects of sin. Obscuring humanity's status as created in God's image leads to abuse of others and even oneself.

17. For elaboration of why this is so, see J. Murray, 1977: 38-39; Allen, 2000: 94.

Protestant denominations of the church, have recognized the inescapable biblical teaching about humanity continuing to be in God's image today. Yet they mistakenly think that to maintain that sin has not damaged God's image is necessarily to be "soft on sin." Accordingly, they teach that while sin has indeed destroyed or damaged much of God's image, some part remains. For example, they may suggest that the "image" aspect of the image remains while the "likeness" aspect is lost or damaged. Or some aspects of the image, so-called "remnants" of the image, are all that remain undamaged.[18] Manufacturing such categories not only lacks biblical warrant (as explained in Ch. 3), but is ultimately unnecessary (see Ch. 5). It is precisely humanity's continuing status as created in God's image that makes sin most sinful.

An important reminder at this point is that humanity's creation in the image of God is first and foremost about God rather than people. Humanity in God's image is about *God* remaining close (i.e., connected) to humanity so that humanity can eventually reflect who *God* is in a God-glorifying way (ultimately at great cost to God). It is not about *people* seeking to be close to God — sin has waylaid that endeavor. Nor is it about *people* abounding in good attributes — sin has undermined that possibility. People are in God's image — God's image is not in people. When commentators reverse the biblical teaching by using this latter expression, it predictably leads to thinking of God's image as damaged, along with everything else that constitutes human beings.[19] While sin may be stronger than people, it is not stronger than God. Recognizing that sin does not damage God or God's image — God's standard for humanity — is completely compatible with the recognition of how terribly sin damages people.

Images of Adam and of "Gods"

Humanity, then, continues to be in God's image, inseparably connected with God and intended by God to have various attributes that somehow reflect God's own. However, sin has prevented those attributes from developing as they should. It is as if humanity has become connected to more than God in ways that have radically affected what humanity is and does.

18. See Berkouwer, 1975: 38, 61-64 and Cairns, 1973: 192 on various weaknesses of this sort of approach.

19. For example, Bruce (1957: 193), when discussing "the divine image in man," unsurprisingly concludes that it is "defaced . . . by reason of sin."

Indeed, humanity does bear the image — evidences being in the image — of things other than God. Humanity bears the image of fallen Adam as well as the image of other "gods." Both warrant attention here.

Image language ties humanity to Adam in Genesis 5 and 1 Corinthians 15. According to Genesis 5:3, Adam fathered a son in his image. The Hebrew expression that appears in Genesis 5:3 regarding the fathering of Seth is similar to the one in 1:26, in that the same terms *demuth* and *tselem* are central. Moreover, in Genesis 5:1 the author has just reaffirmed the creation of humanity in God's image using a shortened form of this expression. So the author is indicating that as humanity is in God's image, so is Seth in Adam's image.

This parallel suggests that there is a connection between Adam and Seth that nothing can break — Adam will always be Seth's father. Moreover, because of this connection the normal expectation is that over time Seth will reflect certain attributes (physical, psychological, functional, etc.) of his father. In the fallen world in which we exist, it may turn out that Seth's actions or personality or appearance hardly at all resembles his father's. But *actual* likenesses are not the point of image language here, as we saw in Chapter 3.[20]

The author has just affirmed humanity's creation in God's image in 5:1, thereby suggesting that what happened in Genesis 1–2 (especially creation in God's image) has continuing relevance for future generations (as Gen. 9:6 makes even clearer). So what does the further image language of 5:3 add? It at least suggests that what happened in Genesis 3–4 also has continuing relevance for future generations. (In 5:4 through the end of the chapter, the author begins the process of tracing out those generations.)

In Genesis 3–4 the author portrays quite vividly that what Seth inherits from Adam involves not just God's good intentions for humanity but also Adam's proclivity to sin.[21] That sin produces rebellion against God

20. Regarding why it is biblically unsound to read the idea of actual physical or other likenesses between Adam and Seth into this passage, see W. Schmidt, 1983: 197; Hughes, 1989: 29; I. Hart, 1995: 321-22; Grenz, 2001: 194; Mays, 2006: 35-36. The image language involves a basic connection of whole persons, not their traits and other attributes — see Purkiser, 1960: 210-11, drawing on Wiley and Culbertson.

21. Many have observed this proclivity as part of being in the image of Adam, e.g., J. Wesley, 1985b: 162; 1985g: 173; Schell, 1901: 168; Hughes, 1989: 29; J. Barr, 1993: 158; Moo, 1996: 534; Barackman, 2001: 283. Thus Maston (1959: 6) refers to this image as the "image of sin." On the implication that God's good intentions for those created in the divine image are also in view here, see Harland, 1996: 197; Bori, 2010: 39; Bosman, 2010: 564.

(Genesis 3) and murder against humanity (Genesis 4). One might naturally expect Seth's life, and by extension everyone's life thereafter (as 1 Corinthians 15 suggests — see below), to be filled with the same. If the *actual* picture temporally and eternally does not end up nearly that bleak, it is only because God's grace — Christ's sacrificial love — intervenes.

In the New Testament, image language again ties humanity to Adam in 1 Corinthians 15. Here what was implicit in Genesis 5 becomes explicit. All people, not just Seth, bear (literally "wear") the image of Adam. As discussion of the parallel terminology regarding people and Christ in Chapter 6 will note, "wearing"/"bearing" an image emphasizes manifesting to some degree what being "in that image" should look like. In this passage, weakness is as much in view as fallenness. The contrast in verse 49 between the "image of the man of dust" (Adam) and the "image of the man of heaven" (Christ) involves the difference between the natural body of "weakness" and the spiritual body of "power" (vv. 43-44).[22]

However, the parallel contrasts between "perishable" and "imperishable" (v. 42) and between "dishonor" and "glory" (v. 43) indicate bearing Adam's image includes humanity's corruption due to sin as well.[23] It need not be one or the other — weakness or fallenness.[24] Bearing the image of Adam entails the expectation that humanity will be like Adam in many ways unless something — or Someone — intervenes (see Ch. 2 on that Someone — that "man of heaven").

There is no reason to exclude any aspect of who Adam was from the general affirmation here that humanity today bears similar traits.[25] Many consider the language of Genesis 5:3 even stronger warrant for this line of thinking. They see the author implying,[26] stating,[27] or even emphasiz-

---

22. Piper (1971: 21) and Gardoski (2007: 29-30) are among those primarily impressed by the finiteness of humanity here.

23. So Augustine, 1960: 103; Kittel, 1964d: 397; Barrett, 1993: 377; S. Wright, 2003: 41; Black, 2006: 191.

24. Accordingly, many simply affirm that Adam (whatever that includes) is in view here, e.g., Godet, 1957: 431; Scroggs, 1966: 88-89; Stuhlmacher, 1994: 136; Thiselton, 2000: 1290.

25. Accordingly, I. H. Marshall (2001: 55) interprets 1 Corinthians 15 as assuming that humanity continues in God's image. Paul's affirmation shortly before that in 11:7 would seem to warrant that assumption.

26. So J. Murray, 1977: 35, 41; Waltke, 1989: 4; Pannenberg, 1991: v. 2, 214; B. Ware, 2002: 20; Garr, 2003: 127, 172; Shults, 2003: 232-33. Clines (1968: 78) originally did not see this affirmation of humanity's continuing status here, but later recognized it as implied (1993: 427).

27. So Chafer, 1947: v. 2, 167; Rad, 1962: 147; 1964: 391; Scroggs, 1966: 13; Ryrie, 1986:

ing[28] that humanity continues in God's image. Tellingly, Genesis explicitly describes the continuation of Adam's line using likeness-image language, located between two post-Fall affirmations of humanity's status in God's image (Gen. 5:1 and 9:6).

The idea is not that Adam's image has replaced God's image, totally or in part.[29] Rather, the point is that humanity is closely enough connected to Adam that the tensions Adam experienced — tensions between being in God's image (Genesis 1), and being weak ("earthy," Genesis 2) and fallen (Genesis 3-4) — are the experience of all of humanity as well.[30] It is not biblically sound to conflate these aspects of human existence in an attempt to resolve the tension by speaking of something like a fallen or damaged image. God's image is not damaged — humanity is fallen, while also continuing to be in God's image, accountable to God's standard. Although there is a tension, it is a biblically sound one.

In its fallen condition, then, humanity has become connected to more than God. People also live bearing the image of sinful Adam. In the process, they become associated with other "gods" as well. People become so involved with those "gods" that they, at least in a metaphorical sense, bear the images of those "gods" too. They become closely connected with them, and they reflect some of their attributes.

So who are these "gods"? In the Bible they often appear as idols or "images" (*tselem/eikon* and various other terms) of supposed deities. Authors in the Bible sometimes acknowledge that such deities are not really gods (referring to them as "no-gods," e.g., Jer. 2:11, or mere blocks of wood, e.g., Isa. 44:19). At other times, authors note that evil spiritual forces can work through such images (e.g., Deut. 32:16-17; 1 Cor. 10:19-20). Elsewhere it becomes apparent that anything can become such an image (see Exod. 20:4, "anything that is in heaven above, or that is on the earth beneath, or that is in the water under the earth"). The key characteristic is that

---

190; Ferngren, 1987: 26; Wenham, 1987: 125-27; Barentsen, 1988: 33; Sarna, 1989: 42; Hamilton, 1990: 256; John Paul II, 1997a: 448-49; 1997b: 526-27; Dumbrell, 2002: 16.

28. Sawyer (1974: 421-22) and Westermann (1994: 464) identify the emphasis as that of the writer of Genesis, whereas in P. Bird, 1981: 138; Mathews, 1995: 170; van Leeuwen, 1997: 645 the emphasis is the author's own conviction about the clarity of what Genesis teaches at this point.

29. Ambrose, 1961: 255-56 and Gerhard, 1962: 63 suggest a total replacement; Brueggemann, 1982: 68 and Frame, 2006: 228 a partial one.

30. Gregory of Nyssa, 1972: 558; A. Strong, 1907: 517; Mathews, 1995: 310; Merrill, 2003: 444 describe these tensions.

it somehow takes God's place in people's lives. Any connection between people and these ungodly images makes people vulnerable to developing attributes like those images.

There are two basic ways that images can take God's place. They can be made by someone other than God, and they can direct worship to something other than God. These two aspects are highlighted together again and again. God warns: "You shall not make for yourself an idol. . . . You shall not bow down to them" (Exod. 20:4-5; Deut. 5:8-9). "You shall make for yourselves no idols . . . to worship at them" (Lev. 26:1). But sadly, all too often someone "makes a god and worships it, makes it a carved image and bows down to it" (Isa. 44:15).

The first form of displacing God, then, is when people rather than God make the images. In Isaiah, for example, variations of the phrase "the work of people's hands" (2:8; 17:8; 37:19) always refer to the making of idols, in contrast with "the work of God's hands" (e.g., the Potter forming the clay into human beings, 64:8).[31] Because God has not made the idols, they are fatally flawed.

Even were people to feel that they need idols/images of God, people simply could not make them. The Bible teaches that there is nothing in the world actually like God to give them a model, as discussed in Chapter 3. Moreover, people have not been able to see God with anything like the clarity necessary to make crafting an adequate representation possible. As Moses reminds the Israelites, "Since you saw no form when the Lord spoke to you at Horeb . . . do not act corruptly by making an idol" (Deut. 4:15-16). A human-made image has nothing to do with God but merely reflects a human perspective (Hos. 13:2). It is "an image formed by the art and imagination of mortals," simply illustrating human "ignorance" (Acts 17:29-30). Only God truly knows what God is like.[32]

The way that King Hezekiah handled the issue of idols illustrates the central concern here. Hezekiah is one of only a few kings whom the Old Testament likens in a favorable way to King David. "He did what was right in the sight of the Lord just as his ancestor David had done" (2 Kgs. 18:3). As the next verse explains, among the right things he did, he "removed the high places, broke down the pillars, and cut down the sacred pole." The

---

31. See discussion in Beale, 2008: 276; Mundle, 1976: 285; Schönborn, 2011: 106-7; Gushee, 2013: 41.

32. For elaboration of this theme, see Rad, 1964c: 382; Berkouwer, 1975: 79; Ferngren, 1987: 24; McFarland, 2005: 18-21; C. Wright, 2006: 173.

first of these is especially significant, for even otherwise-commended kings Asa and Jehoshaphat fell short by not removing the high places (1 Kgs. 15:14; 22:43). Interestingly, chapter 18 later refers to them as the Lord's high places (v. 22). Apparently using idols and idolatrous places "for the Lord" does not solve the problem with idolatry because people rather than God have initiated their construction and remain in control.[33]

At the same time, there is a practical problem with images that people have made: the idea that they could represent God or any deity is laughable! They are not even alive[34] — they have "no breath" (Hab. 2:19). They cannot speak, see, hear, smell, feel, or walk (Deut. 4:28; Ps. 115:5-7; 135:16-17). They are like scarecrows in a field (Jer. 10:5). The commentary in Isaiah 44 is particularly biting. A man takes a piece of wood, burns half of it to cook something, and somehow thinks that the other half can become his savior if he carves it (vv. 16-17). Another person builds the form of a man, but it sits senseless in a shrine somewhere and does nothing (v. 13). Idolatry involves making God into images of people — a far cry from God's decision to make people in the image of God.[35]

The first way that images can take God's place, then, is if someone other than God makes them. The second way is if they direct worship to something other than God.[36] Many of the biblical texts already cited contain this theme. Even images supposedly connected with God can focus worship on themselves rather than on God. While Moses was on the mountain with God, the people held a "festival to the Lord" featuring a golden calf (Exod. 32:5). However, God sees what is really going on: "they

---

33. Asa's and Jehoshaphat's shortcomings here are reminiscent of the shortcoming of King Saul that caused him to lose God's favor and his kingship. Although God had told him to destroy every Amalekite and all their goods (1 Sam. 15:3), Saul decides to spare a small portion of the goods for the purpose of sacrificing to God (v. 15). Because this apparently good use of the goods (i.e., for the Lord) was not initiated by God (v. 22) — nor was the king's assuming a priestly role in sacrifice — Saul's disobedience proved to be disastrous for him (v. 26). So is idolatry, even if the idols are good things that one considers to be in God's best interests. Regarding the "control" issue in idolatry, see Berkouwer, 1975: 81-82; Boer, 1990: 73.

34. On this theme see Dehsen, 1997: 266; Goldingay, 2003: 222; C. Wright, 2006: 173.

35. Regarding God's decision as the alternative to idolatry, see K. Barth, 1958a: 200; Fichtner, 1978: 36; Hoekema, 1994: 67; Watson, 1997: 289; Brueggemann, 1982: 31-32; 1997: 452; Wells, 2004: 25; Schule, 2005: 2; Smail, 2006: 45; van Kooten, 2008: 218; Cortez, 2010: 32.

36. For further discussion of this theme, see Büchsel, 1964: 377; Mundle, 1976: 284; Flender, 1976: 287; Sherlock, 1996: 31-32; Hadley, 1997: 484; Gunton, 2002: 122; Garr, 2003: 164-65.

have cast for themselves an image of a calf, and have worshiped it" (v. 8). They want God to be closer to them — to manifest those traits they value most. In effect, they want to make God in their image, rather than being in God's.[37]

Most images, however, are more directly associated with other "gods." These can be images of deities whom people think are more powerful than God (e.g., idols of Babylonian deities before whom people "fall down and worship" in Isaiah 46:1, 6; or idols of Greek deities that Paul refers to as "objects of worship" in Acts 17:16-23). In fact, anything that people elevate above God — money, sex, power, animals — can be a counterfeit god. There are always plenty of images in the surrounding culture to attract worshipful followers.[38]

What happens when people turn to false gods (i.e., to their images) is that God does not receive all the glory that belongs to God alone. However, God "is to be revered above all gods, for all the gods of the peoples are idols" (1 Chron. 16:25-26); and God's people are to "ascribe to the Lord the glory due his name" (v. 29). While a more detailed discussion of glory must await Chapter 6, the close association between glory and image in the Bible is worth noting here.

Glory has to do with the magnificence and praiseworthiness of God. God intends a related glory for that which is closely connected with God, in God's image — humanity. That glory is manifested concretely in human attributes (traits, functions, etc.) that point to (glorify) God. Whereas the status of being in God's image does not change due to sin, people can lose glory (and gain it through sanctification). God is rightly jealous of the glory that worship should ascribe to no humanly made images, but only to God (Exod. 20:5; Deut. 5:9; 32:16). Idolatry is doubly damaging to God's glory. Not only are counterfeit gods receiving the praise and worship that belong to God, but also those intended to be God's own images, whom God created for God's glory, are the very ones undermining that glory and thereby forfeiting their own.

With all this in mind, Romans 1 becomes a powerful statement on images, including God's image. People have "exchanged the glory of the immortal God for images resembling a mortal human being or . . . ani-

37. Usry and Keener, 1996: 75 and Brenner, 1996: 57 discuss this persistent tendency in humanity.

38. Keller, 2009: xi, applies this recognition to contemporary U.S. society. In some African societies, animals are more likely to be objects of worship than in the U.S. (see Assohoto and Ngewa, 2006: 11-12; Treier, 2008: 179).

mals" (v. 23). They have "worshiped and served the creature rather than the Creator" (v. 25). As a result their thinking has been warped by a "debased mind" (v. 28) and their relationships undermined by doing "things that should not be done" (v. 28). They are "filled with every kind of wickedness" (v. 29). When people worship images of their own making, they lose the glory, including the God-honoring reason, righteousness, relationships, and rulership over creation that God intended them to have because they are in God's image. Such losses will receive more detailed attention in Chapter 5.

Had Paul been thinking that people were no longer fully "in the likeness-image of God," this would have been a likely place to flag that. In Romans 1:23 he uses a rare combination of the terms "image" *(eikon),* "likeness" *(homoioma),* and "human being" *(anthropos)* to describe what people are gaining through idolatry.[39] But instead of using such terms to describe what people are losing in exchange, Paul uses the term "glory" *(doxa).* That is what is at risk where sin is concerned. In fact, he refers to an "image of a corruptible human being" rather than a "corruptible image of a human being" — for sin corrupts people, not images. As he echoes two chapters later, "all have sinned and fall short of the glory of God" (Rom. 3:23). Though all are in God's image and are intended to reflect God's attributes, all in actuality lack the glory God intends them to have. Looking to other images rather than endeavoring to live out the implications of being in God's image has been humanity's downfall.

To be precise, images point to something else, of which they are images. Whether the image is a statue of a "god" or a picture of a "successful" (wealthy, powerful, good-looking, etc.) person, the image in effect encourages people to worship something. When people orient themselves to such objects of worship, they, too, become like and glorify those objects. A powerful dynamic overpowers the dynamic of being in the image of God. People, since they are inescapably in God's image, should exclusively be living out God's intentions for them to reflect godly attributes, to God's glory. Yet they instead live out the implications of their identification with

---

39. In fact, the terms Paul uses for the animal-idols, *peteina, tetrapoda,* and *erpeta,* are the same ones found in the Genesis 1 (Septuagint) creation account, in plural form here as they are there. Even more telling, rather than using the plural "human beings" here to go with the plural animals as objects of idolatry, Paul uses the singular *anthropos,* again reflecting the exact form in which the term appears in Genesis 1. For further discussion of connections between Romans 1 and Genesis 1, see Hyldahl, 1956: 287-88; Wilson, 1973: 359-60; Hooker, 1990: 76-78. Cf. Caneday, 2007: 38.

counterfeit gods. Such is the power and tragedy of sin. People become more like what they worship.[40]

This connection becomes explicit at various points in the Bible. In Psalm 135 the psalmist predicts, "Those who make [idols] and all who trust them shall become like them" (v. 18). So it is no surprise to find in Psalm 115 the recognition that "[t]hose who make [idols] are like them; so are all who trust in them" (v. 8). The author of 2 Kings 17, reviewing the history of God's people, is more specific: "They went after false idols and became false" (v. 15). So is Isaiah 44: A person "makes a god, his idol; he bows down to it and worships. . . . They know nothing, they understand nothing; their eyes are plastered over so they cannot see, and their minds closed so they cannot understand" (vv. 17-18, TNIV). "They" are the counterfeit god and the worshiper alike.

Revelation 13 portrays an ultimate choice that every person must make.[41] People must decide whether they will embrace and live out their status as being in God's image or prefer orienting toward another image instead. Revelation's image *(eikon)* of the beast (associated with Satan, 12:9, 18) epitomizes everything that stands opposed to God. As the first human created in God's image received the breath of life (Gen. 2:7), so the image of the beast receives breath (Rev. 13:15). Whereas being in God's image is most specifically associated with the protection of human life (Gen. 9:6), the beast's image exists for the destruction of human life (Rev. 13:15).

The central issue in Revelation 13 is whom people will worship (v. 15). Those who choose to worship the beast become like the beast — a sort of image of the beast. They literally bear an image of the beast on their right hands or foreheads. (The word for image in vv. 16-17 here, *charagma,* is the same word Paul uses for idol/image in Acts 17:29 referenced above.)

Humanity, then, has indeed not only become connected to but also somewhat reflects — in other words, bears the image of — more than just God. Humanity bears the image of other "gods" as well as the image of fallen Adam. Just as sin in general obscures evidence of being in God's image, so idolatry does the same.[42] People lose sight of the close connection between God and people, and the godly human attributes that God intends

---

40. This idea is elaborated in D. Garland, 1999: 200-1; Lints, 2006a: 222-23; Beale, 2008: 279-82.

41. See, for example, discussions in Krause, 2005: 364; Beale, 2008: 258.

42. For this language, see Hooker, 1990: 83; Reynolds, 2008: 205.

to flow from that connection fail to appear.[43] However, neither people's connection with God, nor the intentions that God has for how people are to reflect God, has changed. People remain in the image of God.

Contrary Voices

In light of how much is at stake, as explained earlier in this chapter and in Chapter 1, it is vital that people not think that God's image has been damaged by sin. Many things about people are badly damaged, but God's image and people's status as created in that image are not. Yet the idea of a damaged image has long been widespread.

Documenting the prevalence of such misunderstanding is important for multiple reasons. The many who take for granted that God's image is undamaged need to see how widely a contrary view is circulating, and thus the urgency of addressing it. Those who have never considered this matter carefully, casually referring to God's image as fully present in one breath and significantly damaged in another, need to recognize the importance of more consistently affirming an undamaged image. Others who intentionally promote the idea that God's image is damaged hopefully will recognize the importance of reconsidering their position and encouraging others to do so as well.

As explained earlier in this chapter, the idea that God's image is not damaged is well grounded not only in the Bible. It is also well represented in the history of Christian commentary on God's image (see especially the section in this chapter on "The Undamaged Image of God"). People who speak of a lost or damaged image often do not argue against the idea of an undamaged image — they simply take for granted that if people are damaged, God's image must be. They overlook the difference between being God's image (as Christ is) and being created according to God's image (specially connected with God and intended to reflect God's attributes, as humanity is).

A four-part chorus of voices has long affirmed a lost or damaged image. Some in this chorus maintain that the image is completely lost. Others suggest that the image is virtually lost. A third group contends that the image is partly lost. And still others insist that at least the appearance of the image

43. Moltmann, 1971: 108-9; Walsh and Middleton, 1984: 64-65; Thiselton, 2000: 834; Ruston, 2004: 278; McFarland, 2005: 18 discuss various aspects of this problem.

(unavoidably an aspect of the term "image") is compromised. Sometimes different theological or cultural assumptions (see Ch. 1), or assumptions that one or more human attributes are what God's image is about (see Chs. 3 and 5), are leading people to these various positions.

In their body of writing, particular authors may use different terms to describe the current state of God's image. In fact, the terms they use may vary even within a particular piece of writing. In the pages that follow, when there is a reference to a particular person affirming that God's image is "lost" or "marred," for instance, the intention is not to claim that this is the only way that the person ever speaks of this image but rather to acknowledge that the person has so spoken in the location noted. Those who have heard this voice may well have been influenced by it and may have in turn passed on that understanding to others. Nevertheless, some of the authors mentioned here would probably be quick to acknowledge that their cited statement is not in line with their best thinking on the subject. They likely would warmly affirm the importance of being consistent regarding the fact that God's image is not damaged.

Only a sample of the voices in each of the four parts of the chorus will be heard below. Even a sample such as this is sufficient to suggest the strength and influence of this chorus. I myself was a member of this chorus until recently. So I identify personally with all below who have inherited a view that is at odds with how the Bible speaks about God's image.

Completely Lost

The most sweeping claim comes from those who maintain that the image is completely lost. This view has been promoted by "many Christian theologians . . . since early times."[44] Early Christian baptismal materials reflect the view of some that the image is lost and needs restoration.[45] One of the most prominent church leaders with this outlook in the earliest centuries of the church was Augustine of Hippo.[46] In a similar vein, Theodore of Mopsuestia writes of humanity losing "the honor and greatness of our image" by accepting in its place "the image of the devil."[47]

44. Towner, 2005: 351.
45. Jervell, 1960: 197-256; R. Jewett, 2007: 529-30.
46. Augustine, 1990: 267. According to Augustine, 1982: ch. 6, sec. 27, "it was this image . . . that Adam lost by his sin."
47. Theodore, 1933: 28; Theodore, 1949: 333; McLeod, 1999: 66-67.

During the Reformation, there was a resurgence of the view that "the image of God may be utterly lost."[48] Martin Luther, for instance, understands God in Genesis to be saying to Adam and Eve: "If you sin, you will lose . . . My image"; and so, concludes Luther, "the image of God was lost."[49] Lutheran theologians Flacius Illyricus and Johann Gerhard affirm the same.[50] In fact, Lutheran theology from the Reformation onward has not only frequently taught that the image of God has been "lost,"[51] but also has often emphasized that it has been "lost entirely."[52] John Wesley echoes this outlook with his insistence that everyone has "totally lost" and "is void of" the image of God.[53] Walter Hilton similarly speaks of sin causing people to "lose the image."[54]

Influential twentieth-century theologians Dietrich Bonhoeffer and Karl Barth voiced similar views. Bonhoeffer laments that God's human creation today "is not his image" and that "the divine image . . . is lost forever on this earth."[55] Among the variety of views concerning the image expressed by Barth, one that impressed itself on many of his colleagues and successors early in his career is that "the image which God in grace had placed upon [humanity] is altogether lost."[56] Theologian Rosemary Radford Ruether observes that this understanding of the image has consistently characterized neo-orthodox Protestant theologians.[57]

More recently, the assertion that humanity has lost the image of God has come from various quarters. Some prominent figures straightforwardly conclude that the image is "lost."[58] Others specify that humanity "lost the

---

48. Ramsey, 1950: 282; similarly according to D. Hall, 1986: 80-81; Horton, 2005: 101; Gonzalez, 2007: 52. McDonald, 2009: 329 documents this outlook in John Owen; and J. Barr, 1993: 162 discusses John Calvin's tendency in this direction.

49. Luther, 1958: v. 1, 63.

50. Olson, 1996: 110-11; Dehsen, 1997: 268; Gerhard, 1962: 36, 62.

51. Feinberg, 1972: 245; Lewis and Demarest, 1994: v. 2, 127.

52. L. Berkhof, 1949: 207-8; Shepherd, 1988: 1019 ("total loss").

53. J. Wesley, 1985b: 162; 1985m: 190; cf. 1985g: 173; 1985k: 295.

54. Hilton, 1908: bk. 2, ch. 4, p. 144.

55. Bonhoeffer, 1959a: 36; Bonhoeffer, 1959b: 270.

56. H. D. McDonald, 1981: 122; J. Barr, 1993: 161. Similarly Brunner, 1947: 95; L. Berkhof, 1949: 208; Jónsson, 1988: 72. For Barth's affirmation that the image has been lost, see K. Barth, 1936: 273.

57. Ruether, 1995: 280-81.

58. Lenski, 1946b: 964; Ramsey, 1950: 263, 278, 280; Crawford, 1966: 223; H. D. McDonald, 1981: 16; O'Brien, 1987: 191; Jónsson, 1988: 12; Patzia, 1990: 76; T. Johnson, 1993: 68; Bell, 1994: 196.

image of God through sin"[59] or through disobedience.[60] Still others focus the time of the loss as occurring at "the Fall."[61] Some see such a loss as implied in the biblical texts, whereas others more forcefully affirm it as "fact."[62]

Plenty of others proclaim the same message, but use slightly different words. Some simply use alternative, generic terms.[63] In harmony with a long rabbinic tradition,[64] they maintain that the image of God is "no longer" present in human beings. Others nuance this view somewhat by suggesting that it is human beings before redemption in Christ who are "not in" the image of God.[65] Such views are not limited to teachers and scholars, but other cultural leaders have appropriated them as well. For example, well-known poet Elizabeth Barrett Browning has lamented the absence of God's image in all of humanity (Christ excepted) in her poem "The Image of God."[66]

Others employ more colorful terms to help drive home the message that the image is completely lost. Some, for example, consider the image to be "obliterated." Gordon Kaufman understands this to be the basic teaching of the church in general.[67] Philip Hughes finds it to be an apt summary of one of John Calvin's primary views; H. D. McDonald considers the same term an apt summary of Karl Barth's teaching; and Göran Collste the same regarding Anders Nygren's.[68]

A similarly vivid way of speaking is to insist that the image has been "destroyed." According to George Forell and Charles Carter, this is a prominent position in "classical Protestantism."[69] Norman Shepherd attributes

59. Kümmel, 1963: 67-69, 86-87; Althaus, 1941: 81-92; Käsemann, 1949: 138; Lohse, 1957: 133; Kaufman, 1956: 157; D. Johnson, 1992: 10. Sands, 2010: 31 claims that this is the New Testament view.

60. Dunn, 1988: 495; Achtemeier et al., 2001: 415.

61. Mueller, 1934: 207; Pieper, 1950: 516 (following Johannes Quenstedt); cf. Robert Dabney, 1878: 293; Augustus Strong, 1907: 517.

62. "Implied": Dunn, 1966: 222; Scroggs, 1966: 70, 90; "fact": Hoeksema, 1966: 211.

63. Chronopoulos, 1981: 6; Eichrodt, 1967: 130; Schilder, 1947 (see analysis in Berkouwer, 1975: 56); Gibbs, 1984: 196.

64. As discussed in Bray, 1991: 204; Scroggs, 1966: 70; and Jervell, 1960: 91.

65. Collste, 2002: 33. Meredith Kline (1980: 33) offers examples. John Strong (2008: 634) sees humanity as "no longer God's image," though some related blessings are accessible through God's people.

66. E. Browning, 1893.

67. Kaufman, 1956: 157.

68. Hughes, 1989: 66; H. D. McDonald, 1981: 122; Collste, 2002: 39.

69. Forell, 1975: 126-27; Carter, 1983a: 198. For example, Arthur Patzia: "In the Fall, however, that image was destroyed" (1990: 76).

it to Lutheran teaching in particular.[70] The idea that the image "can be destroyed" goes back at least as far as the early church father Athanasius and continues today.[71] Roger Ruston and Francisco de Vitoria hear echoes of it in the teachings of the Waldensians and John Wyclif.[72]

Still another way to drive the point home is to insist that humanity has "forfeited the title 'image of God.' "[73] Such a way of speaking typically takes one of two forms. One is that human sin is the perennial cause of this forfeiting.[74] The other is that people have forfeited God's image ever since the Fall (Genesis 3).[75]

Those who maintain that the forfeiting is due to sin have developed a rich vocabulary for making this point. Sin has "effaced the image" with the result that humanity "ceases to image God."[76] Sin is so powerful that it can "mortally wound" and even "erase" the image.[77] As others have put it, "The image has been 'annihilated by sin' and 'extinguished.' "[78] In sum, then, humanity has "sinned away" the image of God.[79]

Those who connect the forfeiting of God's image more to the Fall have similarly developed a dramatic vocabulary in order to underscore how sweeping the impact on the image has been. Noting the connection commonly made between the image and a mirror, Sibley Towner observes that many Christian theologians have understood the Fall in terms of "smashing" the image of God.[80] Others suggest that the Fall "negated" or

---

70. Shepherd, 1988: 1018.

71. See discussion of Athanasius in Maloney, 1973: xiv. For contemporary reaffirmation, see Spanner, 1998: 222; C. Wright, 2004: 121.

72. Ruston, 2004: 81; Vitoria, 1993: 239.

73. Kümmel, 1963: 69, citing in support: K. Schmidt, 1947: 192ff.; Hooker, 1959: 305; Jervell, 1960: 312ff.

74. Lewis and Demarest, 1994: v. 2, 127.

75. H. Carson, 1960: 84. J. Strong (2008: 633; 2005: 97) identifies the decisive point as the tower of Babel incident in Genesis 11 when the image of God was "shattered."

76. Effaced: J. Wesley, 1985n: 354; McKanan, 2002: 149; Horton, 2005: 109; Witherington, 2009: v. 1, 21, 185. Ceases: Walsh and Middleton, 1984: 70. Kittel, 1964c: 393, describes rabbinic support for this latter idea.

77. "Mortally wounded": Mathews's (1995: 165) summary of "the Reformers'" view. "Erased": Kraynak, 2008: 75, citing Cassuto, 1989 in support.

78. "Annihilated": Discussed in L. Berkhof, 1949: 208, with reference to K. Barth, 1936: 273, and in Merriell, 1990: 224, with reference to Aquinas, 1947: pt. I, Q. 93, art. 8. "Extinguished": John Calvin, as discussed in Hughes, 1989: 66.

79. H. D. McDonald, 1981: 38.

80. Towner, 2005: 351.

"wiped out" the image.[81] Meanwhile, Gerhard Kittel cites a millennia-long tradition, reflecting Greek influence, that the image was "taken away" by the Fall.[82]

Virtually Lost

Alongside of those insisting that the image is completely lost can be heard another part of the chorus proclaiming that the image is, more precisely, "virtually lost." Merely a small trace remains. Such a view can be found in Thomas Aquinas, who hears in Augustine an echo of this outlook,[83] as have many others since Aquinas.[84]

This outlook has become much more influential since the Reformation, where it figured prominently in the views of Luther, Calvin, and others. When Luther was not dismissing the image entirely, he characterized it as "almost completely lost" with only "feeble and almost completely obliterated remnants" left.[85] Johann Gerhard similarly admitted that at most a few "little remnants" of the image remain.[86] Calvin more consistently referred to a nearly-lost image of which mere "traces" or a "remnant" or "lineaments" remain.[87] The result has been an understanding, influential in Protestant circles, that sinful human beings have virtually lost God's image.[88] In fact, according to G. C. Berkouwer, such a view appears even to have influenced Immanuel Kant's rationalistic concept of "radical evil" in humanity.[89]

Again, many more colorful terms have helped drive home the message

81. Kaufman, 1956: 165 (negated); Calvin, 1960: bk. III, ch. 2, sec. 12 (wiped out).

82. Wisdom 2:23f., discussed in Kittel, 1964c: 394.

83. Aquinas, 1947: pt. I, Q. 93, art. 8 references Augustine, 1963: bk. 14.

84. Merriell (1990: 224) and Stendahl (1992: 142) hear a similar echo. So do Hughes (1989: 65) and Lewis and Demarest (1994: v. 2, 191), specifically in Augustine's *On the Spirit and the Letter.*

85. Luther, 1958: v. 1, 67. See R. Niebuhr, 1964: 160-61, 269 for a fuller description of Luther's view.

86. Gerhard, 1962, 31.

87. Calvin, 1960: bk. II, ch. 15: sec. 1-4 (nearly lost); 1960: bk. II, ch. 2, sec. 17 (traces); 1948: Gen. 9:6 (remnant); 1948: Gen. 1:26 (lineaments). This last concept in Calvin is analyzed in Zachman, 2007: 64-68.

88. Brunner, 1947: 94-96; Leitch, 1975: 257; Shepherd, 1988: 1019; Hodge, 1982: v. 2, 103.

89. Berkouwer, 1975: 122-24, analyzing Kant, 1793.

that the image is virtually, if not entirely, lost. John Calvin's language is particularly vivid here. In his major work, the *Institutes,* he insists that the image is "mutilated," "almost blotted out," and "all but obliterated."[90] Elsewhere he maintains the image is "almost entirely extinguished" and that any remains are so "maimed that they may truly be said to be destroyed."[91] In multiple works he calls the image "vitiated" and "so corrupted that whatever remains is frightful deformity."[92] The notion of a thorough "corruption" of the image can similarly be found in Martin Luther and in John Wesley.[93]

A number of comparable terms have echoed through the centuries. According to Augustine, not only is the image "worn out" but it can be "so effaced as almost to amount to nothing."[94] Others have similarly affirmed the idea of effacement or near-effacement.[95] Just as pointedly, according to Nestorius the image has been "ruined."[96] In fact, the "ruined image" is the title theme of a chapter in a recent work on theological anthropology.[97]

In other words, it is not unusual for scholars writing about the image today to acknowledge a "radical limitation in the image of God" because they see the image as "greatly damaged" or "spoiled."[98] God's image itself (not just people) has become "fallen" and "sinful."[99] Such an outlook appropriates the historical outlook of Anselm of Canterbury, who lamented that the image of God has been so "wasted away by vices."[100] With so influential a chorus proclaiming that the image of God has been virtually lost in human beings, no wonder a recent popular psychology book like *Overcoming Negative Self-Image* has an entire chapter on the contemporary person titled

---

90. Calvin, 1960: bk. I, ch. 15, sec. 4; bk. I, ch. 15, sec. 4; bk. III, ch. 3, sec. 9.

91. "Extinguished": Calvin, 1994: 481; see further discussion in Hughes, 1989: 66. "Destroyed": Calvin, 1948: Gen. 1:26.

92. "Vitiated": Calvin, 1960: bk. I, ch. 15, sec. 4, and 1948: Gen. 1:26; a term that Louis Berkhof (1949: 204) adopted as his own. "So corrupted": Calvin, 1960: bk. I, ch. 15, sec. 4.

93. Luther, 1958: v. 2, 141 (see discussion in Erickson, 2013: 462); J. Wesley, 1985k: 293.

94. See discussion in Ramsey, 1950: 256, and Collste, 2002: 36 (worn out); Augustine, 1963: bk. 14, sec. 6 (so effaced).

95. Hooker, 1990: 83; Mitton, 1981: 166.

96. Nestorius, 1980: 124. See also L. Berkhof, 1949: 208, with reference to K. Barth, 1936: 273.

97. "Learning from the Ruined Image" (Talbot, 2006).

98. "Radical limitation": D. Johnson, 1992: 10. "Greatly damaged": Boer, 1990: 62; "Spoiled": C. Wright, 2006: 424; World, 2005: par. 93; Hoekema, 1994: 23; Blyden, 1992: 138; Mitton, 1966: 132.

99. Boer, 1990: 87, 90, 102 (fallen); 1990: 70, 85 (sinful).

100. Anselm, 1962 (*Proslogion* 1), quoted in Hughes, 1989: viii.

"Shattered Image." The message to a new generation is that "the image of God has been shattered"[101] — in other words, lost, or at least virtually so.

Partly Lost

There is another section of the chorus whose message concerning the harm done to the image is not quite so sweeping. According to these voices, not all of the image, but a very important part of the image, has been lost. G. C. Berkouwer's book-length historical survey of views concludes that this twofold aspect of the image — part lost and part retained — "constantly comes to the fore" when theologians formulate an understanding of the image for the church.[102] Thomas Smail's book-length analysis concurs, finding this twofold view to be "the mainstream theological tradition" that "started in the early church and continues to this day."[103]

As R. G. Crawford puts it, "Much debate, in our day, has centered around the question — not whether the *imago dei* was lost — but whether it was lost completely."[104] Others have made similar observations.[105] Addison Leitch notes a basic similarity between many Roman Catholic and Protestant views on this score, while Jean Mayland sees something similar in Greek Orthodox outlooks.[106]

In fact, several influential figures in the first five centuries of the church formulated categorical distinctions that have helped shape the intuitions of other parts and eras of the church along the same lines. In the second century, Irenaeus of Lyons divided the image into the "image" proper and the "likeness," the latter of which has been lost due to sin.[107] In the fourth century, Gregory of Nyssa also taught that the full image could not be retained due to sin.[108] Cyril of Alexandria, in the fifth century, promoted various distinctions between aspects of the image. One was the image as

---

101. Anderson and Park, 2003: 28. J. Strong, 2008: 633 also speaks of a "shattered" image.

102. Berkouwer, 1975: 119.

103. Smail, 2006: 202-3.

104. Crawford, 1966: 236.

105. J. Murray, 1977: 40; World, 2005: par. 120; Cortez, 2010: 16-17; Visala, 2014: 109.

106. Leitch, 1975: 257; Mayland, 1999: 61. Cf. Gushee, 2013: 106.

107. Irenaeus, 1867: bk. V, ch. 6); see discussions in McLeod, 1999: 55-57 and H. Reinders, 2008: 233.

108. Gregory of Nyssa, 1972; 1995: 357; see analysis in Maloney, 1973: 139.

what is inseparable from human nature, versus the image as participation in the divine character which humanity has lost through sin.[109]

Such an outlook helped shape some patristic and medieval discussions of the image. Those tended to distinguish between the image as humanity's natural (including rational) endowments — which continue to a significant degree today — and the image (or likeness) as a "superadded gift of righteousness" that was lost in the Fall.[110] Thomas Aquinas in the thirteenth century follows this general framework, distinguishing aspects of God's image that have not been lost (because they belong to the nature of humanity) from supernatural aspects of the image that have been lost and can only be restored in Christ.[111]

Lutheran Scholastics Viktorin Strigel and Johann Quenstedt, and Reformed Scholastics Amandus Polanus and William Bucanus, all maintained versions of the twofold aspect of the image in which part was lost and part was not.[112] So did John Wesley and Jonathan Edwards in some of their eighteenth-century writings.[113] The way was smoothly paved for various Protestant affirmations of this twofold approach in the twentieth century and beyond. Some have maintained two major aspects of God's image, one of which has been lost.[114] Others have defined this image in terms of a long list of human characteristics and indicated that parts of each characteristic have been lost.[115]

The more common approach has been to identify a key aspect or two of God's image that has been essentially lost. Some nominate immortality for this distinction.[116] A larger group focuses specifically on the moral aspect of the image as that which is lost.[117] In a related vein, some others

---

109. Cyril of Alexandria, 2000; see analysis in Burghardt, 1957; Maloney, 1973: 169.

110. Orr, 1948: 58-59.

111. Aquinas, 1947: pt. I, Q. 93, art. 4; Aquinas, 2008: bk. 1, dist. 3; see analysis in Mondin, 1975: 71. Pope John Paul II (1997a: 455) gives testimony to the persistence of this approach in his reference to the remaining and lost aspects of the image in terms of continuing "likeness" and "non-likeness."

112. See discussion in Shults, 2003: 229-30.

113. J. Wesley, 1985d: 410; 1985j: 477; Jn. Edwards, 1982: 35-36.

114. E.g., Bavinck, 1977: 213; Hoekema, 1994: 10. See discussion in Lewis and Demarest, 1994: v. 2, 132, and Chafer, 1947: v. 2, 166.

115. E.g., Grudem, 1994: 444.

116. E.g., Kraynak, 2008: 76. Gill (1978: 395, 449, 468) concurs, adding morality as well.

117. E.g., Orr, 1948: 197; L. Berkhof, 1949: 225-26; Wennberg, 1985: 40. Cf. related views in Kline, 1980: 31; A. Strong, 1907: 515; and even earlier in W. Pope, 1875: v. 1, 424, v. 2, 38. Others say essentially the same thing, though replacing "moral" with a related term such as "functional" (e.g., Hoekema, 1994: 72-73, 85).

indicate that God's image, understood as consisting of relationships, is not completely there in non-Christians. The idea is that since people only completely become God's image as Christians, the image is somewhat lacking or misshapen in nonbelievers.[118]

Emil Brunner, Reinhold Niebuhr, and Helmut Thielicke have developed a somewhat different type of category, though in each case some aspect or dimension of the image is lost or otherwise negated. For Brunner, humanity remains formally in the image of God, as answerable to God. However, regarding the material image of God, which includes people's love toward God and one another, humanity "has lost it wholly — through sin."[119] God's image for Niebuhr includes humanity's natural endowments such as freedom, yet it also includes the virtue of living in accordance with those endowments in faith, hope, and love as God intended — a virtue that humanity can "lose."[120] Thielicke, on the other hand, speaks of two modes of the image in which sin shifts the image into a "negative mode" and the image then becomes a "lost state."[121]

As with those proclaiming that God's image is completely or virtually lost, those maintaining that it is partly lost also have a variety of persuasive ways of conveying their view. A number do so through the language they use to describe the part of the image they consider to be lost. Some speak of the "deprivation of the image of God."[122] Others see a significant aspect of the image as "largely destroyed," "damaged," or "diminished."[123] Still others consider that aspect to be "extinguished" or "obliterated" — "forfeited in the fall."[124] While John Calvin and James Arminius are commonly known for their theological differences, Arminius shared with Calvin the view that humanity has been deprived of at least "a great part of the image of God."[125]

Another group applies even more picturesque language to God's image as a whole to convey their understanding that the image has been

---

118. E.g., Grenz, 1998: 624; Gunton, 1999: 58-59. Cf. Kümmel, 1963: 68.

119. Brunner, 1952: 123, 57-58.

120. R. Niebuhr, 1964: 269-71.

121. Thielicke, 1966: 169-70, 211-12.

122. E.g., Gill, 1978: 480 (deprivation); cf. Hoekema, 1994: 64.

123. For example, "largely destroyed": Orr, 1948: 59; A. Strong, 1907: 516; "damaged": Goodman, 2008: 121; Gardoski, 2007: 21; Mayland, 1999: 61; R. L. Harris, 1980: 768; "diminished": Payne, 1995: 141; B. Ware, 2002: 21-22; World, 2005: par. 30.

124. E.g., Maloney, 1973: 40 (extinguished); Litton, 1960: 119 (obliterated); J. Murray, 1977: 40 (forfeited).

125. Arminius, 1986: 151, 375.

damaged in some way. Some of these speak in terms of a process that has diminished the image. Others speak in terms of the resulting damage with a structural, moral, or visual emphasis.

Those alluding to process see God's image, for example, as "eroded," "reduced," or "impaired" because it has been subject to "degeneration."[126] Due to the Fall, the image has been "diminished."[127] Moreover, sin "disrupts" God's image,[128] causing it to "malfunction."[129] According to such voices, it continues to be possible for the image to be "harmed" and "impoverished"[130] — in other words, subject to "devolution."[131]

Various commentators describe the negative impact on God's image in somewhat structural terms. Stanley Leavy, Ellen Ross, and Philip Hefner all remark that historical Christianity, or at least a major segment thereof, has affirmed over the centuries that the image has been "damaged."[132] Numerous biblical scholars, ethicists, and theologians have made similar affirmations.[133] Others prefer to describe God's image as "bent," "weakened," or "broken."[134] This last term in particular has been a favorite not only of leading Reformed thinkers[135] but also of many others.[136] For instance, Helmut Thielicke talks about "the broken (really fragmented!) *imago Dei.*"[137] Others give the idea of a broken or cracked image much more prominence by using such a term in the title of a book chapter.[138]

---

126. "Eroded": Smail, 2006: 59. "Reduced": C. Wright, 2006: 173; Walton, 2001: 130-31; Boer, 1990: 71. "Impaired": Adamson, 1976: 146; Orr, 1948: 59; Feinberg, 1972: 245; International, 2004: par. 46; Bradley, 2010: 185; T. Peters, 2010: 235, drawing on the Vatican report *Communion and Stewardship.* "Degeneration": Rad, 1964b: 392.

127. John Paul II, 1997a: 455; Ferngren, 1987: 26; McKnight, 2005: 39.

128. Frame, 2006: 229; Thielicke, 1966: 180-81; Reynolds, 2008: 188.

129. Clark, 1984: 73; Clark, 1969: 218-19; Hoekema, 1994: 85.

130. Reynolds, 2008: 192, 193 (harmed); Mondin, 1975: 73, reflecting on the teaching of Thomas Aquinas (impoverished).

131. Lints, 2006b: 4, suggests that it is not uncommon to find reference to the devolution of the image in theological texts.

132. Leavy, 1988: xi; E. Ross, 1990: 102; Hefner, 1984: 335.

133. E.g., Dunn, 1996: 222; Bajema, 1974: 39; Erickson, 2013: 473.

134. Witherington, 2009: v. 1, 20; v. 2, 138 (bent or broken); Merrill, 2006: 200 (weakened). Broken: Orr, 1948: 59; Mitton, 1966: 132; S. Wright, 2003: 42; Driscoll and Breshears, 2010: 138; Koyzis, 2014: 137.

135. According to D. Hall, 1986: 81.

136. According to Crawford, 1966: 236, invoking Baillie, 1939: 102 in support.

137. Thielicke, 1966: 151.

138. For example, Cahill (2006b: "Image . . . Broken") and McKnight (2005: "Cracked Eikons").

Others focus more on the moral or health-related damage the image has endured, though structural implications are intertwined. For example, some see God's image as "perverted."[139] Others find it to be "defiled" or capable of being "warped."[140] Even more consider it to be "corrupted."[141] In fact, Michelle Gonzalez perceives support for a corrupted image "throughout Christian tradition."[142] Meanwhile, Calvin's post-Fall view that "nothing remains after the ruin except what is . . . disease-ridden," "infected," or "tainted with impurity" has attracted significant interest.[143] Others adopt the related terminology of an image that is "twisted," "tainted," "stained," or "blotted."[144]

Augustine and others since have acknowledged the related notion that God's image has been "marred."[145] Some such advocates have portrayed a marring of the image as due to the Fall.[146] Others tend to connect the marring with human sin more generally.[147] Still others explicitly combine the

---

139. Hughes, 1977: 44; Hoekema, 1994: 72, 83, 85; Cahill, 2006b: 70; or, in the view of Zizioulas (1975: 424), as capable of being perverted.

140. E.g., J. Strong, 2008: 633, and Boer, 1990: 36 (defiled); Smail, 2006: 164-65, and Witherington, 2009: v. 1, 20 (warped). On support for the "defiled" image in liberation theology, see Third General Conference, 1979: par. 1142; Hicks, 2000: 145. Relatedly, McReynolds, 2013: 26 speaks of something evil happening to the image at the Fall.

141. Feinberg, 1972: 245; McFadyen, 1990: 43-44; Hoekema, 1994: 23, 26, 31; Sherlock, 1996: 69; Barackman, 2001: 492; Vorster, 2007b: 371; Reynolds, 2008: 196. Similarly Goodman, 2008: 85; Blomberg, 1999: 34; Baker, 1991: 77. Cf. Jastram, 2004: 26; J. Strong, 2005: 98.

142. Gonzalez, 2007: 125.

143. Calvin, 1960: bk. I, ch. 15, sec. 4. See discussions of this aspect of Calvin's view in Phelps, 2004: 358; cf. Hoekema, 1994: 45, with particular reference to Calvin's views in his *Commentary on Genesis* (1948: Gen. 1:26).

144. Plantinga Pauw, 1993: 14 (twisted); McMinn and Campbell, 2007: 351 (tainted); Chafer, 1947: v. 2, 216 (blotted); Bullock, 2012: 86 (stained). Chafer cites William Alexander, 1888: v. 1, 196 in support. The related idea of an "ailing" image is a favored rabbinic term, as noted in Matt, 1987: 83.

145. Machen, 1947: 173; Ecumenical, 2004: 512; Koyzis, 2014: 139; Sunshine, 2013: 77. Also Gardoski, 2007: 17; Boer, 1990: 157; Ferngren, 1987: 30; Feinberg, 1972: 245; Thielicke, 1966: 174; W. Pope, 1875: v. 1, 6. See also discussions in Plantinga Pauw, 1993: 14 and Hughes, 1989: 186.

146. Stott, 1964: 119; *In the Image,* 1967: 67; Schreiner, 1998: 453; Witherington, 2009: v. 1, 185; Hughes, 1989: 28; 1977: 44; 1962: 119; C. Carter, 1983a: 206. Cf. rabbinic support discussed in Flender, 1976: 287-88.

147. M. Smith, 2007: 43; Horton, 2006: 192; 2005: 109; World, 2005: par. 30; Moo, 1996: 534; Ellis, 1996: 173; Sherlock, 1996: 42; Payne, 1995: 141; Grudem, 1994: 449-50;

two ideas;[148] or they even refer to the marring of God's image as something that can continue to get worse.[149]

Instead of (or sometimes in addition to) using primarily structural or moral terms to describe the damage done to God's image, some influential figures use more visual terms. They, with Augustine, indicate that the image has been defaced, deformed, or disfigured.[150] Aquinas and his listeners employ the last two of these;[151] Gregory of Nyssa and his listeners the last.[152] Calvin and his listeners at times invoke all three.[153]

The view that God's image has been defaced "would be endorsed by many thinkers today."[154] Its influence among a wider public has grown through the literature of John Donne, Walter Hilton, and Theodore Maynard.[155] Some connect this defacement with the Fall of the human race in Adam.[156] Others connect it more broadly with sin.[157] Still others emphasize that the defacement continues to worsen with continued sin.[158] That God's

---

Hoekema, 1994: 30; Baker, 1991: 77, 127; C. Carter, 1983b: 247; Flender, 1976: 288; Maston, 1959: 7; Mullins, 1917: 54.

148. Schreiner, 1998: 453; Moo, 1996: 534.

149. Piper, 1989; Smail, 2006: 154.

150. "Defaced": Augustine, 1960: 47; Ramsey, 1950: 256 finds the same outlook in bk. 14, sec. 11 of Augustine's *The Trinity;* Hughes, 1989: 186 locates it in ch. 16 of the same work. "Deformed": Augustine, 1999, as discussed in Hughes, 1989: 65, 186; Aquinas finds this view in Augustine's *The Trinity* (bk. 14), as discussed in Merriell, 1990: 224. "Disfigured": Augustine, 1963: bk. 14, sec. 6; his *Retractions* (1999: n. 97) contains multiple citations to his *Literal Meaning of Genesis* (1982: ch. 6, sec. 27); cf. Soulen and Woodhead, 2006: 4.

151. Aquinas, 1947: pt. I, Q. 93, art. 8; plus see discussion in Merriell, 1990: 224.

152. Gregory of Nyssa, 1972, as interpreted by John Paul II, 1997a: n. 25.

153. Calvin, 1960: bk. I, ch. 15, sec. 4; bk. III, ch. 3, sec. 9; 1948: Gen. 1:26; 1993: Job 14:13-14. Also discussions in Hughes, 1989: 66 and Hoekema, 1994: 45. Towner, 2005: 351, 2001: 27, notes similarly strong defacement language in the Reformation Scots Confession of 1560 (text available at www.creeds.net).

154. Crawford, 1966: 236. For example, Baillie, 1939; Mitton, 1966: 132; Feinberg, 1972: 245; H. D. McDonald, 1981: 39; Towner, 2001: 27; McKanan, 2002: 178-79; J. Strong, 2005: 101-2; Cahill, 2006b: 69; Copeland, 2010: 25; Teel, 2010: 127-28; Koyzis, 2014: 137.

155. Brumble, 1992: 372-73, analyzes its powerful presentation in Donne's "What If This Present" and in Hilton's "Ladder of Perfection." See also Maynard's "The Image of God" (1920: 101).

156. Ryrie, 1986: 192; Ferngren, 1987: 30; Frame, 2006: 228; Chafer, 1947: v. 2, 216 invoking Alexander, 1888: 196 in support. J. Strong (2008: 632) locates the decisive point of defacement somewhat later, in Genesis 11 rather than Genesis 3.

157. Orr, 1948: 197; Bruce, 1957: 193; *In the Image,* 1967: 38; S. Hall, 1995: 41; M. Harris, 2005: 317; Schwöbel, 2006: 56; Gaffin, 2010: 147.

158. Kaufman, 1956: 166; Janzen, 1995: 28; Smail, 2003: 22; 2006: 154.

image is "deformed" and "disfigured" also has continued to have numerous supporters.[159]

Appearance Compromised

Some of the visual references to the damaged image do not clearly indicate that God's image has been partly lost. Instead, they suggest that the image in its entirety is diminished somehow in terms of its appearance. Because the term "image" has a strong visual orientation in many languages, damage done to the appearance of the image is tantamount to damage done to the image itself. Sometimes the term for the visual damage is overtly moral, while at other times the character of this damage is only implicit.

Morally tinged references to the image's damaged appearance include portraying God's image as "blemished," "desecrated," and "naked."[160] Another favorite descriptor for the image is "sullied."[161] Perhaps the most common visual characterization of God's image, though, is that it is "tarnished." People often use that term to describe damage to the image that falls short of completely destroying it.[162] For some, such tarnishing of God's image may be due to the Fall[163] or to sin in general.[164] Others see it as something that worsens with continuing sin.[165]

Sometimes, however, references to the compromised appearance of God's image are less explicit about the damage having any moral aspect. For instance, one way that Aquinas speaks of the image is in terms of it

159. "Deformed": Altmann, 1968: 246-47; Gill, 1978: 521; John Paul II, 1997b: 521; Habermas, 2008: 25; Vorster, 2011: 13 (who attributes this view to virtually all of mainstream Christian theology). "Disfigured": Jas. Edwards, 1991: 218; Mitton, 1966: 132; 1981: 166; International, 2004: par. 46; T. Peters, 2010: 235.

160. LaCugna, 1993: 106, and S. Hall, 1995: 41 (blemished); Sarna, 1989: 13, and Hilkert, 1995: 202 (desecrated); Kline, 1980: 32 (naked).

161. Various early church fathers, as summarized, with examples, in Maloney, 1973: 193. See also C. Carter, 1983a: 206.

162. Eley, 1963: 155; Mayland, 1999: 61; Hoekema, 1994: 15; Breck, 1998: 31; Goldingay, 2003: 223; D. Garland, 1999: 200.

163. LaCugna, 1993: 99; Rae and Cox, 1999: 132; cf. the view of Gregory of Nyssa, discussed in Altmann, 1968: 247.

164. Conn, 1993: 248; Bequette, 2004: 16, invoking Henri de Lubac, 1950: 6 in support; cf. the view of Augustine discussed in Hughes, 1989: 65.

165. Ochs, 2006: 143-44; R. L. Harris, 1980: 768.

being "clouded," "shadowy," "faint," and "darkened."[166] He is joined by some who similarly characterize it as "blackened" or "dim."[167]

Others see more than a dimming here, though, suggesting that God's image is subject to visual disarray. Some, for example, consider God's image "confused."[168] Others see it as "blurred."[169] A number affirm that this blurring originated with the Fall of the human race[170] — a view Ellen Ross finds throughout Christian tradition.[171] Others suggest that this blurring and "blotting out" continue to occur.[172]

Another group of commentators sometimes prefer the stronger notion that God's image is "distorted."[173] Many invoke this term as a way to acknowledge that the image is not entirely lost but it is indeed in serious disarray.[174] This view typically understands such distortion to be the result of sin, whether the focus is on humanity as a whole[175] or on particular people.[176] Some find the idea of a distorted image to be widespread among theologians.[177]

---

166. Aquinas, 1947: pt. I, Q. 93, art. 8 references Augustine, 1963: bk. 14. See Merriell, 1990: 224 and Hoekema, 1994: 37 on this cluster of terms in Aquinas.

167. "Blackened": Gregory of Nyssa, 1987: 63. "Dim": Crawford, 1966: 236 invokes Baillie, 1939 and numerous others in support. See also Orr, 1948: 197; Third General Conference, 1979: par. 1142; cf. Hoekema, 1994: 37 regarding the same term in Aquinas.

168. E.g., Calvin, 1960: bk. I, ch. 15, sec. 4.

169. E.g., Merrill, 2003: 444; Litton, 1960: 119; Ferngren, 1987: 30.

170. E.g., A. A. Jones, 1962: 556; Stark, 2007: 220.

171. E. Ross, 1990: 102.

172. "Blurring": Wolterstorff, 1985: 70. "Blotting out": e.g., Sulentic, 2010: 196, drawing on similar language in Hilkert, 2002: 12, who in turn notes similar language in the U.S. Catholic bishops' pastoral letter "Brothers and Sisters to Us" (National Conference, 1981: 375, 378).

173. Wilson and Blomberg, 1993: 13; Hilkert, 2002: 11-12; Boer, 1990: 64; Baker, 1991: 127; Smail, 2006: 59; Reynolds, 2008: 192; Roberts, 2011: 471. See also the discussion of Calvin's similar view in Torrance, 1952: 46 and Hoekema, 1994: 45.

174. Henry, 1984: 547; Clark, 1984: 74-75; LaCugna, 1993: 106; Wells, 2004: 36; Grudem, 1994: 444; Beale, 2004: 88; Gardoski, 2007: 21; Vorster, 2007b: 327-28.

175. Sidoroff, 1993: 24; Hoekema, 1994: 72; Sherlock, 1996: 42; World, 2005: par. 95; Merrill, 2006: 217; Frame, 2006: 229; Fee, 2007: 487; Rodríguez, 2008: 173; Witherington, 2009: v. 1, 20; Gaffin, 2010: 147. Stark (2007: 220) finds this terminology in the writings of Augustine; S. McDonald (2009: 324) sees it as characteristic of the Reformed tradition generally.

176. Cahill, 1980: 279; Wolterstorff, 1985: 70; McFadyen, 1990: 22; Fedler, 2006: 85; C. Wright, 2006: 172, 424.

177. McLaughlin, 2008: 93 (theologians in general); Vorster, 2011: 13 (mainstream Christian theology).

Other Voices

A chorus of voices, then, has communicated the view that God's image has been completely, virtually, or partly lost, or at least somehow compromised. Many other voices could be added to each of these categories. For instance, there is another array of people who do not explicitly affirm that the image has been lost or damaged, but they maintain that the image must be "restored" (or some variation thereof — see Ch. 7). By speaking in terms of restoring God's image in people, rather than restoring people who are in God's image, they also promote the understanding that God's image itself has been lost or damaged.

The chorus espousing or promoting this view includes theologians, ministry leaders, and numerous others who are influencing the understanding of the clergy and congregations that make up the church. It also includes key bridge people who are helping to shape the direction and impact of various fields essential to human well-being, such as counseling and bioethics.

For example, a widely used book in the training of counselors, *Integrative Psychotherapy,* is based on the notion that the image of God has been damaged in human beings.[178] A similar orientation can be found in the work of a public body charged with developing bioethics policy in the United States, the President's Council on Bioethics. The Council's primary discussion of the image of God in their foundational work on human dignity promotes the understanding that the image has been "lost" or "partially lost."[179] So it is no surprise to find in a popular novel like Morris West's *The Clowns of God* the idea that "what brings us inevitably to the precipice" of destruction as a human race is not just our sin or fallenness. Rather, it is the damaged state of God's image today.[180]

Damaging God's Image

While the Bible consistently avoids indicating that the image of God is either lost or damaged in human beings — now or in any day — all too many people are learning today that such loss or damage has occurred. Admit-

178. McMinn and Campbell, 2007: 351.
179. Kraynak, 2008: 76, 78.
180. West, 1981: 349.

tedly, the Bible does not contain an explicit affirmation that the image of God has *not* been damaged. So the question is really one of discernment. Understanding God's image as undamaged fits best with all the biblical evidence. It also serves the church and world particularly well by not opening the door to the abuses identified in Chapter 1 and by overtly encouraging everyday respect for people different than oneself.

Many of the leading voices cited above may be intending to use God's image in metaphorical ways. The agenda may be to describe in picturesque language the terrible damage that sin has done to human beings. The intended message presumably is that, however close or similar humanity may have originally been to God, that closeness or resemblance has now been lost or at least badly damaged.

Speaking of such matters in terms of damage done to the image of God is understandable, and would even be commendable on rhetorical grounds, if it were not so dangerous in addition to being biblically unsupported. Picturesque language is wonderful as a way to enable people to understand biblical teaching more clearly. However, commentators should avoid it if it leads to a misunderstanding of biblical teaching, particularly teaching that has substantial implications for human well-being.

Whether intended metaphorically, rhetorically, or otherwise, the basic message that many people are receiving today is that God's image is "lost," "obliterated," "destroyed," "forfeited," "shattered," "effaced," "ceased," "mortally wounded," "erased," "extinguished," "annihilated," "sinned away," "smashed," "wiped out," "negated," "taken away" — or else "virtually lost," "mutilated," "almost blotted out," "all but obliterated," "almost entirely extinguished," "maimed," "vitiated," "worn out," "almost effaced," "ruined," "radically limited," "spoiled," "wasted away" — or in any case "partly lost," "eroded," "impaired," "degenerated," "reduced," "diminished," "disrupted," "malfunctioning," "harmed," "impoverished," "damaged," "bent," "weakened," "broken," "cracked," "fragmented," "perverted," "corrupted," "defiled," "warped," "disease-ridden," "twisted," "infected," "tainted," "stained," "blotted," "marred," "defaced," "deformed," "disfigured" — or at the very least "sullied," "blemished," "desecrated," "tarnished," "confused," "blurred," or "distorted."

In light of the biblical teaching that God's image is God's standard for who people are to be, embodied in Christ, the idea that this standard is altered is problematic to say the least. Human accountability to God is at risk — as are human dignity and human destiny, whose magnificence stands or falls with the image itself.

Humanity's creation in the image of God functions in the Bible purely as a way to communicate something positive about who people are, much as the concept of justification does for Christians in the New Testament. Justification involves God graciously seeing Christians as righteous because of their identification with Christ through faith (Rom. 5:1, 18-21). Theoretically, one could say that Christians are justified, but that they have a "damaged justification" — though the Bible never does. Such a way of speaking could be well motivated to guard against the idea that Christians need not take sin seriously. Moreover, one could validly claim that the Bible does not teach per se that a Christian's justification is *not* damaged by sin. Nevertheless, the reason the Bible does not speak about justification as "damaged" is that justification is a concept designed to communicate a positive status. The Bible uses other concepts to describe people's shortcomings.

It is the same with people's status as created in God's image. Speaking of a damaged image may be well motivated and may not directly contradict an explicit teaching in the Bible. However, doing so is at odds with what the term means and how the term is most appropriately used, as suggested by how the Bible's authors consistently use it. Again, the Bible uses other terms to describe people's shortcomings.

Some authors and teachers may attempt to explain theologically how it is possible to talk about a damaged image and still maintain the importance of affirming God-given human dignity and human destiny. However, since the Bible never teaches a damaged image, such attempted reconciliations risk appearing to be more concerned with promoting a constructed theological "system" than affirming biblical teaching (see Ch. 1). For example, if a key reason for respecting and protecting human life and dignity has to do with humanity being created in God's image — and that image is badly damaged — then human life and dignity cannot help but be put at risk in the mind of the average person. Ideas have consequences. While the metaphor of a corrupted or defaced image may be convenient for certain theological purposes, the harm risked by using it far outweighs the gain.

CHAPTER FIVE

Misunderstandings about God's Image

People often think that humanity's creation and continuing existence "in God's image" is about ways that people are currently like God. In the case of Adam and Eve before the Fall, there were all sorts of human attributes that wonderfully reflected God's own attributes. After the Fall those human attributes were severely damaged by sin. So there are two possibilities for people who equate being in God's image with current human attributes. Either God's image is severely damaged by sin, or else the capacity to exercise those attributes is still so intact that having such attributes continues to constitute being in God's image. The previous chapter addressed the first option by discussing why it is important to speak of God's image as the Bible's authors do — without any sense of it being damaged. The present chapter will consider why having particular human attributes cannot be what the Bible means for people to be "in God's image."

A common misunderstanding has been to identify one or more actual human attributes — for example, reason, righteousness, rulership, or relationship — as what constitutes being in God's image. As explained and documented in Chapter 3, however, that is not what the authors of the Bible mean by humanity being in the image of God. In this chapter we will take a look at the actual human attributes that many have used to define God's image, consider how and why these missteps have occurred, and note the harmful consequences of such missteps. This chapter will demonstrate that the godly human attributes that people have today are evidence that God has created humanity in the divine image, but that having those attributes in some measure is not what it means to be in God's image.

First for consideration will be the two attributes that people have most commonly identified with being in God's image throughout the history of the church: reason and righteousness.

Reason and God's Image

While many people have equated being in the image of God with reason (i.e., current rational ability or capacity) alone, others have only partially done so. For some, this partial equation is because they see being in God's image as involving more attributes than just reason. For others, this partial equation results from their separation of the image of God concept into two separate concepts, "image" and "likeness." Initially, our interest here will not be in what such people add to reason, but simply the inclusion of reason itself as at least one aspect of being in God's image.

Identifying people's reason with being in God's image has a long, illustrious history. Many have observed its exceptional influence in the early formative centuries of the church.[1] Important leaders such as Irenaeus, Clement of Alexandria, Origen, Athanasius, Augustine, Cyril of Alexandria, and, somewhat later, John of Damascus, connected reason with God's image.[2] Others have noted that reason remained as the "standard" conception of what constitutes being in God's image in humanity for 1500 years or more[3] up through the time of Aquinas and centuries beyond.[4] Aquinas, greatly influenced by Augustine's understanding of God's image, illustrates the common assumptions that being in God's image is about how people are like God and unlike animals — making reason a prime candidate for what constitutes being in the divine image.[5] In light of this history, it is

1. For example, see McLeod, 1999: 50; Shults, 2003: 224; H. Reinders, 2006: 125-26; Cortez, 2010: 18.

2. On Irenaeus and John of Damascus, see Hodge, 1982: v. 2, 96; on Athanasius, see K. Barth, 1958a: 192; on Clement of Alexandria, Origen, and Cyril of Alexandria, see Maloney, 1973: 72, 167-68 and Windley-Daoust, 2002: 70; on Augustine, see B. Ware, 2002: 15; Collste, 2002: 34; Treier, 2008: 75.

3. For example, G. Peterson, 1996: 51; Grenz, 2001: 143; Van Vliet, 2009: 60.

4. See G. Peterson, 1996: 216; Soulen and Woodhead, 2006: 23; Aquinas, 1947: pt. 1, Q. 14, art. 2; cf. 1947: pt. 1, Q. 93, art. 3, 6-8, where Aquinas often relies on Augustine. See also discussion of Aquinas in Merriell, 1990: 205, 225; Pinckaers, 2005: 156.

5. On being in God's image as how people are like God with reason as the prime example, see Aquinas, 1947: pt. I, Q. 93, art. 2 and the discussion in Mahoney, 2010: 679 (con-

not surprising today to find many explicitly affirming reason as at least a component of being in God's image.[6] Many more assume that a link between people's rational capacity and God's image is a starting point for understanding the image.[7]

"Reason," however, is not as simple a category as it might seem at first glance. Many people use that or another term to refer to a range of mental or spiritual attributes that are broader than the term "reason" technically denotes. For example, some really have in view the idea of knowledge or understanding.[8] Others take the category in the direction of "self-consciousness"[9] or even "self-transcendence."[10] These concepts are closely associated with the general idea of "freedom"[11] — often stated in terms of free will[12] or choice[13] — which many affirm in conjunction with rationality as integral to being in God's image.

---

cerning Aquinas) and Collste, 2002 (concerning Augustine). On having reason as what it means to be in God's image because reason distinguishes people from animals, see Aquinas, 1947: pt. I, Q. 93, art. 6 and discussion in Merriell, 1990: 204-5.

6. For example, J. Wesley, 1985k: 293; Clark, 1969: 218; Mascall, 1974: 33; Shedd, 1980: v. 2, 4; Hughes, 1989: 57; John Paul II, 1997a: 449; Duncan, 2008; Mangano, 2008: 5; Kraynak, 2008: 78-79; Milbank, 2010: 116. See also Ruston, 2004: 209 on John Locke; and Jeeves, 2005: 178 on Descartes and standard Roman Catholic teaching.

7. D. Hall, 1986: 92; Grenz, 2001: 143; and Brink, 2001: 88 all observe that this assumption is automatic for many people.

8. For example, in the early church, see Origen, 1982: 192-93. Cf. Merriell, 1990: 220 on Augustine and Mondin, 1975: 68 on Aquinas. Similarly, see Calvin, 1960a: bk. I, ch. 15, sec. 3. More recent proponents include Litton, 1960: 117 and Gill, 1978: 394. Cf. McCasland, 1950: 86, who connects being in God's image with "intelligence."

9. For example, Maston, 1959: 3; Schleiermacher, 1986: 18; Keil and Delitzsch, 1866: 63-64; Brunner, 1946: 33-35; Chafer, 1947: 181, 184; Litton, 1960: 116-17; McFague, 1993: 123. See discussions in Feinberg, 1972: 240-41; G. Peterson, 1996: 216-17.

10. For example, R. Niebuhr, 1964: 153. See discussions in Phelps, 2004: 349; van Huyssteen, 2006: 132-33.

11. For example, Zizioulas, 1975: 428; Yannaras, 1984: 24; Breck, 1998: 145-46; Dabrock, 2010: 142. See also discussions of Nicholas of Cusa in Carlson, 2008: 104-5; Paul Tillich in Gonzalez, 2007: 75-76; Second Vatican Council's *Gaudium et Spes* in Collste, 2002: 60-61.

12. For example, Gill, 1978: 395-96; Nugent, 1984: 315; D. Hall, 1986: 94; Schillebeeckx, 1990: 230-31; Balswick et al., 2005: 30-31; Vorster, 2011: 22-23. See also discussion of Gregory of Nyssa in Maloney, 1973: 138-39; summary of Descartes in D. Hart, 2009: 225-26; and Grenz's claim (2001: 143) that free will and reason are "universally hailed . . . as marking the divine image." Similarly see Shannon, 2004: 114.

13. For example, McCasland, 1950: 89; Jenkins, 1995: ix; Merrill, 2006: 200; Goodman, 2008: 35-36; Sunshine, 2013: 67. See also discussion of Irenaeus in Osborn, 2003: 256.

Such ways of viewing being in God's image have in common the idea that it is not humanity's physical body that mirrors God's. Rather, a different dimension of human existence, variously called humanity's personhood,[14] soul,[15] mind,[16] or spirit,[17] is what primarily constitutes people's status as created in God's image. So any statement suggesting that "reason" was the dominant understanding of being in God's image in the early centuries of the church or throughout history is really using a code word for a cluster of considerations whose similarity arguably lies more in what they are not than in what they are.

For simplicity's sake, "reason" will serve as the subject of the comments that follow. This does not imply that the differences between reason and these other categories (free will, spirit, etc.) are unimportant. It simply indicates that most of the problems with identifying reason as central to being in God's image apply to all of these commonly connected categories.

As explained in Chapter 1, theological or cultural influences can easily misdirect efforts to formulate an understanding of humanity in God's image. A good example of that is the frequent attempt to define being in God's image in terms of people's rational attributes, spiritual nature, free will, etc. These are indeed excellent human attributes of people today that the Bible's authors discuss. However, there is no biblically sound warrant for using them to define being in God's image, as will be demonstrated shortly. Many things are true of human beings besides

14. Some use the words "person" or "personhood" (e.g., Orr, 1948: 57; Kaufman, 1956: 163-64; Eichrodt, 1967: 126; Lossky, 1985: 137; Fisher, 2005); whereas others refer to "the personal" or "personality" in human beings (e.g., Mullins, 1917: 139; Porteous, 1962: 684; Nellas, 1987: 32; Miley, 1989: 356).

15. For example, Augustine in the *Soliloquies* (see discussion in McCool, 1959: 73-74, Callender, 2000: 25; Drever, 2013: 149), who draws upon Ambrose in the *Hexaemeron* (see discussion in McCool, 1959: 68, 73, and K. Barth, 1958a: 192). Also Calvin, 1960a: bk. I, ch. 15, sec. 3; Gill, 1978: 388; Joas, 2013: 143; Visala, 2014: 103, 117.

16. Some refer to the "mind" (e.g., Sherlock, 1996: 78; Carlson, 2008: 108); whereas others speak in terms of the "intellect" (e.g., Wennberg, 1985: 171; Domingo de Soto in Ruston, 2004: 49). Cf. discussion in Golitzin, 2003: 333-34.

17. Some use the word "spirit" explicitly (e.g., Max Scheler in R. Niebuhr, 1964: 162; Hodge, 1982: v. 2, 96-97; Lewis and Demarest, 1994: v. 2, 209); whereas it is more common simply to connect creation in God's image with the "spiritual" aspect of humanity (see L. Berkhof, 1949: 204; Leitch, 1975: 257; Westermann, 1994: 149; Pannenberg, 1991: v. 2, 180; Gonzalez, 2007: 85; Deane-Drummond, 2012: 945). For support in the formative centuries of the early church, see Thielicke, 1966: 199; Maloney, 1973: xii; Nellas, 1987: 22; cf. Jónsson, 1988: 11-12, who notes the influence of this view "throughout the centuries."

their creation in the image of God. So the key question to ask is not "does it appear biblically sound to see people as (uniquely) rational, spiritual, etc." but, rather, to ask "why should we think that this is what constitutes being in God's image?"[18]

Careful examination reveals that using reason to define being in God's image is more a result of misleading cultural influences in particular than of biblically sound instruction. As it turns out, from well before the beginning of the church there have been powerful cultural influences inclining people's thinking toward viewing reason as the most defining trait of humanity. That mindset has had a formative influence on Christian understanding of being in the image of God.

The influence of Greek philosophy here has been particularly noteworthy.[19] While Plato,[20] Aristotle,[21] and the Stoics[22] differed in many significant respects during the centuries just before Christ, they shared an emphasis on reason as a distinctively important characteristic of humanity. As the church was being born, the Hellenistic Jew Philo worked out many of the implications of this emphasis for such concepts as the image of God in a way that proved quite influential among Jews and Christians alike.[23] One of the earliest Christian theologians, Irenaeus, under the similar influence of Greek philosophy, also promoted an understanding of God's image in which reason is central.[24] With that impetus, and a surrounding culture so impressed by the importance of reason, many other church leaders such as those listed above followed suit (albeit with their

18. Martin Luther (1958: 60-61) and Paul Ramsey (1950: 262) are among many who lament the failure to distinguish these two questions.

19. See discussions in Brunner, 1947: 100; S. Holmes, 2005: 318; Gonzalez, 2007: 5; Cortez, 2010: 19.

20. Regarding Plato's influence on Christian anthropology in general and the concept of humanity in God's image in particular, see R. Niebuhr, 1964: v. 1, 23; Middleton, 2005: 19-20.

21. Aristotle's influence on Christian anthropology and the idea of creation in God's image is noted in Ramsey, 1950: 250-51; Yong, 2007: 172.

22. For Stoicism's exaltation of reason and its connection with understandings of creation in God's image, see McCasland, 1950: 96; Collste, 2002: 85.

23. Lohse (1971: 47-48) and Feinberg (1972: 242) discuss Philo's Jewish impact; for his impact on the church, see Maloney, 1973: 137-38; Børresen, 1982: 360; Bray, 1991: 206. Cf. Jervell, 1960: 52-70 for a fuller discussion of Philo and his impact related to the image-of-God concept.

24. See Brunner, 1947: 99-100; Hoekema, 1994: 34.

own nuances).[25] Plato proved to be particularly influential for Augustine;[26] Aristotle for Aquinas.[27]

In more recent centuries, of particular interest is the way that seeing reason as the essence of being in God's image has gained favor in periods such as the eighteenth-century Enlightenment in Europe, when the appreciation of reason in the broader culture was at its peak.[28] Before and after that century as well, there are ample examples of prominent philosophers such as Descartes, Leibniz, and Hegel who not only have promoted reason in their philosophy but also have advocated it as a way to understand being in God's image.[29] Many theologians and even Bible scholars have followed their lead.[30]

What are we to make of the way that the rise of reason as central to the image-of-God concept has paralleled the valuing of reason in the broader culture? While it should make us suspect that the connection of reason and God's image may well be culturally driven rather than biblically grounded, we need to look to the Bible to see if that suspicion is warranted. It turns out that it is. As Paul notes in a broader context, a Greek preoccupation with "wisdom" is at odds with a biblical outlook (1 Cor. 1:22-23).

Consider the various affirmations of humanity as created in the image of God throughout the Bible. If reason is central to those affirmations, there should be consistent evidence of that in conjunction with all — or at least several — of them. However, many have looked in vain to find them.[31] Particularly in Genesis, the idea of God creating people with the primary intent that they have rational capacity, like God does, appears to be far from the author's mindset. Reading 1:26-27, 5:1, and 9:6 together provides little evidence that the author is trying to make a statement or affirmation about reason.

Genesis 1:26-27 is the first mention of humanity's creation in the image of God in the text of the Bible. God says various things about and to

25. Pannenberg, 1991: v. 2, 206, and G. Peterson, 1996: 215-16, discuss the impact of Greek cultural values on these leaders (as well as Gregory of Nyssa).

26. See McCool, 1959: 76-77; Mahoney, 2010: 678.

27. See R. Niebuhr, 1964: v. 1, 152-53; Hoekema, 1994: 39.

28. As discussed in Ramsey, 1950: 250; Erickson, 2013: 461.

29. Descartes, 1968: 136; Leibniz, 1898: sec. 83; Hegel, 1988: 438. See discussion in G. Peterson, 1996: 217.

30. For documentation and analysis, see Jónsson, 1988: 33-43, 77-91.

31. For instance, K. Barth, 1958a: 108; Thielicke, 1966: 160; K. Peters, 1974: 99; D. Hall, 1986: 92; Ruston, 2004: 56; McFarland, 2005: 1-2; Cortez, 2010: 19; cf. Treier, 2008: 119-20.

adam here and in the following verses. The absence of any overt reference to reason (or the aspects of humanity commonly connected with it, as identified above) suggests that reason is not the author's primary concern here. Because God speaks all of creation into existence out of nothing *(ex nihilo)*, the idea of a shared soul or spirituality between God and people is particularly foreign to the text.[32]

Some have suggested that Genesis 3 lends credence to a special connection between God's image and reason. In that chapter, Adam and Eve become more "like God" by eating the forbidden fruit and thereby coming to "know good and evil." However, this change in humanity is something that the text indicates God does not want. God forbids Adam to eat from the tree of the knowledge of good and evil and says that Adam will die if he does so (2:17). In 3:22-24 it is God's recognition that Adam has gained this knowledge that prompts God to block him permanently from access to the tree of life, so that he will die. If reason is at issue here, then it is not part of the "very good" world, featuring people in God's image, which God originally created (Gen. 1:27, 31).[33]

In Genesis 5:1-2, all that the author mentions in conjunction with God's image is God's blessing and naming of humanity, plus humanity's creation as male and female. Human reason is nowhere to be found here. Verse 3 then refers to Adam fathering Seth in his image — a sort of parallel to God's creation. Neither here, nor in 9:6 where the focus is on being careful not to shed human blood, is there any suggestion that reason is especially in view.

Unsurprisingly, then, in the two New Testament passages most similar to these Genesis texts, reason also appears to play no role. In 1 Corinthians 11:7 Paul offers no definition of the image of God he mentions there. In James 3:9, James identifies the worst people — those one is most likely to curse — as being in God's image. The point seems to be that people are in God's image in spite of how deficient their attributes may be, not because they have good attributes. There is no evidence of reason being an exception to the point James is making.

Other New Testament passages that address humanity's renewal in Christ, however, have suggested to some that reason may be particularly important in God's image after all. If reason were central, though, one would expect to see evidence of that in such passages as Romans 8:29

---

32. See discussion in Horton, 2005: 104; 2006: 183-84.
33. For further discussion on this point, see Ramsey, 1950: 263; Collste, 2002: 85-86.

and 2 Corinthinans 3:18, which talk about Christ's image as the standard according to which people are being conformed/transformed. However, there is no such evidence.

What about the image passages in Colossians and Ephesians? Some claim that these passages associate being "renewed in knowledge" (Col. 3:10) and "renewed in the spirit of your minds" (Eph. 4:23-24) with a renewal of God's image.[34] As we have seen in Chapter 3 and will consider more fully in Chapter 7, however, it is not the image that is being renewed. People are the focus of renewal. The image — here the image of the (Re) Creator Christ — is the fixed standard according to which people are changing. Christ as the image of God (see Ch. 2) manifests knowledge and reason perfectly. God intended people, by creating them in the divine image, to manifest such God-like attributes in an appropriately human way. However, sin has prevented them from doing so.

All people remain in God's image, not because they have wonderful God-like attributes such as reason, but because God's intention that they reflect them to God's glory has not changed. The passages in Colossians 3 and Ephesians 4 do not describe what humanity's creation in the image of God means (God's image involving a special connection with God and a meaningful reflection of God — see Ch. 3). Rather, they depict the breaking of sin's stranglehold on humanity and God's intentions coming to fulfillment in Christ (see Ch. 6).

This distinction between intended versus actual attributes is crucial, for many reasons. We have already seen in Chapter 3 that being in God's image is not about how people today are excellent, how they are like God, or how they are different from animals. Unlike such attributes (or perversions of those attributes), being in God's image is not a matter of degree. Some people are not more in God's image than others are. In other words, being in God's image is not about actual attributes, whether viewed as perverted from some original state or not. The Bible does not use the image-of-God concept in a way that permits such an understanding.

Reason is a good illustration of this. The Bible does not celebrate human reason or understanding, as if it evidences how much like God people are. For instance, the book of Isaiah opens with God lamenting that "Israel does not know, my people do not understand" (1:3). Curiously,

---

34. Examples include Calvin, 1960a: bk. I, ch. 15, sec. 4; Machen, 1947: 175. McCasland, 1950: 88. Merriell, 1990: 204 cites Augustine and Aquinas in support; and Chafer, 1947: v. 2, 163 similarly invokes Richard Watson.

some translations have God saying later in the same chapter something like "Come, let us reason together" (v. 18). However, God is not calling for a discussion but is telling people what they should be doing. Verse 17 contains God's instructions and verse 19 describes the blessings that will accompany obedience. Obedience is rather different from "reasoning together," which is why some recent translations (e.g., the latest NIV) have rendered verse 18 something like "Come now, let us settle the matter." In other words, it is people's own thinking that has gotten them into trouble. So it is not surprising to find later in Isaiah (55:8, 9) God reiterating, "My thoughts are not your thoughts."

This is not merely the perspective of Isaiah. In the Psalms, the psalmist laments that "there is no one who has understanding" (see 14:1-3; 53:1-3) — an observation that Paul echoes in the New Testament (Rom. 3:11). As Paul explains elsewhere, human reasoning is so inept that it does not recognize who God is, particularly who God in Christ is (1 Cor. 1:21). Rather than human wisdom being like God's wisdom, human wisdom is inferior even to God's foolishness, not to mention God's wisdom (v. 25).

Considering reason to be at least a significant aspect of being in God's image, then, can easily reflect an under-appreciation of sin's impact on humanity.[35] Human reason as it exists today is badly perverted.[36] All things considered (as in the perspective of Paul), human reason/understanding/spirituality/etc. is not God-likeness in the meaningful sense of something that is God-glorifying. God intended so much more at creation, and that intention remains steadfast today. That is why humanity remains in God's image. It is not because of how much human reason is like God's reason today.

As already discussed in Chapter 4, humanity's status in the image of God has continued undamaged since the original creation. The Bible shows no recognition of an image damaged by sin. Sin damages people greatly, but they continue straightforwardly in God's image. So it will not work to say that people were originally created with God-like human reason and that sin's perversion of reason means that God's image has been perverted. That would be to force the Bible to say what it does not say (God's image is

---

35. See discussion in Berkouwer, 1975: 51. Kaufman (1956: 159) goes so far as to say that "defining the image in terms of rationality . . . leaves one in the position of being unable to deal with the problem of sin."

36. Ample evidence ranges from everyday life to the great atrocities of history. See Thielicke, 1966: 163; D. Hall, 1986: 111; S. McDonald, 2009: 330.

damaged), based on a logical implication of a concept of God's image (as reason) that the Bible never affirms.

A major reason the Bible's authors do not connect God's image primarily with one or more mental or spiritual capacities is that doing so represents a mind-body or spiritual-physical dichotomy that is foreign to the Bible.[37] As already discussed in Chapter 3, the Bible's authors speak of the whole person (even humanity as a whole), not particular aspects of people, as created in God's image. Accordingly, a dichotomized understanding that privileges the mind or spirit over the body as central to being in God's image is demeaning to the body. The body becomes something that distracts people from more important mental or spiritual endeavors. This can lead to neglect or abuse of the body.[38]

The body is not the only aspect of humanity that suffers when reason gains special status in relation to God's image. The emotional aspect of human existence can readily lose respect as well.[39] So can the relational aspect. In fact, part of the mind itself can decrease in status. Augustine's view illustrates this consequence well: That part of the mind "which is directed to the handling of inferior things is not the image of God."[40] The focus becomes the self-conscious mental life of particular persons, in which the rational, intellectual activity of the human person mirrors reason at work in God.[41]

Some commentators have noted the overly individualistic view of being in God's image implicit here.[42] In fact, such a focus is in danger of eclipsing the importance of particular persons as well. Reason, shared by God and people, becomes what is important in the universe, while the entities that employ it become secondary.[43] Accordingly, John Milton is said to have been nearly as concerned about destroying a fine book as killing a person, because a person has many attributes whereas someone

37. So Berkouwer, 1975: 77; Hoekema, 1994: 41; Strong, 2005: 92; Hopkins, 2005: 186; Cortez, 2010: 21.

38. See discussions in Clines, 1968: 86; D. Hall, 1986: 110; Eilberg-Schwartz, 1996: 44-45; Gushee, 2013: 43.

39. So H. R. Niebuhr, 1996: 42; Hoekema, 1994: 40-41.

40. Augustine, 1963: bk. 12, sec. 10. See discussion in Gonzalez, 2007: 37-38.

41. This is elaborated in Gunton, 2003: 101; Smail, 2006: 84-85; van Huyssteen, 2006: 134.

42. For a discussion of this problem in Augustine, see Vanhoozer, 1997: 164; Gunton, 2003: 102; H. Reinders, 2006: 130-31.

43. This concern is developed further in R. Niebuhr, 1964: 7; Ramsey, 1950: 253; Clines, 1968: 86.

"who destroys a good book, kills reason itself, kills the image of God, as it were in the eye."[44]

Curiously, identifying reason in particular with being in God's image ends up granting image status in ways that would surprise most readers of the Bible. Some especially bright atheists become more in God's image than many followers of Christ.[45] Animals with the most developed reasoning abilities become more in God's image than people whose reason is most impaired.[46] All angels join humans as being in the image of God.[47] Even demons have ample reasoning skills and knowledge, including the knowledge that God exists (James 2:19). Satan is a paramount example of exceptional intellect and a determined will — able to lead the whole world astray, for which Satan is accountable to God (Rev. 12:9).[48] Yet it is not surprising that the Bible does not herald Satan as being in the image of God.

There is much warrant, then, for rejecting the view that reason — current rational ability or capacity — is at least a significant aspect of what being in God's image is. Most importantly, this view does not fit with what the Bible teaches about humanity as created in the image of God. However, we should also note some of the harmful implications of holding this view.

Prominent among them are the implications for those whose reason is badly impaired. If having reason constitutes being in the image of God, then those with little reason are little in God's image. Not only is being "little in God's image" an unbiblical concept, but it leaves those in view without the full dignity and protection that people in God's image warrant. (See Ch. 1 for historical documentation that the theoretical problems in view here have dangerous consequences for real people.)

Those with "little reason" can include, for instance, young children, demented elderly people, or severely mentally disabled adults (whether disabled from birth or injured in a car accident). As already noted in Chapter 1, some Christian leaders have denied that normal protections apply for some such people (e.g., those who are "grossly retarded") because of

---

44. This statement is quoted from Milton's *Areopagitica* at http://en.wikiquote.org/wiki/November_23 (accessed January 4, 2014).

45. So Erickson, 2013: 469. Or, as Brunner (1947: 107) puts it, the rational self becomes God. Cf. Machen, 1947: 170-71 regarding people who have reason without goodness.

46. So Jeeves, 2005: 178; Visala, 2014: 118.

47. W. Pope, 1875: v. 2, 37; Litton, 1960: 1290; Gill, 1978: 392. McLeod, 1999: 74-79, cites other examples of this affirmation.

48. See further discussion in Luther, 1958: 61-62; Ramsey, 1950: 264; Thielicke, 1966: 162; Berkouwer, 1975: 56-57; Jenson, 1999: 55.

the compromise to God's image in their cases.[49] Apparently Martin Luther even advocated drowning a "feebleminded" twelve-year-old child because his limited mental capacities appeared to evidence corruption of his reason and soul.[50] Others have not advocated such actions, but the way they have formulated their support for reason as a hallmark of being in God's image may inadvertently open the door to demeaning people with minimal mental capacities.[51] Sadly, throughout history such image-related demeaning has predictably occurred.[52] Recognizing this harm has encouraged many to speak out against identifying reason as all or part of what it means to be in God's image.[53]

Demeaning those with very little rational capacity can all too easily expand to disrespecting (and much worse) those who have less reason than others according to prevailing cultural standards. Women have sometimes borne the brunt of such image-related discrimination. In some settings, the view has been that men have greater rational capacity than women and thus are more fully in the image of God; therefore, they are more worthy of respect and privilege.[54] Featuring reason as an important aspect of being in God's image can also lead to considering those more educated

49. For Emil Brunner (1952: 57): the protection of being in the image of God "ceases where true human living ceases — on the borderline of imbecility or madness." For Robert Wennberg (1985: 131), reflecting on whether all people are fully in the image of God and so have full moral standing: "the grossly retarded . . . need not be assumed to possess a moral standing as full as that of a normal human adult."

50. Luther (1952: 387) reports this in a write-up of one of his famous "Table Talks." See discussions in Kanner, 1964: 7; Towns and Groff, 1972: 38-39.

51. For example, Aquinas (1947: pt. I, Q. 93, art. 6) argues that beings without rational capacity cannot be in God's image, thereby implying, as H. Reinders (2008: 228) understands him, that those whose capacity is sufficiently damaged are vulnerable to exclusion. Pope John Paul II (1997a: 450), meanwhile, maintains that a person is "made in the image of God insofar as he or she is a rational and free creature" — again, implying that compromised rational capacity could mean compromised status in terms of God's image. The problem here is with the implications of the ideas rather than the authors' intentions (cf. H. Reinders, 2008: 229).

52. See D. Hall, 1986: 108-9; Yong, 2007: 172; Ruston, 2010: 390.

53. For example, J. Reinders, 1997: 199; Moreland and Rae, 2000: 118; Budziszewski, 2002: 30; S. Holmes, 2005: 318; Smail, 2006: 281. See also the Ecumenical Disabilities Advocates Network (2004: 513).

54. See D. Hall, 1986: 109; Sherlock, 1996: 87; van Huyssteen, 2006: 127. Moritz (2009: 142) attributes this view to the apostle Paul based on a biblically unsound impression (see discussion in Chs. 1 and 3) that Paul denies full image-of-God status to women in 1 Corinthians 11.

or "civilized" to be more fully in the image of God, thereby warranting more power and even the right to oppress others.[55] If reason is special because it makes people like God and unlike animals — as is commonly the rationale — then this understanding of being in God's image can lead to exalting people so far above the rest of creation that environmental abuse becomes less offensive.[56]

Since viewing human reason as at least a key aspect of being in God's image can be so harmful, not to mention biblically inaccurate, there must be a better way to understand the significance of reason. Indeed there is, as the conclusion of this chapter will explain.

Righteousness and God's Image

Many others through the centuries have considered righteousness to be even more central to who God is, and so to who people are as created in the image of God. This view has been particularly influential in Reformed theology, as evident in various doctrinal statements.[57] Being created in God's image includes being "good, righteous, and holy" according to the Belgic Confession, "in righteousness and true holiness" according to the Heidelberg Catechism, and "endued with . . . righteousness and true holiness" according to the Westminster Confession.[58] The Lutheran Formula of Concord similarly connects being in God's image with being "pure and holy."[59]

This view reflects the understanding of John Calvin, Martin Luther, and other leaders following in their wake.[60] However, it revives a view that goes back to the earliest centuries of the church.[61] It has also continued to be visible since the Reformation in works of such church leaders

55. For critiques of this tendency, see Cone, 1986: 90-91; García-Rivera, 1995: 99-100.

56. Primavesi (2003: 190) and Horton (2005: 106) elaborate this problem.

57. See discussions in Feinberg, 1972: 242; Lewis and Demarest, 1994: v. 2, 127, 132; Horton, 2005: 101-2.

58. Belgic Confession, art. XIV; Heidelberg Catechism, Lord's Day 3, q. 6; Westminster Confession, ch. IV.2.

59. Formula of Concord, "Epitome," art. I, affirmative 1.

60. Calvin, 1960a: bk. I, ch. 15. sec. 4; bk. II, ch. 2, sec. 12; Luther, 1958: 62-63; similarly Mastricht and Vermigli, as discussed in Horton, 2005: 99-100; and Gerhard, 1962: 37-38. On various Reformed theologians, see H. D. McDonald, 1981: 38; Hoekema, 1994: 71-72.

61. E.g., Clement of Rome, 1891: 70; Gregory of Nyssa, 1972: 533-34; cf. Maloney, 1973: 165, on Cyril of Alexandria and Strong, 1907: 514-15 on the "Latin Fathers."

as John Owen, Jonathan Edwards, and John Wesley.[62] Many affirmations of this outlook appear from the beginning of the twentieth century to the present.[63] For some, this position primarily involves the continuing righteousness or moral capacity (sometimes called "conscience")[64] that characterizes people even in a fallen state. For others, human righteousness was a part of the original creation that has been damaged or lost.

It is not surprising that many people have concluded that righteousness is central to being in the image of God, in light of the common but inadequate assumptions about God's image. Many assume that being in God's image is about how people are excellent, how they are like God, and/or how they are unlike animals. In fact, they often affirm such assumptions directly. Some explicitly acknowledge the assumption about actual likeness to God as the reason they consider righteousness to define what it means to be in God's image.[65] Others explicitly ground their support for this defining role of righteousness in the assumption that being in God's image is about how people are unlike animals.[66]

However, as we saw in Chapter 3, neither likeness to God nor unlikeness to animals is what constitutes being in God's image, whether righteousness or any other human attribute is in view. Accordingly, evidence of greater moral capacity in some animals than in some humans constitutes no threat to the status of humanity in God's image.[67] To maintain that being in God's image is not a matter of people's righteousness is not to suggest that people have no moral capacity. Just as people have rational capacity, they have moral capacity. But that does not mean that either reason or righteousness is what constitutes being in God's image.

If something as basic and significant as humanity's continuing to be in God's image depends on people's righteousness, then righteousness must be an ongoing trait of humanity. Whether construed in terms of actual

62. Owen, 1850a: 146, 155, 1850b: 578; John Edwards, 1982: pt. 1, sec. 5; J. Wesley, 1985c: 184, 1985k: 294; see discussion in S. McDonald, 2009: 325; Jeeves, 2005: 178.

63. E.g., Strong, 1907: 472, 514; Mueller, 1934: 205; Maston, 1959: 3; Purkiser et al., 1960: 214; Ricoeur, 1969: 251; Gill, 1978: 395; Kline, 1980: 31; H. D. McDonald, 1981: 37; Collste, 2002: 164; Duncan, 2008.

64. E.g., see Dabney, 1878: 294; Mullins, 1917: 258; Purkiser et al., 1960: 213; Butler, 1970: Sermon 1, par. 6.

65. E.g., Gregory of Nyssa, 1972: 554; Strong, 1907: 517; Mullins, 1917: 258; Chafer, 1947: v. 2, 168-69; Murphy-O'Connor, 1982: 49.

66. E.g., John Edwards, 1982: pt. 1, sec. 5; Chafer, 1947: v. 2, 1947.

67. See discussion of De Waal, 1997: 216-17, in Jeeves, 2005: 178-79.

capacity for morality or other manifestations of righteousness, that righteousness would presumably be a prominent human characteristic. Yet as we saw in Chapter 4, such a view badly underestimates the tragedy and power of sin. It also is at odds with the direct testimony of the Bible.

According to Psalms 14 and 53, "there is no one who does good" (v. 1). Not even one? "No, not one" (v. 3). The predicament is so bad that people's "throats are open graves" (Ps. 5:9), "under their lips is the venom of vipers" (Ps. 140:3), and "their mouths are filled with cursing and deceit" (Ps. 10:7). In fact, "their feet run to evil, and they rush to shed innocent blood" (Isa. 59:7). Lest anyone think that this is just an Old Testament problem, Paul quotes and affirms these very same descriptions of humanity in Romans 3:10-15. It is tempting, after admitting that people are generally unrighteous, to insist that they at least do some good deeds and thereby "image" something praiseworthy about God. But shortly after the passage in Isaiah that Paul quotes, the text clarifies that "all our righteous deeds are like a filthy cloth" (64:6). Accordingly, explains Paul, people with their self-assumed "righteousness" do not mirror God to God's glory, but instead prompt God's wrath (Rom. 1:18).

People's actual righteousness today (holiness, moral capacity, etc.), then, does not constitute being in God's image. Some who see righteousness as central to being in God's image, though, recognize the ravages of sin. So they suggest that people were originally created to be righteous and thus in God's image, but their righteousness and God's image have been lost or badly damaged. As explained at length in Chapter 4, one major problem with this view is what it says about sin's effect on God's image. The Bible consistently refrains from even a hint that God's image has been damaged — affirming instead that all people continue in God's image. So nothing that has been seriously damaged or lost due to sin, such as human righteousness, can be what constitutes being in God's image.

In light of that, why have many Christian commentators nevertheless concluded that actual righteousness is central to being in God's image? The primary reason has to do with a conflation of terms and ideas. These commentators recognize that people have been badly damaged by sin, so they simply assume that the same applies to God's image.[68] Furthermore, they recognize that people can be restored in Christ, so they simply assume that the image then gets restored as well.[69]

---

68. E.g., Baker, 1991: 78; see other examples in Bray, 1991: 209.
69. E.g., Gill, 1978: 394; Payne, 1995: 152; see other examples in Thiessen, 1949: 220-21.

As discussed in Chapter 4, being in God's image is only one of many things that are true about who people were created to be according to the Bible. Connecting God's image with sin would only make sense if one has smuggled in an understanding of what constitutes that image — something that sin necessarily damages, such as righteousness. However, such understanding is the very thing that should *follow* from what the Bible teaches about the image, not be assumed for some reason at the outset.

The way that those who see righteousness as central to being in God's image read Colossians and Ephesians provides a clue as to what is happening here. In Colossians 3:10, Paul reminds his brothers and sisters in Christ (1:1-2) that they have clothed themselves with the new humanity, "which is being renewed in knowledge according to the image of its creator." By contrasting this with the old humanity "with its practices," Paul signals that the "knowledge" he has in view is something closely connected with righteousness and moral living. This use of "knowledge" corresponds with Paul's and others' use of the term elsewhere.[70]

Although the passage in Colossians indicates that the person is changing, and that the unchanging standard according to which the person is changing is the "image of its creator," many mistakenly read the passage to be saying that the image itself is changing. Probably the best way to account for this misreading is that readers are bringing to the text the idea that God's image is righteousness (and/or reason), which has been badly damaged and so needs restoring. A meaning foreign to the text is thus imposed on the text, causing the reader to confuse what is changing in the verse and what is not. Calvin, for example, brings to the text the assumption that the image is changing, so he states his approach as follows: "The true nature of the image of God is to be derived from what the Bible says of its renewal through Christ."[71] He and others taking this approach then read Colossians 3:10 with the assumption that it is talking about a changing *image* rather than a changing *person*.[72]

Ephesians 4:24 is somewhat parallel to Colossians 3:10. Again the text reminds Christians that they have put off the old humanity, which is morally bankrupt, and have put on the new humanity, "created to be like

70. See Paul's use in Romans 1:21-25; cf. 1 John 2:3-6 and discussion in Frame, 2006: 234-35.

71. 1960: bk. I, ch. 15, sec. 4. See also discussion of his Commentary on Colossians in Driscoll and Breshears, 2010: 118.

72. Other examples include Aquinas, 1947: pt. I, Q. 93, art. 6; Strong, 1907: 516-17; Wilson and Blomberg, 1993: 9; also Kilcrease, 2010: 16, speaking for the Lutheran tradition.

God in true righteousness and holiness." The Colossians 3 term for image, *eikon,* is not present here in Ephesians. Instead God's stated intention is that Christians are "created to be" *kata theon* (according to God). But the parallelism suggests that the concept is the same. As explained in Chapters 2, 3, and 6, when God creates people in the image of God, connection and reflection are in view. A special connection with God is present, and God is intending that people reflect various excellent attributes (traits, capacities, functions, etc.) that will glorify God, because they are to some degree like God's own.

The same misreading sometimes occurs in Ephesians as occurs in Colossians.[73] People mistakenly think that God's image is improving, when it is Christians who are improving instead. If anything, the role that the image concept is playing in this process is even clearer here. Colossians 3 identifies the standard according to which Christians are changing as the image of God in Christ, which the reader only recognizes as specifically Christ by reading beyond the passage in focus here (as already discussed in Ch. 2). Ephesians 4, however, more directly identifies the standard as "God." When Christians become more like God in Christ, as the process of sanctification continues, God is not changing, people are. Or, another way to say essentially the same thing is to affirm that in the sanctification process, God's image is not changing, people are.

Matters of righteousness are indeed explicitly in view in the Colossians and Ephesians passages referring to God's image. However, the absence of references to such matters in the foundational image passages in Genesis 1 and 5 suggests that righteousness is not likely what exclusively defines the image concept. At first glance one might think that the two major "application" passages on the image of God (in Genesis 9 and James 3) point back to matters of righteousness and morality, since they concern killing and cursing. Yet those passages both identify the least righteous people as being in God's image — those whom others are most likely to kill or curse. The point is hardly that people warrant special protection because of their righteousness. The point of those passages appears to be precisely that righteousness is not at issue — *rather,* being in God's image is. The texts contrast the two, rather than equate them.[74]

73. For example, see discussions in J. Wesley, 1985a: 149; Schell, 1901: 166-67; Kline, 1980: 29; Youngblood, 2006: 7; Kaiser, 2008: 40.

74. Berry and Jeeves (2008: 32) are among the many who conclude that there is not "any evidence in Scripture to support the view that the image of God in humans is to be defined in terms of a unique capacity for moral behaviour and moral agency."

The one remaining passage that people occasionally invoke to connect being in God's image with actual righteousness and moral capacity is Genesis 3. In that passage Adam and Eve become more "like God" by obtaining "knowledge of good and evil" (vv. 5, 22). Whether attributes related to reason or those related to righteousness are in view here, the problems with attempting to connect them with being in God's image are the same as noted in the previous section above. The two people already are created in God's image (Genesis 1), so what they are attempting to obtain in Genesis 3 is something different. The text affirms that God wanted people to be in the divine image (Gen. 1:26) but does not want people to obtain the knowledge of good and evil by eating from one particular tree (2:17). The point seems to be to distinguish this knowledge from being in the image, rather than to equate them.[75] Attempts to equate them may well be driven by the inadequate assumption that being in God's image is about how people are actually like God — leading to the biblically unsound conclusion that any way people become more like God makes them more in God's image (cf. Ch. 3).

Commentators sometimes invoke other biblical passages where God's image does not explicitly appear in an attempt to establish actual righteousness as central to being in God's image. For example, some cite Genesis 1:31 — where God sees that all of creation including humanity is "very good" — in support of the idea that humanity's moral goodness is at least a part of what constitutes being created in God's image.[76] Even apart from the question as to whether or not this "very good" has to do with moral goodness or righteousness, this description concerns humanity rather than God's image.

The same problem arises here as in the interpretation of Colossians 3 and Ephesians 4. God created *humanity* (not God's image) as righteous, sin has ravaged that righteousness, and that righteousness is restored in Christ. Conflating people with God's image mutes an important truth. As low as humanity falls, people remain in God's image. The special connection with God continues, and God's wonderful intention for the reflection of God that people are to be is unwavering. Righteousness may be gone, but

75. Whereas van Huyssteen (2006: 143) and Kass (2008: 324-35) appear to overlook this contrast in their attempt to connect moral capacity with creation in God's image, W. Schmidt (1983: 198) and Bray (1991: 207-8) recognize the contrast.

76. For example, see J. Wesley, 1985g: 175; Dabney, 1878: 294; Machen, 1947: 172-73; Pieper, 1950: 516-17.

that is not the end of the story. Being in God's image remains, not only as the basis of an enduring dignity but also as the offer of a glorious destiny.

Elevating righteousness above other aspects of humanity as central to being in God's image introduces a host of problems, some analogous to those observed above in connection with reason. For example, it unbiblically demeans other aspects of humanity, such as the body.[77] It wrongly understands being in God's image as related to a part of what people are and do, rather than the whole (see Ch. 3). Furthermore, since righteousness — even in the form of moral capacity — varies from person to person, viewing being in God's image in terms of righteousness entails that people are in God's image to different degrees, an idea foreign to biblical teaching (again see Ch. 3).

In fact, those deemed to lack righteousness are all-too-easily seen to lack God's image. This implication became explicit in some strands of Jewish teaching and influenced the author of the Apocrypha's *Wisdom of Solomon*.[78] In Christian thinking, it has fueled the idea absent from the Bible that unbelievers are not truly/fully in God's image and the associated implication that some groups or particular people are more in God's image than others are.[79] As Chapter 1 has documented, this idea has invited stereotyping certain (e.g., racial) groups as lacking the morality/righteousness of others, leading to the conclusion that they lack God's image and do not warrant the respect and protection that come with that status.

Discussing being in God's image in terms of clusters of attributes under the broad heading of reason or righteousness does not imply that everyone's view of being in God's image fits neatly into a single category. Needless to say, one can combine any or all of the four clusters of human attributes highlighted in the present chapter — and other attributes as well — to form a distinctive concept of being in God's image. However, doing so compounds the problems that result from considering each attribute individually as what constitutes being in God's image.

Although the present chapter will forgo a repetitious critique of each possible combination of attributes, there is good warrant for pausing at this point to consider the view that a combination of reason and righteousness constitutes being in God's image. This combination (sometimes with ad-

---

77. See discussion in Driscoll and Breshears, 2010: 132.

78. See analysis in Kittel, 1964c: 394; Murphy-O'Connor, 1982: 52.

79. On the difference between Christians and non-Christians, see Aquinas, 1947: pt. I, Q. 93, art. 4; Reinders, 1997: 195; and discussions in Merriell, 1990: 186, and Hoekema, 1994: 36.

ditional human attributes included as well) has had a formative impact on Christian understanding of being in God's image through the centuries. It was influential in the early centuries of the church,[80] with Gregory of Nyssa[81] and Augustine[82] being prominent examples. Its visibility grew in the Roman Catholic Church via Aquinas[83] and in early Protestant accounts of being in God's image.[84] And it persists to the present day.[85]

Some supporters simply find these two (and perhaps other) attributes to be major resemblances between God and humanity, and so equate them with being in God's image. However, there is another more powerful reason that so many have combined these two attributes. Doing so accords with two widely held but erroneous assumptions. It preserves the idea that the benefits of being in God's image continue after the Fall by identifying creation in the image with an exceptional human trait that appears largely to continue after the Fall — reason. Moreover it accounts for the damage of sin and the Fall by identifying creation in the image with another human trait that most obviously sin has decimated — righteousness. The resulting view is that at least one aspect of being in God's image continues in humanity today, whereas in another sense or aspect it does not continue.

An influential figure who pointed the church toward this way of think-

80. For example, Gardoski (2007: 7) discusses it in Justin Martyr's First Apology, and Oduyoye (1982: 46) notes it in the works of Irenaeus and Clement.

81. See Gregory of Nyssa, 1972: 544, 1995: 357, and analysis in R. Niebuhr, 1964: v. 1, 153; Hefner, 1984: 331; D. Hart, 2002: 543.

82. Augustine, 1963: bk. XIV, ch. 4. Although his preoccupation with "reason" in terms of aspects of the mind (memory, understanding, and will) is well recognized, many have also noted how he less directly connects being in God's image with love, virtue, and other righteousness-related attributes. See R. Niebuhr, 1964: v. 1, 158; Hodge, 1982: v. 2, 96; Lewis and Demarest, 1994: v. 2, 131; Sherlock, 1996: 80; G. Peterson, 1996: 216; Phelps, 2004: 353.

83. Aquinas, 1947: pt. I, Q. 93, art. 9; 1947: pt. I, Q. 95, art. 1. Aquinas connects "image" to reason and "likeness" to righteousness, as will be discussed below. See also Merriell, 1990: 188-89; Lewis and Demarest, 1994: v. 2, 126; Ruston, 2004: 56.

84. Major examples include Martin Luther (see discussion of his *Commentary on Genesis* in R. Niebuhr, 1964: v. 1, 161), Philip Melanchthon (see discussion of his doctrine in Lewis and Demarest, 1994: v. 2, 127), John Calvin (1960a: bk. II, ch. 1, sec. 1; cf. discussion in Hoekema, 1994: 42), Jacobus Arminius (1986: 363-64, 712), and John J. Wesley (1985j: 474-75, 1985b: 163; cf. discussion in C. Carter, 1983a: 205). For others, see Hodge, 1982: 98-102.

85. E.g., see Thiessen, 1949: 220; DeWolf, 1953: 205-7; Barabas, 1963: 371; R. Harris, 1980: 768; C. Carter, 1983a: 207, 1983b: 246; Wennberg, 1985: 41; Miley, 1989: 407; Boyce, 1990: 214; Plantinga Pauw, 1993: 12; John Paul II, 1997b: 520; Bequette, 2004: 15. Some, such as Barackman, 2001: 258-59, combine related mental/moral considerations into a personhood-oriented view of being in God's image.

ing was Irenaeus, the first theologian to offer a systematic discussion of God's image. He taught that humanity's creation in God's likeness-image actually has two different aspects, God's image and God's likeness. The first, connected with reason and related capacities, continues after the Fall; the second, connected with righteousness and related capacities, such as relationship with God, is lost after the Fall.[86] On this basis many in the Roman Catholic Church developed the further idea that only being in the image is a natural, intrinsic part of who people are created to be. Being in the likeness was a supernatural gift on top of that, which humanity forfeited due to sin.[87]

By the sixteenth century, biblical scholars had generally recognized the exegetical flaw in the seminal approach of Irenaeus. They recognized that in the Bible "image" and "likeness" are not two separate things associated with humanity, but rather a single concept (see Ch. 3). However, the idea of two different aspects of God's image had become so ingrained that it was difficult in many quarters to conceive of the image otherwise. Humanity's existence in God's image had become a convenient and effective way to communicate the ambiguity of the human condition. God had created people with some attributes that continue to be attractive (at least sometimes) and with other attributes that sin has ravaged or even destroyed. So even without a biblically sound basis for a distinction between two aspects of God's image, the distinction persisted.[88]

With it persisted the equally biblically unsound assumptions, which the original distinction fostered, that being in God's image is a matter of actual human attributes and that at least part of God's image has been lost in the Fall. Protestant leaders largely shared these assumptions, though they reacted against the extrabiblical idea that God added righteousness and other supernatural gifts to humanity's creation in God's image. Protestants tended to favor the more biblically straightforward understanding that Genesis 1:26-27 and 5:1 affirm that being in God's likeness-image is what God directly created people to be.[89]

---

86. On Irenaeus's position, see Brunner, 1947: 93; H. D. McDonald, 1981: 37; Hoekema, 1994: 33-35; Vanhoozer, 1997: 163-64; B. Ware, 2002: 15.

87. For discussions of this Catholic position, see L. Berkhof, 1949: 202, 208; Ramsey, 1950: 260-61; Piper, 1971: 27; Hughes, 1989: 9. An early example of this view is found in the work of Athanasius (especially *On the Incarnation* [1885]; see discussion in Maloney, 1973: 94).

88. On this development, see Westermann, 1994: 148-49; Bray, 2001: 575.

89. This Protestant critique is discussed in Strong, 1907: 521; Brunner, 1952: 77, 94;

Protestants did not object to the idea that likenesses to God such as righteousness were lost or virtually so. However, many rejected the idea that sin has only ravaged part of God's image (whether called the "likeness" or not), while another part remains substantially intact. Humanity in all of its aspects, in their view, is badly damaged by sin.[90] Yet these Protestants were in a bind. On the one hand they knew the Bible teaches that people continue in God's image after the Fall; but they also knew that sin has completely ravaged the human attributes they saw as constituting that image. So as we saw in Chapter 4, some of them developed the idea of small "remnants" of God's image that remain, although virtually all of God's image has been lost.

The idea of remaining remnants of God's image ended up communicating most of the same categories and assumptions the Roman Catholics were affirming — just to a different degree.[91] Many Catholics and Protestants alike appeared to agree that God's image consists of various actual human attributes, such as reason, righteousness, rulership, and/or relationship, some of which have been more or less damaged by sin.[92] This put them at odds with the ways that the Bible speaks about God's image (see Chs. 3 and 4) when it shows no awareness of a damaged image after the Fall and talks as if being in God's image is not a matter of actual human attributes.[93]

This remnants approach also continued the unhelpful conflation of people and God's image. Because many Protestant leaders shared the assumption with their Catholic counterparts that what is true about people is necessarily true of God's image as well, the former maintained that far more damage had to be attributed to God's image than Roman Catholicism generally taught, because of how sweeping the effect of sin is on people.

Litton, 1960: 119-20; R. Niebuhr, 1964: v. 1, 154; J. Murray, 1977: 44-45; Thielicke, 1966: 204-7; Clark, 1984: 57.

90. On this critique, see Machen, 1947: 172; Ramsey, 1950: 282-83; Hughes, 1989: 9.

91. Many Reformed theologians did not intend to carve out part of humanity and designate that as free from sin. However, connecting these remnants with a portion of God's image not destroyed by the Fall communicated that view, as Berkouwer (1975: 128-29) demonstrates. On the resulting structural similarity between many Catholic and Protestant views of being in God's image, see H. Reinders, 2008: 235.

92. See Hoeksema, 1966: 206-7, regarding Protestant support for this approach even where it was somewhat out of line with official church doctrine.

93. For other critiques of the "remnants" approach to God's image, see Brunner, 1947: 105; Ramsey, 1950: 283; Thielicke, 1966: 216; Berkouwer, 1975: 120-22.

They were logically pushed toward the view that God's image has been totally destroyed, as we have seen that many did affirm.

Others, reluctant to contradict the Bible's teaching that being in God's image continues after the Fall, had to contradict the thrust of their own theological view of humanity and sin by admitting that remnants of the image remain. The result is a position that is arguably unsatisfactory on all fronts. It does not accord sufficiently with biblical teaching on humanity's continuation in God's image; it does not sufficiently maintain the thorough impact of sin on humanity; and thus it unbiblically reduces justification in Christ from a complete renewal of people to a partial (albeit substantial) one, restoring whatever has been damaged by sin. As we will see at the end of this chapter, there is a better way of understanding reason and righteousness that does not require jeopardizing either biblical accuracy or theological consistency.

Rulership and God's Image

Relatively recently a different understanding of being in God's image has gained prominence, especially in the area of biblical studies. It focuses on people ruling over creation. Many have observed that right after the creation of humanity in God's image (Gen. 1:27), God tells humanity to "subdue" the earth and "have dominion" over it (v. 28). They therefore conclude that dominion is what constitutes being in God's image.

This view has surfaced at various points in the Christian era, going back to Chrysostom and the School of Antioch in the early church.[94] During the Reformation the Socinians with their Racovian Catechism gained a reputation for this understanding of creation in God's image.[95] However, Calvin also acknowledged a small place for it in his theology, as did Arminius.[96] Many later Arminians in the seventeenth century, among others, affirmed the concept as well.[97] By the end of the twentieth century, many were claiming that this understanding had become the "dominant view" of Old Testament scholars, supported by an "overwhelming majority" — a

94. Chrysostom, 1986: 110; McLeod, 1999: 43-44.

95. On the Socinians' position, see Strong, 1907: 524; L. Berkhof, 1949: 203; H. D. McDonald, 1981: 35; Hodge, 1982: v. 2, 97. On their Catechism (*Racovian*, 1962: 21), see Berkouwer, 1975: 70; Gardoski, 2007: 2; Erickson, 2013: 466.

96. Calvin, 1948 on Gen. 1:26; cf. Hoekema, 1994: 43; Arminius, 1986: 363.

97. Lewis and Demarest, 1994: v. 2, 128.

veritable "consensus."[98] During the first decade of the twenty-first century, others used almost identical language to describe the persistence and even expansion of this consensus.[99]

Those who conclude that this view explains creation in God's image, wholly or in part, often describe humanity using such terms as "royalty" and "rule."[100] They see the key verbs in Genesis 1 — *radah* ("rule over," vv. 26, 28) and *kabash* ("subdue," v. 28) — as words indicating control and authority. For many this understanding reflects an appreciation of the ancient Near Eastern backdrop discussed in Chapters 2 and 3, with its connection between kings and images.[101] Some supporters of this view use the related language of "dominion."[102] Others use the stronger language of "domination" or "subordination."[103] The basic idea is that people are "kings" over creation — or at least "vice-regents" whom God has put in charge.[104] The variation in terminology reflects the variety of supporters.[105]

More than language is at issue here, though. The substance of what "rule" involves is central. For some, a key aspect of creation in God's image is work, which began in the Garden of Eden (Gen. 1:26-30, 2:15) and con-

---

98. "Dominant": Jónsson, 1988: 219; Mathews, 1995: 166. "Overwhelming majority": I. Hart, 1995: 317; Spanner, 1998: 222. "Consensus": G. Peterson, 1996: 219. In a similar vein, see J. Barr, 1993: 158; Ruether, 1995: 272; Clifford, 1995: 183.

99. "Dominant": Yong, 2007: 173; Herring, 2008: 480; Berman, 2008: 22. "Most": Treier, 2008: 120; Cortez, 2010: 22. "Consensus": Shults, 2003: 232; Middleton, 2005: 25. Middleton (2005: 32) also observes the increasing influence of this view among theologians.

100. Pannenberg, 1985: 106; Welker, 1997: 448; Callender, 2000: 29; Beale, 2004: 83; Loader, 2004: 28; Horton, 2005: 105; Duncan, 2008; Roy, 2009: 13; Schmutzer, 2009: 176.

101. This connection is developed most fully in Middleton, 2005: 26-27, 59-60, 88, 145, 204-7. See also Clines, 1968: 97-98; Wilson, 1973: 356; Dumbrell, 2002: 16-17; van Huyssteen, 2006: 120.

102. For example, Mullins, 1917: 259-60; Mueller, 1934: 208; L. Berkhof, 1949: 205-6; Gill, 1978: 396; A. Ross, 1988: 113; Welker, 1997: 448, 1999: 70; Schweiker, 2000: 351; Dempster, 2003: 62; Garner, 2007: 120; Cortez, 2010: 32; Sunshine, 2013: 39-40; Koyzis, 2014: 23.

103. "Domination": Snaith, 1974: 24; Wolff, 1974: 160-62; van Huyssteen, 2006: 155. "Subordination and subduing": Verduin, 1970: 27-28.

104. "Kings": Scroggs, 1966: 13; Wildberger, 1997: 1083; John Paul II, 1997b: 534 (pointing back to Gregory of Nyssa); Schmutzer, 2009: 175-76. "Vice-regents": R. Harris, 1980: 768; Ferngren, 1987: 25-26; Hoekema, 1994: 78-79; Garr, 2003: 169-70; Beale, 2008: 127-28.

105. After identifying Gross (1981: 244-64) as the most complete and important defense of this approach to creation in God's image, Jónsson (1988: 220-21) also cites in support numerous other proponents of this view, as does I. Hart (1995: 317-18) and Middleton (2005: 25-26, 32). This support includes not only biblical studies scholars but some theologians as well — Welker, 1999: 60-73; Dyrness, 1983: 33-34; and others.

tinued beyond (Gen. 3:17-19).[106] Others emphasize in this work a broader responsibility to engage in the formation of culture.[107] For them, creation in God's image provides a "cultural mandate."[108] God endows people with creativity that mirrors God's own.[109] As "created co-creators," they can participate in "artful construction" with God.[110]

In other words, many move away from the oppressive and authoritarian connotations of kingship. They see love and caring as characteristic of the rulership that constitutes humanity in God's image.[111] Many also recognize the centrality of responsibility as well, in which rulership is first and foremost about acting on behalf of God.[112] Rulership, then, becomes more a matter of stewardship.[113] Kingly rule is tempered by priestly service.[114]

The concept of stewardship is appealing here, because it acknowledges God's ownership of creation and people's accountability to the Creator. However, some see in it a preoccupation with the God-human relationship that leaves too undefined humanity's relationship with the nonhuman creation. "Stewardship" can leave the door open to reading human self-interests into God's intentions for the creation, thereby divinely endors-

106. E.g., Wolff, 1974: 160; Greidanus, 1984: 22; I. H. Marshall, 2001: 52; Collste, 2002: 61; Merrill, 2006: 281.

107. E.g., Clarke, 1962: 424-27; W. Power, 1970: 40; K. Peters, 1974: 121; Novak, 2002; Schwöbel, 2006: 50; Mangano, 2008: 9.

108. For use of this term, see Greidanus, 1984: 22; Plantinga, 2002: 31-33; Middleton, 2005: 31-32; Roy, 2009: 13; Koyzis, 2014: 21. Cf. the similar concept in Schrotenboer, 1972: 8-9; P. Marshall, 1985: 21-22; Romanowski, 2001: 36-37.

109. See Purkiser, 1960: 212; Waltke, 1989: 4; Schillebeeckx, 1990: 236-37; Verhey, 2003: 163; Graham, 2006: 280; Reynolds, 2008: 180; Sunshine, 2013: 39-40.

110. The "created co-creator" idea, which the World Council of Churches (2005: par. 91) and the Canadian Council of Churches (2005: 6) connect with being in God's image, is developed in Hefner, 1993: 23-51; Garner, 2007: 209; Jersild, 2008: 44. On "artful construction," see Middleton, 2005: 89; van Huyssteen, 2006: 157; cf. Wolff, 1974: 162.

111. Love: Pannenberg, 1985: 75-76; Clifford, 1995: 186; Towner, 2005: 348; World, 2005: par. 90; van Huyssteen, 2006: 157-58. Caring/compassion: Schillebeeckx, 1990: 237; Welker, 1999: 71; Schweiker, 2000: 351; Verhey, 2003: 97; McConnell, 2006: 121; Moritz, 2009: 144.

112. So Brueggemann, 1982: 32; Birch, 1984: 14; Anderson, 1984: 163; Schillebeeckx, 1990: 245; Pannenberg, 1991: v. 2, 204-5; Schweiker, 2000: 351; Case-Winters, 2004: 818; Merrill, 2006: 136; Mahoney, 2010: 678; Koyzis, 2014: 22; M. Williams, 2014: 85-86.

113. For use of this term in conjunction with being in God's image, see Larkin, 1993: 17-18; O'Mathuna, 1995: 203; Plantinga, 2002: 30-31; Bequette, 2004: 10; International, 2004: pars. 73, 80; McConnell, 2006: 121; Merrill, 2006: 143; Gonzalez, 2007: 149, 164; Mahoney, 2010: 683; Sunshine, 2013: 8; Koyzis, 2014: 23; M. Williams, 2014: 97. Cf. the language of "a trust," e.g., in Fichtner, 1978: 36.

114. On this combination, see Middleton, 2005: 89-90, 207.

ing misuse of the creation. Accordingly, some argue that a more creation-affirming term like "solidarity" or "servant-leadership" better captures what being in God's image entails for humanity.[115] Or at least it provides a necessary supplement to what stewardship necessarily entails.

The ultimate question here, though, is whether or not rulership by any definition is what it means for humanity to be in the image of God. Rulership is somehow associated with God's image in Genesis 1. But if ruling over creation is what creation in God's image means, then rulership would need to be in view in all biblical passages where this image concept appears. That is not the case even in the Old Testament, as many commentators observe.[116]

In Genesis 5:1 God reaffirms the creation of humanity in God's image, but there is no indication that rulership over creation is what is at stake. In verse 3 the image concept may well be extended from Adam to Seth, as we have already discussed in Chapter 3. Again, though, there is no reference to rulership over creation.[117] In Genesis 9:6, the focus is on how humans should handle situations where a human kills a human. The idea of rulership over all creation does not seem to be the point of the author's reference to God's image. Earlier in the chapter there has been some discussion of humanity's relationship to animals and plants. But such relationships are left behind when the author takes up the matter of humanity's status as created in God's image.

Consideration of Psalm 8 can perhaps clarify whether being in God's image and humanity's rulership over creation are largely the same concept. That psalm constitutes an inspiring commentary on humanity's rulership over creation according to God's design in Genesis. Accordingly, some who think that humanity's rulership over creation defines being in God's image assume that Psalm 8 teaches as much.[118] Yet, the terminology of

115. "Solidarity": Clifford, 1995: 184-85; Welker, 1999: 71. "Servant-Leadership": Spanner, 1998: 222-24; C. Wright, 2004: 123.

116. E.g., J. Barr, 1993: 158-59; Watson, 1997: 293; Stendebach, 2003: 394; McFarland, 2005: 2; Bosman, 2010: 567 (drawing on the arguments of Schellenberg, 2009: 111-12 and T. Thompson, 2009). Cf. Niskanen, 2009: 430.

117. One could attempt, with Kline, 1980: 27-28, to find a relevant reference an entire chapter later, where so-called "sons of God" engage in a form of tyrannical rulership. However, both the distance from the image language and the poor reflection on God involved argue against the idea that the author is including this example of rulership to illustrate what being in God's image involves.

118. G. Moore, 1944: 446; Rad, 1964b: 391; Garr, 2003: 220; and Krause, 2005: 361 all see an actual reference to the image of God in Psalm 8, whereas I. Hart, 1995: 320 and Merrill,

God's likeness-image is not even mentioned there.[119] This suggests that while humanity does indeed have an important role to play regarding God's creation, that role is not likely the essence of what being created in God's image entails, even when the Genesis creation account itself is in view as it is in Psalm 8.[120]

In the New Testament, being in God's image appears to be even less associated with the idea of rulership, as many have noted.[121] Several New Testament passages concern the image of God in Christ as a standard according to which Christians are renewed (Col. 3:10; Eph. 4:24; Rom. 8:29; 2 Cor. 3:18). There is no indication in these texts that rulership is primarily in view here, or that humanity's present rulership over God's creation is in view at all.

In James 3 there is a reference to humanity's rulership over the animals shortly before James mentions God's image. But James does not appeal to people to control their tongues as part of their rulership responsibilities in God's image. Rather, in verse 9 James invokes only the creation, in God's image, of those being cursed — with no apparent reference to any rulership on their part. Meanwhile, in 1 Corinthians 11 there is discussion of the relationship of men to women and both to God, but no mention of the rulership over the rest of creation that God gave to male and female together in Genesis 1:27-28. No wonder Calvin observed that if being in God's image is about ways people are like God, many likenesses are better candidates than rulership as far as the relevant biblical texts are concerned.[122]

However, even more important, we have already seen in Chapter 3 that the very idea of people being in God's image because they are somehow currently like God is biblically unsound. Many people preoccupied with defining creation in God's image in terms of likenesses to God conclude that the reason people are in God's image is that they rule over creation like God does.[123] However, as we saw in Chapter 3, substantial biblical ev-

---

2006: 575 less directly claim that Psalm 8 is a "commentary" on the Genesis 1 image-of-God text (similarly Watson, 1997: 294).

119. So observe Berkouwer, 1975: 71 (affirmed in Lewis and Demarest, 1987: v. 2, 136); Mathews, 1995: 162; Kelsey, 2009: v. 2, 923.

120. For affirmation and further discussion of this point, see Erickson, 2013: 468-69.

121. E.g., Shepherd, 1988: 1019; Gunton, 1999: 57; Cortez, 2010: 23-24.

122. Calvin, 1960a: bk. I, ch. 15, sec. 4.

123. E.g., Gregory of Nyssa, 1972: 533; H. W. Robinson, 1926: 164; Verduin, 1970: 20; Walsh and Middleton, 1984: 53-54; Hughes, 1989: 61; Youngblood, 2006: 7-8.

idence indicates that creation in God's image is about God's intentions for humanity, not ways that people are actually like God. So humanity's present rulership over creation cannot be what it means to be in God's image.

Moreover, such an understanding of being in God's image, in terms of particular human attributes, is reductionistic. It fails to recognize that, biblically speaking, people as a whole are in God's image (again see Ch. 3). Being in God's image is not connected merely with one or more aspects of humanity, such as people's function as rulers over creation.[124] Were particular attributes such as ruling (rather than simply being human) to constitute being in God's image, one would expect the Bible to refer to angels as being in God's image as well.[125] In fact, "the ruler of this world" (John 12:31), Satan, along with other "rulers . . . of this present darkness" (Eph. 6:12) could warrant image-related status. However, whether exercised benignly or not, specific attributes like rulership are not what the Bible means by being in God's image. People as a whole are in God's image.

Rulership also cannot be what creation in God's image is primarily about for another reason. According to the Bible, as we saw in Chapter 4, humanity's status as being in God's image is not something that sin has damaged. By contrast, humanity's ability to rule over creation has become so marred and twisted by sin that some would call it "leprous" and "lost."[126] In Bonhoeffer's words, "we do not rule, we are ruled."[127] Although God has always intended for humanity to exercise godly rulership over all creation, Hebrews 2:8-9 explains that this comprehensive rulership is "not yet . . . but we do see Jesus."[128] God's intentions for humanity have already been realized in Christ and will ultimately be realized in humanity through Christ. Human dignity is real today, in part because of human destiny — a glorious eternal life (including rulership over creation) that God offers to all who will accept it. However, it would not amount to much, if anything, were it dependent on the current human rulership attributes of sinful humanity.

124. For further discussion, see A. Strong, 1907: 524; Miley, 1989: 407; Green, 1999: 53-54.

125. McLeod, 1999: 63-64 develops this point, drawing on the work of Theodore of Mopsuestia.

126. See C. Carter, 1983a: 207 (marred); Cortez, 2010: 22 (twisted); Luther, 1958: 66 (leprous); and Buswell's observation (1962: 234) that people cannot even rule themselves.

127. Bonhoeffer, 1959a: 40.

128. On this passage's interpretation of Psalm 8 in a way that connects it more to Christ than to current humanity where God's image is concerned, see Watson, 1997: 295-98; I. H. Marshall, 2001: 49-50.

Support for a rulership concept of what it means today for people to be in God's image can involve more cultural than biblical influence — a problem discussed in general in Chapter 1. Some have observed that an understanding of creation in God's image as rulership can be irresistibly appealing in contemporary societies where pragmatism in general or protecting the global environment in particular are priorities.[129] Cultural biases can work in both directions, though. At one point the view of creation in God's image as rulership was so closely aligned with a theologically suspect school of thought that many rejected the view simply on the basis of guilt by association.[130] The power of such cultural influences underscores the need for biblical grounding to guide the formulation of an understanding of being in God's image.

While viewing actual ability/capacity to rule as what it means to be in God's image is unsound biblically, it can also be dangerous. Not all people have the same ability or capacity to rule, whether that involves political office or personal management of one's own life and work. Accordingly, it becomes all too easy to see some as less in God's image than others, with certain groups lacking the status of being in God's image entirely. Since being in God's image provides a biblical basis for respecting and protecting human beings, as will be discussed in this book's Conclusion, those perceived to lack what is important to being in God's image become subject to demeaning and abuse.

Some people cannot exercise rule in any form, the way that others can, because of mental or physical disabilities. Minority groups subject to colonialism, enslavement, or other oppression cannot do so in the particular ways that those in power value and employ. Stereotyping others (e.g., women) as "unable to rule" can jeopardize their well-being regardless of their actual ability to rule. Such dangers are more than theoretical. Many have suffered as the implications of a wrong understanding of what it means for humanity to be in God's image have played out on the pages of history (see Ch. 1).[131]

As explained in Chapter 3, it makes all the difference to recognize that creation in God's image is about God's intentions for humanity rather than

129. See Jónsson, 1988: 221; J. Reinders, 1997: 190; Erickson, 2013: 467.

130. Hughes (1989: 61) discusses this problem in the era when the above-mentioned Socinians were prominent.

131. Although most of this documentation has already appeared in Chapter 1, Teel (2010: 46-47) and Driscoll and Breshears (2010: 133-34) describe in greater detail why viewing creation in God's image as rulership jeopardizes certain people. Cahill (2006: 211) and Yong (2007: 173) describe ways that the harms described here have actually materialized.

about the attributes that people actually have in this fallen world — or had before the Fall and then largely lost. Nowhere is this more evident than in dealing with two of the biggest debates surrounding the view that being in God's image is about rulership. The first debate is over exactly how rulership is related to being in God's image. The second concerns what is at stake for the natural environment.

The first debate, over the exact connection between rulership and being in God's image, emerges partly from the many difficulties discussed above. If it is so problematic to view rulership as what constitutes creation in God's image, some wonder, then why does God's command to subdue the earth and rule over it follow so closely after God's creation of humanity in the image of God in Genesis 1? Many have responded by suggesting that rulership is not what creation in God's image means; rather, rulership somehow flows from being created in God's image. Several even claim that this view is becoming a "near consensus."[132]

The point here is that just because adjoining verses of the Bible address two matters, those matters are not necessarily the same. Mere proximity does not signify identity.[133] In this case, what separates image and rulership, according to a number of commentators, has to do with God's blessing. God creates humanity in verse 27 in the divine image. Then verse 28 says that God blesses humanity and tells people to exercise rulership over creation. In verse 28 God is speaking to people who already exist in God's image — God is not adding a new status or function to people who are not yet in God's image. Recognizing this says nothing about what being in God's image is; it simply explains why rulership need not be understood as definitive of being in God's image if other references to that in the Bible do not indicate that rulership is central to it.[134]

In light of such observations, many conclude that humanity's rulership over creation is a "consequence" of being in God's image, not the content of being in that image.[135] Others use similar language, calling rulership the

---

132. So Bray, 1991: 197; Grenz, 2001: 197; Smail, 2006: 46-47. Similarly Westermann, 1994: 155.

133. Berkouwer, 1975: 71; Cortez, 2010: 22.

134. So Horst, 1950: 262; Eichrodt, 1967: 127; Miller, 1972: 297: Crouch, 2010: 9.

135. Pieper, 1950: 522; Brunner, 1952: 67; Kidner, 1967: 52; Cook, 1975: 88; Fichtner, 1978: 170; Wenham, 1987: 32; Hamilton, 1990: 137; Pannenberg, 1991: v. 2, 203; Konkel, 1992: 3; Lewis and Demarest, 1994: v. 2, 135; Mathews, 1995: 168; Gardoski, 2007: 7. Jónsson, 1988: 222-23, also discusses other proponents of this view, such as Wildberger (1965) and Jacob (1974).

"expression," "derivative," "result," or another consequence of being in the image.[136] In other words, one might say that being in God's image is the "requisite," "precondition," "presupposition," "cause," "basis," "ground," or "foundation" of humanity's rulership over creation.[137]

As appealing as this construal is, it arguably goes too far in separating rulership from image. While rulership does not appear to define being in God's image, it does appear more integrally connected with it than the idea of "consequence" suggests.[138] In light of all that precedes and follows humanity's creation in the image of God in Genesis, God's many purposes for humanity, including rulership, are constantly implicit in the text. Occasionally they become explicit, as in 1:26 where God proposes to make humanity in God's image "so that they may rule . . ." (NIV).[139] Some translations use "and" to render the conjunction between the statements about image and rule. But this Hebrew conjunction *(we)*, connecting a cohortative verb like "let us make" with a jussive verb, typically expresses a more purposeful "so that" — here, "so that they may rule."[140]

Genesis 1, then, fits the larger pattern of how the Bible's authors use the concept of being in God's image. Humanity's creation in the image of God means that God intends people to reflect various God-honoring attributes. Creation in God's image is about God's intentions, not a statement of current or lost attributes. It encompasses many intended attributes, rulership over creation being one of many.

This understanding of being in God's image, explained in Chapter 3,

136. "Expression": B. Ware, 2002: 16. "Derivative": Orr, 1948: 57. "Result": Maston, 1959: 2; Baker, 1991: 39; B. Childs, 1993: 568; J. Reinders, 1997: 190. Other consequence: Ryu, 1977: 143; J. Murray, 1977: 41; Boyce, 1990: 215.

137. P. Bird, 1981: 140 (requisite); Horton, 2005: 107 (precondition); K. Barth, 1958a: 194 (presupposition); H. D. McDonald, 1981: 36 (cause); Feinberg 1972: 239 (basis), Chafer, 1947: v. 2, 162 (ground); Barentsen, 1988: 32 (foundation).

138. Thielicke, 1966: 157; Clines, 1968: 96; 1993: 427; W. Schmidt, 1983: 198; and Middleton, 2005: 53 all argue that the language of "consequence" is inadequate here — though they go different directions in an attempt to pin down what the closer connection between creation in the image and rulership is.

139. On the idea of "purpose" here, see Piper, 1971: 19; Rad, 1972: 59-60; Wilson, 1973: 356; Flender, 1976: 287; Watson, 1997: 293; Dumbrell, 2002: 16; S. Wright, 2003: 33; C. Wright, 2004: 119. According to Ambrose (1961: 256) and Beale (2004: 81), creating humanity in God's image then becomes the means by which God accomplishes this purpose.

140. With regard to Genesis 1 and God's image, see: I. Hart, 1995: 319-20; van Leeuwen, 1997: v. 4, 645; Stendebach, 2003: v. 12, 394; Middleton, 2005: 53; Towner, 2005: 348; Schmutzer, 2009: 174. Regarding this grammatical construction more generally, see Meek, 1955: 40-43; Lambdin, 1971: 119.

not only clarifies the connection between rulership and God's image, it also provides insight into the environmental implications of humanity's creation in God's image. Many have observed extensive mistreatment of the natural environment in countries where Christianity has historically had influence. Some have suspected that the idea of rulership over creation connected with humanity's biblical status as created in God's image is to blame. They commonly cite an article by Lynn White as key in bringing this matter to the public's attention.[141] White's widely disputed theory is that societies influenced by Christianity have understood humanity's creation in God's image to be about how people are superior to the rest of creation and that creation does not have "any purpose save to serve man's purposes."[142]

The biggest problem with this critique is not the idea that Christianity has had a cultural influence, but the assumption that this influential understanding of being in God's image is truly Christian. As discussed in Chapter 3, creation in God's image is not about attributes that people actually have (rulership or otherwise) and specifically not about ways that people are superior to the rest of creation. Moreover, creation in God's image is not about giving people godlike authority but about making people accountable to God. God intends for people and the rest of creation to exist for the glory of God. Creating humanity in God's image signals that God intends for people to participate in bringing these ends about and that God has given (or will develop in) people the necessary attributes for doing so. Nothing in this picture encourages or even permits neglecting — not to mention abusing — any aspect of creation.

Buttressing the misunderstanding of being in God's image over time has been an inadequate interpretation of the rulership that God intends to develop in people who are in God's image. As noted above, the key verbs in Genesis 1 — *radah* ("rule over," vv. 26, 28) and *kabash* ("subdue," v. 28) — indicate some measure of control and authority. However, separated from the context of being in God's image, these verbs can take on more vio-

141. E.g., Schaeffer, 1970: 12-14; J. Cobb, 1972: 32; Brueggemann, 1982: 32; Wybrow, 1991: 18; G. Peterson, 1996: 223; Hilkert, 2002: 4; C. Wright, 2004: 120.

142. White, 1967: 1205. Others such as Gilkey, 1993: 150-51, have made similar arguments since. See Nash, 1991: ch. 3 for additional examples. However, many — e.g., Pannenberg, 1985: 78; 1991: v. 2, 204; Wybrow, 1991: 33, 166; Haring (2001: 5); Ahiamadu, 2010: 14, 21 — doubt that it is historically accurate to blame Christianity for present-day environmental problems. Shults (2003: 238) notes some others who also consider such blame to be unfounded, including Scott, 1998 and Welker, 1999.

lent and oppressive meanings. Even in other contexts, though, destructive meanings are not necessarily involved. Ruling *(radah)* can be oppressive (e.g., Ezek. 34:4) or it can be associated with furthering righteousness and peace (e.g., Ps. 72:7-8). Even the potentially harsher notion of subduing *(kabash)* the land can primarily refer to liberating it for God-intended purposes (e.g., Num. 32:21-22).[143]

The difference between godly ruling/subduing and ungodly ruling/subduing is the influence of sin. Before the Fall in Genesis, Adam "rules over" all the animals by coming to understand them and naming them (2:20); after the Fall, there is hostility between *adam* (humanity) and the serpent. Before the Fall, Adam is peacefully tilling and keeping the ground (2:15); afterward *adam* is struggling against it (3:17-18).[144] Such difficulty combined with the self-centeredness of sin is a recipe for turning benign ruling and subduing into exploitation. This outcome is understandable, but not what the Bible presents as God's intentions for humanity or the rest of creation. The key here has to do with being in God's image.

God creates humanity in God's image precisely to hold people responsible for carrying out God's agenda.[145] It is God's purposes, not humanity's, that people are to accomplish through ruling and subduing.[146] What this looks like is most evident, as we saw in Chapter 2, in the person of Jesus Christ, who *is* the image of God. In Christ is visible the servant-leader (e.g., Mark 10:43-44), the shepherd who lays down his life for the sheep (e.g., John 10:11).

Accordingly, God castigates some rulers: "you shepherds of Israel who have been feeding yourselves! Should not shepherds feed the sheep?" (Ezek. 34:2). Instead, God insists: "I will feed them with good pasture . . . I will feed them with justice" (vv. 14, 16). There is a parallel between natural and moral goodness here. If people are actually to live in the way

143. For discussion of these terms, see Barr, 1974: 63-64; Gibson, 1981: 80-81; Clifford, 1995: 183-84; Watson, 1997: 293-94; S. Wright, 2003: 33; C. Wright, 2004: 120; 2006: 425-26; Garner, 2007: 124-25; MacDonald, 2008: 324-25; Vorster, 2011: 10.

144. On the contrast between these two settings, see Walsh and Middleton, 1984: 54; Sawyer, 1992: 69-70; Allen, 2000: 81. Pannenberg, 1985: 79 explains this contrast in terms of the difference between responsibility (which God has always intended for humanity) and autonomy (a "modern principle" that "guarantees nature far less protection against its limitless exploitation by human beings than does Christian anthropology").

145. So Towner, 2001: 29; Walton, 2001: 139; Hilkert, 2002: 12-13; van Huyssteen, 2006: 160; Vorster, 2011: 12-13.

146. For elaboration, see Moltmann, 1976: 65; H. D. McDonald, 1981: 35-36; van Leeuwen, 1997: 645; Smail, 2006: 48-49.

God intends for those created in the divine image to live, then they must consistently promote natural and moral goodness, not exploit the human or nonhuman creation for selfish purposes.[147] Knowing what God stands for is crucial in evaluating the merits of being in God's image.[148]

Humanity exists to glorify and be in the image of God, not the other way around. The world does not exist primarily for people; rather, people and the world exist primarily for God. God calls various aspects of creation good in their own right (Gen. 1:4, 12, 18, 21, 25), but humanity is not one of them. Only the combination of humanity and the rest of creation together receives such an affirmation with the words "very good" (v. 31).[149] Humanity's addition to the rest of creation as God sees and intends it makes the rest better, not more oppressed.

As created in the image of God, humanity has a special responsibility for ensuring that this blessed state of the natural world continues. Any special status that creation in God's image confers upon humanity implies no demeaning of anything else.[150] Simply because something is special in a particular way does not mean that other things cannot be special in different ways. If people have invoked humanity's creation in God's image, then, as a justification for environmental exploitation, they are far off course biblically. Any damage they have fostered powerfully illustrates the need for an accurate understanding of what it means to be in God's image (see Conclusion).

Relationship and God's Image

While much Old Testament scholarship has been gravitating toward understanding creation in God's image in terms of rulership, many theologians have inclined toward a different view — that being in God's image is

147. On the relevance of the biblical shepherd motif here, see Brueggemann, 1982: 32-33. Cf. Green, 2011: 273 for a critique of exploitation of nature.

148. If God stands solely for power and control, awareness of that could readily lead those who are in God's image to misuse creation, as Fernandez (2004: 174, 176) and Reynolds (2008: 179) explain.

149. See Spanner, 1998: 217-18, 222-24 for more on the relationship between people and the rest of creation in God's purposes.

150. The idea that certain creatures have special significance, or "speciesism," is discussed in Watson, 1997: 294; C. Wright, 2004: 129. On human uniqueness in biblical perspective, see W. Cobb, 1977: 127; Huebscher, 1988: 14; Bray, 1998: 42.

about relationship.[151] Accordingly, a common contemporary way to categorize approaches to creation in God's image is to identify two particularly popular approaches, one of which is the relational approach.[152] In fact, some consider this approach to be the most popular overall.[153] Although its greatest popularity has been recent, its Protestant roots are in evidence during the Reformation, its Catholic roots reach through earlier figures back at least to Augustine, and its Orthodox roots are traceable to the Cappadocian Fathers.[154]

"Relationship" is a complex term, since it can involve different sorts of associations between different sorts of entities. In the context of humanity in God's image, the relationship most immediately in view is that between people and God. The seminal biblical text in Genesis 1:27 that introduces this relationship connects humanity with God by referring to humanity as created in God's image. Many have seen the God-human relationship as the heart of what it means for people to be in God's image.[155] Others see relationships among people as part of being in God's image also. Either they see such relationships present in the biblical texts referring to God's image (e.g., Gen. 1:27; 9:6; James 3:9), or they consider the relationships among the persons of the Trinity as analogous to what people "image" about God in relationships with other people.[156]

---

151. Erickson (2013: 463) and Cortez (2010: 24) are among those who see "many theologians" in this camp. Some cite a long list of supporters; e.g., Westermann (1994: 1504) cites K. Barth, J. J. Stamm, F. Horst, W. Riedel, F. K. Schumann, W. Vischer, K. Galling, K. Krieger, P. Brunner, W. Rudolph, B. Hessler, T. C. Vriezen, and V. Maag.

152. E.g., Ramsey, 1950: 254; Stendebach, 2003: 393; Hefner, 1984: v. 1, 331; Jónsson, 1988: 223-24; van Leeuwen, 1997: 644; Grenz, 2001: 142; Mitchell, 2013: 88.

153. E.g., Sherlock, 1996: 81. Middleton, 2005: 23 similarly refers to the "pervasiveness" of the approach.

154. Middleton, 2005: 20-21 and Mahoney, 2010: 679 find some support for this approach in the Reformation. Lewis and Demarest, 1994: v. 2, 126 cite the approach in the Franciscan Bonaventure, while Phelps, 2004: 353 and Stark, 2007: 219 see sympathy for this approach much earlier in Augustine. Zizioulas, 1985: 36-40 and J. Reinders, 1997: 202-3 see the image-related teaching of the Cappadocian Fathers such as Gregory of Nyssa as foundational to Greek Orthodox thinking in particular.

155. Those who emphasize the centrality of this relational aspect of being in God's image include Kaufman, 1956: 158; Bonhoeffer, 1959a; Crawford, 1966: 234; Berkouwer, 1975: 59-60, 92-93; Ra. Martin, 1981: 107; Forell, 1982: 24; Navone, 1990: 64; Westermann, 1994: 157-58; Benedict XVI, 1995: 47; Jenson, 1999: 65; Sunderland, 2003: 200; Cahalan, 2004: 73; Canadian, 2005: 4; Mays, 2006: 35; Cortez, 2010: 36; Briggs, 2010: 120; T. Peters, 2010: 219-20; Green, 2011: 274; Thweatt-Bates, 2011: 251-52.

156. Good examples of those who add interpersonal human relationships to relation-

Karl Barth is often credited with bringing particular visibility to the relational understanding of creation in God's image in the last hundred years.[157] He sees humanity as God's "counterpart . . . a Thou that can be addressed by God but also as an I responsible to God."[158] From Genesis 1:27 he also understands humanity's creation as male and female to affirm "man as a genuine counterpart to his fellows."[159] For him, not only are relationships among humans analogous to relationships among God's persons, but humanity's relationship with God is also analogous to relationship within the being of God.[160] Barth developed his view of being in God's image in dialogue with Emil Brunner, whose most influential contribution to the debate was the distinction between "formal" and "material" aspects of God's image.[161] Being in the formal image is the relationship of responsibility toward God in which everyone exists, regardless of their attitude toward God. Being in the material image is the relationship of faith, obedience, and love in which those who are "in Christ" can live.[162]

Understanding being in God's image in terms of relationship means many different things to different people. Some see humanity's relationship with the nonhuman creation to be important, alongside of relationships with God and people.[163] Others agree, but stress the centrality of relationship with God.[164] Some see communication as central to the concept here.[165]

---

ship with God as central to being in God's image include Hilkert, 1995: 200; Thiselton, 2000: 184; Macaskill, 2003: 211; Balswick et al., 2005: 38-40; D. Robinson, 2011: 174; and Breck, 1998: 28-29, who cites in support Greek Orthodox theologians such as Yannaras, Zizioulas, Nissiotis, and Nellas.

157. See Ramsey, 1950: 258; Horst, 1950: 259-70; Jónsson, 1988: 113, 117, 224; J. Barr, 1993: 159, 162; Hoekema, 1994: 50; B. Ware, 2002: 15; Ruston, 2004: 277; H. Reinders, 2008: 238; Treier, 2008: 98.

158. K. Barth, 1958a: 194, 198.

159. K. Barth, 1958a: 184.

160. K. Barth, 1958a: 220.

161. See Hoekema, 1994: 53-54; B. Ware, 2002: 15-16; Smedes, 2014: 196-97.

162. Brunner, 1952: 59-61, 77-78.

163. For example, Hefner, 2000: 73-74; Jeeves, 2005: 183; Towner, 2005: 349; Cahill, 2006b: 67; Gonzalez, 2007: 159-60; Vorster, 2007a: 325; Jersild, 2008: 45; Eibach, 2008: 68; Pineda-Madrid, 2011: 149.

164. For example, Haering, 1915: v. 1, 395-96; Hoekema, 1994: 81; Gunton, 2002: 40-41; 1999: 60.

165. Some — such as A. Murray, 1965: 100; Barentsen, 1988: 36-37; Jenson, 1999: 16, 95; Rogerson, 2010: 185 — affirm this generally, while others (e.g., Vanhoozer, 1997: 177-78) break down the communication in view here into the formal capacity to communicate and the material or actual communication itself.

For others, since God is love, being in God's image is about reflecting or expressing love.[166] Still others emphasize faith or justice as vital to the relationships involved.[167] Many do not see relationship as all that being in God's image entails, though it is a part (generally alongside of one or more of the other human attributes already addressed in this chapter). Some of these advocates include relationship with God with other attributes that constitute being in God's image.[168] Others are more emphatic about adding relationships with people.[169] Still others include the nonhuman creation as well.[170] Definitions of being in God's image that include multiple attributes sometimes construe relationship as taking on a particular form, such as communication.[171]

Most authors use the term "relationship" to refer to actual relationships, rather than mere potential or capacity for relationship or the simple fact of a connection. However, sometimes it is not clear from their description of being in God's image what sort of relationship(s) they envision. Greater clarity generally emerges when they address the impact of sin on God's image. Those for whom sin somehow damages that image or destroys it completely typically have in view people's actual relationships with God, other people, and/or the nonhuman creation. Such actual relationships for them constitute a human "attribute" alongside other attributes such as rulership, righteousness, and reason. The attribute may be understood as completely God-given and God-sustained. Nevertheless it is something

---

166. So H. R. Niebuhr, 1996: 171; Gunton, 1999: 59; 2002: 44; D. Carter, 2003: 83; International, 2004: par. 40; Gonzalez, 2007: 33; P. Peterson, 2008: 33; H. Reinders, 2008: 37-38; Schumacher, 2008: 360. Proponents of this understanding may emphasize people's love for God (e.g., J. Wesley, 1985n: 355; cf. discussion of Gregory of Nyssa in Maloney, 1973: 138-39); or they may also include people's love for one another (e.g., Ramsey, 1950: 259; Welch, 1994: 33; Grenz, 2001: 335; Shults, 2003: 241; Henriksen, 2011: 270) and the rest of creation (e.g., D. Hall, 1986: 107; E. Ross, 1990: 104; McKnight, 2005: 34-35; Reynolds, 2008: 183-84).

167. Faith: see Thielicke, 1966: 194; D. Kelsey, 2009: v. 2, 1027, 1033-34; justice: see Cahill, 2006b: 74.

168. For example, Machen, 1947: 170; Litton, 1960: 117; Rad, 1964b: 390; Thielicke, 1966: 157-58; Mangano, 2008: 8; J. Peterson, 2011: 24.

169. For example, John Paul II, 1997a: 451; Verhey, 2003: 163; Hollinger, 2009: 73.

170. Those who view relationship with the nonhuman creation as a part of being in God's image, either explicitly or in another way connected with a relational understanding of being in God's image, include Ferngren, 1987: 26; Wolff, 1974: 160; Moltmann, 1976: 62; Hoekema, 1994: 82; Bequette, 2004: 8-9; International, 2004: par. 10; McKnight, 2005: 18-19; Reynolds, 2008: 181; Kaiser, 2008: 40; Mahoney, 2010: 681-82; Canceran, 2011: 17.

171. See McFadyen, 1990: 40-41; Schwöbel, 2006: 50; Schmutzer, 2009: 167-68.

that people are able (enabled) to participate in — and can become disabled from participating in (or from participating in well) due to sin.

If all that someone means by associating relationship with image is that people have some connection with God that cannot be damaged and that serves as the basis for human dignity and human destiny, then such a view is in line with the biblically grounded understanding that the present book affirms.[172] Even the idea that people have a "relational capacity" may fit within this understanding, if it is something that sin does not diminish.[173]

However, most relationship-oriented concepts of creation in God's image entail something different. They often describe being in God's image entirely in terms of actual relationships (or relational ability or capacity) with God, people, and/or the rest of creation — all of which sin has damaged. They may instead, with Brunner, see part of the image in terms of a connection unaffected by sin and another part of it in terms of actual relationships that sin does damage. Or they may, as Barth did during his career, begin with a focus on actual relationships virtually destroyed by sin and move toward a more nuanced position under the influence of the way that the Bible invokes the image concept. In all such cases, though, at least some continuing vulnerability to damage on the part of God's image evidences that some sort of actual human "attribute" is or was involved, though other terminology may be used.

A strength of this approach to being in God's image is that it affirms the whole human being as somehow involved with God's image (see Ch. 3) — not just one part, such as reason.[174] However, it reduces what is important

172. For instance, H. Reinders, 2008, with some reliance on Jensen, 1999, develops a view of creation in God's image somewhat similar to the "formal" aspect of the image in Brunner. In this view, God establishes a "relationship" with humanity that is not a function of human attributes. Reinders is particularly clear that this is present even when people "have no awareness of this relationship," e.g., because they are profoundly intellectually disabled (p. 244). Arguably the term "connection" is preferable to "relationship" for denoting the association between God and humanity that does not necessarily involve participation on people's part. "Relationship" then can be used exclusively in its more common sense of an association that can change and can involve degrees — better or worse, closer or more distant, etc.

173. "Relational capacity," as used by King (1965) and many others, may or may not envision actual relationships necessarily flowing from that capacity. Because of the ambiguity of that term, some such as Larkin (1993: 16-17), drawing on D. Hall (1986), make it clear that they understand relationship in terms of actual relationships rather than mere capacity or potential for relationship.

174. See discussions in O'Mathuna, 1995: 201, and Dehsen, 1997: 261.

about people to something they do (i.e., relate), which is problematic.[175] By claiming that being in God's image involves only (some or all of) people's relationships, the approach is at odds with the teaching of the Bible.[176]

A common starting point for justifying the view that creation in God's image is about relationship is Genesis 1:26-27. Right after God creates humanity in the image of God in verse 27, the text also says that God created them male and female. The inadequacy of considering creation as male and female to be the definition of being in God's image will be a topic for discussion later in this chapter.

Some find the image-related material in Genesis 1 to be so meager that they look more to Genesis 2 to find relational material relevant to being in God's image.[177] Genesis 2 does indeed provide a much fuller account of humanity's creation than Genesis 1, but there is no textual evidence that Genesis 2 is addressing the "image" concept. Just because it conveys important information about humanity's relationships with God, one another, and the nonhuman creation does not mean that such relationships constitute the meaning of being in God's image.[178]

The dearth of textual support continues in Genesis 5 and 9. Although Genesis 5:3 and 9:6 refer to Seth as fathered in Adam's image and people created in God's image, the point of those references does not appear to be the relationships involved (other than the basic idea that there are close connections, as discussed in Ch. 3).[179] The status of a connection rather than the content of a relationship similarly appears to be the point of James 3:9 and 1 Corinthians 11:7. New Testament image passages such as Romans 8:29, 2 Corinthians 3:18, and Colossians 3:10 invoke God's image as God's intended standard for human growth, rather than in terms of a relationship. As Chapters 6-7 will discuss, relationships are essential as the source and outworking of that growth, but they do not define the image of Christ according to which or toward which people are growing.

Beyond the lack of textual support, there are numerous other indicators that relationship is not what constitutes being in God's image — at least not relationship in the commonly understood sense of something

---

175. Vorster, 2011: 15 addresses this problem.

176. Among the many who address the exegetical problems with defining humanity's creation in God's image in terms of relationships, see B. Childs, 1993: 568; J. Reinders, 1997: 192; G. Peterson, 2008: 471; Erickson, 2013: 468.

177. For example, see McFadyen, 1990: 31-39; Cortez, 2010: 25.

178. See P. Bird, 1981: 139; Bray, 1991: 223; Watson, 1997: 303.

179. So P. Bird, 1981: 139; Wenham, 1987: 31; Mathews, 1995: 168.

more than the fact of connection. First, as discussed in Chapter 4, the relevant biblical texts suggest that God's image has not been damaged by sin. However, there is ample biblical evidence that sin has damaged all types of human relationships.[180] In the section on image-as-righteousness above, the devastating effects on people's relationships with God and other people have already been noted. The section on rulership above describes the similar effects on people's relationship with the nonhuman creation.

The biblical evidence also indicates that being in God's image is not a matter of degree, varying from person to person the way that relationships do. Those who overlook this consideration (see Ch. 3) tend to justify their view of being in God's image on the inadequate basis that it refers to how people are excellent, how they are unlike animals, or how they are like God — all matters of degree. Explanations of why being in God's image should be understood in terms of relationship commonly bear the marks of this thinking. Barth, for example, describes creation in God's image — so-called "being in encounter" — in terms of four relational excellences, which manifestly differ in degree from person to person.[181] Others appeal to how human relationships differ from animal relationships in order to justify their understanding.[182]

Many more relationship-based views of humanity as created in God's image, though, emphasize how humanity's relationships are like God's.[183] Some of those explicitly draw an analogy between human relationships and relationships within the Trinity.[184] This approach to being in God's image tends to view "image" as a verb rather than a noun.[185] People actually "im-

---

180. See Hoekema, 1994: 84-85, for a summary of this damage, though the Bible consistently presents it as damage to relationships, not to God's image. Lubardic, 2011: 578, drawing on the Greek and Russian Orthodox scholars Lossky, Yannaras, Zizioulas, and Horuzhy, describes as the essence of sin the "fall from person [loving communion] . . . into the individual [autonomic individuality]."

181. K. Barth, 1958a: 250-74, who notes that gladness in relationship is "the *conditio sine qua non* of humanity" (p. 266).

182. E.g., see Boer, 1990: 62; Green, 1999: 54.

183. For example, Thiessen, 1949: 221; Brunner, 1952: 76; Cook, 1975: 90-91; John Paul II, 1997a: 450-51; Gunton, 1999: 58; Grey, 2003: 223; Balswick et al., 2005: 36.

184. For example, Campbell, 1981: 14; Hughes, 1989: 51-52; Stendahl, 1992: 146; K. Douglas, 1995: 76-77; Grenz, 2001: 294; Jastram, 2004: 63; J. Johnson, 2005: 178; Duncan, 2008.

185. D. Hall, 1986: 98 and McMinn and Campbell, 2007: 33 explicitly advocate for the verbal form; McLeod, 1999: 47-48; Plantinga, 2002: 33; Fernandez, 2004: 188; and Fedler, 2006: 82-83 illustrate its use.

age" or "mirror" or "reflect" God today.[186] It is telling, though, that the Bible's authors use a noun instead in all of the central "image" passages (see Ch. 3). The implication is not that how humans relate and how well they image God is unimportant in the Bible. Both are very important; but a careful reading of the Bible suggests that neither is what being in God's image means.[187]

There is an important difference between what something is and what its implications are. As many have observed, God intends good relationships, among other things, to characterize those who are in God's image — whose standard and model is the divine image. In order to have good relationships, God must create people;[188] and those people must have at least the potential ability to relate.[189] Actual relationships involving people then flow from, rather than constitute, what being in God's image is.[190] They are one of the purposes for, and fulfillments of, humanity's creation in God's image.[191]

In other words, people themselves, and not just their relationships, are in God's image (see Ch. 3). Regaining a sense of the importance of community and relationship by critiquing individualistic understandings of the Bible has been an important contribution of recent relational theology. However, focusing exclusively on community rather than also on the members of that community does a different disservice to the Bible. It undermines the appreciation for and protection of each human being that the status of being in God's image explicitly provides. There is an irony in any relational theologies that are so attentive to the importance of "context" that they shortchange the full context of what constitutes a human being. They do this by excluding from being in God's image everything that is significant about people except their relationships.

186. For "mirror" language see Brink, 2001: 116 (drawing upon Calvin) and Smail, 2003: 22; 2006: 153. For "reflect" language see Kyung, 1994: 254; Grenz, 1998: 624; Cortez, 2010: 26.

187. Watson (1997: 304) indicates that in his earlier theological writing (1994: 107-8, 149-51) he viewed relationship as what defines being in God's image — which more careful exegetical study showed to be not in line with the teaching of the Bible.

188. On this distinction, see Piper, 1971: 31; H. Harris, 1998: 226-27; Moreland, 2009: 4-5.

189. On this potential ability as part of what it means to be in God's image, see Mullins, 1917: 54; J. Murray, 1977: 46; Hodge, 1982: v. 2, 96-97; J. Reinders, 1997: 189; I. H. Marshall, 2001: 54; Gardoski, 2007: 9; Gonzalez, 2007: 129.

190. So *The Cloud*, 1981: 122, 194; Bray, 1991: 222-23; Baker, 1991: 39; García-Rivera, 1995: 101; Mathews, 1995: 166; Sherlock, 1996: 37.

191. So Mueller, 1934: 209; Maston, 1959: 5; Gardoski, 2007: 13; Harrell, 2008: 15.

This one-sided focus on community as opposed to particular people is evident in many descriptions of the view that relationship is what constitutes being in God's image. For example, "insofar as man is born an individual, he is not in the image of God." Similarly, "the individual human is incapable of" manifesting God's image. Also, "*I am* not created in the image of God — only *we* are created in the image of God."[192] Yet the Bible associates the term "image" with particular people as well as groups.[193] Most prominently, Christ *is* the image of God (see Ch. 2). Christ is a single being who is relational, but that does not change the fact that it is Christ, and not the relationships in which Christ is engaged, whom the New Testament identifies as the image of God.[194]

Similarly, in Genesis 5:3, the single human being named Seth is what is in the image of his father Adam.[195] In Genesis 9:6 and James 3:9, it is particular people who are being protected because they are in the image of God.[196] Other passages such as 1 Corinthians 11:7 are talking about more than particular human beings — in this case men in general — but even here it is "a man" *(aner)* himself, and not the relationships in which he is engaged, whom Paul identifies with God's image.

Relationships are a vital part of people's lives. However, they can be destructive rather than supportive. Accordingly, it is important not to overlook the protective status or responsibility that being in God's image gives to particular people. Each is unavoidably responsible for his or her own life to some degree. People are not merely the product of whatever relationships are available to them.[197]

Put differently, equating relationships (or relational capacity if that is an attribute damaged by sin) with being in God's image is reductionistic. It fails to recognize that there is much more to human beings and to being

192. The three quotations are from Tavard, 1973: 191; Cortez, 2010: 35; and Johnston, 1998: 138. Similarly, see Brunner, 1952: 64; Sherlock, 1996: 35; Volf, 1998: 183; Grenz, 2002: 54; Stephenson, 2005: 7.

193. See Mathews, 1995: 173; Frame, 2006: 231; and the numerous sources cited regarding this topic in Chapter 3.

194. So Buswell, 1962: 247; B. Ware, 2002: 16.

195. See discussion in Waltke, 1989: 4.

196. So Watson, 1997: 299; B. Ware, 2002: 16; McFarland, 2005: 2.

197. See H. Harris, 1998: 231-32 for an elaboration of this analysis. Also, Bray, 1991: 223 and Wells, 2004: 30, who draw upon Seerveld, 1981: 75 and Dooyeweerd, 1960: ch. 8. Cone (1986: 92-93) notes how even relationships characterized by "freedom" can perpetuate oppression.

in God's image than relationship.[198] Animals engage in relationship, as do Satan and demons.[199] Unless one brings to bear other considerations such as the attributes discussed above (reason, righteousness, etc.), relationship can be oppressive. Many who incline toward the idea that being in God's image somehow involves relationship have become sensitive to the insufficiency of relationship alone as the essence of what creation in God's image entails.[200]

Of even greater concern is the danger to some human beings posed by viewing creation in God's image as relationship. As noted previously, being in God's image is an important biblical basis for respecting and protecting people. However, many who understand being in God's image in terms of relationship do not consider everyone necessarily to be in God's image.[201] For some, people are in God's image "when" they are in appropriate relationships.[202] For others, people are in God's image "insofar as" or "so long as" they are in such relationships.[203]

If a good relationship with God must necessarily be a part of the picture, as is commonly the view, then all non-Christians may lack the status of being in God's image.[204] Not all commentators even see Christians as being in God's image in a complete sense, since that is a status that one "grows into" over time.[205] Accordingly, defenses of a relationship-oriented view of being in God's image often acknowledge that God's

---

198. See elaboration in Clark, 1969: 222. For an example of such reductionistic language, see the claim in Letham, 1990: 70-71 that "our relationship with God is really what we are."

199. See elaboration in Piper, 1971: 32; Larkin, 1993: 19; Hoekema, 1994: 52.

200. For examples, see K. Douglas, 1995: 77; Brink, 2001: 90-91; Gonzalez, 2007: 157. Similarly Stephenson, 2005: 8, drawing upon E. Russell, 2003.

201. Brink, 2001: 116-17 and Cortez, 2010: 26 have both reached this conclusion after studying the literature advocating relationship as definitive of being in God's image. H. Harris (1998: 229), Gushee (2012: 44), and Erickson (2013: 468) note serious problems accompanying the exclusion of some from fully being in God's image.

202. E.g., Ramsey, 1950: 255; Gunton, 1999: 59; Plantinga, 2002: 33.

203. Gregory of Nyssa, 1972: 545; Horst, 1950: 266-67; Bingemer, 1989: 58; Gonzalez, 2007: 156.

204. According to the World Council of Churches (World, 2005: par. 82), only those in communion with Christ "truly image God." For Brunner (1952: 59), addressing one major aspect of being in God's image, one who does not love God "no longer bears the 'image of God.'" Cf. Zizioulas (1985: 15): "From the fact that a human being is a member of the Church, he becomes an 'image of God.'" Cairns (1973: 187, 191) finds this ultimately to be Barth's view.

205. E.g., Graff, 1995: 131-32; Macaskill, 2003: 218; Rogerson, 2003: 28.

image in people is lost,[206] or at least significantly damaged.[207] The door is wide open for protecting some lives more than others, based on assessments of their present or future relationships.[208] (For historical examples, see Ch. 1.)

In light of the disconnects between a relationship-based understanding of being in God's image and the teaching of the Bible, and how problematic this view is for numerous other reasons, its relatively recent popularity suggests that cultural influences may be primarily responsible for its appeal.[209] As discussed in Chapter 1, cultural influences have always made certain views of God's image more intuitively appealing than other views for a while. In the present case, many have attributed the rise of a relationship-oriented understanding of being in God's image in the days of Barth and Brunner to the philosophy of existentialism popular in their day.[210] Others see in their writings the undue influence of the modern notion of an "I-Thou" relationship,[211] or the imposition of other theological commitments that should flow from, not redefine, the biblically based concept of creation in God's image.[212]

Other more recent influences, such as postmodernism's emphasis on socially constructed "realities" (including selves) and increasing sensitivity to people with disabilities, have similarly encouraged understanding being

206. As in D. Hall, 1986: 106; Gonzalez, 2007: 33; Mahoney, 2010: 679. See also Maloney (1973: xiii-xiv), who cites examples from the early church such as Irenaeus and Athanasius; and Fichtner, 1978: 171, who draws on the teaching of the Roman Catholic Church's *Pastoral Constitution on the Church in the Modern World*.

207. As in Boer, 1990: 62; McFadyen, 1990: 20; Baker, 1991: 77; Sherlock, 1996: 42-43; Wells, 2004: 36; Cahill, 2006b; Fedler, 2006: 82-85; Roberts, 2011: 471.

208. For instance, D. G. Jones (1998: 18) supports leaving some human infants to die without treatment on this basis. H. Harris (1998: 232-33) suggests other larger-scale examples involving slaves and women in certain parts of the world.

209. Treier, 2008: 120 accordingly notes that most biblical scholars see this view as a "foreign import." Gonzalez, 2007: 161 adds that theologians supporting a relationship-oriented understanding of being in God's image have often been unduly influenced by "philosophies that predate the Christian tradition."

210. Examples include Piper, 1971: 30-31; Cairns, 1973: 195; Baker, 1991: 112; Lewis and Demarest, 1994: v. 2, 128-30; Gardoski, 2007: 9. Cf. the appeal to Sartre in Zizioulas, 1985: 107 to help define "original sin."

211. So Eichrodt, 1967: 129; P. Bird, 1981: 132; J. Barr, 1993: 160-61; Cortez, 2010: 27; Vorster, 2011: 4, 8; Mouw, 2012: 256. Barth discusses this idea, for example in K. Barth, 1958a: 245.

212. See analysis in Lehmann, 1970: 113; J. Barr, 1993: 162-63; G. Peterson, 1996: 224-25; Crouch, 2010: 8.

in God's image in terms of relationships.[213] So have recent efforts to understand being in God's image in terms of the Trinity, in which contemporary views of human relationships have sometimes influenced the conception of the Trinity that is supposed to serve as the model for human relationships.[214]

Before this section on relationship concludes, there are two particular types of relationship that warrant special comment: parent-child and male-female. Each of these relationships is sometimes considered to be central to what being in God's image means.

Those who see the parent-child relationship as central to being in God's image commonly take their cue from Genesis 5.[215] There, after reaffirming that God created humanity in the divine image (v. 1), the author adds that Adam became the father of a son, Seth, who was in his image (v. 3). Those who see in the Adam-Seth relationship an explanation of what it means to be in God's image readily discard many particulars as incidental. Maleness and shared genetics are set aside as incidental to the deeper point being made.[216] But then why not acknowledge that the parent-child relationship itself is incidental to what being in God's image necessarily involves? After all, the parent-child relationship is not always either referenced or even apparently in view in the various biblical passages about being in God's image. That suggests it is possible to relate the two ideas, but that neither is necessary to define or explain the other.

As discussed earlier (Ch. 3), the deeper point here is that "creation in the image" refers to an intended reflection of various attributes of the Creator (as opposed to the degree to which they currently do reflect those attributes). It calls for good relationships of various sorts, including parent-child. But God intends much more than just good relationships for those who are in God's image. What all is included, and how the New Testament

---

213. Balswick et al. (2005: 31) observe the ways that contemporary philosophical emphases are influencing concepts of creation in God's image in a relational direction. Similarly, see Hentschel, 2008: 48. The influence is not always subtle: note the title of a 2003 book: *Reforming Theological Anthropology: After the Philosophical Turn to Relationality* (Shults). Reynolds (2008: 177) admits that he has formulated a relationship-oriented approach to being in God's image that is "intentionally" constructed in a way that will be especially sensitive to people with disabilities.

214. See analysis in Watson, 1997: 299-300; Kilby, 2000: 432-45.

215. Examples of commentators who identify being sons or children of God as what it means (in full or in part) to be in God's image include Kline, 1977: 257; 1980: 23-24; McDonald, 1981: 41; Curtis, 1992: 390; Walton, 2001: 131; Horton, 2005: 107; 2007: 244; Mangano, 2008: 7-8; Treier, 2008: 191; Schmutzer, 2009: 177; Crouch, 2010: 10.

216. A good illustration is Crouch, 2010: 11.

distinguishes being in God's image from being a child of God, must await Chapter 7's discussion of relationship as part of God's intention. Moreover, there is no indication in the Bible that those who lack or have a diminished degree of parent-child relationships (e.g., child orphans or single adults with no living parents or children) somehow are in God's image to a lesser degree than others are. Such a logical implication would not bode well for the respect people would have for either group.

A second type of relationship that warrants special comment here is the male-female relationship. As noted above, right after God creates humanity in the image of God in Genesis 1:27, the text also says that God created them male and female. Barth asks, "Could anything be more obvious" than that the male-female relationship is "the definitive explanation given by the text itself" regarding what being in God's image means?[217] A number of others have echoed this claim, albeit less brazenly.[218] Still others have found a significant place for this view in their multifaceted understandings of creation in God's image.[219] An exclusively communitarian perspective, in which all people by themselves are devoid of God's image, is sometimes at work here. As one commentator maintains, "it is only through" sexual encounter "that life may be called human, an image of God."[220]

Some supporters would say that they do not literally have in mind a relationship between a male and female, but rather see that relationship as symbolic of other relationships. Where that is the case, then the previous analysis of being in God's image in terms of relationship applies. Others, though, do see the male-female relationship, with its gendered and/ or sexual dimension, to be literally involved. For that view some further comments are in order here.

The reference to male and female in Genesis 1 right after humanity's creation in the image of God leads many commentators to conclude that males and females are both fully in God's image.[221] However, some, often

<hr />

217. Barth, 1958a: 195.

218. E.g., Bailey, 1959: 268; Balthasar, 1967: 206; K. Peters, 1974: 101; P. Jewett, 1975: 33-35; Trible, 1978: 17; Campbell, 1981: 14; Lazenby, 1987: 65; Grenz, 1998: 620-21; 2002: 52; Jastram, 2004: 63; cf. discussion in DeFranza, 2011: 17.

219. Cook, 1975: 91; Hoekema, 1994: 97; Lewis and Demarest, 1994: v. 2, 135; John Paul II, 1997a: 450; Lints, 2006a: 214; Schwöbel, 2006: 50; C. Wright, 2006: 427; Smail, 2006: 44; Mangano, 2008: 5; Hollinger, 2009: 75; Kilcrease, 2010: 28.

220. McFadyen, 1990: 32.

221. Middleton (2005: 206) and Cortez (2010: 16) characterize this as by far the dominant view. Among the innumerable examples are Mueller, 1934: 209; Farley, 1976: 174; Gill,

influenced by misinterpretations of 1 Corinthians 11:7 (see discussion in Chs. 1 and 3), have concluded that females are not in God's image at all[222] — or at least not completely so, as men are.[223]

Understanding the male-female relationship as defining creation in God's image has ambiguous implications for this debate. On the one hand, both males and females would be fully involved in God's image. Yet men by themselves would not be in God's image, nor females by themselves. Such an understanding suggests that living the monastic life with people of a single gender, long revered in the church, disconnects people from being in God's image.[224] The difficulty here is even more acute if the distinctiveness of the male-female relationship has something to do with sexuality or marriage. In that case, sexually abstinent single people might not be in God's image as fully as other people — an idea foreign to the biblical texts. Moreover, those who see the male-female relationship as analogous to the God-human relationship, with both relationships as aspects of being in God's image, may particularly incline toward the view that females in this analogy are not on a par with men in terms of their basic (image-related) status.[225]

An important question here is: To what, exactly, is the male-female relationship referring? Is something other than a relationship between a male and a female in view? It seems quite a stretch to suggest that this relationship (and so being in God's image) somehow includes humanity's

---

1978: 391; Fichtner, 1978: 36; C. Carter, 1983a: 207; Trible, 1978: 18-19; Wenham, 1987: 32-33; Mathews, 1995: 164, 173; Watson, 1997: 299; John Paul II, 1997a: 448; Allen, 2000: 79; I. H. Marshall, 2001: 55-56; Mays, 2006: 36; Frame, 2006: 230; Kaiser, 2008: 40; Schmutzer, 2009: 180.

222. Historical examples include the Encratites (later called Severians), an early Gnostic sect, and much later, Peter Martyr (see A. Strong, 1907: 524; Pieper, 1950: 523-24). More recently, examples of those who conclude Paul teaches in 1 Corinthians 11 that women are not in God's image include McCasland, 1950: 86; Clines, 1993: 427; Collste, 2002: 34; McFarland, 2005: 169. (Clines, 1993: 428 and Goldingay, 2003: 222 imply this understanding.) See Chapter 1 for other examples as well as the harmfulness of claiming that females are not in God's image — or are less so than males.

223. Canceran (2011: 19) finds this view quite common throughout history. McLeod (1999: 59-61, 80-82) discusses it in the early church leaders Diodore, Chrysostom, and Theodoret. Lazenby (1987: 63-64) and Collste (2002: 53-54) describe support for it in Aquinas and other medieval theologians. Litton (1960: 111) and Pannenberg (1991: v. 2, 214-15) see it as Paul's view in 1 Corinthians 11.

224. See Tavard, 1973: 190-91; Hoekema, 1994: 97.

225. Ruether, 1995: 282-84 develops this analysis in dialogue with Karl Barth, Paul Jewett, and Jürgen Moltmann.

relationship with the nonhuman creation. Even seeing the male-female relationship as encompassing the God-human relationship seems far-fetched (unless, as discussed above, only males are like God). The author of Genesis 1 is careful to distance God from the sexuality often associated with other deities.[226] Seeing the male-female relationship merely as representing the person-person relationship might seem less problematic on its face. However, it seems odd that the text would specify gender to define a concept (creation in the image) that does not necessarily involve any consideration of gender.

Barth and others supporting his approach to creation in God's image, though, also have in mind the male-female relationship "imaging" the plurality within God. However, since God is three persons yet one God, the parallels are problematic. God is not two persons, but three; nor are God's persons differently gendered.[227] Human existence can be profoundly embodied in a gendered way without the necessity of implicitly attributing the same to God via the concept of God's image.[228]

Together God's persons make up the single being of God, whereas any male-female combination involves two beings. (Even if "two become one" in marriage, God's image involves more than married people.) No wonder Barth is forced to admit that "the analogy of relation does not entail likeness."[229] However, that should signal that something is amiss here. As we have seen, the Bible portrays humanity as being in the likeness-image of God, not as the analogy of God.

A closer look at the biblical support for understanding creation in God's image in terms of the male-female relationship may help to explain what is amiss. Genesis 1:27 consists of three lines, the first two of which are parallel and expressly concern God's image. The third line then says that

---

226. So Rad, 1972: 60-61; P. Bird, 1981: 156-57. Accordingly, DeFranza (2011: 25) argues against including notions of sexuality in the image-of-God concept.

227. See concern over such disconnects in Wilson, 1973: 357; Berkouwer, 1975: 73; Ruether, 1995: 269; D. T. Williams, 1999: 181-82; Gunton, 1999: 58; Frame, 2006: 231-32.

228. The logic in Grenz, 2001: 294, 303, for instance, appears to be that if embodied and engendered existence are not a part of being in God's image, they lose their importance. However, there is no reason to consider unimportant any aspect of the way God created human beings to be as part of his "very good" creation (Gen. 1:31), whether or not it is part of being in God's image. And in any case, seeing all relationships — among people, within God, between God and people — as sexual relationships (by any definition) is less plausible than seeing sexual relationships as one type of relationship among others. See further discussion on this point in Hughes, 1989: 18-19.

229. Barth, 1958a: 196.

God created humanity male and female. As many have observed, there is little exegetical support for concluding that this third line is a statement of the same idea for the third time.[230] One reason is that the third line in three-line Hebrew poetic units normally serves the purpose of introducing a different idea.[231] Perhaps that explains why one prominent Old Testament scholar, irked by the sweeping claims of Barth's exegesis quoted above, equally brazenly calls it "a particularly ill-judged and irresponsible piece of exegesis."[232]

Several considerations help to explain the reference to male and female in Genesis 1:27. Since the author has just identified humanity per se as created in God's image, further describing humanity as male and female clarifies that both men and women are in God's image. The author thereby makes two affirmations in that single verse. As discussed in Chapter 3, being in God's image is not something merely for human rulers or other special representatives; it involves all of humanity. And it is not men only; women likewise are in God's image.[233] In the context of Genesis as a whole, this last affirmation is necessary lest Genesis 2 leave the impression that it was only the man Adam whom God created in the image of God, with Eve coming later in an unrelated way.

Rather than seeing the third line of Genesis 1:27 as pointing to what precedes, it is just as plausible — many would say more so — to see it as pointing to what immediately follows. What precedes is about God's image; what follows is about people multiplying. Maleness and femaleness are precisely what is required for multiplying.[234] There are different pairs of words that the author could have used to identify maleness and femaleness. *Ish* and *isha* would have been a more social/relational and specifically human pair of terms to use (and in Genesis 2 they do in fact appear in reference to people). However, in Genesis 1 the author instead chooses *zakar*

---

230. E.g., Gregory of Nyssa, 1972: 553-54; P. Bird, 1981: 149-50; 1995: 5-28; Hughes, 1989: 18; Ruether, 1995: 272; Volf, 1996: 173-74; Watson, 1997: 303-4; Cooper, 1998: 256.

231. See analysis of Alter, 1992: 177-78; also affirmed in Middleton, 2005: 49-50; Treier, 2008: 120; Sands, 2010: 36.

232. J. Barr, 1993: 160. The assessment of Barth's position by eminent theologian Wolfhart Pannenberg (1991: v. 2, 205) is similar, if more irenic: "exegetically one can hardly justify his interpretation." On the exegesis, see also Di Vito, 2010: 173.

233. So H. D. McDonald, 1981: 36-37; Pannenberg, 1991: v. 2, 206; Frame, 2006: 231; Merrill, 2006: 203.

234. For this interpretation see, Gregory of Nyssa, 1972: 564; Hughes, 1989: 19; Fatum, 1995: 61-63; Clifford, 1995: 182-84; Ruston, 2004: 280.

and *neqeba,* the same biological/reproductive-related terms the author later uses for animals whose line God wants to preserve from the coming flood in Genesis 6 (v. 19).[235]

The reference to humanity as male and female, then, not only confirms that both Adam and Eve are in God's image but may well also point toward how the influence of that image is to grow. Human multiplying not only expands the scope of God's image (see comments on Genesis 5 below) but it also makes it possible for people to live out some of their God-intended responsibilities as people created in God's image, such as godly care for creation (see final section in this chapter below).[236] In other words, being male and female facilitates being in God's image; it does not constitute it. This understanding guards against the temptation to think of animals as being in God's image simply because they too are male and female.[237]

Beyond Genesis 1 there is little indication that the male-female relationship constitutes being in God's image.[238] As noted above, Genesis 2 and 3 have much to say about relationship but do not connect that with being in God's image. Genesis 5:1-3 associates the maleness and femaleness of humanity even more closely with God's blessing (of fruitfulness — cf. 1:28) than Genesis 1 does. There image language describes the Adam-Seth relationship, hardly a male-female relationship.[239] New Testament passages about God's image (to be discussed in Ch. 6) make no mention of male-female relationship at all. Accordingly, those who understand creation in God's image in terms of the male-female relationship tend to invoke biblical passages about this relationship that have no connection with God's image in an attempt to make their case.[240]

235. So Kline, 1980: 34-35; P. Bird, 1995: 10-11, 22-23; Dumbrell, 2002: 16; Middleton, 2005: 50.

236. See analysis in Wolff, 1974: 162; Loader, 2004: 29; Frame, 2006: 231.

237. As many have noted, being in God's image is something attributed to people only, so it would not make sense to define it exclusively in the exact words that are soon thereafter applied to animals. See P. Bird, 1981: 148-49; J. Barr, 1993: 171; Watson, 1997: 299; Cooper, 1998: 184; I. H. Marshall, 2001: 54; Goldingay, 2003: 222; Mouw, 2012: 256.

238. Many who have studied all of the relevant passages have been impressed similarly (e.g., W. Schmidt, 1983: 194-95; Pannenberg, 1991: v. 2, 205; Frame, 2006: 231).

239. See McLeod, 1999: 48-49 (drawing on Vogels); Bequette, 2004 (drawing on Gregory of Nyssa); Towner, 2005: 348-49.

240. For example, Barth (1958a: 195) suggests that nine passages from the Prophets and two from Revelation, among others, buttress his case, though they in fact make no reference to God's image. Grenz (1998: 621-22) similarly invokes Revelation. Such passages

In the end, a particularly good test for whether or not the male-female relationship is necessarily central to being in God's image is to look at Jesus Christ, whom the New Testament straightforwardly identifies as the image of God (see Ch. 2). There is no evidence in the image-related biblical passages to suggest that the authors are viewing Christ there in terms of a male-female relationship.[241] In fact, when Christians grow to be more in line with God's image (see Chs. 6-7), it is because they are "in Christ." And it is specifically "in Christ" where "there is no longer male and female" (Gal. 3:28).[242]

A Better Understanding of Human Attributes

If actual human attributes such as reason, righteousness, rulership, and relationship are not what constitute being in God's image, what is a better way to understand such attributes and their association with God's image? As explained in Chapter 3, an approach more in line with biblical teaching is to recognize that being in God's image is about humanity's special connection with God, which God *intends* to result in people's reflection of God in many ways. Those intended likenesses include reason, righteousness, rulership, relationship, and many other human attributes that are praiseworthy. But creation in God's image has to do with God's intention for who people should be. In contrast, human attributes as we now experience them are not what constitutes being in God's image — nor are they perversions of what creation in God's image once was.

Humanity in God's image is about connection and reflection — a special connection with God intended to reflect attributes of God, to God's glory and for the flourishing of people as God has always meant them to be. In other words, such attributes are intended consequences of being in God's image.[243] They are among the purposes for which God has created

---

make a strong case for the importance of relationships, including the male-female relationship. However, connecting that to God's image is imposed on the text, not learned from it.

241. See related discussion in Hughes, 1989: 19-20; O'Neil, 1993: 148; Wells, 2004: 35.

242. For further analysis, see Brunner, 1952: v. 2, 65; Witherington, 2009: v. 2, 637; also D. Hart, 2002: 543, who draws on Gregory of Nyssa.

243. Hummel (1984: 86) notes that "theoretically-minded Westerners" are prone to read the Bible's discussion of current human attributes into the definition of God's image rather than recognizing that "the text's interest is almost totally in the image's result, not its content."

humanity. There are so many such attributes, and they vary considerably (at least in degree) from person to person. Accordingly, it is not surprising that the biblical texts referring to God's image do not attempt to describe all of them. In fact, as many commentators have noted, the biblical passages on God's image do not say all that much about what God's image entails.[244] Instead the rest of the Bible is left to explain and illustrate what God intends people to be and do.

Consider first, then, the place of reason in God's purposes. By creating humanity in God's image, God has created an unbreakable connection with humanity, with the intention that humanity would live with rational and spiritual attributes that in some small but wonderful measure reflect God's own. Reason, then, is one of the human attributes that ought to flow from being in the image of God — it is not, in itself, what constitutes being in God's image.[245] It is a particularly strategic capacity since it is a prerequisite for other human attributes that flow from being in God's image, such as rulership[246] and relationship.[247] Because of sin, reason has not developed in people as God intended. That does not mean people are devoid of reason. Rather, it indicates that people's reason is distorted until Christ breaks the power of sin to allow reason to develop and function as God intends.

Having righteousness is similarly not the definition of what it means to be in God's image; rather, righteousness ought to flow from being in God's image.[248] That is God's intention. Righteousness is also an attribute foundational to other attributes that God intends to characterize human beings. For reason or rulership to operate properly, for instance, righteousness must accompany them.[249] While there was a "very goodness" to all of creation in the beginning (Gen. 1:31), human righteousness needed to

244. That is the overall view in J. Barr, 1968; Sawyer, 1974; W. Schmidt, 1983; D. Carson, 2010: 22. Cf. discussion in Jónsson, 1988: 224.

245. For example, see discussion in Wills, 2009: 25. Cf. Barentsen, 1988: 36, who less precisely sees reason as a precondition of all that being in God's image entails.

246. So Gill, 1978: 443; Wennberg, 1985: 37; Treier, 2008: 73; along with other sources cited in the section on rulership above.

247. On reason as a means of knowing God, see Athanasius, 1885: chs. 11, 13; Brunner, 1947: 102-3; Thiessen, 1949: 219; along with other sources cited in the section on relationship above.

248. God's intentions are thus human obligations. This theme is developed in Wilson, 1973: 358; J. Murray, 1977: 38; Hall, 1986: 84; Hughes, 1989: 59.

249. See J. Wesley, 1985d: 409-10; Dabney, 1878: 294; McCasland, 1950: 89; C. Wright, 2006: 426.

develop further to be all that God intended it to be (more on this in Chs. 6-7). Sin not only prevented that development but perverted the original goodness. Because human sin attacks the attributes of God involved in God's image — preventing (for the moment) some aspect of God's intentions from being realized — sin is always basically against God.[250] As David acknowledged to God: "Against you, you alone, have I sinned" (Ps. 51:4).

Rulership, while also not the definition of being in God's image, is something that God intends for people to exercise because they are in the image of God.[251] Reason and righteousness, among other God-honoring attributes, ought to guide rulership since they, too, should flow from being in God's image. As discussed above, rulership will then look like stewardship informed by solidarity and servant leadership, rather than like oppression and exploitation. Although particular human beings can exercise rulership to a degree, as Adam originally did in the Garden of Eden, rulership at its best involves humanity as a whole leading throughout God's creation with all the attributes God has provided.[252] So in a world fragmented by sin, it is not surprising that we do "not yet see" such rulership (Heb. 2:8-9), as discussed above. But once God's people become united in Christ, such rulership becomes possible.[253]

Relationship, meanwhile, is often confused with what it means to be in God's image — perhaps because in its godward form it has to do with a form of connection with God. However, as described above (in this chapter and Ch. 3), the special connection involved in being created in God's image is a fact of creation that sin cannot alter. It assures human dignity and sets the stage for human destiny. In contrast, relationship involves communication, faithfulness, and other qualities that sin does indeed damage.[254] Relationship plays a central role in human existence far beyond any explicit association it has with being in God's image.[255] Where God's image

250. C. Carter, 1983b: 247 develops this theme.

251. So Moritz, 2011: 327. Verhey (2003: 161) uses the language of "vocation" to signify God's intention. Brunner (1952: v. 2, 68) emphasizes that people exercise rulership because they are (already) in God's image.

252. See Walsh and Middleton, 1984: 55; Jónsson, 1988: 222.

253. For further development, see D. Johnson, 1992: 12.

254. Some, such as Brunner (1952: 59-60), use the term "relationship" but have in mind "connection" in the more narrow sense. Others use alternate terms as broad as relationship that lead them to include more elements of actual relationship in the concept of creation in God's image than is warranted. E.g., Calvin (1960a: bk. II, ch. 2, sec. 1) speaks of "participation in God"; John Paul II (1997b: 519) of a "bond with God."

255. One can develop a biblically sound anthropology that is quite relational without

is concerned, relationship has to do with God's intentions, rather than the actual relationships that everyone has today with God, with other people, and with the nonhuman creation. Actual God-honoring relationships flow from being in God's image, to the degree that sin does not interfere. They are not per se what is in God's image; people are.[256]

People have many God-given attributes, including relationship. As Christ through the Spirit breaks the power of sin in people's lives, those attributes, in special ways unique to each individual and community — and impossible to anticipate fully — reflect the attributes of God to God's glory.[257] With John, Christians acknowledge that "what we will be has not yet been revealed"; yet they can also affirm with confidence that when Christ finally returns "we will be like him" (1 John 3:2). That is the destiny of humanity created in God's image.

---

imposing on the Bible a definition of being in God's image that is exclusively relational. See Treier, 2008: 197.

256. Relational accounts of being in God's image that are biblically grounded gravitate toward this recognition. For example, Lints (2006a) generally understands being in God's image in terms of relationship, yet at one point he speaks of the "relational dynamic that connects image (person) to original (God)" (p. 209, parentheses his). This statement reflects a recognition that there is a meaningful distinction between people and their relationships, with being in God's image attaching more precisely to the former.

257. See Thielicke, 1966: 176-77; Roy, 2009: 15; Sexton, 2010: 197. Hilkert (2002: 6-7) and Witherington, 2009: v. 2, 643 explore the role that gender plays in how people uniquely manifest the range of attributes God intends in those who are created in the divine image.

PART III

Human Destiny

CHAPTER SIX

Humanity's Renewal in God's Image: Primary Voices

God created humanity to be in the image of God. As explained in Chapter 3, being in the image of God involves special connection and intended reflection. God's special connection with people is the source of their dignity and helps explain their destiny. God's intention that people reflect numerous divine attributes is the source of their destiny and helps explain their dignity. Sin has badly damaged people by rendering them incapable of living out God's intention for them. God's intention (for what the reflection should look like) has not changed due to sin, nor has the fact that people are specially connected with God. In other words, sin has not damaged what being in God's image constitutes. Sin has damaged people, but not God's image (see Ch. 4).

So it is people, not God's image, that need changing. In fact, they so thoroughly need changing that their renewal amounts to a new creation. God's provision for that is Jesus Christ, who is the image of God. Christ reveals what it looks like to be intimately connected with God and to reflect all of the godly attributes God intends for humanity to reflect. As discussed near the end of Chapter 2, Christ as the image of God and humanity's creation according to the image of God are profoundly related. As this chapter will demonstrate, so are humanity's creation according to God's image and humanity's renewal according to Christ, God's image.[1] Christ is both the standard and the enabler of who people are to be, as created in God's image.

---

1. On the continuity of New Testament renewal with the Old Testament concept of humanity created in God's image, see Maston, 1959: 9; Watson, 1997: 282-83; International, 2004: par. 11.

There are three central New Testament passages that describe human-ity's renewal in (i.e., according to, *kata*) God's image in Christ. Three other passages echo the first three in ways that clarify some of the implications involved. The three central passages use different expressions to identify the renewal taking place in Christ, but the concept is the same in all three cases. It is the idea that people are being liberated from sin to fulfill all that God intends them to be as human beings created in the image of God. In the Incarnation the true identity and content of God's image has been revealed as nothing less than the very person of Christ (2 Cor. 4:4; Col. 1:15). So the New Testament presents humanity's renewal as taking place according to the image of God in Christ — or according to the image that is Christ, or simply, according to the image of Christ.[2] In Romans 8:29 the focus is the image of God's son; in 2 Corinthians 3:18 it is the Lord's image; and in Colossians 3:10, the image of the one who (re)created the new humanity.

People in Christ now have a more specific orientation than toward the generic image of God — their standard and aspiration is now specifically the image of Christ (who is God). They are renewed according to (Col. 3:10) — and thereby conformed to (Rom. 8:29) — and thus transformed into (2 Cor. 3:18) — Christ's image. None of these expressions suggests a changing image; it is people who are changing according to an unchanging image. The problem with humanity is that people have never been able to fulfill what God intends for those created in the divine image. In Christ, now they are increasingly able actually to become what they are supposed to be: like God in Christ (Eph. 4:24; 1 John 3:2), bearing Christ's image (1 Cor. 15:49).

However, the connection with Christ involved in bearing Christ's im-age is so intimate that the New Testament often speaks (in various terms) simply of conforming to *Christ* rather than conforming to the *image of Christ*. These are not two different ideas, but a single concept. Conforming to the image of Christ essentially means conforming to the image that is Christ — specifically conforming to the image of God that is Christ — with people's special connection with God and God's intended reflection of God particularly in view.

As explained in Chapter 2, Christ demonstrates what it means to be God's image; and Christ calls people to follow. Christ as the image of God

2. On the image of Christ and the image of God as essentially the same thing, see Piper, 1971: 22-23; Furnish, 1984: 215; D. Kelsey, 2009: v. 2, 999.

lives without the shackles of sin, free to be all that God intends. Christians, in Christ, will ultimately also become free of sin and able to be all that God intends for humanity. Nevertheless, they will remain human. So even when they become God's image in Christ after Christ's return, they will not become all that Christ is as God's image, for Christ is both divine and human. Rather, in Christ people gain the opportunity to realize their specifically human destiny — to become truly human.

The Primary Passages

It will be instructive to examine separately each of the six passages identified above, beginning with the three primary statements about humanity's renewal according to God's image in Christ. Nevertheless, as image-related topics arise prominently in the discussion of a particular passage, the relevant contribution of the other passages warrant consideration at the same time.

Romans 8

In Romans 8, Paul presents the big picture of what renewal in God's image is all about — where it ultimately ends. God has determined that Christians will "be conformed to the image" of Christ, *the* son of God (v. 29), which includes membership in God's family (v. 29) and glorification (v. 30). Paul signals the crucial importance of the image concept here by interrupting his summary description of what God has done for Christians (foreknew, predestined, called, justified, glorified) with an explanation of the central role that the image of Christ plays in all of this.[3] Christians become the human image of God in Christ by becoming conformed to Christ. As always, the idea of image here evokes elements of connection and reflection. Ultimately, Christians will not have merely the sort of connection and reflection consisting primarily of God's intention at creation. Rather, they will experience an intimate connection with God in Christ and will actually reflect God's attributes to the full extent that human beings can do so, for sin will be gone.

Paul here is describing the nature of Christians' connection with God

---

3. See discussion in Moo, 1996: 534.

in general and with Christ in particular. He could have simply stated that Christians will become "the same form as" *(symmorphous)* God. But he knows that this conforming involves a process that God put in place before humanity's creation and is bringing to completion in Christ. It involves humanity's creation according to the image *(eikon)* of God and is fulfilled as people identify with Christ, God's *eikon* of God, to the glory of God. Christians, then, more specifically become "the same form as" Christ, and even more specifically become the same form as Christ in Christ's capacity as the image of God. In Paul's words, Christians become conformed to the image that is God's son *(symmorphous tes eikonos tou huiou autou)*.[4]

The "foreknew . . . glorified" sequence in which Paul locates reference to the divine image, then, suggests that he has in mind a fulfillment of humanity's creation in God's image.[5] The concept of election/predestination (v. 29), which is closely related to the concept of intention that is integral to creation in God's image, reinforces this impression. So does the immediately preceding discussion of the joint fallenness of humanity and the rest of creation, which harkens back to early Genesis.[6] According to Paul in verse 3, humanity becoming the likeness of God in Christ also flows from God in Christ becoming the likeness of humanity (see Ch. 2 for the rich connection between the Incarnation and the image of God).

The focus in Romans 8:29 is not so much on how Christians are currently changing in accordance with God's image in Christ.[7] Rather, the focus is more eschatological.[8] Human destiny — the fulfillment of God's intentions for humanity — is in view. The stated purpose of humanity conforming to God's image is that Christ may be "the firstborn *(prototokos)* within a large family." Christ as *prototokos* (see Ch. 2), when connected

---

4. Many, such as Scroggs, 1966: 69; Hughes, 1989: 27; Fitzmyer, 1993: 525; and Byrne (1996: 272), see this to be the most accurate translation of the Greek text and best explanation for what would otherwise be a needless repetition of the idea of form/image. If one prefers a translation of "Christ's image" over the "image that is Christ," the meaning here is ultimately the same. Describing people in terms of Christ's image, since Christ is God, is still to identify them with God's image, but God's image as that can only be understood and experienced in Christ.

5. So Bruce, 1963: 176; Moo, 1996: 534; Gunton, 1999: 58-59; Grenz, 2001: 225-26, 231-32; 2004: 622.

6. See discussion in Moritz, 2011: 324 (election) and in Keck, 2005: 210 and Sexton, 2010: 203 (creation).

7. Hoekema, 1994: 24 and Byrne, 1996: 273 are among the many who note the difference between Romans 8:29 and 2 Corinthians 3:18 in that regard.

8. See Moo, 1996: 534-35 and Grenz, 2001: 229 for further development of this theme.

with Christ as image in Colossians 1, refers not just to Christ before the creation of the world but also to Christ's resurrection. Similar ("first fruit") language appears in the image-of-Christ discussion in 1 Corinthians 15, where Paul connects bearing Christ's image with the certainty of bodily resurrection.

Accordingly, it is not surprising that the word *symmorphous* appears elsewhere in the New Testament only in Philippians 3:21. There Paul explains that in the glorification involved in resurrection, Christ will "transform the body of our humiliation that it may be conformed to the body of his glory." For Paul, conforming to Christ is something that is accomplished in the end, when all aspects of the person are glorified, including the body. Nevertheless Christians do not merely wish for this; it is a "sure thing," a "done deal." Many commentators see Paul signaling this assurance through his use of past-referring verbs here: not only *foreknew, predestined, called,* and *justified,* but also *glorified.* Christians can endure the worst suffering that the world can inflict (vv. 18-23, 33-36) because they can rely on this entire sequence, including their ultimate glorification. At the start of verse 29 the word *hoti* (because) literally presents this sequence — especially conforming to (the image of) Christ — as the reason for Christians' confidence. They can know that for them all things will work together for good (v. 28).[9] Christ as firstborn is not only preeminent over but also in solidarity with humanity.

Misunderstanding the first verbs in the sequence, *foreknew* and *predestined,* is easy to do. Paul here is not talking about a decision of God to include some and exclude others, regardless of their wishes. Rather, Paul is talking about God's determination to provide a glorious destiny for those whom God knows are to constitute God's family. This is not the knowledge of one actually experiencing intimacy with an existing person (as when "Adam knew Eve," Gen. 4:1). The people God is foreknowing here do not even exist at the time of foreknowing. Rather, this is the knowledge that particular people will exist in the future, and for them God has a plan that will conform them to God's image, Christ.[10]

The completion of that conforming, glorification, is "about to be revealed to us" (v. 18). It will occur at the point of bodily resurrection, as

---

9. On this theme here, see Cairns, 1973: 49; R. Jewett, 2007: 529. Blackwell, 2011: 159 adds that the verbs here, while referring to the past, also convey a sense that what has been assured from long ago will in fact be completed in the future.

10. So Achtemeier, 1985: 144; Byrne, 1996: 272; Witherington, 2009: v. 2, 322-23.

noted above, and will include the fulfillment of God's intentions for people to reflect God-in-Christ in many ways.[11] Not merely outward action but also personal character is in view here.[12] The process and content of glory will be elaborated below in relation to 2 Corinthians 3:18, where glory plays a more prominent role.

Implicit in this discussion of Romans 8 is the understanding that conforming to God's image, Jesus Christ, involves the whole person — particularly since conforming is not completed until the resurrection of the body.[13] Moreover, the entirety of justified humanity (i.e., followers of Christ), not just particular people, is the subject of the conforming here. This is a both/ and, not an either/or. Particular people experience particular "sufferings" (v. 18) and "weaknesses" (v. 26); and when the Spirit helps (e.g., by interceding in prayer; vv. 26-27), specific people and trials are involved. Yet just as there is one image, Jesus Christ, so there is one humanity being conformed to that image.[14]

There are many indications of this community focus in the text. The nouns and pronouns throughout this part of Romans 8 are plural. Paul has in mind "all of us" (v. 32), meaning all whom God justifies on the basis of Christ's death, resurrection, and ascension (vv. 33-34). In verse 30, Paul includes all such people in the overall process of calling, justifying, and glorifying. Conforming to Christ's image is about God generating "a large family" (v. 29), not just a large number of unrelated individuals. This is essential, for the very idea of being a family underscores that there are implications for people's relationships with one another, not just for their individual relationships with the family's head.

This combined focus on particular people and yet also on those who love God in Christ as an integrated whole is consistent with references to God's image throughout the Bible.[15] A good example is in Colossians 3, where the Colossians are reminded that they have stripped off the old humanity with its practices (v. 9) and have clothed themselves with the new humanity, "which is being renewed . . . according to the image of its creator" (v. 10). The focus is the singular *"anthropos"* (often translated

---

11. See Murray, 1968: 319; Piper, 1971: 21-22; Berkouwer, 1975: 109; Fitzmyer, 1993: 525; Mangano, 2008: 170.

12. So Hodge, 1950: 285; Grenz, 2001: 230; D. Kelsey, 2009: v. 2, 954.

13. Among the many who understand the whole person to be in view here, see Byrne, 1996: 268; Keck, 2005: 217; Witherington, 2009: v. 1, 238-39.

14. See Grenz, 2004: 623; D. Kelsey, 2009: v. 2, 953; Kilcrease, 2010: 33.

15. As Cairns, 1973: 52; Walsh and Middleton, 1984: 86; and Vorster, 2011: 20 observe.

"man," or else "self" to be more gender neutral), together with its practices (which vary from person to person). This terminology suggests to each recipient of the letter that the author is addressing that person particularly. Moreover, the very renewing of the new humanity argues against equating this humanity with Christ and thus an exclusively corporate understanding, for Christ needs no renewal. Christ instead is the image, the standard, according to which every Christian's new humanity experiences renewal.

Yet there is at the same time a profoundly corporate sense in which the family of believers has stripped off the old humanity and clothed themselves with the new humanity. The very singularity of the reference to humanity *(anthropos)* here also indicates that people in some sense are discarding an old version of humanity (or *adam,* to use the Hebrew Old Testament equivalent of *anthropos*) in favor of a new humanity (a new *adam*). Although the process of renewal takes time, all believers are developing in the same direction toward a complete unification in Christ, the ultimate *adam* (recall discussion of 1 Cor. 15:45-49 in Ch. 2).[16]

"In that renewal there is no longer Greek and Jew . . ." (Col. 3:11). The greater the renewal, the more that people move away from their individualism to recognize and live out their new corporate humanity. At the end of humanity's renewal, the conformation of all Christians to Christ's image is complete and the corporate aspect of God's image comes to the fore. However, the charge to move in that direction comes initially to particular people who must embrace this image — this corporate destiny — as their own.[17] Moreover, bodily resurrection, while occurring simultaneously for everyone, will be recognizably unique for each person.

Ephesians 4 echoes Colossians 3 by reminding readers that they have put away the old humanity (v. 22) and clothed themselves with the new humanity through a process of renewal designed to make them like God (vv. 23-24). In Ephesians, this discussion flows from instruction on spiritual gifts and the body of Christ. That instruction has a corporate goal since the gifts and parts of the body are to work together toward unity and maturity (v. 13). Yet each gift and part is important for a different reason and Christ uniquely empowers each. Verses 4-7 strike the balance: "There is

---

16. On the corporate dimension of God's image as connected with Adam and Christ as representatives or models of humanity, see Dunn, 1988: 495; 1996: 222-23.

17. Schweizer, 1982: 197 sees a focus on individual persons as central here; Ra. Martin, 1981: 107 emphasizes the corporate dimension; O'Brien, 1987: 190-91 affirms both. Bonhoeffer, 1959b: 272 describes the movement away from individualism.

one body. . . . But each of us was given grace according to the measure of Christ's gift."[18]

Particular people are indeed in God's image, as Chapter 3 explains. Human life and human dignity depend upon that, as the Conclusion will elaborate. The conforming, transforming, and renewing of people according to Christ's image profoundly affects each person even without regard for their relationships with others.[19] However, biblically, people are always envisioned in those relationships because that is how God has created and called them to live. Some commentators describe humanity according to Christ's image in terms of community;[20] others, in terms of communion, corporate reality, solidarity, or simply church.[21] By whatever name, this communal aspect of humanity in God's image is particularly easy to neglect in cultures preoccupied with individuals and their rights, and so requires explicit attention.

Who exactly is this community? God has created all humanity in the image of God — specially connected with God and intended by God to reflect various godly attributes to God's glory. However, sin impedes the fulfillment of those intentions. In the Incarnation, Christ comes to remove sin, establishing the opportunity for a much closer connection between humanity and God and personally reflecting the attributes of God that humanity ought to embody. Since sin is precisely the reason that God's intentions for humanity in God's image have not been fulfilled, only those in whom sin has been eliminated can fulfill God's intentions. Those are the members of Christ's body whom God is conforming, transforming, and renewing according to the image of Christ. Most commentators appropriately consider this body and image of Christ to involve only Christians. They are the "saints" (*hagioi*, holy ones) of Romans 8:27-28 "who love God."[22] Even if every member of humanity does not fulfill humanity's

18. C. E. Lincoln, 1990: 287; O'Brien, 1999: 331; Hoehner, 2002: 610 are all impressed by the balance here.

19. For further development of the importance of not minimizing the connection of particular people and God's image here, see Pannenberg, 1991: v. 2, 199.

20. E.g., Clines, 1968: 103; Grenz, 2001: 334; 2002: 54; Green, 2011: 277.

21. E.g., Zizioulas, 1975: 442-43 (communion); S. Wright, 2003: 43 (corporate reality); McFarland, 2005: 54 (solidarity); Bonhoeffer, 1959b: 274 (church).

22. See discussion in Barth, 1958a: 203-5; Wild, 1985: 137; Hoekema, 1994: 89; Middleton, 2005: 17. While some suggest that even non-Christians must be regarded as members of Christ's body and so Christ's image (e.g., McFarland, 2005: 59), that idea tends to be based on a conflation of Christ as "head over all things" (Eph. 1:22) and Christ as head of the church/body, as if they are referring to the same things. That Christ's body is specifically

destiny, humanity itself fulfills that destiny. The Pilgrims who sailed across the Atlantic Ocean to establish a colony at Plymouth, Massachusetts are appropriately said to have fulfilled their destiny, even though not every Pilgrim survived the journey.

2 Corinthians 3

If Romans 8 presents the big picture of where renewal in God's image ultimately ends, 2 Corinthians 3 describes the process of how people get there. Whereas Romans 8 shows the church, Christ's body, as conformed to Christ's image once glorification is complete, 2 Corinthians 3 explains that Christians "are being transformed into the same image from one degree of glory to another" (v. 18). This process of increasing glory (sanctification) begins for believers even before death and resurrection.

In line with consistent biblical teaching described above, the process involves both particular Christians and the church as a whole. The reference to different degrees of glory signals that different people are at different stages of transformation and that the Spirit works in them accordingly. However, the emphatic "we all" *(hemeis pantes)* as the subject of verse 18, and the focus on one image, that of Christ, are reminders of the movement toward corporate unity underway here.[23]

Outside the Bible, it is common for two accusatives, x and y, to follow the active verb "transform" *(metamorphoo)* — something transforms x into y. However, this verb appears in the New Testament only as a passive verb, in a way that nuances its meaning. Simply suggesting that Christians (x) are transformed into y ("the same image" — *ten auten eikona*) risks the unnuanced misinterpretation that Christians are being changed into something they presently have no connection with.[24]

Paul's only other use of *metamorphoo* comes in Romans 12:2, where he is concerned about people who are conformed to "the pattern of this world." He wants them instead to be formed differently — to be "trans-

---

"the church" is straightforwardly affirmed in various New Testament texts (e.g., Eph. 1:22-23; 5:23; Col. 1:18, 24; cf. 1 Cor. 12:27-28). Affirming this is not to denigrate non-Christians or nonhuman creatures in any way; it is simply to acknowledge that their dignity and destiny, such as they are, lie elsewhere than as the body of Christ.

23. On the corporate dimension here, see Grenz, 2001: 250-51; S. Wright, 2003: 40-41.

24. For further detail, see Robertson, 1923: 486; Lenski, 1946b: 949; Blass, 1961: sect. 159(4); M. Harris, 2005: 315.

formed." Although care is necessary when translating compound verbs, the sense in this case appears to combine the meaning of *meta* ("after," when followed by an accusative) and *morphoo* (to form). People are to be formed after (conformed to) something other than the world. In 2 Corinthians 3:18, Paul more fully explains that they are to be formed after Christ's image. The process of forming in view here culminates in people being fully conformed to Christ's image (Rom. 8:29). This passage in 2 Corinthians 3 describes both Christians being (trans)formed "after" or "according to" Christ's image and what Christians will ultimately be transformed into.

It is acceptable simply to maintain the more common terminology of Christians being transformed "into" Christ's image. After all, people now are not God's image but are en route to becoming God's image — they are "in God's image" (see Ch. 3).[25] Nevertheless, one must remember that this means Christians are already becoming better able to fulfill the divine intentions that have always marked their lives as created in God's image.

Paul describes Christ's image as the "same image" in 2 Corinthians 3:18, indicating that he has just referred to an image. The immediately previous word, the verb meaning "seeing as though reflected in a mirror" *(katoptridzomenoi)*, contains the idea of an image that is "seen" (cf. below regarding the related idea of "reflected"). What is seen here is "the glory of the Lord."

Just a few verses later, Paul clarifies what he has in mind. People need to be "seeing the light of the gospel of the glory of Christ, who is the image of God" (4:4). As already discussed in Chapter 2, while people are in the image of God, Christ *is* the image of God. Christ's connection with God is far more intimate; and, with no sin involved, Christ's attributes are an actual reflection of God's. People need transformation from their current fallen/unglorified state — in the image of God yet bearing the image of Adam (see Ch. 4). They need to be transformed so that they can actually and completely bear the image of Christ as God always intended for them to do. The image of Christ is full of glory. As people are transformed, they change "from one degree of glory to another" (3:18) until their glorification is complete with resurrected bodies (see below).

Since what people are seeing is the glory of the Lord, which Paul goes on to describe more completely as "the glory of God in the face of Je-

---

25. On 2 Corinthians 3:18 as a confirmation that people are not God's image but can become God's image, ultimately, in Christ, see International, 2004: pars. 12-13; M. Harris, 2012: 64-65.

sus Christ" (4:6), one could say that Christ is the mirror reflecting God's glory (in line with Hebrews 1; see Ch. 2).[26] However, it is important not to press any metaphor farther than the author intends. The main point here seems to be that when one looks to Christ, the image of God, one sees God's glory that God intends for Christians to manifest as well once they are transformed.[27] Christ (or the image that is Christ) is the standard. Sin prevents Christians from living according to that standard. So Christians need transformation in order to become the same image that Christ is.[28]

Becoming all that the image of Christ entails, then, requires "transforming." The Gospels use this verb to describe Christ's Transfiguration (Mark 9:2; Matt. 17:2), suggesting that powerful change is involved. The only other New Testament use of this verb is in the challenge of Romans 12:2 to be "transformed" by "renewing" (the same two verbs used to connect people with Christ's image in 2 Cor. 3:18 and Col. 3:10). Transforming, like renewing, refers to a process of change in 2 Corinthians, as both the present tense of the verb and the resulting degrees of glory underscore.[29]

Significantly, it is people who are changing. They are the subject of the passive verb "being transformed." No image is changing. The image, here Christ's image, is the fixed standard according to which people are changing. This is an important observation, because of how often commentators claim that God's image is changing (see Ch. 7). The increase in people's glory manifests the change they are undergoing. Although Chapter 2 has already discussed the difference between image and glory in relation to Christ, the distinction warrants further attention here.

The image-glory passage in 2 Corinthians runs from the mention of "glory" in 2 Corinthians 3:7 to the reference to what is "visible" in 4:11. In 3:7, Paul introduces glory by talking about how visible it was on the face of Moses, who represented the "ministry of condemnation" (v. 9). However, now there is a "greater glory" present in the "ministry of justification" (3:9-10). This observation underscores an important feature of glory: its variability. Glory can differ from person to person and can be more in some and less in others. It can also change for particular people.

---

26. So Watson, 1997: 282, 301; D. Kelsey, 2009: v. 2, 998.

27. See Thrall, 1994: 284-85; Lambrecht, 1999: 56; M. Harris, 2005: 315; Morgan, 2010: 170.

28. For this as the reference of "same," see Lenski, 1946b: 950; Scroggs, 1966: 69; Stanley, 1984: 129; Barrett, 1993: 125; Painter, 2001: 48; Collste, 2002: 33; Matera, 2003: 102; Smail, 2003: 23; Litwa, 2008: 118.

29. On this theme, see Lenski, 1946b: 949; Furnish, 1984: 241; Martin, 1986: 72.

Whereas the glory visible on Moses faded (v. 13), the glory that Christians have is increasing. They are being transformed "from one degree of glory to another" (v. 18).[30]

Paul explains the need for this transformation in Romans 1. People have lost God's glory. They "have exchanged the glory of the immortal God for images resembling a mortal human being" or animals (v. 23). As many have noted, Paul here is confirming the diagnosis of Psalm 106:20 ("They have exchanged the glory of God for the image of an ox") in language that points back to God's intentions for humanity in Genesis 1.[31] The truth, among other things, is that God deserves worship and glory from people created to be in God's image. But people have "exchanged the truth about God for a lie and worshiped and served the creature rather than the Creator" (v. 25).

The reason that Paul characterizes this as a lie rather than merely a bad choice is that it contradicts God specifically at the point of what God intends in terms of images. God does not want images reflecting human desires to direct worship away from God. God has created people according to the divine image — to reflect godly attributes — so that people will direct worship Godward, resulting in God's glory (and by extension people's). However, people have abandoned that glory and are contradicting who they are created in God's image to be. Image and glory are meant to be together as they are in Christ, not separated as they are in fallen humanity.

One loses an important aspect of the intended contradiction here by mistakenly thinking that Romans 1 teaches that people have lost both the image and glory of God.[32] There is no indication here that people have lost God's image (see discussion in Ch. 4), only that they have lost God's glory.[33] Overlooking the important difference between image and glory, then, is one of the primary reasons that some commentators conclude that God's image, like God's glory, has been lost or damaged in humanity.

Equating image and glory in 2 Corinthians 3:18 leads to the view that

30. For an elaboration of these changes and this contrast, see Hughes, 1989: 26-27; Thrall, 1994: 286; Hafemann, 1996: 408; Grenz, 2001: 248-49; M. Harris, 2005: 316-17.

31. These connections are developed in Hooker, 1990: 81-82; Collins, 1999: 409-10; Green, 2011: 277.

32. Examples of those who suggest this include Kümmel, 1963: 68, drawing on Althaus, 1941; Bell, 1994: 196; Ecumenical, 2004: 512.

33. Examples of those who put the focus on glory rather than image in terms of what is lost include Pope, 1875: v. 2, 18; Murphy-O'Connor, 1982: 82; Mathews, 1995: 164, 170-71.

Paul just as well could have written that Christians are being transformed "from one degree of image to another."[34] However, such a view undermines the crucial New Testament idea that the image (of Christ) is a standard according to which Christians are being transformed — not a changing target. In this very verse, Paul contrasts humanity's changing glory with the unchanging standard of Christ's image. These concepts are not identical or interchangeable.[35] Various discussions of 1 Corinthians 11:7 also essentially equate image and glory, leading to the conclusion that people who have lost God's glory have also lost God's image.[36] It is telling, though, that Paul never reaches that conclusion himself. Instead he uses the two terms in distinctly different ways.

Equating image and glory, and so concluding that God's image is damaged or lost in humanity, has a long history. Paul inherited a Jewish tradition that viewed righteousness and thus glory as essential to being in God's image. Image and glory had become almost synonymous, with both considered lost or badly damaged in the Fall.[37] Consequently, it is understandable to read that view into Paul's writings.[38] Paul, however, often reworked inherited or culturally influential ideas in light of God's revelation in the Old Testament and in Christ; and this is a case in point. For Paul and other New Testament authors, it is accurate to say that image and glory are closely "linked."[39] However, that is because glory so aptly helps to explain how transformation into Christ's image progresses, not because they are the same thing.[40] Christ overcomes sin, enabling the transformation that people require due to the ravages of sin and modeling what the end result will look like (see Ch. 2). Glory in people grows as

34. So Kittel, 1964d: 397; cf. the similar view in Scroggs, 1966: 99, 104.

35. For further development of this observation, see Furnish, 1984: 216; D. Garland, 1999: 200.

36. So Gill, 1978: 479; Kline, 1980: 31.

37. On this tradition as a backdrop to Paul, see Jervell, 1960: 100-104; Scroggs, 1966: 64-65; Wilson, 1973: 360; Conzelmann, 1975: 188.

38. As already explained in Chapter 4, some early church leaders recognized as unbiblical the claim that humanity lost God's image. However, they devised an equally unbiblical separation of image and likeness in order to equate only likeness with glory, and argue that humanity has lost that. The history of this discussion well illustrates the problem of completely separating terms that the Bible connects as well as equating terms that the Bible significantly distinguishes.

39. So, for example, Wilson and Blomberg, 1993: 9; Mathews, 1995: 171-72; I. H. Marshall, 2001: 59.

40. This perspective is well developed in Bray, 1991: 204-5, 219-21.

they grow increasingly like Christ, reflecting the attributes of God and glorifying God in the process.[41]

Christians are drawing closer to Christ, experiencing what it means to be "in" Christ, and thereby sharing in Christ's glory. Glory then ends up working in two directions. On the one hand, God's glory is transforming Christians to manifest attributes reminiscent of who God is and for what God stands. Christ himself gives an example in one of his prayers: "The glory that you have given me I have given them, so that they may be one, as we are one" (John 17:22). This is God's glory — the same glory that God intended to share with humanity at creation;[42] however, now it is conveyed to Christians as Christ's own.[43]

On the other hand, the manifesting of such relational and other attributes in turn brings more glory *(doxa)* to God. These may be attributes, for instance, of the mind (Rom. 15:6), of righteousness (2 Cor. 9:13; 1 Pet. 2:12), of service (Acts 21:20; 1 Pet. 4:11), or of the body, particularly through enduring suffering (1 Cor. 6:20; 1 Pet. 4:16). Through all these God can be glorified *(doxadzetai).*[44] In fact, glorifying God in this way has always been the divine intention behind creating humanity in the image of God.[45]

Christians will not experience the fullness of glory before death or Christ's return. However, they experience — and God receives — degrees of this glory even now as people are transformed into Christ's image from one degree of glory to another.[46] Hymn-writer Charles Wesley conveys the desire of the Christian who has this understanding:

In me, Lord, thyself reveal,
Fill me with a sweet surprise;

41. On Paul's similar view of glory in 1 Corinthians 11:7, involving people's manifestation of godly attributes to the honor of God, see Feuillet, 1975: 160; Godet, 1957: 120; Barentsen, 1988: 34-35; Thiselton, 2000: 835.

42. For elaboration, see Calvin, 1960a: bk. II, ch. 12, sec. 6; Dunn, 1988: 495; Beale, 2008: 131; Schmutzer, 2009: 175.

43. So Furnish, 1984: 216; Shults, 2003: 240-41; Vorster, 2011: 20.

44. See Murphy-O'Connor, 1982: 83-84; Fee, 1987: 516; Beale, 2008: 282; Witherington, 2009: v. 1, 22.

45. For elaboration, see Grudem, 1994: 440-41; C. Wright, 2006: 404-5; Kilcrease, 2010: 27.

46. On this "already but not yet" aspect of glory, see Kittel, 1964e: 250-51; Moltmann, 1985: 225, 227; Schnackenburg, 1992: 160; G. Peterson, 1996: 225; Shults, 2003: 237; Gardoski, 2007: 31-36; Horton, 2006: 193.

Let me thee when waking feel,
Let me in thy image rise. . . .

O that I might know thee mine!
O that I might thee receive!
Only live the life divine,
Only to thy glory live![47]

This backdrop sheds some helpful light on the meaning of one of the words in 2 Corinthians 3:18 that appears only here in the Bible. Paul writes about Christians who are "seeing the glory of the Lord as though reflected in a mirror." Here "seeing . . . as though reflected in a mirror" translates the verb *katoptridzomenoi,* which is in the middle voice. Because of the ideas of seeing and reflecting bound up with the mirror idea embedded in this verb, many people debate whether Paul is saying here that people are seeing the Lord's glory or reflecting it.

Favoring the translation of "reflecting" is understandable.[48] In verse 7 Paul refers to Moses reflecting God's glory on his face. According to verse 13, Moses wore a veil over his face to prevent the Israelites from seeing that the glory was fading. Paul then relocates the veil metaphor, indicating that a veil has covered the hearts/minds of unbelievers ever since and prevents them from seeing the truth of the gospel (vv. 14-15). When one turns to the Lord, says Paul, the veil is removed (v. 16). Because Paul says that new believers have "unveiled faces," some see Paul returning to the original metaphor of the veil over Moses' face. Just as Moses once reflected the Lord's glory, now Christians do. Yet others maintain that removing the veil in unbelievers enables them to see rather than to reflect.

The overall argument of 3:18–4:6 suggests that Paul intends both.[49] Seeing comes first, followed by reflecting, as was the case with Moses. The verb in question, then, is probably best translated as "seeing," with the notion of "seeing something as in a mirror" included.[50] Then the transforming

---

47. C. Wesley, 1889.

48. E.g., Lenski, 1946b: 948; Barth, 1958a: 204; Berkouwer, 1975: 111; Schweizer, 1982: 64; Bray, 1991: 217.

49. As early as Chrysostom (see Barrett, 1993: 124-25), some commentators have seen evidence of both meanings in the single verb — e.g., Sherlock, 1996: 58-59; D. Garland, 1999: 199; Painter, 2001: 48; N. Wright, 1992a: 185. However, even if that is not an accurate rendering, both ideas are at least present in the single verse — see Wilson, 1973: 358.

50. Furnish, 1984: 214 presents more detailed Greek and Latin evidence, and Thrall,

subsequent to that in verse 18 conveys the idea of reflection; and Christ is the image (of God) where people see the reflection of God's glory (as Paul in chapter 4 goes on to clarify — see below).[51] It would seem odd to suggest that transformation takes place after something is reflected. Normally reflection would follow or be concurrent with transformation.[52]

Paul's argument does not primarily maintain the similarity of present believers and Moses; rather, it contrasts them. Paul emphasizes this contrast in verses 7-11 before introducing the veil metaphors. Moses had only occasional access to God and God's glory, whereas Christians are continually seeing the Lord's glory (as the present tense of *katoptridzomenoi* underscores). The limited similarity present is between Moses removing the veil (that separated him from God), whenever they met (Exod. 34:34), and the veil separating unbelievers and God now needing removal as well. However, people cannot simply take off the veil the way Moses did. This removal and the transformation that follows "comes from the Lord" (2 Cor. 3:18).[53] Even more pointed is the contrast here between unbelieving Israelites and believing Christians. That contrast is largely lost, though, if the translation describes unbelievers as nonseeing (3:14; 4:4) and believers as reflecting rather than seeing.[54]

Paul continues the veil metaphor in chapter 4 and clarifies what he has just said in 3:18: "[T]he god of this age has blinded the minds of unbelievers, so that they cannot see the light of the gospel of the glory of Christ, who is the image of God" (4:4).[55] People see through their faces, and the veil that lies between their faces and Christ's must be removed. People need "the light of the knowledge of the glory of God in the face of Christ" (v. 6). Removing the veil is about gaining the ability to see with the face

---

1994: 294-95 further Old Testament evidence, which provide linguistic support for this conclusion. N. Wright, 1992a: 185 (similarly Hafemann, 1996: 411-12) summarily concludes that "linguistic evidence favours the meaning 'behold as in a mirror.'"

51. On Christ as the mirror (or mirror-image) highlighted in the gospel, see Furnish, 1984: 239; Thrall, 1994: 292-94; Witherington, 1995: 382; Lambrecht, 1999: 55-56; Grenz, 2001: 247; M. Harris, 2005: 315.

52. For further development of this observation, see Hughes, 1962: 117; Barrett, 1993: 125; Thrall, 1994: 291; Matera, 2003: 97; M. Harris, 2005: 314.

53. Cairns, 1973: 48 and Watson, 1997: 301 compare Moses and Christians in terms of the veil and its removal.

54. So Ra. Martin, 1986: 71; Grenz, 2001: 246-47.

55. D. Kelsey, 2009: v. 2, 1000 and Minor, 2009: 79 describe how Paul uses the beginning of chapter 4 to explain what he has just affirmed in summary fashion at the end of chapter 3.

as well as the heart (God makes "light shine in our hearts," v. 6). Once believers can see Christ — can see what being God's image is intended to look like — then the transformation and reflecting can begin.

That Christians see God's glory in the face of Christ, rather than as some abstract radiance, suggests that Christ serves as God's image and the standard for humanity in very concrete human terms — as concrete as a face. Accordingly, the transformation into that same image and the increase in glory that Christians experience should be concretely evident. As God undermines the influence of sin and the god of this age in the Christian's life, God's intentions for humanity can be fulfilled. The unsuppressed attributes that ought to characterize those created in God's image can become visible. Moses had a visible glory — how much more Christians.[56]

In fact, as soon as the image/glory statement of 2 Corinthians 3:18 concludes, Paul adds a "therefore" and launches into some concrete attributes of character and living that he and his co-workers have experienced. They "do not lose heart" (4:1) because God's glory is increasing in them, not fading away as for Moses. They "have renounced the shameful things that one hides" (v. 2) and instead face the suffering of this world head on, "afflicted in every way, but not crushed . . ." (vv. 8-9). Through ongoing transformation into the same image of God that Christ has demonstrated, Paul celebrates that "we are always being given up to death for Jesus' sake, so that the life of Jesus may be made visible in our mortal flesh" (v. 11).[57]

The human attributes that God intends as a reflection of divine attributes are a particular tribute to God in circumstances where human ability apart from Christ is least able to account for what people are doing. The mere "clay jars" that people are do not detract from God's glorious image in Christ precisely because they lack glory in themselves (v. 7). What is essential is their special connection with God.[58] With God's transforming power at work in and through them (v. 7), they grow from one degree of glory to another, until ultimately they reach "an eternal weight of glory

---

56. Thrall, 1994: 285; D. Kelsey, 2009: v. 2, 1001-2; and Gushee, 2012: 108 further develop the idea that increasing glory means the increasing manifestation of God-glorifying attributes.

57. On the image of Christ as especially including godly living and being in the face of suffering and death, see Chapter 5; also Painter, 2001: 49-50; Grenz, 2001: 249.

58. Lenski, 1946b: 950 and Vorster, 2011: 19-20 note that in Christians, good traits are godly traits. They develop from a connection with God.

beyond all measure" (v. 17). In the process, this all works "to the glory of God" (v. 15).

This divine power has several aspects to it. Most importantly, as just noted, there is one God, and something can only become God's image when God makes it so.[59] In themselves, people have no lasting significance.[60] In 2 Corinthians, Paul explicitly states that transformation into Christ's image "comes from the Lord."[61] Romans 8 communicates a similar view by locating humanity's conforming "to the image of his [God's] son" in the context of God's foreknowing, predestining, calling, justifying, and glorifying.[62] Colossians 3 identifies those renewed according to Christ's image as "God's chosen ones."[63]

The Spirit in particular, though, provides the power for the transformation necessary if people are to become Christ's image.[64] As 2 Corinthians 3:17 indicates, "The Lord [who removes the veil that separates people from God] is the Spirit." Accordingly, transformation into the image of Christ "comes from the Lord, the Spirit" (v. 18).[65] While this is the Lord's/God's doing, the Spirit is God's agent, of sorts, to work this transformation.[66] More precisely, the text suggests that the Spirit is the source of this transformation, leaving the door open for some sort of involvement on the part of the people experiencing this transformation (see below).[67]

59. On this theme, see Chapter 4; also Irenaeus, 1867: 99; Patzia, 1990: 76; Gunton, 1999: 59.

60. On this theme related to God's image, see Thielicke, 1966: 152; Mitton, 1981: 165; Pannenberg, 1985: 53; 1991: 228, 275; Vorster, 2011: 19.

61. On "the Lord" here as referring to the God of Paul's Scriptures, the Old Testament, see Furnish, 1984: 211-12.

62. For elaboration, see Piper, 1971: 22; Byrne, 1996: 268.

63. For elaboration on this and the parallel passage in Ephesians, see O'Brien, 1999: 331-32.

64. Whether the Spirit's involvement is greater in this transformation into the image of Christ than was the case in humanity's original creation has been the subject of some debate. On the debate between John Calvin (1960b: 338-40) and John Owen (1850b: 284-85) on this score, see Prins, 1972: 43; S. McDonald, 2009: 327-28, 333.

65. On the different possible translations here, but the primacy of the Spirit in any case, see Piper, 1971: 23; Furnish, 1984: 216, 235-36; Barrett, 1993: 126; Thrall, 1994: 287; D. Kelsey, 2009: v. 2, 1000; M. Harris, 2012: 65.

66. The idea of the Spirit as God's "agent" who does this "work" is developed in Lenski, 1946b: 951; Hoekema, 1994: 86; Lambrecht, 1999: 56; Gardoski, 2007: 31; Yong, 2007: 191. Similarly Barth, 1958a: 204.

67. According to 2 Corinthians 3:18, this transformation is "from" *(apo)* the Spirit, as opposed to, e.g., "by" *(hupo)* the Spirit. See Lenski, 1946b: 950; Fichtner, 1978: 66.

"The Spirit gives life" (v. 6), and "where the Spirit of the Lord is, there is freedom" (v. 17) — in contrast to Moses' "ministry of death" and "condemnation" (vv. 7, 9).[68]

In Romans 8, leading up to the discussion of conformation to Christ's image, Paul also identifies the Spirit as the source of freedom (v. 2) and life (v. 6) in contrast to the Mosaic law (v. 3). Whereas elsewhere he describes transformation into Christ's image as a process of glorification culminating in the transformation of the body, in verse 23 he refers to that glorification process as "the first fruits of the Spirit" leading to "the redemption of our bodies." The Spirit's work of transformation into Christ's image includes the total person.[69] Yet it becomes evident in specific human mental, moral, relational, and other attributes (vv. 4, 5, 13-16, 26).[70] Once the transformation is complete with the glorification of the body, even right rulership over creation will be possible (vv. 19, 23).

Noting the important role of the Spirit here is in no way to detract from the centrality of Christ for the image of God. As discussed in Chapter 2, without Christ becoming the likeness of humanity, defeating sin, and demonstrating God's intentions for humanity as created in the divine image, people could never live out humanity's destiny to become the image of God.[71] The only place that the veil separating people from God can be removed, so that transformation into Christ's image can begin, is "in Christ" (2 Cor. 3:14). Being "in Christ" must precede becoming Christ's image, for the process of becoming Christ's image only begins by gaining an intimate connection with God.[72] So it is inescapably "through Christ" that people become Christ's image.[73] Christ, working through the Spirit, is the source and the means of their transformation;[74] and it is inseparably "with Christ"

68. For more on this contrast, see Thrall, 1994: 287; Grenz, 2001: 251; Gardoski, 2007: 31.

69. The notion that people (not just particular attributes) are the focus of the Spirit's work is commonly assumed; see, e.g., J. Wesley, 1985f: 200; Gerhard, 1962: 62; Maloney, 1973: 181; Shults, 2003: 240; Krause, 2005: 365.

70. On such specific outworkings of the Spirit's work in humanity related to Christ's image, see Wesley, 1985d: 410-11; Cairns, 1973: 44; M. Harris, 2005: 318.

71. The centrality of Christ here is summarized in Horst, 1950: 270; R. Niebuhr, 1964: 266; Hughes, 1985: 20; Navone, 1990: 66; Ja. Edwards, 1991: 218; Sidoroff, 1993: 24; Hoehner, 2002: 611; R. Jewett, 2007: 529-30.

72. See M. Barth, 1974a: 70; Scroggs, 1966: 69; Ecumenical, 2004: 512; McFarland, 2005: 166.

73. So D. Garland, 1999: 200; Witherington, 2009: v. 2, 788.

74. Thompson, 2005: 28-29 (source); Witherington, 2009: v. 1, 21-22 (means). Early

that this renewal takes place. As Colossians 3 emphasizes, "in that renewal [according to Christ's image] . . . Christ is all and in all" (vv. 10-11).[75]

Crucial, then, is the work of God, including all persons of the Trinity, in the renewal, conformation, and transformation of humanity into God's image in Christ. Nevertheless, people also play a necessary role in that process. God's work does not render human effort unnecessary; rather, it enables it.[76] God is the initiator — the creator and renewer. Humanity is simply the responder; but response is necessary.[77] In 2 Corinthians 4, as discussed above, Paul describes in great detail the extensive effort that is involved in living out the transformation described at the end of the previous chapter.

In Colossians and Ephesians, the close relationship between divine and human effort to facilitate renewal in Christ is even more explicit. God in Christ offers a new humanity, "which is being renewed in[to] knowledge according to the image of its creator" (Col. 3:10). Christians "clothed" themselves with it after they "stripped off" the old humanity with its practices (v. 9).[78] As the parallel language of Ephesians reminds Christians: To have "learned Christ" correctly (4:20) you must have learned "to put away your former way of life," your old humanity, and "to clothe yourselves" with the new humanity (vv. 22-24).[79] This clothing metaphor, among other insights related to renewal according to Christ's image, warrants further consideration here.

Colossians 3

There is an old humanity *(anthropos)* that Christians have stripped off and a new humanity that they have put on, according to Colossians 3:9-10.

Greek Church leaders such as Irenaeus discuss at length Christ's work in this regard through the Spirit; see Maloney, 1973: 195.

75. As will be considered further in relation to Colossians 3 below, humanity's renewal involves the incorporation of believers into Christ's body; e.g., see Patzia, 1990: 251.

76. On this theme, see Smalley, 1984: 146; Witherington, 2009: v. 1, 20, 248.

77. Boer, 1990: 11, 83, 85, 93 describes the place of human response in transformation into Christ's image.

78. On human effort and the holiness necessarily involved in renewal according to the image of Christ, see Wesley, 1985e: 275. For similar discussion in Aquinas, see Mondin, 1975: 72-73; Merriell, 1990: 183.

79. For elaboration, see Stott, 1979: 182. Collins, 1999: 572 explores the same idea in the image passage near the end of 1 Corinthians 15.

As already discussed in Chapters 3 and 4, the subject here is not merely individual "selves." It is also humanity in a corporate sense, whether the entire human race in Adam or the church in Christ.[80] Paul is saying that the entire body of Christians has put off the old humanity and put on the new. The language of "wearing" is similar to the language of "bearing" in 1 Corinthians 15:49 (see below). In 1 Corinthians 15 Paul describes people, all of whom are in God's image. However, apart from Christ they are the "old humanity" whose identity is bound up with Adam, with all his shortcomings.[81] In fact, they bear the image of Adam. That means the same weakness and corruption that characterized fallen Adam, including a perishable body, will continue to characterize everyone unless something (or Someone) intervenes.

When people turn to Christ, however, Christians strip off that old humanity, that old and corrupting identity, and clothe themselves with a new identity, a new humanity. The distinctive feature of that new humanity is that the power of sin has been broken in Christ. All that will now be possible must unfold over time as people are renewed according to the image of Christ. That image is the God-glorifying standard of the very being and life of Christ (see Ch. 2). Only after Christ's return will renewal be complete (1 Corinthians 15), though this fulfillment begins to appear even now in the renewal of the "new humanity" that Christians already wear.

The four verses leading up to verses 9-10 provide ample documentation of what the old humanity looks like.[82] It includes "fornication, impurity, passion, evil desire, and greed (which is idolatry)" (v. 5); disobedience toward God (v. 6); and "anger, wrath, malice, slander, and abusive language" (v. 8). Verse 9 then singles out lying as if it is specially connected somehow with the renewal about to be discussed, while verse 10 singles out knowledge as what especially results from that renewal. Indeed, these are the two central problems highlighted in Genesis 3, where Adam and Eve, created in God's image, embrace the lie (v. 4) of the serpent and grasp at the wrong knowledge — knowledge that God does not want them to have (vv. 5-6, 22).

These connections, plus the reference to "image" *(eikona)* and the Creator *(tou ktisantos),* suggest that humanity and God's image are very much

---

80. See Grenz, 2001: 255-58; S. Wright, 2003: 40.

81. On the old man as a way of being and doing, see W. Pope, 1875: v. 1, 425; Grenz, 2001: 254-55.

82. For discussion of each sin here, see I. H. Marshall, 2001: 64-65.

in Paul's mind here.[83] People started off quite well, in God's image (Gen. 1:27, 31). In Adam, though, people also reoriented toward another image, allowing sinful being and doing to become the standard, to the dishonor of God. Sin covered people like the veil of 2 Corinthians 3:14-16, which can only be set aside in Christ. In Colossians 3 Paul reminds Christians that they have taken off the old humanity, the covering of sin that defined who they were and how they lived, preventing them from being who God intended them to be at creation. They have clothed themselves with the new humanity in its place.

As noted in Chapter 4, there is a "you" here whom Paul is addressing who is not identical with either the old or new humanity. "You" once wore the old humanity, took it off, and put on the new. This "you" refers to people created in God's image, sidetracked from God's purposes by donning the "old humanity."[84] However, God has now launched this same plural "you" on a new course, attired with a new humanity, which will progressively become all that God intends for people to be (involving even more than Adam had at creation, as will be discussed in Ch. 7).[85] "You" refers to those who are undergoing renewal according to the image of God in Christ, which is the divine image that God intends for humanity ultimately to be and bear.

The present-tense verb here (*anakainoumenon,* "being renewed") likely signifies the same sort of continuous, progressive change as the present-tense verb in 2 Corinthians 3:18 ("being transformed," discussed above).[86] Its passive voice is a reminder that people, despite their involvement in undressing and dressing, are not the agents of their own renewal. They are "being renewed," with God as the implicit renewer.[87]

The expression "the image of God in Christ" warrants further explanation here. The text of Colossians 3:10 calls the standard of renewal the "image of its creator" (*eikona tou ktisantos auton,* literally "image of the one who created it"), with "it" referring to the new humanity with which Christians have clothed themselves. The first question, then, is who created the new humanity? In the New Testament, the verb here is normally

---

83. See Lightfoot, 1927: 213-14; Machen, 1947: 175; Scroggs, 1966: 69; Murray, 1977: 40; H. D. McDonald, 1981: 16; Gardoski, 2007: 32.

84. Boer, 1990: 83 develops this continuity in greater detail.

85. On this idea in Colossians, see Lohse, 1971: 143; Grenz, 2001: 257.

86. Piper, 1971: 23 and Dunn, 1996: 222 address the progressive nature of what is happening in both passages.

87. Patzia, 1990: 76 develops this theme.

associated with God as creator (see the close parallels in Rom. 1:25; Eph. 3:9; but also Matt. 19:4; Mark 13:19; 1 Cor. 11:9; 1 Tim. 4:3; 1 Pet. 4:19; Rev. 4:11; 10:6). If God is the creator of Colossians 3:10, then the standard of renewal here is the image of God, which 1:15 has just identified as Christ.[88]

Nevertheless, some commentators going back at least to Chrysostom have insisted that the reference here to the creator has Christ in view, at least primarily. Sometimes when a New Testament author uses the verb *ktizo*, particularly when Christians are the subject, the reference to Christ is indeed unmistakable. For example, Ephesians 2:10 refers to Christians as "created in Christ Jesus." Creation is God's work, but it is God in Christ who is specifically involved in human re-creation. In fact, Christ's involvement in creation extends to everything created. This understanding is especially evident in Colossians, which teaches that all things were created through Christ (Col. 1:16). Colossians 1 uses the same verb *ktizo* to affirm this, while Hebrews 1:2 and John 1:3 use different verbs to similarly affirm Christ as the one through whom God created everything. If Christ is the creator of Colossians 3:10, then the standard of renewal here is the image of Christ.

Setting up an either/or between God and Christ when it comes to the re-creation of humanity, though, creates a false dichotomy. The creator here may well be God, but in the context of Colossians the author likely is specifically thinking of God in Christ. Accordingly, we can state the standard for renewal as either Christ or the image of Christ without significantly affecting the meaning.[89] As explained earlier, when it comes to the image of God and humanity's re-creation, either wording conveys the same standard.[90]

This standard involves many things, a few of which are mentioned in Colossians 3. Verse 10 indicates that renewal according to the image of God in Christ involves renewal "into full knowledge" *(eis epignosin)*. This knowledge is one of many attributes that God intends for humanity to have as a result of being created in the divine image. Sadly, Adam and Eve

---

88. Those who support this interpretation include Lightfoot, 1927: 214; Scroggs, 1966: 69-70; Lohse, 1971: 142; Schweizer, 1982: 198; O'Brien, 1987: 191. Acknowledging Christ as the image is at least preferable to equating Christ with the new humanity (as, e.g., in Kümmel, 1963: 68-69; Ra. Martin, 1981: 107-8), since the new humanity "is being renewed" — something that is not true of Christ.

89. So Wilson, 1973: 358; Mitton, 1981: 165.

90. This understanding underlies the discussions in Orr, 1948: 279; O'Brien, 1987: 191; McFarland, 2005: 49; D. Kelsey, 2009: v. 2, 946.

believed the serpent's lie that God did not want them to have knowledge like God has, so on their own they grabbed for what they thought to be desirable knowledge. They did gain some autonomy-related knowledge. However, in the process they severely damaged their relationship with God, who intended them to have true/full knowledge rather than autonomy. People's sinful self-centeredness prevented them from developing the God-intended attribute of ongoing knowledge that can come only from God as part of "knowing God." As with all attributes that God intends to flow from creation in the divine image, once sin is removed in Christ then God's intentions can actually be fulfilled.

Humanity's distinctive identity as created in God's image has never changed. A special connection between God and people and God's intention that people should reflect certain divine attributes to God's glory remained even after the Fall; and both remain after redemption by Christ. Being free from sin, Christ demonstrates not only God's intentions but also their actual fulfillment (see Ch. 2). In Christ, Christians are much more able to live out God's intentions. Most importantly, they need fuller knowledge — knowledge of how God wants them to be and to live — for that to occur. Accordingly, God breaks the power of sin over people, which is when they strip off the old humanity and clothe themselves with the new. At that point, a renewal process begins involving the increasing fulfillment of God's intentions for people as they learn more about how they can reflect and glorify God.

There is much to this knowledge, so the text of 3:10 does not identify it as mere "knowledge" *(gnosis)* but "full knowledge" *(epignosis)*. Paul has already used this concept in 1:6 to describe a small part of this knowledge, the full knowledge (full knowing, *epegnote*) of God's grace that one understands and experiences at the point of salvation. Christians do not gain all aspects of knowledge at once, but the text says that they are renewed "into" it.

A few verses after the introduction of the concept in 1:6, Paul elaborates on what this knowledge involves for Christians.[91] It is knowledge of God (1:10) and knowledge of God's will (1:9). Knowledge of God means more than information, but includes intimate personal connection as well.[92] Knowledge of God's will includes knowledge of God's intention for how people are to reflect who God is and what God does.[93] These elements of

91. For more on Paul's use of *epignosis* here, see Piper, 1971: 23; Grenz, 2001: 256-57.
92. See S. Wright, 2003: 39-40; Gardoski, 2007: 32-33.
93. See Lohse, 1971: 143; I. H. Marshall, 2001: 63; Vorster, 2011: 20.

connection and reflection explain why full knowledge is necessarily associated with humanity's renewal according to God's image. Since God's image in Christ is specifically in view, Paul goes on to clarify that the knowledge involved here is knowledge of Christ, "in whom are hidden all the treasures of wisdom and knowledge" (2:2). Such knowledge is a far cry from philosophy "according to human tradition" (2:8), the autonomous thinking ("empty deceit") that led Adam and Eve astray in Eden.[94]

Full knowledge, then, is just one aspect of (and a means of access to) all that God intends for humanity in Christ. In the immediate context of Colossians 3:10, Paul particularly has in mind being free from what characterized the "old humanity" discussed above. Plus he goes on to describe the "new humanity" in terms of the unity (v. 11), compassion, kindness, humility, meekness, patience (v. 12), forgiveness (v. 13), love (v. 14), peace, and thankfulness (v. 15) that God intends for people to reflect.[95] Each of these attributes is underscored and developed throughout the New Testament. For example, 1 Corinthians 12:13 and Galatians 3:28-29 elaborate on the unity in Colossians 3:11 that overcomes the deepest apparent distinctions among people such as Greek versus Jew and slave versus free.[96]

Paul's characterizing the image of God in Christ mentioned in 3:10 as a fixed standard that is guiding the renewal taking place is significant. There is no image changing here — people as the new humanity are changing according to what the image is and requires. As noted above, this is consistent with the rest of the Bible's teaching that when humanity fell in early Genesis, God's image did not change, people did. God's image, including God's intentions and standards, remains as constant as God is over time. Humanity, though, changes, first for the worse and later, in Christ, for the better. Misunderstanding on this point has led to several problematic ideas: that God's image is about ways that people are like God (e.g., beings who have knowledge or reason, see Chs. 3 and 5), that God's image has been damaged by sin (see Ch. 4), and that this image must change (i.e., be restored; see later in this chapter). The Bible affirms none of these views, but instead conveys a different understanding.

People have always been, and continue to be, in God's image. Christians, now reoriented to God's image in Christ, can fully become what

---

94. This contrast is noted in Lightfoot, 1927: 213; D. Kelsey, 2009: v. 2, 947.

95. For discussion of each virtue here, see I. H. Marshall, 2001: 65-66.

96. For more on this attribute in Colossians 3, see Maston, 1959: 10; Krause, 2005: 366.

God has created and is renewing them to be. In line with the core biblical meaning of being "in" or "according to" the image of God, they have an intimate connection with Christ,[97] and in Christ they increasingly reflect God's own attributes, to God's glory.[98] Being a Christian, then, involves having a commitment to the person and pattern of Christ.[99] It requires being the person and living the life that echoes Christ's own.[100]

This is not merely imitation, as one person might imitate another; rather, the connection aspect of being in the image of God in Christ is crucial here. We have seen in Chapter 3 (and will see further in the Conclusion) the related notion that who people are, in God's image, has huge implications for how others must treat them. People cannot kill (Gen. 9:6) or curse (James 3:9) others since such behavior violates the image-related status of their victims. One is addressing God whether one curses God or curses someone in God's image, because of the connection between the two. It is a contradiction to curse one and not the other: "Does a spring pour forth from the same opening both fresh and brackish water? Can a fig tree ... yield olives?" (James 3:11-12). Sin, then, involves people in the contradiction of treating others as something that they are not.

The contradiction of sin, however, becomes even more personal when it involves people in doing something that contradicts who they themselves are. When they become Christians, they do not merely take on a new resolve to be better people. They are "born again," as Jesus described it (John 3:3-7). "There is a new creation" (2 Cor. 5:17). Colossians 3 describes this in terms of a "new humanity" with which people have clothed themselves. The very life and person of Christ is alive in them. Paul can say that "it is no longer I who live, but it is Christ who lives in me" (Gal. 2:20) — or simply that "living is Christ" (Phil. 1:21). The renewal of Christians is according to the image of God in Christ because it is actually Christ who is alive in them.

Sin in non-Christians is bad enough — sometimes because it involves harming someone in God's image (the one sinned against), and always because the one who sins contradicts what God intends people to be as

97. On this theme, see Scroggs, 1966: 105; Liefeld, 1997: 114; S. Wright, 2003: 31-32.
98. On this theme, see Schnelle, 1996: 100; Frame, 2006: 229.
99. For the language of "pattern," see Oduyoye, 1982: 48; Dunn, 1996: 221; Barackman, 2001: 347; S. Holmes, 2005: 319.
100. Chapter 2 of the present work develops the idea of Christ as standard. Regarding the appropriate human response to that, see Berkouwer, 1975: 102; Ja. Edwards, 1991: 218; Byrne, 1996: 268; Black, 2006: 191; Steenberg, 2009: 9.

created in the divine image.[101] Sin in Christians, though, is an even bigger contradiction.[102] How can one live contrary to Christ when one's life *is* Christ? In effect, Paul is saying to Christians in Colossians and his other letters: You must "be who you are." The indicative is inseparable from the imperative.[103] Christians have become (have put on) the new humanity and so they must live as such. The classic formulation of this affirmation in Paul's writings is Rudolf Bultmann's "Become what you are!" *(Werde, der du bist)*. That formulation may invite misinterpretation, though, by apparently suggesting that one is not something yet but must become it. Paul's argument is somewhat different. He exhorts believers to *be* what they already are. Just as it is grammatically preposterous to state that people are other than they are, so it is preposterous morally and otherwise when such is the case.[104]

In Colossians 3, since Christians have clothed themselves with the new humanity (v. 10), Paul reminds them to "clothe yourselves with compassion . . ." (v. 12) and to "clothe yourselves with love" (v. 14). Such things are not separate from their new humanity but are precisely what this humanity looks like (to the extent that the dirt of sin does not still render their new clothing unrecognizable). Ephesians 4 echoes this perspective by talking about "putting away" falsehood (v. 25), which is simply a part of what "putting away" the old humanity (v. 22) entails.[105]

Images or standards according to which one lives have power to shape identity. False images can foster false identities. Apart from Christ, although people are in God's image, the false images of Adam (1 Cor. 15:49, as discussed in Ch. 3) and the world have obscured people's true identity. According to Romans, people have given up the glory that ought to accompany who they are in God's image in exchange for various forms of worldly image (*eikonos*, 1:23). They are conformed to the world (12:2) rather than conformed to God's image in Christ (8:29).[106]

---

101. As Karl Barth puts it: Because of who God has created people to be in God's image, "sin is not a possibility but an ontological impossibility. . . . [A man who sins] chooses his own impossibility" (1958b: 136). Cf. Wesley, 1985g: 175.

102. See, for example, Patzia, 1990: 76, 251; Hoehner, 2002: 610.

103. On the relation between the indicative and the imperative in the context of God's image, see Thielicke, 1966: 152; Schnackenburg, 1991: 201; O'Brien, 1999: 333.

104. For an elaboration of this dynamic as central to the "reality-bounded" ethics of Paul and, indeed, the New Testament more broadly, see Kilner, 1992: 20-26, 53-69.

105. On the indicative and imperative in the image-related teaching of Colossians and Ephesians, see Thielicke, 1966: 152; Grenz, 2001: 251-52; 2004: 624; S. Wright, 2003: 42.

106. This contrast is developed further in Beale, 2008: 282.

So people need for their sin, which fosters and is fostered by false images, to be removed. Only then can all that they were created to be in God's image — and are now re-created to be according to God's image in Christ — become manifest. That is the "making new" of Colossians 3:10. It is not a renewal of something old. The old humanity is gone — Christians have stripped it off. Instead, the new humanity is becoming in substance what it already is in status. Christians are being transformed (2 Cor. 3:18) until even their very bodies are resurrected and glorified. The future completion of this renewal process is so certain (Rom. 8:29-30 and here below) that it is a part of who Christians are even now. That indicative, which includes even the future, grounds the numerous imperatives of how Christians are to be and live now.[107]

The Primary Echoes

While the passages in Romans, 2 Corinthians, and Colossians are the most developed biblical statements about humanity's re-creation in the image of God in Christ, there are three other passages that echo the first three in ways that clarify some of the implications involved. Again, it will be instructive to examine each of these passages separately. Nevertheless, as image-related topics arise prominently in the discussion of a particular passage, we will consider the contribution of other passages to that topic at the same time.

Ephesians 4

In the latter part of Ephesians there is a passage that appears to be a shortened version of the Colossians passage, with several alterations to suit the purposes of Ephesians.[108] It echoes a number of the image-related themes in the three passages that we have already examined. The focal verses remind Christians that they were taught to "put away" their former way of life, their old humanity (*anthropos,* v. 22), to be "renewed" in the spirit of their minds (v. 23), and to "clothe" themselves with the new humanity *(an-*

---

107. On the eschatological nature of the indicative, see Kittel, 1964d: 397; Clines, 1968: 102-3; Grenz, 2001: 240.

108. For a discussion of the background issues here, see C. E. Lincoln, 1990: 272-74.

thropos), "created according to the likeness of God in true righteousness and holiness" (v. 24).

In light of the close parallels to Colossians 3 here, many commentators understandably see a reference to the likeness-image of God in Ephesians 4:24.[109] However, no noun for likeness or image actually appears in Ephesians 4. Instead the text simply says that the new humanity has been created "according to God" *(kata theon),* in line with the unique purposes of Ephesians. Therefore, simply equating the passages in the two epistles is unwarranted.[110]

The two epistles and other image-related passages in the New Testament speak similarly about the human predicament without Christ. The "old humanity" of Ephesians 4:22 is reminiscent of the "old humanity" of Colossians 3:9 and even, to a degree, the "image of Adam," the *choikos anthropos* ("earthy humanity") of 1 Corinthians 15:49. In such passages, the word "creation" does not appear with the old humanity, for the latter involves humanity's sin nature, which is not God's intention in creation.[111] Creation in God's image is the divine intention.

Sin, like the veil in 2 Corinthians 3:14-15, prevents people from recognizing Christ. (Satan is also involved as an encourager of this blindness, according to 2 Cor. 4:4.) Sin "covers" humanity, affecting the being and lifestyle of the one who wears it.[112] It blocks the fulfillment of God's intentions, humanity's God-glorifying attributes, such that the glory that should radiate from those in God's image does not.[113] This covering requires removal. Ephesians and Colossians indicate that Christians have "put off" the old humanity that holds sin in place. Simply putting off the old and putting on the new does not mean that all sin disappears. There is still a process of renewal that must proceed in the new humanity, as discussed above regarding the Colossians passage (cf. Eph. 4:23); but that renewal can only proceed once sin has been redressed.

This clothing imagery is helpful as long as it does not conjure up the idea that sin only lies on the surface of human existence. It permeates hu-

---

109. E.g., Barabas, 1963: 370; Piper, 1971: 24; M. Barth, 1974: 509; Mitton, 1981: 164-65; Hodge, 1982: v. 2, 101.

110. For an overview of differences, see Best, 1998: 432.

111. See Schnackenburg, 1991: 200; Hoehner, 2002: 611.

112. For classical discussions, see Gregory of Nyssa, 1954: 148-49; Origen, 1982: 193-94. More recently, see Grenz, 2001: 260.

113. On this theme see Cairns, 1973: 46-47; Reitman, 2010: 125.

man existence and requires purging of the entire human being.[114] What needs removal is nothing less than a form of humanity itself *(anthropos)*. Yet people are not giving up their entire identity in the process. There is "someone" there who puts off the old humanity and puts on the new.[115] That someone is the person (again viewed communally and not just in terms of each person separately) as originally created in God's image. Adam and Eve quickly put on a counterfeit humanity — a costume of sorts, the "old humanity" — and now people must put it off and put on the "new humanity" — which will make possible the fulfillment of God's intentions even beyond who Adam and Eve originally were.

Since Ephesians 4:24 affirms that the new humanity has been created, it is not indicating that Christ per se is the new humanity. However, the introduction to this passage in verses 20-21 suggests a close connection between the two.[116] It describes the mandate to put away the old humanity and put on the new as the "truth [that] is in Jesus" (v. 21). Christians are not just people who have met Christ; they are those who have also "learned Christ" (v. 20). The new humanity is a way of being and living that follows the pattern of Christ's humanity (note the reference to "Jesus" in verse 21, emphasizing the focus on Christ's humanity here). Nevertheless, it is also Christ as God who is the standard of humanity.[117] Ephesians 4 ends and the next chapter begins with the summary statement: "Therefore be imitators of God" (5:1) by following the example of Christ (5:2). The destiny of humanity is ever the reflection of God-glorifying attributes.

Ephesians 4:24 encapsulates all this by recalling that the new humanity has been created *kata theon,* according to God — according to (the standard of) God in Christ, as the context clarifies. "God" here has a similar meaning to "the image of God" in Colossians 3:10.[118] "God" in Ephesians 4:24 refers to the divine intentions for being and living in the same way that "Christ" does just four verses earlier.[119]

Ephesians 4 provides insight beyond Colossians 3 regarding what

---

114. On purging, see Hart, 2002: 549; on the related theme of deliverance, see Reitman, 2010: 123, 129.

115. For further discussion, see M. Barth, 1974: 539; Best, 1998: 438-39.

116. M. Barth, 1974: 539; Best, 1998: 440; and Grenz, 2001: 262-63 provide differently nuanced perspectives here.

117. See Berkouwer, 1975: 101-2; A. T. Lincoln, 1990: 287-88; O'Brien, 1999: 332.

118. So Lightfoot, 1927: 214; Gerhard, 1962: 35-36; Best, 1998: 437.

119. For more on the meaning of *kata theon,* see Wild, 1985: 135; O'Brien, 1999: 332; Grenz, 2001: 263.

these intentions include. As discussed above, a key contribution of Colossians on this score is the important place of the reflected attribute of "full knowledge" in enabling Christians to recognize God's other intentions for them as they are renewed according to the image of God in Christ. Awareness of the importance of such knowledge is evident in Ephesians 4 as well.[120] Christians are to be "renewed in the spirit of your minds" (v. 23). Paul underscores the importance of this by separately identifying it as something that apparently must be in place, once the old humanity is gone, if the new humanity is to be put on appropriately.

Paul goes on to explain, though, that if full knowledge is foundational, true righteousness and holiness are also vital in renewal according to God's image in Christ — in re-creation according to God. People must not only recognize the good but also live it. Living in righteousness and holiness *(dikaiosune kai hosioteti)* is a summary statement of what living in accordance with God's intentions entails. It is "according to God" in that this same pair of traits is connected with God in the Old Testament (e.g., Deut. 32:4), with God's Incarnation in Christ (e.g., Luke 1:75), and with God in the end times (e.g., Rev. 16:5).[121]

The word pair as a whole suggests virtuous living in accordance with God's will. Righteousness, often a relational term in Paul, can also refer to actions (and even be translated as justice, see Rom. 6:13, 18-20; 2 Cor. 6:7, 14; Phil. 4:8). Holiness often refers to an inner attitude, though it also suggests separation from that which is unholy. The overall idea is a unified being and doing that glorifies God.[122] The requirement that this righteousness and holiness be "in truth" underscores the crucial connection between righteousness/holiness and God in Christ in Ephesians 4:24. Paul has just said that "truth is in Jesus" in verse 21, so the righteousness and holiness in view here are in Christ, not in oneself (cf. 2:8-10) or in the "trickery" and "craftiness" of false teachers (cf. 4:14).[123]

This emphasis on true righteousness and holiness in Ephesians, while a good summary statement of God's intentions for humanity, also appears to reflect the particular challenges facing the Ephesian church. If Rev-

---

120. On the connection between Ephesians and Colossians regarding knowledge and God's image, see A. T. Lincoln, 1990: 287.

121. Best, 1998: 437-38 and Grenz, 2001: 263-64 offer further documentation.

122. For further discussion of these terms in conjunction with God's image, see M. Barth, 1974: 510-11; Schnackenburg, 1991: 201; O'Brien, 1999: 332-33; Vorster, 2011: 20.

123. On the significance of truth in this context, see Hodge, 1982: v. 2, 101; Schnackenburg, 1991: 201-2; Gardoski, 2007: 34.

elation 2:1-7 (addressed to the church at Ephesus) is an indication of a longstanding problem in Ephesus,[124] a growing weakness of the Ephesians may have involved doing their works of righteousness and holiness in a way separated from a fervent love for God in Christ. In fact, the very last words of the epistle to the Ephesians are an appeal for "an undying love for our Lord Jesus Christ," perhaps suggesting that some were losing their initial love. Even a simple exhortation to "speak the truth" in response to doctrinal "trickery" (4:14) becomes in Ephesians a reminder to "speak the truth in love" (4:15).

Although the Ephesians were adept at spotting doctrinal error (Rev. 2:2, 6), they were more concerned about conforming to right doctrine than to the person of God. They were doing good "works" (commended in Rev. 2:2) but they were not doing works closely enough associated with God to please and glorify God (2:5). So in Ephesians 4:24, Paul appears to cut to the heart of the matter and rephrase the image-of-God-in-Christ concept in terms of the necessity of being and living "according to God" in true righteousness and holiness.

Whether this or other circumstances in Ephesus lie behind the emphasis on being and living "according to God," the importance of being like God is a major theme in Ephesians. That theme helps account for the unique way that Ephesians words the image-of-God-in-Christ concept. Ephesians 4 begins with the idea of God's standard, begging Christians to "lead a life worthy of the calling to which you have been called" (v. 1). The chapter continues the theme in verse 15 by requiring Christians to "grow up in every way into" Christ. At the conclusion of chapter 4, Christians are exhorted to act "as God in Christ has" (v. 32). The summary (*oun,* "therefore") in 5:1 is that Christians are to "be imitators of God," living "as Christ" did (v. 2).[125] In this context, 4:24 provides the reason for being and living like God: God has created the new humanity to be like God. That is the divine intention.

God's intention is that humanity become, not God, but like God, reflecting God — the fulfillment of what God had in mind by creating human-

124. Revelation may have been written as much as thirty-five years or more after Ephesians, so problems existent during the writing of Revelation may not have been present during the writing of Ephesians. However, the evidence noted here suggests that the problem highlighted in Revelation as the characteristic problem of the Ephesian church was already present in incipient form at the writing of Ephesians.

125. On the importance of understanding "like God" in terms of "like God in Christ," even in Ephesians, see Berkouwer, 1975: 101-2; O'Brien, 1987: 191; Hoekema, 1994: 330, 62.

ity in the first place according to the divine image. Describing this idea as *theosis* (literally, "deification"), as some theologians do, may inadvertently run the risk of giving some people a mistaken impression on this score.[126] There is a glorious truth here — that through incorporation into Christ and receiving God's Spirit, Christians can share, by grace, in the very life of God. At the same time, people will not become God. It will be clear in the eternally future heaven who is worshiping whom.[127]

God has indeed given Christians "precious and very great promises, so that [they] . . . may become participants of the divine nature" (2 Pet. 1:4). However, in light of biblical teaching as a whole, the eschatological nature of such promises probably points more to such divine attributes as imperishability (not able to die) — something that did not characterize Adam and Eve — than to becoming God per se.[128] As the discussion above suggests, this participation in the divine nature also includes other attributes involving resemblances to God in character as well as action, which manifest the life of God within.[129]

Such reflection of God does not merely involve particular people but also has a community dimension to it (as matters related to God's image always do).[130] Christians' likeness to God must include "one another" (v. 2), for "there is one body" (v. 4). Living "according to God" (v. 24) logically entails *(dio)* that "all of us" (v. 25) do so.

Living "according to God" is closely related to the language of conformation in Romans 8:29 and the ideas of "following" and "obeying" God

126. The *theosis* terminology is that of Breck (2003: 29) and Lubardic (2011: 530, who in turn is summarizing the teaching of Lossky, Yannaras, Zizioulas, and Horuzhy). Maloney (1973: 170) suggests the divinity of humanity in related terms: "God became man in order that men might become gods." Breck as well as Harrison (2010: 193) helpfully explain *theosis* more in terms of sharing in the life (energies, attributes) of God than as signifying that people actually become God.

127. For more on this point, see Cairns, 1973: 50-51; Smalley, 1984: 146; International, 2004: par. 94; Horton, 2007: 267-307; Van Vliet, 2009: 62; Witherington, 2009: v. 2, 738-39, 757.

128. Even the passages addressing people as the future likeness-image of God in Christ do not suggest that they become God. See Scroggs, 1966: 88 on 1 Corinthians 15:49 and Schnackenburg, 1992: 158-59 on 1 John 3:2.

129. So Packer, 2003: 56; van Huyssteen, 2006: 320; Witherington, 2009: v. 1, 198-99; v. 2, 737; cf. De Smedt and De Cruz, 2014: 150. Thus Blackwell, 2010: 304 (drawing on Finlan, 2008; Litwa, 2008; and Gorman, 2009) summarizes the legitimate heart of the *theosis* idea as follows: "Believers do not become gods themselves, but rather they become like God through a participation in him, such that they reflect divine attributes."

130. Noted in M. Barth, 1974: 592.

so common in the Bible.[131] Such language primarily has to do with God's intentions, rather than providing (fully) accurate descriptions of present realities. However, the ultimate fulfillment of these intentions at the completion of humanity's glorification is certain (see discussion of Romans 8 above). Then it may truly be said that Christians are like God in Christ (1 John 3:2), fully bearing Christ's image (1 Cor. 15:49). It is to these last two eschatological passages related to the image of God that we now turn.

1 Corinthians 15

In 1 Corinthians 15 Paul has much to say about bodily resurrection. He locates it in the context of an entire way of being and living that God has always intended for people from before humanity's creation in the divine image.[132] First, to establish that bodily resurrection is indeed possible, Paul notes that Christ rose bodily from the dead (vv. 12-20). Then he explains that Christ was just the first fruits of God's intentions, and that Christians will also be raised bodily (vv. 20-22, though it is not explicit until verses 35ff. that the body is involved).

Paul's concern here is not just to make a statement about resurrection. Resurrection is the culmination of an entire trajectory of life that either goes the way of Adam or the way of Christ. In Adam, there is only death — ultimately nothing to live for except one's own pleasure (vv. 22, 32). People in this mindset lack knowledge of God, says Paul (v. 34). He echoes here the need for the first fruits of renewal, "full knowledge," involved in re-creation according to God's image in Christ (see discussion of Col. 3:10 above). Such knowledge gives Christians the confidence that how they are living now is a part of a story that will end victoriously. Accordingly, Paul's "therefore" (hoste) statement that concludes the teaching of 1 Corinthians 15 reads: "Therefore, my beloved, be steadfast, immovable, always excelling in the work of the Lord, because you know that in the Lord your labor is not in vain" (v. 58).

The trajectory of life in Christ begins when people first "belong" to Christ, and it runs through their resurrection (v. 23) and beyond, when they will fully "bear the image of Christ" — actually manifesting the heav-

---

131. See Clines, 1968: 103; M. Barth, 1974: 588-89.

132. On the connection of 1 Corinthians 15:49 and Genesis 1 concerning God's image, see N. Wright, 2005: 28; T. Peters, 2010: 220-21.

enly humanity/*anthropos* of Christ as opposed to the earthy humanity/*anthropos* of Adam (v. 49). Colossians 3:10 unpacks in more detail what people need in order to reach this glorious conclusion. Christians must clothe themselves with the new humanity, which is being renewed in knowledge according to the image of its creator.[133] Resurrection and glorification are included in such a trajectory; indeed, they are its very goal. However, they are not the entire trajectory. The trajectory begins before natural death, when Christians are still suffering with the limits and sinfulness of fallen humanity (i.e., bearing the image of Adam).

Like so much in Paul's theology, the trajectory of what bearing Christ's image involves is something that begins now but is not completed until glorification after death. It is both "already" and "not yet." Even after Christians decide to put off the old humanity, aspects of Adam's image (some elements of finiteness as well as all elements of fallenness) continue. For Paul, that means "I die every day!" (1 Cor. 15:31) — hardly a description of one untouched by the death that attends bearing the image of Adam. Yet Paul knows where the trajectory is surely headed — toward a complete bearing of Christ's image, including the experience that "Death has been swallowed up in victory" (v. 54).

From the chapter as a whole it appears that Paul's primary concern is the resurrected body.[134] After spending fourteen chapters addressing all sorts of ways that Christians should be living out who they are in Christ, Paul here adds more information about what this new existence will involve after Christ's return. Christians will have a "spiritual" *(pneumatikon)* body rather than their current "natural" *(psychikon)* body (v. 44).[135] An important question here, though, is whether Paul only has the body in view in the contrast between Adam and Christ in verse 49, or whether the "image of Adam" and the "image of Christ" mentioned there involve more.

---

133. The metaphor of wearing is present here in 1 Corinthians 15:49 as well, with Paul using the verb *phoreo* rather than *phero* (to bear or carry) — see Thiselton, 2000: 1289-90. Moo (1996: 534) prefers the related sense of "imprint."

134. So Byrne, 1996: 269; D. Garland, 2003: 736-37.

135. At the heart of the *pneumatikon/psychikon* distinction is the contrast between supernatural and natural life. Translating 1 Corinthians 15 using spiritual versus natural terminology regarding death and the human body (so NIV, ESV, etc.) is preferable to using spiritual versus physical terminology (so NRSV), since the spiritual, resurrected body can have physical substance, as suggested by Jesus' resurrected body. The resurrected Jesus said to the disciples, "Touch me and see; for a ghost does not have flesh and bones as you see that I have" (Luke 24:39).

Verse 48 suggests that the body is a particular application of a broader truth. Paul writes: As was the one *(anthropos)* of dust, so are those who are of the dust; and as is the one *(anthropos)* of heaven, so are those who are of heaven. Translations typically supply the present-tense verbs here, but there are no verbs at all in the original. A timeless principle is involved, which is as true right now as it will be throughout eternity. Because of this principle, those who are "of heaven" must have bodies "of heaven," so-called spiritual bodies. However, the same principle applies to all aspects of who people are, and Paul demonstrates ample awareness of that in other passages concerning God's image in Christ (see above).

In verse 49, then, references to the image *(eikon)* of Adam and the image *(eikon)* of Christ most immediately have in view their respective bodies. However, Paul assumes that image involves more than the body. The image of God is about all human attributes that are a reflection of God's attributes. Nowhere will Christians' reflection of Christ be more evident than when they have spiritual bodies like Christ does — an attribute that also facilitates the intimate connection involved in bearing the image of God in Christ.[136] This reflection will be visible in many other ways as well. Again verse 48: As is the *anthropos* of heaven (Christ as human), so ultimately are Christians. That includes many ways of being like Christ in character and behavior.[137]

All likenesses to Christ in those connected to Christ (i.e., all reflections of Christ) glorify God. With the addition of each likeness comes increasing glory. So the process that extends from the point of becoming a Christian to glorification of the resurrected body is a process of transformation into God's image in Christ "from one degree of glory to another" (2 Cor. 3:18). The resurrection of the body is a huge, final step in that process, since all bodies have a particular form of glory (vv. 40-41). The difference in glory between the "natural" and "spiritual" body is so great that when God transforms the former into the latter, dishonor itself becomes glory (vv. 42-43).

This context helps with a translational challenge central to verse 49. Is the final verb descriptive and future — is Paul saying that Christians will bear the image of Christ? Or is that verb hortatory, with Paul exhorting Christians by saying "Let us bear the image of Christ"? The difference is

---

136. On the connection involved here in bearing Christ's image, see Scroggs, 1966: 84-85; Grenz, 2001: 235; D. Kelsey, 2009: v. 2, 951.

137. On other reflections of God's attributes involved here, besides the glorified body, see Fee, 1987: 794; D. Kelsey, 2009: v. 2, 951; Witherington, 2009: v. 1, 202, 242.

a single letter in the Greek (omicron vs. omega), with both verbal forms sounding very similar in verbal reading. Since the image of Christ in this particular verse and chapter is focused primarily on the spiritual body, Paul can hardly be saying that Christians should bear (put on?) a spiritual body now. Paul makes it clear in verses 22, 42-44, and 50-51 that he is contrasting two things: humanity's present existence with a natural body and Christians' future existence (after Christ's return) with a spiritual body. Christians cannot have a spiritual body now.[138] Nor is it for Christians to change their type of body. They will "be changed" (*allagesometha*, v. 51) — God will do the changing.[139] It would not make sense, then, for Paul to exhort Christians to have a spiritual body now.

Nevertheless, quite a few older manuscripts of the New Testament have the hortatory version of verse 49.[140] Is there a plausible and powerful reason why people making early copies of the New Testament might have recorded the verb as hortatory-present rather than descriptive-future, perhaps even unconsciously? Indeed there is. It is the very structure of Paul's argument regarding the resurrection of human bodies in verses 12-58. There are three points here where Paul introduces a new descriptive passage by referring to what someone says. In verse 12 he asks, "How can some of you say there is no resurrection of the dead?" In verse 35 he then adds, "But someone will ask, 'How are the dead raised?'" And in verse 50 he clarifies: "What I am saying, brothers and sisters, is this. . . ." After each of these three statements there is a lengthy descriptive passage. The first concludes with an exhortation in verse 34, as is typical of Paul: "Come to a sober and right mind, and sin no more." The third concludes with another exhortation in verse 58: "Be steadfast, immovable, always excelling in the work of the Lord." So readers/copiers expect to read an exhortation in verse 49.

Paul is indeed giving his readers an exhortation of sorts; but it is an exhortation, in effect, simply to accept his teaching on this point — to understand rightly — rather than his more common exhortation to do or be something. The problem Paul is addressing here is not fundamentally one of action or character. It is the claim that some people are making, that "there is no resurrection of the dead" (v. 12). This is not merely one

---

138. For examples of that rationale and conclusion, see Godet, 1957: 431-32; Conzelmann, 1975: 288; Barrett, 1993: 377.

139. E.g., see Grenz, 2001: 239-40; D. Garland, 2003: 738.

140. See documentation in Collins, 1999: 572 and Thiselton, 2000: 1288-89, which indicates to some commentators that an element of exhortation is somehow involved here; e.g., see Scroggs, 1966: 89; Hays, 1997: 273-74; Collins, 1999: 570; Thiselton, 2000: 1289.

mistaken idea among the hundreds of ideas that constitute Christian faith. Everything hinges on it. If it is true, then Paul must admit that everything he is saying and doing is worthless: "our proclamation has been in vain and your faith has been in vain" (v. 14).

Accordingly, he addresses in detail both parts of the issue in question: Is there a resurrection of the dead? (v. 12); and if there is, with what kind of body are people raised? (v. 35). He makes the strongest arguments he can to answer the first question and then exhorts people to "come to a sober and right mind" (v. 34). The response he is looking for is right understanding. The right response to the second question, though, is not simply to accept that people will be raised, but to understand more specifically what the resurrected body will be like. Paul makes two attempts to convince his readers that people will have spiritual bodies like the resurrected Christ does: verses 35-49 and verses 50-58. The implicit exhortation to readers in verse 49 is simply to rightly understand that resurrected bodies will be spiritual bodies like Christ's.

Although it is understandable that readers and copiers would expect something with hortative force here, Paul really hasn't finished his defense of the spiritual body yet. Verses 50-57 are a clarification of what he has just argued ("What I am saying . . . ," v. 50). The exhortation comes in verse 58. In other words, the exhortation in verse 34 concludes Paul's response to the question about whether people are raised bodily from the dead; and the exhortation in verse 58 concludes Paul's response to the question about what kind of body the resurrection body will be. Everything in verses 35-57 (including v. 49) is essentially a description of what Paul wants his readers to understand, so that they will know that their "labor is not in vain" (v. 58).

In the end, the overall meaning is little affected regardless of which way one translates the last verb in verse 49.[141] There are ample grounds in Paul's letters and other New Testament writings to conclude that the image of Christ includes both the body and other aspects of who people are. While the glorification of the body will take place at the end of Christians' transformation into Christ's image, from one degree of glory to another, other aspects of renewal begin long before then. Christians are created in God's image and are being transformed according to God's image in

141. For background discussion that leads to this conclusion, see Fee, 1987: 794-95; B. Childs, 1993: 584-85; Thiselton, 2000: 1288-89. Nevertheless, translators must go one way or the other and often go with the NRSV decision to translate the verb descriptive and future "we will bear the image." Similarly, Hafemann, 1996: 418.

Christ. Admittedly, they may not yet be the image of God in Christ fully and are unable yet to fully become so. However, Paul understandably urges them to reflect God now to the extent that they can in light of their new humanity. While such exhortation may be more implicit than explicit in 1 Corinthians 15:49, we have seen that it is more explicit elsewhere in the Pauline letters, as it is in the first letter of John.

1 John 3

John does not use the same image *(eikon)* language that Paul does. Nevertheless, there is at least an echo of the biblical likeness-image concept in 1 John 3:2.[142] John writes to fellow Christians that when God is revealed, Christians will be like God, for they will see God truly. As previously noted (and elaborated below), this is one of the clearest statements in the Bible about the impossibility of describing fully what it means for Christians to be the likeness-image of God in Christ. However, it also echoes Paul's confidence in Romans 8 that Christians will in fact end up conformed to Christ's image once their glorification is complete.

Evident are the telltale indications that the biblical image-of-God concept is in view here: connection and reflection. John opens the verse by noting a particularly intimate connection with God that Christians have: "We are God's children." This affirmation is also reminiscent of Romans 8, where Paul describes becoming (conformed to) Christ's image partly in terms of being God's children. However, while Christians' identity as God's children is assured, the consummation of being fully adopted by God awaits the future point of bodily redemption (Rom. 8:23). Then, because of the intimate connection between Christians and God, and the bondage of sin being removed, God intends for Christians to become like God in so many ways that they will warrant the simple description "like [*homoioi*] God."

There is some debate over whether John is lifting up God or Christ as the standard for humanity to be like. Ultimately, it is both. 1 John 3:2 begins by affirming that Christians are children of God, so Christ in particular is not the focus. Christians are siblings, not children, of Christ. The next affirmation is also about Christians: what they will be is not yet manifest. The third affirmation responds to that, though, by noting that something will appear at some point, and seeing whatever that is will have a transforming

---

142. On the connection with Genesis 1 here, see Barclay, 1976: 75; Strecker, 1996: 89.

effect on Christians. It would seem odd to say that seeing what Christians have become is what will transform Christians. In other words, it is more likely that the third affirmation is introducing a new subject whose manifestation will cause transformation.

The expression here "when he [or it] is revealed" *(ean phanerothe)* is identical to the expression just three verses earlier, which refers to the return of Christ; so that is likely also its meaning in 3:2.[143] John sometimes moves very quickly and subtly between the Father and the Son as the main subject when he refers to God. This is a good illustration of that.[144] Much in this verse applies to God in general.[145] The aspiration to be like God, for example, is rooted in the very being of humanity at creation. Nevertheless, for John as for other New Testament authors, God is now God in Christ. Both the broader concept of God and the specific reference to Christ are not far away, even when the author makes a reference to the Father.

The central idea in 3:2, then, is that transformation occurs in Christians when they see Christ "as he is."[146] The idea is similar to what Paul expresses in 2 Corinthians 3:18, as discussed above.[147] Paul notes that Christians, seeing the glory of the Lord as though reflected in a mirror, are being transformed into that image from one degree of glory to another. Seeing causes transformation. However, what Paul describes as happening presently by degrees, based on seeing only indirectly, becomes complete transformation in John when Christians see God in Christ directly. As Paul puts it in another context (1 Cor. 13:12), "now we see in a mirror, dimly, but then we will see face to face."

The point of 1 John 3:2 is not to identify all that ultimately being like God will include. In fact, John maintains here that such understanding is not available to humanity yet, for "what we will be has not yet been revealed."[148] Even the lack of being recognized, though, is a part of Chris-

---

143. On Christ as central here, see I. H. Marshall, 1978: 172; Keener, 2005: 19. R. Brown, 1982: 394 notes other supporters of this view, including Bultmann, Dodd, and Houlden.

144. For further discussion, see I. H. Marshall, 1978: 172.

145. On God as the primary focus of this verse, see R. Brown, 1982: 394-95, invoking Plummer, Schneider, and others in support.

146. So Gregory of Nyssa, 1987: 70; Brooke, 1912: 82; Bonhoeffer, 1959b: 273; Smalley, 1984: 147; Strecker, 1996: 88. The causality involved here, though, is not clear to all; e.g., see R. Brown, 1982: 396; Painter, 2002: 221.

147. For more on the similarity between Paul and John on this point, see I. H. Marshall, 1978: 172-73; Keener, 2005: 16.

148. On this theme, see Berkouwer, 1975: 105; Beyreuther and Finkenrath, 1976: 503; Smalley, 1984: 146; 2007: 139.

tians' limited likeness to Christ before death. As John explains in the previous verse: "The reason the world does not know us is that it did not know him" — the same statement about Christ that John included in the opening of his gospel (John 1:10).

Other New Testament chapters discussing humanity's renewal according to God's image in Christ (e.g., Colossians 3 and Romans 8) contain similar affirmations. Not until Christ returns will Christians be revealed — "in glory" (Col. 3:4; Rom. 8:19). Yet this new humanity is being renewed in God's image even now, because Christians have a particularly special connection with God in Christ: they are God's children (1 John 3:2).

God intends this new humanity, created according to (the image of) God (in Christ), to begin reflecting godly attributes. As noted above, Ephesians summarizes those attributes in terms of "righteousness and holiness," just as John summarizes them here in terms of purity. John's argument is that God in Christ is pure; and Christians do not merely wish, they "know" *(oidamen)*, that they will be like Christ. So purity should characterize all Christians now (v. 3). Even though their transformation is not yet complete, the fact that it will certainly be so in the future means that it ought to proceed as much as possible in the present. The glory that comes from reflecting God's attributes increases throughout the Christian's life. Nevertheless, glorification will not be complete until the glorification of the body when Christ returns.[149]

In several ways, then, the primary New Testament voices build on the Old Testament. Humanity indeed was originally created in God's image — specially connected with God and intended to reflect God — but humanity also became enslaved and covered by sin. However, Christ has enabled Christians to cast off the old humanity — including the bondage of sin — and to put on a new identity — the new humanity. Christians thereby have a closer connection with God and can increasingly reflect God's attributes. Nevertheless, they will not fully become the image of God in Christ until Christ returns, people are raised from the dead, and sin is removed completely. At that point Christians will have as intimate a connection with God, and be as magnificent a reflection of God, as is humanly possible. They will at last no longer just be *in* the image of God, they will fully *be* the image of God, in Christ.

---

149. On 1 John 3:1-3 and the themes of purity and glory, see I. H. Marshall, 1978: 172; Smalley, 1984: 148; T. Johnson, 1993: 68; Kruse, 2000: 116.

CHAPTER SEVEN

Humanity's Renewal in God's Image: Recurring Themes

At various points in Chapter 6, the discussion has already gathered together insights from multiple New Testament passages on humanity's renewal according to God's image in Christ. There remain several overarching themes that warrant special attention. They include the place of God's image in eternity and destiny, the difference between people and God's image in the process of renewal, and the centrality of connection and reflection in what God's image entails.

Eternity and Destiny

Many commentators have rightly noted that humanity's renewal according to God's image in Christ accomplishes what God originally intended for Adam and Eve in Eden.[1] However, far more than a return to Eden is involved here. God's image is forward-looking by its very nature.[2] It is primarily about God's eternal purposes for humanity — not merely current attributes, whether those like God's or those unlike animals' (see Ch. 3). God's purposes involve much more for humanity than is evident in the initial creation.[3]

---

1. E.g., Gregory of Nyssa, 1972: 586; A. M. Ramsey, 1949: 151; Cairns, 1973: 200; Grenz, 2004: 624; Witherington, 2009: v. 1, 239.

2. For further development of the eschatological character of God's image, see Fichtner, 1978: 172; Tracy, 1983: 248; Hefner, 1984: 336-37; Junker-Kenny, 2001: 81; Shults, 2003: 235-37 (who invokes Irenaeus, Athanasius, Herder, Schleiermacher, Irving, Troeltsch, and Moltmann in support); G. Peterson, 2008: 472; Sexton, 2010: 200 (echoing Grenz, 2001: 240); Vorster, 2011: 21; Lubardic, 2011: 530.

3. Haering, 1915: 391 similarly speaks in terms of purpose; Thielicke, 1966: 172 in terms

As discussed in Chapter 2, Christ is the image of God and has always been so. Humanity's creation in (according to) the image of God has always had the image of Christ — the image of God that is Christ — as its model and goal.[4] Today is no different. People learn far less about what being God's image entails by looking to Adam and Eve than they do by looking to Christ.[5]

The New Testament is more concerned about Christians focusing on becoming conformed to the image of Christ (Rom. 8:29) than about pointing people back to Adam. Part of the backdrop to Romans 8 is Romans 5, where Paul does not merely explain a parallel between Adam and Christ. He in effect insists that Christ rather than Adam should "much more surely" be humanity's concern (vv. 15, 17). Even before he sinned, Adam did not have the same lasting righteousness that a regenerated, justified Christian has.[6] In Christ, the old *adam* is not being made better, but a new humanity is created for the purpose of a much greater renewal (Col. 3:9-10).[7] As Paul clarifies shortly after the image passages in 2 Corinthians 3 and 4, "in Christ there is a new creation" (5:17). The old humanity has been crucified and buried (Rom. 6:4-6).[8] All of humanity and the nonhuman creation have a great stake in that renewal.[9]

Before Adam and Eve sinned, they were not yet fulfilling all that God ultimately intended for humanity. They still needed to move from simple righteousness to confirmed righteousness — not just eating from the tree of life but also bypassing and leaving behind the tree of the knowledge of good and evil to do so. They also needed the same sort of "spiritual body"

---

of promise; Hughes, 1989: 410-11 in terms of design; Grenz, 2001: 181 (invoking Dorner) in terms of destination.

4. For more on this theme, see Orr, 1948: 269-70; Bruce, 1957: 194; I. H. Marshall, 2001: 60; S. Holmes, 2005: 319; Smail, 2006: 63; Mangano, 2008: 170.

5. So Thomas, 1949: 160; Pannenberg, 1985: 51 (invoking Calvin and Luther); Boer, 1990: 160; Watson, 1997: 292-93; Shults, 2003: 239-40; Witherington, 2009: v. 1, 198; Gaffin, 2010: 137.

6. Litton, 1960: 120; Thielicke, 1966: 154; Baker, 1991: 78-79; and Hoekema, 1994: 82 develop this theme in terms of righteousness, while McFadyen, 1990: 275 develops it in terms of freedom and Pannenberg, 1991: v. 2, 212-14 in terms of righteousness, eternal life, and knowledge.

7. For elaboration, see Wilson, 1973: 359; Nellas, 1987: 38-39; Ellacuría, 1993: 585; Sherlock, 1996: 49; Hicks, 2000: 156; Grenz, 2002: 47-48.

8. So Schweizer, 1982: 198; Witherington, 2009: v. 1, 199.

9. See McFadyen, 1990: 46 and Yong, 2007: 191 on humanity; Thompson, 2005: 29 and Cahill, 2006b: 77 on the nonhuman creation.

that Christ gained after his resurrection — which 1 Corinthians 15 includes as part of what it means to bear the image of God in Christ.[10] A kingdom of people with spiritual bodies is not a new idea introduced as a result of the Fall. Rather, it is a kingdom that God prepared for humanity "from the foundation of the world," as Christ explains it to his fellow resurrected brothers and sisters at the final judgment in Matthew 25:34. So the renewal that people undergo in Christ is partly a return to how God created Adam and Eve in Eden (the "re" in renewal), and partly something more (the "new" in renewal).

Simply being created in God's image has never enabled people actually to reflect the entire range of God's attributes that God intends — in terms of body, righteousness, reason, relationships, rulership, and other attributes. There have been various ways that people have been like God to some degree, particularly before the Fall. However, even pre-fallen humanity required transformation according to the image of Christ from one degree of glory to another, to echo 2 Corinthians 3:18. In some respects, as with bodily transformation, that would likely have taken place in a moment. However, in other respects, where living out God's intentions required growth, people would have needed to grow over time. Even Jesus grew in wisdom (Luke 2:52) and in obedience (Heb. 5:8) during his sin-free human life.

Living according to God's image has always been about a trajectory guided by God's intentions to be fulfilled only in Christ, not about a set of attributes to which humanity needs to return.[11] In Christ people indeed undo the setbacks of the Fall; but such restoration enables development and is not an endpoint.[12] Hence, the change that 2 Corinthians 3:18 envisions is not just about restoring humanity as created in Eden but also about moving forward to previously unknown levels of glory, with a focus on Christ rather than the original Adam.[13] A similar outlook is visible in other New Testament passages on humanity's renewal according to God's image in Christ.[14]

---

10. Litton, 1960: 117 and Kline, 1980: 31 discuss the different stages of righteousness, while Vos, 1972: 169 and Grenz, 2001: 236-37 (cf. 2004: 623) discuss the "spiritual body."

11. The necessity of Christ's further work beyond the original creation is developed in Nellas, 1987: 38.

12. So Shepherd, 1988: 1019; Hoekema, 1994: 26; Wilkins, 1997: 116-17; Wells, 2004: 38.

13. On this focus in 2 Corinthians 3, see Thielicke, 1966: 181; Murphy-O'Connor, 1982: 54; Dunn, 1996: 222; Frame, 2006: 235.

14. See Clines, 1968: 102 on Romans 8; Schweizer, 1982: 198 and J. Barr, 1993: 164 on

Nevertheless, from creation onward humanity has the full status of being created in God's image. Humanity has a special connection with God, and God intends humanity to be a meaningful reflection of who God is and what God does. That status is not affected by sin, as Chapter 4 has demonstrated. So the fact of humanity's existence in God's image is not what changes in Christ; rather, in Christ people put on a "new humanity" in which there is no bondage to sin. People are now freed to "be who they are." As in various aspects of Paul's (and others') theology, the imperative — the challenge to be or do something — rests on the indicative — who people in fact already are by virtue of creation and redemption.[15] God has created people with the intention that they reflect various godly attributes of being and action, and in Christ the fulfillment of that intention is now possible.[16]

Accordingly, renewal in God's image has a "not yet" as well as an "already" character to it.[17] The status of being clothed in the new humanity is already a reality for people alive today, with huge implications (see Conclusion). However, the fulfillment of actually exercising all the attributes that God intends for humanity has not yet come to be. Even for Christians, the "not yet" has only *begun* to become "already." The culmination of that process will be the return of Christ when people experience bodily resurrection.[18] This understanding is so securely rooted in a variety of New Testament texts that it accords with either of the competing translations of 1 Corinthians 15:49 discussed in Chapter 6.[19]

The spiritual body of the resurrection is only one of the many attri-

---

Colossians 3; M. Barth, 1974: 508, Schnackenburg, 1991: 200, and Best, 1998: 435 on Ephesians 4; Bray, 1991: 208 and Black, 2006: 190 on 1 Corinthians 15.

15. On the indicative and the imperative in relation to God's image, see Tracy, 1983: 248; Richard, 1986: 165-66; Gushee, 2012: 109. Martin Luther King Jr. speaks of this imperative in terms of "oughtness" (see discussion in Wills, 2009: 24).

16. Regarding implications for being, see D. Robinson, 2011: 169. Regarding implications for action, see Lohse, 1971: 142-43; Teel, 2010: 95. Regarding both, see Hoekema, 1994: 28; McFadyen, 1990: 18; Duncan, 2008; D. Carson, 2010: 23.

17. Calvin, 1960: bk. I, ch. 15, sec. 4 describes this tension in terms of "now" vs. "in heaven"; Thielicke, 1966: 180 in terms of "present" and "future"; Flender, 1976: 288 in terms of "now" and "still to be." Wild, 1985: 135-36 speaks of particular believers "growing into" what is already the corporate reality of the church's status "in Christ."

18. So Ja. Edwards, 1991: 218 and Schnelle, 1996: 100 (Christ's return); and Schreiner, 1998: 453 and Green, 2011: 298 (bodily resurrection).

19. Those who concur on this point include Shults, 2003: 239-40, who translates 1 Corinthians 15:49 as a description of the bearing/fulfilling God's image that will follow resurrection, and Fee, 1987: 795, who translates it as challenging Christians to start bearing/fulfilling God's image now to the degree possible.

butes that God intends for humanity to manifest. A wide range of attributes is in view, as this chapter will discuss below. All of these attributes have a forward-looking character to them, in that God intends more for them than can be manifested in humanity's finite and fallen state.[20] Some of the attributes themselves suggest that no definitive list of attributes is possible from the vantage point of the present. For instance, God intends for humanity to have freedom to be and do more in the future than others have been and done in the past.[21] Some would refer to such freedom in terms of the creativity that God intends humanity to express.[22] By their very nature, freedom and creativity are constantly opening up previously unimagined vistas bounded only by God's intentions and glory.[23]

Appropriately recognizing the eternal context of God's image can be a source of great encouragement. It has always been humanity's destiny to progress from one degree of glory to another.[24] Without any eternal awareness at all, it is tempting to see humanity in its sinfulness as a rather disappointing reflection of God. With an "overrealized eschatology" such as plagued the Corinthians of New Testament fame, the idea that all of God's redeeming and renewing intentions for humanity are somehow already fulfilled is similarly discouraging.[25] The "already" is indeed wonderful, but the "not yet" is truly inspiring.

This inspiring future aspect of being in God's image is captured well in the concept of "destiny."[26] From the Latin *destinare* ("to make firm, establish, settle"), destiny suggests a future that is sure. In the words of Danish poet Inger Christensen:

20. See Boer, 1990: 68; Shults, 2003: 237-38; Ecumenical, 2004: 516; van Huyssteen, 2006: 141-42.

21. So Tracy, 1983: 249; Hümmel, 1984: 92; McFadyen, 1990: 41; Reynolds, 2008: 182. On the related idea of the unknowable character of both God and humans in the image of God, see Woodhead, 2006: 238.

22. E.g., Carlson, 2008: 23, 32-33, 81-82, 114-15 (drawing on the work of Gregory of Nyssa, Giovanni Pico della Mirandola, and Giordano Bruno); Reynolds, 2008: 182.

23. On glory — first God's and then derivatively humanity's — as the defining summary of God-intended attributes, see Chapters 2 and 6; J. Murray, 1968: 319 notes the preeminence of Christ here.

24. Hughes, 1989: 9 develops this theme in terms of destiny.

25. Wilson and Blomberg, 1993: 13 reflect on the first discouragement; Schnelle, 1996: 99-100 on the second. For more on overrealized eschatology, see Fee, 1987: 795.

26. For examples of destiny language to convey the future aspect of being in God's image, see Haering, 1915: v. 1, 393-94; Moltmann, 1984: 15-16; Vanhoozer, 1997: 165; Horton, 2005: 95; 2006: 182-83; Sexton, 2010: 193 (echoing Grenz, 2001: 280); Henriksen, 2011: 270.

Imago Dei — the goal of human life.
The most important is not what we are
but what we well
might be
Maybe
cannot be as yet
but can and shall become.[27]

It is tempting to think that being created in God's image secures humanity's dignity in the past and present, while being renewed according to God's image in Christ secures Christians' destiny in the future. However, dignity and destiny are as interdependent as they are distinct. While people may more commonly associate image-related dignity with humanity's creation, destiny predates even creation, rooted as it is in God's foreknowledge: "Those whom he foreknew he also predestined to be conformed to the image" of Christ (Rom. 8:29). People may also more commonly associate image-related destiny with humanity's future bodily resurrection. Nevertheless, dignity follows even resurrection as God's people live out the dignity of God-glorifying rulership as God's image in Christ "forever and ever" (Rev. 22:5).

Dignity and destiny intertwine not only temporally but also logically. As important as creation is in establishing human dignity, it is human *destiny* that ensures human dignity. Because God offers to all, through Christ, a destiny in which human dignity becomes gloriously visible, humanity gains a dignity even now simply by being the recipient of such an amazing offer.[28] Moreover, it is no accident that Christ takes on human form to make this destiny possible. Dignifying people by creating them in the divine image ensured that, when it became necessary, God would pay the ultimate price of the humiliation of the Incarnation and death on a cross (Phil. 2:6-8) in order to secure human destiny.[29]

27. Poem reprinted in Aargaard, 1982: 358.

28. In the Bible, the term "glory" in conjunction with God's image serves as a strong link between dignity and destiny. While glory commonly accompanies the reflection of divine attributes involved in human destiny, the very terms for glory (e.g., *kabod* in Hebrew) suggest the idea of dignity — see Rad, 1964b: 391.

29. This point is developed in Chapter 2. For more on how dignity depends on destiny and destiny depends on dignity, see Eibach, 1976: 91-93; Nellas, 1987: 36-37; Hilkert, 1995: 195-96; Reinders, 1997: 200-201; 2006: 123; Watts, 2006: 249; Henriksen, 2011: 267-68;

This destiny is in some sense available to all of humanity, for God has created all and does not want anyone to perish (2 Pet. 3:9). In that sense, God intends for all to reflect God-glorifying attributes. God has created all according to the divine image and wants all actually to become God's image in Christ.[30] However, many members of the human race — those wearing the "old humanity" in Adam according to Colossians 3, Ephesians 4, and 1 Corinthians 15 — reject this destiny. Only the church, the body of Christ, has "put on" the "new humanity" and goes on to fulfill God's purposes for humanity in Christ. They are the people who live out the destiny that God intends for humanity created in the divine image.

As noted in the earlier discussion of Romans 8:29 (see Ch. 6), just as the Pilgrims fulfilled their destiny — though every individual among them did not survive — so humanity's destiny is sure even if some members abandon ship. Those who are now undergoing renewal according to Christ's image — the image of God in Christ — can have confidence regarding their destiny. Christ has already demonstrated — through life, death, resurrection, and glorification — what the trajectory of being in God's image entails.[31] Moreover, Christ is the "first fruits" of the fulfillment of God's intentions for humanity. To a large degree, Christ's history is humanity's destiny,[32] and humanity's destiny in Christ is the confirmation and assurance of human dignity.[33]

Humanity's destiny entails glory — participating in the glory of Christ.[34] That glory is not just some sort of amorphous glow, but involves specific attributes that will in some measure be like God's and will glorify God (cf. discussion of glory in Ch. 2).[35] Those include the various attributes highlighted in Chapter 5. For instance, such mental/spiritual attributes as freedom and responsible choice are a part of human destiny

---

D. Robinson, 2011: 174-75. On the related idea of creation in God's image involving an interplay between dignity and vocation, see Sands, 2010: 36.

30. For more on this theme, see Oberdorfer, 2010: 238.

31. See Brunner, 1947: 112; Pannenberg, 1991: v. 2, 219-20; Vanhoozer, 1997: 173; S. Wright, 2003: 42.

32. So Witherington, 2009: v. 1, 20. Similarly Bonhoeffer, 1959b: 274; Hughes, 1989: 36; Schnelle, 1996: 102; Vanhoozer, 1997: 165; S. Wright, 2003: 42; McFarland, 2005: 53; Vorster, 2011: 19.

33. See Moltmann, 1984: 16; Hilkert, 1995: 202.

34. On glory and humanity's destiny, see Hughes, 1989: 27; Mathews, 1995: 171; Schnelle, 1996: 98-99; Watson, 1997: 298; Gaffin, 2010: 146.

35. For elaboration, see Moltmann, 1976: 68; Grenz, 2001: 238-39; Erickson, 2013: 471.

in Christ.[36] So is righteousness,[37] including moral character and personal integration/integrity.[38] Human destiny similarly includes godly rulership over creation.[39] Moreover, a love relationship with God and others[40] — an eternal fellowship and community[41] — is an integral aspect of that destiny. The final section of this chapter will have more to say about such attributes.

People and Image

Being in God's image, then, is not primarily about how people are presently like God. Rather, it is about a destiny in which God intends that humanity will manifest attributes resembling God's, in appropriate measure, to God's glory. It is that goal, exemplified in the very person of Christ, that is God's image. Sin has no more altered that goal than it has altered Christ — which explains why the Bible never teaches that sin has destroyed or damaged God's image (see Ch. 4). If God's image is not damaged, then it does not need restoration. *People* are badly damaged by sin and need restoration, but that is not true of God's image. People continue to be created according to God's image without qualification. The agenda for who people are to become has not changed.

Just as no biblical texts indicate that God's image has been damaged, the Bible never indicates that God's image is restored in Christ (see detailed consideration of the relevant texts in Chs. 4 and 6). In light of how much is at stake here, as explained in Chapter 1 and the Conclusion, it is vital that people not consider God's image to be damaged by sin and in need of restoration. Many things about people are badly damaged, but their status as created in God's image is not. Nevertheless, the idea of a damaged image that can be restored in Christ has long been widespread.

36. So Brunner, 1947: 98, 106; Moltmann, 1976: 66-67; Sherlock, 1996: 56-57; Cone, 1997: 137.

37. See Haering, 1915: v. 1, 399; Chafer, 1947: 172; Black, 2006: 191-92.

38. On character, see Cairns, 1973: 60; on integration, see Pannenberg, 1985: 142.

39. K. Barth, 1958a: 206 and Pannenberg, 1985: 531 develop this aspect of human destiny.

40. On relationship and destiny, see Berkouwer, 1975: 59 and Fichtner, 1978: 36; on love and destiny, see Brunner, 1947: 106 and D. Robinson, 2011: 175.

41. On fellowship and destiny, see Moltmann, 1976: 63 and Pannenberg, 1991: v. 2, 180, 227, 231; on community and destiny, see Grenz, 2001: 272, 303 and Wills, 2009: 159-60 (drawing on Martin Luther King).

Documenting the prevalence of such misunderstanding is important, for multiple reasons. Those who take for granted that God's image requires no restoration need to see how widely a contrary view is circulating, and thus the urgency of addressing it. Those who have never considered this matter carefully, casually referring to God's image as fully present in one breath and in need of restoration in another, need to recognize the importance of more consistently affirming an undamaged image. Others who intentionally promote the idea that God's image is damaged by sin and restored in Christ hopefully will recognize the importance and value of reconsidering their view and encouraging others to do so as well.

As explained in Chapter 4, the idea that God's image is not damaged and so needs no restoration is well grounded in the teaching of the Bible. It is also well represented in the history of Christian commentary on God's image. People who speak of a lost/damaged and restored image often do not argue against the idea of an undamaged image — they simply take for granted that if people are damaged and need restoration, the same goes for God's image. They overlook the difference between *being* God's image (as Christ is) and *being created and restored according to* God's image (as humanity is — specially connected with God and *intended* to reflect God's attributes).

Many influential voices have maintained that God's image has been lost or damaged. Some claim that humanity therefore needs that image restored. Others argue essentially the same thing, but in different words. In their body of writing, particular authors may use different terms to describe the current or ideal state of God's image. In fact, the terms they use may vary even within a particular piece of writing. In the pages that follow, when a citation documents someone as affirming that God's image needs "restoration" or "repair," the intention is not to claim that this is the only way that the commentator ever speaks about human fallenness and renewal — just that the commentator has so spoken in the venue noted. Those who have heard this voice may well have been influenced by it and may have in turn passed on that understanding to others. Nevertheless, some of the authors mentioned here might well acknowledge that their cited statement is not in line with their best thinking on the subject. Those authors would probably warmly affirm the need to be consistent in affirming that God's image is neither damaged nor in need of restoration.

Only a sample of the relevant voices will be heard below. Even a sample such as this is sufficient to suggest the strength and influence of these voices.

A number of commentators explicitly affirm the importance of "restoring" God's image and that such restoration can indeed take place in

Christ.[42] Some find this notion to be widespread.[43] One way to popularize the idea has been through published prayers such as that by the poet John Donne, which implores God to "restore Thine image."[44] Such prayers flow readily from the view that Christ's redemptive sacrifice has made possible the restoration of God's image.[45] Some emphasize that this restoration takes place gradually.[46] Others focus on its completion. The idea is that complete restoration of God's image takes place in Christ.[47] It will be completed only after death.[48]

Many of the common inadequate assumptions about God's image discussed in Chapter 3 have understandably led people to assume that God's image has been damaged and needs restoration. What is a little surprising is that some commentators refer to the actual New Testament texts that speak of God's image in Christ and claim to see there a restoration of "the image" rather than the person. Some see this throughout such passages.[49] Others see it specifically in Colossians 3:10.[50] More see it in both Colossians 3:10 and Ephesians 4:24.[51] Still others find it in Romans 8:29, 1 Corinthians

42. For example, Horst, 1950: 270; Maston, 1959: 11; Hoeksema, 1966: 209; Kittel, 1964d: 397; Cahill, 1980: 279, 2006b: 55; A. T. Lincoln, 1990: 287; Sherlock, 1996: 72; International, 2004: par. 51; Garner, 2007: 111; Yong, 2007: 189 (following John Swinton); Witherington, 2009: v. 1, 20; v. 2, 788; Driscoll and Breshears, 2010: 138; Bullock, 2012: 85. Bonhoeffer (1959b: 272) adds the unusual claim that Christ has restored the image of God in everyone (i.e., "in all that bears a human form").

43. Brumble, 1992: 373 traces it through a wide range of literature; Conn, 1993: 247 notes its influence in the medieval monastic movement; Altmann, 1968: 247 sees it as something that Scholastics like Aquinas and reformers like Luther and Calvin held in common.

44. E.g., Donne, 1896a: 172-73, at the conclusion of his poem "Good Friday, 1613, Riding Westward."

45. So Hilton, 1908: bk. 2, ch. 1, p. 136; Maston, 1959: 12; A. Murray, 1965: 102; Shepherd, 1988: 1020; Boer, 1990: 36; Hoekema, 1994: 10; Wells, 2004: 36; Cahill, 2006b: 75; Reynolds, 2008: 199. Ferngren (2009: 102), drawing on Stroumsa, 1990: 30, finds ample support for this view in the early church.

46. For example, Calvin, 1960: bk. III, ch. 20, sec. 45; Hoekema, 1994: 47.

47. So A. Strong, 1907: 515; Kilcrease, 2010: 33.

48. So Luther, 1958: 64-65; Hümmel, 1984: 92; Wilson and Blomberg, 1993: 9; Wilkins, 1997: 116; Vorster, 2011: 19.

49. E.g., Hoekema, 1994: 22-27; S. Wright, 2003: 35.

50. E.g., Gerhard, 1962: 36; Kilcrease, 2010: 33.

51. Pannenberg, 1991: v. 2, 210-12 finds substantial evidence of this outlook in Reformation and post-Reformation theology. More recent examples include Barabas, 1963: 371; A. T. Lincoln, 1990: 287; Patzia, 1990: 251. Pieper, 1950: 518-19 even claims that "Col. 3:10 and Eph. 4:24 distinctly state that it [God's image] is being restored in the believer."

15:49, and 2 Corinthians 3:18 as well.[52] As detailed in Chapters 4 and 6 of the present work, however, none of those passages talk about a changing image. Instead they all talk about *people* changing in accordance with a standard (the image of Christ) that is not changing.

"Restoration" is not the only common way that people speak about reversing the supposed damage to God's image. Some speak instead (or in addition) about the "renewal" of God's image.[53] The main idea is that God renews this image through Christ.[54] Less common are a variety of other terms that implicitly or explicitly refer to getting back a lost image. This way of speaking may assert that Christians "recover," "regain," or "reclaim" God's image,[55] or it may indicate that God's image is "re-created" or "recuperated" in humanity.[56] Others use terms that suggest more an improvement in a damaged image than reclaiming something lost. According to this understanding, God's image must be "repaired," "redeemed," or "redone" in Christians.[57] Still others use language that focuses more on the process of renewal in which God's image is "evolving," "moving," "developing," or even "becoming."[58] In this process, the image is being "perfected."[59]

Most of these terms are apt descriptions of redeemed people, who are changing. However, as we have seen, they are not accurate descriptions of God's image, which is not changing. In light of the fact that no New Testament texts talk about a changing image, then, it is a little surprising that some commentators claim that the New Testament texts referring to God's

52. E.g., Kittel, 1964d: 396-97; Eichrodt, 1967: 130. Smail, 2003: 23 focuses primarily on 2 Corinthians 3:18.

53. For example, John Paul II, 1997b: 521; Barackman, 2001: 491; Middleton, 2005: 17; Witherington, 2009: v. 2, 642, 788.

54. So K. Barth, 1958a: 200; Cairns, 1973: 195; Chestnut, 1984: 113; Sherlock, 1996: 50.

55. Recover: e.g., Merton, 1981: 123; Vorster, 2011: 19. Regain: e.g., Brunner, 1952: v. 2, 53; Wells, 2004: 38; Visala, 2014: 109. J. Wesley uses both terms often (recover: 1985n: 358; 1985o: 310; 1985h: 209, 214; regain: 1985a: 143; 1985b: 163; 1985h: 214). Ferngren (2009: 102), drawing on Stroumsa, 1990: 49, finds ample support for the idea of reclaiming the image of God in the early church.

56. Recreated: e.g., Bonhoeffer, 1959b: 270. Recuperated: e.g., Origen, as discussed in Maloney, 1973: 73-74.

57. Repaired: e.g., Vorster, 2011: 18; Gushee, 2012: 107. Redeemed: e.g., Lints, 2006a: 219; Witherington, 2009: v. 2, 737. Redone: e.g., Fichtner, 1978: 65.

58. Evolving: e.g., Pannenberg, 1985: 50-51 (drawing on Ficino and Herder) and De Smedt and De Cruz, 2014: 148. Moving: e.g., Cortez, 2010: 17. Developing: e.g., Mahoney, 2010: 682 (drawing on Catholic doctrine since Vatican II). Becoming: T. Peters, 2010: 223.

59. So Gill, 1978: 396; Wilson and Blomberg, 1993: 9; John Paul II, 1997b: 521; Pinckaers, 2005: 157 (drawing on Aquinas); Ciampa and Rosner, 2010: 825.

image in Christ actually affirm a "renewal" or "transformation" of the image itself (much as others affirm a "restoration" — see above). Some assert this of all such New Testament texts.[60] Others make the claim in relation to Colossians 3:10 or Ephesians 4:24.[61] Still others make it regarding Romans 8:29 or 2 Corinthians 3:18.[62] Such claims are illustrations of reading ideas into the text rather than drawing ideas out of the text — a misstep not uncommon in discussions of God's image (recall Ch. 1).

Reading ideas into New Testament texts causes additional reading into the text of the Old Testament. Some commentators suggest that simply because New Testament texts supposedly teach that the image is changing, the Old Testament must teach that the image has suffered damage. Some understand this damage in terms of the complete loss of God's image.[63] For others, the same logic causes them to conclude without Old Testament textual evidence that God's image must be "canceled" or "marred."[64]

Many other commentators are not so explicit about the logic that leads them from the New Testament back to the Old Testament. Nevertheless, they similarly assert the position that what is damaged in the Old Testament is restored in the New Testament. For some of them, a completely lost image is restored.[65] For others, this lost image is regained, gotten back, recovered, or renewed.[66] For some, the image that is restored has been only marred rather than lost.[67] Others basically agree, although they refer to this partial loss in terms of an image that is corrupted, defaced, or

60. E.g., Cairns, 1973: 51; Sherlock, 1996: 73; Frame, 2006: 229.

61. E.g., Blomberg, 1999: 35 (Col. and Eph.); Cortez, 2010: 17 (Col.).

62. E.g., Mangano, 2008: 12 (Rom.); Cortez, 2010: 17 (2 Cor.).

63. Examples include L. Berkhof, 1949: 204; Gerhard, 1962: 62; Crawford, 1966: 233. Shepherd (1988: 1019) sees this as a common Lutheran understanding, while Pannenberg (1991: v. 2, 215) attributes it to "older Protestant" commentators in general.

64. Calvin, 1996: 50 (canceled); Hoekema, 1994: 30 (marred). Schell (1901: 166) uses similar language: "To prove that man has fallen from the image of God, I have but to prove that this image is restored to man when he is redeemed in Christ Jesus."

65. E.g., H. D. McDonald, 1981: 16; O'Brien, 1987: 191; Patzia, 1990: 76, 251; T. Johnson, 1993: 68; R. Jewett, 2007 (drawing on Jervell, 1960). See *The Cloud,* 1981: 70 for a discussion of this view in Irenaeus. D. Hall, 1986: 80-81 sees its influence in "the Protestant Reformers"; and Lewis and Demarest, 1994: v. 2, 127 note its influence among Lutherans in particular.

66. Regained: e.g., Brunner, 1952: v. 2, 53. Gotten back: e.g., Dunn, 1988: 495. Recovered: Achtemeier, 2001: 415 (also Gonzalez, 2007: 29 formulates the view of Irenaeus in this way). Renewed: Jónsson, 1988: 12 (drawing on Brunner; similarly Witherington, 2009: v. 2, 757, who uses the term "effaced" rather than lost).

67. E.g., W. Pope, 1875: v. 1, 6; Hughes, 1962: 119; Stott, 1964: 119; Boer, 1990: 157; Schreiner, 1998: 453.

deformed.[68] For some, only the appearance of the image that is restored has been compromised. However, because the term "image" has a strong visual orientation in many languages, damage done to the appearance of the image is tantamount to damage done to the image itself. Commentators typically describe such damage by claiming that God's image, restored in Christ, has been tarnished or distorted.[69]

The idea that in Christ God's damaged image can be restored is problematic first and foremost because of its lack of biblical support. Nevertheless, it also has the many other problems associated with the idea that God's image is damaged in the first place (see Ch. 4). Prominent among them is the implication that people can be in God's image to different degrees.[70] Since human dignity is a function of being in God's image, a decreasing and increasing image suggests that human dignity itself is a variable characteristic. Those who are least in God's image thereby become least protected from the killing and other abuse that being in God's image is supposed to protect people from (see Ch. 3). The danger here becomes particularly pointed when people are not recognized to be "persons"[71] or even "human beings"[72] until their status as being in God's image is sufficiently restored.

Connection and Reflection

Sin, then, damages people rather than God's image, and the restoration that takes place in Christ involves people rather than God's image. In

68. E.g., Hoekema, 1994: 23, 85 (corrupted); Orr, 1948: 266 (defaced); Altmann, 1968: 246-47 (deformed).

69. E.g., D. Garland, 1999: 200 (tarnished); Witherington, 2009: v. 1, 238 (distorted).

70. For the idea that the damaged image is only partly restored, by degrees, even in Christians, see Thielicke, 1966: 180; Merriell, 1990 (drawing on Aquinas); Pannenberg, 1991: v. 2, 216-17; Hoekema, 1994: 28.

71. For example, Fletcher (1954: 221-22) argues that people "become persons" and fully warrant image-of-God status when various "qualities of personal stature" have sufficiently developed.

72. For example, Herder (1800: 229), who exercised significant influence on later discussions of God's image such as Pannenberg's and Grenz's, maintained that "[w]e are not yet human beings, but are daily becoming so." D. Kelsey (2009: v. 2, 904) finds this influence "very troubling" in Grenz (see, e.g., Grenz, 2001: 179-80): "The entirety of human history, then, [is] not in fact a history of actual human beings, in actual human communities, actually in the image of God. . . . So why treat them as having the dignity, and deserving the respect, of ends in themselves, and not merely as means to our own ends?"

fact, more than restoration is taking place in Christ — there is a forward-looking, eternal dimension to God's image that goes beyond restoration of what once was. With that framework in mind, we can now focus more specifically on what it means for humanity to be renewed according to God's image in Christ. As has always been the case regarding being in God's image (see Ch. 3), connection and reflection are central.

Connection

Through a careful analysis of Colossians 1:15, 2 Corinthians 4:4, and Hebrews 1:3 in particular, Chapter 2 has already demonstrated that special connection with God is one central aspect of Christ being God's image. Chapter 6 has documented through detailed consideration of Romans 8:29, 2 Corinthians 3:18, and Colossians 3:10, among other passages, that humanity's renewal according to God's image in Christ is also about a special connection — about literally being "in" Christ.

Admittedly, there are significant differences in how image-of-God language applies to humanity and how it applies to Christ. Christ, both as human and divine, is God's image. Humanity will never be God, though Christ eternally is. Even as human, Christ is undamaged by sin, so Christ *actually* manifests in being and action everything of God that God intends for humanity to reflect as God's image. However, sin has damaged humanity terribly, such that many of God's intentions for humanity, established at the creation of humanity in God's image, *cannot actually* be fulfilled in people at present.

To the extent that the influence of sin in people diminishes, the fulfillment of those intentions can begin. Nevertheless, complete fulfillment — complete conforming to (Romans 8), transforming into (2 Corinthians 3), and renewal according to (Colossians 3) God's image — must await resurrection and glorification following Christ's return. In other words, Christ *is* God's image, whereas humanity is only *in* (or *according to*) God's image until the glorification after bodily resurrection, when those in Christ will finally *become* and *bear* God's image.

Focusing exclusively on these differences between Christ and humanity (i.e., between Christ and other human beings) can lead to neglecting their common orientation toward God's image. As discussed in greater detail in Chapter 2, there are at least three major problems with overly separating Christ and humanity when it comes to God's image.

First, doing so often reflects the assumption that being in God's image is primarily about how people are actually like God. This book has argued in great detail that actual likeness to God is not what humanity's existence in God's image is all about. Being in God's image is about a special connection with God and the intended reflection of God. Whereas for Christ, with no sin present, the intended and actual are identical, there is a huge disconnect due to sin between what God intends people to reflect and what they actually reflect. That explains how people can continue to be in God's image even in their sin, according to the Bible's consistent language. No image of God is damaged by sin, because neither the fact of people's special connection with God nor what God *intends* them to reflect has changed. God is at work conforming Christians — those wearing the new humanity — to the same image that Christ is (see discussion of 2 Cor. 3:18 in Ch. 6).

There are two other problems with overly separating Christ and humanity when it comes to God's image. One involves the way that doing so overlooks how the New Testament repeatedly draws on the creation and redemption language and themes of Genesis. The image of God/Christ passages in 2 Corinthians 3–4, Colossians 3, and Hebrews 1, plus the Christ-as-Second-Adam passages (see Ch. 6), build on the Old Testament image-of-God concept in a transformative way.

The remaining problem is that separating Christ and humanity regarding God's image neglects the common language that the Bible uses to describe the divine intentions involved in each case. God intends for people and Christ both to manifest the glory of God in specific ways. Those ways include attributes reflecting who God is and what God does, such as reason/wisdom, righteousness, rulership, and relationship/family (more on such attributes below).

Rather than being separated, then, Christ as the image of God and humanity in the image of God are profoundly associated. As detailed in Chapter 2, although humanity in general does not see Christ until after the Incarnation, Christ has always been God's image from before the creation of humanity. That is to say, the standard for what humanity was to be — an understanding of what the humanity of Christ entails — existed before God created Adam/*adam*. Although the Second Adam in his redemptive work as Jesus Christ is a fulfillment of who God has always intended people to be, that is not because Christ becomes something new. Christ is the same yesterday, today, and forever (Heb. 13:8). Christ becoming flesh and blood is not a new initiative developed by God to restore a wayward humanity. Christ has always been the image of God, the standard of humanity, and the perfect lamb whose blood redeems believers. For this redemptive task Christ "was destined before the foundation of the world, but was revealed at the end of the ages" (1 Pet. 1:20).

Humanity and Christ are both specially connected to God — humanity in God's image and Christ as God's image. The fulfillment of humanity actually becoming God's image requires union with Christ. Some commentators use related concepts such as identification or representation, but the core idea here is that there is an intimate connection with God in Christ that gives people a distinctive identity.[73] Renewal according to God's image in Christ involves fulfilling God's intention at creation, when God first created humanity in God's image. In other words, the image of God in the Old and New Testament and the image of (God in) Christ in the New Testament are essentially the same,[74] reflecting the oneness of God and Christ.

Humanity's renewal according to God's image in Christ, then, is rooted in connection with God through Christ. It also involves reflection of God through Christ — fulfilling God's intention for humanity through Christ by reflecting appropriate divine attributes. Such reflection begins in the present and it reaches its fullness in the future.

Reflection in the Present

As has been the case since the beginning, God intends for people to be like God — to reflect attributes of God — to the glory of God. What they have not been able to be and do on their own, especially since the Fall, they are now increasingly able to be and do in Christ. At issue here are various attributes such as reason, righteousness, rulership, and relationship, which Chapter 5 has already discussed. The point is not that humanity apart from Christ has none of these attributes to any degree, but that the growth of such attributes is badly stunted in sinful people. Whatever attributes do exist often glorify people rather than God.

In Romans 8, between discussions of Christ becoming the likeness of humanity and humanity becoming the likeness of Christ, Paul contrasts two ways of reflecting attributes. There are those "who live according to the flesh" and those "who live according to the Spirit" (v. 5). Both groups

---

73. On identification, see Kline, 1980: 26; on representation, see A. Ross, 1988: 113.
74. So Chafer, 1947: v. 2, 162; Kline, 1980: 24; D. Hall, 1986: 86; Treier, 2008: 76.

may be exercising some reason, following some moral guidelines, managing their lives and environment to some degree, and maintaining relationships somewhat well. Nevertheless, "the mind that is set on the flesh is hostile to God . . . and cannot please God" (vv. 7-8). Regardless of the degree to which people have various attributes, then, there is a fundamental need for people to put on the new humanity — to break free from the power of sin through identification with the death and resurrection of Christ. Doing so is essential if people are to experience renewal according to the image of God in Christ (see discussion of Colossians 3 in Ch. 6), both in the future (see below) and in the present.[75]

As has always been the case, God intends for people today to reflect attributes of God.[76] However, in Jesus Christ humanity receives a clearer understanding of what that can look like.[77] People are to follow the example and pattern of Jesus.[78] In Jesus they see modeled not only excellence in the abstract, but also what that looks like in a fallen world. Before attributes excel in the new heaven and earth, they grow in the midst of weakness and suffering.[79]

Not only the life of Jesus, but also his earthly teaching — and the teaching of the rest of the written word of God — help fill out the picture of what God intends for human attributes to include.[80] Even the Bible as a whole can only convey general descriptions of attributes, plus illustrations in particular times and places. It remains for all of history, with its great diversity of cultures, to display the complete picture of what the fulfillment of creation in God's image, of God's intended reflection of the divine in humanity, entails.[81] Accordingly, God's image in Christ, as God intends it, is far more than what any particular person could be. Fully appreciating that image requires understanding it in its corporate completeness, involving all of redeemed humanity.[82]

75. On the insufficiency of even excellent human attributes apart from Christ, see D. Hall, 1986: 78; Clemens, 2004: 20.

76. See Piper, 1971: 25; Hoekema, 1994: 89.

77. See Maloney, 1973: xv; Grudem, 1994: 445.

78. On example, see O'Mathuna, 1995: 204; on pattern, see Erickson, 2013: 472.

79. This theme is developed at length in Bonhoeffer, 1959b, e.g., 271-72.

80. Recall the discussion in Chapter 1 here about the Genesis text merely opening the door to an idea whose content the entire Bible is intended to flesh out. Also see Calvin, 1960: bk. III, ch. 6, sec. 1; I. H. Marshall, 2001: 63-65; Witherington, 2009: v. 1, 19-20.

81. So van Huyssteen, 2006: 157; Treier, 2008: 181-82; Rogerson, 2010: 192.

82. McFarland, 2005: 57, 165 and Mouw, 2012: 265-66 elaborate on this theme.

While sin temporarily has impeded the realization of God's intentions for humanity to reflect God, there have always been hints of what godly attributes could look like in a human being. The wisdom of Solomon (1 Kgs. 10:23-24), the righteousness of Daniel (book of Daniel, e.g., 6:22), the relationship that David had with God (numerous Psalms; cf. Acts 13:22), and the rulership of Josiah (2 Kgs. 22-23; esp. 23:25) come readily to mind. So do the excellences of many others such as Ruth (book of Ruth) and Esther (book of Esther). Like all good gifts (James 1:17, e.g., wisdom, v. 5), these attributes come from God, manifesting the divine intention for those created in God's image. People created in the image of God typically have such attributes in some measure[83] — though the ravages of sin constrain them severely (recall Ch. 3).

The way out of this constraint is Christ. The four attributes most often associated with the image of God (see Ch. 5) provide just a few of the many illustrations of the renewal God intends for Christians. One of those four is a cluster of mental, volitional, and spiritual attributes often grouped under the heading of reason. Christians experiencing renewal according to the image of God in Christ can have the mind of Christ (1 Cor. 2:16).[84] As Colossians 3:10 observes, that renewal has especially to do with knowledge.[85] This knowledge goes far beyond mere information (see discussion of Colossians 1–3 and 2 Corinthians 3–4 in Ch. 6). It fosters a host of moral, relational, and other attributes in people, including a strengthening of the conscience.[86]

Such knowledge is closely associated with wisdom, godly will, and freedom.[87] Some would add even the ability to do better arithmetic.[88] According to Ephesians 4:23-24, renewal "in the spirit of your minds" must take place, once the old humanity is put away, so that people can appropriately put on the new humanity, created to be like God. Ephesians labels this entire process "learning Christ" (v. 20), for humanity's renewed rational/spiritual attribute is an important part of what renewal according to God's image in Christ entails.

---

83. Wills, 2009: 152-55 explores the implications of this for human community in the work of Martin Luther King Jr.

84. On the renewed mind, see P. Ramsey, 1950: 257; Stott, 1979: 183.

85. On the renewal of knowledge, see Clark, 1984: 14-15; Dunn, 1996: 221-22.

86. For elaboration, see H. Carson, 1960: 84; Schweizer, 1982: 197.

87. On wisdom see Mangano, 2008: 171-72; on godly will, Torrance, 1952: 80 and McFarlane, 1999: 101; on freedom, Sherlock, 1996: 161.

88. E.g., Clark, 1969: 219.

A second illustration of this renewal involves humanity's renewal in righteousness. As Ephesians 4:24 affirms, living in righteousness and holiness is a summary statement of what reflecting godly attributes entails. The word pair as a whole suggests virtuous living in accordance with God's will (see discussion in Ch. 6). Righteousness, often a relational term in Paul, can also refer to actions (and even be translated as justice, see Rom. 6:13, 18-20; 2 Cor. 6:7, 14; Phil. 4:8).[89] Holiness often refers to an inner attitude, though it also suggests separation from that which is unholy.[90] The overall idea is a unified being and doing that glorifies God. Such righteousness and holiness include the renouncing of "shameful things" (2 Cor. 4:2). As the "therefore" of 2 Corinthians 4:1 indicates, this renouncing is one implication of the image-related transformation described at the end of 2 Corinthians 3.

The human attribute of righteousness is necessarily dependent on the close relationship between God and people. That relationship has been badly damaged by sin and can only be restored through Christ's death and resurrection. In Christ, reflecting God's attributes is increasingly possible for people as they appropriate Christ's righteousness and live out its implications according to the model of God in Christ, by the power of the Holy Spirit.[91]

For the apostle John, living out the implications of image-related righteousness requires that people "purify themselves" (1 John 3:3). His exhortation reflects the view that becoming Christ's image is a future certainty for Christians, though not yet a fully lived reality (recall discussion in Ch. 6). John's argument is that God in Christ is pure; and Christians do not merely wish — they *know* — that they will be like Christ (v. 2). Knowledge leads to purity, one of the many ways that reason and righteousness, along with other human attributes, are interconnected.[92]

Being and living like Christ, then, are inextricably bound together in God's intention for those who will become Christ's image. As the influence

89. See Hoeksema, 1966: 209; Clark, 1984: 14-15; Kilcrease, 2010: 26; in addition to sources cited in Chapter 6.

90. See Wesley, 1985m: 194; Witherington, 2009: v. 2, 549; in addition to sources cited in Chapter 6.

91. For a fuller discussion of the involvement of both divine empowerment and human effort, see the discussion of 2 Corinthians 3 in Chapter 6 of the present work; cf. H. D. McDonald, 1981: 16 (drawing on Machen); McFarlane, 1999: 100-101; O'Brien, 1999: 333.

92. Woodhead, 2006: 236-37 uses the related language of sanctification. On purification related to Christians as Christ's image, see Calvin, 1960: bk. I, ch. 15, sec. 4; T. Johnson, 1993: 68-69; Kruse, 2000: 116.

of sin over Christians decreases in Christ, the character of Christ develops within them. They increasingly are able to manifest the virtues of Christ, to God's glory.[93] Jane Parker Huber, in her hymn "God, You Spin the Whirling Planets," captures the longing of people created in God's image to be able to reflect godlike virtues:

> We, created in your image
> Would a true reflection be
> Of your justice, grace, and mercy
> And the truth that makes us free.[94]

Ethical behavior is not merely the product of externally imposed mandates; it flows from virtues that glorify God because they are like God's own. God manifests such virtues in Christ and produces them in Christ-followers as well.[95]

A third illustration of humanity's renewal according to God's image in Christ involves rulership over aspects of God's creation. Although God intended humanity to exercise stewardship informed by solidarity and servant leadership in the world, people in their sinfulness have often had a destructive impact instead. In Christ, with the power of sin broken, fulfillment of the divine intention signaled in creating humanity in God's image is now possible. Rulership increasingly becomes care, not tyranny, whether in large public projects with great environmental impact or in personal gardening.[96] Through renewal according to Christ's image, those who follow Christ become more interested in serving than in being served by the creation — more devoted to restoring it than dominating it.[97] Rulership increasingly becomes more redemption and liberation than exploitation and oppression.[98]

Nevertheless, God's full intention for humanity's rulership will not be fulfilled until after Christ's return. From the perspective of eternity, God has subjected "all things to them [humanity], God left nothing outside their

---

93. On character and Christ's image, see McCasland, 1950: 88; Grudem, 1994: 445; Witherington, 2009: v. 1, 22-23; on virtues and Christ's image, see A. T. Lincoln, 1990: 288-89.

94. Huber, 1978. For discussion, see Towner, 2001: 27.

95. For more on this theme, see Mitton, 1981: 166; Kruse, 2000: 116; Horton, 2005: 97; Witherington, 2009: v. 1, 22.

96. On care, see Hoekema, 1994: 88; on gardening, see Guroian, 2006: 48.

97. Witherington, 2009: v. 2, 738 and Kilcrease, 2010: 26 develop this theme.

98. E. Johnson, 1992: 73 and Gonzalez, 2007: 150 develop this theme.

control. As it is, we do not yet see everything in subjection to them, but we do see Jesus" (Heb. 2:8-9). Because Jesus has demonstrated rulership over creation as God's image (see discussion in Ch. 2), there is assurance that people will be able to reflect godly rulership once they are conformed to Christ's image as described in Romans 8:29.

Leading up to verse 29 in Romans 8, Paul has just commented on the dreadful impact that sin has had upon creation: "The creation was subjected to futility" (v. 20). Nevertheless there is hope. Because of Christ, the painfulness is not that of final death but the pain of straining toward new life. As Paul puts it, "The whole creation has been groaning in labor pains until now" (v. 22). Christians share in that groaning as they long for the future redemption of their bodies (v. 23).

Christians are being transformed according to God's image in Christ, from one degree of glory to another, until they reach complete glorification (2 Cor. 3:18). Accordingly, "the creation waits with eager longing for the revealing of the children of God . . . in hope that the creation itself will be set free from its bondage to decay and will obtain the freedom of the glory of the children of God" (Rom. 8:19-21). In Christ people will reflect God's marvelous ability to rule, as joint heirs with Christ (v. 17).[99] However, there will only be limited progress in that direction until sin is no more.

A fourth human attribute, relationship, also provides a biblically affirmed illustration of the reflection of God that Christians can ultimately become in Christ. In those who are conforming to Christ's image, relationships with God, other people, and the rest of creation are undergoing renewal. Christ as God's image leads by example here in all three realms, as discussed in Chapter 2.[100] Improved relationships with the nonhuman creation are what renewed rulership is all about (see above).

Improved relationships with God develop in everything from inclinations of thought and will, to prayer, to obedience in word and deed, to worship, resulting in peace and a genuine sharing of life with God.[101] It is people's relationship with God that is changing, in accordance with the standard of Christ; that standard (i.e., the image of God in Christ) is not changing. Those who understand God's image to be defined by actual re-

99. So Buswell, 1962: 234; Hughes, 1989: 412-13; D. Johnson, 1992: 12; Schreiner, 1998: 454.

100. For further discussion of this point, see Fedler, 2006: 87-88.

101. These themes are developed in Maloney, 1973: 157; Hughes, 1989: 412-13; E. Ross, 1990: 103; Hoekema, 1994: 86-87; McFarland, 2005: 165-66.

lationship rather than intended relationship logically tend to overlook this important distinction.[102]

Meanwhile, improved relationships with people become visible in everything from seeking social justice and meeting the needs of those who are most needy, to forgiveness and prayer for even one's enemies, to using one's gifts and abilities in the service of others.[103] The result is the unity that comes from rejoicing and mourning with all without regard to the social categories like race, class, and gender that divide people.[104] As Colossians 3:11 explains, "in that renewal ['according to the image,' v. 10], there is no longer Greek and Jew, circumcised and uncircumcised, barbarian, Scythian, slave and free." Instead there is a great array of relational attributes reflecting Christ and glorifying God (see Ch. 6 regarding "glory" in 2 Cor. 3:18).

Some commentators emphasize the parent-child relationship as central to what being in God's image entails. There is some biblical warrant for associating the two, as long as they are not equated, and the focus remains on God's intention in Christ rather than who people already are (see Ch. 5). In the image-related description of Christ as "the reflection of God's glory and the exact imprint of God's very being" (see Ch. 2 on Heb. 1:3), Christ is also described as God's "Son" (v. 2). When Christians ultimately become conformed to the image of God's Son, they will be a large family together with Christ; they will be God's children too (Rom. 8:29).[105] Hebrews draws the same conclusion, locating a description of Christians as "God's children" (2:10) right after the description of Christ (1:1–2:9). "Jesus is not ashamed to call them brothers and sisters . . . for the one who sanctifies and those who are sanctified all have one Father" (2:11). When John echoes image language in 1 John 3:2 (see Ch. 6), he similarly calls Christians "God's children."[106]

---

102. Berkouwer, 1975: 45 and Painter, 2001: 53-54 are among many examples cited earlier in this chapter of those who, because of their view of God's image as actual relationships, attribute the change here to a change in the image itself rather than a change in the people who are experiencing renewal according to God's image in Christ.

103. These themes are developed in Hoekema, 1994: 87; Gunton, 1999: 61; World, 2005: par. 83, Painter, 2001: 46.

104. On such image-related unity, see Hughes, 1989: 412-13; E. Ross, 1990: 112; McFarland, 2005: 7; Witherington, 2009: v. 2, 55.

105. For elaboration, see Kline, 1980: 24, 30; Byrne, 1996: 269; S. Wright, 2003: 41.

106. For the association of being an image and being a child in the New Testament (though a tendency to conflate them), see Cairns, 1973: 52-59; Boer, 1990: 11; and the title of Smail's 2006 book on God's image, *Like Father, Like Son.*

The emphasis in such passages is on God as the source of people's lives.[107] Being a child involves dependence and intimacy.[108] Those are among the many characteristics that God intends for people to have. However, there is much more to God's image than this. God's image should not be reduced to the parent-child relationship, any more than parent-child relationships should be reduced to the concept of God's image.[109] The association of the two simply helps to convey some aspects of what God intends for people ultimately to reflect as God's image in Christ.

One of the attractions of understanding image solely in terms of relationship is that referring to all people as God's children can communicate the significance of human life more easily than appealing to the image of God. Particularly in light of the oppressive misuse of appeals to God's image (see Ch. 1), the employment of this strategy has not been surprising.[110] There is some biblical warrant for it, in that the Gospel of Luke echoes Genesis 5:1-3 by identifying Adam as "son of God" (Luke 3:38).

However, as one reads further into the New Testament, the soundness of this strategy becomes more questionable. While Paul and James affirm that all people are created in God's image, there are also indications that thinking of all people as God's children is not completely accurate. John observes that being a child of God is not simply a function of being born human. Rather, people must receive and believe Christ in order to "become children of God" (John 1:12).

Already in the Old Testament Adam's creation as son of God had given way to the recognition that being a child of God really required more than just being a person. A special relationship with God was necessary. In the exodus, the Israelites had such a relationship, called collectively by God "my firstborn son" (Exod. 4:22; similarly Hos. 11:1). Later God calls them "children of the Lord your God" (Deut. 14:1). After a period of abandoning God again, God promises that they will again be called "children of the living God" (Hos. 1:10).

In the New Testament, though, Paul has to clarify that merely being a Jew "by flesh" is insufficient for truly being a child of God. In his words: "It is not the children of the flesh who are the children of God, but the

107. So Aquinas, 1947: pt. I, Q. 33, art. 4; Mathews, 1995: 170.

108. On this theme, see Berkouwer, 1975: 103.

109. On the importance of not conflating these terms, see W. Schmidt, 1983: 197.

110. Examples include Thurman, 1949: 49; King, 1991a: 255; Paris, 1985: 10; Wills, 2009: 27-28. Even Karl Barth (1958b: 134) refers at one point to "every man" being the brother of Christ.

children of the promise are counted as descendants" (Rom. 9:8). He goes
on in verses 25-26 to quote the Hosea 1:10 passage, introducing it with
the clarification that children of the promise are Christians "whom [God]
has called, not from the Jews only but also from the Gentiles" (v. 24). To
be sure, he uses the statement of one of the Athenians' poets — that "we
are God's offspring" (Acts 17:28-29) — to argue against inanimate images
adequately representing who God is.[111] However, even the term he affirms,
offspring *(genos),* is a more generic term than the more personal term he
normally uses to refer to children *(tekna)* of God. He is adapting popular
Greek terminology of the day for apologetic purposes.

Jesus himself made a distinction between those who were the children
of God and those who were the children of the devil instead (John 8:42-
44) — a distinction that John later develops in his letters (e.g., 1 John 3:10).
In light of New Testament teaching, then, maintaining that being in God's
image means being a child of God is problematic. All people are in God's
image, but only Christians are God's children in the fullest sense.[112] In
Christ, though, as God's intentions for humanity are increasingly fulfilled,
the dependency and intimacy of being God's child increasingly constitute
an appropriate way to describe one aspect of renewed humanity.

One of the most prominent ways that the New Testament speaks of
the relational aspect of humanity's renewal according to God's image is in
terms of love *(agape).* Love is something that God initiates. In light of the
special connection that humanity has with God, as created in God's image,
God's intention that humanity experience such love is not surprising. After
explaining God's plans for humanity, including conformation to Christ's
image (Rom. 8:29-30), Paul asks, "What then are we to say about these
things?" (v. 31). His answer is to describe the lengths to which God has
gone in Christ (vv. 32-34) to ensure that nothing can "separate us from
the love of Christ" (v. 35). Indeed, "neither death, nor life, nor angels, nor
rulers, nor things present, nor things to come, nor powers, nor height, nor
depth, nor anything else in all creation, will be able to separate us from
the love of God in Christ Jesus our Lord" (vv. 38-39). Christians experience this love directly from God and mediated through fellow members
of God's family.[113]

Christians then respond by directing such love back toward God and

---

111. See W. Pope, 1875: 426; L. Berkhof, 1949: 202; Buswell, 1962: 236.

112. For further considerations on this theme, see Baker, 1991: 39-40.

113. Schnackenburg, 1992: 159 and Yong, 2007: 189 develop the implications of this.

others.[114] Complete conformation to Christ's image in Romans 8:29 entails not only experiencing God's love but also loving God in return (v. 28). After Colossians 3:10 says that Christians have clothed themselves with the new humanity, "which is being renewed in knowledge according to the image of its creator," the following verses spell out what that looks like. The climax comes in the command of verse 14: "Above all, clothe yourselves with love, which binds everything together in perfect harmony."

Similarly, after the echo of this image-related teaching in Ephesians 4:24, the remainder of the chapter goes on to describe what those who are "like God" should *not* be like, followed by the conclusion: "Therefore be imitators of God, as beloved children, and live in love, as Christ loved us" (5:1-2). The implications of the image-related echo in 1 John 3:2 follow the same pattern. John describes what Christians should not be like (vv. 3-10), concluding: "for this is the message you have heard from the beginning, that we should love one another" (v. 11).[115]

Love fulfills all that the moral law requires, according to Paul (Rom. 13:9-10), in harmony with Jesus (Matt. 22:37-40). Much of the Bible fleshes out what love looks like concretely. Nowhere is it more powerfully demonstrated than in the face of suffering. "No one has greater love than this, to lay down one's life" (John 15:13). How does God demonstrate love toward people? According to Romans 5:8, the answer is that "while we still were sinners Christ died for us." The true character of love appears in the face of suffering and death.

Suffering per se is not a godly attribute and is not part of God's standard for what those in the divine image should experience and reflect. Rather, *exercising love in the face of* suffering is. Equating suffering with being godly is to invite justifying oppression and abuse on the grounds that they will be good for oppressed and abused people (see Ch. 1). Because love is for the glory of God, love (i.e., self-giving *agape* love) in the face of suffering is about bearing suffering in place of others where possible, not about causing the suffering of others.[116]

---

114. On the place of love in humanity's renewal according to God's image in Christ, see Cairns, 1973: 44; Hoekema, 1994: 86; Smail, 2003: 27; Reynolds, 2008: 195-96; Witherington, 2009: v. 1, 23.

115. For more on love and image in these echo passages, see Hoekema, 1994: 22 (Ephesians) and Berkouwer, 1975: 116 (1 John). On love as the church living in a way that glorifies the relational Trinity, see Grenz, 2001: 294; Sexton, 2010: 193-94, 199.

116. On this theme, see Plantinga, 2002: 34 and Teel, 2010: 165 (who draws on the related work of Cannon, Williams, Douglas, Copeland, and Townes).

Reflection in the Future

Reason, righteousness, rulership, and relationship, then, are prime examples of human attributes that God has always intended to reflect God's own attributes and that are central to what God is renewing in Christ. This renewal is already underway for Christians, so it is possible for these attributes to improve considerably before death or Christ's return. Nevertheless, the renewal of these attributes will not be complete — nor will they entirely glorify God — until after the full glorification of Christians. Then entirely new attributes will join renewed existing attributes to fill out the picture of God's intention for humanity in the image of God. Prominent among those new attributes will be imperishability and the spiritual body.

Many commentators have observed that there is some sort of association between God's image and the impossibility of dying — commonly called "immortality,"[117] although "imperishability" is a more precise term for it. In view is not just being *able not to die* (the narrow sense of "immortal," which was true of Adam before the Fall). Also at issue here is being *not able to die* (imperishability), which was not true of Adam before the Fall. The fact that Adam and Eve died demonstrates that they were able to die, and so were not yet imperishable. Nevertheless, some commentators, assuming that being imperishable is at least a part of what it means to be in God's image, reach a problematic conclusion. They suggest that, since humanity has obviously been subject to death since the Fall, all people must have lost God's image at the Fall.[118] However, the Bible teaches that people continue to be in God's image — that God's image is not lost — as demonstrated at length in Chapter 4. So there must be something wrong with the notion that all who are in God's image are, or were ever, imperishable. A consideration of Genesis 1–3 can illuminate what the problem here is.

When God creates Adam, God warns him that he will die if he eats from the tree of the knowledge of good and evil (2:17). In other words, humanity even before the Fall can die; people are not imperishable. The idea that people cannot die (i.e., will not die even if they oppose God) appears instead in the mouth of the lying serpent: "You will not die" (3:4).

---

117. For example, Mullins, 1917: 260; Litton, 1960: 117; Purkiser, 1960: 213; Shedd, 1980: v. 2, 4.

118. Examples of this assumption and conclusion include Luther, 1958: 65; L. Berkhof, 1949: 205; Gerhard, 1962: 46; Gill, 1978: 396; Kraynak, 2008: 76.

Needless to say, Adam and Eve do eat from the forbidden tree, and God pronounces a sentence of death (3:19). God had provided from the outset the possibility of attaining imperishability. God had created the tree of life (2:9), whose fruit humanity was not forbidden to eat. However, once God had determined that imperishability in such a fallen condition would not be good for humanity, God sent *adam* out of Eden and prevented any return lest *adam* "take also from the tree of life, and eat, and live forever" (3:22). In other words, humanity had not yet obtained imperishability, even though humanity was in God's image.

As a result, today "it is [the King of kings and Lord of lords — v. 15] alone who has immortality [not to mention imperishability]" (1 Tim. 6:16). The only way to gain imperishability is from God. Whereas the first *adam* failed to overcome death, God sent from heaven a second *adam* (1 Cor. 15:47) whose resurrection demonstrated that even death had been defeated (vv. 20-26). By rising with Christ from death, those who bear Christ's image (v. 49) at that point will become the first members of the human race to ever "put on imperishability" (v. 54). Thus "the Spirit is saying to the churches. . . . To everyone who conquers, I will give permission to eat from the tree of life" (Rev. 2:7). Those who demonstrate by their godly love that God's intended reflection of divine attributes is taking place in them (vv. 4-5) will experience the complete fulfillment of God's intention after their resurrection, including imperishability.

Imperishability, then, is something that God *intended* to characterize humanity, not something that has ever *actually* characterized humanity. So imperishability is not a human attribute that partially defines what being in God's image is, any more than the actual presence of any human attribute helps define being in God's image. Creation in God's image is instead defined by a special connection that people have with God, and God's intention that people be/become a meaningful reflection of God, with the humanity of Christ as the model and goal. Unlike attributes such as reason, righteousness, rulership, and relationship — which God made operative in people right from the beginning and begins renewing in Christ as soon as people commit their lives to Christ — imperishability never characterized Adam and Eve in Eden, nor does it characterize Christians today. Adam and Eve had to survive the ravages of the temptation before God would have given them the opportunity to eat from the tree of life forever; and Christians must survive the ravages of death before they can partake of the glorious fruit throughout eternity.

The Apocrypha's Wisdom of Solomon contains a pithy statement that may convey a similar outlook.[119] Its usual translation says that "God created us for incorruption, and made us in the image of his own eternity" (2:23). Since humanity was not incorruptible in Eden and did in fact end up in serious corruption, the first expression here may well mean that incorruption was one *purpose* for which God created humanity. God intended human righteousness and related undefiled attributes. Although sin intervened and brought lasting corruption, God's intention for humanity has never changed. Accordingly, image-of-God language appropriately comes to the author's mind here. Humanity in God's image has to do with imperishability as well as incorruption, but by way of God's intention for humanity, not as a description of what humanity has ever actually been. Humanity, though in God's image, is not yet imperishable. However, since imperishability is part of God's intention for humanity as a reflection of God, it will ultimately characterize those who are completely renewed according to God's image in Christ.

To avoid confusion on this matter, several distinctions are helpful. Imperishability is not the same thing as having a future, knowing about or desiring eternal life, or continuing a conscious existence. Regarding the first, creation in God's image is indeed immediately associated with God's command to "multiply," "fill the earth," and "have dominion" (Gen. 1:28).[120] However, because sin intervenes, so does death. People actually have a future, but it entails death. Imperishability remains intention, not actuality. Secondly, people's knowledge of and desire for eternal life may be actual. However, just because one knows about or desires something, one does not necessarily have it.[121] Imperishability is an excellent example of that.

The third helpful distinction here has to do with the difference between imperishability and continued conscious existence.[122] All people have continued conscious existence. As for those who reject God and so must endure God's wrath, the book of Revelation indicates that "the smoke

---

119. For discussion of this passage in relation to God's image, see McCasland, 1950: 91-92; John Paul II, 1997b: 520.

120. Schwöbel, 2006: 50 discusses this future orientation in conjunction with God's image.

121. Gregory of Nyssa (see discussion in Maloney, 1973: 140-42) appears to overlook this distinction. Sawyer, 1992: 71 makes the more modest claim (without explicit textual warrant) that knowing about the possibility of immortality is a component of what it means to be God's image. God's image as knowledge is critiqued here in Chapter 5.

122. For more on this distinction, see Brunner, 1952: v. 2, 68-69; Carter, 1983a: 206; Boyce, 1990: 215.

of their torment goes up forever and ever" (Rev. 14:11). Jesus similarly warned that some people would be consigned to "eternal fire" (Matt. 18:8; 25:41). However, this is an eternal experience of *death,* as opposed to the eternal *life* that God promises to those committed to Christ. Whereas all people will experience natural death unless Christ returns before they die — thus they are not imperishable — there is a spiritual life, ultimately with a spiritual body (1 Cor. 15:44), that constitutes eternal life.[123]

Christians can begin to experience this eternal life even now. God is protecting them from losing eternal life, that is, from spiritual death. In John 10:28-29, "perishing" entails being snatched out of God's hand, which God will not allow to happen. John 17:3 offers an even more explicit definition: "This is eternal life, that they may know you, the only true God. . . ." Only believers have eternal life and will not die, in the sense of ceasing to have an intimate "knowing" relationship with God. Nevertheless, even Christians will die naturally, and God-intended imperishability will only become actual for them after death and resurrection.

Like imperishability, the resurrected, spiritual body is part of the reflection of God that God intends for humanity's eternal future. While reflecting God's attributes begins even while living in the fallen world, the spiritual body is a second aspect of bearing the image of God in Christ that is not yet part of humanity's experience. The spiritual body is the primary focus, for example, of Paul's discussion of Christ's image in 1 Corinthians 15. The resurrection of Christ's body as a "spiritual body" (v. 45) is one way that Christ is the standard, the model, the "first fruits" of the fulfillment of God's intention for humanity (vv. 20-23). Christians will most fully exhibit whose image they are — bearing (literally, wearing) Christ's image (v. 49) — when their "flesh and blood" (v. 50) is "changed" at the return of Christ (v. 51). For the dead that will mean resurrection and transformation; for those living that will mean natural bodies of dishonor and weakness changing into spiritual bodies of glory and power (v. 43).[124]

Before physical death, according to Romans 8:23, Christians "have the

123. As noted in the Chapter 6 discussion of 1 Corinthians 15, using the contrasting terminology of spiritual/natural regarding death and the human body (so NIV, ESV, etc.) is preferable to spiritual/physical (so NRSV), since the spiritual, resurrected body can have physical substance, as will be discussed here shortly. Also, the generalization about people dying is not meant to imply that God cannot translate a living person directly to heaven in exceptional situations, as in the case of Elijah (2 Kgs. 2:11).

124. On the spiritual body as one aspect of bearing the image of God in Christ according to 1 Corinthians 15, see Scroggs, 1966: 104; Gushee, 2012: 107.

first fruits of the Spirit." They can begin the process of increasing Christ-likeness. Because their bodies are "dead because of sin" (8:11), though, Paul adds in 8:23 that they must "wait for adoption, the redemption of our bodies." Bodily redemption is something no one has or sees yet (8:25). Only by undergoing that can Christians become fully conformed to the image of God in Christ and together constitute a large eternal family with Christ as the firstborn (8:29).[125] As Paul similarly describes this process in Philippians 3:21, Christ "will transform the body of our humiliation that it may be conformed to the body of [Christ's] glory."[126]

The explicit inclusion of the human body as an aspect of God's image in Christ is further evidence that the whole person, not merely the non-bodily aspects of humanity, is associated with God's image.[127] Moreover, not just individuals, but also all of Christ's brothers and sisters together in resurrected glory as God's family, will ultimately constitute that image.[128] And Christ, as the firstborn, is the pattern. Christ is not God's image merely as a disembodied spirit who appears and disappears on earth. Rather, a human body — the incarnation of God — is a distinctive feature of who Christ is.[129]

Perhaps more strikingly, Christ's bodily existence does not end at the crucifixion. There is a true bodily resurrection, which means that Christ continues to have bodily form. In Christ, "the whole fullness of deity dwells [not 'dwelled'] bodily" (Col. 2:9).[130] Moreover, as a "spiritual" body, Christ's resurrected body should not be contrasted with his "physical" body, as if there can be no material dimension to that which is spiritual. "Touch me and see," says the risen Christ in Luke 24:39, referring to his resurrected body as "flesh and bones."

There is no difficulty, then, with understanding the whole human being including the body as involved in the image-of-God concept. Never-

---

125. For elaboration, see Scroggs, 1966: 103-4; Cairns, 1973: 44-45; Dunn, 1973: 137; Stott, 2001: 252; and the expanded discussion in Chapter 6 of the present work.

126. On the connection of this passage with the spiritual human body as an aspect of Christ's image, see J. Murray, 1968: 319; Stott, 1988: 123; Barackman, 2001: 283.

127. See L. Berkhof, 1949: 204-5; Cairns, 1973: 47; Gill, 1978: 393; Barackman, 2001: 347; Witherington, 2009: v. 1, 239; Koyzis, 2014: 136.

128. Cf. Häring, 2001: 8.

129. Irenaeus developed this theme early in the church's history. See Maloney, 1973: 36-37; Osborn, 2003: 256. For Christ's resurrection body as the pattern for humanity's, see D. Kelsey, 2009: v. 2, 1025.

130. On Colossians 2:9 and God's image, see McFarland, 2005: 24-25; Witherington, 2009: v. 2, 123.

theless, one must recognize that humanity's creation in this image involves God's intention for what ought to be and will ultimately be, rather than simply aspects of humanity as those currently are. God has intended from the beginning much more for humanity's bodily existence than what people have ever experienced in their bodies. Even Jesus' bodily existence before his death was nothing special. As the suffering servant whom Isaiah foresaw, "he had no form or majesty . . . nothing in his appearance that we should desire him" (Isa. 53:2).[131]

God intended so much more for the human body. After resurrection, Christ's body can still be touchable flesh and bones, and Christ can still eat food (Luke 24:43). Yet Christ can appear and disappear in ways that suggest his body is not bound by physical limitations the way that people's bodies are. Because Christ as God's image serves as the pattern for people in God's image to become the image of God in Christ, people's spiritual bodies apparently will share such attributes — fulfilling God's intention from the beginning.

Even without the Fall, there would have been the need for a form of the "changing" that Paul says that living Christians will undergo when Christ returns.[132] God would have changed physical bodies into spiritual bodies that could assume physical dimensions but would not have been limited by them. The original earth, as will be the case with the new earth in Revelation, would have been sufficient space for everyone since space itself would not have been a constraint — or else the earth itself could have been changed. The removal of the possibility of death would have been part of the "changing," even as it will be removed when every Christian's "perishable body puts on imperishability" at the fulfillment of God's purposes for humanity (1 Cor. 15:54).

Paul does not teach that the spiritual body is something completely unconnected with the natural body. Instead, it is something in continuity with the natural body, though the result of a profound transformation. Accordingly, Paul can say that "this perishable body must put on imperishability" (1 Cor. 15:53). This is the fulfillment of God's intention for embodied humanity in God's image. In fact, the body has always been in view from the very beginning when the Bible speaks of humanity's creation in God's image, simply because it is part of being human.

In Genesis 1 there is no suggestion that God is creating only a part of

131. Hughes, 1989: 29 develops this theme.
132. So Litton, 1960: 116.

humanity in God's image. Rather, humanity itself, *adam,* is in God's image (v. 27). Part of the same statement and verse is the acknowledgment that male and female are included in this humanity — suggesting to some that bodily matters are indeed in view here. When Genesis 2 describes in greater detail what God actually did following the decision in Genesis 1:26 to create humanity in the divine image, the first thing mentioned is God forming Adam's body (2:7).[133]

Accordingly, describing humanity using a concrete term like *tselem/* image and another visual term like *demuth/*likeness is hardly surprising.[134] (See detailed discussion of these terms in Ch. 3.) Whatever is involved, it appears to include the body. A teaching of the famous rabbi Hillel well illustrates this Old Testament understanding. He explained that if people responsible for images of kings keep them washed, how much more must people keep those in God's image (i.e., themselves) washed.[135]

As discussed in Chapter 3, the reference to Seth as made in Adam's image (Gen. 5:3) follows the restatement of humanity as created in God's image (5:1). Some commentators find here an emphasis on the physical aspect of images.[136] Others are more cautious regarding this text, at least about invoking it to suggest that God's image is *primarily* about the body.[137] Many also find in Genesis 9:6 — where there is a reference to murder as a violation of those created in God's image — an implication that the body is somehow involved in God's image.[138]

Seeing in these Genesis texts the idea that being in God's image is

133. Regarding gender and the body in Genesis 1, see Matt, 1987: 76 and Teel, 2010: 39. Teel there adds more regarding how Genesis 2 expands on Genesis 1 concerning the relevance of the body here.

134. On the connection of these two terms with the human body, see Miller, 1972: 291-92; Tigay, 1984: 170; Watson, 1997: 288-89; Dumbrell, 2002: 16; Middleton, 2005: 25; Mangano, 2008: 3.

135. Leviticus Rabbah 34:3. See discussions of this in G. Moore, 1944: 447; Tigay, 1984: 170; Matt, 1987: 76.

136. McCasland, 1950: 89-90; Brumble, 1992: 372. More cautiously, Porteous, 1962: 683; Tigay, 1984: 173; Mangano, 2008: 3 suggest that the text at least warrants not excluding the body from the concept of God's image.

137. Clines (1968: 57-58) is cautious regarding the view of Gunkel, 1964: 112; J. Barr (1993: 158) regarding the similar views of Eberhard Jüngel and others; cf. similar discussion in O'Mathuna, 1995: 201.

138. E.g., L. Berkhof, 1949: 205; Thielicke, 1966: 160-61; Gill, 1978: 392-93. See also the review of Humbert's position in Jónsson, 1988: 103. As Kass (1990: 38; 2003: 186; 2008: 325) puts it, "God's image is tied to blood, which is the life."

primarily about the body is going too far (see more below). Nevertheless, these texts together suggest the idea that the body is part of a larger whole. Creation in God's image includes the whole person — or viewed corporately, includes all of humanity.[139] There is no dichotomy of body and spirit here.[140] There is a union or, better, a unity of the person here.[141] People do not have bodies; they are bodies (though not just bodies).[142] In other words, as noted earlier in Chapter 3, the concept of God's image includes the body, along with every other aspect of being human as God intends it.[143] Even many inclined to include other aspects of humanity more directly in the image-of-God concept recognize that it is only with and through the body that people are in God's image.[144]

Understating or overstating the place of the body in God's image is easy to do. Many understate it by suggesting that the body is really not part of being in God's image at all. Several commentators see this as the view instinctively held by most Christians.[145] Others find that many, even most, theologians affirm this view.[146] Exclusion of the body from God's image is prominent in the Alexandrian school of the early church (Clement, Origen, Athanasius, Basil, Gregory Nazianzen, Gregory of Nyssa, Cyril, etc.).[147] The writings of commentators such as Augustine and Calvin also appear to reflect it.[148]

People exclude the body for different reasons. Many theologians ex-

---

139. For a "whole person" view of God's image, see Piper, 1971: 18 (invoking Rad in support); Wenham, 1987: 30; Westermann, 1994: 149-50; Hoekema, 1994: 68. Sherlock, 1996: 75 extends the reference to humanity as a whole.

140. On dichotomy, see Leitch, 1975: 256-57.

141. On union, see Mondin, 1975: 67-68 (invoking Aquinas); McFarland, 2005: 1-2 (invoking Irenaeus). On unity, see J. Murray, 1977: 39; Shepherd, 1988: 1019; Dumbrell, 2002: 16.

142. So Reynolds, 2008: 181. Zizioulas, 1975: 423 accordingly notes that the body is inseparable from the person and thus from God's image.

143. Hughes (1989: 12) discusses this view in Rad; Westermann (1994: 150) in Wilderberger and Stamm; Hoekema (1994: 68) in Bavinck. See also Clines, 1968: 91.

144. So Mueller, 1934: 207; Pieper, 1950: 521; Litton, 1960: 116; D. Hall, 1986: 70 (echoing Simpson, 1952: v. 1, 484).

145. So H. D. McDonald, 1981: 34-35. Similarly, Wilson and Blomberg, 1993: 8; Treier, 2008: 124.

146. Many: Westermann, 1994: 150; van Huyssteen, 2006: 161. Most: Middleton, 2005: 24-25.

147. For examples, see H. W. Robinson, 1926: 165; Maloney, 1973: 165; McLeod, 1999: 50-51.

148. See Augustine, 1991: bk. II, ch. 27 (and discussion in Hughes, 1989: 11); Augustine

clude the body from being in God's image because they consider attempting to represent God by any physical object to be the essence of idolatry. They assume on this basis that God's image must involve only the nonmaterial aspects of humanity.[149] Biblically, though, there is a great difference between idols and the image of God, as previously discussed here (Ch. 4).

Meanwhile, some individuals and traditions tend to devalue the human body per se, so it would be hard for them to conceive of the body as having any place in God's image.[150] Others divorce the body from God's image because they are so impressed by how inferior and corruptible the body is, compared to the soul.[151] For some such observers, the body is mere "slime," "clay and gore," or even worse: "a filthy bag of excrement and urine" — though more subtle language is normally used in devaluing the body.[152]

Such descriptions are a far cry from the glory of who God is. Because so many people assume that being in God's image has to do with how people are actually like God (see Ch. 3), it makes sense that they exclude the human body from the concept of the image.[153] Human bodies, some point out, are more like animals than like God. If such commentators assume that being in God's image has to do with how people today are actually unlike animals (see Ch. 3), their conclusion that the body is far removed

---

1963: bk. 12, sec. 7.12 (and discussion in Stark, 2007: 218). Also Calvin, 1960: bk. I, ch. 15, sec. 3, who rejects Osiander's inclusion of body and soul in the concept of God's image.

149. E.g., R. L. Harris, 1980: 768; Lewis and Demarest, 1994: v. 2, 145; Sherlock, 1996: 75. Frame, 2006: 229 attributes this view to "some theologians," whereas Teel, 2010: 42 finds that "theologians have consistently" held this view.

150. On Manichean and Platonic influences, see Litton, 1960: 110-11; on the asceticism that influenced Origen and Augustine, see Middleton, 1994: 11; cf. McGinn, 1985: 328; McLeod, 1999: 51. Teel, 2010: 38 describes the persistence of this low view of the body throughout the history of the church and how this view has biased Christians toward excluding the body from God's image.

151. For example, Origen (see Hughes, 1989: 10), Ambrose (see Tavard, 1973: 106), A. Strong, 1907: 523, 991, and others in Teel, 2010: 42.

152. Ambrose (1961: 259) and Origen (numerous citations in Maloney, 1973: 71) both use "slime" terminology. Ferngren, 1987: 39-40 and Dodds, 1968: 29 document the still-more-colorful language referenced here. Eilberg-Schwartz, 1996: 52 describes in less pejorative terms the problem that many have with connecting the human body and God's image in any way.

153. Examples include Ambrose, 1961: 256-58; Augustine, 1949: 99-100; Arminius, 1986: 363; Strong, 1907: 515; Mullins, 1917: 257; Machen, 1947: 169; Clark, 1984: 6; Miley, 1989: 406; Jenkins, 1995: ix; Gardoski, 2007: 24. On the broader trend that such examples illustrate, see Berkouwer, 1975: 75; also Clines, 1968: 59, who adds the examples of H. H. Rowley, P. G. Duncker, F. Festorazzi, and U. Cassuto.

from that image comes as no surprise.[154] A more biblically grounded view that creation in God's image is about God's intentions for humanity, rather than descriptions of who people currently are, has huge implications for the body here (see below).

While many understate the place of the body in God's image, others overstate it. In fact, some see the view that the body is the primary content of God's image as the most influential view in recent decades.[155] Many supporters of this view understand the Hebrew terms for image and likeness to be emphasizing the physical.[156] However, even they rarely deny all nonphysical aspects of God's image. They may be reacting against an overspiritualizing of the concept rather than attending sufficiently to the way that the Hebrew terms refer to the whole person in the text.[157]

In the view of many commentators, some biblical texts suggest that God has — or at least can have — some sort of form.[158] If that is true of God, then God's image including human bodily form would come as no surprise. Claiming that God has something like a physical body, though, is not necessary in order to maintain that people in all aspects of their being (including bodies) are in God's image.[159] The point is not that everything

154. Examples include Ambrose, 1961: 256; Luther, 1958: 57; Clark, 1969: 216; Boyce, 1990: 213; Koyzis, 2014: 137.

155. Scroggs, 1966: 12 attributes this view to "the majority of exegetes" (similarly see Clines, 1968: 56, citing Stamm). Miller, 1972: 292-93 sees it as "widely accepted." Crouch, 2010: 7 maintains that it is still the "dominant view."

156. E.g., Overstreet, 2005: 66-67 stands in a long line of scholars beginning with Theodor Noldeke and Hermann Gunkel at the beginning of the twentieth century (as discussed in Jónsson, 1988: 44 and Westermann, 1994: 149-50, who also notes the support of Gerhard von Rad and Walther Zimmerli) and continuing mid-century through Paul Humbert and L. Koehler (as discussed in Clines, 1968: 56; W. Schmidt, 1983: 194; Jónsson, 1988: 101-3) as well as C. R. Smith, 1951: 29-30 (as discussed in H. D. McDonald, 1981: 34; Sherlock, 1996: 74). On Mormon support for the primacy of the human body in God's image, see Richards, 1958: 16-17; Erickson, 2013: 461.

157. See Barth, 1958a: 193-94; Clines, 1968: 58.

158. For example, Augustine, 1991: bk. I, ch. 17; Porteous, 1962: 683; Miller, 1972: 292; Kline, 1980: 30; Waltke, 1989: 3-4; McLeod, 1999: 47; Overstreet, 2005: 68-70. They point to such passages as Numbers 12:8, where God says that Moses, unlike various prophets, "beholds the form of the Lord."

159. On the problem with basing conclusions about the human or divine body on the anthropomorphic and theomorphic language of the Bible, see Gill, 1978: 393; Ferngren, 1987: 25; Hughes, 1989: 12-13; van Leeuwen, 1997: 644; P. Peterson, 2008: 470. On the specific problems this introduces regarding the sexuality of God, see Eilberg-Schwartz, 1996: 48; P. Peterson, 2008: 472.

about people is or will be like God. Rather, being in God's image means that people have various attributes that are similar to God's in a particularly human way.

Some would go so far as to equate erect posture with godlikeness.[160] That is probably going too far, especially since various animals also stand up on two legs.[161] Nevertheless, people do use their bodies to carry out attributes such as ruling and relating that may have some resemblance to God's ruling and relating. People's use of their bodies for these purposes need not imply that God requires body parts to fulfill the same purposes.[162] For instance, people see with their eyes and hear with their ears. God also sees and hears, but not because God has physical body parts. God also understands, but not by using a physical brain. When people do such things in an embodied way, it does not mean that God has a body, but that people do have bodies. People are in God's image — they have a connection with God and are intended to be a reflection of God — as embodied beings and not apart from their bodies.[163] Virtually everything that a person is requires a body (though not only a body) to express it.[164]

While the natural body is therefore important already, the transformed spiritual body will only be more so. Many human attributes such as rulership and relationship will be greatly facilitated by a glorious spiritual body, compared to a dishonorable natural body. Since the reflection of God central to being in God's image has more to do with intended future likeness rather than actual present likeness,[165] viewing the body as included in

---

160. E.g., Augustine, 1991: bk. I, ch. 17; Thiessen, 1949: 291; Orr, 1948: 56; Jónsson, 1988: 107 (discussing the view of Ludwig Kohler). Some connect erect posture in this context with looking up to God (e.g., Gill, 1978: 393); others with wide vision (e.g., Brunner, 1947: 388); others with moral uprightness (see discussion in Erickson, 2013: 461); others with rulership over the rest of creation (see analysis of the views of Lactantius, Kohler, Jüngel, and numerous others in Pannenberg, 1991: v. 2, 207).

161. E.g., chickens and kangaroos. For a critique of bodily erectness as a feature of God's image, see Chafer, 1947: v. 2, 161-62; Gerhard, 1962: 49-50 (discussing Bernard of Clairvaux's critique); Pannenberg, 1991: v. 2, 219.

162. See Gerhard, 1962: 50-51 (reflecting on Bucanus); Conzelmann, 1975: 186 (emphasizing the face); Gill, 1978: 393; Grudem, 1994: 448; Ulmer, 2005: 17-18.

163. Clines, 1968: 87; Konkel, 1997: 969; and Treier, 2008: 193 emphasize the connection aspect here.

164. See discussion in Ryrie, 1986: 191; Matt, 1987: 76; McLeod, 1999: 68; Teel, 2010: 126-27; Gonzalez, 2007: 163.

165. For more on this theme, see Bavinck, 2004: 577-78; Pannenberg, 1991: v. 2, 217; Mouw, 2012: 265-66.

God's image makes particularly good sense. After all, Christ has a spiritual body even today. As Christ *is* the image of God, so will Christ's family be, after their renewal according to God's image.

Living in the Image of God

Nothing less than liberation and devastation are at stake when discussing humanity in the image of God. What opens the door to devastation is conceiving of God's image in terms of present human attributes (traits, functions, capacities, etc.) that are like God's. Such attributes vary between people and over time, and sin damages them. Since being in God's image provides a biblical foundation for respecting and protecting human life and dignity, a damaged image means that the basis for this respect and protection is damaged. It is hard for that not to translate, in the average mind, to less respect and protection.

As Chapter 1 has demonstrated, that is exactly what has often happened historically. Impoverished and disabled people, victims of the Nazi holocaust, Native American groups, enslaved Africans and their descendants, and women, among others — not to mention the natural environment — have suffered the devastating results. Ideas have consequences, even when the best motivations lie behind those ideas. How different is the biblical outlook that God's image has more to do with who God is — it is, after all, the image *of God* — than about who people are!

Ultimately, the image of God is Jesus Christ. People are first created and later renewed according to that image. Being in the image of God involves connection and reflection. Creation in God's image entails a special connection with God and also God's intention that people be a meaningful reflection of God, to God's glory. Renewal in God's image entails a more intimate connection with God through Christ and an increasingly actual reflection of God in Christ. Connection with God is the foundation of human dignity. Reflection of God is the aspiration of human destiny. All of humanity participates in human dignity. All of humanity is offered human destiny, though some embrace it while others choose a subhuman destiny instead.

While the Bible does not contain an explicit affirmation that the image of God has *not* been damaged, there is never the slightest suggestion that damage has occurred. The Bible simply and consistently refers to humanity as "in God's image" both before and after the Fall. People are severely damaged by sin, but God's image — the standard and goal of their existence — does not change. This makes sense because neither God's connection (as opposed to relationship) with people, nor God's intention for people, is damaged by the Fall.

The absence of any indication in the Bible that God's image can be damaged should give one pause. The question is really one of wisdom. Would the church be wise to follow the Bible's lead by *not* suggesting that the image has been damaged? Arguably, yes, it would. It would similarly be wise not to suggest that God's image is any particular human attribute, any group of attributes, or the entire set of human attributes, as those actually exist, either currently or before the Fall. Although those who propose such views may be able to constrain the harmful implications of those views by invoking other biblical ideas, history demonstrates that many others will not be so theologically sophisticated.

As important as it is to avoid paving the way for future devastation through unwise communication about God's image, it is just as important to harness the power of humanity as created in God's image to inspire Christian outreach and engagement. The limited motivation in many churches and believers to communicate the good news of the gospel through words and actions testifies that something is missing.

As just noted, humanity's creation in God's image means, first of all, that humanity has a special connection with God. The human race as a whole and each human being have this connection. Particular human attributes are not the focus, but whole persons and humanity as a whole are in view. The connection is sufficiently close that abusing, especially killing, a human being is to abuse God. Herein lies ultimate human dignity. People cannot add to or subtract from this dignity in themselves or in others, since being in God's image is not an attribute that anyone or anything can cultivate or diminish. Special connection with God is simply an undeserved gift (albeit a special kind of gift, as will be noted shortly).

Secondly, humanity's creation in God's image means that God intends humanity to be a reflection of God, to God's glory. This intention, from before the foundation of the world, has included Christians eternally living with and glorifying God by manifesting attributes that reflect God's own. Hardly had God created humanity when people decided to prefer their own way over God's, and sin prevented the fulfillment of God's intention. People remained in God's image — they were still intended to reflect God-glorifying attributes and thus still connected with God in a special way. Human dignity was not weakened; however, the fulfillment of actually becoming God's image — human destiny itself — could not occur without the removal of sin. Christ as savior breaks the power of sin; however, Christ as the image of God not only demonstrates God's special connection and thus commitment to humanity but also reveals much of God's intention for humanity's reflection of God.

The exciting implications of all this for how best to view and act toward people could fill many more books. Some of these implications have to do with those being acted upon. What does it mean for them to be in God's image? Other implications deal with those doing the acting. What does being in God's image involve for them? Some summary observations regarding both will pave the way for some final comments concerning a way forward.

Being Viewed as in God's Image

In Chapter 1 we have already noted many historical examples of the inspirational potential of the idea that all people are in God's image. People should be viewed certain ways precisely because they are in the image of God.

For instance, human life has great significance on these very grounds.[1] Many people use some term such as "dignity" to describe the special significance that comes from being in God's image.[2] This is not the dignity

1. E.g., Fedler's statement (2006: 81) that humanity's creation in the image of God "highlights the high view of human life held by God." Similarly, see Sherlock, 1996: 158. Such creation justifies human existence (Barth, 1958a: 183). Sarna (1989: 11) sees humanity's privileged "unique relationship with God" rooted in the details of the language used to describe humanity's creation in God's image. See also Thomas, 1949: 161-62; Baker, 1991: 119-20; Konkel, 1992: 1.

2. E.g., Pope, 1875: v. 1, 424; McCasland, 1950: 94; Bajema, 1974: 30; Fichtner, 1978: 170; Tracy, 1983: 244-45; Benedict XVI, 1995: 45; Sherlock, 1996: 160-61; Baker, 1991: 120; Grudem, 1994: 449-50; Bayertz, 1996: xiii-xiv; Bray, 1998: 42; Allen, 2000: 83; Walton, 2001: 137; Kass, 2003: 187; Shannon, 2004: 114; Bequette, 2004: 8; McMinn and Campbell, 2007: 27; Garner, 2007: 233-34; Neuhaus, 2008: 227; Reynolds, 2008: 186; Henriksen, 2011: 266-67; Schönborn, 2011: 31; Vorster, 2011: 16; Reiss, 2011: 181; Mitchell, 2013: 91. See also

that varies according to circumstances ("circumstantial dignity"), but the dignity that necessarily accompanies being human ("humanity's dignity"). To reflect that distinction, some people refer to such dignity as "natural" or "inherent."[3] The danger of such language is that it can imply that dignity is intrinsic to humanity without any necessary reference to God.[4] Such is not the case with the dignity resulting from creation in God's image. This dignity is "given," "imparted," "conferred," "bestowed" by God.[5] As a "received" dignity, it is an "alien" dignity that becomes humanity's dignity by God's design.[6] It is a gift of God's grace.[7] However, it does not come without requirements. So in that sense it has an element of loan as well as gift to it. There is something that must in some sense be accounted for or repaid (though not in kind).[8] Being created in God's image has great benefits, but it comes with God's great expectations (see below).

The dignity of all who are in God's image, humanity's dignity, neither depends on particular human attributes nor diminishes due to sin. Discussions of such dignity reveal how easy it is — once one unwisely concludes that sin has damaged God's image — to conclude that humanity's dignity is damaged as well.[9] With this dignity diminished, so is the mandate to respect and protect people (more below). Creation in God's image arguably can provide a more solid basis for human significance than other historical attempts can,[10] precisely because human limitations cannot weaken it. This dignity is as unshakable as God.

Another way that people acknowledge the special significance that

Robinson, 2011: 9, 166-67, drawing on the work of Augustine as well as Balthasar and Barth. For Aquinas's view, see Maritain, 1947: 32 and Merriell, 1990: 237.

3. Natural: Aquinas, 1947: pt. I, Q. 93; art. 3. Inherent: Rodríguez, 2008: 173; Bradley, 2010: 185; Vorster, 2011: 22. Sunshine, 2013: 15 uses the related language of "intrinsic" dignity.

4. On this danger, see Black, 2006: 180; Gushee, 2012: 52-53.

5. Pellegrino, 2006: 253; Kesich, 1975: 13 (given); Hailer and Ritschl, 1996: 96 (imparted); Schwöbel, 2006: 53 (conferred); Mott, 1982: 46-47 (bestowed; similarly Cahill, 1980: 280; Roy, 2009: 11).

6. G. Kelsey, 1965: 73 (received); Thielicke, 1966: 180 (alien). Thus, where there is no God imparting such dignity to humanity, as in classical Confucianism, "it is unrealistic to hope for protection of human dignity for every individual" (Lo, 2009: 175-76).

7. John Paul II, 1997a: 454 (gift); Budziszewski, 2002: 30 (grace).

8. On human life as loan as well as gift, see Kilner, 1992: 67.

9. E.g., A. Murray, 1965: 103; Third General Conference, 1979: 170 (par. 331); Pinckaers, 2005: 162 (reflecting Aquinas).

10. E.g., see Ferngren, 1987: 34; Schulman, 2008: 10; cf. P. Peterson, 2008: 36; Orr, 1948: 34.

comes from being in God's image is to refer to humanity's great "worth."[11] Others similarly cite humanity's special "value."[12] The danger with such economic language is that it implicitly puts people on a scale with all other things, albeit much higher on the scale than most other things. The problematic implication is that a large enough number of anything else on the scale has the same value as a person.[13] To avoid this implication, people commonly revert to the expression that people have "infinite" value or worth.[14] However, that way of speaking can so easily imply that human beings rival God in their worth — what exceeds infinity? — and that such worth is therefore inherent in humanity rather than derivative from God.[15]

Accordingly, some prefer a more modest and less quantitative term that overtly connects humanity and God. Many adopt the concept of "sanctity."[16] The term "sacredness," though, accomplishes the same thing with such added benefits as suggesting an unchanging connection to God rather than a process of sanctification or a set of morally admirable traits.[17] Being created in God's image, then, means that all people have a sacredness to them independent of any actual attributes. A person cannot be demeaned even in another person's thoughts without that constituting an unholy affront to God.

Since God's image has a corporate dimension to it and is not just something true of particular people by themselves, humanity's existence in God's image entails that everyone has this special significance of sa-

11. So Maston, 1959: 12; King, 1965; Verhey, 2003: 91; World, 2005: par. 117; Driscoll and Breshears, 2010: 115; Reiss, 2011: 181.

12. Gibbs, 1984: 186; Oduyoye, 1995: 175; Moreland and Rae, 2000: 338-39; World, 2005: par. 85; Merrill, 2006: 296; Goodman, 2008: 67.

13. On the "deeper irreducibility" of humanity, which this implication violates, see Graham, 2006: 278.

14. E.g., Maston, 1959: 13, 15; Kidner, 1967: 51; Sarna, 1989: 12; Painter, 2001: 45; Breck, 2003: 27; Kepnes, 2004; World, 2005: pars. 45, 119; P. Peterson, 2008: 37.

15. E.g., Hailer and Ritschl, 1996: 96; P. Ramsey, 1950: 277. On the dangers of ascribing "absolute value" to human life, see Sherlock, 1996: 172; cf. Spanner (1998: 216), who is worried about the demeaning of nonhuman life that this view may unconsciously promote.

16. Gelernter (2008: 404) goes so far as to suggest " 'human sanctity' means 'created in God's image.' " See also Porteous, 1962: 683; Walton, 2001: 134; Kass, 1990: 38; 2003: 187; C. Wright, 2006: 423.

17. Those preferring "sacredness" include Chafer, 1947: v. 2, 168; Stendahl, 1992: 143; Breck, 1998: 9; Gushee, 2012: 19, 52-53; Erickson, 2013: 473. Cf. Taylor, 1992: 19; Ferngren, 1987: 27, 42. Also, the "sanctity of life" term suggests only the abortion debate in the minds of so many people that an alternative term with similar meaning can connect better with a wider range of life-related issues.

credness. There is a basic equality among members of the human community.[18] This does not mean that people consider everyone to be equal or identical in every respect.[19] Rather, it suggests "that they deal with each person as uniquely sacred and ignore all claims to special sanctity."[20] As disabilities ethicist Hans Reinders observes, humanity's creation in God's image signifies that "in the loving eyes of God . . . there are no marginal cases of being 'human.'"[21] People who are socially marginalized need not define themselves by their circumstances or the demeaning viewpoint of those who would oppress them.[22] With the notion of equality comes the idea of a basic unity.[23] All people together have a common origin and purpose.

The equality and unity that ought to characterize humanity as a whole become more understandable and achievable within the church. Here Christians are increasingly fulfilling God's intentions for them according to the image of Christ. Christ is the common source and goal of who they are.[24] There is an equality here of significance — of sacredness — that does not deny differences but celebrates them as a means of strengthening life together.[25]

Being Treated as in God's Image

People who are viewed in terms of the dignity, sacredness, equality, and unity grounded in their identity as being in God's image will be treated

18. Maston, 1959: 13; G. Kelsey, 1965: 87; Moltmann, 1976: 62; 1984: 11; Plantinga Pauw, 1993: 14; H. R. Niebuhr, 1996: 178; Habib, 1998: 36-37; Kass, 2003: 183; Ruston, 2004: 271 (drawing upon Pope Leo XIII's *In Plurimis*); Fedler, 2006: 82; Gonzalez, 2007: 128; Vorster, 2007a: 325-26; Goodman 2008: 43; Gushee, 2012: 46-47; Koyzis, 2014: 22.

19. So Behr-Sigel, 1982: 374; Greidanus, 1984: 15; Jastram, 2004: 73.

20. H. R. Niebuhr, 1996: 155; cf. discussion in Hicks, 2000: 118. Vorster (2011: 22) calls this "fundamental" equality; C. Wright (2006: 423), "radical" (root) equality.

21. R. K. Reinders, 2006: 124; H. Reinders, 2008: 119. Sawyer (1992: 72) notes that "even disobedient, humiliated, struggling men and women . . . demand our reverence and respect" because they are in the image of God.

22. This theme is developed in Hilkert, 2002: 12; Hopkins, 2005: 41, 185.

23. See G. Kelsey, 1965: 87; Goldfeld, 2011: 51; Mouw, 2012: 263.

24. See H. Carson, 1960: 85; Clines, 1968: 103; Fichtner, 1978: 171; McFarland, 2005: 5-6; Krause, 2005: 366. Also recall that the New Testament teaching about being Christ's image typically addresses a plurality of believers rather than particular persons.

25. Brunner, 1952: v. 2, 66; Konkel, 1992: 1; McFarland, 2005: 55, 64 develop this theme.

in certain ways. People will treat them with respect.[26] By treating those created in the image of God in a particular way, one treats the Creator in that same way.[27] Accordingly, some would even say that reverence or veneration is due toward other people.[28]

Respect and reverence, though, can mean a lot or a little, depending on how concrete a difference they make in how people act. One way for them appropriately to mean a lot is for them to undergird specific human rights. Human rights refer to what people ought to receive or be protected from by virtue of being people. People are in the image of God, which means that how they are treated and to what they have access matters greatly. Because they are in God's image, they have dignity and sacredness that warrant according them human rights.[29] In that sense, ultimately, rights "are by the *imago* anchored in the structure of the universe."[30] Not surprisingly, many denominational documents and theological commentators emphasize the direct connection between human rights and humanity's creation in the image of God.[31] Sometimes they focus on the way that Genesis 9 underscores the importance of protecting people from physical assault (especially murder). They also commonly note James's warning not to assault people with words.

26. John Paul II, 1979: 68; Third General Conference, 1979: 129 (pars. 38-40); Ra. Martin, 1988: 119; Breck, 1998: 146; Watts, 2006: 251; Reynolds, 2008: 185; Goodman, 2008: 149. Cf. Gelernter, 2008: 399.

27. On this point regarding respect, see Chafer, 1949: v. 2, 168; Sawyer, 1992: 71-72; Grudem, 1994: 449-50.

28. E.g., Sawyer, 1992: 72 (reverence); McFarland, 2005: 30 (veneration, drawing on John of Damascus' *On the Divine Images*).

29. So Moltmann, 1976: 59, 72; 1984: 12, 17; Third General Conference, 1979: 189 (par. 475); Hilkert, 1995: 194-95; International, 2004: par. 22; Stackhouse, 2005: 27; van Huyssteen, 2006: 161; Bradley, 2010: 183; Marshall, 2001: 61-63. Cf. Wills, 2009: 113 on Martin Luther King Jr.; and Mahoney, 2010: 682 on Vatican II.

30. Thomas, 1949: 163. Cf. Greidanus, 1984: 14.

31. As Ruston, 2004: 270 documents: "In the twentieth century it became routine in papal and conciliar documents to link the possession of rights with the image and likeness of God in all human beings" — e.g., see *Pacem in Terris,* par. 3; *Gaudium et Spes,* pars. 29, 68; *Octagesima Adveniens,* par. 17; *Laborem Exercens,* pars. 1, 13, 33, 112, 125; *Sollicitudo Rei Socialis,* pars. 29, 30; and "it is now commonly used in this way in the social doctrine of many other denominations" (e.g., see the Church of Scotland's *Report 2000* "Human Rights" document [pars. 2.8, 6.2] and the Methodist Conference 2003 "Church and Society" document [par. 6]). Regarding Christian theologians across denominational lines, see Habib, 1998: 36; also Tracy, 1983: 242-43; Richard, 1986: 165-70; Stendahl, 1992: 143; Rakestraw, 1992: 402; van Huyssteen, 2006: 317; Roy, 2009: 12, 15.

Nevertheless, it is important to keep rights closely tied to a clear sense of the dignity/sacredness of all people. Otherwise, rights claims can degenerate into mere assertion of self with no regard for others.[32] Human rights are really God's rights over humanity more than one person's rights over another. God is every person's creator, so God is the one to direct how people treat one another.[33] Being in God's image, people draw their significance from God's connection with them and from the divine reflection God intends them to be, not merely from any attributes they may have per se (however excellent those are). In other words, people have rights, but they do not have a right to those rights. Those rights flow from the God-given dignity and sacredness rooted in creation in God's image.

Just as humanity is not merely a collection of separate people but is also an interrelated whole, so humanity's status as created in God's image has implications for the whole together. God has a connection with humanity as a whole; and God intends divine attributes to be reflected in humanity corporately, not just in particular people. God intends justice to be a hallmark of human society, as it is of God's own character.[34] Just treatment of all requires taking account of personal and societal relationships in which people live, rather than merely viewing people as individuals. Where there is injustice, liberation from that oppression is what humanity's status in God's image mandates.[35]

While people never warrant less than what justice requires, they frequently warrant more — they warrant love. Love is God's ultimate intention for relationships of people with one another and with the natural world as well.[36] Love involves giving more than the minimum required

32. So Kilner, 1992: 25; Sherlock, 1996: 170-71; Walton, 2001: 138-39; Watts, 2006: 248.

33. On this theme, see Moltmann, 1976: 59; 1984: 17; Mott, 1982: 52-53; Roy, 2009: 12; Gushee, 2012: 52.

34. Regarding the connection of justice with God's image, see Wolterstorff, 1985: 70; D. C. Jones, 1994: 83; Beisner, 1994: 64-65; Oduyoye, 2001: 76; World, 2005: par. 119; Stackhouse, 2005: 38; van Huyssteen, 2006: 315; Gonzalez, 2007: 126-27, 132, 160; Bradley, 2010: 189-90; Mitchell, 2013: 87.

35. See Thomas, 1949: 162-63; Moltmann, 1976: 60-61; Tracy, 1983: 248-49; Plantinga Pauw, 1993: 14; Fields, 2001: 98; Ruston, 2004: 272 (discussing the teaching of Leo XIII); Barilan, 2012: 66; and sources on freedom/liberation cited in Chapter 5.

36. So G. Kelsey, 1965: 77-78; Goodman, 2008: 149; Henriksen, 2011: 271. As Calvin (1960a: bk. III, ch. 7, sec. 6) puts it: "there is but one way in which to achieve what is not merely difficult but utterly against human nature: to love those who hate us. . . . It is that we remember not to consider men's evil intention but to look upon the image of God in them."

and requires more than utilitarian maximizing of social benefit.[37] It generates true solidarity, fellowship, interdependence, inclusive community, and unified mission.[38] Such social blessings are as much human rights as are personal protections and provisions.[39] Again, the reason that people warrant love is not that people are so lovable in themselves, but that love is the appropriate way to treat those in God's image.

Perhaps the most obvious way to violate justice and love is to destroy someone who is in God's image.[40] Nicholas Rowe's *Tamerlane* laments war precisely because it

> . . . Lays waste the noblest work of the creation,
> Which wears in vain its Maker's glorious image.[41]

Genesis 9:6 explicitly invokes humanity's status as created in God's image in conjunction with forbidding murder.[42] Destroying someone in God's image, in light of God's connection with humanity, is tantamount to attacking God personally.[43] The "shedding of blood" here (whether literally or by extension) may encompass all life-threatening or bloody violations of a person.[44]

---

37. See Benedict XVI, 1995: 45; Verhey, 2003: 162.

38. On solidarity and God's image, see Tracy, 1983: 247; on fellowship and God's image, see Mahoney, 2010: 682; on interdependence and God's image, see W. Cobb, 1977: 134. Regarding God's image as inclusive community, see World, 2005: par. 128; Hopkins, 2005: 184-85; Wills, 2009: 155 (summarizing the view of Martin Luther King Jr.); Bradley, 2010: 185. Cf. World, 2005: pars. 123, 126 on unified mission.

39. So Moltmann, 1976: 61-67; 1984: 17; Roy, 2009: 15.

40. See Hughes, 1989: 67 (discussing John Calvin's view); John Paul II, 1997b: 538; Vorster, 2011: 22.

41. See Rowe (1966: Act 1, Scene 1), reflecting revisions included in the version available to John Wesley (1985i: 156).

42. Miller, 1972: 300-301; Aalders, 1981: 187-88; Barentsen, 1988: 33-34; Hamilton, 1990: 315; Benedict XVI, 1995: 45; van Leeuwen, 1997: 645; Callender, 2000: 29-30; Walton, 2000: 39; van Huyssteen, 2006: 120; Bori, 2010: 39; Bosman, 2010: 564; Highfield, 2010: 21. Accordingly, notes Sarna (1989: 62): "unlike the law collections of the ancient Near East, the Bible never imposes the death penalty for crimes against the property of one's fellow." See below for the view that this passage primarily identifies those inflicting punishment as the ones who are created in God's image. As some here (e.g., Aalders) have argued, both views may be valid, particularly if verse 6b provides an image-based rationale for the entirely of vv. 1-6a.

43. Priest, 1988: 145; Harland, 1996: 204; Mulzac, 2001: 75; Garr, 2003: 161; Merrill, 2006: 152, 342; Roy, 2009: 11.

44. Bajema, 1974: 31; Ferngren, 1987: 38 (discussing Clement); Sawyer, 1992: 71; D. S. Williams, 1993: 146; Balswick et al., 2005: 161; World, 2005: 119; Gonzalez, 2007: 126-27.

According to James 3:9, violations of people created in God's image can include even abusing them using words alone.[45]

There are many arenas where treating people correctly as created in God's image is particularly important in light of the historical abuses documented in Chapter 1. For example, the existence of all humanity in God's image offers a potent rallying cry for respecting and protecting even the weakest and most marginalized of human beings.[46] God would have people attend to the needs of those who are impoverished precisely because they are in God's image.[47] Impoverished people are not more important than others; however, their special degree of need means that the equal regard due to all who are in God's image requires a special degree of care toward them.[48] Since both particular people and humanity as a whole are in God's image, addressing poverty must take place at both a personal and structural level.[49]

Similarly, people with special needs due to disabilities warrant special care and welcome. They have an image-based dignity that does not waver, regardless of their ability or potential ability.[50] Christ, God's image, models God's embrace of disability on the cross and through a resurrected but wounded body.[51] All humanity shares in such woundedness and vulnerability in a variety of forms — physical, mental, moral, spiritual — without losing the dignity of being created in the image of God.[52] Whoever would treat those with disabilities as God does must view them in terms of their destiny as well as their dignity — in terms

45. Grenz, 2001: 203-4; S. Wright, 2003: 34-35; D. Kelsey, 2009: v. 2, 938.

46. So John Paul II, 1979: 63; Hoekema (discussing Calvin), 1994: 44; Hilkert, 1995: 192; 2002: 11; Oduyoye, 1995: 184; Painter, 2001: 45; Walton, 2001: 138; Soulen, 2006: 108; Bazzell, 2012: 232; Gushee, 2012: 108. See Bullock, 2012: 14 regarding homeless people in particular.

47. See Calvin, 1960a: bk. III, ch. 7, sec. 6, with support from Wolterstorff, 1985: 69 and Hughes, 1989: 67; also King, 1965; Brueggemann, 1982: 24-25; Hopkins, 2005: 185-86; Roy, 2009: 11-12.

48. On preferential attention to those who are poor, see Third, 1979: 265 (par. 1142); Gutiérrez, 1988: 168; Jónsson, 1988: 189; McFarland, 2005: 76.

49. Regarding the structural dimension, see Fernandez, 2004: 99-100; World, 2005: par. 34; Hopkins, 2005: 184.

50. Painter, 2001: 45; Walton, 2001: 138; Soulen, 2006: 108; Yong, 2007: 173; Schulman, 2008: 8-9; Neuhaus, 2008: 227; Bray, 1998: 50; Rodríguez, 2008: 50; McReynolds, 2013: 35-36.

51. Eiesland, 1994: 90, 99-100; Ecumenical, 2004: 512; World, 2005: par. 84; Yong, 2007: 174-75; Reynolds, 2008: 207; D. Kelsey, 2009: v. 2, 1018-19.

52. Sherlock, 1996: 172-74; Reynolds, 2008: 186-88.

of God's intention for them to be a divine reflection as well as their special connection with God.[53] Their glorious renewal according to God's image in Christ is sure if they are believers and still offered to them if they are not (yet).[54]

Because people in their entirety, including their bodies, are in God's image, particular bodily characteristics never warrant ascribing greater worth to one race or ethnicity than another.[55] Slavery is a particularly outrageous example of making unwarranted distinctions.[56] Theologian Leonard Verduin says it well: "[T]o make a slave of a fellow image-bearer is a contradiction in terms."[57] It is a violation of how God intends one person in the divine image to behave toward another and thus is an offense against God.[58] Not just reconciliation but racial solidarity is the goal, in which appreciation of the diversity of God's purposes for humanity in God's image is the norm.[59] Affirming humanity's creation in God's image is a powerful way to mobilize the church to oppose racism in word and deed.[60] With due appreciation for the evil involved here, Christians will not be satisfied with bandaging the wounded but will insist on transforming the social practices and structures that perpetuate racism.[61]

The same goes for overcoming the oppression of women. People, male and female alike, are created in God's image — not because women have the same attributes as men but because of God's connection with them and the divine reflection God intends them to be.[62] Because demeaning

53. On the implications for the church's involvement here, see D. G. Jones, 1998: 8; World, 2005: pars. 109, 119; Reynolds, 2008: 226.

54. For more on this theme, see Reynolds, 2008: 186, 207. No wonder R. K. Reinders (2006: 133-39) contends that a secular outlook cannot provide comparable warrant for the special care due to people with disabilities.

55. So Maston, 1959: 3, 15; G. Kelsey, 1965: 72; H. S. Smith, 1972: viii; Cone, 1986: 93-94; 1997: 137-38; Bernal, 1993: 58; Lutheran, 1994: 29; Ellis, 1996: 148; C. E. Lincoln, 1999: 16-17; Fields, 2001: 59; Trotman, 2003: 102; Hopkins, 2005: 159; C. Wright, 2006: 423; Roy, 2009: 11-12; Teel, 2010: 171.

56. See Blyden, 1992: 138; Ruston, 2004: 270; Teel, 2010: 124; Copeland, 2010: 24; Erickson, 2013: 473.

57. Verduin, 1970: 37, though his view of being in God's image is somewhat different from the view advocated here.

58. Trotman, 2003: 102; Teel, 2010: 37.

59. Usry and Keener, 1996: 110; Harrell, 2008: 19, 22; Bradley, 2013: 152.

60. Fields, 2001: 61; Rodríguez, 2008: 11; Teel, 2010: 158-59.

61. Oduyoye, 1982: 47; Emerson and Smith, 2000: 18, 118, 171.

62. See Horowitz, 1979: 177; Fulkerson, 1997: 107, 114; Oduyoye, 2001: 72; Z. Moore, 2003: 111-12; Lowry, 2012: 15. Accordingly, Abetz (2010: 15-16) argues that the proper re-

women is an affront to people in God's image, it is an offense against God.[63] Moreover, men and women alike participate in renewal according to God's image in Christ.[64] To oppress women is for the body of Christ to forfeit much of the blessing of diversity and interdependence that God has intended to characterize humanity in the divine image from the beginning.[65] Women warrant far better treatment.[66] They must be treated with the dignity, rights, love, and all other blessings appropriate for those created, and called to renewal, in God's image.[67] The church is to lead the way in responding to this challenge, within its walls and in its public engagement.[68]

Recognizing that people are in God's image also has profound implications for communicating with those who are not Christians.[69] They are still fully in the image of Adam, subject to the sinfulness of the "old humanity." As also in God's image, they are connected with God and warrant great respect in any interaction with them.[70] However, the magnificent eternity designed for those in Christ is not theirs (yet). They cannot fulfill the divine intentions for all who are in God's image. Their pursuit of their own priorities and disregard for the gift of being in the divine image grieves God. They need to put off the old humanity and put on the new, thereby beginning the process of renewal according to God's image in Christ. The more that Christians appreciate their own status and purpose as they undergo renewal in this image, the greater the impetus for them to do all they can to help others recognize the same dignity and realize the same destiny.[71]

sponse to privileging males because they supposedly better image a God with masculine characteristics is not merely to demonstrate that God has feminine characteristics as well.

63. E. Johnson, 1992: 9; D. S. Williams, 1993: 146.

64. On the *imago Christi* theme and women, see Pineda-Madrid, 2011: 91, 135.

65. Oduyoye, 1995: 181; Bray, 1998: 42; International, 2004: par. 36; Hopkins, 2005: 114.

66. For further implications of women and men as equally in God's image, see Horowitz, 1979: 175; B. Childs, 1985: 189; Jónsson, 1988: 185-86; Hamilton, 1990: 138; Tepedino, 1993: 226; Ruether, 1995: 268; Oduyoye, 1996: 170; 2001: 114-15; Verhey, 2003: 207; Ruston, 2004: 280; Hopkins, 2005: 34; Gonzalez, 2007: 144-45.

67. So Horowitz, 1979: 175; Aronson, 1984: 19; Grant, 1989: 208 (drawing on Katie Cannon); Tepedino and Ribeiro, 1993: 223; Hilkert, 1995: 192; Roy, 2009: 11-12.

68. See Ross, 1990: 101; B. Childs, 1993: 585; P. Hunter, 1993: 195; Oduyoye, 2001: 69; B. Ware, 2002: 21; Rodríguez, 2008: 173; Roy, 2009: 15.

69. For more on the implications for evangelism, see Wesley, 1985k: 303; Hilkert, 1995: 194.

70. As Old Testament scholar and missiologist C. Wright (2006: 423) observes, "the validity of evangelism in principle does not legitimize any and every method of evangelism in practice."

71. For elaboration, see Buswell, 1962: 254; Baker, 1991: 127.

Because all people are in God's image, and God has created them to fulfill the divine intention for that image, there is reason to think that at least some of them are capable of understanding and responding to the gospel with the help of the Holy Spirit.[72] There are also grounds for expecting there to be some resonance in non-Christians with the idea that people have an innate dignity, even if the source of that dignity is unclear to them.[73] Only Christians, though, are in the process of conforming to the image of God in Christ, to the increasing glory of God. This helps explain the biblical teaching that, while Christians are to view and treat all people with respect and love as created in God's image, they have a special godly responsibility toward fellow Christ-followers.[74]

Being in God's Image

Recognizing that another person or group is in God's image, then, has huge implications. So does recognizing oneself as created in God's image. Most discussion about the implications of being in God's image centers on who we see others to be; however, in some ways who we understand ourselves to be is more important. Being in God's image offers little protection to people from someone who is not disposed to recognize their God-related status. When someone duly appreciates his or her own existence as created in God's image, the groundwork is in place for that person to learn to view and treat everyone as created in God's image.

Jesus highlights this difference in Luke 10. Whereas the man questioning him is preoccupied with the status of others ("Who is my neighbor?" — v. 29), Jesus was more concerned with the questioner's own status (was he *being* a [good] neighbor? — v. 36).[75] Similarly, people should not be so preoccupied with the question of whom the category of "in God's image" includes that they fail to consider carefully what it means for they themselves to be in God's image. In fact, those who follow Jesus and so become free to fulfill God's intention for those in the divine image are uniquely

72. So Maston, 1959: 8; Boer, 1990: 114-15, 121; Wilson and Blomberg, 1993: 13; Ellis, 1996: 43; Erickson, 2013: 473.

73. See H. McDonald, 1981: 16-17; C. Wright, 2006: 450; R. K. Reinders, 2006: 125.

74. So Calvin, 1960a: bk. III, ch. 7, sec. 6, elaborating on the biblical backdrop to Galatians 6:10.

75. For more on this dynamic in the image-of-God concept, see P. Ramsey, 1950: 278; O'Mathuna, 1995: 205.

suited to grow in their appreciation of others in God's image.[76] They learn to love persons for their very existence, rather than for the attributes of their existence (the specifics of who they are and what they do). They can then empower people to love themselves and others by helping them to recognize everyone as created in God's image.[77]

The implications for pastoral care and counseling are immense.[78] Even the weakest person — morally, emotionally, spiritually — has a special connection with the God of the universe. Moreover, God intends for that person increasingly to become a meaningful reflection of God en route to a glorious eternal life as the image of God in Christ. Neither that connection nor that intention is damaged by sin — which means the status of being in God's image is not damaged. Sin has indeed damaged the person and prevented the fulfillment of what being in God's image ought to entail. However, people's existence as created in God's image can give them meaning and hope even in the depth of despair.[79] The special connection and intended reflection that constitute being in God's image are God's enduring promise to them that so much more is possible if they are willing to let God break the power that sin has over them.

In the life of Christ, believers can glimpse what they can surely become because of who God has already created them to be (see Ch. 2). They can be confident that when they see Christ more clearly and their transformation is complete, they will truly be like Christ (see Ch. 6). Through Christ they can now increasingly experience the renewal of attributes such as reason, righteousness, rulership, and relationship (see Ch. 5) with new knowledge and holiness as special evidence of that (see Ch. 6).

They can also look forward to experiencing other aspects of renewal according to God's image in Christ that they cannot experience until after death or Christ's return (see Ch. 7). Christians struggling with the many limitations of their bodies can particularly rejoice that their future spiritual

---

76. See Maston, 1959: 14; S. McDonald, 2009: 330 (discussing Owen, 1850-1855b).

77. On the place of loving in God's image, see Foltz, 2001: 330; P. Peterson, 2008: 37 (discussing Soelle, 1984). On empowering to love, see Ross, 1990: 103 (drawing on the work of Zizioulas).

78. For more on this theme, see Welch, 1994: 36-38; Reitman, 2010; Robinson, 2011: 162.

79. See Krause, 2005: 367; Goodman, 2008: 148; D. Carson, 2010: 23; Reitman, 2010: 125. Also Schönborn (2011: 42), who affirms the teaching of John Paul II (1980: 585) that only because of creation in the image and likeness of God does humanity have meaning in this world.

bodies will overcome the oppression of such limitations. Those devitalized by a broader range of life's threats can rejoice in their coming imperishability (see Ch. 7). Unbelievers can receive the good news that all of this is for them as well if they enter into renewal according to the image of God in Christ by committing themselves to Christ.

Much is lost when pastors, counselors, and other ministers do not encourage and challenge hurting people with the glorious truth that they are created, and continue, in God's undamaged image. People need to hear the message that, like many others, they may be flawed in terms of rational, moral, relational, and/or other attributes. However, their special connection with God and intended reflection of God — their existence in God's image — is not about their current limited attributes. Despite all that is wrong with them, their existence in God's image is a constant that has not deteriorated, for it is more about God than about people.[80] It is God's pronouncement voiced in Genesis 1:26 before the beginning of the creation of humanity, and it is God's commitment recorded in Romans 8:29. God has determined that the implications of humanity's creation in God's image will be fulfilled regardless of what that costs God — even if God's own child must die to break the power of sin. What wonderful news that is for many people![81]

Not surprisingly, effective ministry flows from recognizing oneself and those among whom one is ministering as, together, in God's image.[82] That recognition fosters humility in the one ministering.[83] It also engenders a sense of responsibility to reflect God's character and priorities well.[84] Image-inspired ministry involves speaking constructively and working for the liberation of others from oppression.[85] It entails acting redemptively. For example, overcoming racism is not just a matter of recognizing that

---

80. Like the very person of God, the image of God remains "untarnished by the tragic" (Reynolds, 2008: 187).

81. For example, a clear sense of identity as created in God's image has played an important role in the struggles of African Americans according to Mayland, 1999: 62; Teel, 2010: 165. See also Chapter 1.

82. See Maston, 1959: 14; D. Hart, 2009: 17-18; cf. Goodman, 2008: 68 for this modeled in Jesus Christ. Regarding implications for Christian social work, see Hodge and Wolfer, 2008 and Pooler, 2011: 444-46.

83. Ross, 1990: 107; Graham, 2006: 277.

84. Bray, 1998: 51; Grenz, 2001: 15 (drawing on Howe, 1995); McMinn and Campbell, 2007: 26-27.

85. On the grounding of speaking constructively in Colossians 3, see H. Carson, 1960: 84; M. Barth, 1974: 511. On working for liberation from oppression, see Cone, 1986: 93; Japinga, 1999: 90-92; Garner, 2007: 129, 132.

people who are "different" are in God's image. It includes living out one's status as created in God's image in a way that allows God to overcome one's self-centeredness and enables seeking the well-being of all as God does.[86] Similarly, overcoming gender bias requires more than acknowledging women as created in God's image. It also necessitates men understanding and living more fully the implications of their own creation in God's image.[87] People who humbly and gratefully see themselves as being in God's image have so much more to offer the world as a result, in terms of social transformation as well as personal redemption and liberation.[88]

One area of life where being in God's image has major implications is humanity's relationship with the natural world. Being in God's image gives humanity a special dignity, but that in no way logically implies that the rest of creation has such a low status that exploitation by people is acceptable.[89] Rather, as explained in Chapter 5, God intends humanity in the divine image to act toward the creation as God would act. Such "rulership" over the nonhuman creation, on both a personal and societal level, will then look like caring stewardship informed by solidarity and servant leadership, rather than like oppression and exploitation. People in God's image also have a responsibility, delegated by God, to maintain proper order in human society.[90] Humanity has often not fulfilled its God-given responsibilities to God's creation. In Christ people are not relieved from such worldly responsibilities but restored to them.[91]

A Better Way Forward

Recognizing all people as created in the image of God, then, has huge implications for how people should understand themselves, as well as how

---

86. So Oldham, 1924: 265; Teel, 2010: 168; cf. Baker, 1991: 126, and Lutheran, 1994: 36-37 for the connection of this idea with Colossians 3.

87. So Oduyoye, 2001: 105; cf. p. 65 on Jesus Christ as the model for this.

88. See W. Barr, 1982: 484; Hopkins, 2005: 185.

89. See Case-Winters, 2004: 818 (discussing Hefner's work); Sands, 2010: 39-40; Green, 2011: 273; Vorster, 2011: 22.

90. Many commentators see in Genesis 9:6 a mandate for people, who are in God's image, to hold murderers accountable — and not just a mandate not to destroy someone created in God's image. E.g., Clines, 1968: 78-79; 1993: 427; Tigay, 1984: 174, 177-78; D. Williams, 1999: 187; Garr, 2003: 162-63. However, as Wolff (1974: 164) notes, this power to rein in harm is not unlimited.

91. So Moritz, 2009: 139; cf. S. Wright, 2003: 42.

they should view and treat others. Such is the case in every sphere of life. Consider, for instance, the realm of bioethics, which concerns matters of right and wrong, good and bad, where life and health are at issue. Many of its challenges have to do with assisted procreation, abortion, human experimentation, stem cell research, access to healthcare, end-of-life treatment, genetic intervention, cybernetic enhancement, and other ways to restore or improve human beings. The magnitude of these challenges to human and environmental well-being is staggering, yet the silence and inaction of most churches in this arena is distressing.[92]

Prominent among the causes for this lack of engagement is an inadequate understanding of what it means for humanity to be in God's image.[93] Every human being has a great stake in these matters — especially those considered most expendable in their societal settings. Those most likely to be killed or verbally abused are those whom people would most like to be rid of or those whose elimination would be most socially beneficial. Biblical writers invoke the image of God precisely to uphold the life and well-being of such "marginal" and "dispensable" people — though all other people benefit from the same respect and protection in the process.

The church's uneven track record in affirming and living these teachings has been troubling enough with regard to such moral challenges as racism, sexism, poverty, and disability. But the stakes are only growing with the rapid growth of powerful biotechnologies. It used to be that sick people would die when an illness proceeded to a certain point. Now technology can keep people alive for many more years, even decades. Either overtreatment or undertreatment can result, with accompanying violations of dignity and life. Similarly, it used to be that genetic deficiencies in a family would lead to bodily problems generation after generation that could not be altered. Now technology is developing the ability not only to correct problems for all future generations but also to design people's bodies genetically to suit personal or societal preferences — or to replace

---

92. This problem, and the need for a more influential role for teaching on the image of God as a result, are discussed in P. Peterson, 2008: 28; Reinders, 1997: 199. Charles Colson and Nigel Cameron (2004: 20-21) are concerned that churches are "sleeping through another moral catastrophe . . . [for which] our churches are ill-prepared."

93. Part of the problem is simply the need to work out the implications of what it means for humanity to be in God's image in the face of new challenges — see Hall, 1986: 63. However, a more serious difficulty arises when people's understanding of being in God's image is not fully in line with what the authors of the Bible say about it.

human bodies entirely with computerized robotics. The challenges to human life and dignity are increasingly profound.

So many churches' pessimism or apathy about such matters suggests that some key aspect of biblical teaching is not doing its job. It is as if the ultimate biblical basis for ethical engagement on which other biblical exhortations depend — humanity's creation and renewal in God's image — has become largely inoperative somehow. It is hard to imagine a more effective way to undermine this crucial teaching than reducing God's image to one or more particular attributes that people have, such as reason, righteousness, rulership, or relationship. If being in God's image is about people actually having (as opposed to God intending) such particular traits or abilities, then the door is open wide to demeaning those who lack those traits or abilities — or who have them to a lesser degree than others do. Understanding God's image in terms of current attributes also fosters the idea that God's image is damaged, since sin has damaged all human attributes.

Indeed, as noted in Chapter 4, people in churches today are often learning that God's image is "lost," "obliterated," "destroyed," "forfeited," "shattered," "effaced," "ceased," "consumed," "erased," "extinguished," "annihilated," "smashed," "wiped out," "negated," "taken away" — or else "virtually lost," "mutilated," "almost blotted out," "all but obliterated," "almost entirely extinguished," "maimed," "vitiated," "worn out," "almost effaced," "ruined," "radically limited," "spoiled," "wasted away" — or in any case "partly lost," "eroded," "impaired," "degenerated," "reduced," "diminished," "disrupted," "malfunctioning," "harmed," "impoverished," "damaged," "bent," "weakened," "broken," "fragmented," "perverted," "corrupted," "warped," "disease-ridden," "twisted," "infected," "tainted," "blotted," "marred," "defaced," "deformed," "disfigured" — or at the very least "sullied," "blemished," "tarnished," "confused," "blurred," or "distorted."

It is no wonder that people have little inspiration for offering others the respect and protection that should accompany being in God's image. That image is in shambles. It offers little inspiration for people to be more than they are. Before it can do that, supposedly, it must be "restored," "renewed," "recovered," "regained," "gotten back," "re-created," "recuperated," "repaired," "redeemed," "redone," "evolved," "moved," "developed," "perfected," or "transformed" (see Ch. 7). Since this is a process that will be far from complete in this world, being in God's image remains far from the inspiration that God purposed it to be from before the beginning of creation and still desires it to be.

Of course, many of those promoting the idea of a badly damaged image in need of massive restoration may intend to speak of God's image in more of a metaphorical than a literal sense. The concern may be to describe in graphic language the terrible damage that sin has done to human beings. The intended message presumably is that, however close humanity may have originally been to God, that closeness has now been lost or is at least badly damaged.

Speaking of such matters in terms of damage done to the image of God is understandable and would even be commendable on rhetorical grounds, were it not so dangerous (Ch. 1) in addition to being biblically unsupported (Ch. 4). Vivid language is wonderful as a way to enable people to understand biblical teaching more clearly. However, it must be avoided if it leads to a misunderstanding of biblical teaching, particularly teaching that has huge implications for human well-being.

No wonder Christians are not consistently motivated to stand up and speak out for human life, dignity, and sacredness grounded in God's image. No wonder the church has such a checkered record with regard to racism, sexism, poverty, disability issues, and care for the natural environment. No wonder the church is not devoting more effort to understanding and engaging daunting challenges, such as those of bioethics. A primary biblical basis for advocacy and action in the face of such challenges, according to the teaching of many, has been significantly undermined — or so people are hearing.

The vitally important affirmation that every human being is truly/fully "in the image of God" is not the only biblical basis for advocacy and action, so the church has hardly been unengaged with the world. Nevertheless, this great biblical affirmation is among the most foundational and powerful bases for such engagement. With this affirmation not very prominent in the consciousness of the church, the urgency of engaging what ultimately depends upon all people being created in the undamaged image of God is correspondingly weak.

Many of those cited here as promoting the idea of a lost or damaged image would probably be quick to point out that they *do* in fact urge the church to engage the great ethical challenges of our day. The idea that any aspect of their writing and teaching could unintentionally be helping to undermine the importance or urgency of that engagement would be very painful for them to contemplate — as it was for me personally. This analysis is offered in the hope that concern for godly moral engagement will help prompt a fresh look at the relevant biblical writings and a revival of an understanding of God's image that has surfaced repeatedly throughout the history of the church.

This analysis is intended as a message of hope, not of despair — of better possibilities for the future, not mere regret for the past. God has created humanity with a God-related significance that is wonderful indeed. All people are created in the image of God! And the biblical writings, under God's superintending hand, consistently never even suggest that this image has been damaged or lost, despite the grave harm that sin has caused to human beings themselves.

Humanity's creation in the image of God gives no one the slightest saving merit before God — that comes only through Jesus Christ. But creation in the divine image does say a lot about why God has gone to such great lengths to reach and restore people in Christ — and why the church should do so as well. Moreover, it speaks volumes about how all people are to treat one another (and why), while God's restoring initiatives continue in their midst.

Without seeing humanity as created in the undamaged image of God — specially connected to God and intended to meaningfully reflect many God-glorifying attributes — there are ample grounds for pessimism regarding bioethical and other challenges. Far less than is needed can be expected from the church even in terms of reaction to the most glaring problems, not to mention proactive engagement with the entire range of challenges.

However, if the church's inspiration and rallying cry is the creation of all humanity in God's image, there is great hope for so much more. The church can become widely known as the champion of all human beings. After all, those the church would champion are in God's image. In fact, the church itself is being renewed in God's image. The church will continue to call all people to renounce their sin and follow Christ, for renewal according to God's image in Christ is the glorious fulfillment of what only began at creation. At the same time, the church can help show people the extent of God's love by the way that Christians uphold the life and dignity of all — even the down and dejected, the needy and neglected, the ruined and rejected.

Elaborating many of the exciting implications of this understanding of humanity in God's image must await future work on the part of many; however, that endeavor will be well worth the effort. At issue is nothing less than the dignity and destiny of humanity.

References Cited

Aagaard, Anna Marie. 1982. "Imago Dei." *Mid-Stream* 21: 350-58.

Aalders, G. Charles. 1981. *Genesis.* Translated by William Heynen. Vol. 1. Bible Student's Commentary. Grand Rapids: Zondervan.

Abanes, Richard. 1996. *American Militias: Rebellion, Racism & Religion.* Downers Grove, IL: InterVarsity Press.

Abetz, Katherine. 2010. "Identity for Women: A Proposal for the Gendered *imago Dei* Based on 1 Corinthians 11:1-16." *Pacifica* 23, no. 1: 15-32.

Abon-Assaf, Ali, Pierre Bordreuil, and Alan R. Millard. 1982. *La Statue de Tell Fekherye et son Inscription Bilingue Assyro-araméenne.* Paris: Recherche sur les Civilisations.

Achtemeier, Paul J. 1985. *Romans.* Interpretation. Atlanta: John Knox.

Achtemeier, Paul J., Joel B. Green, and Marianne Maye Thompson. 2001. *Introducing the New Testament: Its Literature and Theology.* Grand Rapids: Eerdmans.

Adamson, James B. 1976. *The Epistle of James.* New International Commentary on the New Testament. Grand Rapids: Eerdmans.

Ahiamadu, Amadi. 2010. "A Critical Assessment of the Creation Mandate in Genesis 1:26-28 and Its Human Rights Implications for Nigeria." In *Genesis,* ed. Athalya Brenner et al., pp. 13-24. Minneapolis: Fortress.

Albrektson, Bertil. 1976. *History and the Gods.* Lund, Sweden: Gleerup.

Alexander, William L. 1888. *A System of Biblical Theology.* Vol. 1. Edinburgh: T. & T. Clark.

Allen, Ronald B. 2000. *The Majesty of Man.* 2nd ed. Grand Rapids: Kregel.

Alter, Robert. 1992. *The World of Biblical Literature.* San Francisco: Basic Books.

Althaus, Paul. 1941. "Das Bild Gottes bei Paulus." *Theologische Blatter* 20: 81-92.

Altmann, Alexander. 1968. "Homo Imago Dei in Jewish and Christian Theology." *Journal of Religion* 48, no. 3: 235-59.

Ambrose. 1961. *Hexameron, Paradise, and Cain and Abel.* Translated by John J. Savage. New York: Fathers of the Church, Inc.

Amundsen, Darrel W. 1996. *Medicine, Society, and Faith in the Ancient and Medieval Worlds*. Baltimore: Johns Hopkins University Press.

Anderson, Neil T., and Dave Park. 2003. *Overcoming Negative Self-Image*. Ventura, CA: Regal.

Angerstorfer, Andreas. 1984. "Gedanken zur Analyse der Inscrift(en) der Beterstatue vom Tel Fecherije." *Biblische Notizen* 24: 7-11.

Anselm. 1962. *Basic Writings: Proslogium, Mologium, Gaunilo's In Behalf of the Fool, Cur Deus Homo*. Translated by Sidney Deane. Chicago: Open Court.

Antone, Hope S. 2007. "Reminiscing 25 Years of IGI, 20 Years of AWRC." *In God's Image* 26: 1.

Aquinas, Thomas. 1947. *Summa Theologica*. Translated by Fathers of the English Domincian Province. Vol. 1. New York: Benziger.

———. 2008. "Commentary on the Sentences of Peter Lombard." In *On Love and Charity: Readings from the "Commentary on the Sentences of Peter Lombard,"* trans. Peter Kwasniewski. Washington, DC: Catholic University of America Press.

Arellano, Luz Beatriz. 1994. "Women's Experience of God in Emerging Spirituality." In *Feminist Theology from the Third World*, ed. Ursula King, pp. 318-39. Maryknoll, NY: Orbis.

Arminius, Jacobus. 1986. *The Works of James Arminius*. Translated by James Nichols. Vol. 2. Grand Rapids: Baker.

Armistead, W. S. 1903. *The Negro Is a Man: A Reply to Charles Carroll's Book*. Tifton, GA: Armistead & Vickers.

Aronson, David. 1984. "Creation in God's Likeness." *Judaism* 33, no. 1: 13-20.

Arx, Urs von. 2002. "The Gender Aspects of Creation from a Theological, Christo-logical, and Soteriological Perspective: An Exegetical Contribution." *Anglican Theological Review* 84, no. 3: 519-54.

Assmann, Jan. 2000. *Herrschaft und Heil*. Munich: Hanser.

Assohoto, Barnabe, and Samuel Ngewa. 2006. "Genesis." In *Africa Bible Commentary*, ed. Tokunboh Adeyemo, pp. 9-84. Grand Rapids: Zondervan.

Athanasius of Alexandria. 1885. *Athanasius De Incarnatione*. Translated by Archibald Robertson. London: D. Nutt.

Attridge, Harold W. 1989. *The Epistle to the Hebrews*. Edited by Helmut Koester. Hermeneia. Philadelphia: Fortress.

Augustine of Hippo. 1949. *The Confessions*. Translated by Edward B. Risey. New York: Carlton House.

———. 1960. *On the Psalms*. Translated by Scholastica Hebgin and Felicitas Corrigan. Vol. 1. London: Newman Press.

———. 1963. *The Trinity*. Translated by Stephen McKenna. Washington, DC: Catholic University of America Press.

———. 1982. *The Literal Meaning of Genesis*. Translated by John Taylor. Vol. 1. New York: Newman Press.

————. 1990. *Sermons*. Edited by John E. Rotelle, translated by Edmund Hill. Vol. 1, Part 3. Brooklyn, NY: New City Press.

————. 1991. "Two Books on Genesis Against the Manichees." In *Saint Augustine on Genesis*, trans. Roland Teske, pp. 45-141. Fathers of the Church 84. Washington, DC: Catholic University of America Press.

————. 1999. *The Retractations*. Translated by Mary Inez Bogan. Washington, DC: Catholic University of America Press.

Bailey, Derrick S. 1959. *The Man-Woman Relation in Christian Thought*. London: Longmans.

Baillie, John. 1939. *Our Knowledge of God*. New York: Scribner.

Bajema, Clifford E. 1974. *Abortion and the Meaning of Personhood*. Grand Rapids: Baker.

Baker, William H. 1991. *In the Image of God: A Biblical View of Humanity*. Chicago: Moody.

Balswick, Jack O., Pamela Ebstyne King, and Kevin S. Reimer. 2005. *The Reciprocating Self: Human Development in Theological Perspective*. Downers Grove, IL: Inter-Varsity Press.

Balthasar, Hans Urs von. 1967. *A Theological Anthropology*. New York: Sheed and Ward.

Barabas, Steven. 1963. "Image of God." In *Zondervan Pictorial Bible Dictionary*, ed. Merrill C. Tenney, pp. 370-71. Grand Rapids: Zondervan.

Barackman, Floyd H. 2001. *Practical Christian Theology*. 4th ed. Grand Rapids: Kregel.

Barclay, William. 1976. *The Letters of John and Jude*. 2nd ed. Daily Study Bible. Philadelphia: Westminster.

Barentsen, Jack. 1988. "The Validity of Human Language: A Vehicle for Divine Truth." *Grace Theological Journal* 9, no. 1: 21-43.

Barilan, Yechiel M. 2012. *Human Dignity, Human Rights, and Responsibility*. Cambridge, MA: MIT Press.

Barnes, Gilbert H., and Dwight L. Dumond, eds. 1965. *Letters of Theodore Dwight Weld, Angelina Grimke Weld, and Sarah Grimke, 1822-1844*. Vol. 1. Gloucester, MA: Peter Smith.

Barr, James. 1968. "The Image of God in Genesis — A Study in Terminology." *Bulletin of the John Rylands Library* 51: 11-26.

————. 1974. "Man and Nature: The Ecological Controversy and the Old Testament." In *Ecology and Religion in History*, ed. David Spring and Eileen Spring, pp. 48-75. New York: Harper & Row.

————. 1993. *Biblical Faith and Natural Theology*. Oxford: Clarendon.

Barr, William R. 1982. "Life: Created in the Image of God." *Mid-Stream* 21 (October): 473-84.

Barrett, C. K. 1993. *The First Epistle to the Corinthians*. Black's New Testament Commentary. Peabody, MA: Hendrickson.

Barth, Karl. 1936. "The Doctrine of the Word of God." In *Church Dogmatics*. Vol. 1, pt. 1. Edinburgh: T. & T. Clark.

————. 1958a. "The Doctrine of Creation." In *Church Dogmatics,* ed. Geoffrey W. Bromiley and Thomas F. Torrance. Vol. III, pt. 1. Edinburgh: T. & T. Clark.

————. 1958b. "The Doctrine of Creation." In *Church Dogmatics,* ed. Geoffrey W. Bromiley and Thomas F. Torrance. Vol. III, pt. 2. Edinburgh: T. & T. Clark.

Barth, Markus. 1974. *Ephesians 1–3.* Anchor Bible Commentary. New York: Doubleday.

Barth, Markus, and Helmut Blanke. 1994. *Colossians: A New Translation with Introduction and Commentry.* Translated by Astrid B. Beck. New York: Doubleday.

Bavinck, Herman. 1977. *Our Reasonable Faith.* Grand Rapids: Baker.

————. 2004. *Reformed Dogmatics: God and Creation.* Grand Rapids: Baker Academic.

Bayertz, Kurt. 1996. "Human Dignity: Philosophical Origin and Scientific Erosion of an Idea." In *Sanctity of Life and Human Dignity,* ed. Kurt Bayertz, pp. 73-90. Dordrecht: Kluwer.

Bazzell, Pascal D. 2012. "Toward a Creational Perspective on Poverty: Genesis 1:26-28, Image of God, and Its Missiological Implications." In *Genesis and Christian Theology,* ed. Nathan MacDonald et al., pp. 228-41. Grand Rapids: Eerdmans.

Beale, Gregory K. 2004. *The Temple and the Church's Mission.* Downers Grove, IL: InterVarsity Press.

————. 2008. *We Become What We Worship.* Downers Grove, IL: IVP Academic.

————. 2011. *A New Testament Biblical Theology.* Grand Rapids: Baker Academic.

Beare, Francis W. 1982. *The Gospel According to Matthew.* San Francisco: Harper & Row.

Beckwith, Roger. 1978. "The Bearing of Holy Spirit." In *Man, Woman and Priesthood,* ed. Peter Moore, pp. 45-62. London: SPCK.

Behr, John. 2013. "The Promise of the Image." In *Imago Dei: Human Dignity in Ecumenical Perspective,* ed. Thomas Albert Howard, pp. 15-37. Washington, DC: Catholic University of America Press.

Behr-Sigel, Elisabeth. 1982. "Woman Too Is in the Likeness of God." *Mid-Stream* 21: 369-75.

Beisner, E. Calvin. 1994. "Justice and Poverty: Two Views Contrasted." In *Christianity and Economics in the Post-Cold War Era,* ed. Herbert Schlassberg, Viney Samuel, and Ronald Sider. Grand Rapids: Eerdmans.

Bell, Richard H. 1994. *Provoked to Jealousy: The Origin and Purpose of the Jealousy Motif in Romans 9–11.* Wissenschaftliche Untersuchungen zum Neuen Testament 63. Tübingen: J. C. B. Mohr (Paul Siebeck).

Belleville, Linda L. 1995. *2 Corinthians.* IVP New Testament Commentary Series 8. Downers Grove, IL: InterVarsity Press.

Benedict XVI (Joseph Ratzinger). 1995. *In the Beginning . . . .* Translated by Boniface Ramsey. Grand Rapids: Eerdmans.

Bequette, John P. 2004. *Christian Humanism: Creation, Redemption, and Reintegration.* Lanham, MD: University Press of America.

Berkhof, Hendrikus. 1979. *Christian Faith.* Translated by Sierd Woodstra. Grand Rapids: Eerdmans.

Berkhof, Louis. 1949. *Systematic Theology.* Grand Rapids: Eerdmans.

Berkhofer, Robert F., Jr. 1978. *The White Man's Indian.* New York: Alfred A. Knopf.

Berkouwer, G. C. 1975. *Man: The Image of God.* Grand Rapids: Eerdmans.

Berman, Joshua A. 2008. *Created Equal: How the Bible Broke with Ancient Political Thought.* Oxford: Oxford University Press.

Bernal, Martin. 1993. "Black Athena: Hostilities to Egypt in the Eighteenth Century." In *The "Racial" Economy of Science: Toward a Democratic Future,* ed. Sandra Harding, pp. 47-63. Bloomington: Indiana University Press.

Bernhardt, Karl H. 1956. *Gott und Bild.* Berlin: Evangelische Verlagsanstalt.

Berry, R. J., and Malcolm Jeeves. 2008. "The Nature of Human Nature." *Science & Christian Belief* 20, no. 1: 3-47.

Best, Ernest. 1998. *Ephesians.* International Critical Commentary. Edinburgh: T. & T. Clark.

Beyreuther, Erich, and Gunter Finkenrath. 1976. *"Homoios."* In *New International Dictionary of New Testament Theology,* 2:500-505. Grand Rapids: Zondervan.

Bingemer, Maria Clara. 1989. "Reflection on the Trinity." In *Through Her Eyes: Women's Theology from Latin America,* ed. Elsa Tamez, pp. 56-80. Maryknoll, NY: Orbis.

Birch, Bruce C. 1984. "In the Image of God." *Sojourners* 13, no. 1: 10-15.

Bird, Michael F. 2009. *Colossians and Philemon: A New Covenant Commentary.* New Covenant Commentary Series. Eugene, OR: Cascade.

Bird, Phyllis A. 1981. " 'Male and Female He Created Them': Gen 1:27b in the Context of the Priestly Account of Creation." *Harvard Theological Review* 74, no. 2: 129-59.

———. 1995. "Sexual Differentiation and Divine Image in the Genesis Creation Texts." In *The Image of God: Gender Models in Judaeo-Christian Tradition,* ed. Kari Elisabeth Børresen, pp. 5-28. Minneapolis: Fortress.

———. 1997. *Missing Persons and Mistaken Identities: Women and Gender in Ancient Israel.* Minneapolis: Fortress.

Black, C. Clifton. 2006. "God's Promise for Humanity in the New Testament." In *God and Human Dignity,* ed. Kendall Soulen and Linda Woodhead, pp. 179-95. Grand Rapids: Eerdmans.

Blackwell, Ben C. 2010. "Immortal Glory and the Problem of Death in Romans 3:23." *Journal for the Study of the New Testament* 32, no. 3: 285-308.

———. 2011. *Christosis.* Tubingen, Germany: Mohr Siebeck.

Blass, Friedrich, Albert Debrunner, and Robert Funk. 1961. *A Greek Grammar of the New Testament and Other Early Christian Literature.* Chicago: University of Chicago Press.

Blomberg, Craig L. 1992. *Matthew.* New American Commentary 22. Nashville: Broadman.

———. 1999. *Neither Poverty nor Riches: A Biblical Theology of Material Possessions.* Grand Rapids: Eerdmans.

Blyden, Edward W. 1992. "The African Problem and the Method of Its Solution." In *African-American Social and Political Thought 1850-1920,* ed. Howard Brotz, pp. 126-39. New Brunswick, NJ: Transaction.

Bock, Darrell L. 1994. *Luke 9:51–24:53*. Baker Exegetical Commentary on the New Testament. Grand Rapids: Baker Books.

Bockmuehl, Markus. 1997. "'The Form of God' (Phil. 2:6): Variations on a Theme of Jewish Mysticism." *Journal of Theological Studies* 48, no. 1: 1-23.

Boer, Harry R. 1990. *An Ember Still Glowing: Humankind as the Image of God*. Grand Rapids: Eerdmans.

Bonhoeffer, Dietrich. 1959a. *Creation and Fall: A Theological Interpretation of Genesis 1–3*. Translated by John C. Fletcher and Kathleen Downham. New York: Macmillan.

————. 1959b. *The Cost of Discipleship*. Translated by Reginald H. Fuller. London: SCM.

Bori, Pier C. 2010. "Ad Imaginem Dei." In *In the Image of God*, ed. Alberto Melloni and Riccardo Saccenti, pp. 39-44. Berlin: Lit.

Bornkamm, Gunther. 1975. *Jesus of Nazareth*. New York: Harper & Row.

Børresen, Kari Elisabeth. 1982. "The Imago Dei: Two Historical Contexts." *Mid-Stream* 21: 359-65.

————. 1995. "God's Image, Man's Image? Patristic Interpretation of Gen. 1,27 and 1 Cor. 11,7." In *The Image of God: Gender Models in Judaeo-Christian Tradition*, ed. Kari Elisabeth Børresen, pp. 187-209. Minneapolis: Fortress.

Bortone, Pietro. 2010. *Greek Prepositions from Antiquity to the Present*. New York: Oxford University Press.

Bosman, Hendrik. 2010. "Humankind as Being Created in the 'Image of God' in the Old Testament: Possible Implications for the Theological Debate on Human Dignity." *Scriptura* 105: 561-71.

Botman, H. Russel. 2006. "Covenantal Anthropology: Integrating Three Contemporary Discourses of Human Dignity." In *God and Human Dignity*, ed. R. Kendall Soulen and Linda Woodhead, pp. 72-86. Grand Rapids: Eerdmans.

Bowery, Anne-Marie. 2007. "Monica: The Feminine Face of Christ." In *Feminist Interpretations of Augustine*, ed. Judith Chelius Stark, pp. 69-95. University Park: Pennsylvania State University Press.

Boyce, James P. 1990. *Abstract of Systematic Theology*. Escondido, CA: Den Dulk Christian Foundation.

Bradley, Anthony B. 2010. *Liberating Black Theology*. Wheaton, IL: Crossway.

Bradley, Anthony B., ed. 2013. *Aliens in the Promised Land*. Phillipsburg, NJ: P&R Publishing.

Bradshaw, Jeffrey M. 2010. *In God's Image and Likeness*. Salt Lake City: Eborn Publishing.

Branick, Vincent P. 1985. "The Sinful Flesh of the Son of God (Rom 8:3): A Key Image of Pauline Theology." *Catholic Biblical Quarterly* 47, no. 2: 246-62.

Bray, Gerald L. 1991. "The Significance of God's Image in Man." *Tyndale Bulletin* 42, no. 2 (November): 195-225.

————. 1998. "God and Our Image." In *Grace and Truth in the Secular Age,* ed. Timothy Bradshaw, pp. 41-51. Grand Rapids: Eerdmans.

————. 2001. "Image of God." In *New Dictionary of Biblical Theology,* ed. T. Desmond Alexander and Brian S. Rosner, pp. 575-76. Downers Grove, IL: InterVarsity Press.

Breck, John. 1998. *The Sacred Gift of Life: Orthodox Christianity and Bioethics.* Crestwood, NY: St. Vladimir's Seminary Press.

————. 2003. *God with Us: Critical Issues in Christian Life and Faith.* Crestwood, NY: St. Vladimir's Seminary Press.

Brenner, Athalya. 1996. "The Hebrew God and His Female Complements." In *Reading Bibles, Writing Bodies: Identity and the Book,* ed. Timothy Beal and David Gunn, pp. 56-71. London: Routledge.

Briggs, Richard S. 2010. "Humans in the Image of God and Other Things Genesis Does Not Make Clear." *Journal of Theological Interpretation* 4, no. 1: 111-26.

Brink, Paul A. 2001. "Selves in Relation: Theories of Community and the *Imago Dei* Doctrine." In *The Re-Enchantment of Political Science,* ed. Thomas W. Heilke and Ashley Woodiwiss, pp. 85-120. Lanham, MD: Lexington Books.

Brooke, Alan E. 1912. *A Critical and Exegetical Commentary on the Johannine Epistles.* International Critical Commentary. Edinburgh: T. & T. Clark.

Brooks, George E. 1967. "The American Frontier in German Fiction." In *The Frontier Re-examined,* ed. John McDermott, pp. 155-67. Urbana: University of Illinois Press.

Brooks, James A. 1991. *Mark.* New American Commentary 23. Nashville: Broadman.

Brown, Colin. 1991. "Trinity and Incarnation: In Search of Contemporary Orthodoxy." *Ex Auditu* 7: 83-100.

Brown, Francis, S. R. Driver, and Charles A. Briggs, eds. 1966. *A Hebrew and English Lexicon of the Old Testament.* Oxford: Oxford University Press.

Brown, Peter. 1992. *Power and Persuasion in Late Antiquity.* Madison: University of Wisconsin Press.

Brown, Raymond E. 1982. *The Epistles of John.* Anchor Bible Commentary. New York: Doubleday.

Browning, Elizabeth Barrett. 1893. *The Image of God: The Poems of Elizabeth Barrett Browning.* New York: Frederick Warne & Co.

Browning, Robert. 2004. *Christmas Eve.* 10th ed. Project Gutenberg. http://www.gutenberg.org/cache/epub/6670/pg6670.html.

Brownson, Orestes. 1861. "Slavery and the War — Part II." *Brownson's Quarterly Review.* www.orestesbrownson.com/203.html.html.

Bruce, F. F. 1957. *The Epistles to the Ephesians and Colossians.* Grand Rapids: Eerdmans.

————. 1963. *The Epistle of Paul to the Romans.* Vol. 12. Tyndale New Testament Commentary. Grand Rapids: Eerdmans.

————. 1964. *The Epistle to the Hebrews.* New International Commentary on the New Testament. Grand Rapids: Eerdmans.

Brueggemann, Walter. 1982. *Genesis.* Atlanta: John Knox.

————. 1997. *Theology of the Old Testament.* Minneapolis: Fortress.

Brumble, H. David. 1992. "Imago Dei." In *A Dictionary of Biblical Tradition in English Literature*, ed. David L. Jeffrey, pp. 372-73. Grand Rapids: Eerdmans.

Brunner, Emil. 1946. "Nature and Grace." In *Natural Theology*, ed. Peter Fraenkel. Edinburgh: J. & J. Gray.

———. 1947. *Man in Revolt: A Christian Anthropology*. Philadelphia: Westminster.

———. 1952. *The Christian Doctrine of Creation and Redemption*. Translated by Olive Wyon. Philadelphia: Westminster.

Bruns, Roger. 1971. "Anthony Benezet's Assertion of Negro Equality." *The Journal of Negro History* 56 (July): 230-38.

Buber, Martin. 1958. *I and Thou*. Translated by Ronald Smith. New York: Scribner.

Buchanan, George W. 1972. *Hebrews*. Anchor Bible Commentary. New York: Doubleday.

———. 1996. *The Gospel of Matthew*. Mellen Bible Commentary New Testament. Lewiston, NY: Mellen Biblical.

Büchsel, Friedrich. 1964. "εἴδωλον." In *Theological Dictionary of the New Testament*, ed. Gerhard Kittel, 2:375-78. Grand Rapids: Eerdmans.

Budziszewski, Jay. 2002. "The Second Tablet Project." *First Things* 124: 23-31.

Bullock, Annie Vocature. 2012. *Real Austin: The Homeless and the Image of God*. Eugene, OR: Cascade.

Burghardt, Walter. 1957. *The Image of God in Man According to Cyril of Alexandria*. Washington, DC: Catholic University of America Press.

Buswell, J. Oliver. 1962. *A Systematic Theology of the Christian Religion*. Vol. 1. Grand Rapids: Zondervan.

Butler, Joseph. 1970. *Butler's Fifteen Sermons Preached at Rolls Chapel and a Dissertation of the Nature of Virtue*. Edited by T. A. Roberts. London: SPCK.

Byrne, Brendan. 1996. *Romans*. Sacra Pagina. Collegeville, MN: Liturgical Press.

Cahalan, Kathleen A. 2004. *Formed in the Image of Christ: The Sacramental Moral Theology of Bernard Häring*. Collegeville, MN: Liturgical Press.

Cahill, Lisa Sowle. 1980. "Toward a Christian Theory of Human Rights." *The Journal of Religious Ethics* 8: 277-301.

———. 2006a. "Bioethics, Relationships and Participation in the Common Good." In *Health and Human Flourishing*, ed. Carol Taylor and Roberto Dell'Oro, pp. 207-22. Washington, DC: Georgetown University Press.

———. 2006b. "Embodying God's Image: Created, Broken, and Redeemed." In *Humanity Before God*, ed. William Schweiker, Michael Johnson, and Kevin Jung, pp. 55-77. Minneapolis: Fortress.

Cairns, David. 1973. *The Image of God in Man*. Revised. London: Collins.

Callender, Dexter E., Jr. 2000. *Adam in Myth and History*. Winona Lake, IN: Eisenbrauns.

Calvin, John. 1948. *Commentary on Genesis*. Translated by John King. Grand Rapids: Eerdmans.

————. 1960a. *Institutes of the Christian Religion.* Translated by Ford Battles. Philadelphia: Westminster.

————. 1960b. *The First Epistle of Paul the Apostle to the Corinthians.* Translated by John Farmer. Edinburgh: Oliver & Boyd.

————. 1993. *Sermons on Job.* Edinburgh: Banner of Truth Trust.

————. 1994. "On the Divinity of Christ." In *Calvini Opera 47.* Geneva: Droz.

————. 1996. *2 Corinthians and Timothy, Titus & Philemon.* Translated by Thomas A. Smail and David Torrance. Grand Rapids: Eerdmans.

Cameron, Nigel M. de S. 1989. *Complete in Christ.* London: Marshall Pickering.

Campbell, Cynthia M. 1981. "Imago Dei Reconsidered: Male and Female Together." *Journal for Preachers* 4, no. 2: 9-14.

Canadian Council of Churches, Commission on Faith and Witness. 2005. *Becoming Human: On Theological Anthropology in an Age of Engineering Life.* Toronto: C.C.C.

Canceran, Delfo. 2011. "Image of God: A Theological Reconstruction of the Beginning." *Asia Journal of Theology* 25, no. 1: 3-23.

Caneday, Ardel B. 2007. "They Exchanged the Glory of God for the Likeness of an Image: Idolatrous Adam and Israel as Representatives in Paul's Letter to the Romans." *Southern Baptist Journal of Theology* 11, no. 3: 34-45.

Cannon, Katie G. 1988. *Black Womanist Ethics.* Atlanta: Scholars Press.

Carlson, Thomas A. 2008. *The Indiscrete Image.* Chicago: University of Chicago Press.

Carr, Anne E. 1993. "The New Vision of Feminist Theology." In *Freeing Theology: The Essentials of Theology in Feminist Perspective,* ed. Catherine Mowry LaCugna, 5-29. New York: HarperCollins.

Carroll, Charles. 1969. *"The Negro a Beast" or "In the Image of God."* Reprint. Miami: Mnemosyne.

Carson, Donald A. 1988. *Matthew, Mark, Luke.* Edited by Frank E. Gaebelein. Vol. 8. The Expositor's Bible Commentary. Grand Rapids: Zondervan.

————. 2010. *The God Who Is There: Finding Your Place in God's Story.* Grand Rapids: Baker.

Carson, Herbert M. 1960. *The Epistles of Paul to the Colossians and Philemon.* Tyndale New Testament Commentary. Grand Rapids: Eerdmans.

Carter, Charles W. 1983a. "Anthropology." In *A Contemporary Wesleyan Theology,* ed. Charles W. Carter, pp. 191-232. Grand Rapids: Zondervan.

————. 1983b. "Hamartiology." In *A Contemporary Wesleyan Theology,* ed. Charles W. Carter, pp. 233-82. Grand Rapids: Zondervan.

Case-Winters, Anna. 2004. "Rethinking the Image of God." *Zygon* 39: 813-26.

Cassuto, Umberto. 1989. *From Adam to Noah: A Commentary on the Book of Genesis I–VI (Pt. 1).* Translated by Israel Abrahams. Jerusalem: Magnes Press, Hebrew University.

Catholic Conference Administrative Board. 1987. "The Many Faces of AIDS: A Gospel Response." Washington, DC: U.S.C.C. http://old.usccb.org/sdwp/international/mfa87.shtml.

Chafer, Lewis S. 1947. *Systematic Theology*. Dallas: Dallas Seminary Press.

Channing, William E. 1836. *Slavery*. 4th ed. Boston: James Monroe.

———. 1841. "Spiritual Freedom." In *The Works of William E. Channing*, 4:67-103. Boston: James Monroe.

Charlesworth, J. H. 1990. "The *Beth Essentiae* and the Permissive Meaning of the Hiphil (Aphel)." In *Of Scribes and Scrolls*, ed. Harold W. Attridge, John J. Collins, and Thomas Tobin, pp. 67-78. Lanham, MD: University Press of America.

Childs, Brevard S. 1985. *Old Testament Theology in a Canonical Context*. Philadelphia: Fortress.

———. 1993. *Biblical Theology of the Old and New Testament*. Minneapolis: Fortress.

Childs, James M. 1982. "On Seeing Ourselves: Anthropology and Social Ethics." *Word & World* 2, no. 3: 225-33.

Chronopoulos, Isaiah. 1981. "Restoring God's Icon." *Epiphany* 2, no. 1: 5-6.

Chrysostom, John. 1862. "Homily VIII on Genesis 1." In *Patrologia Graeca 53*, ed. Jacques P. Migne, pp. 69-76. Paris: Imprimerie Catholique.

———. 1999. *Homilies on Genesis 1–17*. The Fathers of the Church 74. Washington, DC: Catholic University of America Press.

Ciampa, Roy E., and Brian S. Rosner. 2010. *The First Letter to the Corinthians*. Pillar New Testament Commentary. Grand Rapids: Eerdmans.

Clanton, Jann Aldredge. 1990. *In Whose Image? God and Gender*. New York: Crossroad.

Clark, Gordon H. 1969. "The Image of God in Man." *Journal of the Evangelical Theological Society* 12, no. 4: 215-22.

———. 1984. *The Biblical Doctrine of Man*. Trinity Paper 7. Jefferson, MD: Trinity Foundation.

Clarke, W. Norris. 1962. "Technology and Man: A Christian Vision." *Technology and Culture* 3, no. 4: 422-42.

Clement of Rome. 1885. *Recognitions*, in *Ante-Nicene Fathers*, vol. 8, ed. Philip Schaff. Grand Rapids: Christian Classics Ethereal Library. www.ccel.org/schaff/anf08 .pdf.

———. 1891. "Epistle to the Corinthians." In *The Apostolic Fathers*, ed. J. B. Lightfoot. London: Macmillan.

Clifford, Anne M. 1995. "When Being Human Becomes Truly Earthly: An Ecofeminist Proposal for Solidarity." In *In the Embrace of God: Feminist Approaches to Theological Anthropology*, ed. Ann O'Hara Graff, pp. 173-89. Maryknoll, NY: Orbis.

Clines, David J. A. 1968. "The Image of God in Man." *Tyndale Bulletin* 19: 53-103.

———. 1993. "Image of God." In *Dictionary of Paul and His Letters*, ed. Gerald F. Hawthorne and Ralph P. Martin, pp. 426-28. Downers Grove, IL: InterVarsity Press.

Cobb, John B. 1972. *Is It Too Late? A Theology of Ecology*. Beverly Hills, CA: Bruce.

Cobb, William D. 1977. "Romantic Revolt and Moral Autonomy." *Encounter* 38: 125-35.

Cohen, William B. 2003. *The French Encounter with Africans: White Response to Blacks, 1530-1880*. Bloomington: Indiana University Press.

References Cited

Collins, Raymond F. 1999. *First Corinthians.* Sacra Pagina 7. Collegeville, MN: Liturgical Press.

Collste, Göran. 2002. *Is Human Life Special?* Bern: Peter Lang.

Colson, Charles W., and Nigel M. de S. Cameron, eds. 2004. *Human Dignity in the Biotech Century.* Downers Grove, IL: InterVarsity Press.

Comte-Sponville, André. 2006. *The Little Book of Atheist Spirituality.* Translated by Nancy Houston. New York: Viking.

Cone, James H. 1979. "The White Church and Black Power." In *Black Theology: A Documentary History,* ed. James H. Cone and Gayraud Wilmore, Vol. 1, 1966-1979, pp. 112-32. Maryknoll, NY: Orbis.

———. 1986. *A Black Theology of Liberation.* 2nd ed. Maryknoll, NY: Orbis.

———. 1997. *Black Theology and Black Power.* Maryknoll, NY: Orbis.

Conn, Joann Wolski. 1993. "Toward Spiritual Maturity." In *Freeing Theology: The Essentials of Theology in Feminist Perspective,* ed. Catherine Mowry LaCugna, pp. 235-59. New York: HarperCollins.

Conzelmann, Hans. 1975. *1 Corinthians.* Translated by James W. Leitch. Hermeneia. Philadelphia: Fortress.

Cook, James I., ed. 1975. *Grace Upon Grace.* Grand Rapids: Eerdmans.

Cooper, John W. 1998. *Our Father in Heaven: Christian Faith and Inclusive Language for God.* Grand Rapids: Baker Books.

Copeland, M. Shawn. 2010. *Enfleshing Freedom: Body, Race, and Being.* Minneapolis: Fortress.

Cortez, Marc. 2010. *Theological Anthropology.* London: T. & T. Clark.

Cracroft, Richard H. 1967. "The American West of Karl May." *American Quarterly* 19: 249-58.

Cranfield, C. E. B. 1977. *The Gospel According to Mark.* Cambridge: Cambridge University Press.

———. 1985. *A Critical and Exegetical Commentary on the Epistle to the Romans.* International Critical Commentary. Edinburgh: T. & T. Clark.

Crawford, Robert G. 1966. "Image of God." *Expository Times* 77, no. 8: 233-36.

Crosby, John F. 2006. "The Witness of Dietrich von Hildebrand." *First Things* 169 (December): 7-9.

Crouch, Carly L. 2010. "Genesis 1:26-27 as a Statement of Humanity's Divine Parentage." *Journal of Theological Studies* NS 61: 1-15.

Curtis, Edward M. 1984. *Man as the Image of God in Genesis in the Light of Ancient Near Eastern Parallels.* Ann Arbor, MI: University Microfilms.

———. 1992. "Image of God (OT)." In *The Anchor Bible Dictionary,* 3:389-91. New York: Doubleday.

Cyril of Alexandria. 2000. "Commentary on John." In *Cyril of Alexandria,* trans. Norman Russell, pp. 96-129. Oxford: Routledge.

Dabney, Robert L. 1878. *Systematic Theology.* 2nd ed. St. Louis: Presbyterian Publishing Co.

Dabrock, Peter. 2010. "Drawing Distinctions Responsibly and Concretely: A European Protestant Perspective on Foundational Theological Bioethics." *Christian Bioethics* 16 (April): 128-57.

Daly, Mary. 1975. *The Church and the Second Sex.* New York: Harper & Row.

Davids, Peter H. 1989. *James.* New International Biblical Commentary. Peabody, MA: Hendrickson.

Davies, W. D., and Dale C. Allison. 2004. *Matthew: A Shorter Commentary.* Edited by Dale C. Allison Jr. London: T. & T. Clark International.

Davies-John, Elisabeth. 2003. "Disabled and Made in the Image of God." In *Growing into God,* ed. Jean Mayland, pp. 121-24. London: Churches Together in Britain and Ireland.

Davis, David B. 2001. *In the Image of God.* New Haven: Yale University Press.

———. 2008. *Inhuman Bondage: The Rise and Fall of Slavery in the New World.* New York: Oxford University Press.

Davis, Ellen F. 2009. *Scripture, Culture, and Agriculture.* Cambridge: Cambridge University Press.

Deane-Drummond, Celia. 2012. "God's Image and Likeness in Humans and Other Animals: Performative Soul-Making and Graced Nature." *Zygon* 47 (December): 434-48.

DeBoer, Willis P. 1976. "Calvin on the Role of Women." In *Exploring the Heritage of John Calvin,* ed. David Holwerda, pp. 236-72. Grand Rapids: Baker.

De Cruz, Helen, and Yves De Maeseneer. 2014. *"Imago Dei:* Evolutionary and Theological Perspectives." *Zygon* 49 (March): 95-100.

DeFranza, Megan K. 2011. "Sexuality and the Image of God: Dangers in Evangelical and Roman Catholic Theologies of the Body." *Africanus Journal* 3, no. 1: 16-25.

Dehsen, Christian D. von. 1997. "The Imago Dei in Genesis 1:26-27." *Lutheran Quarterly* 11: 259-70.

Dempster, Stephen G. 2003. *Dominion and Dynasty.* New Studies in Biblical Theology. Downers Grove, IL: IVP Academic.

Den Boer, Willem. 1979. *Private Morality in Greece and Rome.* Leiden: Brill.

Descartes, Rene. 1968. *Discourse on Method and the Meditations.* Translated by F. E. Sutcliffe. New York: Penguin.

De Smedt, Johan, and Helen De Cruz. 2014. "The *Imago Dei* as a Work in Progress: A Perspective from Paleoanthropology." *Zygon* 49 (March): 135-56.

de Waal, Frans. 1997. *Good Natured: The Origin of Right and Wrong in Humans and Other Animals.* Cambridge, MA: Harvard University Press.

DeWolf, L. Harold. 1953. *A Theology of the Living Church.* New York: Harper & Row.

Di Vito, Robert. 2010. " 'In God's Image' and 'Male and Female': How a Little Punctuation Might Have Helped." In *God, Science, Sex, Gender,* ed. Patricia Beattie Jung and Aana Marie Vigen, pp. 167-83. Urbana: University of Illinois Press.

Diodore. 1860. "Fragmenta in Genesin." In *Patrologia Graeca 33,* ed. Jacques P. Migne, pp. 1562-80. Paris: Imprimerie Catholique.

Dixon, Lorvaine. 2003. "Made in the Image of God: A Womanist Perspective." In *Growing into God*, ed. Jean Mayland, pp. 113-20. London: Churches Together in Britain and Ireland.

Dodds, E. R. 1968. *Pagan and Christian in an Age of Anxiety*. Cambridge: Cambridge University Press.

Dohmen, Christoph. 1983. "Die Statue von Tell Fecherije und die Gottebenbildlichkeit des Menschen." *Biblische Notizen* 22: 91-106.

Donne, John. 1609-1610. "Holy Sonnet 15 (in the Westmoreland Sequence)." www .sonnets.org/donne.htm.

————. 1896a. "Good-Friday, 1613, Riding Westward." In *Poems of John Donne*, ed. Edmund K. Chambers, 1: 172-73. London: Lawrence & Bullen.

————. 1896b. "To the Countess of Huntingdon." In *The Poems of John Donne*, ed. Edmund K. Chambers. Vol. 2. London: Lawrence & Bullen. http://www.bartleby .com/357/133.html.

Dooyeweerd, Herman. 1960. *In the Twilight of Western Thought*. Philadelphia: Presbyterian and Reformed Publishing Co.

Douglas, Kelly Brown. 1995. "To Reflect the Image of God: A Womanist Perspective on Right Relationship." In *Living the Intersection: Womanism and Afrocentrism in Theology*, ed. Cheryl J. Sanders, pp. 67-77. Minneapolis: Fortress.

Douglass, Frederick. 1992a. "Speech on the Dred Scott Decision." In *African-American Social and Political Thought 1850-1920*, ed. Howard Brotz, pp. 247-62. New Brunswick, NJ: Transaction.

————. 1992b. "The Nature of Slavery." In *African-American Social and Political Thought 1850-1920*, ed. Howard Brotz, pp. 215-20. New Brunswick, NJ: Transaction.

————. 1994. "Narrative of the Life of Frederick Douglass, an American Slave." In *Autobiographies: Frederick Douglass*, pp. 1-102. New York: Library of America.

Dover, Kenneth J. 1974. *Greek Popular Morality in the Time of Plato and Aristotle*. Oxford: Basil Blackwell.

Downey, Glanville. 1965. "Who Is My Neighbor? The Greek and Roman Answer." *Anglican Theological Review* 47: 3-15.

Drever, Matthew. 2013. "Redeeming Creation: Creatio *ex nihilo* and the *Imago Dei* in Augustine." *International Journal of Systematic Theology* 15, no. 2: 135-53.

Driscoll, Mark, and Gerry Breshears. 2010. *Doctrine: What Christians Should Believe*. Wheaton, IL: Crossway.

Dumbrell, William J. 2002. *The Faith of Israel: A Theological Survey of the Old Testament*. 2nd ed. Grand Rapids: Baker Academic.

Duncan, J. Ligon, III. 2008. "Biblical Manhood and Womanhood: The Big Picture — Genesis 1:26-27" (March 12). http://www.downloadpreken.com/artikelen/ A348.pdf.

Dunn, James D. G. 1973. "I Corinthians 15:45 — Life-Giving Spirit." In *Christ and Spirit in the New Testament*, ed. Barnabas Lindars, Stephen S. Smalley, and C. F. D. Moule. Cambridge: Cambridge University Press.

————. 1988. *Romans*. Word Biblical Commentary 38A. Dallas: Word Books.

————. 1996. *The Epistles to the Colossians and to Philemon*. New International Greek Testament Commentary. Grand Rapids: Eerdmans.

Dyck, Arthur J. 1990. "The Image of God: An Ethical Foundation for Medicine." *Linacre Quarterly* 57 (February): 35-45.

Dyrness, William A. 1983. *Let the Earth Rejoice*. Westchester, IL: Crossway.

Eagleson, John, and Philip Scharper, eds. 1979. *Puebla and Beyond*. Translated by John Drury. Maryknoll, NY: Orbis.

Eastman, Henry P. 1905. *The Negro, His Origin, History and Destiny: Containing a Reply to "The Negro a Beast."* Boston: Eastern.

Ecumenical Disability Advocates Network. 2004. "A Church of All and for All: An Interim Statement." *International Review of Mission* 93 (370/371) (October): 505-25.

Edwards, James. 1991. *Romans*. New International Biblical Commentary. Peabody, MA: Hendrickson.

Edwards, Jonathan. 1982. *Freedom of the Will*. Edited by Arnold S. Kaufman and William K. Frankena. New York: Irvington.

Eibach, Ulrich. 1976. *Medizin und Menschenwurde*. Wuppertal: Theologischer Verlag R. Brockhaus.

————. 2008. "Protection of Life and Human Dignity: The German Debate between Christian Norms and Secular Expectations." *Christian Bioethics* 14, no. 1: 58-77.

Eichrodt, Walther. 1967. *Theology of the Old Testament*. Translated by J. A. Baker. Vol. 2. Old Testament Library. Philadelphia: Westminster.

Eiesland, Nancy L. 1994. *The Disabled God*. Nashville: Abingdon.

Eilberg-Schwartz, Howard. 1996. "The Problem of the Body for the People of the Book." In *Reading Bibles, Writing Bodies: Identity and the Book,* ed. Timothy Beal and David Gunn, pp. 34-55. London: Routledge.

Eley, Ann Salliss. 1963. *God's Own Image*. Luton, UK: White Crescent.

Ellacuría, Ignacio. 1993. "The Crucified People." In *Mysterium Liberationis: Fundamental Concepts of Liberation Theology,* ed. Ignacio Ellacuría and Jon Sobrino, pp. 580-603. Maryknoll, NY: Orbis.

Ellingworth, Paul. 1993. *The Epistle to the Hebrews*. New International Greek Testament Commentary. Grand Rapids: Eerdmans.

Elliot, John H. 1993. "The Rediscovery of America." *New York Review of Books* 40: 36-41.

Ellis, Carl F., Jr. 1996. *Free at Last? The Gospel in the African-American Experience*. Downers Grove, IL: InterVarsity Press.

Eltester, Friedrich-Wilhelm. 1958. *Eikon im Neuen Testament*. Berlin: Verlag Alfred Töpelmann.

Emerson, Michael O., and Christian Smith. 2000. *Divided by Faith: Evangelical Religion and the Problem of Race in America*. New York: Oxford University Press.

Erickson, Millard J. 2013. *Christian Theology*. 3rd ed. Grand Rapids: Baker.

Evans, Craig A. 1990. *Luke.* New International Biblical Commentary. Peabody, MA: Hendrickson.

Farley, Margaret A. 1975. "New Patterns of Relationship: Beginnings of a Moral Revolution." *Theological Studies* 36: 627-46.

———. 1976. "Sources of Sexual Inequality in the History of Christian Thought." *Journal of Religion* 56, no. 2: 162-76.

Fatum, Lone. 1995. "Image of God and Glory of Man: Women in the Pauline Congregations." In *The Image of God: Gender Models in Judaeo-Christian Tradition,* ed. Kari Elisabeth Børresen, pp. 50-133. Minneapolis: Fortress.

Faus, José I. G. 1993. "Anthropology: The Person and the Community." In *Mysterium Liberationis: Fundamental Concepts of Liberation Theology,* ed. Ignacio Ellacuría and Jon Sobrino, pp. 497-521. Maryknoll, NY: Orbis.

Fedler, Kyle D. 2006. *Exploring Christian Ethics.* Louisville: Westminster John Knox.

Fee, Gordon D. 1987. *The First Epistle to the Corinthians.* New International Commentary on the New Testament. Grand Rapids: Eerdmans.

———. 2007. *Pauline Christology.* Peabody, MA: Hendrickson.

Feinberg, Charles L. 1972. "Image of God." *Bibliotheca Sacra* 129: 235-46.

Fernandez, Eleazar S. 2004. *Reimagining the Human: Theological Anthropology in Response to Systemic Evil.* St. Louis: Chalice.

Ferngren, Gary B. 1987. "The Imago Dei and the Sanctity of Life: The Origins of an Idea." In *Euthanasia and the Newborn,* ed. R. C. McMillan, 23-45. Dordrecht: D. Reidel.

———. 2009. *Medicine & Health Care in Early Christianity.* Baltimore: Johns Hopkins University Press.

Feuillet, A. 1975. "La dignite et la rôle de la femme d'après quelques textes pauliniens Comparison avec L'Ancien Testament." *New Testament Studies* 21 (January): 157-91.

Fichtner, Joseph. 1978. *Man in the Image of God.* New York: Alba House.

Fields, Bruce L. 2001. *Introducing Black Theology.* Grand Rapids: Baker Academic.

Finlan, Stephen. 2008. "Can We Speak of Theosis in Paul?" In *Partakers of the Divine Nature: The History and Development of Deification in the Christian Traditions,* ed. Michael Christensen and Jeffrey Wittung, pp. 68-80. Grand Rapids: Eerdmans.

Fisher, Christopher L. 2005. "Animals, Humans and X-Men: Human Uniqueness and the Meaning of Personhood." *Theology and Science* 3: 291-314.

———. 2010. *Human Significance in Theology and the Natural Sciences.* Eugene, OR: Pickwick.

Fitzmyer, Joseph A. 1981. *The Gospel According to Luke (x–xxiv).* Anchor Bible Commentary 28A. New York: Doubleday.

———. 1993. *Romans.* Anchor Bible Commentary. New York: Doubleday.

Fleischer, Manfred P. 1981. "Are Women Human? The Debate of 1595 Between Valens Acidalius and Simon Gediccus." *Sixteenth Century Journal* 12: 107-20.

Flender, Otto. 1976. "*Eikon*." In *New International Dictionary of New Testament Theology*, 2: 286-88. Grand Rapids: Zondervan.

Fletcher, Joseph. 1954. *Morals and Medicine*. Princeton: Princeton University Press.

Foltz, Bruce V. 2001. "Hidden Patency: On the Iconic Character of Human Life." *Christian Bioethics* 7, no. 3: 317-31.

Forell, George W. 1975. *The Protestant Faith*. Philadelphia: Fortress.

Frame, John M. 2006. "Men and Women in the Image of God." In *Recovering Biblical Manhood and Womanhood*, ed. John Piper and Wayne Grudem, pp. 228-36. Wheaton, IL: Crossway.

France, R. T. 2002. *The Gospel of Mark*. New International Greek Testament Commentary. Grand Rapids: Eerdmans.

Frankfort, Henri. 1954. *The Art and Architecture of the Ancient Orient*. Harmondsworth, UK: Penguin.

Fulkerson, Mary McClintock. 1997. "Contexting the Gendered Subject: A Feminist Account of the Imago Dei." In *Horizons in Feminist Theology: Identity, Tradition, and Norms*, ed. Rebecca S. Chopp and Sheila Greene Davaney. Minneapolis: Fortress.

Furnish, Victor P. 1984. *II Corinthians*. Vol. 32A. Anchor Bible Commentary. Garden City, NY: Doubleday.

Gaffin, Richard B., Jr. 2010. "The Glory of God in Paul's Epistles." In *The Glory of God*, ed. Christopher W. Morgan and Robert A. Peterson, pp. 127-52. Wheaton, IL: Crossway.

García-Rivera, Alex. 1995. *St. Martin de Porres*. Maryknoll, NY: Orbis.

Gardoski, Kenneth M. 2007. "The Imago Dei Revisted." *Journal of Ministry and Theology* 11, no. 2: 5-37.

Garland, David E. 1998. *Colossians and Philemon*. NIV Application Commentary. Grand Rapids: Zondervan.

———. 1999. *2 Corinthians*. New American Commentary 29. Nashville: Broadman & Holman.

———. 2003. *1 Corinthians*. Baker Exegetical Commentary on the New Testament. Grand Rapids: Baker.

Garland, Robert. 1995. *The Eye of the Beholder*. Ithaca, NY: Cornell University Press.

Garner, Stephen R. 2007. "Transhumanism and the *Imago Dei*." PhD Dissertation, New Zealand: University of Auckland.

Garnet, Henry H. 1999. "Henry Highland Garnet Urges Slaves to Resist." In *African-American Social and Political Thought 1850-1920*, ed. Howard Brotz, pp. 295-98. New Brunswick, NJ: Transaction.

Garr, W. Randall. 2000. " 'Image' and 'Likeness' in the Inscription from Tell Fakhariyeh." *Israel Exploration Journal* 50, nos. 3-4: 227-34.

———. 2003. *In His Own Image and Likeness: Humanity, Divinity, and Monotheism*. Leiden: Brill.

Gayman, Dan. 1994. *The Two Seeds of Genesis 3:15*. Revised. Schell City, MO: Church of Israel.

References Cited

Geldenhuys, Norval. 1951. *Commentary on the Gospel of Luke.* New International Commentary on the New Testament. Grand Rapids: Eerdmans.

Gelernter, David. 2008. "The Irreducibly Religious Character of Human Dignity." In *Human Dignity and Bioethics,* ed. the President's Council on Bioethics, pp. 387-405. Washington, DC: U.S. Government.

Genovese, Eugene D. 2000. "The Legal Basis for Mastery." In *Major Problems in African American History,* ed. Thomas Holt and Elsa Brown, 1:224-33. New York: Houghton Mifflin.

Gerhard, Johann. 1962. "The Image of God." In *The Doctrine of Man in Classical Lutheran Theology,* ed. Herman Preus and Edmund Smits, trans. Mario Colacci, pp. 25-66. Minneapolis: Augsburg Fortress.

Gess, Johannes. 1976. *"Charakter."* In *New International Dictionary of New Testament Theology,* ed. Colin Brown, 2:288-89. Grand Rapids: Zondervan.

Gibbs, Jeffrey. 1984. "The Grace of God as the Foundation for Ethics." *Concordia Theological Quarterly* 48: 185-201.

Giblin, Charles H. 1971. " 'The Things of God' in the Question Concerning Tribute to Caesar (Lk 20:25; Mk 12:17; Mt 22:21)." *Catholic Biblical Quarterly* 33 (October): 510-27.

Gibson, John C. L. 1981. *Genesis.* Edinburgh: Saint Andrew.

Gilkey, Langdon. 1993. *Nature, Reality, and the Sacred: The Nexus of Science and Religion.* Minneapolis: Fortress.

———. 1994. "Nature as the Image of God: Signs of the Sacred." *Theology Today* 51, no. 1: 127-41.

Gill, John. 1978. *A Complete Body of Doctrinal and Practical Divinity; Or, a System of Evangelical Truths, Deduced from the Sacred Scriptures.* Grand Rapids: Baker.

Gillman, Florence Morgan. 1987. "Another Look at Romans 8:3: 'In the Likeness of Sinful Flesh.' " *Catholic Biblical Quarterly* 49, no. 4: 597-604.

Glaude, Eddie S., Jr. 2000. *Exodus: Religion, Race, and the Nation in Early Nineteenth-Century Black America.* Chicago: University of Chicago Press.

Godet, F. 1957. *Commentary on the First Epistle of St. Paul to the Corinthians.* Vol. II. Classic Commentary Library. Grand Rapids: Zondervan.

Goldfeld, Naomi Vogelmann. 2011. "The Divine Image in All Humankind." *Dialogue & Alliance* 25, no. 1: 51-55.

Goldingay, John. 2003. "Image, Likeness (of God)." In *The Westminster Theological Wordbook of the Bible,* ed. Donald E. Gowen, pp. 222-23. Louisville: Westminster John Knox.

Golitzin, Alexander. 2003. "The Image and Glory of God in Jacob of Serug's Homily, 'On That Chariot That Ezekiel the Prophet Saw.' " *St. Vladimir's Theological Quarterly* 47, no. 3-4: 323-64.

Gonzalez, Michelle A. 2007. *Created in God's Image: An Introduction to Feminist Theological Anthropology.* Maryknoll, NY: Orbis.

Goodman, D. C. 2008. *The Identities of God and Man.* Denton, TX: Jakes Books.

Gorman, Michael. 2009. *Inhabiting the Cruciform God.* Grand Rapids: Eerdmans.

Gossett, Thomas F. 1997. *Race: The History of an Idea of America.* New York: Oxford University Press.

Gould, Stephen J. 1993. "American Polygeny and Craniometry before Darwin." In *The "Racial" Economy of Science: Toward a Democratic Future,* ed. Sandra Harding, pp. 84-115. Bloomington: Indiana University Press.

Graff, Ann O'Hara. 1995. "Strategies of Life: Learning from Feminist Psychology." In *In the Embrace of God: Feminist Approaches to Theological Anthropology,* ed. Ann O'Hara Graff, pp. 122-37. Eugene, OR: Wipf & Stock.

Graham, Elaine L. 2006. "The 'End' of the Human or the End of the 'Human'? Human Dignity in Theological Perspective." In *God and Human Dignity,* ed. Kendall Soulen and Linda Woodhead, pp. 263-81. Grand Rapids: Eerdmans.

Grant, Jacqueline. 1989. *White Women's Christ and Black Women's Jesus.* Atlanta: Scholars Press.

Green, Joel B. 1997. *The Gospel of Luke.* New International Commentary on the New Testament. Grand Rapids: Eerdmans.

―――. 1999. "Scripture and the Human Person: Further Reflections." *Science and Christian Belief* 11, no. 1: 51-63.

―――. 2011. "Humanity — Created, Restored, Transformed, Embodied." In *Rethinking Human Nature,* ed. Malcolm Jeeves, 271-94. Grand Rapids: Eerdmans.

Greenfield, Jonas C., and Aaron Shaffer. 1983. "Notes on the Akkadian-Aramaic Bilingual Statue from Tell Fekkerye." *Iraq* 45, no. 1: 109-16.

Gregory of Nyssa. 1954. *The Beatitudes.* Translated by Hilda C. Graef. New York: Newman.

―――. 1972. "On the Making of Man." In *Dogmatic Treatises,* ed. Philip Schaff, pp. 527-86. Grand Rapids: Eerdmans.

―――. 1987. *Commentary on the Song of Songs.* Translated by McCambley Casimir. Brookline, MA: Hellenic College Press.

―――. 1993. "Homily 4 on Ecclesiastes." In *Gregory of Nyssa, Homilies on Ecclesiastes,* ed. Stuart Hall, pp. 72-84. Berlin: Walter de Gruyter.

―――. 1995. "On Virginity." In *Gregory of Nyssa: Dogmatic Treatise,* ed. Philip Schaff and Henry Wall, trans. William Moore and Henry A. Wilson. Vol. 5. Nicene and Post-Nicene Fathers. Peabody, MA: Hendrickson.

Greidanus, Sidney. 1984. "Human Rights in Biblical Perspective." *Calvin Theological Journal* 19: 5-31.

Grenz, Stanley J. 1994. *Theology for the Community of God.* Nashville: Broadman & Holman.

―――. 1998. "Theological Foundations for Male-Female Relationships." *Journal of the Evangelical Theological Society* 41 (December): 615-30.

―――. 2001. *The Social God and the Relational Self.* Louisville: Westminster John Knox.

―――. 2002. "The Social God and the Relational Self: Toward a Theology of the

Imago Dei in the Postmodern Context." *Horizons in Biblical Theology* 24, no. 1: 33-57.

―――. 2004. "Jesus as the *Imago Dei:* Image-of-God Christology and the Non-Linear Linearity of Theology." *Journal of the Evangelical Theological Society* 47, no. 4: 617-28.

Grey, Mary. 2003. "Created in the Image — The Suffering, Broken Body of Christ, the Church." In *Growing into God,* ed. Jean Mayland, pp. 223-34. London: Churches Together in Britain and Ireland.

Gropp, Douglas M., and Theodore J. Lewis. 1985. "Notes on Some Problems in the Aramaic Text of the Hadd-Yith'i Bilingual." *Bulletin of the American Schools of Oriental Research* 259: 45-61.

Gross, Walter. 1981. "Die Gottebenbildlichkeit des Menschen in Kontext der Priester-scrift." *Theologische Quartalschrift* 161: 244-64.

Grudem, Wayne A. 1994. *Systematic Theology: An Introduction to Biblical Doctrine.* Grand Rapids: Zondervan.

Gundry, Robert H. 1993. *Mark: A Commentary on His Apology for the Cross.* Grand Rapids: Eerdmans.

Gunkel, Hermann. 1964. *Genesis.* Göttingen: Vandenhoeck & Ruprecht.

Gunton, Colin E. 1999. "Trinity, Ontology, and Anthropology: Towards a Renewal of the Doctrine of the Imago Dei." In *Persons, Divine and Human,* ed. Colin E. Gunton and Christoph Schwöbel, pp. 47-61. Edinburgh: T. & T. Clark.

―――. 2002. *The Christian Faith: An Introduction to Christian Doctrine.* Malden, MA: Blackwell Publishers.

―――. 2003. *The Promise of Trinitarian Theology.* Edinburgh: T. & T. Clark.

Guroian, Vigen. 2006. *The Fragrance of God.* Grand Rapids: Eerdmans.

Gushee, David P. 2012. *The Sacredness of Human Life.* Grand Rapids: Eerdmans.

Guthrie, George H. 1998. *Hebrews.* NIV Application Commentary. Grand Rapids: Zondervan.

Gutiérrez, Gustavo M. 1988. *A Theology of Liberation.* Revised. Maryknoll, NY: Orbis.

―――. 1993. *Las Casas: In Search of the Poor of Jesus Christ.* Maryknoll, NY: Orbis.

Habermas, Ronald T. 2008. *Introduction to Christian Education and Formation.* Grand Rapids: Zondervan.

Habib, Gabriel. 1998. "The Universality of Human Rights." *Christian Social Action* (December): 36-37.

Hadley, Judith M. 1997. *"Atsab."* In *New International Dictionary of Old Testament Theology and Exegesis,* ed. Willem A. VanGemeren, 3: 483-84. Grand Rapids: Zondervan.

Haering, Theodore. 1915. *The Christian Faith: A System of Dogmatics.* Translated by John Dickie and George Ferries. London: Hodder & Stoughton.

Hafemann, Scott J. 1996. *Paul, Moses, and the History of Israel.* Peabody, MA: Henrickson.

―――. 2000. *2 Corinthians.* NIV Application Commentary. Grand Rapids: Zondervan.

Hagner, Donald A. 1990. *Hebrews*. New International Biblical Commentary. Peabody, MA: Hendrickson.

Hailer, Martin, and Dietrich Ritschl. 1996. "The General Notion of Human Dignity and the Specific Arguments in Medical Ethics." In *Sanctity of Life and Human Dignity*, ed. Kurt Bayertz, pp. 91-106. Dordrecht: Kluwer.

Hall, Douglas J. 1986. *Imaging God: Dominion as Stewardship*. Library of Christian Stewardship. Grand Rapids: Eerdmans.

Hall, Sewell. 1995. "They Shall See His Face." In *In His Image: The Implication of Creation*, ed. Ferrell Jenkins, pp. 39-51. Temple Terrace: Florida College.

Hamilton, Victor P. 1990. *The Book of Genesis: Chapters 1–17*. New International Commentary on the Old Testament. Grand Rapids: Eerdmans.

Hands, Arthur R. 1968. *Charities and Social Aid in Greece and Rome*. Ithaca, NY: Cornell University Press.

Häring, Hermann. 2001. "From Divine Human to Human God." In *The Human Image of God*, ed. Hans-Georg Ziebertz, Friedrich Schweitzer, Hermann Häring, and Don Browning, pp. 3-28. Leiden: Brill.

Harland, P. J. 1996. *The Value of Human Life*. Leiden: E. J. Brill.

Harrell, Joan R. 2008. "A Womanist Perspective: *Imago Dei* in Black and White." *Liturgy* 23, no. 3: 15-24.

Harrelson, Walter. 1980. *The Ten Commandments and Human Rights*. Philadelphia: Fortress.

Harrington, Daniel J. 1991. *The Gospel of Matthew*. Sacra Pagina 1. Collegeville, MN: Liturgical Press.

Harris, Harriet A. 1998. "Should We Say That Personhood Is Relational?" *Scottish Journal of Theology* 51, no. 2: 214-34.

Harris, Murray J. 2005. *The Second Epistle to the Corinthians: A Commentary on the Greek Text*. New International Greek Testament Commentary. Grand Rapids: Eerdmans.

———. 2010. *Colossians and Philemon*. Exegetical Guide to the Greek New Testament. Nashville: B & H Academic.

———. 2012. *Prepositions and Theology in the Greek New Testament*. Grand Rapids: Zondervan.

Harris, R. Laird. 1980. "*Tselem*." In *Theological Wordbook of the Old Testament*, 2:767-68. Chicago: Moody.

Harrison, Nonna Verna. 2010. *God's Many-Splendered Image*. Grand Rapids: Baker.

Hart, David B. 2002. "The Mirror of the Intimate: Gregory of Nyssa on the Vestiga Trinitatis." *Modern Theology* 18, no. 4: 541-61.

———. 2009. *Atheist Delusions: The Christian Revolution and Its Fashionable Enemies*. New Haven: Yale University Press.

Hart, Ian. 1995. "Genesis 1:1–2:3 as a Prologue to the Book of Genesis." *Tyndale Bulletin* 46, no. 2: 315-36.

Hartin, Patrick J. 2003. *James*. Sacra Pagina 14. Collegeville, MN: Liturgical Press.

References Cited

Hays, Richard B. 1997. *First Corinthians*. Interpretation. Louisville: John Knox.

Hefele, Karl J. 1877. *Concilengeschichte*. Vol. 3. Freiburg: Herder.

Hefner, Philip J. 1984. "The Creation." In *Christian Dogmatics*, ed. Carl E. Braaten and Robert W. Jenson, pp. 265-359. Philadelphia: Fortress.

———. 1993. *The Human Factor: Evolution, Culture, and Religion*. Minneapolis: Fortress.

———. 2000. "Imago Dei: The Possibility and Necessity of the Human Person." In *The Human Person in Science and Theology*, ed. Niels H. Gregersen, Willem Drees, and Ulf Gorman, 73-94. Edinburgh: T. & T. Clark.

Hegel, G. W. F. 1988. *Lectures on the Philosophy of Religion*. Edited by Peter Hodgson. Berkeley: University of California Press.

Henriksen, Jan-Olav. 2011. "The Erotic Self and the Image of God." In *In Search of Self: Interdisciplinary Perspectives on Personhood*, ed. J. Wentzel van Huyssteen and Eric P. Wiebe, pp. 256-72. Grand Rapids: Eerdmans.

Henry, Carl F. H. 1973. "Man." In *Baker's Dictionary of Theology*, ed. Everett Harrison, p. 339. Grand Rapids: Baker.

———. 1984. "Image of God." In *Evangelical Dictionary of Theology*, ed. Walter Elwell, pp. 545-48. Grand Rapids: Baker.

Hentschel, Justin. 2008. "The Movement of the Image of God from a Structural to Relational Model as a Shift from Bounded Set to Centered Set." ThM Thesis, Dallas: Dallas Theological Seminary.

Herder, Johann G. 1800. *Outlines of a Philosophy of the History of Man*. Translated by T. Churchill. New York: Bergman.

Herring, Stephen L. 2008. "A 'Transubstantiated' Humanity: The Relationship Between the Divine Image and the Presence of God in Genesis i 26f." *Vetus Testamentum* 58: 480-94.

Hicks, Douglas A. 2000. *Inequality and Christian Ethics*. Cambridge: Cambridge University Press.

Highfield, Ron. 2010. "Beyond the 'Image of God' Conundrum: A Relational View of Human Dignity." *Christian Studies* 24 (January): 21-32.

Hildebrand, Dietrich von. 1934. "Der Kampf um die Person." *Der Christliche Ständestaat* 6 (January 14): 3-6.

Hilkert, Mary Catherine. 1995. "Cry Beloved Image: Rethinking the Image of God." In *In the Embrace of God: Feminist Approaches to Theological Anthropology*, ed. Ann O'Hara Graff, pp. 190-205. Eugene, OR: Wipf & Stock.

———. 2002. "Imago Dei: Does the Symbol Have a Future." *The Santa Clara Lectures* 8, no. 3.

Hilton, Walter. 1908. *The Scale (or Ladder) of Perfection*. Westminster, UK: Art and Book Company.

Hitler, Adolf. 1939. *Mein Kampf*. New York: Reynal & Hitchcock.

Hittinger, F. Russell. 2013. "Toward an Adequate Anthropology: Social Aspects of *Imago Dei* in Catholic Theology." In *Imago Dei: Human Dignity in Ecumenical*

Perspective, ed. Thomas Albert Howard, pp. 39-78. Washington, DC: Catholic University of America Press.

Hodge, Charles. 1950. *Commentary on the Epistle to the Romans.* Grand Rapids: Eerdmans.

─────. 1976. *Commentary on the First Epistle to the Corinthians.* Grand Rapids: Eerdmans.

─────. 1982. *Systematic Theology.* Grand Rapids: Eerdmans.

Hodge, D. R. and T. A. Wolfer. 2008. "Promoting Tolerance: The Imago Dei as an Imperative for Christian Social Workers." *Journal of Religion & Spirituality in Social Work: Social Thought* 27, no. 3: 297-313.

Hoehner, Harold W. 2002. *Ephesians: An Exegetical Commentary.* Grand Rapids: Baker Academic.

Hoekema, Anthony A. 1994. *Created in God's Image.* Grand Rapids: Eerdmans.

Hoeksema, Herman. 1966. *Reformed Dogmatics.* Grand Rapids: Reformed Free Publishing Association.

Hollinger, Dennis P. 2009. *The Meaning of Sex.* Grand Rapids: Baker.

Holman, Susan R. 2001. *The Hungry Are Dying.* Oxford: Oxford University Press.

Holmes, Oliver W. 1901. "Oration, 1855." In *The New England Society Orations,* ed. Cephas Brainerd and Eveline Warner Brainerd, 2:271-302. New York: The Century Co.

Holmes, Stephen R. 2005. "Image of God." In *Dictionary for Theological Interpretation of the Bible,* ed. Kevin Vanhoozer. Grand Rapids: Baker Academic.

Hooker, Morna Dorothy. 1960. "Adam in Romans 1." *New Testament Studies* 6, no. 4: 297-306.

─────. 1990. *From Adam to Christ: Essays on Paul.* Cambridge: Cambridge University Press.

─────. 1991. *The Gospel According to Saint Mark.* London: Hendrickson.

Hopkins, Dwight N. 2005. *Being Human: Race, Culture, and Religion.* Minneapolis: Fortress.

Hornung, Erik. 1967. "Der Mensch als 'Bild Gottes' in Ägypten." In *Die Gottebenbildlichkeit des Menchen,* ed. Oswald Loretz, pp. 123-56. Munich: Kosel.

Horowitz, Maryanne Cline. 1979. "The Image of God in Man — Is Woman Included?" *Harvard Theological Review* 72 (October): 175-206.

Horst, Friedrich. 1950. "Face to Face: The Biblical Doctine of the Image of God." trans. John Bright. *Interpretation: A Journal of Bible & Theology* 4: 259-70.

Horton, Michael S. 2005. *Lord and Servant: A Covenant Christology.* Louisville: Westminster John Knox.

─────. 2006. "Image and Office: Human Personhood and the Covenant." In *Personal Identity in Theological Perspective,* ed. Richard Lints, Michael S. Horton, and Mark R. Talbot, pp. 178-203. Grand Rapids: Eerdmans.

─────. 2007. *Covenant and Salvation: Union with Christ.* Louisville: Westminster John Knox.

References Cited

Hosmer, William. 1853. *Slavery and the Church*. Auburn, NY: W. J. Moses.

Howe, Leroy T. 1995. *The Image of God: A Theology of Pastoral Care and Counseling*. Nashville: Abingdon.

Howington, Arthur F. 1975. "Not in the Condition of a Horse or an Ox." *Tennessee Historical Quarterly* 34: 249-63.

Huber, Jane Parker. 1978. *God, You Spin the Whirling Planets*. Hymn. http://people .bethel.edu/~kisrob/papers/noosphere/page40.htm.

Huebscher, Joe. 1988. "Created in the Image of God." *ETS — 0414*. Portland, OR: Theological Research Exchange Network.

Hughes, Philip E. 1962. *Paul's Second Epistle to the Corinthians: The English Text with Introduction, Exposition and Notes*. New International Commentary on the New Testament. Grand Rapids: Eerdmans.

————. 1977. *A Commentary on the Epistle to the Hebrews*. Grand Rapids: Eerdmans.

————. 1985. "The Christology of Hebrews." *Southwestern Journal of Theology* 28, no. 1: 19-27.

————. 1989. *The True Image: The Origin and Destiny of Man in Christ*. Grand Rapids: Eerdmans.

Hull, John M. 2001. "Blindness and the Face of God: Toward a Theology of Disability." In *The Human Image of God*, ed. Hans-Georg Ziebertz, Friedrich Schweitzer, Hermann Häring, and Don Browning, pp. 215-30. Leiden: Brill.

Hultgren, Arland J. 2011. *Paul's Letter to the Romans: A Commentary*. Grand Rapids: Eerdmans.

Humbert, Paul. 1940. *Études sur le récit du paradis et de la chute dans la Genèse*. Neuchâtel: Université de Neuchâtel.

Hummel, Horace D. 1984. "The Image of God." *Concordia Journal* 10: 83-93.

Hunter, David G. 1992. "The Paradise of Patriarchy: Ambrosiaster on Woman as (Not) God's Image." *Journal of Theological Studies* 43: 447-69.

Hunter, Patricia L. 1993. "Women's Power — Women's Passion." In *A Troubling in My Soul*, ed. Emilie M. Townes, 189-98. Maryknoll, NY: Orbis.

Hyldahl, Niels. 1956. "A Reminiscence of the Old Testament at Romans I.23." *New Testament Studies* 2 (May): 285-88.

"Image of God Source of Oppression, Says Consultation." 1981. *The Ecumenical Review* 33 (January): 77.

In the Image of God. 1967. Merrimac, MA: Destiny Publishers.

International Theological Commission. 2004. "Communion and Stewardship: Human Persons Created in the Image of God." http://www.vatican.va/roman _curia/congregations/cfaith/cti_documents/rc_con_cfaith_doc_20040723 _communion-stewardship_en.html.

Irenaeus of Lyons. 1867. "Against Heresies, Book V." In *Ante-Nicene Christian Library: Translations of the Writings of the Fathers down to A.D. 325*, ed. Alexander Roberts and James Donaldson. Vol. IX. Edinburgh: T. & T. Clark.

Jacob, Edmond. 1974. *Theology of the Old Testament*. London: Hodder & Stoughton.

Janzen, J. Gerald. 1995. "Imaging God in Dust." *Living Pulpit* 4, no. 2: 28-29.

Japinga, Lynn. 1999. *Feminism and Christianity*. Nashville: Abingdon.

Jastram, Nathan. 2004. "Man as Male and Female: Created in the Image of God." *Concordia Theological Quarterly* 68, no. 1: 5-96.

Jeeves, Malcolm. 2005. "Neuroscience, Evolutionary Psychology, and the Image of God." *Perspectives on Science and Christian Faith* 57, no. 3: 170-86.

Jenkins, Ferrell. 1995. "Introduction." In *In His Image: The Implication of Creation*, ed. Ferrell Jenkins, ix-x. Temple Terrace: Florida College.

Jenkins, William S. 1935. *Pro-Slavery Thought in the Old South*. Chapel Hill: University of North Carolina Press.

Jennings, Theodore W. 2003. "Theological Anthropology and the Human Genome Project." In *Adam, Eve and the Genome: The Human Genome Project and Theology*, ed. Susan Brooks Thistlethwaite, pp. 93-111. Minneapolis: Fortress.

Jenson, Robert W. 1999. *Systematic Theology*. Vol. II. New York: Oxford.

Jersild, Paul. 2008. "Rethinking the Human Being in Light of Evolutionary Biology." *Dialog* 47: 37-52.

Jervell, Jacob. 1960. *Imago Dei*. Göttingen: Vandenhoeck & Ruprecht.

Jewett, Paul K. 1975. *Man: Male and Female*. Grand Rapids: Eerdmans.

Jewett, Paul K., with Marguerite Shuster. 1996. *Who We Are: Our Dignity as Human*. Grand Rapids: Eerdmans.

Jewett, Robert. 2007. *Romans: A Commentary*. Hermeneia. Minneapolis: Fortress.

Joas, Hans. 2013. *The Sacredness of the Person: A New Genealogy of Human Rights*. Translated by Alex Skinner. Washington, DC: Georgetown University Press.

John Paul II. 1979. "Opening Address at the Puebla Conference." In *Puebla and Beyond*, ed. John Eagleson and Philip Scharper, pp. 57-71. Maryknoll, NY: Orbis.

———. 1980. "Homily for the Mass at Le Bourget." *Documentation Catholique* 1788 (June 15).

———. 1997a. "On the Dignity and Vocation of Women." In *The Theology of the Body: Human Love in the Divine Plan*, pp. 443-92. Boston: Pauline Books and Media.

———. 1997b. "The Gospel of Life." In *The Theology of the Body: Human Love in the Divine Plan*, pp. 493-582. Boston: Pauline Books and Media.

Johnson, David H. 1992. "The Image of God in Colossians." *Didaskalia* 3, no. 2: 9-15.

Johnson, Elizabeth A. 1984. "The Incomprehensibility of God and the Image of God Male and Female." *Theological Studies* 45, no. 3: 441-65.

———. 1992. *She Who Is: The Mystery of God in Feminist Theological Discourse*. New York: Crossroad.

Johnson, Janelle. 2005. "Genesis 1:26-28." *Interpretation: A Journal of Bible & Theology* 59, no. 2: 176-78.

Johnson, Luke T. 2006. *Hebrews: A Commentary*. Louisville: Westminster John Knox.

Johnson, Thomas F. 1993. *1, 2, and 3 John*. New International Biblical Commentary 17. Peabody, MA: Hendrickson.

Johnston, Kristin K. 1998. "Over All Creation." *Currents in Theology of Mission* 25: 137-41.

Jones, A. A. 1962. "Image." In *New Bible Dictionary,* ed. J. D. Douglas, p. 556. Grand Rapids: Eerdmans.

Jones, D. Gareth. 1998. "Infanticide: An Ethical Battlefield." *Science and Christian Belief* 10 (April): 3-19.

————. 2002. "Biomedical Manipulation: Arguing the Case for a Cautiously Optimistic Stance." *Perspectives on Science and Christian Faith* 54, no. 2: 93-102.

Jones, David C. 1994. *Biblical Christian Ethics.* Grand Rapids: Baker.

Jónsson, Gunnlaugur A. 1988. *The Image of God: Genesis 1:26-28 in a Century of Old Testament Research.* Coniectanea Biblica 26. Stockholm: Almqvist & Wiksell.

Junker-Kenny, Maureen. 2001. "The Image of God — Condition of the Image of the Human." In *The Human Image of God,* ed. Hans-Georg Ziebertz, Friedrich Schweitzer, Hermann Häring, and Don Browning, pp. 73-82. Leiden: Brill.

Kaiser, Walter C. 2008. *The Promise-Plan of God: A Biblical Theology of the Old and New Testaments.* Grand Rapids: Zondervan.

Kanner, Leo. 1964. *A History of the Care and Study of the Mentally Retarded.* Springfield, IL: Thomas.

Kant, Immanuel. 1793. *Die Religion Innerhalb der Grenzen der Blossen Vernunft. Die Metaphysik der Sitten.* Frankfurt: Reclam-Universität Bibliothek.

Kapparis, Konstantinos. 2002. *Abortion in the Ancient World.* London: Duckworth.

Käsemann, Ernst. 1949. "Eine Urchristliche Taufliturgie." In *Festschrift für Rudolf Bultmann,* ed. Ernst Wolf, pp. 133-48. Stuttgart: Kohl.

Kass, Leon R. 1990. "Death with Dignity and the Sanctity of Life." *Commentary* 89, no. 3: 33.

————. 2003. *The Beginning of Wisdom: Reading Genesis.* New York: Free Press.

————. 2008. "Defending Human Dignity." In *Human Dignity and Bioethics,* ed. the President's Council on Bioethics, pp. 387-405. Washington, DC: U.S. Government.

Kaufman, Gordon D. 1956. "The Imago Dei as Man's Historicity." *Journal of Religion* 36, no. 1: 157-68.

Keck, Leander E. 2005. *Romans.* Abingdon New Testament Commentary. Nashville: Abingdon.

Keener, Craig S. 1999. *A Commentary on the Gospel of Matthew.* Grand Rapids: Eerdmans.

————. 2005. *1-2 Corinthians.* New Cambridge Bible Commentary. New York: Cambridge University Press.

Keil, Karl, and Friedrich Delitzsch. 1866. *The Pentateuch.* Translated by James Martin. Edinburgh: T. & T. Clark.

Keller, Timothy. 2009. *Counterfeit Gods.* New York: Dutton.

Kelsey, David H. 2009. *Eccentric Existence: A Theological Anthropology.* Louisville: Westminster John Knox.

Kelsey, George D. 1965. *Racism and the Christian Understanding of Man*. New York: Charles Scribner's Sons.

Kepnes, Steven. 2004. "Adam/Eve: From Rabbinic to Scriptural Anthropology." *The Journal of Scriptural Reasoning* 4 (October).

Kesich, Veselin. 1975. "The Biblical Understanding of Man." *Greek Orthodox Theological Review* 20: 9-18.

Kidner, Derek. 1967. *Genesis: An Introduction and Commentary*. Vol. 1. Tyndale Old Testament Commentary. Leicester, UK: InterVarsity Press.

Kilby, Karen. 2000. "Perichoresis and Projection: Problems with Social Doctrines of the Trinity." *New Blackfriars* 81, no. 957: 432-45.

Kilcrease, Jack. 2010. "Kenosis and Vocation: Christ as the Author and Exemplar of Christian Freedom." *Logia* 19, no. 4: 21-33.

Kilner, John F. 1992. *Life on the Line*. Grand Rapids: Eerdmans.

———. 2011. *Why the Church Needs Bioethics: A Guide to Wise Engagement with Life's Challenges*. Grand Rapids: Zondervan.

King, Martin Luther, Jr. 1965. "The American Dream." Sermon July 4, Ebenezer Baptist Church, Atlanta. http://www.sweetspeeches.com/s/309-martin-luther-king-jr -the-american-dream#.

———. 1968. *Where Do We Go from Here?* Boston: Beacon.

———. 1991a. "A Christmas Sermon on Peace." In *A Testament of Hope: The Essential Writings of Martin Luther King Jr.*, ed. James Washington, pp. 253-58. San Francisco: HarperCollins.

———. 1991b. "The American Dream." In *A Testament of Hope: The Essential Writings of Martin Luther King Jr.*, ed. James Washington, pp. 208-16. San Francisco: HarperCollins.

———. 1991c. "The Ethical Demands for Integration." In *A Testament of Hope: The Essential Writings of Martin Luther King Jr.*, ed. James Washington, pp. 117-25. San Francisco: HarperCollins.

Kirk-Duggan, Cheryl A. 1993. "African-American Spirituals." In *A Troubling in My Soul*, ed. Emilie M. Townes, pp. 150-71. Maryknoll, NY: Orbis.

Kistemaker, Simon J. 1997. *2 Corinthians*. Grand Rapids: Baker Academic.

Kittel, Gerhard. 1964a. "Δόξα in the LXX and Hellenistic Apocrypha." In *Theological Dictionary of the New Testament*, ed. Gerhard Kittel, 2:242-45. Grand Rapids: Eerdmans.

———. 1964b. "Images of Gods and Men in Judaism and Christianity." In *Theological Dictionary of the New Testament*, ed. Gerhard Kittel, 2:383-88. Grand Rapids: Eerdmans.

———. 1964c. "The Divine Likeness in Judaism." In *Theological Dictionary of the New Testament*, ed. Gerhard Kittel, 2:392-95. Grand Rapids: Eerdmans.

———. 1964d. "The Metaphorical Use of Image in the NT." In *Theological Dictionary of the New Testament*, ed. Gerhard Kittel, 2:395-97. Grand Rapids: Eerdmans.

———. 1964e. "The NT Use of *Doxa*, II." In *Theological Dictionary of the New Testament*, ed. Gerhard Kittel, 2:247-51. Grand Rapids: Eerdmans.

Kleinknecht, Hermann. 1964. "The Greek Use of Eikon." In *Theological Dictionary of the New Testament*, ed. Gerhard Kittel, 2:388-90. Grand Rapids: Eerdmans.

Kline, Meredith G. 1977. "Creation in the Image of the Glory-Spirit." *Westminster Theological Journal* 39, no. 2: 250-72.

———. 1980. *Images of the Spirit*. Baker Biblical Monograph. Grand Rapids: Baker.

Klug, Eugene F. A. 1984. "The Doctrine of Man: Christian Anthropology." *Concordia Theological Quarterly* 48, no. 2-3: 141-52.

Koehler, Ludwig. 1948. "Die Grundstelle der Imago-Dei-Lehre, Gen 1:26." *Theologische Zeitschrift* 4: 16-22.

Koehler, Ludwig, and Walter Baumgartner. 2001. *The Hebrew and Aramaic Lexicon of the Old Testament*, rev. Walter Baumgartner and Johann Stamm, trans. M. E. J. Richardson. Leiden: Brill.

Koester, Craig. 2001. *Hebrews*. New York: Doubleday.

Konkel, August H. 1992. "Male and Female as the Image of God." *Didaskalia* 3, no. 2: 1-8.

———. 1997. "dmh." In *New International Dictionary of Old Testament Theology and Exegesis*, 1:967-70. Grand Rapids: Zondervan.

Köstenberger, Andreas J., Scott Kellum, and Charles L. Quarles. 2009. *The Cradle, the Cross, and the Crown: An Introduction to the New Testament*. Nashville: B. & H. Academic.

Koyzis, David T. 2014. *We Answer to Another: Authority, Office, and the Image of God*. Eugene, OR: Pickwick.

Krause, Deborah. 2005. "Keeping It Real: The Image of God in the New Testament." *Interpretation: A Journal of Bible & Theology* 59, no. 4: 358-68.

Kraynak, Robert P. 2008. "Human Dignity and the Mystery of the Human Soul." In *Human Dignity and Bioethics*, ed. the President's Council on Bioethics, pp. 61-82. Washington, DC: President's Council.

Kreitzer, Larry. 1989. "Christ and Second Adam in Paul." *Communio Viatorum* 32, no. 1: 55-101.

Kruse, Colin J. 2000. *The Letters of John*. Grand Rapids: Eerdmans.

Kudlien, Fridolf. 1970. "Medical Ethics and Popular Ethics in Greece and Rome." *Clio Medica* 5: 91-121.

Kuitert, Harry. 1972. *Signals from the Bible*. Grand Rapids: Eerdmans.

Kümmel, Werner Georg. 1963. *Man in the New Testament*. Translated by John Vincent. Revised and Enlarged. Philadelphia: Westminster.

Kyung, Chung Hyun. 1990. *Struggle to Be the Sun Again: Introducing Asian Women's Theology*. Maryknoll, NY: Orbis.

———. 1994. "To Be Human Is to Be Created in God's Image." In *Feminist Theology from the Third World*, ed. Ursula King, pp. 251-58. Maryknoll, NY: Orbis.

LaCugna, Catherine Mowry. 1993. "God in Communion with Us." In *Freeing Theology:*

The Essentials of Theology in Feminist Perspective, ed. Catherine Mowry LaCugna, pp. 83-114. New York: HarperCollins.

Lakey, Michael J. 2010. *Image and Glory of God.* New York: T. & T. Clark.

Lambdin, Thomas O. 1971. *Introduction to Biblical Hebrew.* New York: Charles Scribner's Sons.

Lambrecht, Jan. 1999. *Second Corinthians.* Vol. 8. Sacra Pagina. Collegeville, MN: Liturgical Press.

Lane, William L. 1974. *The Gospel According to Mark.* New International Commentary on the New Testament. Grand Rapids: Eerdmans.

————. 1991. *Hebrews 1-8.* Word Biblical Commentary 47a. Nashville: Thomas Nelson.

Larkin, Lucy. 1993. "Douglas John Hall — The Stewardship Symbol and the Image of God." *Theology in Green* 3, no. 7: 13-19.

Las Casas, Bartolome de. 1958. "Tratado Comprobatorio del Imperio Soberano y Principado Universal que los Reyes de Castilla y Leon Tienen sobre las Indias." In *Obras Escogidas,* ed. Juan Perez de Tudela Bueso, 5: 350-423. Madrid: Atlas.

Laws, Sophie. 1993. *The Epistle of James.* Black's New Testament Commentary. Peabody, MA: Hendrickson.

Lazenby, Henry F. 1987. "The Image of God: Masculine, Feminine, or Neuter?" *Journal of the Evangelical Theological Society* 30: 63-70.

Leavy, Stanley A. 1988. *In the Image of God: A Psychoanalyst's View.* New Haven: Yale University Press.

Lehmann, Paul L. 1970. "Karl Barth and the Future of Theology." *Religious Studies* 6, no. 2: 105-20.

Leibniz, Gottfried W. 1898. *The Monadology.* Translated by Robert Latta. Oxford: Clarendon.

Leitch, Addison H. 1975. "Image of God." In *The Zondervan Pictorial Encyclopedia of the Bible,* ed. Merrill C. Tenney, pp. 256-58. Grand Rapids: Zondervan.

Lenski, Richard C. H. 1946a. *The Interpretation of St. Luke's Gospel.* Minneapolis: Augsburg Fortress.

————. 1946b. *The Interpretation of St. Paul's First and Second Epistle to the Corinthians.* Columbus, OH: Wartburg Press.

————. 1946c. *The Interpretation of the Epistle to the Hebrews and of the Epistle of James.* Columbus, OH: Wartburg Press.

Letham, Robert. 1990. "The Man-Woman Debate: Theological Comment." *Westminster Theological Journal* 52: 65-78.

Levenson, Jon D. 1994. *Creation and the Persistence of Evil.* Princeton: Princeton University Press.

Lewis, Gordon R., and Bruce A. Demarest. 1987. *Integrative Theology.* 3 vols. Grand Rapids: Zondervan.

Lichtheim, Miriam. 1976. *Ancient Egyptian Literature.* 2 vols. Berkeley: University of California Press.

Liefeld, Walter L. 1997. *Ephesians*. IVP New Testament Commentary. Downers Grove, IL: InterVarsity Press.

Lightfoot, J. B. 1927. *Saint Paul's Epistles to the Colossians and to Philemon*. London: Macmillan.

Lincoln, Abraham. 1953. "'Speech at Lewistown, Illinois' (August 17, 1858)." In *The Collected Works of Abraham Lincoln*, ed. Roy Basler, 2:544-47. New Brunswick, NJ: Rutgers University Press.

Lincoln, Andrew T. 1990. *Ephesians*. Word Biblical Commentary 42. Nashville: Thomas Nelson.

Lincoln, C. Eric. 1999. *Race, Religion, and the Continuing American Dilemma*. 2nd ed. New York: Hill & Wang.

Lincoln, C. Eric, and Lawrence H. Mamiya. 1990. *The Black Church in the African-American Experience*. Durham, NC: Duke University Press.

Lints, Richard. 2006a. "Imaging and Idolatry. The Sociality of Personhood in the Canon." In *Personal Identity in Theological Perspective,* ed. Richard Lints, Michael S. Horton, and Mark R. Talbot, pp. 204-25. Grand Rapids: Eerdmans.

————. 2006b. "Introduction: Theological Anthropology in Context." In *Personal Identity in Theological Perspective,* ed. Richard Lints, Michael S. Horton, and Mark R. Talbot, pp. 1-10. Grand Rapids: Eerdmans.

Litton, Edward A. 1960. *Introduction to Dogmatic Theology*. London: James Clarke.

Litwa, M. David. 2008. "2 Corinthians 3:18 and Its Implications for Theosis." *Journal of Theological Interpretation* 2, no. 1: 117-33.

Lloyd, Genevieve. 1984. *The Man of Reason: "Male" and "Female" in Western Philosophy*. Minneapolis: University of Minnesota Press.

Lo, Pilgrim W. K. 2009. "Human Dignity — A Theological and Confucian Discussion." *Dialog* 48: 168-78.

Loader, William. 2004. *The Septuagint, Sexuality, and the New Testament*. Grand Rapids: Eerdmans.

Lohse, Eduard. 1957. "Imago Dei bei Paul." In *Libertas Christiana: Festschrift für Friedrich Delekat,* ed. Ernst Wolf and Walter Matthias, pp. 122-35. Munich: Kaiser.

————. 1971. *Colossians and Philemon*. Translated by William R. Poehlmann and Robert J. Karris. Hermeneia. Philadelphia: Fortress.

Lombardo, Paul A. 2008. *Three Generations, No Imbeciles: Eugenics, the Supreme Count, and Buck v. Bell*. Baltimore: Johns Hopkins University Press.

Long, Thomas G. 1997. *Hebrews*. Interpretation. Louisville: John Knox.

Lossky, Vladimir. 1985. *In the Image and Likeness of God*. Crestwood, NY: St. Vladimir's Seminary Press.

Lowry, Noelle Z. 2012. "The Image of God in Humanity: Fleshing Out the Bare Bones of Marital Oneness." *Priscilla Papers* 26, no. 4 (November): 13-15.

Lubac, Henri de. 1950. *Catholicism*. Translated by Lancelot Sheppard. New York: Longmans, Green & Co.

Lubardic, Bogdan. 2011. "Orthodox Theology of Personhood: A Critical Overview." *Expository Times* 122, nos. 11-12: 521-30; 573-81.

Luther, Martin. 1952. *Colloquia Mensalis*. London: Du-Gard.

—. 1958. *Luther's Works*. Edited by Jaroslav Pelikan, translated by George Schick. St. Louis: Concordia.

Lutheran Church–Missouri Synod, Commission on Theology and Church Relations. 1994. "Racism and the Church: Overcoming the Idolatry." February.

Luz, Ulrich. 2001. *Matthew 21–28*. Translated by James E. Crouch. Hermeneia. Minneapolis: Fortress.

Maag, Victor. 1954. "Sumerische und Babylonische Mythen von der Erschaftung des Menschen." *Asiatische Studien* 8: 85-106.

—. 1955. "Altestamentliche Anthropogonie in ihrem Verhältnis zur altorientalischen Mythologie." *Asiatische Studien* 9: 15-44.

Macaskill, Donald. 2003. "Human Individuality and Inclusive Community: Concepts of Self, Vocation, and *Imago Dei*." In *Growing into God*, ed. Jean Mayland, pp. 211-20. London: Churches Together in Britain and Ireland.

MacDonald, Nathan. 2008. "The *Imago Dei* and Election: Reading Genesis 1:26-28 and Old Testament Scholarship with Karl Barth." *International Journal of Systematic Theology* 10, no. 3: 303-27.

Machen, John G. 1947. *The Christian View of Man*. Grand Rapids: Eerdmans.

Mahoney, Jack. 2010. "Evolution, Altruism, and the Image of God." *Theological Studies* 71: 677-701.

—. 2011. *Christianity in Evolution*. Washington, DC: Georgetown University Press.

Maldonado-Torres, Nelson. 2008. *Against War*. Durham, NC: Duke University Press.

Maloney, George A. 1973. *Man, the Divine Icon*. Pecos, NM: Dove Publications.

Mangano, Mark J. 2008. *The Image of God*. Lanham, MD: University Press of America.

Mann, C. S. 1986. *Mark*. Anchor Bible Commentary 27. New York: Doubleday.

Maritain, Jacques. 1947. *The Person and the Common Good*. Translated by John Fitzgerald. New York: Scribner.

Marsh, Charles. 2005. *The Beloved Community: How Faith Shapes Social Justice, from the Civil Rights Movement to Today*. New York: Basic Books.

Marshall, Christopher D. 2001. *Crowned with Glory & Honor*. Telford, PA: Pandora.

Marshall, I. Howard. 1978. *The Gospel of Luke*. New International Greek Testament Commentary. Grand Rapids: Eerdmans.

—. 2001. "Being Human: Made in the Image of God." *Stone-Campbell Journal* 4, no. 1: 47-67.

Marshall, Paul. 1985. *Thine Is the Kingdom*. Grand Rapids: Eerdmans.

Martin, Ralph P. 1981. *Colossians and Philemon*. New Century Bible Commentary. Grand Rapids: Eerdmans.

—. 1983. *Carmen Christi: Philippians ii.5-11 in Recent Interpretation and in the Setting of Early Christian Worship*. Grand Rapids: Eerdmans.

—. 1986. *2 Corinthians*. Word Biblical Commentary 40. Waco, TX: Word Books.

————. 1988. *James*. Word Biblical Commentary 48. Waco, TX: Word Books.

————. 1996. "Image." In *New Bible Dictionary,* ed. D. R. W. Wood and I. Howard Marshall. 3rd ed. Leicester, UK/Downers Grove, IL: InterVarsity Press.

Martin, Robert K. 2002. "Encountering God in the Image of Christ: Iconic Leadership." *Journal of Religious Leadership* 1, no. 1: 83-100.

Mascall, E. L. 1974. *The Importance of Being Human.* Westport, CT: Greenwood Press.

Maston, T. B. 1959. *The Bible and Race.* Nashville: Broadman.

Matera, Frank J. 2003. *II Corinthians: A Commentary.* New Testament Library. Louisville: Westminster John Knox.

Mathews, Kenneth A. 1995. *Genesis 1–11:26.* Nashville: Broadman & Holman.

Matt, Hershel J. 1987. "Fading Image of God? Theological Reflections of a Nursing Home Chaplain." *Judaism* 36, no. 1: 75-83.

Matter, E. Ann. 2000. "Christ, God, and Women in the Thought of St. Augustine." In *Augustine and His Critics,* ed. Robert Dodaro and George Lawless, pp. 164-75. New York: Routledge.

————. 2007. *"De cura feminarum:* Augustine the Bishop, North African Women, and the Development of a Theology of Female Nature." In *Feminist Interpretations of Augustine,* ed. Judith Chelius Stark, pp. 203-14. University Park: Pennsylvania State University Press.

Maxwell, John F. 1975. *Slavery and the Catholic Church.* London: Barry Rose.

Mayland, Jean. 1999. "Made and Re-Made in the Image of God." *Modern Believing* 40, no. 3: 59-65.

————. 2003. "Introduction." In *Growing into God,* ed. Jean Mayland, pp. 1-21. London: Churches Together in Britain and Ireland.

Maynard, Theodore. 1920. "The Image of God." In *The Last Night and Other Poems,* pp. 101-2. New York: Frederick A. Stokes.

Mays, James L. 2006. "The Self in the Psalms and the Image of God." In *God and Human Dignity,* ed. Kendall Soulen and Linda Woodhead, pp. 72-86. Grand Rapids: Eerdmans.

McCasland, S. Vernon. 1950. " 'The Image of God' According to Paul." *Journal of Biblical Literature* 69 (June): 85-100.

McClendon, James W. 1991. "Philippians 2:5-11." *Review & Expositor* 88, no. 4: 439-44.

McConnell, Walter. 2006. "In His Image: A Christian's Place in Creation." *Asian Journal of Theology* 20: 114-27.

McCool, Gerald A. 1959. "The Ambrosian Origin of St. Augustine's Theology of the Image of God in Man." *Theological Studies* 20: 62-81.

McDonald, Hugh D. 1981. *The Christian View of Man.* Westchester, IL: Crossway.

McDonald, Suzanne. 2009. "The Pneumatology of the 'Lost' Image in John Owen." *Westminster Theological Journal* 71, no. 2: 323-35.

McDonough, Sean M. 2009. *Christ as Creator.* Oxford: Oxford University Press.

McFadyen, Alistair I. 1990. *The Call to Personhood.* Cambridge: Cambridge University Press.

McFague, Sallie. 1993. *The Body of God.* Minneapolis: Fortress.

McFarland, Ian A. 2005. *The Divine Image.* Minneapolis: Fortress.

McFarlane, Graham W. P. 1999. "Strange News from Another Star." In *Persons, Divine and Human,* ed. Colin E. Gunton and Christoph Schwöbel, pp. 98-119. Edinburgh: T. & T. Clark.

McGinn, Bernard. 1985. "The Human Person as Image of God: Western Christianity." In *Christian Spirituality,* ed. Bernard McGinn and John Meyendorff, pp. 312-30. New York: Crossroad.

McKanan, Dan. 2002. *Identifying the Image of God.* New York: Oxford University Press.

McKenna, John E. 2008. *The Great AMEN of the Great I-AM.* Eugene, OR: Wipf & Stock.

McKitrick, Eric L., ed. 1963. *Slavery Defended.* Englewood Cliffs, NJ: Prentice-Hall.

McKnight, Scot. 2005. *Embracing Grace.* Brewster, MA: Paraclete.

————. 2011. *The Letter of James.* New International Commentary on the New Testament. Grand Rapids: Eerdmans.

McLaughlin, Elizabeth W. 2008. *Engendering the Imago Dei.* Ann Arbor, MI: UMI Microform.

McLeod, Frederick G. 1999. *The Image of God in the Antiochene Tradition.* Washington, DC: Catholic University of America Press.

McMinn, Mark R., and Clark D. Campbell. 2007. *Integrative Psychotherapy.* Downers Grove, IL: InterVarsity Press.

McReynolds, Kathy. 2013. "A Historical and Literary Exploration of Key Passages in Genesis." *Journal of the Christian Institute on Disability* 2, no. 2: 25-36.

Meconi, David V. 2000. "*Grata Sacris Angelis:* Gender and the Imago Dei in Augustine's *De Trinitate* XII." *American Catholic Philosophical Quarterly* 74, no. 1: 47-62.

Meek, Theophile J. 1955. "Result and Purpose Clauses in Hebrew." *Jewish Quarterly Review* 46, no. 1: 40-43.

Melchert, Christopher. 2011. "God Created Adam in His Image." *Journal of Qur'anic Studies* 13, no. 1: 113-24.

Melick, Richard R., Jr. 2010. "The Glory of God in the Synoptic Gospels, Acts, and the General Epistles." In *The Glory of God,* ed. Christopher W. Morgan and Robert A. Peterson, pp. 79-106. Wheaton, IL: Crossway.

Merriell, Donald J. 1990. *To the Image of the Trinity.* Belgium: Universa.

Merrill, Eugene H. 2003. "Image of God." In *Dictionary of the Old Testament: Pentateuch,* ed. Desmond Alexander and David W. Baker, pp. 441-45. Downers Grove, IL: InterVarsity Press.

————. 2006. *Everlasting Dominion.* Nashville: Broadman & Holman.

Merton, Thomas. 1981. *The New Man.* New York: Farrar, Straus & Giroux.

Mettinger, Tryggve N. D. 1974. "Abbild oder Urbild? Imago Dei in traditionsgeschichtlicher Sicht." *Zeitshrift für fie Alttestamentliche Wissenschaft* 86: 403-24.

Mexico Conference. 1993. "Final Document on Doing Theology from Third World

Women's Perspective." In *Feminist Theology from the Third World,* ed. Ursula King, pp. 35-44. Maryknoll, NY: Orbis.

Meyer-Wilmes, Hedwig. 1987. "Women's Nature and Feminine Identity." In *Women, Work, and Poverty,* ed. Elizabeth Schüssler Fiorenza and Anne E. Carr, pp. 93-101. Edinburgh: T. & T. Clark.

Middleton, J. Richard. 1994. "The Liberating Image? Interpreting the *Imago Dei* in Context." *Christian Scholar's Review* 24, no. 1: 8-25.

————. 2005. *The Liberating Image: The Imago Dei in Genesis 1.* Grand Rapids: Brazos Press.

Milbank, John. 2010. "The Mystery of Reason." In *The Grandeur of Reason,* ed. Peter Candler Jr. and Conor Cunningham, pp. 68-117. London: SCM.

Miley, John. 1989. *Systematic Theology.* Vol. 1. Peabody, MA: Hendrickson.

Millard, Alan R., and Pierre Bordreuil. 1982. "A Statue from Syria with Assyrian and Aramaic Inscriptions." *Biblical Archaeologist* 45, no. 3: 135-41.

Miller, J. Maxwell. 1972. "In the 'Image' and 'Likeness' of God." *Journal of Biblical Literature* 91, no. 3: 289-304.

Minor, Mitzi L. 2009. *2 Corinthians.* Smith & Helwys Bible Commentary. Macon, GA: Smyth & Helwys.

Mitchell, Alan C. 2007. *Hebrews.* Sacra Pagina 13. Collegeville, MN: Liturgical Press.

Mitchell, C. Ben. 2013. "The Audacity of the *Imago Dei:* The Legacy and Uncertain Future of Human Dignity." In *Imago Dei: Human Dignity in Ecumenical Perspective,* ed. Thomas Albert Howard, pp. 79-112. Washington, DC: Catholic University of America Press.

Mitton, C. Leslie. 1966. *The Epistle of James.* Marshall's Study Library. Grand Rapids: Eerdmans.

————. 1981. *Ephesians.* New Century Bible Commentary. Grand Rapids: Eerdmans.

Moltmann, Jürgen. 1971. *Man: Christian Anthropology.* London: SPCK.

————. 1976. "Christian Declaration on Human Rights." *Reformed World* 34, no. 2: 58-72.

————. 1984. *On Human Dignity.* Translated by M. Douglas Meeks. Philadelphia: Augsburg Fortress.

————. 1985. *God in Creation.* San Francisco: Harper & Row.

Mondin, Battista. 1975. *St. Thomas Aquinas' Philosophy in the Commentary to the Sentences.* The Hague: Martinus Nijhoff.

Montefiore, Hugh. 1964. *A Commentary on the Epistle to the Hebrews.* New York: Harper & Row.

Moo, Douglas J. 1996. *The Epistle to the Romans.* New International Commentary on the New Testament. Grand Rapids: Eerdmans.

Moore, George F. 1944. *Judaism.* Cambridge, MA: Harvard University Press.

Moore, Zoë Bennett. 2003. "'One Ladies' One Normal: Made in the Image of God — Issues for Women." In *Growing into God,* ed. Jean Mayland, pp. 103-12. London: Churches Together in Britain and Ireland.

Moreland, J. P. 2009. *The Recalcitrant Imago Dei*. London: SCM.

Moreland, J. P., and Scott B. Rae. 2000. *Body and Soul: Human Nature & the Crisis in Ethics*. Downers Grove, IL: InterVarsity Press.

Morgan, Christopher W. 2010. "Toward a Theology of the Glory of God." In *The Glory of God*, ed. Christopher W. Morgan and Robert A. Peterson, pp. 153-88. Wheaton, IL: Crossway.

Moritz, Joshua M. 2009. "Animals and the Image of God in the Bible and Beyond." *Dialog* 48, no. 2: 134-46.

————. 2011. "Evolution, the End of Human Uniqueness and the Election of the Imago Dei." *Theology & Science* 9, no. 3: 307-39.

Morris, Leon. 1992. *The Gospel According to Matthew*. Pillar New Testament Commentary. Grand Rapids: Eerdmans.

Mott, Stephen C. 1982. *Biblical Ethics and Social Change*. New York: Oxford University Press.

Moule, C. F. D. 1965. *The Gospel according to Mark*. Cambridge: Cambridge University Press.

Mounce, Robert H. 1991. *Matthew*. New International Biblical Commentary. Peabody, MA: Hendrickson.

————. 1995. *Romans*. New American Commentary 27. Nashville: Broadman & Holman.

Mouw, Richard. 1983. *When the Kings Came Marching In*. Grand Rapids: Eerdmans.

————. 2012. "The *Imago Dei* and Philosophical Anthropology." *Christian Scholar's Review* 43, no. 3: 253-66.

Mueller, John T. 1934. *Christian Dogmatics*. St. Louis: Concordia.

Mullins, Edgar Y. 1917. *The Christian Religion in Its Doctrinal Expression*. Philadelphia: Judson Press.

Mulzac, Kenneth. 2001. "Genesis 9:1-7: Its Theological Connections with the Creation Motif." *Journal of the Adventist Theological Society* 12, no. 1: 65-77.

Mundle, Wilhelm. 1976. *"Eidolon."* In *New International Dictionary of New Testament Theology*, 2:288-89. Grand Rapids: Zondervan.

Murphy-O'Connor, Jerome. 1982. *Becoming Human Together*. Wilmington, DE: Michael Glazier.

Murray, Andrew. 1965. *With Christ in the School of Prayer*. Old Tappan, NJ: Fleming H. Revell.

Murray, John. 1968. *The Epistle to the Romans*. Grand Rapids: Eerdmans.

————. 1977. "Man in the Image of God." In *Collected Writings of John Murray*, 2:34-46. Edinburgh: Banner of Truth Trust.

Nash, James A. 1991. *Loving Nature: Ecological Integrity and Christian Responsibility*. Nashville: Abingdon.

Navone, John J. 1990. "The Image and Glory of God." *Homiletic and Pastoral Review* 91, no. 1: 64-67.

Nellas, Panayiotis. 1987. *Deification in Christ: Orthodox Perspectives on the Nature of the Human Person.* Translated by Norman Russell. Crestwood, NY: St. Vladimir's Seminary Press.

Nestorius of Constantinople. 1980. "First Sermon Against the Theotokos." In *The Christological Controversy,* ed. Richard A. Norris, pp. 123-30. Philadelphia: Fortress.

Neuhaus, Richard J. 2008. "Human Dignity and Public Discourse." In *Human Dignity and Bioethics,* ed. President's Council on Bioethics, pp. 215-28. Washington, DC: U.S. Government.

Niebuhr, H. Richard. 1996. *Theology, History, and Culture.* New Haven: Yale University Press.

Niebuhr, Reinhold. 1964. *The Nature and Destiny of Man.* Vol. 1. New York: Charles Scribner's Sons.

Niehaus, Jeffrey J. 2008. *Ancient Near Eastern Themes in Biblical Theology.* Grand Rapids: Kregel.

Niskanen, Paul. 2009. "The Poetics of Adam: The Creation of *Adam* in the Image of *Elohim.*" *Journal of Biblical Literature* 128, no. 3: 417-36.

Nixon, R. E. 1962. "Glory." In *New Bible Dictionary,* ed. J. D. Douglas, pp. 472-73. Grand Rapids: Eerdmans.

Nolland, John. 1989. *Luke 18:35–24:53.* Word Biblical Commentary 35c. Dallas: Word Books.

———. 2005. *The Gospel of Matthew: A Commentary on the Greek Text.* New International Greek Testament Commentary. Grand Rapids: Eerdmans.

Novak, Michael. 2002. "Another Islam." *First Things* (November). http://www.firstthings.com/article/2007/01/-another-islam-43.

Nugent, Christopher. 1984. "The Face as Theology." *Theology Today* 41: 314-20.

O'Brien, Peter T. 1987. *Colossians, Philemon.* Word Biblical Commentary 44. Nashville: Thomas Nelson.

———. 1999. *The Letter to the Ephesians.* Pillar New Testament Commentary. Grand Rapids: Eerdmans.

———. 2010. *The Letter to the Hebrews.* Pillar New Testament Commentary. Grand Rapids: Eerdmans.

Oberdorfer, Bernd. 2010. "Human Dignity and 'Image of God.'" *Scriptura* 204: 231-39.

Ochs, Peter. 2006. "The Logic of Indignity and the Logic of Redemption." In *God and Human Dignity,* ed. Kendall Soulen and Linda Woodhead, pp. 143-60. Grand Rapids: Eerdmans.

O'Donovan, Oliver. 1986. *Resurrection and Moral Order.* Grand Rapids: Eerdmans.

Oduyoye, Mercy Amba. 1982. "In the Image of God: A Theological Reflection from an African Perspective." *Bulletin of African Theology* 4, no. 7: 41-54.

———. 1995. *Daughters of Anowa: African Women and Patriarchy.* Maryknoll, NY: Orbis.

———. 1996. "Spirituality of Resistance and Reconstruction." In *Women Resisting Violence: Spirituality for Life,* ed. Mary John Mananzan et al., pp. 161-71. Maryknoll, NY: Orbis.

————. 2001. *Introducing African Women's Theology*. Sheffield, UK: Sheffield Academic Press.

O'Faolain, Julia, and Lauro Martines. 1973. *Not in God's Image: Women in History from the Greeks to the Victorians*. New York: Harper & Row.

Oldham, J. H. 1924. *Christianity and the Race Problem*. London: SCM.

Olson, Oliver K. 1996. "Flacius Illyricus, Matthias." In *The Oxford Encyclopedia of the Reformation*, ed. Hans Hillebrand, 2:110-11. New York: Oxford University Press.

O'Mathuna, Donal P. 1995. "The Bible and Abortions: What of the 'Image of God'?" In *Bioethics and the Future of Medicine*, ed. John F. Kilner, Nigel M. de S. Cameron, and David L. Schiedermayer, pp. 199-211. Grand Rapids: Eerdmans.

O'Neill, J. C. 1999. "If God Created Adam in His Own Image, in the Image of God Created He Him, How Is Christ the Image of God?" *Irish Biblical Studies* 21, no. 2: 79-87.

O'Neill, Mary Aquin. 1993. "The Mystery of Being Human Together." In *Freeing Theology: The Essentials of Theology in Feminist Perspective*, ed. Catherine Mowry LaCugna, pp. 139-60. New York: HarperCollins.

Origen. 1982. *Homilies on Genesis and Exodus*. Translated by Ronald E. Heine. Washington, DC: Catholic University of America Press.

Orr, James. 1948. *God's Image in Man, and Its Defacement in the Light of Modern Denials*. Grand Rapids: Eerdmans.

Osborn, Eric F. 2003. "Irenaeus: Rocks in the Road." *Expository Times* 114, no. 8: 255-58.

Otto, Eberhard. 1971. "Der Mensch als Geschöpf und Bild Gottes in Ägypten." In *Probleme biblischer Theologie*, ed. Hans Wolff, pp. 335-48. Munich: Kaiser.

Otto, Randall E. 1992. "The Imago Dei as Familitas." *Journal of the Evangelical Theological Society* 35 (December): 503-13.

Overstreet, R. Larry. 2005. "Man in the Image of God: A Reappraisal." *Criswell Theological Review* 3, no. 1: 43-70.

Owen, John. 1850-1855a. "Christologia." In *The Works of John Owen*, ed. William Goold, Vol. 1: 1-272. London: Johnstone & Hunter.

————. 1850-1855b. "Pneumatologia." In *The Works of John Owen*, ed. William Goold. Vol. 3. London: Johnstone & Hunter.

Owen-Ball, David T. 1993. "Rabbinic Rhetoric and the Tribute Passage (Mt. 22:15-22; Mk. 12:13-17; Lk. 20:20-26)." *Novum Testamentum* 35: 1-14.

Packer, J. I. 2003. "Reflected Glory." *Christianity Today* 47, no. 12: 56.

Painter, John. 2001. "Outward Decay and Inward Renewal: A Biblical Perspective on Aging and the Image of God." *Journal of Religious Gerontology* 12, no. 3-4: 43-55.

————. 2002. *1, 2, 3 John*. Sacra Pagina 18. Collegeville, MN: Liturgical Press.

Pannenberg, Wolfhart. 1985. *Anthropology in Theological Perspective*. Translated by Matthew J. O'Connell. Philadelphia: Westminster.

————. 1991. *Systematic Theology*. Translated by Geoffrey Bromiley. Vol. 2. Grand Rapids: Eerdmans.

Paris, Peter J. 1985. *The Social Teaching of the Black Churches*. Philadelphia: Fortress.

Patzia, Arthur G. 1990. *Ephesians, Colossians, Philemon.* New International Biblical Commentary. Peabody, MA: Hendrickson.

Pauw, Amy Plantinga. 1993. "Personhood, Divine and Human." *Perspectives* 8, no. 2: 12-14.

Payne, Leanne. 1995. *The Broken Image.* Grand Rapids: Baker.

Pelikan, Jaroslav. 1978. "*Imago Dei:* An Explication of Summa Theologiae, Part I, Question 93." In *Calgary Aquinas Studies,* ed. Anthony Parel. Toronto, Canada: Pontifical Institute of Medieval Studies.

Pellegrino, Edmund. 2006. "Toward a Richer Bioethics: A Conclusion." In *Health and Human Flourishing,* ed. Carol Taylor and Roberto Dell'Oro, pp. 247-69. Washington, DC: Georgetown University Press.

Peña, Milagros. 2007. *Latina Activists Across Borders.* Durham, NC: Duke University Press.

Penning, Guido. 2007. "Ethics Without Boundaries: Medical Tourism." In *Principles of Health Care Ethics,* ed. Richard E. Ashcroft, Angus Dawson, Heather Draper, and John R. McMillan, pp. 505-10. 2nd ed. Chichester, UK: John Wiley & Sons.

Peters, Karl E. 1974. "The Image of God as a Model for Humanization." *Journal of Religion and Science* 9 (January): 98-125.

Peters, Ted. 2010. "Can We Enhance the Imago Dei?" In *Human Identity at the Intersection of Science, Technology, and Religion,* ed. Nancey Murphy and Christopher Knight, pp. 215-38. Burlington, VT: Ashgate.

Peterson, Gregory R. 1996. "Are We Unique? The Locus Humanus, Animal Cognition and the Theology of Nature." Ph.D. Dissertation, Denver, CO: The Iliff School of Theology and the University of Denver (Colorado Seminary).

———. 2008. "Uniqueness, the Image of God, and the Problem of Method: Engaging van Huyssteen." *Zygon* 43, no. 2: 467-74.

Peterson, James C. 2011. "*Homo Sapiens* as *Homo Dei:* Paleoanthropology, Human Uniqueness, and the Image of God." *Toronto Journal of Theology* 27 (March): 17-25.

Peterson, Paul S. 2008. "The Unquantifiable Value of 'Imago Trinitatis': Theological Anthropology and the Bioethical Discourse on Human Dignity." *Human Reproduction and Genetic Ethics* 14, no. 2: 27-38.

Phelps, Matthew P. 2004. "Imago Dei and Limited Creature: High and Low Views of Human Beings in Christianity and Cognitive Psychology." *Christian Scholar's Review* 33, no. 3: 345-66.

Pieper, Franz. 1950. *Christian Dogmatics.* Translated by Theodore Engelder. 4 vols. St. Louis: Concordia.

Pierce, Brian. 1992. "Bartolomé de Las Casas and Truth: Toward a Spirituality of Solidarity." *Spirituality Today* 44: 4-19.

Pigeaud, Jackie. 1997. "Les Fondements philosophiques de l'éthique médicale." In *Médecine et morale dans l'Antiquité,* ed. Hellmut Flasher and Jacques Jouvanna, pp. 255-96. Geneva: Hardt Foundation.

Pinckaers, Servais. 2005. "Aquinas on the Dignity of the Human Person." In *The Pinck-*

aers Reader: Renewing Thomistic Moral Theology, ed. John Berkman and Craig Steven Titus, trans. Mary Noble, Craig Steven Titus, Michael Sherwin, and Hugh Connolly, pp. 144-63. Washington, DC: Catholic University of America Press.

Pineda-Madrid, Nancy. 2011. *Suffering and Salvation in Ciudad Juárez.* Minneapolis: Fortress.

Piper, John. 1971. "The Image of God: An Approach from Biblical and Systematic Theology." *Studia Biblica et Theologica* 1 (March): 15-32.

————. 1989. "Male and Female He Created Them in the Image of God." *Desiring God.* http://www.desiringgod.org/resource-library/sermons/male-and-female-he-created-them-in-the-image-of-god.

Plantinga, Cornelius, Jr. 2002. *Engaging God's World: A Christian Vision of Faith, Learning, and Living.* Grand Rapids: Eerdmans.

Plischke, Hans. 1951. *Von Cooper bis Karl May: Eine Geschichte des völkerkundlichen Reise- und Abenteuerromans.* Düsseldorf: Droste.

Polkinghorne, John. 2006. "Anthropology in an Evolutionary Context." In *God and Human Dignity,* ed. Kendall Soulen and Linda Woodhead, pp. 89-103. Grand Rapids: Eerdmans.

Pooler, David K. 2011. "Professional Flourishing: Re-visioning Self-Care Using *Imago Dei.*" *Social Work and Christianity* 38 (Winter): 440-52.

Pope, Stephen J. 1993. "Proper and Improper Partiality and the Preferential Option for the Poor." *Theological Studies* (June): 242-71.

Pope, William B. 1875. *A Compendium of Christian Theology.* 2nd ed. 2 vols. New York: Phillips & Hunt.

Porteous, N. W. 1962. "Image of God." In *The Interpreter's Dictionary of the Bible,* ed. George A. Buttrick, 2: 682-85. New York: Abingdon.

Posey, Walter. 1952. *The Presbyterian Church in the Old Southwest.* Richmond, VA: John Knox.

Power, Kim. 1996. *Veiled Desire: Augustine on Women.* New York: Continuum.

Power, William L. 1970. "The Imago Dei and Man Come of Age." *Illiff Review* 27: 35-41.

————. 1997. "*Imago Dei — Imitatio Dei.*" *International Journal of Philosophy of Religion* 42: 131-41.

President's Council on Bioethics. 2008. *Human Dignity and Bioethics.* Washington, DC: President's Council.

Price, Daniel J. 2002. *Karl Barth's Anthropology in Light of Modern Thought.* Grand Rapids: Eerdmans.

Priest, James E. 1988. "Gen. 9:6: A Comparative Study of Bloodshed in Bible and Talmud." *Journal of the Evangelical Theological Society* 31: 145-51.

Primavesi, Anne. 2003. "Made and Remade in the Image of God." In *Growing into God,* ed. Jean Mayland, pp. 187-91. London: Churches Together in Britain and Ireland.

Prins, Richard. 1972. "The Image of God in Adam and the Restoration of Man in Jesus Christ: A Study in Calvin." *Scottish Journal of Theology* 25: 32-44.

Purkiser, W. T., ed. 1960. *Exploring Our Christian Faith.* Kansas City, MO: Beacon Hill.

Putz, Oliver. 2009. "Moral Apes, Human Uniqueness, and the Image of God." *Zygon* 44 (September): 613-24.

Racovian Catechism. 1962. Lexington, KY: Theological Library Association.

Rad, Gerhard von. 1962. *Old Testament Theology.* Translated by D. M. G. Stalker. Vol. 1. Edinburgh: Oliver & Boyd.

———. 1964a. "*Kabod* in the OT." In *Theological Dictionary of the New Testament,* ed. Gerhard Kittel, 2:238-42. Grand Rapids: Eerdmans.

———. 1964b. "The Divine Likeness in the OT." In *Theological Dictionary of the New Testament,* ed. Gerhard Kittel, 2:390-92. Grand Rapids: Eerdmans.

———. 1964c. "The Prohibition of Images in the OT." In *Theological Dictionary of the New Testament,* ed. Gerhard Kittel, 2:238-42. Grand Rapids: Eerdmans.

———. 1972. *Genesis.* Old Testament Library. Philadelphia: Westminster.

Rae, Scott B., and Paul M. Cox. 1999. *Bioethics: A Christian Approach in a Pluralistic Age.* Grand Rapids: Eerdmans.

Rakestraw, Robert V. 1992. "The Persistent Vegetative State and the Withdrawal of Nutrition and Hydration." *Journal of the Evangelical Theological Society* 35 (September): 389-405.

———. 1997. "Becoming Like God: An Evangelical Doctrine of Theosis." *Journal of the Evangelical Theological Society* 40 (June): 257-69.

Ramsey, A. Michael. 1949. *The Glory of God and the Transfiguration of Christ.* London: Longmans, Green & Co.

Ramsey, Paul. 1950. *Basic Christian Ethics.* Louisville: Westminster John Knox.

Reimers, David M. 1965. *White Protestantism and the Negro.* New York: Oxford University Press.

Reinders, Hans S. 2006. "Human Dignity in the Absence of Agency." In *God and Human Dignity,* ed. Linda Woodhead and R. Kendall Soulen, 121-39. Grand Rapids: Eerdmans.

———. 2008. *Receiving the Gift of Friendship: Profound Disability, Theological Anthropology, and Ethics.* Grand Rapids: Eerdmans.

Reinders, Johannes. 1997. "Imago Dei as a Basic Concept in Christian Ethics." In *Holy Scriptures in Judaism, Christianity and Islam,* ed. Hendrik Vroom and Jerald Gort, pp. 187-204. Amsterdam: Rodopi.

Reiss, Moshe. 2011. "Adam: Created in the Image and Likeness of God." *Jewish Bible Quarterly* 39 (July): 181-86.

Reitman, James S. 2010. "God's 'Eye' for the *Imago Dei:* Wise Advocacy Amid Disillusionment in Job and Ecclesiastes." *Trinity Journal* 31 NS: 115-34.

Reule, George. 1971. "Christology of Philippians 2:5-11." *Springfielder* 35, no. 2: 81-85.

Reynolds, Thomas E. 2008. *Vulnerable Communion: A Theology of Disability and Hospitality.* Grand Rapids: Brazos Press.

Rice, David. 1956. *Slavery Inconsistent with Justice and Good Policy.* Lexington: University of Kentucky Library Association.

Richard, Lucien. 1986. "Toward a Renewed Theology of Creation: Implications for the Question of Human Rights." *Église et Théologie* 17: 149-70.

Richards, LeGrand. 1958. *A Marvelous Work and a Wonder.* Salt Lake City: Deseret.

Richardson, Kurt A. 1997. *James.* New American Commentary. Nashville: Broadman & Holman.

———. 2004. *Imago Dei:* Anthropological and Christological Modes of Divine Self-Imaging." *The Journal of Scriptural Reasoning* 4 (October).

Ricoeur, Paul. 1965. *History and Truth.* Translated by Charles Kelbley. Evanston, IL: Northwestern University Press.

———. 1969. *The Symbolism of Evil.* Translated by Emerson Buchanan. Boston: Beacon.

Ridderbos, Herman. 1975. *Paul: An Outline of His Theology.* Translated by John De Witt. Grand Rapids: Eerdmans.

Rist, John M. 1982. *Human Value: A Study in Ancient Philosophical Ethics.* Leiden: Brill.

Roberts, Jason P. 2011. "Emerging in the Image of God to Know Good and Evil." *Zygon* 46 (June): 471-81.

Robertson, Archibald T. 1923. *A Grammar of the Greek New Testament in the Light of Historical Research.* New York: Hodder & Stoughton.

Robinson, Dominic. 2011. *Understanding the "Imago Dei": The Thought of Barth, Von Balthasar and Moltmann.* Burlington, VT: Ashgate.

Robinson, H. Wheeler. 1926. *The Christian Doctrine of Man.* Edinburgh: T. & T. Clark.

Rodríguez, Rubén Rosaria. 2008. *Racism and God-Talk: A Latino/a Perspective.* New York: University Press of America.

Rogerson, John W. 2003. "Made in the Image and Likeness of God." In *Growing into God,* ed. Jean Mayland, pp. 25-30. London: Churches Together in Britain and Ireland.

———. 2010. *A Theology of the Old Testament.* Minneapolis: Fortress.

Romanowski, William D. 2001. *Eyes Wide Open: Looking for God in Popular Culture.* Grand Rapids: Brazos.

Ross, Allen P. 1988. *Creation and Blessing.* Grand Rapids: Baker.

Ross, Ellen M. 1990. "Human Persons as Images of the Divine." In *The Pleasure of Her Text,* ed. Alice Bach, pp. 97-116. Philadelphia: Trinity Press.

Rowe, Nicholas. 1966. *Tamerlane.* 3rd ed. Philadelphia: University of Pennsylvania Press.

Roy, Steven C. 2009. "Embracing Social Justice: Reflections from the Storyline of Scripture." *Trinity Journal* 30: 3-48.

Ruchames, Louis. 1967. "The Sources of Racial Thought in Colonial America." *The Journal of Negro History* 52 (October): 251-72.

Ruether, Rosemary Radford. 1974. "Misogynism and Virginal Feminism in the Fathers of the Church." In *Religion and Sexism,* ed. Rosemary Radford Ruether, pp. 150-83. New York: Simon & Schuster.

———. 1995. "Imago Dei, Christian Tradition and Feminist Hermeneutics." In *The*

Image of God: Gender Models in Judaeo-Christian Tradition, ed. Kari Elisabeth Børresen, pp. 267-91. Minneapolis: Fortress.

———. 2007. "Augustine: Sexuality, Gender, and Woman." In *Feminist Interpretations of Augustine,* ed. Judith Chelius Stark, pp. 47-67. University Park: Pennsylvania State University Press.

Rumscheidt, H. Martin. 1972. *Revelation and Theology: An Analysis of the Barth-Harnack Correspondence of 1923.* Cambridge: Cambridge University Press.

Russell, Edward. 2003. "Reconsidering Relational Anthropology: A Critical Assessment of John Zizioulas's Theological Anthropology." *International Journal of Systematic Theology* 5, no. 2: 168-86.

Russell, Letty M. 1985. "Introduction: Liberating the Word." In *Feminist Interpretation of the Bible,* ed. Letty M. Russell, pp. 11-18. Philadelphia: Westminster.

Ruston, Roger. 2004. *Human Rights and the Image of God.* London: SCM.

———. 2010. "Image of God and Natural Rights: A Dual Inheritance." In *In the Image of God,* ed. Alberto Melloni and Riccardo Saccenti, pp. 383-90. Berlin: Lit.

Ryrie, Charles C. 1986. *Basic Theology.* Wheaton, IL: Victor Books.

Ryu, Tongshik. 1977. "Man in Nature: An Organic View." In *The Human and the Holy: Asian Perspectives in Christian Theology,* ed. Emerito P. Nacpil and Douglas J. Elwood, pp. 139-53. Maryknoll, NY: Orbis.

Sands, Paul. 2010. "The Imago Dei as Vocation." *Evangelical Quarterly* 82, no. 1: 28-41.

Sarna, Nahum M. 1989. *The JPS Torah Commentary: Genesis.* Philadelphia: Jewish Publication Society.

Sawyer, John F. A. 1974. "Meaning of Bselem Elohim (In the Image of God) in Genesis I–XI." *Journal of Theological Studies* 25, no. 2: 418-26.

———. 1992. "The Image of God, the Wisdom of Serpents and the Knowledge of Good and Evil." In *A Walk in the Garden,* ed. Paul Morris and Deborah Sawyer, pp. 64-73. Sheffield, UK: Sheffield Academic Press.

Schaeffer, Francis A. 1970. *Pollution and the Death of Man.* Wheaton, IL: Tyndale.

Schell, William G. 1901. *Is the Negro a Beast? A Reply to Chas. Carroll's Book.* Moundsville, WV: Gospel Trumpet Publishing Company.

Schellenberger, Annette. 2009. "Humankind as the 'Image of God': On the Priestly Predication (Gen. 1:26-27; 5:1; 9:6) and Its Relationship to the Ancient Near Eastern Understanding of Images." *Theologische Zeitschrift* 65: 97-115.

Schilder, Klaas. 1947. *Heidelbergsche Catechismus.* Vol. 1. Goes: Oosterbaan & Le Cointre.

Schillebeeckx, Edward. 1990. *Church: The Human Story of God.* New York: Crossroad.

Schleiermacher, Friedrich. 1986. *The Christian Faith.* Translated by H. R. Macintosh and J. S. Stewart. Edinburgh: T. & T. Clark.

Schmidt, Alvin J. 1989. *Veiled and Silenced: How Culture Shaped Sexist Theology.* Macon, GA: Mercer University Press.

Schmidt, Karl L. 1947. "Homo Imago Dei im Alten und Neuen Testament." *Eranos-Jahrbuch* 15: 149-95.

Schmidt, Werner H. 1964. *Die Schöpfungsgeschichte der Priesterschrift.* Neukirchen-Vluyn: Neukirchener Verlag.

———. 1983. *The Faith of the Old Testament: A History.* Translated by John Sturdy. Philadelphia: Westminster.

Schmutzer, Andrew J. 2009. *Be Fruitful and Multiply: A Crux of Thematic Repetition in Genesis 1–11.* Eugene, OR: Wipf & Stock.

Schnackenburg, Rudolf. 1965. *The Moral Teaching of the New Testament.* New York: Herder & Herder.

———. 1991. *Ephesians: A Commentary.* Translated by Helen Keron. Edinburgh: T. & T. Clark.

———. 1992. *The Johannine Epistles.* Translated by Reginald and Ilse Fuller. New York: Crossroad.

Schneider, Johannes. 1967. "Homoiosis." In *Theological Dictionary of the New Testament,* ed. Gerhard Kittel and Gerhard Friedrich, 5:190-91. Grand Rapids: Eerdmans.

Schnelle, Udo. 1996. *The Human Condition: Anthropology in the Teachings of Jesus, Paul, and John.* Translated by D. C. Denn Jr. Minneapolis: Fortress.

Schönborn, Christoph C. 2011. *Man, the Image of God.* Translated by Henry Taylor and Michael Miller. San Francisco: Ignatius.

Schreiner, Thomas R. 1998. *Romans.* Baker Exegetical Commentary on the New Testament. Grand Rapids: Baker Books.

Schrotenboer, Paul. 1972. *Man in God's World: The Biblical Idea of Office.* Toronto: Wedge.

Schüle, Andreas. 2005. "Made in the Image of God: The Concepts of Divine Images in Gen. 1–3." *Zeitschrift für die Alttestamentliche Wissenschaft* 117: 1-20.

Schulman, Adam. 2008. "Bioethics and the Question of Human Dignity." In *Human Dignity and Bioethics,* ed. President's Council on Bioethics, 3-18. Washington, DC: President's Council.

Schumacher, Michele M. 2008. "Ecclesial Existence: Person and Community in the Trinitarian Anthropology of Adrienne von Speyr." *Modern Theology* 24 (July): 359-85.

Schweiker, William. 2000. "The Image of God in Christian Faith: Vocation, Dignity, and Redemption." In *Christianity in Jewish Terms,* ed. Tikva Frymer-Kensky et al., pp. 347-56. Boulder, CO: Westview.

Schweizer, Eduard. 1982. *The Letter to the Colossians.* Translated by Andrew Chester. Minneapolis: Augsburg.

Schwöbel, Christoph. 2006. "Recovering Human Dignity." In *God and Human Dignity,* ed. R. Kendall Soulen and Linda Woodhead, pp. 44-58. Grand Rapids: Eerdmans.

Scott, David. 2008. "Racial Images in John Wesley's Thoughts Upon Slavery." *Wesleyan Theological Journal* 43 (September 1): 87-100.

Scott, Peter. 1998. "Imaging God: Creatureliness and Technology." *New Blackfriars* 29: 260-74.

Scroggs, Robin. 1966. *The Last Adam.* Oxford: Basil Blackwell.

Seerveld, Calvin. 1981. "A Christian Tin-can Theory of Man." *Journal of the American Scientific Affiliation* 33, no. 2: 74-81.

Seneca, Lucius. 1995. "On Anger." In *Moral and Political Essays,* ed. John Cooper and J. F. Procope, pp. 1-116. Cambridge: Cambridge University Press.

Sexton, Jason S. 2010. "The Imago Dei Once Again: Stanley Grenz's Journey Toward a Theological Interpretation of Genesis 1:26-27." *Journal of Theological Interpretation* 4, no. 2: 187-205.

Shannon, Thomas A. 2004. "Grounding Human Dignity." *Dialog* 43, no. 2: 113-17.

Sharp, Donald B. 1995. "A Biblical Foundation for an Environmental Theology: A New Perspective on Genesis 1:26-28 and 6:11-13." *Science et Esprit* 47, no. 3: 305-13.

Shedd, William G. T. 1980. *Dogmatic Theology.* Nashville: Thomas Nelson.

Shepherd, Norman. 1988. "Image of God." In *Baker Encyclopedia of the Bible,* ed. Walter A. Elwell, 1:1017-20. Grand Rapids: Baker.

Sherlock, Charles. 1996. *The Doctrine of Humanity.* Downers Grove, IL: InterVarsity Press.

Shults, F. LeRon. 2003. *Reforming Theological Anthropology: After the Philosophical Turn to Relationality.* Grand Rapids: Eerdmans.

Sidoroff, Matti. 1993. "Man as the Icon of God." *Greek Orthodox Theological Review* 38: 24-25.

Simpson, Cuthbert A. 1952. "The Book of Genesis: Exegesis." In *Interpreter's Bible,* 1:465-829. Nashville: Abingdon.

Smail, Thomas A. 2003. "In the Image of the Triune God." *International Journal of Systematic Theology* 5 (March): 22-32.

―――. 2006. *Like Father, Like Son.* Grand Rapids: Eerdmans.

Smalley, Stephen S. 1984. *1, 2, 3 John.* Word Biblical Commentary 51. Waco, TX: Word Books.

―――. 2007. *1, 2, 3 John.* Revised. Word Biblical Commentary 51. Nashville: Thomas Nelson.

Smedes, Taede A. 2014. "Emil Brunner Revisited: On the Cognitive Science of Religion, the *Imago Dei,* and Revelation." *Zygon* 49 (March): 190-207.

Smith, C. Ryder. 1951. *The Bible Doctrine of Man.* London: Epworth.

Smith, Gerrit. 1859. *Three Discourses on the Religion of Reason.* New York: Ross & Tousey.

Smith, Goldwin. 1863. *Does the Bible Sanction American Slavery.* Cambridge: Sever & Francis.

Smith, H. Shelton. 1972. *In His Image, But . . . Racism in Southern Religion, 1780-1910.* Durham, NC: Duke University Press.

Smith, Matthew L. 2007. *In His Image.* Bloomington: Author House.

Smith, Robert H. 1988. *Matthew.* Augsburg Commentary of the New Testament. Minneapolis: Augsburg.

Snaith, Norman. 1974. "The Image of God." *Expository Times* 86: 24.

Soelle, Dorothee, with Shirley A. Clayes. 1984. *To Work and to Love: A Theology of Creation*. Philadelphia: Fortress.

Soskice, Janet Martin. 2011. "Imago Dei and Sexual Difference: Toward an Eschatological Anthropology." In *Rethinking Human Nature*, ed. Malcolm Jeeves, pp. 295-306. Grand Rapids: Eerdmans.

Soulen, Kendall. 2006. "Contextualizing Human Dignity." In *God and Human Dignity*, ed. Kendall Soulen and Linda Woodhead, pp. 1-24. Grand Rapids: Eerdmans.

Spanner, Huw. 1998. "Tyrants, Stewards — or Just Kings?" In *Animals on the Agenda*, ed. Andrew Linzey and Dorothy Yamomoto, pp. 216-24. Urbana: University of Illinois Press.

Spicq, Ceslas. 1982. *Notes de Lexicographie Neo-Testamentaire*. Vol. 3: Supplement. Göttingen: Vandenhoeck & Ruprecht.

Squire, Aelred. 1951. "The Doctrine of the Image in the *De Veritate* of St. Thomas." *Dominican Studies* 4: 164-77.

Stackhouse, Max L. 2005. "Why Human Rights Needs God: A Christian Perspective." In *Does Human Rights Need God?* ed. Elizabeth Bucar and Barbara Barnett, pp. 25-40. Grand Rapids: Eerdmans.

Stanley, David M. 1984. "Imitation in Paul's Letters: Its Significance for His Relationship to Jesus and to His Own Christian Foundations." In *From Jesus to Paul*, pp. 127-41. Waterloo, ON: Wilfrid Laurier University Press.

Stark, Judith Chelius. 2007. "Augustine on Women: In God's Image, but Less So." In *Feminist Interpretations of Augustine*, ed. Judith Chelius Stark, pp. 215-41. University Park: Pennsylvania State University Press.

Steenberg, Matthew C. 2009. *Of God and Man*. London: T. & T. Clark.

Stein, Murray. 2008. " 'Divinity Expresses the Self . . .' An Investigation." *Journal of Analytical Psychology* 53: 305-27.

Stein, Robert M. 1992. *Luke*. Edited by David Dockery. New American Commentary 24. Nashville: Broadman & Holman.

Stendahl, Krister. 1992. "Selfhood in the Image of God." In *Selves, People and Persons*, ed. Leroy S. Rouner, pp. 141-48. Notre Dame: University of Notre Dame Press.

Stendebach, F. J. 2003. "Tselem." In *Theological Dictionary of the Old Testament*, ed. G. Johannes Botterweck, Helmer Ringgren, and Heinz-Josef Fabry, trans. Douglas W. Stott, 12:386-95. Grand Rapids: Eerdmans.

Stephenson, Bret. 2005. "Nature, Technology and the *Imago Dei*: Mediating the Nonhuman Through the Practice of Science." *Perspectives on Science and Christian Faith* 57, no. 1: 6-12.

Stott, John R. W. 1964. *The Epistles of John*. Grand Rapids: Eerdmans.

———. 1979. *The Message of Ephesians*. Bible Speaks Today. Leicester, UK: InterVarsity Press.

———. 1988. *The Letters of John: An Introduction and Commentary*. Vol. 19. Tyndale New Testament Commentary. Downers Grove, IL: InterVarsity Press.

Strecker, Georg. 1996. *The Johannine Letters.* Translated by Linda M. Maloney. Hermeneia. Minneapolis: Fortress.

Strong, Augustus H. 1907. *Systematic Theology.* Valley Forge, PA: Judson Press.

Strong, John T. 2005. "Israel as a Testimony to YHWH's Power: The Priest's Definition of Israel." In *Constituting the Community,* ed. John T. Strong and Steven Tuell, 89-106. Winona Lake, IN: Eisenbrauns.

———. 2008. "Shattering the Image of God: A Response to Theodore Hiebert's Interpretation of the Story of the Tower of Babel." *Journal of Biblical Literature* 127, no. 4: 625-34.

Stroumsa, G. G. 1990. *"Caro salutis cardo:* Shaping the Person in Early Christian Thought." *History of Religions* 30: 25-50.

Stuhlmacher, Paul. 1994. *Paul's Letter to the Romans.* Translated by Scott J. Hafemann. Louisville: Westminster John Knox.

Sulentic, Alison McMorran. 2010. "Harry Potter and the Image of God: How House-Elves Can Help Us to Understand the Dignity of the Person." In *The Law and Harry Potter,* ed. Jeffrey Thomas and Franklin Snyder, pp. 189-207. Durham, NC: Carolina Academic Press.

Sullivan, John E. 1963. *The Image of God: The Doctrine of St. Augustine and Its Influence.* Dubuque, IA: The Priory Press.

Sumner, Charles. 1860. "The Barbarism of Slavery." Lecture delivered to the United States Senate June 4. http://medicolegal.tripod.com/sumnerbarbarism.htm.

Sunderland, Chris. 2003. "Human Nature and the Image of God — Social and Biological Factors." In *Growing into God,* ed. Jean Mayland, pp. 192-200. London: Churches Together in Britain and Ireland.

Sunshine, Glenn. 2013. *The Image of God.* Lavergne, TN: Every Square Inch.

Talbot, Mark R. 2006. "Learning from the Ruined Image: Moral Anthropology After the Fall." In *Personal Identity in Theological Perspective,* ed. Richard Lints, Michael S. Horton, and Mark R. Talbot, pp. 159-77. Grand Rapids: Eerdmans.

Tanner, Kathryn. 1994. "The Difference Theological Anthropology Makes." *Theology Today* 50, no. 4: 567-79.

———. 2010. *Christ the Key.* Cambridge: Cambridge University Press.

Tavard, George H. 1973. *Woman in Christian Tradition.* Notre Dame: University of Notre Dame Press.

Taylor, Philip. 1992. "Image-Bearers as Caregivers." *Didaskalia* 3, no. 2: 16-23.

Teel, Karen. 2010. *Racism and the Image of God.* New York: Palgrave Macmillan.

Tepedino, Ana Maria, and Margarida L. Ribeiro. 1993. "Women and the Theology of Liberation." In *Mysterium Liberationis: Fundamental Concepts of Liberation Theology,* ed. Ignacio Ellacuría and Jon Sobrino, pp. 221-31. Maryknoll, NY: Orbis.

Tertullian. 2002. *De Cultu Feminarum.* Translated by S. Thelwell. http://www.ccel.org/ccel/schaff/anto4.iii.iii.i.i.html.

The Cloud of Unknowing. 1981. New York: Paulist.

The Covenant, the Sword, and the Arm of the Lord. 1995. "What We Believe." In *Ex-*

tremism in America: A Reader, ed. Lyman T. Sargent, pp. 329-30. New York: New York University Press.

Theodore of Mopsuestia. 1933. *Commentary of Theodore of Mopsuestia on the Lord's Prayer and on the Sacraments of Baptism and the Eucharist.* Translated by Alphonse Mingana. Cambridge: Heffer & Sons.

———. 1949. *Les Homélies Catéchétiques de Theodore de Mopsueste.* Translated by Raymond Tonneau and Robert Devreese. Vatican City: Vaticana.

Thielicke, Helmut. 1966. *Theological Ethics.* Edited by William H. Lazareth. Vol. 1. Philadelphia: Fortress.

Thiessen, Henry C. 1949. *Introductory Lectures in Systematic Theology.* Edited by Vernon D. Doerksen. Grand Rapids: Eerdmans.

Third General Conference of the Latin America Episcopate. 1979. "The Final Puebla Document." In *Puebla and Beyond,* ed. John Eagleson and Philip Scharper, pp. 122-285. Maryknoll, NY: Orbis.

Thiselton, Anthony C. 2000. *The First Epistle to the Corinthians.* New International Greek Testament Commentary. Grand Rapids: Eerdmans.

Thomas, John N. 1949. "'What Is Man': The Biblical Doctrine of the Image of God." *Interpretation: A Journal of Bible & Theology* 3, no. 2: 154-63.

Thompson, John L. 1988. "*Creata ad Imaginem Dei, Licet Secundo Gradu:* Woman as the Image of God According to John Calvin." *Harvard Theological Review* 81 (April): 125-43.

Thompson, Marianne. 2005. *Colossians and Philemon.* Two Horizons New Testament Commentary. Grand Rapids: Eerdmans.

Thompson, Thomas L. 2009. "*Imago Dei:* A Problem in Pentateuchal Discourse." *Scandinavian Journal of the Old Testament* 23: 135-48.

Thornwell, James H. 1850. *The Rights and Duties of Masters.* Charleston, SC: Walker & James.

Thrall, Margaret E. 1994. *The Second Epistle to the Corinthians.* Vol. 1. International Critical Commentary. London: T. & T. Clark.

Thurman, Howard. 1949. *Jesus and the Disinherited.* Nashville: Abingdon.

Thweatt-Bates, Jennifer. 2011. "Posthuman Selves: Bodies, Cognitive Processes, and Technologies." In *In Search of Self: Interdisciplinary Perspectives on Personhood,* ed. J. Wentzel van Huyssteen and Eric P. Wiebe, pp. 243-55. Grand Rapids: Eerdmans.

Tigay, Jeffrey H. 1984. "The Image of God and the Flood: Some New Developments." In *Studies in Jewish Education and Judaica in Honor of Louis Newman,* ed. Alexander M. Shapiro and Burton I. Cohen, pp. 169-82. New York: Ktav.

Torrance, Thomas F. 1952. *Calvin's Doctrine of Man.* London: Lutterworth.

Towner, Wayne S. 2001. *Genesis.* Westminster Bible Companion. Louisville: Westminster John Knox.

———. 2005. "Clones of God." *Interpretation: A Journal of Bible & Theology* 59, no. 4: 341-56.

Towns, Elmer L., and Roberta L. Groff. 1972. *Successful Ministry to the Retarded.* Chicago: Moody.

Tracy, David. 1983. "Religion and Human Rights in the Public Realm." *Daedalus:* 237-54.

Treier, Daniel J. 2008. *Introducing Theological Interpretation of Scripture: Recovering a Christian Perspective.* Grand Rapids: Baker Academic.

Trible, Phyllis. 1978. *God and the Rhetoric of Sexuality.* Philadelphia: Fortress.

Trinkaus, Charles. 1995. *In Our Image and Likeness: Humanity and Divinity in Italian Humanist Thought.* Vol. 1. Notre Dame: University of Notre Dame Press.

Trotman, Arlington. 2003. "Black People Made in the Image of God." In *Growing into God,* ed. Jean Mayland, pp. 93-102. London: Churches Together in Britain and Ireland.

Ulmer, Kenneth. 2005. *In His Image: An Intimate Reflection of God.* New Kensington, PA: Whitaker House.

Umar, Muhammad S. 2004. "Image of God: A Note on Scriptural Anthropology." *The Journal of Scriptural Reasoning* 4 (October).

Usry, Glenn, and Craig S. Keener. 1996. *Black Man's Religion.* Downers Grove, IL: InterVarsity Press.

Vainio, Olli-Pekka. 2014. "*Imago Dei* and Human Responsibility." *Zygon* 49 (March): 121-34.

Vanhoozer, Kevin. 1997. "Human Being, Individual and Social." In *The Cambridge Companion to Christian Doctrine,* ed. Colin E. Gunton, pp. 158-88. Cambridge: Cambridge University Press.

Van Bavel, Tarcisius J. 1989. "Woman as the Image of God in Augustine's *De Trinitate* XII." In *Signum Pietatis,* ed. A. Zumkeller, pp. 267-88. Würzburg: Augustinus-Verlag.

Van Huyssteen, J. Wentzel. 2006. *Alone in the World?* Grand Rapids: Eerdmans.

Van Kooten, George H. 2008. "Image, Form, and Transformation: A Semantic Taxonomy of Paul's 'Morphic' Language." In *Jesus, Paul, and Early Christianity,* ed. Rieuwerd Buitenwerf, Harm Hollander, and Johannes Tromp, pp. 213-42. Leiden: Brill.

Van Leeuwen, Raymond C. 1997. "Form, Image." In *New International Dictionary of Old Testament Theology and Exegesis,* ed. Willem A. VanGemeren, 4: 643-48. Grand Rapids: Zondervan.

Van Vliet, Jason. 2009. *Children of God: The Imago Dei in John Calvin and His Context.* Göttingen: Vandenhoeck & Ruprecht.

Verduin, Leonard. 1970. *Somewhat Less Than God.* Grand Rapids: Eerdmans.

Verhey, Allen. 2003. *Reading the Bible in the Strange World of Medicine.* Grand Rapids: Eerdmans.

Veyne, Paul. 1990. *Bread and Circuses.* Translated by David Pearce. London: Penguin.

Visala, Aku. 2014. "*Imago Dei,* Dualism, and Evolution: A Philosophical Defense of the Structural Image of God." *Zygon* 49 (March): 101-20.

Vitoria, Francisco de. 1917. "On the Indians." In *De Indis et De Iure Belli Reflectiones,* 115-87. Washington, DC: Carnegie Institution.

———. 1993. "On the American Indians." In *Vitoria: Political Writings,* ed. Anthony Pagden and Jeremy Lawrence, pp. 231-92. Cambridge: Cambridge University Press.

Vogels, Walter. 1994. "The Human Person in the Image of God (Gen 1,26)." *Science et Esprit* 46, no. 2: 189-202.

Volf, Miroslav. 1996. *Exclusion and Embrace: A Theological Exploration of Identity, Otherness, and Reconciliation.* Nashville: Abingdon.

———. 1998. *After Our Likeness: The Church and the Image of Community.* Grand Rapids: Eerdmans.

Völkl, Richard. 1961. *Christ und Welt mach dem Neuen Testament.* Würzburg: Echter.

Voltaire [François Marie Arouet]. 1880. *Le Sottisier.* Paris: Librairie des bibliophiles.

———. 1961. "Septième Lettre d'Amabed." In *Les Lettres d'Amabed.* Paris: Éditions universitaires.

Vorster, Nico. 2007a. "A Theological Evaluation of the South African Constitutional Value of Human Dignity." *Journal of Reformed Theology* 1: 320-39.

———. 2007b. "The Value of Human Life." *Ecumenical Review* 59: 363-83.

———. 2011. *Created in the Image of God.* Eugene, OR: Pickwick.

Vos, Geerhardus. 1972. *The Pauline Eschatology.* Grand Rapids: Eerdmans.

Vriezen, Theodor C. 1943. "La création de l'homme d'après l'image de Dieu." *Oudtestamentische Studien* 2: 87-105.

Walsh, Brian J., and J. Richard Middleton. 1984. *The Transforming Vision.* Downers Grove, IL: InterVarsity Press.

Walters, Jerome. 2001. *One Aryan Nation Under God.* Naperville, IL: Sourcebooks.

Waltke, Bruce K. 1989. "Relating Human Personhood to the Health Sciences: An Old Testament Perspective." *Crux* 23 (3): 2-10.

Waltke, Bruce K., and M. O'Connor. 1990. *An Introduction to Biblical Hebrew Syntax.* Winona Lake, IN: Eisenbrauns.

Walton, John H. 2001. *Genesis.* NIV Application Commentary. Grand Rapids: Zondervan.

Walton, John H., Victor H. Matthews, and Mark W. Chavalas. 1994. *The IVP Bible Background Commentary.* Downers Grove, IL: InterVarsity Press.

Ware, Bruce A. 2002. "Male and Female Complementarity and the Image of God." *Journal for Biblical Manhood and Womanhood* 7: 14-23.

Ware, Timothy. 1979. *The Orthodox Way.* London: A. R. Mowbray & Co.

Watson, Francis. 1994. *Text, Church and World.* Edinburgh: T. & T. Clark.

———. 1997. *Text and Truth: Redefining Biblical Theology.* Grand Rapids: Eerdmans.

Watts, Fraser. 2006. "Human Dignity: Concepts and Experience." In *God and Human Dignity,* ed. R. Kendall Soulen and Linda Woodhead, pp. 247-62. Grand Rapids: Eerdmans.

Weems, Renita J. 2003. "Re-reading for Liberation: African American Women and the Bible." In *Feminist Interpretation of the Bible and Hermeneutics,* ed. Silvia Schroer and Sophia Bietenhard, pp. 19-32. London: Sheffield Academic Press.

Weinandy, Thomas G. 2000. *Does God Suffer?* Notre Dame: University of Notre Dame Press.

Weinstein, Donald, and Rudolf M. Bell. 1982. *Saints and Society: Two Worlds of Western Christendom, 1000-1700.* Chicago: University of Chicago Press.

Welch, Edward T. 1994. "Who Are We? Needs, Longings, and the Image of God in Man." *The Journal of Biblical Counseling* 13 (Fall): 25-38.

Welker, Michael. 1999. *Creation and Reality.* Translated by John Hoffmeyer. Minneapolis: Fortress.

———. 2006. "Theological Anthropology Versus Anthropological Reductionism." In *God and Human Dignity,* ed. R. Kendall Soulen and Linda Woodhead, pp. 319-30. Grand Rapids: Eerdmans.

Wells, Paul. 2004. "In Search of the Image of God: Theology of a Lost Paradigm?" *Themelios* 30, no. 1: 23-38.

Welz, Claudia. 2011. "Imago Dei: References to the Invisible." *Studia Theologica* 65 (January 1): 74-91.

Wenham, Gordon J. 1987. *Genesis 1–15.* Word Biblical Commentary 1. Waco, TX: Word Books.

Wennberg, Robert N. 1985. *Life in the Balance.* Grand Rapids: Eerdmans.

Wernow, Jerome R. 1995. "Saying the Unsaid: Quality of Life Criteria in a Sanctity of Life Position." In *Bioethics and the Future of Medicine,* ed. John F. Kilner, Nigel M. de S. Cameron, and David L. Schiedermayer, pp. 93-111. Grand Rapids: Eerdmans.

Wesley, Charles. 1889. "Omnipresent God! Whose Aid." Hymn 287. In *A Collection of Hymns for the Use of the People Called Methodists,* ed. John Wesley. London: Wesleyan-Methodist Book-Room. www.ccel.org/w/wesley/hymn/jwg0287.html.

Wesley, John. 1985a. "Awake, Thou That Sleepest." In *The Works of John Wesley: Sermons I,* ed. Albert Outler, pp. 142-58. Nashville: Abingdon.

———. 1985b. "Heavenly Treasure in Earthen Vessels." In *The Works of John Wesley: Sermons IV,* ed. Albert Outler, pp. 161-67. Nashville: Abingdon.

———. 1985c. "Justification by Faith." In *The Works of John Wesley: Sermons I,* ed. Albert Outler, 181-99. Nashville: Abingdon.

———. 1985d. "On the Fall of Man." In *The Works of John Wesley: Sermons II,* ed. Albert Outler, pp. 400-412. Nashville: Abingdon.

———. 1985e. "On the Sabbath." In *The Works of John Wesley: Sermons IV,* ed. Albert Outler, 267-78. Nashville: Abingdon.

———. 1985f. "On Working Out Our Own Salvation." In *The Works of John Wesley: Sermons III,* ed. Albert Outler, pp. 199-209. Nashville: Abingdon.

———. 1985g. "Original Sin." In *The Works of John Wesley: Sermons II,* ed. Albert Outler, pp. 170-85. Nashville: Abingdon.

———. 1985h. "Salvation by Faith." In *The Works of John Wesley: Sermons I,* ed. Albert Outler, pp. 109-30. Nashville: Abingdon.

———. 1985i. "The Deceitfulness of the Human Heart." In *The Works of John Wesley: Sermons IV,* ed. Albert Outler, pp. 149-60. Nashville: Abingdon.

———. 1985j. "The End of Christ's Coming." In *The Works of John Wesley: Sermons II*, ed. Albert Outler, pp. 471-84. Nashville: Abingdon.

———. 1985k. "The Image of God." In *The Works of John Wesley: Sermons IV*, ed. Albert Outler, pp. 290-303. Nashville: Abingdon.

———. 1985l. "The Lord Our Righteousness." In *The Works of John Wesley: Sermons I*, ed. Albert Outler, pp. 444-65. Nashville: Abingdon.

———. 1985m. "The New Birth." In *The Works of John Wesley: Sermons II*, ed. Albert Outler, pp. 187-201. Nashville: Abingdon.

———. 1985n. "The One Thing Needful." In *The Works of John Wesley: Sermons IV*, ed. Albert Outler, pp. 351-59. Nashville: Abingdon.

———. 1985o. "The Witness of Our Spirit." In *The Works of John Wesley: Sermons I*, ed. Albert Outler, 299-313. Nashville: Abingdon.

———. 2011. *Thoughts Upon Slavery*. Charleston, SC: Nabu Press.

West, Morris L. 1981. *The Clowns of God*. New York: William Morrow & Co.

Westcott, Brooke Foss. 1950. *The Epistle to the Hebrews*. Grand Rapids: Eerdmans.

Westermann, Claus. 1974. *Creation*. Translated by John Scullion. Philadelphia: Fortress.

———. 1994. *Genesis 1–11: A Continental Commentary*. Translated by John J. Scallion. Minneapolis: Fortress.

White, Lynn, Jr. 1967. "The Historical Roots of Our Ecologic Crisis." *Science* 155 (March): 1203-7.

Wilckens, Ulrich. 1967. "*Charakter* in the New Testament." In *Theological Dictionary of the New Testament*, ed. Gerhard Kittel and Gerhard Friedrich, 9:421-22. Grand Rapids: Eerdmans.

Wild, Robert A. 1985. "'Be Imitators of God': Discipleship in the Letters to the Ephesians." In *Discipleship in the New Testament*, ed. Fernando F. Segovia, pp. 127-43. Philadelphia: Fortress.

Wildberger, Hans. 1965. "Das Abbild Gottes Gen 1:26-30." *Theologische Zeitschrift* 21: 245-59, 481-501.

———. 1997. "Tselem/Image." In *Theological Lexicon of the Old Testament*, ed. Ernst Jenni and Claus Westermann, trans. Mark Biddle, 3:1080-85. Peabody, MA: Hendrickson.

Wilkins, Michael J. 1997. *In His Image: Reflecting Christ in Everyday Life*. Colorado Springs, CO: NavPress.

Williams, David T. 1999. "Who Will Go for Us (Is 6:8): The Divine Plurals and the Image of God." *Old Testament Essays* 12: 173-90.

Williams, Delores S. 1993. "A Womanist Perspective on Sin." In *A Troubling in My Soul*, ed. Emilie M. Townes, pp. 130-49. Maryknoll, NY: Orbis.

Williams, Michael D. 2013. "First Calling, Part II: The *Imago Dei* and the Order of Creation." *Presbyterian* 39, no. 2: 75-97.

Williams, R. J. 1972. "Scribal Training in Ancient Egypt." *Journal of the American Oriental Society* 92: 214-21.

Wills, Richard W., Sr. 2009. *Martin Luther King Jr. and the Image of God.* New York: Oxford University Press.

Wilson, R. Ward, and Craig L. Blomberg. 1993. "The Image of God in Humanity: A Biblical-Psychological Perspective." *Themelios* 18, no. 3: 8-15.

Wilson, S. G. 1973. "New Wine in Old Wineskins: Image of God." *Expository Times* 85: 356-61.

Windley-Daoust, Susan. 2002. *The Redeemed Image of God.* Lanham, MD: University Press of America.

Winslow, Donald F. 1965. "Gregory of Nazianus and Love for the Poor." *Anglican Theological Review* 47: 348-59.

Witherington, Ben, III. 1995. *Conflict and Community in Corinth: A Socio-Rhetorical Commentary on 1 and 2 Corinthians.* Grand Rapids: Eerdmans.

———. 2009. *The Theological and Ethical Thought World of the New Testament.* Downers Grove, IL: InterVarsity Press.

Wolff, Hans W. 1974. *Anthropology of the Old Testament.* London: SCM.

Wolterstorff, Nicholas. 1985. "Worship and Justice." *Reformed Liturgy & Music* 19, no. 2: 67-71.

Woodhead, Linda. 2006. "Apophatic Anthropology." In *God and Human Dignity,* ed. R. Kendall Soulen and Linda Woodhead, pp. 233-46. Grand Rapids: Eerdmans.

World Council of Churches. 2005. *Christian Perspectives on Theological Anthropology.* Faith and Order Paper 199. Geneva: W.C.C.

Wright, Christopher J. H. 2004. *Old Testament Ethics for the People of God.* Downers Grove, IL: InterVarsity Press.

———. 2006. *The Mission of God.* Downers Grove, IL: InterVarsity Press.

Wright, N. T. 1986. *Colossians and Philemon: An Introduction and Commentary.* Vol. 12. Tyndale New Testament Commentary. Downers Grove, IL: InterVarsity Press.

———. 1992a. *The Climax of the Covenant.* Minneapolis: Fortress.

———. 1992b. *The New Testament and the People of God.* Minneapolis: Fortress.

———. 2005. *Paul: Fresh Perspectives.* London: SPCK.

Wright, Stephen I. 2003. "The Phrase 'Image of God' in the New Testament." In *Growing into God,* ed. Jean Mayland, pp. 31-44. London: Churches Together in Britain and Ireland.

Wybrow, Cameron. 1991. *The Bible, Baconianism, and Mastery over Nature.* New York: Peter Lang.

Yannaras, Christos. 1984. *The Freedom of Morality.* Translated by Elizabeth Breire. Crestwood, NY: St. Vladimir's Seminary Press.

Yong, Amos. 2007. *Theology and Down Syndrome.* Waco, TX: Baylor University Press.

Yorke, Gosnell L. O. R. 1995. "Biblical Hermeneutics: An Afrocentric Perspective." *The Journal of Religious Thought* 52, no. 1: 1-13.

Youngblood, Ronald. 2006. "Genesis: Study Notes." In *TNIV Study Bible,* pp. 6-86. Grand Rapids: Zondervan.

Zachman, Randall C. 1990. "Jesus Christ as the Image of God in Calvin's Theology." *Calvin Theological Journal* 25, no. 1: 45-62.

————. 2007. *Image and Word in the Theology of John Calvin*. Notre Dame: University of Notre Dame Press.

Zaru, Jean. 1994. "The Intifada, Nonviolence, and the Bible." In *Feminist Theology from the Third World*, ed. Ursula King, pp. 230-35. Maryknoll, NY: Orbis.

Zeskind, Leonard. 1986. *The "Christian Identity" Movement*. New York: National Council of Churches.

Zizioulas, John D. 1975. "Human Capacity and Human Incapacity: A Theological Exploration of Personhood." *Scottish Journal of Theology* 28, no. 5: 401-47.

————. 1985. *Being as Communion*. New York: St. Vladimir's Seminary Press.

Index of Names and Subjects

Bultmann, Rudolf: and new humanity, 259

Cahill, Lisa Sowle: and colonization, 23; and Nazi Germany, 21; and women, 14
Calvin, John: and body, 306; and human/animal distinction, 109; and image completely lost view, 162; and image partly lost view, 168, 170-71; and image virtually lost view, 164-65; and likeness-image concept, 127; and righteousness, 189, 192; and rulership, 199, 203; and women, 34-35
Carr, Anne: and feminist theology, 16
Carroll, Charles: influence of book *The Negro as Beast*, 25-27
Carter, Charles: and image completely lost view, 162
Channing, William Ellery: as author of *Slavery*, 11; and war against God, 117
Children: of devil, 297; of God, 77-78, 81, 145, 271, 273, 294-98; and parent-child relationship, 222; and reason, 186
Christ. *See* Jesus Christ
Christensen, Inger: and dignity, 278-79
Christian tradition: and image partly lost view, 166-68, 171; and image's appearance compromised view, 173; and image virtually lost view, 165; and reason, 178, 196; and relationship, 211; and righteousness, 189-91, 196; and rulership, 199; and understanding of humanity, 6-10; and women, 32-35
Chrysostom: and Colossians 3:10, 255; and rulership, 199; and women, 32
Church, the, 68, 75-76, 298; in Christ, 77, 140, 144, 240-41, 253, 277, 280, 300; and image completely lost view, 160, 162-63, 174; and image damaged view, 142, 149-50, 174, 328-30; and image partly lost view, 166, 174; and image undamaged view, 175, 312, 329-30; and likeness-image

concept, 90, 100, 107, 126-28, 245; and natural environment, 16, 329; and people with disabilities, 20, 329; and physical body, 303, 306-7; and reason, 48, 178-81, 195-99; and relationship, 219-20, 223; and righteousness, 178, 189-90, 195-99; and slavery, 14, 24-25; and understanding of humanity, 6-10, 18-19, 82, 86, 105, 283-84, 316-17, 321, 322, 327-29; and women, 30-35
Clement of Alexandria: and body, 306; and distinction between image and likeness, 127; and reason, 178
Clement of Rome: and caring for those in need, 7-8
Clifford, Anne: and women and patriarchy, 14
Clines, D. J. A.: and prepositions in Genesis 1, 89
Collste, Göran: and image completely lost view, 162
Community: of believers, 138, 277; in Colossians 3, 144, 253; and connection, 85-88; and corporate aspect of God's image, 85-87, 118, 122, 240-41, 262, 286, 306, 315-16; and destiny, 239, 281; in Ephesians 4, 145; and godly attributes, 290-91, 318; and love, 318-19; over-emphasis on, 118, 217-18, 222, 286; and reflection, 230, 265; and relationship, 217-18, 222; in Romans 10, 238-42; in 2 Corinthians 3, 242
Conformation: in Ephesians 4, 264; to image of Christ, 8, 42, 53, 67, 70, 72, 74-75, 89, 91-92, 115, 123, 132, 135, 142, 184, 234, 252, 259, 275, 288, 294-95, 323; in Romans 8, 77-78, 81, 235-42, 250-51, 271, 275, 279, 287, 294-95, 297-98, 303; to world, 259
Connection: in ancient Near East, 120; of Christ with God, 61-69, 72, 78-79, 121, 132, 143, 242; corporate dimension of, 85-88; to evil powers, 59, 118; and kings, 55-58; of people with

Index of Biblical Passages